SOCIAL
PSYCHOLOGY

SOCIAL PSYCHOLOGY
A Sociological Approach

GEORGE J. McCALL
J. L. SIMMONS

With glossary prepared by Nola Simmons

The Free Press
A Division of Macmillan Publishing Co., Inc.
NEW YORK

Collier Macmillan Publishers
LONDON

The Free Press
A Division of Macmillan Publishing Co., Inc.
866 Third Avenue, New York, N.Y. 10022

Collier Macmillan Canada, Ltd.

Library of Congress Catalog Card Number: 81-67552

Printed in the United States of America

printing number
1   2   3   4   5   6   7   8   9   10

Library of Congress Cataloging in Publication Data

McCall, George J.
    Social psychology, a sociological approach.

    Includes bibliographies and indexes.
    1. Social psychology. I. Simmons, J. L. (Jerry L.),
1933-   . II. Title.
HM251.M38   302   81-67552
ISBN 0-02-920640-5   AACR2

Copyright Acknowledgments

To W. G. and Nina McCall, true parents,
and
to Earl and Lola Simmons, vagabond spirits.

Contents

CONTENTS

CONTENTS

CONTENTS

CONTENTS

xiii

CONTENTS

CONTENTS

Part IV. The Web   423

Preface and Acknowledgments

This book presents a thoroughly sociological approach to social psychology. It is definitely not another even-handed compound of psychology and sociology in the recently fashionable "convergent" tradition nor is it one more "symbolic interactionism" or "role-theory" book, although we are fully sympathetic to both. *Social organization, social process,* and the *social character of the individual* are instead the resounding themes of this book, in the tradition of Georg Simmel, Robert E. Park, Everett C. Hughes, and their followers. Indeed, the texture and flavor of this book most nearly resemble those of textbooks on the social psychology of organizations—not as confined to bureaucracies and voluntary associations, but here covering the entire range of social organizations, from the planetary level down to fleeting encounters.

We believe the book to be directly responsive to the concerns of many—expressed most forcefully by Liska (1977)—that social psychology might "soon disappear as a distinct area of interest within sociology unless more of the implicitly social psychological research being done in the various 'sociology of' subfields is in the future interpreted in terms of its relevance to social psychological processes and not exclusively in terms of its relevance to those particular social structures in which it is situated" (Boutilier, Roed, and Svendson, 1980). This book attempts to review and to integrate many social psychologies—of language and communication, youth and aging, sex roles and politics, work and stratification, social movements and mass behavior, cities and community, bureaucracy and total institutions, family and small groups, relationships and marriage, gatherings and encounters, and many others.

Social psychology is not presented here as the study of how individuals' behaviors and characteristics are influenced by other persons and by social roles nor even as the study of social interaction, although both these aspects (House, 1977) play a vital part in our treatment of social psychology. Rather, this book considers that the classical subject matter of social psychology is defined by the more fundamental question: what is the nature of the relation of the individual to Society, to the organized web of social life? Our characterization of that relation emphasizes and elaborates a manifold reciprocity between self and society. First, like Cooley and many others, we consider that the character of the individual and of Society are twin-born—joint products of the same social process. Second, like Simmel and so many others, we hold that the character of social process is, in turn, jointly influenced by both the individual and Society. These classic principles are endorsed not only by interactionists and role

PREFACE AND ACKNOWLEDGMENTS

theorists but also by virtually all sociologists; they have in fact animated much of the very best sociological theory and research over the past half-century. The aim of this book is a full and consistent formulation of the wealth of sociological ideas and findings that specify and substantiate these two principles.

A brief overview of the organization of the book may cast some light on the general nature of that formulation.

Part I introduces the student to social psychology and develops fundamental concepts. More specifically, Chapter 1 places sociological social psychology within the broader intellectual history of social psychology and goes on to set forth classic principles in a preliminary box-and-arrow model. Chapter 2 imparts basic sociological ideas concerning the social nature of the individual, including those of reference-group theory, symbolic interactionism, role theory, self theory, and exchange theory. Chapter 3 acquaints the student with fundamental concepts regarding the nature of any social organization, identifies variable features, and characterizes the fundamental varieties of organizations and their interorganizational relations. Chapter 4 reviews and refines the preliminary model of relations among individual, social organization, and social process.

Part II is devoted to clarifying the idea of social process—one relatively unfamiliar to many students. Chapters 5 through 9 analyze the tactics of both the organization and the individual in the shaping of five basic social processes: recruitment, socialization, interaction, innovation, and social control. Chapter 10 details how the interrelations among these five processes constitute an endlessly looping system shaping individuals' roles and careers as well as the organization's division of labor and collective action. Chapter 11 sensitizes the student to the overriding contextual influences of social change.

Part III applies the now fully articulated general model to a series of distinct varieties or levels of social organization, demonstrating how the character of an organization distinctively alters the character of various social processes—which in turn affects the nature of the individual's role and career and, thereby, his individual character. These chapters contain a great deal of fundamental organizational analysis and findings from a wide range of sociological specializations. Worldwide and international organizations are considered in Chapter 12, and societal-level organizations—speech communities, age-sex structures, polities, economies—are examined separately in Chapters 13 through 16. Diffuse collectivities, such as masses, publics, and social movements, are treated in Chapter 17. Several types of communities are analyzed in Chapter 18, and associations (bureaucracies, voluntary associations, total institutions) are the subject of Chapter 19. Groups, relationships, and encounters—the most familiar organizational levels in social psychology and in everyday life—are analyzed in Chapters 20 through 22. By taking up these levels last, we have sacrificed immediacy of appeal. However, we believe that this price is more than compensated for by increased student appreciation of how profoundly such face-to-face organizations are shaped by the multiplicity of larger organizations within which they are embedded.

Part IV returns to the original focus on the relation between the individual and the entire dense network of interrelated organizations of all levels and varieties: Society, the organized web of social life. Chapter 23 examines the various means by which both individuals and organizations cope with and manage these multiple role involvements. Implications for self and Society are then delineated in one last fine-tuning of the model.

The distinctive content features of this book stem significantly from the fullness and consistency of our formulation of the classic sociological approach to social psychology. The formulation is a full one in several senses.

1. Six lines of influence are here regarded as central to social psychology. Whereas every formulation gives due attention to the influence of Society (and perhaps even of social process) upon the individual, this formulation comparably examines the influence of the individual directly upon social process and indirectly upon Society, as well as the reciprocal direct influences between Society and social process.
2. In considering the influence of Society upon the individual, attention is given to the separate effects of organizational membership, role, and career.
3. All the levels and varieties of social organizations comprising Society receive comparable attention, as do a full range of basic social processes.
4. Interorganizational relations, fundamental to the concept of Society as the web of organized social life but too seldom considered in social psychology, receive extensive treatment.
5. The formulation is fully sociological in content and flavor. Considerations of social organization and social process predominate throughout; the conception of a social organization is a full-bodied one (careful not to overemphasize the aspect of social structure); and a fully sociological view of the individual is maintained—a Meadian social self adjusting multiple role-identities through interplay of the "I" and the "me" to achieve character and become a person.

Similarly, the formulation is a consistent one in several important senses.

1. One fundamental model of relations among the individual, the social, and the processual aspects is applied at each level of social organization, from the entire web of Society down to fleeting relationships and encounters.
2. One single framework is employed in characterizing each of the many diverse varieties and levels of organizations, and likewise a single framework is used in characterizing each of the diverse social processes.
3. The various social processes are not viewed in isolation but are shown to comprise an interlinked system of basic organizational processes encompassing recruitment, socialization, interaction, innovation, social control, role-making, career development, and logistical management.
4. Roles and careers are treated not as two distinct social products but as two aspects of a single resultant of social process.

Even though thoroughly sociological in its formulation, the conventional coverage of this book is greater than may be apparent. Despite a table of contents that differs sharply from those of many other textbooks in social psychology, little that is of social psychological significance is actually omitted. In a sort of figure-ground reversal, many topics which might be chapter headings in other books (topics such as altruism or person perception) become recurrent threads running through our parts and chapters, often under more sociological nomenclature.

Even in such cases, however, the sources drawn upon in this book are predominantly sociology journals and books, tapping to some degree nearly every subfield within the discipline; psychological literature is cited only where most appropriate. Even such staunch macrosociologists as Otis Dudley Duncan and Peter M. Blau are cited more frequently than any individual psychologist, and such fields as anthropology, political science, gerontology, and sociolinguistics are drawn upon as saliently as psychology.

The form and style of this book have been dictated by its one overriding aim: to produce a thorough student comprehension of fundamental princples as these apply distinctively at each organizational level. The presentation is self-consciously cumulative and progressive, building a steadily deeper appreciation of key concepts and principles and of their intricately connected implications. Formal devices include an extensive glossary and a considerable number of figures, charts, and tables displaying important connections—in many cases a progressive *series* of charts making directly visible such cumulative developments. Certain chapters (particularly Chapters 4 and 10) and sections of chapters (for example, the final section of Chapter 16, pulling together the separate societal-level chapters) are clearly marked as occasions of cumulative review and progressive integration of ideas. Nearly every chapter concludes with a carefully constructed summary to rehearse the student on its essential argument.

Stylistically, substantial reliance is placed on concrete examples and illustrations drawn from contemporary life that are meaningful in the life experience of most college students. The book does also draw upon and cite a large number and variety of theoretical and research sources, yet—unlike some other textbook styles—it does not generally dwell at length on how a study arrived at its conclusions nor on how any sustained line of research unfolded through a process of criticisms, replications, and qualifications. To do so would in this case, we are convinced, have disrupted the narrative flow of the development and defeated our central aim.

For those instructors wishing to communicate to students more of the scientific research base upon which sociological social psychology rests, we have appended to each chapter a discussion of various works suggested for additional reading; judicious assignments of outside readings from these lists may often suit the instructor's needs and purposes. In the near future we hope to prepare a companion volume of selected readings designed specifically to communicate the research base of sociological social psychology.

Some years ago, at the promptings of Alexander J. Morin and Howard S. Becker, the senior author (McCall) devised the basic framework of this book. The detailed elaboration of that framework has itself been a demanding and challenging process of

PREFACE AND ACKNOWLEDGMENTS

integrating a range of sociological literatures. Many friendly hands have joined in this work; chief among these were, at various points in time, Norman K. Denzin, Michal M. McCall, and William L. Erickson. Helpful in other ways have been many students in social psychology classes at various universities, responding to presentations of these developing materials.

It took Gladys Topkis, our editor, to extricate the project from its seemingly endless development. Her dedication, wit, and editorial skills soon elicited a completed statement of this sociological formulation. It was at that point that the history of collaboration between the two authors came to cross that of this project. Fortuitous external events provided the opportunity to resume direct collaboration, and this book is the result.

Virtually a cliché in acknowledgments sections is some nod to the forbearance of the author's family having made possible the completion of the book. Only authors can truly know how great a contribution such forbearance actually makes in trying to garner precious blocks of consecutive hours for the library and the typewriter. We are thus uncommonly grateful to our children—Sarah and Grant; Christopher and David—and to our wives—Nancy Shields and Nola Simmons—for their gracious tolerance. Working wives both, Nola has kindly and effectively prepared the glossary for this book and Nancy has contributed helpful technical insights. And both literally and allegorically, they baked the cookies, brewed the coffee and the tea.

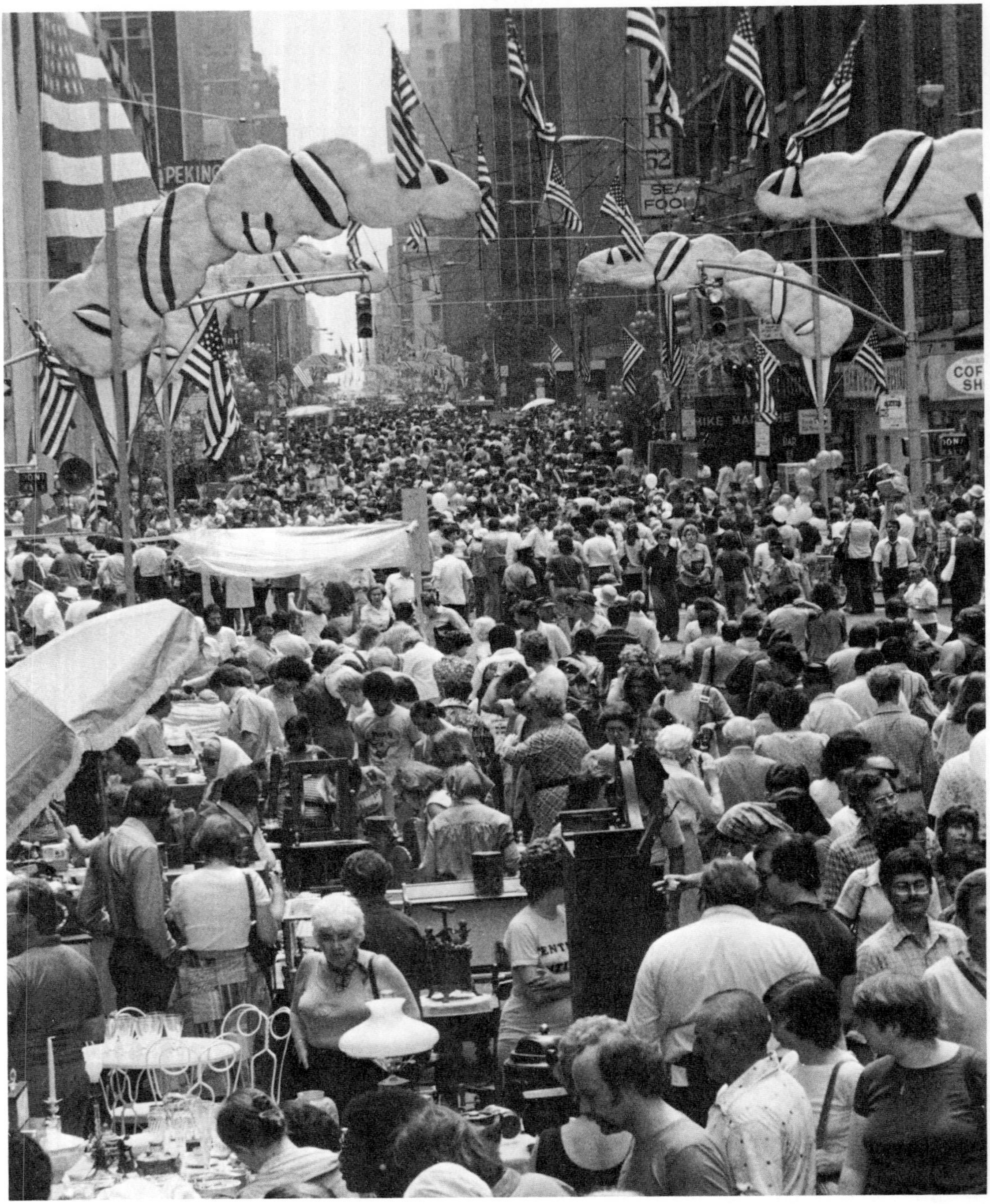

Photo courtesy of United Nations/M. Tzovaras

Approaches: An Introductory Note to the Student Reader

What is worthwhile about studying social psychology? Certainly there are many men and women who have lived full and productive lives without ever having heard of the subject. To be sure, social psychology does not provide all the answers one might like to have on hand for the very real business of living. But if sociological social psychology will not dispel all the mysteries surrounding human beings making their way through their social universe, it can at least light some candles along the way to illuminate some important and sometimes curious phenomena.

So what might a person gain from the study of this book? First, the reader can make acquaintance with an important part of our common intellectual heritage. In these pages one can get at least a brief glimpse of some ideas that have become part of the very vocabulary of modern thinking, such as "role," "organization," "community," and "relationship." Knowing more about such terms and the conceptual understandings behind them increases one's literacy and sophistication.

Second, a careful study of these pages will increase one's understanding of phenomena that, understood or not, make up a good deal of daily social living. Some degree of such knowledge is required more and more in a growing number of occupational fields—from business administration and nursing to social work and policing.

Third, there is intellectual curiosity, which can be pleasant and rewarding in itself. One might find it interesting to contemplate the profound interdependence of all the human beings on this planet, or the subtle pair relationships that tend to preoccupy us all, or the ways in which recruitment processes continue to operate throughout each person's life, or the curious "steppingstone" impacts of social change. Human beings and their organizations can be fascinating creatures in and of themselves.

Fourth, the investment of some time and energy in the study of this book can yield

APPROACHES: AN INTRODUCTORY NOTE TO THE STUDENT READER

some very practical dividends. After all, each person *lives* in a social world, peopled with other human beings and a welter of social organizations, from the government and the school to the community and the roommate. With the knowledge of this book, one can do better in his or her own social psychological "career."

The reader is no stranger to the phenomena examined in this book because they pertain to the very fabric of human life. But often one can gain a new insight into something quite familiar simply by getting some distance from it and viewing it from a different angle or a new perspective. It is our purpose to provide some of these angles and perspectives.

From the dim beginnings of history, in every society, we find men and women struggling to understand such things as human nature and its relations to society and the rest of the cosmos. Libraries are crammed with both nonfiction and dramatic books on these great subjects, and the bulk of the current research being done around the world has some bearing upon them. The focus of our study, therefore, is not new.

All of these attempts to make coherent the nature of human beings in society—from early myths to modern researches—can be roughly located somewhere along a range of approaches running from the physicalistic and biological up to the philosophical and spiritual. Each approach has its basic (often buried and implicit) premises, each has made its contributions, and each is not wholly exclusive of the others. Each approach colors, influences, and perhaps determines the very questions that are asked—as well as those that are never asked.

The *physicalistic/biological approach* has irrefutably established that the biological aspects of human beings influence both individuals and social organizations. A man in his eighties usually does not have the physiological vigor of a man in his twenties, a successful songwriter cannot function during cardiac arrest, toxins tend to lower the emotional level of a person, and (despite all commercial claims to the contrary) a woman's "mood," behavior, and even appearance tend to vary across the phases of her menstrual cycle. Even a slave camp or a totalitarian regime must take account of the fact that people need some food and sleep in order to continue being functional. All organizations that involve much of their members' time must make some provision for bathrooms and places to sit down.

These and a host of other biological influences upon social behaviors can be demonstrated, and such research has led to many improvements in human life. However, this biological approach too often misses the other side of the flow: how social factors impinge upon biological conditions. A social shock may throw off a woman's menstrual cycle; the loss of an expected Emmy award might plunge a songwriter into despair and cardiac stress; organizational decisions can produce high toxin levels, depressing body functions.

This two-way street of influences is slowly becoming better recognized, especially among leading-edge researchers and practitioners (for instance, in holistic medicine, nutrition research, epidemiological studies of social factors in disease, and psychosomatic research). In this book we will not lose sight of the fact that humans are "based" in a biological organism.

2

Approaches: An Introductory Note to the Student Reader

The *psychological approach* focuses on the individual as a unit and inquires into the internal workings of that unit and its stimulus-response exchanges with its environment, particularly with other such individual psychological units. From this perspective, social structures and organizations tend to be shadowy and less real than the persons who comprise their ranks.

This psychological approach has produced many insights into human behavior as well as a great deal of fascinating reading. We have learned much about how psychological traits relate to one another, how individuals react under stress, how many aspects of human sexuality are affected, and so on. But the social side of mankind—real to every person walking the streets of life—seems to float above and beyond the grasp of the psychological perspective. Still, as one looks around a classroom, one does see individuals as well as the class; the individual will never be lost sight of in this book.

The *sociological approach* emphasizes the group framework within which human living is carried on. Conversely from the psychological approach, here the individual often becomes something of a shadowy stick-figure, less real than the relationships, groups, and organizations of which he or she is a part. For certain analytic purposes, such as the study of populations and public opinion analyses, this can be a very useful emphasis. Sociologists have contributed greatly in a wide variety of fields, ranging from government and industry to the family and urban processes. Sociologists have particularly shed light on "emergent" social phenomena that cannot be traced back to the level of the individual and that display an independent existence, such as societies, ceremonies, ethnic traditions, and social realities in general. We will have a good deal more to say about such social realities in this book.

The *anthropological approach* has produced some of the most provocative data of recent times and has helped to break up many culture-bound fixed ideas about human nature and social institutions. Cross-cultural studies have served an invaluable function by demonstrating that a certain given is not some immutable "mother nature" truth but only a local social, psychological, and sometimes even biological habit. Because of the work done within the anthropological approach, the present book is less bound up in the tunnel vision of a particular place, station, and time than it otherwise might have been.

Finally, there is a deep, rich *philosophical approach* to humanity and its social travails. This broad perspective ranges from the cynical to the whimsical to the mystical and transcendental, and it includes some of the greatest works and most highly recognized thinkers in human history. There is no attempt to evaluate these works here, but many individuals have found answers—at least for themselves—somewhere within this perspective. Works from this perspective will not be entirely ignored in the present book.

We must emphasize two points concerning each of the broad perspectives on social man sketched above. First, each of them contains a great range of specific viewpoints within itself. The psychological approach, for instance, ranges from stark laboratory experimentalism with animals to quite rich and complex social psychological subapproaches. Likewise, sociology ranges from vast and sweeping sociocultural/historical theories, from which the individual has virtually disappeared, to subapproaches where individuals are held to generate all social reality.

Second, most researchers and practitioners cannot be easily categorized into one single perspective. There are, for example, both transcendental biologists and biological mystics. And the ordinary worker in these fields borrows what he finds useful, no matter where it came from. The various approaches are usually a matter of emphasis.

If one were to draw a model of the overlapping premises and concerns of each of the broad approaches, one would find *social psychology* in the intersection. Particularly, as the name implies, social psychology occupies an area where sociology and psychology overlap. This intersection seems the most vital to fundamental human concerns because this is "where we live" and, to borrow a term from computer language, this is the "address" of most human events.

Of course, any of the broad approaches could address this intersection, emphasizing only its own premises, variables, and questions. A religious philosopher might develop a "spiritualistic social psychology" or a biologist might develop a "physiological social psychology." Indeed, each of these might be very fascinating but each would reflect the blind spots and tunnel visions of the parent approach from which it sprang. Similarly, a psychiatrist or an economist, for example, might elect to address this intersection. Yet neither is likely to have had any formal education in psychology, sociology, or anthropology; psychiatric training is almost exclusively medical, focused on the anatomy and physiology of disordered human functioning, and the training of economists places far greater emphasis on applied mathematics than on social science knowledge.

We have studied to some extent each of the broad approaches sketched above, but most particularly psychology and sociology. We have chosen here to emphasize the sociological approach because (1) no existing textbook of social psychology seems to treat both the individual and social organizations as socially real; and (2) we have found within the sociological approach a set of concepts, premises, and questions that can especially enrich our understandings of social psychology.

Of course, this set of concepts, premises, and questions does not cover all there is to human beings and their societies. There are, for example, cosmic questions from the field of physics, on the one hand, and from the fields of religion, on the other, that we do not undertake to treat. But whatever the ultimate nature of human beings and the universe, individuals and organizations will be found to play central parts in the human drama that is the stuff of this book and so are worthy of a close examination.

First, in this agenda, we need to see where sociological social psychology came from. In the process of reconstructing this clamorous bit of intellectual history, we can already begin to learn some things about our own individual lives.

PART I

HUMAN BEINGS IN SOCIETY

Marketplace negotiation is remarkably similar to many of our daily exchanges and interactions.

CHAPTER 1

Social Psychology

As an area of intellectual inquiry, social psychology has had a peculiar history and is surprisingly difficult to characterize or define. It is obviously an important area: several thousand persons identify themselves as professional social psychologists, and courses labeled ''social psychology'' are taught in most American colleges and universities. Several scientific journals of social psychology are published, and textbooks in social psychology abound. But relatively few of these textbooks or professional social psychologists seem to agree upon a definition of the term itself. Rather, there seem to be a number of somewhat distinct social psychologies, sometimes having little more in common than the label ''social psychology'' and a concern with the broad question: *What is the social nature of man?*

This lack of conceptual unity is reflected in the history of social psychology as an academic ''discipline.'' It remains the case even today that the great majority of social psychologists have received their degrees in either psychology or sociology, merely specializing in social psychology as a subarea within one of these broader and well-established disciplines. The implications of this fact are recognized (and deplored) by many scholars.

> ''Sociological'' social psychologists stress the importance of group variables, while ''psychological'' social psychologists stress the importance of individual variables. Imperialistic tendencies are common. Some sociologists would go so far as to claim that most mental disease is a product of disturbed social connections, while some psychologists would claim that wars are the direct result of aggressive tendencies of paranoid persons. . . . The field has suffered because of the tendency of its workers to ''choose'' sides rather than to work with the data of both sociology and psychology simultaneously. To account fully and

accurately for [social behavior] it is necessary to have a dual orientation rather than two orientations [Meltzer, 1961: 43, 47].

In keeping with this evaluation of social psychology, in the mid-1950s and 1960s several universities created autonomous departments or Ph.D. programs in social psychology, with the aim of developing such a dual orientation—a social-psychological, not a psychological or a sociological, orientation. By the 1970s, however, almost all of these new departments and programs had been disbanded or subsumed under the original sociology or psychology departments. Although some impressive beginnings had been made toward the development of a convergent approach, the marriage of disciplines proved unworkable.

It is therefore perhaps more realistic to view social psychology not as a distinct discipline but as a single name for subfields within the two parent disciplines. This view is engagingly expressed by Theodore Newcomb.

> The history of social psychology may be likened to the digging of a tunnel. Sociologists did the first digging, starting from their own side of the mountain. Their information as to what lay on the psychological side of the mountain was necessarily limited and was mainly applied by way of speculation and analogy. The psychologists, who started burrowing somewhat later, had a vague sense of direction, but no map of the terrain where they needed to emerge. The two tunnels have been a-building for more than a half-century now, and they are still nowhere near meeting [Newcomb, 1948: 169–170].

Appropriately, the first two textbooks in social psychology appeared within months of each other in 1908, one by a sociologist (E. A. Ross) and one by a psychologist (William McDougall). Until very recently, when the push for a convergent orientation emerged, virtually all textbooks could be unmistakably classified as either psychological or sociological in nature.

It is important, at this point, then, to attempt to characterize social psychology as it has traditionally been viewed in psychology and in sociology. Such characterization in a few paragraphs is necessarily oversimplified; we do not suppose that the following are fully accurate accounts of the views of any particular social psychologist within either tradition. However, these sketches will enable us to emphasize some of the important divergences and parallels between the psychological and the sociological traditions of social psychology.

THE PSYCHOLOGICAL TRADITION

Traditionally, psychological social psychology might be described as "an attempt to understand and explain how the thought, feeling, and behavior of individuals are influenced by the actual, imagined, or implied presence of other human beings" (Allport, 1968: 3). The basic explanatory concept to account for individual thought, feeling, and behavior is the *personal trait* or characteristic disposition of the individual, such as rigidity, intelligence, or hostility. The individual's various traits are organized into a complex functioning entity known as the *personality,* which conditions the activation of any single trait. These traits are largely acquired—through a process of *learning,* that is, through the "conditioning" effects of favorable and unfavorable experiences with the stimulus objects of one's environment, especially other persons. For example, a person's learning history may have resulted in the formation of a trait of hostility. This trait may in turn condition his attitudes toward a large number of stimulus objects—for example, Jews. His anti-Semitic attitude is triggered by rather simple stimulus features (*cues*) that he has learned to associate with this category of objects, cues such as complexion, accent, or last name. Once triggered, this attitude then conditions his thought, feeling, and behavior toward the encountered object.

The focus on individual traits, reinforcement learning, simple stimulus features, and individual behavior lends itself to, and facilitates, controlled laboratory experiments as the basic method of research in psychological social psychology.

THE SOCIOLOGICAL TRADITION

One of the earliest sociological textbooks in social psychology crisply expressed that tradition's definition of the subfield: "Social psychology is the study of social interaction. It is based upon the psychology of group life. It begins with an interpretation of group-made types of human reactions, of communication, and . . . actions" (Ellwood, 1925: 16). Within this tradition, the core concepts are *social positions,* such as policeman or mother, and *social situations,* such as pounding the beat or breakfast. In group life, any person occupying a specified social position is provided with a recipe for his conduct in any specified social situation. The group-made recipe for "mother," for instance, contains ideas, feelings, and behaviors appropriate to her conduct in the social situation of "breakfast." Such a recipe for conduct, known as a *social role,* is the key explanatory concept in this tradition.

The individual has a considerable number of social roles, corresponding to the numerous social positions he occupies and referring to many of the social situations in which he finds himself. His set of social roles is organized in complex ways, as for instance by order of importance, into a *social self,* the integrative entity of the person. Social roles are seen as having been acquired through *socialization,* a process by which the group imparts its various recipes to the individual. A given role, or situational recipe for conduct, is triggered by the *meaning* of the person's immediate social environment. For example, if an off-duty policeman strolling with his family in the park on Sunday sees a youth tinkering with a car and interprets this behavior as an attempted theft, the role of policeman-witnessing-a-crime will come into play and he will take action in this light. The details of the action he takes will, however, be determined by the further actions of the suspicious youth—denial, flight, resistance, and so on. These actions of the youth in turn are conditioned by the social role that he adopts in the situation—tinkerer or thief—which may depend in part on whether he interprets our hero as being a policeman or a mere Sunday stroller. The role that each adopts and the actual conduct of each party depend in good part on the role and conduct of the other party. This mutual dependency of action is the *social interaction* that sociological social psychologists seek to study and explain. They seek to explain the lines of action (the respective *interactive roles*) of the parties in a joint act such as the police–citizen example.

The emphasis of this traditional approach on "group-made" factors, such as social positions, social roles, meanings, and socialization, does not lend itself so neatly to laboratory manipulations and experimentation. Research in this tradition instead has relied more heavily on questionnaire and interview methods for identifying and tracing the effects of "group-made" factors.

COMPARISON OF TRADITIONAL APPROACHES

In briefly describing each of the two major traditions in social psychology, we have identified two important contrasts between them.

First, we have seen that the psychological tradition emphasizes the individual while the sociological tradition emphasizes the "group." The former seeks to explain individual behaviors, the latter to explain social interaction; the former seeks to explain by means of individual traits acquired through learning, while the latter seeks to explain by means of social roles acquired through socialization.

Second, the two traditions differ in their characteristic styles of research. The assumptions of the psychological tradition encourage laboratory experimentation, whereas the sociological emphasis on "group-made" factors leads to survey research and other field methods.

Although these contrasts are very important and have doubtless contributed heavily to the continuing divergence between psychological and sociological practitioners (Stryker, 1977), the two traditions also exhibit striking parallels in their approaches to social psychology, as shown in Figure 1–1.

In each case, the basic explanatory concept is a type of *disposition* toward action located in the person, either a trait representing an individual disposition or a social role representing a sociocultural disposition. In each case these dispositions are organized into some type of integrative entity at the core of the person, that is, a personality or a social self. In each case these dispositions are viewed not as innate but as having been acquired, either through stimulus-response learning from one's experiences with other persons or through socialization—the purposive collective transmission of cultural wisdom and folly—conducted by the various groups in one's environment. In each case these dispositions are thought to be triggered by features of the environment, either a simple physicalistic environment (cues, especially the behavior or appearance of other individuals) or a more complex social environment (meanings of persons, acts, and situations).

These important parallels have permitted social psychologists of either tradition to envision a common field of social psychology. In fact, the parallels have become recognized more and more in the past few years, enabling social psychologists to borrow more freely from each tradition. This borrowing can be seen most readily in recent textbooks of social psychology. Virtually all textbooks published in the past

Social Psychology

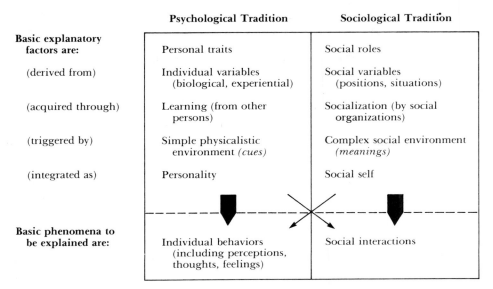

	Psychological Tradition	Sociological Tradition
Basic explanatory factors are:	Personal traits	Social roles
(derived from)	Individual variables (biological, experiential)	Social variables (positions, situations)
(acquired through)	Learning (from other persons)	Socialization (by social organizations)
(triggered by)	Simple physicalistic environment *(cues)*	Complex social environment *(meanings)*
(integrated as)	Personality	Social self
Basic phenomena to be explained are:	Individual behaviors (including perceptions, thoughts, feelings)	Social interactions

FIGURE 1-1. **Parallels and Divergences between the Psychological and Sociological Traditions in Social Psychology**

decade, whether written by psychologists or by sociologists, now, for instance, tend to define social psychology as the study of social interaction. The major differences among types of textbooks are now to be found in the relative weight given to (1) more thoroughly individual or more thoroughly social types of explanatory concepts; and (2) laboratory experimental or field research methods.

However, this recent convergence between the two traditions has proven rather strained and artificial; as noted, the marriage has failed in practice. Despite some parallels, deep divergences have remained between the two approaches involving fundamentally different assumptions about the nature of human beings in society. Indeed, these divergent assumptions pose fundamentally different questions defining the very content of social psychology.

This book examines the fundamentally *sociological* content of social psychology, leaving to others the more frequently promoted psychological and convergent approaches. Through this sociological approach, an additional understanding of the human condition may be reached, as we shall see.

THE INDIVIDUAL AND SOCIETY

The defining question of sociological social psychology is: *What is the nature of the relation between the individual and society?* This question was approached in several important ways by early sociologists before a formulation that seemed generally satisfactory was found.

HUMAN BEINGS IN SOCIETY

One early approach greatly emphasized the primacy of the individual. The so-called *phenomenological* approach, put forward by Charles Horton Cooley, among others, held that, for practical purposes of human action, society existed in the mind of the individual, in the form of his ideas of what he and other persons were like and of the relations among these persons.

> So far as the study of immediate social relations is concerned the personal idea is the real person. That is to say, it is in this alone that one man exists for another, and acts directly upon his mind. My association with you evidently consists in the relation between my idea of you and the rest of my mind. If there is something in you that is beyond this and makes no impression on me it has no social reality in this relation. *The immediate social reality is the personal idea. . . .* Society, then, in its immediate aspect, *is a relation among personal ideas.* In order to have society it is evidently necessary that persons should get together somewhere; and they get together only as personal ideas in the mind. . . . Society exists in my mind as the contact and reciprocal influence of certain ideas named "I," Thomas, Henry, Susan, Bridget, and so on. It exists in your mind as a similar group, and so in every mind. . . .

> In saying this I hope I do not seem to question the independent reality of persons or to confuse it with personal ideas. The man is one thing and the various ideas entertained about him are another; but the latter, the personal idea, is the immediate social reality, the thing in which men exist for one another, and work directly upon one another's lives. Thus any study of society that is not supported by a firm grasp of personal ideas is empty and dead—mere doctrine and not knowledge at all [Cooley, 1902: 118–119, 123–124; emphasis in original].

In this approach, we have not Jack and Jill, but rather Jack's ideas of Jill and Jill's ideas of Jack forming immediate social reality.

The contrary early approach of *group determinism* emphasized instead the primacy of society. Georg Simmel, for example, held that the individual represented essentially the unique intersection of the groups to which he belonged. The relevant characteristics of the individual are actually a sum of the characteristics of members of those various groups and are uniquely his only in that no other individual is a member of exactly the same set of groups.

> As individuals, we form the personality out of particular elements of life, each of which has arisen from, or is interwoven with, society. . . . The groups with which the individual is affiliated constitute a system of coordinates, as it were, such that each new group with which he becomes affiliated circumscribes him more exactly and more unambiguously. To belong to any one of these groups leaves the individual considerable leeway. But the larger the number of groups to which an individual belongs, the more improbable is it that other persons will exhibit the same combination of group-affiliation, that these particular groups will "intersect" once again [Simmel, 1955: 140–141; originally published 1922].

That is, if we knew enough about Jack's and Jill's group memberships, we would essentially know Jack and Jill and could predict their conduct.

A third approach, *interactionism,* takes the individual and society as equally basic and primary, viewing society as a stage or an arena and individuals as players on or in it. The stage setting constrains the character the individuals can assume, but the individuals can also affect the character of the stage, redesigning the sets, as it were. As Herbert Blumer put it,

> First, . . . the organization of a human society is the framework inside of which . . . acting units develop their actions. . . . Social organization enters into action only to the extent to which it shapes situations in which people act, and to the extent to which it supplies fixed sets of symbols which people use in interpreting their situations. . . . Second, such organization and changes in it are the product of the activity of acting units and not of "forces" which leave such acting units out of account [Blumer, 1962: 189–190].

The shaping situation is Jack and Jill sent for water. However, as acting units, these two might well redesign this scene for romantic or other purposes.

Each of these approaches has contributed lasting insights to sociological social psychology which cannot be ignored in this book. However, yet a fourth approach to the question of the individual and society has won the broadest support as a general formula. This *social process* approach, also enunciated by Cooley and Simmel, holds that society and the individual are merely two sides of the same coin, and that that primary coin is social process—the dynamic and evolutionary flow of human life itself, giving shape and substance to both persons and social groupings. Neither, say, the unhappiness of a marriage nor that of its two members is primary, but rather it is the unhappy course of events of married life that is basic and primary—failures in the social processes of marital recruitment, socialization, interaction, or social control.

> A separate individual is an abstraction unknown to experience, and so likewise is society when regarded as something apart from individuals. The real thing is Human Life, which may be considered either in an individual aspect or in a social, that is to say general, aspect; but is always, as a matter of fact, both individual and general. In other words, "society" and "individuals" do not denote separable phenomena, but are simply collective and distributive aspects of the same thing, the relation between them being like that between . . . the army and the soldiers, the class and the students, and so on. This holds true of any social aggregate, great or small. . . . So far, then, as there is any difference between the two, it is rather in our point of view than in the object we are looking at. . . .

> The organic view stresses both the unity of the whole and the peculiar value of the individual, explaining each by the other. What is a football team without a quarterback? Almost as useless as a quarterback without a team. A well-developed individual can exist only in and through a well-developed whole, and *vice versa* [Cooley, 1902: 36–37].

Thus, Cooley would have us see, for instance, that Jack and Jill's adventures on the hill affect the reputation and well-being not only of the two individuals but also of the larger community that sent them there.

This book basically adopts a combination of the social process and the interactionism approaches; that is, social process simultaneously affects the character of the individual and the character of society, *and* the character of individuals and of society jointly affect the character of social process. We shall come to see that within this formula the important insights of the first two approaches can be retained as well.

But first, a terminological problem must be clarified. When these early writers employed the term society, they did not intend it in the modern anthropological sense of some particular society, such as the Hopi or the Japanese, as distinct from other comparable societies. Rather, these early writers meant Society in the abstract, with a capital S—the web of organized social life in general. For purposes of analysis, modern sociologists do not ordinarily study this web in its entirety but break it down into smaller pieces for closer examination, with the aim of eventually putting all the pieces together again. Accordingly, through most of this book we will address not the entire web of organized social life (Society) but these smaller pieces known as "social organizations," ranging from national economies through communities and corporations down to pair relationships and encounters. Thus, in this modern scheme, the central question of sociological social psychology becomes one of the nature of the relation between the individual and social organizations.

Let us, then, reword our basic formula accordingly and sketch a picture of it (Figure 1–2) to establish more firmly the approach of this book. *Social process simultaneously affects the character of individuals and the character of social organizations,* and, in turn, *the character of individuals and that of social organizations jointly affect the character of social process.*

How would a social psychologist employ the framework depicted in Figure 1–2? One focus of research has been the influence of organizational elements, such as division of labor, on personal stability and change. For example, a large number of studies have shown that a change in occupational position has sweeping effects on a person's own self-concept. Conversely, social psychological research has also examined the influence of the individual upon the shape and performance of an organization. Numerous studies have shown, for example, that changes in top management personnel have altered the very character and fate of an organization. Social processes, such

FIGURE 1-2. Relations between the Individual and a Social Organization

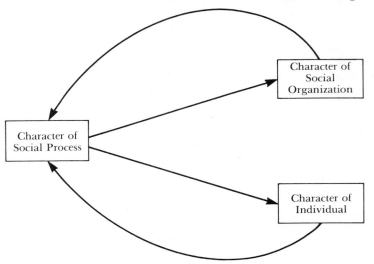

as recruitment or socialization, have been shown to be the medium through which these influences are transmitted. For instance, researchers have found that (contrary to some student views) the socialization process of schools and prisons differs sharply, leading to distinctively different impacts on the character of their respective "inmates." Similarly, individuals holding extremely discrepant personal viewpoints greatly distort the interaction process within small groups, thereby dramatically altering the group itself.

Without totally abandoning the experimental method favored by psychologists or the survey method developed by sociologists, this approach to social psychology centrally relies on the more naturalistic methods of observation for the study of organizational process and structure.

But before we draw out further implications of the approach depicted in Figure 1-2, we must clarify the character of the individual (in Chapter 2), the character of social organizations (in Chapter 3), and the character of social processes (in the chapters of Part II).

SUMMARY

Social psychology arose independently within sociology and within psychology, and these two distinctive traditions have remained fairly separate for the most part. The psychological tradition has emphasized the influence of other persons on individual functioning, whereas the sociological tradition has focused on the study of social interaction. The more thoroughly individualistic tradition of psychology has emphasized personality (as a structure of personal traits), reinforcement learning, simple stimulus features, and laboratory experimentation. The more thoroughly social tradition of sociology has placed its emphasis on "group-made" factors—social self (as a structure of social roles), socialization, meanings—and on questionnaire and interview methods of research.

Despite these deep divergences, the two traditions do display certain abstract parallels in their explanatory schemas, each invoking some type of acquired action-disposition, viewed as under the control of some sort of integrative personal structure yet triggered by some features of the environment. These highly abstract parallels have permitted some cross-fertilization between the two traditions and, recently, the preliminary development of a convergent approach to social psychology. That this convergence is a strained and somewhat artificial one is evidenced by the general failure of joint departments and programs to survive their decade of trial.

At root, the two traditions pose fundamentally different questions. The defining question of sociological social psychology concerns the nature of the relation between the individual and society. Four general answers were proposed by early sociologists. The phenomenological approach emphasized the primacy of the individual, while the group determinism approach held that society is more basic than the individual. The interactionism approach regarded the two as equally basic and primary, while the social process approach held that social process is primary, with society and the individual emerging as simply the collective and the distributive aspects of the social process of human life. This book adopts a combination of the latter two approaches, reformulated to accommodate the modern sociological practice of analyzing society into a constituent web of social organizations.

Social process simultaneously affects the character of individuals and the character of social organizations, and, in turn, the character of individuals and that of social organizations jointly affect the character of social process. Research within this fundamentally sociological approach to social psychology emphasizes the more naturalistic research methods of field observation for the study of organizational process and structure, together with the survey research and experimental methods of the convergent and traditional approaches.

SUGGESTIONS FOR ADDITIONAL READING

The intellectual history of social psychology remains without any truly adequate account. Gordon W. Allport reviews "The Historical Background of Modern Social Psychology" (in Gardner Lindzey and Elliot Aronson, eds., *The Handbook of Social Psychology,* Vol. I, 2nd ed. Reading, Mass.: Addison-Wesley, 1968). Dorwin Cartwright's "Contemporary Social Psychology in Historical Perspective" (*Social Psychology Quarterly,* 1979, 42: 82–93) deals more forthrightly with the two traditions and with the mid-century push for a convergent approach.

Perhaps the most cogent comparison of the two traditions in the contemporary period is to be found in Sheldon Stryker's "Developments in 'Two Social Psychologies': Toward an Appreciation of Mutual Relevance" (*Sociometry,* 1977, 40: 145–160). The outstanding development of the convergent approach is surely the textbook by Paul F. Secord and Carl W. Backman (*Social Psychology,* 2nd ed. New York: McGraw-Hill, 1974).

In the wake of the collapse of the movement for joint programs and departments, there has arisen a tidal wave of ferment and unrest among social psychologists. In their review of this "literature of crisis and self-criticism," Robert G. Boutilier, J. Christian Roed, and Ann C. Svendsen ("Crises in the Two Social Psychologies: A Critical Comparison," *Social Psychology Quarterly,* 1980, 43: 5–17) note substantial unrest within both traditions. For the most part, however, this unrest has centered on a loss of faith in the paradigm of psychological social psychology. See, for example, Lloyd H. Strickland, Frances E. Aboud, and Kenneth J. Gergen, eds., *Social Psychology in Transition* (New York: Plenum Press, 1976); Nigel Armistead, ed., *Reconstructing Social Psychology* (Baltimore: Penguin Books, 1974); and Alan C. Elms, "The Crisis of Confidence in Social Psychology" (*The American Psychologist,* 1975, 30: 967–976).

Through the 1970s, psychological social psychology moved away from traits and attitudes toward an emphasis on "intra-individual processes," such as attribution and person perception. Cognitive theories emphasizing active information-processing and symbolic representation systems have become widely accepted. Meanings, perceptions, and interpretations are more important in contemporary psychology. The powerful influence of the individual's real-life social matrix is more often conceded, and the likelihood that situational factors typically outweigh individual factors is now widely contemplated within psychological social psychology. Methodologically, these scholars have become rather disillusioned with laboratory experimentation and have developed a new interest in research in natural settings (see, for example, Leonard Bickman and Thomas Henchy, eds., *Beyond the Laboratory: Field Research in Social Psychology*. New York: McGraw-Hill, 1972).

An appreciation of the fundamental character of the various research methods in social psychology—experimentation, questionnaire and interview survey research, observation—can be readily obtained from any good textbook on methods of research (for example, Claire Selltiz, Lawrence S. Wrightsman, and Stuart W. Cook, *Research Methods in Social Relations,* 3rd ed., New York: Holt, Rinehart, and Winston, 1976). A better grasp of the naturalistic field methods characteristic of the sociological social psychology approach examined in this book can be obtained through a reading of Leonard Schatzman and Anselm Strauss's *Field Research: Strategies for a Naturalistic Sociology* (Englewood Cliffs, N.J.: Prentice-Hall, 1973) or our own earlier book (McCall and Simmons, *Issues in Participant Observation: A Text and Reader*. Reading, Mass.: Addison-Wesley, 1969).

Photo courtesy of Satoru Tsufura, Fieldston Lower School, the Ethical Culture Schools

In order to play together, children must communicate their individual assumptions and reach shared definitions of the situation.

CHAPTER 2

The Social Nature of Human Beings

What are the underlying assumptions of sociology regarding the nature of human beings?

If there is one thesis with which all sociological social psychologists would agree, it is that human nature is not inherent in the individual specimen of *Homo sapiens* but is somehow brought about in him by Society (that is, by social organizations).

> Man is not born human. It is only slowly and laboriously, in fruitful contact, cooperation, and conflict with his fellows, that he attains the distinctive qualities of human nature [Park, 1915: 9]

> Man does not have [human nature] at birth; he cannot acquire it except through fellowship, and it decays in isolation [Cooley, 1909: 30].

From time to time sociologists have been able to study those rare individuals who have been reared in profound social isolation—chained to a bed, locked in a closet, or wandering in the forest (for example, K. Davis, 1947). True to the sociological maxim, these "feral children" have been found to lack many of those mental processes, sentiments, and behavioral dispositions people ordinarily associate with the phrase "human nature."

These isolated individuals were found lacking in the most basic interpersonal skills, such as the abilities to joke, flirt, negotiate, or carry on a normal conversation. They were unable to make light switches or can openers work. They lacked such sentiments as sympathy and such attributes as courtesy. They might desire to breed, but they lacked any conception of marriage; they might eat but never dine; they could seek shelter but not make a home; they had wants but no long-term aspirations. They had no conception of "personal appearance." In short, they were unable to function in society.

In this chapter we will examine some of the most important sociological ideas about the social nature of the individual and his functioning. We do so in order to better understand (1) what is meant by the "character" of the individual; and (2) how it is that individual character can be affected by social organizations through the medium of social process.

INDIVIDUAL ATTRIBUTES

Sociologists share with psychologists a deep interest in certain familiar mental and behavioral attributes displayed by human individuals, such as memory, emotion, attitudes, and the like. Unlike psychologists, however, sociologists quite uniformly hold that any individual attribute is subject to the influence of social organizations.

Physical Characteristics. Virtually any bodily state can be influenced by social organizations. For example, one's adrenalin level might be elevated by a letter from the draft board or Internal Revenue Service; being jilted by her fiancé might throw off a woman's menstrual cycle.

Appearance. How one looks, smells, feels, and sounds to others can be influenced by social organizations. In one family the daughter is made pleasingly plump, while in another the daughter is made stringently slim. The grooming practices and dietary preferences of ethnic communities affect the odor of perspiration.

Personal style. The demeanor, mannerisms, communicative idiom, and expressive manner of the individual are all influenced by social organizations. For example, a soldier literally relaxes or comes to attention on command, employs a military jargon, and sprinkles his speech with "sirs."

Perceptions. What the individual perceives and what he pays attention to are heavily influenced by social organizations. Cosmetics executives discern many subtle shades of lipstick; a garage mechanic notices many distinct varieties of rattles and knocks.

Memory. The accuracies and distortions of individual memory are influenced by social organizations. Following her boss's tantrum, a secretary may forget to file the company taxes, misremember a caller's name, but remember to unplug the coffee pot. A mother can accurately recall the precise birthweights of all her grown children but "remembers" their school grades as having been higher than they were.

Feelings and emotions. The individual's emotional reactions to any object or event can be influenced by social organizations. For example, some married women view with alarm any attractive female in their husbands' offices, and a Social Security increase engenders joy among recipients but resentment among employers.

Attitudes, opinions, judgments, and evaluations. How the individual evaluates a given object or event is influenced by social organizations. Attitudes toward marijuana are highly responsive to peer-group cultures, and one's opinion on the Palestine question often reflects one's political party affiliation.

Interests, goals, desires, wants, and plans. What the individual strives to attain or obtain is influenced by social organizations. Madison Avenue can successfully promote a new product, a candidate, or even a war. The well-raised Russian strives to be a good socialist and the well-raised Afghan takes pride in being a faithful Muslim.

Acts and habits. What an individual does—now and/or recurrently—is influenced by social organizations. A good deal of any person's daily round is established by the demands of his or her organizational memberships—job, family, and friendship circles. The housewife cooks supper for her family as part of her role; she makes pizza habitually, because the family prefers it to fish.

Skills and abilities. What the individual is able to do well, poorly, or not at all is influenced by social organizations. A native Bushman cannot type, an Andes porter can carry heavy jugs upon his head, and a Viking youth could catch a spear with either hand.

Personal resources. The resources an individual can mobilize for action (knowledge, intelligence, beauty, wealth, possessions, opportunities) are influenced by social organizations. Shifts in the job market can drastically affect a breadwinner's opportunities, and on-the-job training might enable a paramedic to save his child's life in an emergency. More exotically, through such futuristic technologies as genetic engineering and bionics, social organizations can influence such deeply personal features as life span, types of illness, private fantasies, heart beat, and even the DNA structure of the cells.

At a minimum, then, all these sorts of personal attributes, influenced by social organizations, must be included in what we mean by the character of the individual. But how does the individual obtain this character? The answer starts with the central concept of social role.

SOCIAL ROLES

As we shall see in Chapter 3, a social organization is not homogeneous but is structurally differentiated. That is, baseball teams are made up not simply of baseball players but of pitchers, catchers, outfielders, and so on; train crews are made up not simply of railroaders but of engineers, conductors, and brakemen. Within any organization various *positions* may be recognized—a concept on which we shall elaborate in the next chapter, but one that is familiar enough in ordinary life. In sociology, such organizational positions are conventionally referred to as *social positions*.

HUMAN BEINGS IN SOCIETY

All of us have come to learn quite a lot about many social positions we have contact with. We may know a good deal about quarterbacks, bus drivers, bank tellers, or nurses. This knowledge is of two kinds. One kind is quite generalized, covering the characteristic traits, habits, skills, and so on, of quarterbacks or bank tellers. The second kind of knowledge is more situational, covering how a quarterback or a bank teller will act, think, and feel in one situation as opposed to another. For example, we know that a quarterback likes to call a pass play when his team is near midfield but a running play when it is near its own goal line. Thus, we have *expectations* about known social positions. We anticipate what kind of person a quarterback will be—clever, knowledgeable, authoritative, decisive, a bit of a gambler. We also anticipate what he would do, think, or feel in a given type of situation. These general and situational anticipations make life easier for us—easier to play football against a quarterback or drive on the same street with a bus driver.

This rewarding consequence of informed expectations is in fact so valuable to us that we often get angry or upset when our expectations about a social position are violated—when a quarterback, bus driver, or bank teller crosses up our expectations by acting ''uncharacteristically.'' We often protest or even retaliate in some fashion. Sociologists would say that we ''exert negative sanctions.'' This kind of response indicates that our expectations are *normative* as well as anticipatory. That is, we not only believe that the bus driver will act a certain way but also feel that he *should* act this way.

If we reward him sufficiently for doing so and punish him sufficiently for not doing so, it is quite likely that he will typically do, feel, think, or look as we expect him to—an instance of what sociologists call a ''self-fulfilling prophecy'' (Merton, 1957; Jones, 1977). This self-reinforcing aspect of expectations is in good part responsible for the fact that we are indeed able to know a great deal about bus drivers, nurses, and other social positions.

The expectations people hold regarding a social position constitute a *social role*. As noted, any social organization encompasses more than one social position. A basketball team of, say, sixteen players contains only five positions; two or three players share any one position, in some alternating fashion. No matter who happens to be playing that position at any particular moment, the other players hold certain expectations concerning the position of, say, strong forward or point guard. That is, a person becomes subject to ''role expectations'' not as an individual but by virtue of occupying a particular social position.

Such role expectations vary, however, in two important ways: (1) in the extent to which they have been communicated to the position occupant; and (2) in the degree of consensus or agreement by others concerning the expectations held toward a position. A role expectation may be clearly or only vaguely communicated to the occupants of, say, position *A* by the occupants of the other positions. Moreover, that expectation may be more or less consensual; for example, the occupants of position *A* may or may not accept that communicated expectation or perhaps the occupants of position *A* (or of position *B,* for that matter) cannot agree to view that position in the same way. Needless to say, those expectations that are clear and consensual are more likely to exert the self-fulfilling effect we have mentioned.

The Social Nature of Human Beings

A social position (*A*) always exists within a network of related positions, and the occupants of each of the other positions hold expectations toward position *A*. Such expectations may diverge one from the other, and indeed may even prove competing or conflicting. In some cases, the incompatible expectations stem from occupants of two or more different social positions. For example, a customer may expect the bank teller to be sociable whereas her supervisor expects her to be businesslike. In other cases, the incompatible expectations may stem from a single related position. The bank teller's supervisor may expect her to answer all phone calls promptly and yet to service all her customers at the window immediately. In either case, such competing or conflicting expectations naturally tend to diminish the force of their self-fulfilling properties.

The social role for a position is, then, some aggregate of the expectations held toward that position by the occupants of all the other positions within that network, with the expectations of some weighing more than others. Expectations carried over from the person's past position experiences may also be included in this aggregate, as we shall see.

To the extent that the various role expectations comprising a social role are clear, consensual, and compatible, these expectations tend to be self-fulfilling in nature. A cardinal principle of sociological social psychology is that *an individual tends to become the kind of person he is expected to be* as an occupant of a social position *with a consistently and clearly defined social role.*

HUMANS AS SOCIAL BEINGS: OTHERS AND REFERENCE PROCESSES

But of course, thrusting upon the individual a set of normative social expectations concerning his or her personal attributes would not produce those attributes unless that person decided, or was constrained, to *comply* with those expectations. But why would one comply? Why doesn't a person just do as he or she pleases?

Sociologists point to the solid biological fact that humans are (and always have been) one of the relatively rare mammals that are *social-living,* whose adult members sleep and forage for existence in close proximity and in sustained interaction with other adults the year around (Wynne-Edwards, 1962). The members of all such species are highly interdependent for survival, whether in terms of defense, foraging, child-rearing, or other functions. Not fortuitously, members of any social-living species also prove to be *psychologically* interdependent. Emotional dependence is most readily demonstrated; in the face of fear, discomfort, boredom, or joy, any social-living animal reliably seeks social contact with his fellows for the physical and behavioral comfort and nurturance they can provide. Deprived of such social contact and emotional nurturance, a young social animal fails to display the normal developmental pattern—physically, emotionally, and intellectually (Hebb, 1955); Harlow and Harlow, 1962). Those of his fellows who provide the individual with such psychological support become his *significant others* (M. H. Kuhn, 1964); indeed, Cooley (1909) believed that it is through interaction with significant others—people with whom the individual has deep personal bonds—that one acquires those sentiments and traits we consider to be "human nature." In the bizarre world of the Nazi concentration camp (Bettelheim, 1943), some inmates were even driven to reliance on and slavish identification with their captors in the absence of alternative significant others. Among *all* social-living animals, the individual's alertness to and emotional dependence on the signals of approval, acceptance, recognition, cooperation, and tolerance by his significant others are clearly marked (e.g., Fox, 1971).

Over and above these primordial interdependencies of all social-living species stands the more distinctively human interdependency of the social division of labor (Durkheim, 1933). Capitalizing on the economic efficiencies of job specialization and economic exchange, human populations have elaborated the division of labor to such lengths that no single individual, group, or even community in the modern world can be regarded as self-sufficient, in the sense that it could long survive on its own resources (O. D. Duncan, 1964). In fact, there is a planetary level of human interdependence, as we will see in Chapter 12.

In view of these primordial and cultural interdependencies, other persons largely limit what an individual is able or permitted to do. Without the cooperation, approval, or at least tolerance of others, the individual is largely powerless to pursue his own interests. Therefore, he very much wants at least *some* others to view him appropriately and favorably.

> In human society every act of every individual tends to become a gesture, since what one does is always an indication of what one intends to do. The consequence is that the individual in society lives a more or less public existence, in which all his acts are anticipated, checked, inhibited, or modified by the gestures and the intentions of his fellows. It is in this social conflict . . . that human nature and the individual may acquire their most characteristic and human traits [Park, 1927: 738].

> Human behavior is fundamentally neither reflexive, instinctive, nor even habitudinal merely, but conventional and rational, that is to say, governed by rules, codes, and insitutions; controlled by fashion, etiquette, and public opinion. . . . Conduct is that form of behavior we expect in man when he is conscious of the comment that other men are making, or are likely to make, upon his actions [Park, 1931: 36].

The individual's desire for others to view him appropriately and favorably is complicated by the fact that these other persons do not comprise a homogeneous set. Instead, they represent a diverse plurality of organizations and individuals—each pursuing different interests, each imposing different codes and role expectations, each sponsoring a distinctive perspective on the social world, each making distinctive comment on the individual's actions.

Reference-group theory (Hyman and Singer, 1968) attempts to set forth the principles underlying the individual's differential receptivity to these various organizations and individuals and his differential use of the perspectives on the social world that each of these sponsors (Shibutani, 1955). A *reference group* is an organization or person that has in some fashion *impressed* the individual, in either a positive or a negative manner, which that person then employs as a basis for self-evaluation and attitude formation. It should be emphasized that a reference group need not be an organization in which he holds membership, and a reference other (Schmitt, 1972) need not be a person with whom he shares a personal relationship. A youth from the poor section of town will demonstrably be influenced by his neighborhood peers, but he may also aspire to the manners and the standards of the country-club set.

Reference-group selection is not a passive or automatic process; the person does some choosing in terms of his or her own predispositions. For example, parents are continually surprised and sometimes shocked when they learn whom their children are adopting as reference others—Luke Skywalker, Charles Manson, Billy Graham, or the old recluse living next door.

There are two ways in which the individual uses a reference group or reference other. First, he uses them in developing and imposing standards of belief, feeling, and conduct. Social reality is highly ambiguous, and the "social validation" of a viewpoint provided by a reference group or reference other is often sorely needed by the individual. Second, he uses them as a source of comparison for measuring and judging himself and other persons (including the reference other). The individual's sense of self-worth greatly depends on this use of reference groups and reference others. In real life, a single reference group is commonly used by the person for both of these functions—normative and comparative—but sometimes for only one of them. A boy may pattern his speech after Muhammad Ali but judge his school grades in comparison with his own sister.

The organizational complexity of Society virtually forces the social individual to choose and rely upon reference groups and reference others in order to overcome the difficulties of maintaining necessary social supports. The basic sociability and interdependence of human beings are major factors in the individual's readiness to comply, at least to some extent, with the set of normative social expectations brought to bear on him through his social roles.

HUMANS AS COGNITIVE BEINGS: THE SELF[1]

As implied by his engagement in these reference-group processes, the human being is very much a thinker, a creature of symbolic proclivities far exceeding those of other species. Human beings dream and scheme, envision and imagine, anticipate and reminisce. From these symbolic abilities a number of crucial social psychological principles can be extracted—principles that give rise to the very nature and content of social reality. These principles were first set forth by George Herbert Mead in a series of brilliant works (1932, 1934, 1938).

1. *Man is a thinker, a planner, a schemer.* He continuously constructs plans of action (what Mead called "impulses") out of bits and pieces of plans left lying around by his culture, fitting them together in endless combinations of the larger patterns and motifs that the culture presents as models. This ceaseless planning is carried on at all levels of awareness, not always verbally but always conceptually, not always in words but

---

[1] This section is based on McCall and Simmons (1978), pp. 52–60, 64–65, 83–84.

always in meanings. Part of the story of Jack and Jill would therefore be Jack's subjective musings about Jill and his inner thoughts about the journey up the hill.

2. *Things take on meaning in relation to plans.* The meaning of any "thing" (as a bundle of stimuli, in Mead's sense) can be taken as its implications for the plans of action man is always constructing. Its meaning can be thought of as the answer to the question, "Where does it fit into the unfolding scheme of events?" If a plan of action is visualized in the form of a flow chart, things may be regarded as the nodes or points at which choices must be made between alternative courses of action: "Where do we go from here?" It can be seen from this description that the same "thing" can present different *meanings* relative to different plans of action. An ordinary beer bottle, for instance, can mean two very different things, depending on whether one is contemplating a cool drink or barroom violence. But to the extent that we have all absorbed the same plans of action from the culture, the thing can yet have consensual meaning. A beer bottle, after all, is still a beer bottle, whatever our momentary proclivities may be. Thus, for both Jack and Jill, the hill might represent either an arduous climb or an opportunity to be alone, away from their families, but it remains a hill.

3. *We act toward things in terms of their meaning for our plan of action.* Otherwise stated, the execution of our plan of action is contingent upon the meaning *for that plan* of every "thing" we encounter. If we bend down to pick up a stick and that stick turns out to be a dead snake—or vice versa—the chances are that the original plan of action will be suspended and superseded by some other plan. Jack might be happy about the pail as an opportunity for covertly holding hands, or he might view it as a chance to show off his strength to Jill, or he might kick it resentfully as being part of an encumbering chore to be gotten over speedily so that he can lie around the house.

4. *Therefore, we must identify every "thing" we encounter and discover its meaning.* We have always to be identifying (categorizing, naming) the "things" we encounter and interpreting (construing, reconstructing) them to determine their meanings for our plans of action. Until we have made out the identity and meaning of a thing vis-à-vis our plans, we have no bearings; we cannot proceed effectively. In the case of those distinctive "things" that are other human beings, the principal categories employed in identifying persons are social positions such as husband, major general, third baseman, first violinist, Lutheran, Irishman, Fuller Brush man, "young man of great promise," or plant manager. By identifying persons in terms of their social positions, we are afforded "lead time" in coping with them, for we may know what implications people in such positions have for our plans of action and we can modify our conduct accordingly. It should also be noted here that social roles contain within them distinctively social plans of action; for example, the role of mother may contain within it the social plan for preparation and staging of the social event called "breakfast." For this reason Jack and Jill must each determine whether the other is romantically available, if each is considering a romantic plan of action.

5. *For social plans of action, the meanings of "things" must be consensual.* If a plan of action involves more than one person and we encounter a "thing" whose meaning for this plan of action is unclear—not consensual among those involved—the meaning

must be hammered out by collective effort in the give-and-take of social interaction. A strolling couple, for example, encountering a sudden rain shower, can define the falling droplets as a threat to their clothing or as a romantically adventurous walk in the rain. Being the product (or object) of this collective effort, the consensually arrived-at meaning is a "social object," according to Mead. This meaning will seldom be clear and identical in the minds of all concerned, yet it will still be consensual in the pragmatic sense that the understanding will at least be sufficiently common to permit the apparent mutual adjustment of individual lines of action, whether in cooperation or conflict. Each member of the strolling couple will yet retain his or her own version of the event. In that most important case of persons as "things," the collective process of establishing the meaning of a person crucially involves arriving at *some* consensual identification of that person's current and latent social role. In order to proceed with *any* scenario, Jack and Jill must arrive at some minimal agreement on the "real" nature of their trip up the hill.

6. *The basic "thing" to be identified in any situation is the person himself.* For each individual actor there is one key "thing" whose identity and meaning must be consensually established before all else—namely, oneself. "Who am I in this situation? What implications do I have for the plans of action, both active and latent, of myself and of the others?" The answers to these questions, if *consensually* arrived at as described above, constitute the "character" of that person in that situation. Self qua character, then, is not only a personal thing but also a social object, in Mead's sense. Among all the possibilities, Jack and Jill—through the give-and-take of their interaction—must arrive at the part each will play before they can proceed with "their story."

According to Mead, the individual achieves selfhood at that point at which he first begins to act toward himself in more or less the same fashion in which he acts toward other people. When he does so, he is said to be "taking the role of the other toward himself." It is important not to become confused by this phrase. The individual, John Doe, *is* still himself, and others act with respect *to* him. But when he too begins to act toward John Doe in some similar fashion, he can be said to be serving *in the role of* an other toward himself. It is still he who is doing this responding, even though he is also the object toward which he is responding. In other words, he is now "self-conscious." This reflexiveness is what William James (1890) meant when he wrote that the self as subject and the self as object—the "I" and the "me"—are distinct but inseparable.

Mead used the terms "I" and "me" in a similar but importantly different sense. Both James and Mead took over Kant's definition of the "I" as the essentially unknowable active agent of the personality—that which does the thinking, the knowing, the planning, the acting. Whereas James meant by the "me" all those aspects of the personality that the "I" knows and cares about, Mead meant something rather different. By the "me," Mead meant all those *perspectives* on himself that the individual has learned from others—the *attitudes* that the "I" assumes toward his own person when he is taking the role of the other toward himself (as discussed above regarding reference-group processes).

If the "I" and the "me" constitute the totality of the self, this self is best seen in what Mead called the "inner forum," the silent internal conversation that is continually going on inside the human being. But we should not think of this conversation as a simple dialogue between something called the "I" and something called the "me." Ordinarily, one's mind is reacting to what one is saying or thinking as one is saying or thinking it. One monitors oneself throughout the process and from multiple perspectives and contexts. The "me" consists merely of the accumulated frames of reference in terms of which the mind appraises and evaluates and monitors the ongoing thought and action of its own person, the "I."

Sociologists emphasize the profound importance of this continual self-appraisal, carried on in terms of standards internalized from significant others and reference groups but individually elaborated. As Mead and others have suggested, this process is the basis for that intelligent, controlled, socialized behavior of which we are so proud, the singular accomplishment of the human species.

> One thing that distinguishes man from the lower animals is the fact that he has a conception of himself, and once he has defined his role he strives to live up to it. He not only acts, but he dresses the part, assumes quite spontaneously all the manners and attitudes that he conceives as proper to it. Often enough it happens that he is not fitted to the role which he chooses to play. In any case, it is an effort for any of us to maintain the attitudes which we assume; all the more difficult when the world refuses to take us at our own estimates of ourselves. Being actors, we are consciously or unconsciously seeking recognition, and failure to win it is, at the very least, a depressing, often a heartbreaking, experience. . . .
>
> The consequence of this, however, is that we inevitably lead a dual existence. We have a private and a public life. In seeking to live up to the role which we have assumed, and which society has imposed upon us, we find ourselves in a constant conflict with ourselves. Instead of acting simply and naturally, as a child, responding to each natural impulse as it arises, we seek to conform to accepted models, and conceive ourselves in some one of the conventional and socially accepted patterns. In our efforts to conform, we restrain our immediate and spontaneous impulses and act, not as we are impelled to act, but rather as *seems appropriate and proper to the occasion.*
>
> Under these circumstances our manners, our polite speeches and gestures, our conventional and proper behavior, assume the character of a mask. . . . In a sense, and in so far as this mask represents the conception which we have formed of ourselves, the role we are striving to live up to, this mask is our "truer self," the self we should like to be. So, at any rate, our mask becomes at last an integral part of our personality; becomes second nature. We come into the world as individuals, achieve character, and become persons [Park, 1927: 738–739; emphasis added].

These remarks on the self by Park suggest that there is more than a little of the theatrical in ordinary human conduct. Indeed, this idea has been a prevalent theme in sociological social psychology, from Mead's early writings on role down to the more recent elaborate "dramaturgical" frameworks (Goffman, 1959b; Brissett and Edgley, 1974).

The key concepts in theatrical performance are character, role, and audience. The first two are very closely intertwined and must be carefully differentiated. In the fullest sense, a *character* is a person with a distinctive organization of such personal characteristics as appearance, mannerisms, habits, traits, and motives. A *role,* on the other hand, is the characteristic and expectable conduct truly expressive of that character. If the actor's performance (all those actions that can be construed as relevant to the role) is congruent with that role, the audience of relevant others attributes to him the corresponding character. The audience is satisfied with the conduct and is absorbed in the emergent dramatic reality. If, however, the actor's performance is incongruous, his audience regards him as "out of character."

Of course, the success or failure of a performance is not entirely in the hands of the actor himself. The props and supporting cast can often make or break an actor's performance, whatever his own ability. In an important sense, then, the success of an actor's performance depends on whether or not each entire *scene* of the play is well-staged, is brought off as socially real.

In this dramaturgical analogy, even the audience is a factor in the performer's success. No matter how brilliant the script, characters and their roles are always largely implicit; much of the art of acting and directing lies in fleshing out the skeletal anatomy of characters and roles as they are suggested in the meager lines and stage directions. Audiences, as well as actors, differ widely in their ability to see plausible characters and roles in what are merely parts, in their ability to clothe these parts with dramatic reality. The same performance may strike one audience as overdrawn and entirely unconvincing, yet it may impress a more naïve audience as nightmarishly gripping.

All of this is theater, yet it serves to illuminate much of real-life social conduct. If each of us has a part to play in the larger drama of social life, in terms of the position we occupy in the web of social organizations, we must first conceive the role implicit in that position and perform in a manner expressive of that role if we are at last, in Park's terms, "to achieve character and become persons."

From this dramaturgical perspective, what we have been referring to as the "I," the active agent of the self, can be thought of as the *performer*. And the "me" can profitably be thought of as the very important internal *audience* of that performer. If a performer is successful, he is never seen by his audience as an "actor" but as the character he strives to represent. There is, then, yet a third aspect of the social self, the self as "*character*."

Following Goffman's brilliant work (1959b: 80–81, 253–255), we recognize three aspects of the social self:

1. the self as performer (the active aspect)
2. the self as audience to that performer (the evaluative aspect)
3. the self as character performed (the communicated aspect).

We must recognize that the person does not think about himself abstractly but rather thinks *something about* himself, about his thoughts, actions, and other personal characteristics. He develops quite specific and concrete images, attitudes, opinions, expectations, standards, and feelings toward his own person, just as he does toward other persons. Because any of these other persons plays a number of somewhat divergent social roles, our individual's conceptions of that other person are likely to be somewhat role-specific; he may think differently about his boss as a golfer or mother than as an employer. Similarly, our individual's conceptions of his *own* person are likely to be role-specific (McCall and Simmons, 1978; Stryker, 1968; Burke, 1980). A *role-identity* is his imaginative view of himself as an occupant of a particular social position. Or, to put it in dramaturgical terms, a role-identity may be defined as the character and the role an individual devises for himself as an occupant of that position. These role-identities provide plans of action for the self as performer, evaluative standards for the self as audience, and communicable personal qualities for the self as character.

Each individual has, of course, a good many such role-identities—at least one for each social position he occupies, aspires to occupy, or has considered occupying. A person's set of role-identities is organized in complex fashion. The most distinctive aspect of this organization is the hierarchical arrangement of role-identities in terms of their individual prominence in the person's considerings about himself. Some of his identities are more important to him than others, and the contents of these more prominent identities lend continuity and direction to the person's life. This prominence hierarchy of identities (sometimes called the "ideal self") is not the sole personal determinant of conduct, however, for if it were, only the most prominent role-identities would ever be performed. Indeed, organizations and other people frequently cajole and badger individuals into performing roles that may *not* be prominent in the person's own self-concerns.

Other factors, closely linked to the person's short-run life situation, very often cause less prominent role-identities to become temporarily quite salient ("up front") in the person's actions. We must therefore be careful to distinguish the very fluid *hierarchy of salience* (sometimes called the "situational self") from the relatively enduring *hierarchy of prominence* of role-identities (the ideal self). For example, a man's work role as manager might be most prominent, yet his mother's illness may prompt his family role as son temporarily to overshadow all his other role-identities.

At any rate, it should be recognized that *self-appraisal* and *self-judgment,* like social appraisal and social approval or disapproval from others, are very significant factors in determining whether an individual will comply with the social expectations incumbent upon him by virtue of occupying a set of social positions.

HUMANS AS RATIONAL BEINGS: "ECONOMIC MAN" AND SOCIAL TRANSACTIONS

We have emphasized that the human individual is a creature of countless impulses—constantly thinking, planning, scheming—but that most of these impulses are in the end not acted upon but are inhibited or suppressed by self or others. On what basis are some of an individual's multitudinous impulses (plans of action) selected for actual performance?

Sociologists consider that, for the most part, that basis is *rational choice from the person's viewpoint,* a cognitive (if not always conscious) deliberation regarding alternative actions. People choose among alternative plans of action on the basis of the expected consequences of each alternative. That is to say, they weigh the expected outcomes or payoffs of those alternative plans of action. According to the concept of rationality, no rational actor would choose an action which he expects to have a "worse" outcome, all things considered, than the expected outcomes of his alternative possibilities. "Better" is to be preferred over "worse," and "more" over "less." Of course, full rationality would require consideration of all empirically possible alternatives as well as a complete knowledge of the contingencies and consequences of each. Needless to say, this is impossible. Instead, people display "bounded rationality" (Simon, 1957), considering at any time only a limited subset of all possible alternatives and then choosing on the basis of less than complete knowledge. Therefore, one does not ordinarily maximize payoffs but one optimizes (or at least "satisfices") them. That is, one does not ordinarily choose the absolutely "best" possible action but only the best relative to one's limited set of alternatives (or at least chooses one that is "good enough").

Man's less than total rationality reflects the fact that while he has potentially unlimited wants and impulses, he has limited abilities and resources, including time, to pursue them. *Economic rationality* is a matter of optimizing (or at least satisficing) a set of wants in the face of finite resources. An economically rational actor, in principle, will allocate his resources among alternative projects in such a way as to expect to "do pretty well" for as many as possible of his numerous wants. Indeed, it is on such a criterion of economic rationality that the individual is generally thought to choose among plans, roles, and identities.

Any action consequence that satisfies some want or interest is a *benefit*. Many actions or performances are gratifying in themselves in that they bring various bodily pleasures or relieve certain bodily discomforts or afford a sense of pleasure in exercising competence. Making a good pot of coffee, landing an airplane, and getting the monthly bank statement balanced are gratifying in themselves. That such performances are enjoyable in themselves is indicated by the fact that people are willing to incur certain costs simply to be allowed to perform them. Some will put up with aches and pains to climb a mountain.

Other performances may be gratifying mainly because they gain us certain benefits that in turn are useful to us in pursuing our various endeavors. Money, labor, information, material goods, privileges, favors, social status, and more may be helpful in carrying out our enterprises. As a consequence, these acquire a certain value of their own, and we may be willing to incur certain costs simply to acquire them.

Aside from *intrinsic* gratifications gained in performances and *extrinsic* gratifications gained through performances, the most distinctively human type of benefit is *role-support,* the communicated support accorded by one's audience for one's claims concerning one's role-identity. Because both others and self constitute important audiences, we should distinguish social support from self-support, within this broader category of role-support. To gain role-support of either variety, an individual is willing to incur certain costs. A dancer will arduously practice for weeks to win that eventual applause from her audience, and some wives will cook for many hours to elicit a brief "Good meal!" from their husbands.

Costs include not only the expenditure of a scarce resource such as time, energy, and material possessions, but also "opportunity costs," the forgoing of benefits from alternative actions that might have been taken. To gain the benefits of beach living, one must forgo the potential benefits of the Rocky Mountain lifestyle.

An economically rational actor is one who chooses on the basis of his or her own benefit–cost analysis of alternative plans of action. If we define *profit* as the benefits of an action minus the costs of that action, we may characterize an economically rational actor as one who chooses among alternatives on the basis of *his or her own* analysis of the comparative expected profitability of those alternatives.

Any act produces benefits and costs for other persons as well as for the performer. This ripple effect of action consequences is yet another important source of human interdependence; within any situation, *A*'s choices have consequences for *B*, while *B*'s choices have consequences for *A*. There are two modes of social transaction in the face of this interdependence—behavior exchange and behavior coordination (Kelley and Thibaut, 1978). *Behavior exchange* is a trade. In this mode, each performer chooses on the basis of his own individual benefit/cost ratio, bargaining where he must, in a classic "I'll scratch your back if you'll scratch mine" fashion. *Behavior coordination,* on the other hand, is a joint venture. In the behavior coordination mode, each performer chooses on the basis of the *joint* consequences of their respective actions, conferring (rather than bargaining) on joint alternatives. The lawyer confers with his client regarding their strategy, but he bargains with the other side. Parents confer with each other about their child's education and bargain with him about washing the dishes.

Exchange

Social exchange theories (Homans, 1974; Chadwick-Jones, 1976; Emerson, 1976) envision a market for the trading of performances, in which each participant gives some of his resources to another in return for somewhat different resources from the other. This market relies upon "shopping around," "making deals," "haggling," and "driving a hard bargain." Each participant considers the benefits and the costs to himself of any potential exchange, relative to alternative possible exchanges, and decides whether this exchange would be sufficiently profitable to him. From such a perspective, social interaction takes on an aspect of a *bargaining* process of bids and counterbids leading to an eventual agreement on a "rate of exchange" or to a breakoff of negotiations. In every human encounter, the participants bargain over the kinds and quantities of benefits that each will give (or permit) the others in return for the kinds and amounts he hopes to receive (or be permitted).

This bargaining is ordinarily quite subtle and smooth, but it may become quite obvious and uncertain of outcome. The routine daily give-and-take exchanges between marital partners, for example, might require no words at all, but a contemplated move might invoke explicit and even heated negotiations over the allocation of rooms in the new house. The bargaining process is not entirely ruthless or unprincipled but is conducted with at least one eye toward certain rules of the marketplace. One such rule seems to be that the obtained benefits of each party must be at least somewhat comparable *within each category of benefit:* extrinsic benefits for extrinsic, intrinsic for intrinsic, role-support for role-support (McCall and Simmons, 1978: 151). For example, an exchange of sex for money is generally frowned upon.

Perhaps the most widely discussed rule of social exchange is the norm of *distributive justice,* which specifies that a fair exchange between two persons is one in which the outcomes for each participant are directly proportional to his or her investments. Violations of this norm are viewed as exploitations and ripoffs and lead to tension, dissatisfaction, and a desire for change.

Obviously, social comparisons of the sort entailed by the norm of distributive justice typically involve reference others or reference groups, which (in their comparative function) serve as a standard or point of comparison against which the individual may measure the adequacy of his outcomes.

Coordination

Joint ventures are at least as important as trades. Human beings must rely on coordination and cooperation, as well as exchange, to accomplish the business of living. A person who is not responsive to other people's outcomes can scarcely function in any social setting. Such a stark individualist may not be bothered by this incapacity, but at that moment he tends back toward "feral man" (those profoundly isolated individuals discussed at the beginning of this chapter).

No one takes into account the interests of all other beings, and no one always subordinates his personal interests to those of others. However, at the very least, human interdependence leads a person to consider benefits and costs for his significant others along with his own. In the very process of being a mother, a woman considers her child as well as herself; an employer must pay some heed to the interests of his employees as well as his profit ledger.

Indeed, many common social realities are joint ventures, as Mead has already shown us. A party can exist only through the actions of guests; a wedding only through the arrival of the bride and groom; a band only through the coordinated performances of its players.

Whether through trade or joint venture, the individual's compliance with his set of social expectations will be influenced by his appraisal of the benefits and costs for self and others.

HUMANS AS ACTIVE BEINGS: SOCIAL INTERACTION[2]

According to Mead, any act of any animal consists of three components or stages:

1. There are in the animal *impulses* (incipient acts) seeking enactment.
2. The animal then encounters *stimuli* favoring one or another of these incipient acts.
3. There follows a *response* to these stimuli in terms of the favored impulse.

[2] This section is based on McCall and Simmons (1978), pp. 78, 121-154.

Acts, in this view, are present in latent form in the animal and are *released*, not "stimulated," by configurations of stimuli that the animal *seeks out* in order to fulfill these impulses or incipient acts. A hungry person does not simply salivate at the sight of food but actively explores the refrigerator. The animal is thus not a passive robot merely reacting to the environment of stimuli but an active agent seeking to *act upon* that environment or, as Mead would say, to *create* the objects of his environment, in the sense, previously noted, that plans of action confer meaning on "things." Acts create objects; that is, meaningless "things" are converted to meaningful "objects" through acts. For example, the act of chopping vegetables and placing them in an attractive bowl before the supper guests creates the object "salad."

The action *situation* in which an individual finds himself at a given moment is comprised of some configuration of "things." The meaning or significance of that situation—what sociologists call the *definition of the situation*—depends on the active and latent plans of action of the individual. A hotdog cart on a footpath in the park may be defined as a chance to get a bite or as an irritating obstacle, depending on whether the person is a hungry stroller or a jogger.

Social acts, involving the coordinated activity of more than one performer, require the fitting together of the individual lines of action of those participants (Stokes and Hewitt, 1976). This in turn requires some shared or social definition of the situation—some consensual agreement regarding the nature of the objects these participants encounter. If individual acts generate objects, *social acts* generate *social objects*.

By what means do the participants in a social act construct a social definition of the situation and join together their individual lines of action?

First, consider the matter of constructing a social definition of the situation. One pair of cognitive processes and one pair of expressive processes are involved in this construction.

Cognitive Processes in Social Acts

Cognitive processes have to do with judging the meaning of those key "things" in a situation that are the participants themselves. Thus, this pair of processes has a certain logical priority in the development of a definition of the situation. Working from subtle clues and tentative impressions, each participant attempts to discern the identities of all the others.

Imputation of Role to Other. A person's identities are not ordinarily to be directly perceived but are to be inferred from his appearance and, especially, his actions. The man in blue uniform may not be a policeman but an actor or a bus driver; the man in shirtsleeves may not be a customer but a captain of detectives. Even sexual identification is subject to error and deception. Identities are seldom simply read off from a person's appearance but must be inferred from visible clues and from his behaviors.

When we use a person's behaviors as the basis for our inferences about his identities, we are employing the process of *role-taking*. The distinctiveness of role-taking as a perceptual process lies in its aim, which is to discover not the qualities of a person but the role he is performing and, thereby, his present identities. One is trying to see through the other's specific acts to discover the line of action that gives them direction, coherence, and meaning.

> Behavior is said to make sense when a series of actions is interpretable as indicating that the actor has in mind some role which guides his behavior. . . . The isolated action becomes a datum for role analysis only when it is interpreted as the manifestation of a configuration. The individual acts as if he were expressing some role through his behavior and may assign a higher degree of reality to the assumed role than to his specific actions. The role becomes the point of reference for placing interpretations on specific actions, for anticipating that one line of action will follow upon another, and for making evaluations of individual actions. For example, the lie which is an expression of the role of friend is an altogether different thing from the same lie taken as a manifestation of the role of confidence man. . . . The unity of a role cannot consist simply in the bracketing of a set of specific behaviors, since the same behavior can be indicative of different roles under different circumstances. The unifying element is to be found *in some assignment of purpose or sentiment to the actor*. Various actions by an individual are classified as intentional and unintentional (relevant and irrelevant) on the basis of a role designation. . . . Role-taking involves selective perception of the actions of another and a great deal of selective emphasis, organized about some purpose or sentiment attributed to the other [Turner, 1962: 24, 28; emphasis in original].

In trying to discern Other's role, then, Person imputes to Other certain purposes or motives in the light of which Other's conduct appears to Person as a recognizable line of action. ''The key to person perception lies in our attention to what he is *trying to do*'' (Allport, 1961: 520).

Improvisation of a Role for Self. Once Person has discovered what he (rightly or wrongly) conceives to be Other's current role, he modifies his own line of action on the basis of what he perceives Other's implications to be for Person's manifest and latent plans of action. That is, having imputed a role to Other, Person devises (or improvises) his own role in the light of what Other's imputed role means for Person.

This description must not be taken to imply that Other's role *determines* Person's role in the simple sense that he is thereby led to play the corresponding counterrole. Instead, Person devises his own role in terms of how he can best make use of Other's line of action; if Other's imputed role happens to be one that is unfavorable to Person's plans, Person devises his own role in terms of how he can induce Other to *change* his line of action to one more compatible for cooperative joint ventures or more profitable to Person in terms of exchange.

Other, meanwhile, must also attempt to discern Person's role (and consequently, to modify his own). Once Other has imputed a role to Person, Other can proceed to devise and revise his own role.

If the parties are to achieve even rudimentary accomodation in the situation, each party's improvised role must be at least roughly in line with the role imputed to him by the other parties—otherwise the encounter has gone amiss. In all but the most standardized situations, this rough correspondence may be quite problematic. The chances of crossing one another up are substantial, especially in those cases where one is reluctant to go along with other's role or with the role other imputes to one. Person's imputed and improvised roles somehow must be squared with one another, through communication with Other, who faces these same problems.

Expressive Processes in Social Acts

Communication takes place through processes of overt expression that are active attempts to affect situations in order to align the imputations and improvisations of *every* participant.

Presentation of Self. The first of these expressive processes is the selective presentation of self, the tactics of which have been thoroughly explored by Erving Goffman (1959b). By carefully controlling his expressive behaviors Person can convey to Other an image of the character he desires to assume in the situation. If this control is exercised skillfully, if Person's performance thoroughly sustains his role and character, Other will likely go along with this expressed identity. In effect, then, an individual's presentation of self tends to become a self-fulfilling image.

Other will be motivated from his own plans of action either to endorse or to doubt Person's expressed identity. In the latter case, Other may seek disproving evidence within the situation itself and sometimes even by pursuing external sources.

Through skillful presentations of self, however, Person virtually constrains Other to accept Person's claim to character and to conduct himself toward Person in the fashion appropriate when in the presence of such a character. That is, when an individual "makes an implicit or explicit claim to be a person of a particular kind, he automatically exerts a moral demand upon the others, obliging them to value and treat him in the manner that persons of this kind have a right to expect" (Goffman, 1959b: 13). By conducting oneself as if one were a certain kind of person, the individual exerts leverage on others to *act toward oneself* as if one were that kind of person and thus to support one's performance and one's claims. If a person claims to be a writer or an expert fisherman or a topflight golfer and if nothing about his talk or performance enables others to dispute that claim, they are most likely to go along, at least publicly, with his claim to that identity in the situation.

Altercasting. The second expressive process, that of "altercasting" (Weinstein and Deutschberger, 1963, 1964) resembles presentation of self in its form but differs in its point of application. That is, not only does Person's performance express an image of who he is, but it also simultaneously expresses an image of who Person takes *Other* (or "alter") to be. This image, too, has a tendency to become self-fulfilling, for Person acts toward Other as if Other were indeed the sort of individual that Person takes him to be, and Person may continue to do so regardless of what Other actually does. The enthusiastic salesman may treat an individual as if this other were an eager customer; the protestations and denials of Other may be interpreted as merely coy expressions of eagerness, thus confirming the salesman's image of Other. In fact, casting him in this manner may actually lead Other eventually to adopt this role of eager customer. Therein lies the utility of this expressive process.

Yet neither presentation of self nor altercasting necessarily or automatically brings the roles and characters that Person devises for himself into line with those imputed to him by Other. These processes only serve to express to Other the role that Person has imputed to Other and the role that Person has devised for himself. Other may not even "read" these expressive messages correctly, for it is a long leap from expressions sent to impressions received. And whether accurately read or not, Person's expressed roles for self and Other may not be acceptable to Other in terms of Other's own plans of action.

In such a case, Person's expressive processes only suggest to Other the direction in which Person would like to modify the roles of each party. Other, in turn, will employ these processes to indicate to Person the somewhat different direction in which *he* would like to modify the roles. If neither party is willing to give on these issues, both will continue to talk right past each other, acting profitlessly on incompatible bases.

Typically, however, the two parties will negotiate some sort of consensus, each acceding somewhat to the other's conceptions, though seldom in equal degree. Labeling theorists (for example, Schur, 1971) have emphasized such inequalities between the altercasting by social control agents (such as policemen or psychiatrists) and the presentation of self by private citizens in delicate encounters. Even there, however, the supposedly delinquent or insane person will seldom simply acquiesce in the agent's altercasting but will continue to present a more favorable character, seeking against heavy odds to negotiate a more desirable definition.

Negotiation of Identities

This emergent definition of the role and character of each participant is not executed in a single step but is the eventual result of a complex process of negotiation. Agreement must first be reached simply on the broad outlines of who each party is (in terms of social positions such as doctor, lawyer, and Indian chief) before bargaining or conferring can begin on the specific contents of the present behavior of the participants.

At every stage of the negotiation, the moves of each party, motivated by hopes of joint action and/or by benefit–cost considerations, take the form of insinuations about identities—a debate or an argument over who each person is. The tactics of rhetorical persuasion or dramatic arts are more evident than are those of the marketplace. Each move is presented as a change (or a refusal to change) in the presentation of self or in altercasting. If the move is in a direction acceptable to the other party, he will alter his own expressive behavior in a manner that tacitly signals his concurrence and his concession (or perhaps signals his demand for still further concessions in the same directon from his partner). If the move is not acceptable, it is countered by a studied and emphatic persistence in his line of altercasting and presentation of self.

The negotiation is basically a process of settling which, how many, and how much of his salient role-identities each person will be allowed to incorporate into his performance. Weinstein and Deutschberger (1964) have pointed out that there are not one but two bargains to be struck in this connection, one with oneself and one with alter. Person must, first of all, somehow reconcile the role he improvises for himself (in response to the role he has imputed to Other) with the demands of his own salience hierarchy. One is seldom allowed by others to perform exactly the role one would prefer most. Second, Person must also reconcile his improvised role toward Other with demands of *Other's* salience hierarchy. The content of one or more of Other's salient role-identities may dictate that Person act toward Other in an altogether different fashion than is indicated by Person's own improvised and expressed role.

The first stage in this process, as mentioned, is to negotiate the identities of each participant, to come to an agreement simply upon the relevant social positions to which each person belongs for purposes of the present encounter. This agreement represents essentially a working agreement from which basis the parties continue to bargain or confer, negotiating the specifics of their lines of action. The form of such a working agreement is schematically represented in Figure 2–1.

A working agreement can be said to exist when the cognitive processes of one person, with respect to social identities, are not in gross conflict with the expressive processes of the other person. It exists, that is, when the altercasting of one party is not greatly inconsistent with the improvised role of the other party *and* when the presentation of self by one party is not in conflict with the role imputed to him by the other. Such a working agreement, in which the expressive processes of one party are in rough agreement with the cognitive processes of the other and vice versa, constitutes the "definition of the situation." In routine and standardized encounters, such as those between a checkout clerk and customers or between a receptionist and callers, this agreement is readily attained. In repeat encounters between mutually acquainted persons, their previous working agreement may be virtually taken for granted—at least

FIGURE 2-1. The Working Agreement

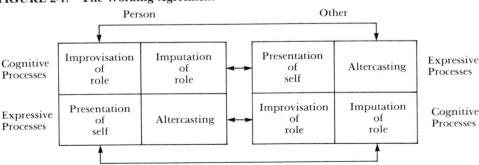

Source: McCall and Simmons, 1978: 139.

until something goes awry or one party "pushes" for a redefinition of the agreement. However, the attainment of such a "definition of the situation" does not necessarily settle the matter of identities and the meaning of persons for the duration of the encounter. Typically, it is only a beginning, an agreement on which the parties can stand while they continue to work out the finer points of their roles and characters as they proceed through that social situation.

Negotiation of Lines of Action

The establishment of identities within social interaction is usually little more than a necessary prerequisite to the execution of other social tasks. Many complex activities are carried on in the presence of other people, and in most instances these activities (rather than the establishment of identities) are the main focus of the interaction. The negotiation of identities is the first task of interaction and, although it is never completely settled, it ordinarily fades into the background as a working agreement on the basis of which the participants can turn to the main business of the interaction—building canoes, making love, or eating dinner.

To begin with, they must come to some sort of agreement on the *task focus* of the interaction. Many possible tasks or social activities are open to persons with given sets of identities; they must decide not only who they are but what they are doing there. Two friends, for example, convened for a sociable evening together, must choose among many possible activities: conversation around the kitchen table, fishing, bowling, miniature golf, a game of cards, and so on. For the sake of illustration, they eventually choose to go bowling. Having done so, they must proceed to make a host of further collective decisions to implement this chosen task focus and specify it into meshing lines of action. Tacitly or explicitly, decisions must be reached on who will drive them to the bowling alley, who will pay for the rented shoes, who will bowl first, who will keep score, who will buy the beer, and so forth.

Every one of these decisons on the task and its specifications into behavior has significance in relation to various gratifications and identities, benefits and costs, for the participants. Consider, for example, a person's appraisals of extrinsic benefits and costs. The decision to do the driving or the scoring implies a certain amount of labor and risk. Monetary considerations are involved in deciding whose car will be used, who will rent the shoes and buy the beer, and how many lines they will bowl. Aside from actual expeditures, there is the matter of forgoing opportunities for earning money. Status is also involved in the decisions on who will drive, who will bowl first, and so on.

These same negotiations also have implications for intrinsic gratifications. Who will have the pleasure (if it be such) of driving and scoring? Shall athletic pleasures be allowed to prevail over opportunities for rest and relaxation? Perhaps the cool night air at the ball park would be more desirable than the stuffy atmosphere of the bowling alley. Shall the person spurn the sense of competence he obtains through miniature golf in favor of the lesser sense of competence that arises from his less adequate performance at bowling?

The gratifications of role-support are also involved in these decisions. Does the decision to bowl or to buy the beer agree with the person's conceptions of himself? If so, is such a decision more gratifying in terms of role-support than the decision to play cards or to discuss the latest international crisis would be?

One's performance and that of Other must be considered in terms of all such benefits and costs in order to determine its overall "profitability." Buying the beer costs money but brings status, provides a refreshing drink, and is perhaps congruent with one's conception of self as friend. Is it, on balance, worth doing? This consideration underlies our every act; these complex calculations, though they may be "rational," are seldom very conscious or deliberate. If an act, whether one's own or Other's, does not appear to be sufficiently profitable for one's own individual *or joint* concerns, one will, other things being equal, propose some more desirable alternative. In the light of emerging conditions, one has to strike a bargain, not only with oneself but also with Other, as to what one is willing to settle for in the interaction. If two parties cannot agree upon a pair of lines of action sufficiently profitable to each, they may break off negotiations, departing for more profitable alternative interactions. Most often, however, they do strike some adequate behavior exchange or behavior coordination.

A behavior exchange can be achieved in either of two ways. First, the participants may compromise on the roles they would ideally like to perform in the situation. If one person wants to play cards and the other wants to bowl, they may compromise by playing a couple of hands before going out to bowl. Or, second, they may strike a bargain not in terms of the present situation but in terms of a *series* of situations. That is, they may agree to bowl tonight on the implicit promise of playing cards on some future occasion. This negotiation of a bargain for the current occasion in terms of promises for different bargains in subsequent interactions might well be called "trading in futures," to borrow a phrase from the commodities market.

Behavior coordination is achieved not through compromise or trade but through conferring upon possible lines of joint action which would be responsive to joint rather than strictly individual concerns. This mode of social transaction harkens back to the basic human interdependencies at the biological, psychological, sociological (and perhaps even "spiritual") levels.

Whichever the mode of resolution, such a transaction constitutes a "social act" and may generate any number of "social objects." We wish to emphasize that every social act invariably generates two broad and important types of social object—the characters of the participating individuals and a social organization (that is, a purposeful fitting together of individual lines of action). A wedding, for example, creates not only a "bride" and a "groom" but also a "marriage." An election creates not only a "president" but also an "administration." Individuals playing chess games in particular sequences create not only a "tournament" but also a "champion" and a "runner-up." The more enduring the social act, the more enduring are both the social organization and the characters of its participants.

SUMMARY

Human nature is not in-born but is developed in the individual by social organizations. The entire range of individual attributes—physical, mental, emotional, and behavioral—is (1) subject to influence by social organizations; and (2) included in the concept of the "character" of the individual.

An individual tends to become the kind of person he is expected to be as an occupant of a social position with a consistently and clearly defined social role. His innate sociability, as well as his physical, psychological, and economic dependence on other persons, are major factors motivating him to comply with at least those role expectations sponsored by his significant others and his reference groups.

Self-awareness and self-control afford an effective mechanism for either compliance or noncompliance with role expectations. Self-appraisal and self-judgment may be as significant in framing individual conduct as social approval or disapproval, yet the individual's conception of self stems importantly from the "social looking-glass" of others' reactions to his attributes. Accordingly, self-appraisal and self-judgment tend to correlate with the social appraisal and the social approval/disapproval of his significant others. Therefore, self-judgment, like social approval or disapproval from others, tends to motivate the individual toward compliance with role expectations.

Besides approval and disapproval, a wide range of other benefits and costs can be conferred or imposed by others, who may employ these to motivate the individual to comply with their expectations of him. The benefit/cost outcome to the individual of any of his acts is bound up with the benefits and costs to others. This interdependence of outcomes may be managed more or less rationally through the social transactions of exchanges or joint ventures. In either case, his compliance with role expectations will be influenced by his appraisal of the benefits and costs for himself and for others.

Individuals' contributions to any social or joint act are thus negotiated through imputation of roles to others and improvisation of roles for self and through the expressive processes of presentation of self and altercasting. The first task of social interaction is the negotiation of identities, although the principal focus of interaction is the execution of some social activity (requiring negotiation of specific lines of action). From any social act there emerge both the characters of the individual participants and a social organization, that is, a purposeful fitting together of individual lines of action.

SUGGESTIONS FOR ADDITIONAL READING

As noted in Approaches, attempts to pin down what is "human nature" long preceded anything that might be considered social science. But perhaps few events had greater impact on such analysis than the discovery of "feral children," that is, children who had had little or no social rearing. Roger Shattuck's *The Forbidden Experiment: The Story of the Wild Boy of Aveyron* (New York: Farrar, Straus, and Giroux, 1980) is a fascinating account of the dramatic impact on intellectual society of this discovery. A general account of a contemporary American case is Eleanor Craig, *One, Two, Three: The Story of Matt, A Feral Child.* (New York: McGraw-Hill, 1978).

Even today no topic is more controversial than the biological roots of human nature. Currently, this controversy centers on "sociobiology," the view that the distinguishing features of human nature are genetically determined (Edward O. Wilson, *On Human Nature,* Cambridge: Harvard University Press, 1978, and *Sociobiology: The New Synthesis,* Cambridge: Harvard University Press, 1975). Many scholars dispute this view bitterly; see, for example, Ashley Montagu, ed., *Sociobiology Examined* (New York: Oxford University Press, 1980). The view perhaps most congenial to the approach of this chapter is the counterargument (Peter J. Wilson, *Man: The Promising Primate,* New Haven: Yale University Press, 1980) that it is the fundamental existential *circumstances* of human life that lead everywhere to the development of universal human nature.

In this chapter we have asserted that any individual attribute may be influenced by social organizations. As we proceed through the chapters of Part III, we shall show more specifically how various organizations accomplish these feats. Meanwhile, the interested reader may wish to consult other sociological accounts of some of these influences. Some useful readings include: Basil Bernstein, "Some Sociological Determinants of Perception," *British Journal of Sociology,* 1958, 9:159–174; Mark Zborowski, "Cultural Components in Response to Pain," *Journal of Social Issues,* 1952, 8:16–30; Theodore D. Kemper, *A Social Interactional Theory of Emotions,* New York: Wiley-Interscience, 1978; and James T. Borhek and Richard F. Curtis, *Sociology of Belief,* New York: Wiley-Interscience, 1975.

Many of the ideas in this chapter regarding the social self and social interaction are more fully developed in our earlier book, McCall and Simmons, *Identities and Interactions* (second ed.) (New York: Free Press, 1978) and in Jerold Heiss, *The Social Psychology of Interaction* (Englewood Cliffs, N.J.: Prentice-Hall, 1981). The historical development of such ideas is carefully examined in Sheldon Stryker's *Symbolic Interactionism: A Social Structural Version* (Menlo Park: Benjamin/Cummings, 1979). A more direct exposure to the research base underlying these ideas is presented in Chad Gordon and Kenneth J. Gergen, eds., *The Self in Social Interaction,* vol. 1 (New York: Wiley, 1968).

The social self is usefully studied in Morris Rosenberg's *Conceiving the Self* (New York: Basic Books, 1979) and in Theodore Mischel, ed., *The Self: Psychological and Philosophical Issues* (Oxford: Blackwell, 1977). Important analyses of social interaction are provided by Randall Stokes and John P. Hewitt ("Aligning Actions," *American Sociological Review,* 1976, 41:838–849) and by Erving Goffman in a series of works (*The Presentation of Self in Everyday Life,* Garden City, N.Y.: Doubleday, 1959; *Interaction Ritual,* Garden City, N.Y.: Doubleday, 1967; *Strategic Interaction,* Philadelphia: University of Pennsylvania Press, 1971).

The sociological concepts of "social construction of reality" and of "negotiated social order" are further developed in Peter L. Berger and Thomas Luckman, *The Social Construction of Reality* (Garden City, N.Y.: Doubleday, 1966) and in Stanford M.

The Social Nature of Human Beings

Lyman and Marvin B. Scott, *The Drama of Social Reality* (New York: Oxford University Press, 1975).

The social psychological implications of role theory are examined in Bruce J. Biddle, *Role Theory: Expectations, Identities, and Behaviors* (New York: Academic Press, 1979). Sociological works on reference-group processes are paralleled by psychological works on "social comparison theory"; see, for example, Jerry Suls and Richard F. Miller, *Social Comparison Processes: Theoretical and Empirical Perspectives* (New York: Halsted Press, 1977). The theory of behavior exchange and behavior coordination is best developed in Harold H. Kelley and John W. Thibaut, *Interpersonal Relations: A Theory of Interdependence* (New York: Wiley-Interscience, 1978). A wider view of social transactions is presented in Bruce Kapferer, *Transaction and Meaning: Directions in the Anthropology of Exchange and Symbolic Behavior* (Philadelphia: Institute for the Study of Human Behavior, 1976).

Photo courtesy of U.N. Canadian Government Travel Bureau

Thanks to coordinated collective effort, these four fishermen will haul in enough herring for all.

CHAPTER 3

The Nature of Social Organizations

What is this thing called a "social organization"? And how does it so demonstrably influence, color, shape, and sometimes even dominate the personal lives of individuals?

An airport taxi picks up three unacquainted passengers—a weightlifter, a fireman, and a doctor. On the way into town, they chance to observe another car swerve across the highway, roll down an embankment, and begin to burn. The cab driver halts and radios for emergency assistance while the passengers leap out to do what they can. The weightlifter wrenches open the car's badly smashed door and extricates the injured driver; the fireman attacks the flames to prevent an explosion; the doctor gives emergency medical treatment to the injured man. Together, these individual lines of action add up to an effective rescue operation; an impressively functioning rescue team has emerged through unthinking individual responses to an accidental situation by a fortuitously selected set of persons. At a crude and temporary level, a rudimentary "social organization" has developed.

Much more often, however, rescue teams and any other type of social organization emerge through much more purposive transactions involving joint venture. That is, neither the persons nor the lines of action involved in organized effort are left to chance but are purposefully and collectively arrived at.

Every social organization has a natural history—the sequence of its "birth" and developmental course through time—which is a fascinating subject in itself. In its beginnings, an organization is no more than an impulse in someone's mind: a man drinking coffee in a Paris café, a woman watching an all-male line at the voting booth, an engineer daydreaming about having his own company, a young doctor thinking about all the upsets stemming from unplanned pregnancies among her patients, or a young man deciding he would like to get married and start raising a family.

45

Some sort of organization emerges in the empirical world only after some form of joint activity is worked out with others, even if it is only some friends "talking it over." The actual "birth" of the organization may be marked by a very mundane, even trivial, event such as renting a small office space or posting a notice for a meeting.

At this stage, organizations are quite fluid; any early member may have tremendous influence upon its entire content, structure, and future course. Also at this stage, the life of the organization is very precarious; the majority of organizations die during this phase.

If the organization survives these formative stages, it goes through growth and stabilization phases, becoming an accepted part of the social scene. Somewhere along the line in this early period it becomes a *social reality* that others can perceive. Thus, individuals *create* organizations which then subsequently impinge upon a larger number of individuals. As time goes on, such organizations become more and more "real"—a very part of the fabric that new generations come to experience as social reality. For instance, "the United States of America" is now a very solid reality but its very name was once only an idea in the minds of a few colonial men.

A crucial point here is that while early members share in the actual collective formation of the organization, subsequent recruits and nonmembers face the already existing social reality of a going concern. A youth now joins rather than forms the Boy Scouts, and an intellectual now might react to the tenets of the already well-established communist party.

THE IDEA OF SOCIAL ORGANIZATION

A social organization, then, is a distinct kind of joint venture—one in which not all the eventual participants were necessarily involved in its original formation.

Any social organization displays aspects both of unity and of diversity. The aspect of unity is one of *collectivity,* that is, the sense of comprising one social unit, to which the participating individuals "belong" or of which they are "members." The aspect of diversity is that of a *social structure,* a differentiated pattern in which members not only play distinctive parts in a "division of labor," but also occupy distinct, though interdependent, social positions. A social organization is not merely a collectivity but a structured collectivity. The kitchen of a restaurant, for instance, is a rather complex organization of distinct interdependent roles and sharply differentiated social positions, with the head chef "on top" and the potwasher "at the bottom." Hundreds of small, often complex actions dovetail and mesh together so as to wine and dine a large volume of customers in a very short period of time. Without this structuring, the kitchen would be chaos and the workers would be a mob (W. F. Whyte, 1949). Working as a team, however, the employees produce the reality of a functioning restaurant. Such teamwork (Goffman, 1959b) also produces the subjective awareness among the workers that together they comprise a collectivity over and above individual realities and pursuits.

Collectivity

A social organization is a distinct kind of joint venture, arising for the purpose of producing some type of "collective good."

A collective good (Olson, 1971) is any good that, if any one person benefits from it, its benefits cannot feasibly be withheld from at least some other persons. The benefits of citizenship are an example; no one citizen's rights are diminished by the fact of another's citizenship. All citizens in a town can gain some benefit from the civic clean-up campaign, in the form of lowered disease risks and a beautified landscape for all. As another example, one member's enjoyment of a pair-relationship does not diminish (and may even enhance) the potential enjoyment of the other member.

A *pure* collective good is one from which all of its consumers receive exactly equal benefits. Often, however, even with a truly collective good its various consumers receive unequal benefits. For example, everyone in town receives some protection from fire through the establishment of a fire station (a collective good), but those whose property is located nearer the station obviously receive more of this protection than those whose property is farther away. In fact, most truly collective goods are impure to some degree, many significantly so. An individual good, at the other extreme, is any good that can be enjoyed by one person only. If one child eats the remaining cookies, the other children go without. In poker and in competitive sports, one person's winnings entail losses by all others.

Social organizations produce a variety of both collective and individual goods, yet it is the production of collective goods that is their distinguishing feature. Collective goods, like any other goods, do not simply exist in nature but must be produced through human efforts and, therefore, entail human costs. Establishing a fire station, for example, involves producing not only a building, specialized equipment, and trained manpower, but also fire-fighting behaviors in the face of great danger and discomfort. The costs of producing such a good are not merely a matter of money and scarce materials but also involve an expenditure of time, of "blood, sweat, and tears," and of opportunities forgone. The costs of producing any good are partly organizational costs of administration or decision making and partly more direct operating costs.

Organizational costs arise from the often considerable collective effort necessary to decide: (1) how much of the good to produce (how many and what kinds of fire stations); (2) how to cover the costs of production (who will provide how much money for bricks, who will lay the bricks, who will polish the fire truck, who will carry the hose into burning buildings); and (3) how to distribute the benefits produced (to whose houses will the station be closest). *Operating costs* of production are incurred in the carrying out of these decisions, in directly producing the good (in actually buying and laying bricks, polishing trucks, and hosing down fires). The inescapable occurrence of both organizational and operating costs in all human endeavors is how and why it might, for example, "cost" the taxpayers $2.50 to "spend" $1.00 on city renovations.

There is a major dilemma concerning the production of collective goods that does not arise in the production of individual goods. Although some set of individuals may share an interest in consuming the good, they do not necessarily share an interest in paying the costs of its production. By the very definition of a collective good, its production will benefit each of these individuals, regardless of how it gets produced and paid for. Consequently, each hopes that someone else will pay for its production; each hopes for a "free ride." The townspeople desire good schools, well-maintained streets, and adequate police protection, but a sizable proportion of these hopeful beneficiaries will bitterly oppose any local tax increases to pay for them. In consequence, the bond issue may not pass and the fire station may not be built or, if built, may be so under-budgeted that it proves faulty and inadequate.

How is this dilemma ever resolved? To do so ordinarily requires that each potential consumer bear a share of the costs of production proportionate to his share in the collective good. In other words, *collective action,* a joint or social act, is required in order to produce a collective good. To bring about such collective action ordinarily requires offering *selective sidepayments* as individual incentives, as Olson (1971) has so brilliantly shown. These sidepayments (1) are separate from and additional to the individual's share in the collective good; and (2) take the form of selective sanctions—rewards or punishments, depending on one's contributions in cost-sharing. In content, such sidepayments may include material goods, such as money, a chic office, or expense writeoffs, but they may also include rank and privileges, authority over others, or affection and esteem. If executives were not preferentially rewarded, few would take the responsibility, and if citizens were not punished for tax evasion, how many would pay their share of taxes? It is in these ways that selective sidepayments help to bring about collective action leading to production of a collective good.

These selective sidepayments, then, constitute a third, additional cost of producing a collective good, beyond the organizational and operating costs already mentioned. The existence of such selective sidepayments for participation in collective action exerts a profound impact on the social structure of an organization, as we shall now see.

Social Structure

An organization is a unitary collectivity, yet it also displays a diversity that is crucial to any understanding of it. Even in the most rudimentary organizations, the membership is internally differentiated in terms of function, activity, and position. From the level of the government on down to the family, no two members perform exactly the same roles or occupy exactly the same positions. Members are *organized* to facilitate coordinated actions. This organizing may come about through negotiation, through the accidents of happenstance, through an order from above, or in some other way, but it is always to be found.

All those joint ventures that are social organizations involve different actions by various participants. This follows from the fact that individuals differ in capabilities, willingness, and interests. In a wedding, some must play the parts of preacher, bride, groom, and guests, and these positions are not interchangeable. In the restaurant, there must be a cook, waiters and waitresses, dishwashers, and paying customers, and these positions too are not readily interchangeable. A glance at these examples will show (1) the fundamental differentiation of the participants; and (2) the fundamental interdependence of the positions. And although Sally might take Mary's place as bride, no bride could ever change places with the groom.

How members relate to one another is affected more by the role expectations held toward their positions than by the personal attributes of the occupants. For the sake of organizational efficiency, these expectations include provisions for the routine handling of recurrent situations. The preacher presides at many weddings, and the waitress again and again serves up food to customers. A part of almost any organizational role is the carrying out of recurring actions which mesh together with the recurring acts of others within the structure. These roles are differentially valued for their respective contributions to collective action and are thus accorded differing sidepayments. No one would argue that the skipper and the cabin boy should receive equal rewards, although both might enjoy the collective good of the fresh salt air at sea.

In view of the above considerations, we shall regard a social organization as *a structured collectivity undertaking collective action to produce a collective good.*

CHARACTERISTICS OF ORGANIZATIONS

The characteristics of any organization are significantly rooted in the personal attributes of those individuals who comprise that organization. Of primary significance in this regard are, first, the *interests* (goals, plans, wants, needs) and, second, the *capacities* (skills, resources) of those individuals.

Interests

The production of a collective good is the fundamental function of any social organization. For a good to be collective, it must satisfy some interest shared by a number of individuals. According to MacIver (1937), an organization

> is likely to be formed wherever people recognize a like, complementary, or common interest sufficiently enduring and sufficiently distinct to be capable of more effective promotion through collective action, provided their differences outside the field of this interest are not so strong as to prevent the partial agreement involved in its formation [MacIver, 1937: 252].

Social organization thus rests on one or more *collective interests,* that is, on a common interest, on like interests, or on complementary interests exhibited by two or more persons.

Collective Interests. A *common* interest is one whose satisfaction constitutes a *pure* collective good, that is, one from which consumers receive equal benefits. "Only when men identify themselves with some inclusive indivisible unity of their fellows, or with

some cause that pertains equally to all who seek it, does the truly common interest reveal itself.'' (MacIver, 1937: 31). Only a team can win, and each member shares equally in the victory, even though some members may receive additional individual recognition for their personal contributions. Similarly, freedom is a common interest often promoted by political activists.

Like interests are essentially parallel personal interests, the cooperative pursuit of which may prove mutually beneficial in varying degrees to the several individuals. For example, three struggling lawyers may form a cooperative law office to lower the overhead costs for each and thus enhance the profitability of their individual practices.

Complementary interests are unlike but reciprocal interests and thus are mutually beneficial, as when one person has an interest in talking and another in listening.

Although an organization initially may be formed primarily to promote one type of collective interest, it will ordinarily come to generate still other collective interests. Consider, for example, an athletic team.

> Obviously the members get an individual or private satisfaction through belonging to it. Membership in the team, for example, satisfies their like interests of recreation and physical exercise, perhaps brings some distinction with it; it also satisfies the like and the complementary interest of companionship. But it has a further interest for its members. They want the team to succeed not simply because it redounds to their credit as individuals. They want it to succeed also for the credit of the team or for the credit of the college. Their individual interests merge in this inclusive interest. If a player does badly he is still gratified that the team wins; if he shines, he is still distressed that the team loses. Each has in degree the sense of the whole. Each shares a common interest [MacIver, 1937: 255].

A collective interest, of whatever type, is one in which satisfaction of interest for one person does not necessarily diminish satisfaction of interest for others. That is, a collective interest is any interest the satisfaction of which is, at least weakly, a collective good. Whereas the satisfaction of like or complementary interests represents a true but impure collective good, the satisfaction of a common interest represents a pure collective good. Hence, every organization tends eventually to cultivate a common interest. It is this common interest that in turn tends to hold together a further complex web of like and complementary interests. For example, friendships and small exchange circles will develop among the members of the athletic team.

Special Interests. In no organization are all of the interests among members only collective interests. Some will be special interests, meaning that satisfaction for one member will necessarily diminish the satisfaction for other members.

Competing interests occur when several members want the same good but there is not enough of that good available to *fully* satisfy the wants of all of them. If one team member gets newspaper coverage as the star of the game, this automatically relegates all others to the background. *Conflicting* interests, on the other hand, are such that if the interest of one member is satisfied, the interest of another member cannot be satisfied in *any* degree. In a presidential election, as one candidate wins, the rival candidates lose.

The Nature of Social Organizations

Although such competing and conflicting interests among members of an organization can be very divisive, normally they are kept within limits. First, these special interests are frequently outweighed by collective interests. Second, in many cases, special interests—for instance, competition for prestige or promotion—depend for their very possibility on the continued existence of the organization. In other words, competing and conflicting interests must be accommodated to collective interests, and especially to the common interest.

> It is worth observing that every [organization], seeking its own preservation or expansion, endeavors in various ways to cultivate the common interest. For example, it devises symbols of its unity and keeps them before the attention of its members. There is a multitude of ways in which the common interest is emphasized—slogans, appellations of brotherhood, emblems, flags, festivals, parades, processions, initiation rites, rallies, intergroup competitions, and so on, all designed to evoke or sustain the *esprit de corps* of the members, to make them feel their solidarity [MacIver, 1937: 257].

Resources

To undertake collective action, an organization must possess at least some resources—human, and perhaps material—in order to pay the three types of costs of producing a collective good. For either the human or the material resources, both the quantity and the quality of resources are important, often crucial, considerations.

Human Resources. The quantity of human resources refers, in the first instance, to the *number of members* an organization has. For many collective tasks (for example, building a pyramid, raising money, pressuring Congress, fighting a battle), larger numbers of members tend to increase the efficacy of collective action, both by simply increasing the number of workers and by increasing the likelihood that within the membership some especially effective contributions will be found. Moreover, the larger the membership, the more specialized (and thereby the more efficient) the division of labor may become.

On the other hand, this well-documented relationship between organizational size and organizational complexity (for example, Pugh et al., 1969) has been shown to create difficulties as well. Organizational costs of production (decision-making costs) increase geometrically with the number of persons involved in a decision. Generally, the greater the organizational size, the smaller the proportion of members involved in making a collective decision and the greater the proportion of members whose interests may be harmed. Furthermore, greater organizational complexity increases the need for communication among members in order to coordinate their specialized contributions. Every growing organization must come to grips in some way with this problem of communication within its differentiated membership.

A second aspect of the quantity of human resources refers to the *degree of participa-*

tion in collective action by members, regardless of their number. In some organizations, members devote most of their individual energies, time, and personal resources to the organization and its collective actions; individual interests correspond closely to collective interests. The life of a monk in a cloistered monastery exemplifies this type. But in other organizations—such as a gun club—members ordinarily contribute very little of their time, energy, and resources; only a segment of an individual's interests corresponds to the collective interests, and participation is segmental. To increase the quantity of their human resources, organizations usually promote increased participation and involvement among their members.

The quality of an organization's human resources is a matter of the capacities and incapacities of its members to contribute to collective action. Organizational success in collective action depends heavily on the abilities (intelligence, strength, discipline), skills (clerical, mechanical, communicative), and personal resources (knowledge, experience, appearance, contacts) of its members. Of course, only some of any member's abilities, skills, and resources are relevant to the organization's collective interests and collective actions. Just as the interests among members may be collective or special, other attributes of members may represent collective resources (relevant to collective interests) or special resources (relevant to special—that is, personal—interests).

Material Resources. Frequently, various material resources such as money, facilities, equipment, food, special clothing, or materials are also required in order to produce a collective good—particularly to pay for operating costs of its production. But material resources may also be necessary to pay for organizational costs; for example, telephone charges, postage, travel costs, or rent for a meeting hall. Finally, selective sidepayments to members may take the form of selectively distributing material collective resources, as in the forms of salaries or wages, expense accounts, and other material privileges.

In some cases, an organization's material resources may be contributed by its members, either as outright transfers of ownership (donations) or as use contributions (the temporary loan of a member's home, truck, or chain saw). In other cases, an organization's material resources may be earned—obtained from nonmembers as a result of members' collective actions, such as fund-raising activities, grant-proposal writing, collective investment of contributed resources, or the selling of goods and services to customers.

As with human resources, both the quantity and the quality of material resources will condition the scope and success of collective action. For example, a crucial difference between a major political party and a minor party is in the material resources of each, such as funding for television spots, postage for mail campaigns, availability of jet airplanes for stumping, and so on. Every organization—from governments on down to pair relationships—needs human and material resources in order to function at all. And the greater the quantity and quality of those resources, the better the organization is likely to fare in its social environment.

Culture

Every social organization evolves its own shared culture. Through their collective interests and collective actions, the members come to inhabit a distinctive little world (Blumer, 1962). To the varying degrees of their participation, some members virtually dwell in this world while others merely visit. The objects constituting that little world are the social objects generated by their social acts, and these represent the objects of their collective interests. Insofar as this little world is distinctive, outsiders do not find it entirely meaningful; they do not fully understand the language, thought, feelings, and actions of the members. That is to say, outsiders do not fully share the culture of that organization. At least half of the overheard conversation in a law office or medical clinic makes little sense to the person in the waiting room, and the gestures and activities of a Tibetan priest would leave the Western observer utterly baffled.

Organizational members tend to employ distinctive *words and phrases* to describe features of their little world, or at minimum give distinctive new meanings to familiar words. ''Angel'' means one thing in the Catholic sections of New Mexico, but quite another in the world of off-Broadway. Members share distinctive *beliefs* about the objects and events within their world, often amounting to a rather elaborate lore and mystique concerning the central objects and happenings. Outsiders are likely to regard these beliefs as mainly folklore and superstition. Members also share some sense of the history of their little world, a history which outsiders see as heavily embroidered with legend and myth.

By virtue of collective interests, members share certain *values* which are bound up with those interests. ''Values are banners under which one can fight (however mildly), being bound up with man's vision of the good life through his conceptions of the beneficial. . . . A value represents a slogan capable of providing for the rationalization of action by encapsulating a positive attitude toward a purportedly beneficial state of affairs'' (Rescher, 1969: 9). Outsiders, however, may experience difficulty in identifying what the values are, and tend to regard them as odd and misguided at best.

Flowing from collective interests and shared values are social *norms,* ''conceptions of right and wrong, proper and improper, acceptable and unacceptable, moral and immoral, legal and illegal, legitimate and illegitimate, conventional and unconventional, tolerable and intolerable, suitable or unsuitable'' (J. Bernard, 1962: 42). ''Enacted norms'' are deliberately created by explicit collective decision. ''Crescive norms'' emerge through members' interactions and only come to be (collectively) discovered. The category of crescive norms includes customs, mores, and conventions.

> *Custom* is the broadest category; it refers to any norm coming down from the past that regulates fairly fundamental forms of behavior, such as the sexual or racial division of labor, the timing of life rhythms, the use of ceremony or ritual, and the like. *Mores . . .* represent a special kind of custom, one that has especially strong sanctions behind it, with a great deal of emotion associated with it, feelings of right and wrong, moral and immoral. Violating the mores is more shocking than is behavior which is merely not customary. Eating human flesh, for example, or nudism, or infanticide. *Convention . . .* refers to norms regulating the

amenities . . . in clothing, house furnishings, ornaments, entertaining, dress, speech, "social life," the arts. . . . It reflects the very ethos of a group, that is, the relative position assigned to one individual in relation to another. . . . All three kinds of crescive norms may deal with the same kinds of behavior. . . . The mores regulate who may sleep with whom and custom fixes the times when people sleep; convention tells what kinds of clothing, both for people and for beds, is proper [Bernard, 1962: 50–54; emphasis in original].

Some norms apply to every member of the organization; these we shall call *membership norms*. Other norms apply only to those persons who occupy a particular social position; such *positional norms* are an integral part of the role expectations discussed in Chapter 2.

Every organization will be found to have both general membership norms and positional norms. These often become so taken for granted that they are somewhat invisible to the membership and can be easily seen only by newcomers and outsiders. The strength of these norms is such that many an organization, when facing a drastically changed environment, simply shatters rather than change its ways.

When members very pointedly and very formally act in compliance with a norm of any kind, such performance is referred to as *ritual,* emphasizing its symbolic and conventional character. Complex social performances incorporating numerous rituals in a conventional ordering are *ceremonies*. Ritual and ceremony display members' respect for the common interest of the organization. Every organization, from the largest to the smallest and most fleeting, develops a culture of its own—a fabric of shared meanings which generate a common reality for its members.

Division of Labor

For the members of a collectivity to undertake collective action, their individual lines of action must be both differentiated and coordinated. To operate an old-fashioned steamboat, for example, one person must steer, one must stoke and regulate the engine, and one must delve the depths, all in close coordination.

Such differentiation of action, to prove effective, must bear some relationship to the differential distribution of collective human resources (knowlege, skills, experience) within the membership. In the steamboat example, things would work out best for the organization if the member with the greatest mechanical skill handled the engine and the one most familiar with the peculiarities of the river did the steering. There is a (far from perfect) tendency to match competencies with positions, and in fact the point at which organizations go awry can often be traced to a gross violation of this principle. The accompanying coordination of action must rest heavily on the sense of collectivity that is engendered by collective interests and by shared cultural understandings.

In turn, the division of labor tends to become routinized—if not institutionalized—into a structure of social roles, thus engendering within the organizational culture both social objects (social positions) and specialized norms (role expectations). The structured network of role relationships interconnecting the various social posi-

FIGURE 3-1.   An Example of an Organization Chart (for a Business Company)

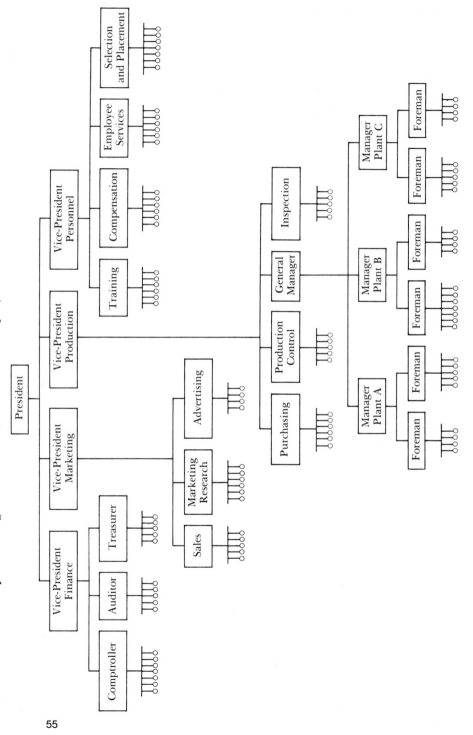

Source: Porter, Lawler, and Hackman, 1975: 76. Reproduced with permission.

tions rather fully prescribes how individual lines of action are to be specialized and coordinated. A commonly encountered skeletal display of this structure is the organizational chart, emphasizing the coordination of the contributions of the various social roles (see Figure 3-1). The *role structure* of an organization constitutes its primary social structure.

Social Differentiation

In addition to such primary, functional differentiation among members of a collectivity, a secondary, more interpersonal differentiation arises.

Suborganizations. *Collective* secondary differentiation takes the form of suborganizations within the larger organization. Suborganizations may be "official"—that is, prescribed in the role structure itself. Examples include such suborganizations as departments, divisions, branches, and authorized committees. "Unofficial" suborganizations, such as factions and cliques, *arise* to supplement the primary and official structures. Examples include voting coalitions within the board of directors, conspiratorial alliances among assembly-line workers, office cliques, filibuster factions in legislatures, and covert sexual liaisons. Within the organizational culture, some unofficial suborganizations may be viewed as legitimate or at least may be recognized as de facto, while others may be viewed as illegitimate and potentially troublesome to organizational functioning.

Whether official or unofficial, suborganizations cohere around *special interests* shared by some but not all members of the larger organization. Some of these special interests may have been brought into the organization by individual members, and others may have been created within the organization through the division of labor and its attendant selective sidepayments.

Dimensional Structures. *Individual* secondary differentiation of the membership takes the form of rank-ordering individuals along evaluative interpersonal dimensions. Such dimensions may include:

1. *power:* the ability to influence others through one's control of human and/or material collective resources
2. *authority:* the ability to influence others through the rights normatively invested in one's position in the role structure
3. *leadership:* the performance of key acts that greatly advance collective action (for example, by making a significant suggestion) or greatly enhance the sense of collectivity (for example, by helping the members to release tensions in a difficult situation)
4. *status:* worthiness based on the extent to which one's attributes, role, and/or actions are recognized as contributing to the collective interests
5. *affect:* the degree to which one is liked or disliked, based on the perceived extent

to which one's attributes and/or actions contribute to the more individual, special interests of the members

6. *communication rank:* the extent and frequency of receiving and initiating communications with other members

7. *conformity:* the extent to which one conforms to the norms of the organization and of one's position.

Each of these rank-orderings constitutes a dimensional social structure. Social scientists constantly make reference to such dimensional social structures as the power structure, status structure, communication structure, and so on.

An individual's position in such dimensional social structures is a function of the relevance of his personal attributes to collective and special interests, in the degree to which the division of labor reflects and enhances that relevance. Since many of these structures rest on similar factors and are mutually reinforcing, it should not be surprising that most dimensional structures tend to be closely correlated (Secord and Backman, 1974). The major exception is the affect structure, which in many organizations tends to be uncorrelated with any other. Also, in most organizations the conformity structure tends to have a U-shaped relationship to other structures—conformity being highest among members in the middle range of other structures and lowest among those at the top and bottom. Again, although not all of these dimensions of individual secondary differentiation are well-developed in every social organization, every organization does notably display some dimensional social structures. In fact, which of these dimensional structures are better developed is an important clue to any organization's character.

When we speak of a ''structured collectivity'' in our definition of a social organization, the term is meant to refer not only to the existence of a primary structure (division of labor or role structure) but also to the existence of various secondary structures (suborganizations and dimensional social structures) within the collectivity. The organizational chart may show the primary structure, but, as every member knows, it does not begin to tell the full story of what goes on within the organization, how it holds together, or how its work actually gets done. To understand these matters, we must invoke knowledge of the secondary social structures—both suborganizations and dimensional structures.

ORGANIZATIONAL ATTRIBUTES

No two social organizations can exert exactly the same influence on an individual or on social processes. Organizations differ in their ''character,'' and it is the character of the organization that determines the nature of its influences.

Every organization displays the five broad features reviewed above: interests, resources, culture, division of labor, and social differentiation. The organizational attributes which define the character of any particular social organization are to be found in certain variable details of these universal features. Just as the endless diversity of human faces consists in combinations of variable details of certain universal features (eyes, ears, nose, mouth, brows, and chin), the endless diversity of social organizations consists in combinations of variable details of the broad organizational features of interests, resources, culture, division of labor, and social differentiation.

Sociologists find it useful to characterize an organization through answers to a series of questions concerning the details of these broad organizational features. These questions include the following:

> What is the nature and content of each of these features as they are exhibited by the particular organization?
>
> To what degree are these various features elaborated, that is, developed in greater or lesser detail?

FIGURE 3-2. Organizational Attributes as Specifications of General Organizational Characteristics

	Nature, Content	Elaboration	Formalization	Shape	Demandingness
INTERESTS					
Common	?	?	?	NA	NA
Like	?	?	?	NA	NA
Complementary	?	?	?	NA	NA
Competing	?	?	?	NA	NA
Conflicting	?	?	?	NA	NA
RESOURCES					
Human	?	NA	NA	NA	NA
Material	?	NA	NA	NA	NA
CULTURE					
Language	?	?	?	NA	NA
Beliefs	?	?	?	NA	NA
Values	?	?	?	NA	NA
Norms	?	?	?	NA	?
Rituals	?	?	?	NA	NA
DIVISION OF LABOR					
Social positions	?	?	?	NA	NA
Social roles	?	?	?	NA	?
Role structure	?	?	?	?	NA
SOCIAL DIFFERENTIATION					
Suborganizations	?	?	?	?	NA
Dimensional structures	?	?	?	?	NA

Note: NA indicates not applicable.

To what degree are these various features formalized, that is, recognized, referred to, and understood by the membership in a standard and uniform manner?

[Regarding primary and secondary structural features] What is the shape of these structures? (For example, "tall" structures have many power levels relative to number of members, while "flat" structures have relatively few.)

[Regarding membership and positional norms] What is the degree of demand with which the organization exerts claims on a member's life? (For example, the priestly order requires more from the priest than the Rotary Club demands from a Rotarian.)

The applicability of these descriptive questions regarding the range of organizational features is summarized in Figure 3–2.

VARIETIES OF ORGANIZATIONS

Endless diversity notwithstanding, some important general varieties of organizations can be distinguished, each of which exerts characteristically different influences upon the individual and upon social processes. For our purposes, seven general varieties will be distinguished, primarily on the basis of their organizational scope. Organizational scope is itself a complex function of the number of members, geographical extent, degree of member participation, and duration. The seven varieties of organizations distinguished here are presented in descending order of organizational scope.

Societal-Level Structures

Colloquially speaking, the largest-scope social organization to which an individual ordinarily relates is a "society," a concept closely related to the modern ideal of a nation-state. The ideal of a nation-state is a collectivity that is (1) distinctive and homogeneous with respect to language, culture, and ethnicity; and (2) unified and autonomous territorially, politically, and economically. Whereas the ideal of the nation-state presumes that linguistic, cultural, ethnic, political, and economic boundaries are (in general) geographically coincident, the empirical situation is that such boundaries are actually fuzzy and cross-cutting. A "society" is thus hard to find, although its various overlapping components (which we shall call "societal-level structures") can be roughly identified in the real world. Therefore, such societal-level structures are the organizations of greatest scope that will be dealt with in this chapter.

Perhaps the most basic societal structure is the *speech community,* the collectivity comprised of all those persons who speak a given language; an example would be the English-speaking world. Although a speech community may be culturally diverse in many ways, each speech community does tend to have associated with it a somewhat distinctive *age-sex structure*—that is, an articulated system of social positions and social roles based on the individual attributes of age and sex.

Another identifiable societal-level structure is the *polity,* or political organization. In modernized areas of the world, the polity tends to take the form of a ''state''—a centralized authority claiming political sovereignty and a monopoly on the legitimate use of force within its territorial boundaries. Each polity tends to have associated with it an *economy,* a social organization to produce and distribute services and material goods. Although an economy can be analyzed in a number of useful ways, as sociologists we shall primarily consider an economy to be a structure of occupations.

If we know something of the speech community, age–sex structure, polity, and economy to which an individual belongs, we will in most cases know a good deal about that individual.

Diffuse Collectivities

Within societal-level structures, the organizations of greatest scope are, typically, diffuse collectivities—large in both membership size and geographical extent, but of variable duration and characterized by mostly indirect interaction among members. Generally the largest and most enduring of these diffuse collectivities are masses. A *mass* is essentially a collectivity organized as an audience to some (singular or recurring) event of common interest—such as a television show, the World Series, the stock market, or a moon shot—through some medium of mass communication.

A *public* is a mass that is interested in, divided over, and striving to influence decision makers concerning some specific issue that is to be decided, such as an election or Congressional action on building more nuclear plants.

A *social movement* is a diffuse collectivity acting with some continuity to promote or resist some specific broad social change, such as the status of women or blacks.

Diffuse collectivities touch the lives of all, members or not, and are a paramount aspect of modern social life.

Communities

Generally smaller in scope is the community, a relatively large and clearly bounded (nondiffuse) collectivity in which the individual finds (1) his significant others—mate, kin, friends, associates, and eventual graveside mourners; as well as (2) his major social institutions—church, school, health care, bank, newspaper, retail establishments, and so on. In other words, the community is that subsocietal collectivity within which the individual conducts his major life activities. The community type that immediately comes to mind is the geographical or *local community,* in which membership is determined by place of residence. Despite high geographical mobility in modern times, great numbers of people still do conduct their major life activities within the bounds of a single local community, whether it is Poughkeepsie, Paris, or a Punjab village.

Ethnic categories may also constitute communities; we not infrequently see references to "the Polish community," "the Chinese community," or "the Puerto Rican community" in the United States. And indeed, many members of such ethnic categories do find all their significant others and all their social institutions within the bounds of their ethnic fellows, so that we may properly speak of the *ethnic community.*

Similarly, religious affiliation may define communities—for example, the Jewish community, the Amish community, the Catholic community—in the same full sense of the term. Again, even today, the *religious community* remains a vigorous type of social organization.

Finally, one's occupation—especially if it is a profession or craft—may define a collectivity having many of the characteristics of a community; examples include the military community, the criminal community, and the medical community. With the increasing professionalization of the labor force, the so-called *occupational community* has emerged as a significant social form.

Associations

More specialized, limited-purpose organizations of comparatively large size (whether of national, regional, or local extent) will be treated here as associations.

In this book, all those associations in which a significant proportion of the membership receives salary or wages for organizational participation will be considered *bureaucracies,* on the ground that most such organizations display rigorous authority structures and elaborate rules and regulations. The degree of "bureaucratization" of these bureaucracies, of course, varies widely. Bureaucracies will include, then, such organizations as governmental agencies, business firms, religious organizations, school systems, universities, and hospitals.

Voluntary associations, on the other hand, may have a few salaried functionaries, but are numerically dominated by unpaid volunteer members. Examples include local churches, charitable service organizations, citizen action committees, the PTA, and the Izaak Walton League. When America is spoken of as a nation of joiners, the reference is to joining voluntary associations.

A final type of association is the *total institution,* an organization in which its clients' lives are almost completely controlled by the organization's staff. Total institutions may be either special types of bureaucracies (mental hospitals, prisons, convents, military boot camps) or special types of voluntary associations (radical communes, such as the People's Temple commune at Jonestown).

Groups

Groups are generally smaller organizations (having from three or four members up to around forty) with less specialized purposes and functions. "Formal groups," such as a work group within a factory, are rather officially established for one broad central purpose. "Informal groups," such as a friendship circle, are not established but simply evolve, through and for informal social interaction. In either case, however, the group typically serves a number of interpersonal functions for its members.

A group on which an individual heavily depends for satisfaction of a wide variety of important interpersonal needs, such as his family, is a "primary group." Groups on which the members are less broadly dependent, such as an incidental golf foursome or a joint investment group, are "secondary groups."

All groups (and especially small groups) are likely to display (1) extensive personal knowledge about each member by each member; (2) reliance on informal role differentiation; and (3) wide consensus among the members.

Relationships

An interpersonal relationship (or "dyad") is, in essence, a two-person group—formal or informal, primary or secondary—and displays all the characteristics of a group. However, relationships demand separate treatment in this book because of certain distinctive organizational dynamics resulting from their peculiar vulnerability. Unlike any other enduring social organization, a relationship is necessarily terminated by the departure of any single member.

The study of interpersonal relationships—friendship, marriage, parent/child, doctor/patient—has been a central concern in both sociological and psychological social psychologies.

Encounters

A final variety of social organization is the social act itself, the organization inherent in a direct, face-to-face *encounter* among persons. The number of participants is generally quite small, and the duration of an encounter is ordinarily a matter of minutes or hours. But despite the almost trivial scope, an encounter is the fundamental unit of collective action and, therefore, the basic building block for organizations of more impressive scope.

Each of these seven general varieties of social organization exerts characteristically differing influences on individuals and on social processes, as we shall show in the chapters of Part III.

RELATIONS AMONG ORGANIZATIONS

No social organization functions independently of other organizations; indeed, the Society of which older sociologists so frequently spoke refers to the dense and multidimensional web of interrelations among the countless number of specific social organizations.

As any organization looks at its environment, it sees not only people, buildings, geographical terrain, and meteorological conditions but—most vividly—*other organizations*. A wholesale firm, for example, is dependent on a swarm of other corporations—its suppliers, its customers, transportation firms, and so on—as well as regulatory agencies, labor unions, insurance companies, and trade associations.

Power and dependency relations with external organizations vitally impinge upon the collective actions of any organization (Evan, 1972), requiring it to bargain, negotiate, and confer with other organizations in social-exchange and joint-venture transactions. The whole range of conflict and cooperation strategies may be observed in these interorganizational transactions and maneuverings, quite analogous to the interactive negotiations between persons (Aldrich, 1979).

Sociological investigations of interorganizational relations have emphasized particularly the impact on the organization of the stability (Burns and Stalker, 1961) and the complexity (Lawrence and Lorsch, 1967) of its organizational environment. A simple, stable environment facilitates development of a more fixed and elaborated role structure. A complex or rapidly changing environment tends to induce a more fluid division of labor. For example, the roles in farming tend to be established far more stably than those in a leading-edge electronics firm.

A distinctive aspect of interorganizational relations is that one variety of organization may be nested or *embedded* within another; a bureaucracy such as a factory, for example, may have embedded within it—as suborganizations—a number of formal and informal groups (committees, task forces, factions, cliques). A state will have many communities embedded within it, and these will in turn have many families, firms, and associations embedded within them. From the standpoint of the embedded organization, the larger organization within which it is lodged is effectively an external organization—perhaps the most immediate and critical feature of the embedded organization's environment. The interorganizational bargaining and negotiation, conflicts and cooperations, are not confined to organizations of the same variety or scope. An embedded work group, for example, is necessarily engaged in just such a give-and-take with the larger bureaucracy in which it is lodged.

Because so many organizations are embedded and because an understanding of their environments is so critical to an understanding of any organization, the chapters of Part III will be sequenced in diminishing order of organizational scope, so that the reader will gain a greater appreciation of the environment of embedded organizations. Like persons, social organizations must adapt their character to the presses of their organizational environments. Since shifts in organizational character entail changes in the influences on individuals and social processes, we shall always need to consider the environment of any organization.

THE SOCIAL PSYCHOLOGICAL RELEVANCE OF ORGANIZATIONS

An individual lives virtually his entire life within social organizations; his biography could essentially be written as a history of his organizational involvements (Tausky, 1970). Consider, for the moment, bureaucracies alone. In any modernized society, the life of an individual is marked by bureaucratic membership and nonmembership roles from birth to death. Chances are that you were born in a hospital, were educated in a school system, are now employed by a business firm or agency, borrowed money for your present car from a financial institution, were (or will be) licensed by state bureaus to marry or to drive a car, and upon your death will be finally ministered to by a mortuary, a church, and a law firm. Similar birth-to-death sequences of organizational involvements could be sketched for both larger and smaller organizations, from national economies and communities, on the one hand, to small groups and pair relationships, on the other. Nearly all personal problems, challenges, opportunities, and constraints arise through one's life-course involvements with social organizations of some kind.

Going back now to the social nature of human beings as described in Chapter 2, the reader should note that it is by social organizations that a person is subjected to social roles—expectations about his various individual attributes. Organizations also serve as reference groups and contain significant others on whom one's identity depends; thus, organizations serve as important anchors for self-conception and self-appraisal. Organizations are vital direct sources of both benefits and costs; moreover, a person's more emergent benefit/cost transactions with others tend to occur within social organizations and sometimes create new ones. In this way, organizations serve as primary arenas for social interaction, providing both opportunities for and constraints upon negotiation of the social reality of one's personal character.

For all these reasons, the character and life course of any individual cannot be truly understood without close consideration of the many social organizations with which one must deal. Each of these organizations exerts a somewhat different influence on the individual. These influences vary, depending on the general organizational variety (or level of organizational scope), the pattern of organizational attributes, and the interorganizational context—in short, depending on the character of a particular organization. This organizational character shapes not only the contours of a person's social position and social role, but also his ''degrees of freedom'' in seeking to embrace, compromise, or evade these role expectations.

SUMMARY

A social organization is a type of joint venture in which not all the participants were necessarily involved in its original formation. It is always a structured joint activity undertaken to produce some type of collective good.

In its aspect of unity, an organization is a collectivity—a set of persons sharing the sense of participating in a joint venture. To produce a collective good ordinarily requires collective action (that is, a sharing in the costs of production proportional to one's share in the collective good). To bring about collective action, selective sidepayments are ordinarily necessary. In its aspect of diversity, an organization is a social structure—a differentiated pattern in which members occupy distinctive positions and perform distinctive but interdependent roles. A social organization thus may be defined as ''a structured collectivity undertaking collective action to produce a collective good.''

The Nature of Social Organizations

The core features of any social organization are its collective and special interests, its human and material resources, its culture, its division of labor, and its social differentiation (suborganizations and dimensional social structures). In characterizing a particular organization, one would want to know the nature and content, degree of elaboration, and degree of formalization of each of these features. Regarding the organization's structural features, one would want to know the shape of the structure; regarding its cultural norms, one would want to know their degrees of demandingness.

Seven general varieties of social organizations are distinguished, in descending order of organizational scope: societal-level structures, diffuse collectivities, communities, associations, groups, relationships, and encounters.

Organizations, like persons, are widely and profoundly interdependent and are engaged in a range of interorganizational transactions. The functioning and fate of any organization is greatly influenced by its environment—particularly by its relations to other organizations. One especially relevant relation is that of "nesting"; an organization may essentially be embedded within another organization of greater scope.

The social psychological relevance of social organizations is manifold. The individual lives virtually his entire life within organizations. Nearly all his personal problems, challenges, opportunities, and contraints are organizationally engendered. It is by social organizations that the individual is subjected to social roles—expectations about his various individual attributes. Moreover, organizations also serve as reference groups, as anchors for self-conception and self-appraisal, as sources of a wide range of shaping benefits and costs, and as arenas for social interaction in which the social reality of personal character is negotiated. The character of any particular organization critically shapes not only the contours of a person's social position and social role but also his degrees of freedom in seeking to embrace, compromise, or evade these role expectations.

SUGGESTIONS FOR ADDITIONAL READING

In our personal lives, we most often view social organizations "from the bottom up," from the perspective of a quite ordinary member. Yet, perhaps without realizing it, each of us has also had some experience as an organizational manager—at least in small peer groups, pair relationships, and encounters. Nothing makes the complex character of an organization more real to us than assuming the viewpoint of top management responsible for the organization's fate. Theodore Caplow's little book *How To Run Any Organization: A Manual of Practical Sociology* (New York: Holt, Rinehart, and Winston, 1976) is eminently successful in placing the reader in the boots of the top manager, and making the reality of organizational functioning, crisis, and change vivid and immediate. Moreover, the management principles taught there will prove useful to the reader in his personal life, as he moves into leadership positions in a variety of organizations, from families, groups, and local associations to corporations and social agencies.

At the other extreme of social order, we recommend Thomas C. Schelling's *Micromotives and Macrobehavior* (New York: Norton, 1978), which analyzes an enormous variety of highly patterned social orders that are not quite social organizations—audiences in lecture halls, lines outside movie theaters, and gaggles of pedestrians trying to cross a busy street. Although these are not joint ventures, and hence not organizations, they (as well as many other social orders) are shown to be distinctive social transactions in the face of interdependence of individual outcomes.

A readable guide through the complexities of the organizational attributes discussed in this chapter is Mary Zey-Ferrell's *Dimensions of Organizations: Environment, Context, Structure, Process, and Performance* (Santa Monica, California: Goodyear, 1979). Doubtless the most innovative strand of organizational theory and research today concerns organizational environments and interorganizational relations; the outstanding account of these ideas is Howard E. Aldrich's *Organizations and Environments* (Englewood Cliffs, N.J.: Prentice-Hall, 1979). Organizational processes—the focus of Part II of our book—are usefully discussed in Marvin E. Olsen's *The Process of Social Organization,* 2nd ed. (New York: Holt, Rinehart, and Winston, 1978) and in Karl E. Weick's *Social Psychology of Organizing,* 2nd ed. (Reading, Mass.: Addison-Wesley, 1979).

SOME
GUIDING
PRINCIPLES

An essential responsibility of this book is to develop progressively the core model of social psychology introduced at the end of Chapter 1. As the reader's familiarity with various major topics deepens, the core model with which we began can be further refined and elaborated and, hence, become more illuminating. Now that the reader has acquired a deeper understanding of the character of the individual and that of social organizations, we take this opportunity to introduce the first of these progressive refinements in our model of the relation between the individual and a social organization.

Through Chapters 2 and 3, we have begun to see that the link between the individual and an organization lies in his *organizational role*—a key concept that appeared nowhere in the original model (see Figure 1-2). We shall show, however, that organizational roles are central indeed to any sociological formulation of social psychology. This centrality is exhibited literally in the refined model depicted in Figure 4-1, which indicates that an individual's organizational role mediates between the various influences of his own individual character, the character of the social organization, and the character of social process. Three guiding principles of social psychology are reflected in this refined model and need to be stated clearly here.

FIRST PRINCIPLE

The first of these guiding principles is that *the character of the individual's organizational role affects both the character of the individual and the character of the organization.* In Chapter 2 we noted the sociological tenet that an individual tends to become the kind of person he or she is expected to be as an occupant of any particular role; army officers tend to become stern and authoritative whereas artists tend to become sensitive and somewhat eccentric. In Chapter 3 we saw that a functioning social organization of any kind is, at root, nothing other than a system of interdependent organizational roles; it is scarcely surprising, then, that the character of any of these roles—from the highest to the most lowly—directly affects the overall character of the organization. The tone and texture

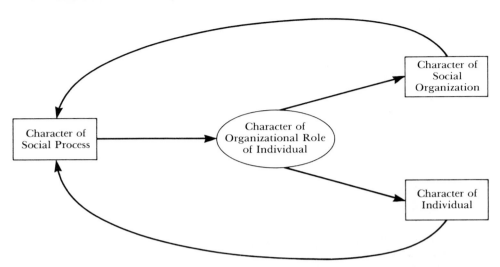

FIGURE 4-1.   **Organizational Role as Key Linkage among Individual, Organization, and Social Process**

of a scout troop, for example, may be effectively set as much by the line of action of the newest tenderfoot as by the role performance of the scoutmaster.

The personal and organizational consequences of organizational roles are topics of extensive research in social psychology as we will see in the remaining chapters of this book. Most often when we speak of organizational roles, we have in mind *membership* roles, that is, roles played only by a member of the structured collectivity (such as president, sergeant, freshman, parishioner, foreman, quarterback). But there are also a number of important *nonmembership* organizational roles, which may be either "manifest" or "latent," depending on the individual's awareness of his relation to the organization.

Manifest nonmembership roles include such organizational roles as admirer, supporter, and beneficiary on the positive side and detractor, opponent, and victim on the negative side. Even *latent* nonmembership roles—for instance, indirect beneficiary or indirect victim—are of vital importance in the "ecological order" of human society (Park, 1939; McCall, 1964). Such manifest and latent nonmembership roles, no less than membership roles, may have a profound impact on both the individual and the organization.

One example of such a manifest nonmembership role were Ralph Nader's activities in the 1960s as critic of General Motors and other corporations. Nader's actions had profound effects on GM's engineering and production standards and, reciprocally, provoked the company to undermine his credibility through a personal smear campaign. All of this subsequently catapulted Nader into the national spotlight and created for him a novel role-career as America's leading consumer advocate.

Some Guiding Principles

Latent nonmembership roles may exist without the direct awareness of either party, where an individual nonmember is bound to an organization in a relationship of mutual influence. A small military group embedded in a government bureau may bring anonymous death to a village thousands of miles away. A group of Arab businessmen may set in motion a sequence of events which brings prosperity several years later to a Scottish town they had never heard of. A physics student writes a paper which, through an improbable chain of events, eventually permits India to develop its own atomic bomb. In all of these cases, either party may have no knowledge that the other party even exists.

Taking into account this variety of membership and nonmembership roles, manifest and latent, it may be said without exaggeration that each individual plays *some role* in relation to every organization. It is this fact that renders meaningful the classical question regarding the nature of the relation between the individual and Society (in the sense of the web of organized social life in general).

SECOND PRINCIPLE

The second guiding principle is that *the character of organizational processes determines the nature of individuals' organizational roles* (which, in turn, simultaneously affect the character of the individuals and the character of the organization). That is to say, organizational roles—whether membership or nonmembership in type—do not simply exist in or around an organization; instead, they *develop*. Individual lines of action are mutually adjusted, fit together in a division of labor, through differentiation and coordination of various interests and resources. Organizational roles develop in this fashion through the functioning of certain *organizational processes* such as recruitment, socialization, interaction, innovation, and social control.

The contributions made by these five basic organizational processes to the development of individuals' organizational roles have been examined in many social psychological studies to be reviewed in Part II. Although each of these five processes distinctively influences the character of organizational roles, contemporary scholarship has been concerned also with how they interlace to form a ''role-making'' system of influences—a major topic throughout Part II and the principle focus of Chapter 10 in particular.

THIRD PRINCIPLE

The third guiding principle is that *the character of the individuals and that of the organization jointly affect the character of the organizational processes* of recruitment, socialization, interaction, innovation, and social control. The operation of such organizational processes could hardly be unaffected by the interests, resources, and tactics of the individuals and of the organization. In recruitment, for example, a storefront church may rely on tactics of spiritual conversion while an army may rely on forcible conscription; we may expect the character of the recruitment process for IBM to differ from that for Hell's Angels, and for a college-trained engineer as compared with a high-school dropout. The character of the individual often casts a long shadow on organizational functioning; both the gifted and the retarded student can strain the organizational processes of a school class, as can the bored, the hostile, or the manipulative student. As a great many social psychological studies have demonstrated, the individual is never the passive object of organizational processes but is an active participant employing varied countertactics of his own.

The one element of our model not yet examined in detail is that of social process, a concept with which many students are relatively unfamiliar. A general introduction to the concept of social process in organizational life is provided on page 75, and in the chapters of Part II we examine the five basic organizational processes—recruitment, socialization, interaction, innovation, and social control—and discuss the general character of each, how each is affected by the individual and by the organization, and the contribution each process makes to the development of an individual's organizational role.

SUGGESTIONS FOR ADDITIONAL READING

The model of social psychology as refined and elaborated in Figure 4–1 has considerable currency, particularly in the study of organizational behavior. An excellent presentation and discussion of this model—although in the narrower context of associations only—is to be found in Lyman W. Porter, Edward E. Lawler III, and J. Richard Hackman, *Behavior in Organizations* (New York: McGraw-Hill, 1975).

The principle that the character of the individual's organizational role affects the character of the individual as well as that of the organization is developed quite thoroughly and persuasively in Anselm L. Strauss, *Mirrors and Masks: The Search for Identity* (New York: Free Press, 1959). The antecedents of that work are still very much worthwhile: Everett C. Hughes' "Institutional Office and the Person" (reprinted in Hughes, *The Sociological Eye: Selected Papers,* Chicago: Aldine-Atherton, 1971: 132–140). Concerning our discussion of nonmembership organizational roles, the reader who may be unacquainted with the very illuminating example of Ralph Nader's role relative to General Motors may wish to examine Thomas Whiteside's *The Investigation of Ralph Nader: General Motors versus One Determined Man* (New York: Arbor House, 1972).

How basic organizational processes give rise to organizational roles is reviewed and synthesized in George Graen, "Role-Making Processes within Complex Organizations" (pp. 1201–1245 in Marvin D. Dunnette, ed., *Handbook of Industrial and Organizational Psychology,* Chicago: Rand McNally, 1975). The concept of role-making was introduced by Ralph H. Turner in his article "Role-taking: Process versus Conformity" (pp. 20–40 in Arnold M. Rose, ed., *Human Behavior and Social Processes,* Boston: Houghton Mifflin, 1962). The related concept of "situational adjustment" advanced by Howard S. Becker ("Personal Change in Adult Life," *Sociometry*, 1964, 27: 40–53) warrants further attention for its bearing on this principle.

How the character of organizational processes is affected jointly by the nature of individuals and of the organization is nowhere more discernible than in the case of socialization. In their valuable article, "Toward a Theory of Organizational Socialization" (*Research in Organizational Behavior*, 1979, 1: 209–264), John Van Maanen and Edgar H. Schein have analyzed the contingent pairings of organizational and individual tactics in socialization and have related these to structural features of organizations. Similarly instructive is the analysis of the innovation and social control processes in Richard Hawkins and Gary Tiedeman, *Creation of Deviance: Interpersonal and Organizational Determinants* (Columbus, Ohio: Merrill, 1975).

As a general introduction to the concept of organizational processes, we may recommend Marvin E. Olsen's *The Process of Social Organization,* 2nd ed. (New York: Holt, Rinehart, and Winston, 1978).

PART II

BASIC SOCIAL PROCESSES

One can safely assert that there are complex interrelationships between social organizations and the individuals within them. But this still leaves the important question of how such mutual influences are transmitted. More specifically, through what medium do such transmissions of influence travel? Through what processes does a wailing infant become an American, a young man learn to run a company, a couple work out their differences so they can remain together, a doctor transform his textbook learning into an active practice, and an agency keep its employees from simply walking off with its materials and suborning the clients for their own profit and amusement?

These and a multitude of other shaping effects are created through the *basic social processes* of recruitment, socialization, interaction, innovation, and social control. In the chapters of Part II we will be examining each of these as components of the social process, but they are not actually separable in real life. For example, no socialization occurs without some interaction; there is usually some recruitment aspect to any interaction; socialization usually has some forward-looking social control features; live interaction almost inevitably involves some innovation; and so on. In any social activity one can find each of these processes woven together (although of course one may predominate on a given occasion), and they are basic in that they occur in all human societies, at all historical times, and at all organizational levels.

These basic processes are often thought of far too narrowly—recruitment being considered only in beginnings, social control only as deterrence, and innovation only as grand invention, for example. But when one looks, one finds these processes everywhere in social living. The reader might enjoy spotting them in his or her own life situations over, say, the next week to see their pervasiveness and become sensitized to their workings. In order to round out our view of these processes, their impacts upon the establishment of roles and upon the course of organizational careers are examined, and finally the processes are considered in the context of social change. We should emerge from Part II with a far deeper understanding of how organizations and individuals "get together." There is both a logical and an empirical sequence in the workings of these five basic processes, and the beginning of this natural sequence is recruitment.

The Army uses the symbol of Uncle Sam to appeal to a potential recruit's sense of duty and patriotism.

CHAPTER 5

Recruitment

How do individuals become members of organizations? And how do organizations gain memberships?

The answer, in both cases, is through the organizational process of recruitment. Through recruitment, a youth becomes a member of the Third Army, a bisexual becomes part of the San Francisco gay community, a girl achieves the status of "young married," and a retiree finds himself one of the "regular crowd" who drink coffee together at the local coin shop. How one ends up in his or her own organizational "niches"—and changes from niche to niche throughout one's life career—entails, first of all, recruitment.

Recruitment is the process through which individuals' participation in a social organization is *determined*. As one examines the phenomenon of recruitment in social life, one begins to see that a very large number of organizational and individual activities bear directly or indirectly upon it. A good deal of interpersonal communication concerns recruitment; public relations and advertising are in large matter involved with recruitment; entire industries, such as education, clothing, and cosmetics, are in good part dependent upon it. Recruiting is a deep and continuing aspect of human life.

At first glance, the recruitment process appears complex and multifaceted, but it can be understood by isolating some of its basics. The first two of these aspects are *selection* and *placement*. Selection concerns which individuals, if any, will act as members of the collectivity. Placement concerns which positions in the various social structures of the organization will be occupied by these individual members.

As the term selection implies, membership in a collectivity is always selective—no organization includes all human beings. From the organization's viewpoint, some individuals are highly desirable for membership, others are acceptable, and some are undesirable. For the organization, then, selection is a process of obtaining desirable members while avoiding undesirable members. Similarly, from an individual's viewpoint, membership in a particular organization may be personally desirable, tolerable, or undesirable. For the individual, selection is a process of obtaining desirable memberships and avoiding undesirable memberships. As Groucho Marx once remarked, "I wouldn't join any organization that would have me for a member."

Whenever an individual joins an organization, he enters not just a collectivity but a structured collectivity. Thus, a person is never recruited simply into membership but always into some organizational position and role as well. One is recruited as a "newlywed," not just a "married"; as a helper, carpenter, or electrician, not just a construction worker. No organization is so unstructured that it does not have an internal pattern of positions, and an individual is always recruited for some position, not just membership, even if the position is no more specific than "new member." Therefore, placement is simultaneous with selection and is of equal importance. Organizations recruit role occupants, such as treasurer, janitor, and client, and individuals seek organizational positions and roles.

It is also important to bear in mind that the recruitment process does not terminate upon an individual's entry into membership and a social position. Recruitment is actually an ongoing, never-ending organizational process for both the organization and the individual. Almost from the first moment of entrance into the organization, the individual is looking around for further opportunities and the organization is evaluating him or her with an eye toward other positions.

Selection—the sorting out of desirable and undesirable members—is a continuous business for any organization. Steps must be taken recurrently to retain desirable members for the collectivity and to eject undesirable members. Similarly, individuals must continually strive to maintain their desirable memberships and to relinquish their undesirable memberships. Placement, too, is continuous. Occupants may be recruited *out of,* as well as into, organizational positions—through promotion, demotion, or lateral transfer. Thus, both the organization and the individual member must take continual action concerning ongoing placement, each striving to "do better." The individual's movement through a series of organizational positions, through ongoing recruitment, constitutes his *organizational career,* a matter of great moment to both the organization and the individual (and extensively studied by sociological social psychologists).

Figure 5-1 summarizes these points concerning selection and placement. Selection (indicated by heavy arrows) is a question of membership in the collectivity. An individual may or may not be selected, and once selected may or may not be subsequently "selected out" of the collectivity. Placement (indicated by light arrows) is a question of position within the social structures of the organization—both primary (role structure) and secondary (suborganizations and dimensional structures). Since placement, like selection, is never settled once and for all, the individual member is likely (over time) to occupy a series of positions comprising his organizational career.

Recruitment

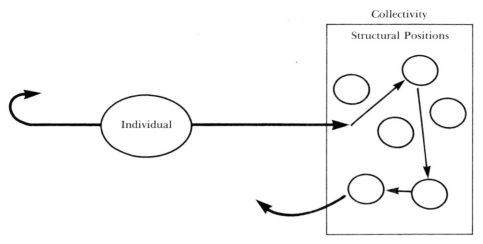

Collectivity

Structural Positions

Individual

FIGURE 5-1. Selection and Placement Processes

THE BASIS OF RECRUITMENT

The basis on which the question of membership for an individual is determined may be either ascriptive or voluntary.

Ascriptive Recruitment

In ascriptive recruitment, the organization holds membership "rights" to an individual (and/or vice versa), which may be backed by "legitimate" force or threat. Which individuals an organization holds such rights to is determined by a wide range of individual characteristics.

When a child is born into a particular family, for example, that family has ascriptive rights to claim this child as a member. This usually means that a particular speech community (such as English-speaking people), a polity (say, the United States), and an age-sex structure (for instance, the cohort of American girls born in the early 1970s) also lay ascriptive claims on the child. Most communities to which the family belongs (local, ethnic, religious) also claim the individual by virtue of birth to one of its members. If the family belongs to a church that practices infant baptism or similar procedures, the church may also claim the child. Even some occupational structures (for example, caste systems) may claim her at birth. And should the child be born in a hospital, this bureaucracy will claim her as a client.

Birth rights are not the only ascriptive basis for organizational claims. For example, *developmental characteristics* of the individual, such as attaining a certain age or failing to attain certain abilities, may give organizations a claim to his membership. The school system, the army, and institutions for the developmentally disabled are clear examples of such organizations. The individual's *behavior* may afford some organizations, such as the criminal justice system, the civil courts, or mental hospitals, the right to demand his participation. Even *events that merely happen to* the individual may generate ascriptive claims. For example, being severely injured in an automobile accident may give a hospital emergency room rights to claim him as a client. Being graduated from college gives the alumni association the right to claim him as a member. By virtue of *joining one organization,* the individual becomes subject to the rightful claims of still other organizations. By entering into a marriage, for example, one may rightfully be claimed by the spouse's family. By taking a job with a particular company, one may be claimed by a particular labor union.

In many of these cases, the organization's rights to claim the individual are recognized by the law of the polity and thus are backed by the legitimate potential use of force by the polity on behalf of the claimant organization. In other cases, such as street gangs and disreputable labor unions, the ascriptive "rights" claimed by the organization are not recognized by the polity—although the claims may be backed by the use or threat of force by the organization itself. In the case of some religious organizations, the threat may not be one of force but of eternal damnation of the individual or his kin. It should be noted that even though an organization may hold membership rights to an individual, the organization may choose not to exercise these rights. Membership may be withheld or withdrawn from individuals whom the organization finds to be undesirable; thus, selection is an aspect even of ascriptive recruitment.

Finally, there is the point that ascriptive claims may be held—and exercised—by the individual upon the organization as well. The ancient notion of birthright, for example, implies that the individual too has a right to membership in his family, his nation-state, and so on. Similarly, at age five a child receives the right to schooling, and being severely injured confers a right to medical treatment.

Voluntary Recruitment

In voluntary recruitment, neither the organization nor the individual has any special rights concerning membership. Under these circumstances, the recruitment process displays an additional aspect before selection and placement. This prior aspect is *attraction,* the process of generating a set of membership possibilities. For the organization, attraction is a matter of generating a set of candidates from which to select members. For the individual, attraction amounts to generating a set of membership offers or options from which to select. In attraction, each party is essentially seeking to make its favorable features widely known so as to stimulate an appreciable number of applicants or offers.

For organizations, this is largely a matter of "public relations"—the techniques of image management or "presentation of self" in a manner that attracts applicants, customers, monies, and in general produces a favorable climate of opinion. This mat-

Recruitment

ter has two aspects: (1) actively seeking to avoid unfavorable publicity by avoiding unpopular actions and/or controlling information about unpopular actions taken; and (2)
obtaining favorable publicity by promoting one's publicly favored actions or presenting one's actions in a good light. There is now sprawling public relations, advertising,
and marketing industry involved in such public image management, and its clientele
includes firms, celebrities, foundations, churches, and presidential candidates. More
direct attraction overtures by organizations to individuals may be made through
public meetings and sponsored events, direct-mail campaigns, and soliciting referrals
from other organizations. In the modern social ''marketplace,'' organizations spend
substantial resources on the business of attraction.

For the individual also, attraction is essentially a ''public relations'' matter of
favorable presentation of self as described in Chapter 2, a process of ''impression
management'' in which the individual attempts to control the information about
himself that an organization might receive. Unfavorable information may be carefully
omitted, hidden, denied, or made the subject of elaborate excuses or justifications; active efforts are made to emphasize (if not exaggerate) those personal attributes that one
believes would be viewed favorably. Specific alternative membership possibilities may
be obtained through some of the same tactics employed by organizations—advertising,
direct-mail campaigns, and use of broker agencies. Most often, however, the individual obtains his membership possibilities by responding directly to the attraction
efforts already made by organizations. That is to say, having become favorably aware
of an organization or an organizational position, he applies to the organization for
possible membership. By some means, formal or informal, the individual lets it be
known that he or she is available—for a job, a sale, a membership in the club, a relationship, or whatever the recruiting situation may be.

Attraction, by either an organization or an individual, is a matter of making
known what that organization or individual has to offer—what possible benefits could
be obtained in terms of joint ventures and exchanges. Voluntary recruitment is essentially a *social-exchange process,* as described in Chapter 2. Through attraction tactics,
each party communicates what benefits it could provide the other; through selection
tactics, each party communicates what benefits it wants from the other in return.
Therefore, some balance between attraction and selection must be worked out, as
every recruiter and every ''single'' discovers. If a bargain satisfactory to both parties
can be struck, each party selects the other and the individual becomes a member. If
the attraction is not mutual, the eventual selection will not be mutual, and the individual will not become a member.

Various attraction/selection dilemmas arise in this exchange process (Porter,
Lawler, and Hackman, 1975: ch. 2). First, for either party, its own attraction and
selection activities are somewhat incompatible. If selection is pressed too far (making
heavy demands for benefits), attractiveness suffers; if attraction is pressed too far (only
presenting possible benefits), selection suffers (obtaining too little information about
benefits that might be obtained). Second, the attraction efforts of one party are in conflict with the selection efforts of the other. For example, if a company is too selective,
its attractiveness—and therefore its number of recruits—may suffer, but if it heavily

stresses attraction, it may get flooded with unqualified recruits and customers. In attraction, either party tends to be motivated to put the most favorable face on itself, emphasizing all that it *could* provide. The other party, in its selection efforts, seeks instead to learn both the positive and the negative attributes—the real story—in order to determine what it *would* get from the first party.

ORGANIZATIONAL AND INDIVIDUAL INTERESTS

The exchange of benefits between organization and individual is important not only in voluntary but also in ascriptive recruitment. If the organization expects to derive no benefit from an individual's membership, it will withhold membership even if it holds rights to that individual's participation. Similarly, no organizational position is totally without benefits to its occupant; even a slave, prisoner, or conscripted soldier at least receives minimal sustenance. If the individual benefits are too few, he will withhold his actual participation in the collective action (perhaps at the cost of his life) even if he cannot escape membership. Both voluntary and ascriptive recruitment, then, are matters of social exchange and differ only in the means by which membership possibilities are identified.

Organizational Recruitment Interests

When a pool of potential recruits has been identified (on the basis of ascriptive rights or through voluntary attraction), the organization must obtain further information about each of these potential members in order to make its selection. The recruitment interest of the organization in an individual depends heavily on its perceptions of the individual's personal attributes—appearance, style, skills, resources, goals, attitudes, habits. The membership norms and, especially, the positional norms (role expectations) provide a fairly specific set of organizational expectations concerning the pattern of personal attributes that a new position occupant should display. These normative expectations constitute the selection criteria against which potential recruits are compared and thus guide the nature of the information-gathering procedures. Such procedures may be highly formalized or quite informal, lengthy or brief, but they always exist in the recruitment process—and at all levels of organizations, from the government civil service on down to the neighborhood gang of boys or a pair of potential lovers.

Ability criteria, for example, lead the organization to inquire into the potential recruit's training credentials and performance record. Testimonials may be sought, and the potential recruit may be required to undergo direct tests of ability. Motivational and attitudinal criteria may also dictate direct tests, the providing of character references, and inquiry into past performance. Again, such screenings may be highly formalized, as with the extensive tests and personal dossiers involved in obtaining a security-clearance job, or they may be as informal as the simple questions "Where are you from?" or "That looks like a good dirt bike; can you ride it?" More purely social criteria (such as appearance, style, ethnicity, family background, social connections) typically dictate some type of personal interview in addition to historical backgound checks. If the person's attributes meet one or more of the organization's expectations (and hence appear potentially useful in satisfying some collective interest), the organization may view him as a potential collective resource of some value.

In absolute terms, of course, virtually no individual is without some small potential value to any organization. However, selection is based not on absolute value but on *relative value.* First, the potential usefulness of the individual or the position must be weighed relative to the potentially costly consequences of other, less desirable attributes. Second, the value of the potential resource must be compared to that of existing actual resources. Third, the potential value of the individual must be assessed relative to the potential value of other possible recruits.

A baseball team, for example, may learn of a youngster with great power-hitting ability but may not be interested in recruiting him. First, he may also be known to strike out frequently, to have a poor throwing arm, and to be injury-prone; that is to say, some of his other attributes may outweigh his valued attributes. Second, the team may be loaded with power hitters already and thus may have relatively little need for another. Third, the team may know of another youngster with good power who strikes out less often and has a better arm. Whether an organization views a potential member as desirable, acceptable, or undesirable thus depends on the value of that person's attributes relative to his negative attributes, existing collective resources, and alternative potential members, as well as to the organization's perception of its relative needs.

The fact that a potential recruit's value is relative to these other factors leads to some interesting "supply and demand" situations. If more teachers are graduated than there are teaching jobs, schools can be very selective; if there is more demand for computer personnel than the supply of applicants, companies must concentrate on attraction and cannot be too concerned with possible costly attributes. If a person already has many friends and memberships, he or she can be choosy about new ones; but if new in town, he or she is likely to be less discriminating, at least at first. In Alaska, where there are far more males than females, any woman is far more likely to be recruited for a relationship than in Washington, D. C., where there are more females than males.

Individual Recruitment Interests

A parallel account can be sketched for the individual. That is, the recruitment interest of an individual in obtaining a position within an organization depends on his perceptions of the attributes of that organizational position in relation to his personal interests and resources. The fact that the individual's criteria for joining are not as coherent as the organization's does not mean that they are any less real. Indeed, the individual often has more at stake, with regard to his or her role-identities, than the organization has. A writer, for example, has more riding on having a story accepted than the magazine has in looking for good material. A child moving into a new neighborhood may have more concern over being accepted by the neighborhood play group than the group has over gaining one more member. Even when the individual is being eagerly sought by the organization, recruitment will have at least as much impact on the individual's personal life as on the organization's future development.

The individual's expectations concerning the pattern of organizational attributes that a position of this type should display tend not to be as well specified or as stable as the organization's expectations about the atttributes of position occupants, since the latter rest on an organizational culture. The individual may hold very naîve expectations, based on Hollywood depictions of youthful bull sessions, or he may hold well-grounded expectations based on previous participation in similar organizations. Whatever the basis of his expectations concerning a particular type of position, these serve as his selection criteria against which position possibilities of this type are matched. His normative expectations thus guide his information-gathering efforts about opportunities. If the person's expectations are grossly unrealistic, the realities of the opportunity marketplace may provide a rude awakening and expectations will have to be realigned with existing possibilities.

If the person considers a position to be potentially useful in the pursuit of some joint venture or personal interest, he or she will view the organizational position favorably. But this is not the end of his evaluations. An individual always evaluates a potential organizational position relative to its costly attributes, to his existing personal resources, and to alternative potential positions. This may be done consciously or impulsively, but some such evaluating always occurs. A young engineer may learn of a high-paying job but may not be interested in applying for it. First, the job is with a firm with poor advancement prospects and is located in an undesirable region. Second, he already has a lucrative job. Third, he has learned of a comparable job in his favorite city. Whether an individual views a potential organizational position as desirable, acceptable, or undesirable thus depends on its assessed relative personal value.

Relations Between Recruitment Interests

Since recruitment is a social-exchange process, its outcome hinges on the relationship between the organization's interest in the individual and the individual's interest in the organizational position. At a given time, these respective levels of interest may be *congruent* (e.g., each finds the other desirable) or *discrepant* (the organization views the individual as desirable while the individual sees the organizational position as undesirable or vice versa). The next moves of each party depend on this relationship between their levels of interest (exhibited in Figure 5–2).

Individual Views Organizational Position as:

Organization Views Individual as:	Desirable	Acceptable	Undesirable
Desirable	Congruent Interests: both highly interested Superior Deal	Discrepant Interests: *O* interested *I* highly interested	Discrepant Interests: *O* uninterested *I* highly interested
Acceptable	Discrepant Interests: *O* highly interested *I* interested	Congruent Interests: both interested Standard Deal	Discrepant Interests: *O* uninterested *I* interested
Undesirable	Discrepant Interests: *O* highly interested *I* uninterested	Discrepant Interests *O* interested *I* uninterested	Congruent Interests: both uninterested No Deal

FIGURE 5-2.   Relations between Recruitment Interests of Organization and of Individual

ORGANIZATIONAL AND INDIVIDUAL TACTICS

Let us first consider congruent interests, which are more straightforward than discrepant interests.

Congruent-Interest Tactics

In the case where each party considers the other to be *undesirable,* negotiations are simply terminated, and each ceases to regard the other as a viable alternative. Statistically, this is probably the most common attraction-selection outcome in social life. Most individuals and organizations become rather skilled at quickly checking out possibilities of potential memberships and end the majority of such "negotiations" at an early stage by mutual consent.

When each party views the other as being *acceptable,* negotiations also tend to be relatively simple. For a given position, such as professor, any organization has a basic standard offer—some standard share in the collective goods and some standard package of selective sidepayments (a certain established salary, office arrangement, teaching load, committee load). Similarly, among actual and potential occupants of that position there tends to be some corresponding basic standard concerning what an individual should normally bring to and put into the performance of that role. And

85

when the parties see one another as acceptable, each tends to make to the other the basic standard offer and each is likely to accept, resulting in what we might call a "standard deal."

Behaviorally, one party makes an explicit offer and the other makes an explicit acceptance, with the cross-offer and cross-acceptance remaining implicitly couched within the explicit ones. An employer, for example, offers a contract, the terms of which set forth not only what the organization offers but also what the employee will contribute in return. By applying for a position, an individual is effectively offering his services and resources, leaving the organization to accept or reject. An organization may also make the first contact, offering a position which the individual must accept or reject.

In the case of ascriptive recruitment, it is generally the organization that makes the first move, "offering" a position by notifying the individual that the organization has exercised its right to his participation. This sort of "draft" procedure implicitly carries with it the offer of basic standard benefits and the demand for basic standard participation by the individual; the draftee accepts this offer by reporting and signing up.

When each party regards the other as *desirable,* each offers the other more than the standard deal. These extra benefits (inducements) are tendered to repay the other for the extraordinary benefits a party considers it would derive from the individual's participation in this organization. With each offering extra inducements, an agreement in which each party receives more than the standard deal is likely to be reached quickly. In these circumstances, both parties are also most likely to regard the potential mutual involvement as a joint venture. In such a situation of mutual desirability, rules are likely to be bent, standard requirements waived, and any oppositions swept aside in a by-pass of normal routines. Both sides will tend to work cooperatively to "close the deal." If subsequent events should prove that the deal was less than desirable, each side may fall back on the legalities of the standard rules—for example, the fine print in the contract or the state laws governing a marriage.

Discrepant-Interest Tactics

Discrepant interests are encountered perhaps more often than congruent interests and are, in any case, much more interesting. An important sociological principle underlying this greater fascination is the *principle of least interest* (Waller, 1938), which holds that the party having the lower level of interest in the other party has less to lose and can therefore more readily dictate the terms of any agreement between them. For example, if a television series is eager to retain a star because of his popularity but the star is not very interested in continuing the show, the star is in a position to drive a hard bargain. If Jack is more interested in Jill than Jill is in Jack, Jill can dictate more of the terms of their journey up the hill.

In situations of discrepant interests, then, the general strategy of the more interested party is to strive to make itself more attractive to the other—in other words, to eliminate or at least reduce the discrepancy and thereby escape the operation of the principle of least interest. Of course, the general strategy of the less interested party is to try to maintain the interest discrepancy and the accompanying power advantage.

Nonnegative Interests. In those cases where one party is desirable and the other is merely acceptable, the party with less interest in the other is in a position to drive a hard bargain, holding out for still further inducements. A limit to such bargaining, however, resides in one of the attraction/selection dilemmas mentioned above; if the holdout party becomes excessive in demands for inducements, its own attractiveness tends to suffer, perhaps to the point at which that party is no longer seen as desirable (at which point the power advantage and the inducements disappear).

If it is the organization that must offer inducements (the selective sidepayments discussed in Chapter 3), these inducements can be drawn from the collectivity and/or from the social structure. Within the collectivity a variety of human and material resources are to be found, access to which may be offered to the potential recruit. The social structure affords direct social rewards of position (such as status, power, and authority) as well as various role privileges and perquisites accompanying the position; a higher than standard position may be offered, or rapid advancement promised, or additional role privileges offered. For example, a keenly sought executive may be offered stock-buying privileges, a lush expense account, and assistance from the firm's tax consultants, in addition to the standard benefits.

The individual seeks to elicit organizational inducements that are personally valuable to him—without having to increase his own offer of standard participation—by tactfully communicating why he places so little relative value on the offered organizational position. He may point out the offsetting negative attributes of the position, the kinds of benefits he is already obtaining elsewhere, and the benefits he believes he could obtain from available alternative positions. In doing so, he implicitly communicates to the organization the sorts of inducement to which he might respond favorably. This must usually be done with some delicacy and aplomb, lest the person be redefined as offensive and undesirable.

If, on the other hand, it is the individual who must offer inducements to the organization, two possible targets must be distinguished. First, he may offer to contribute more than the standard personal resources toward satisfying one or more of the collective interests—for example, by putting in more hours, taking a lower salary, making larger donations, or by obtaining extra skills. Second, in the individual counterpart to the organization's selective sidepayments, he or she may offer to contribute personal resources toward satisfying the personal special interests of individuals already within the organization. Such offers may be either direct or veiled and promissory, and are usually directed toward persons who occupy ''gatekeeper'' positions in the organization, such as purchasing agents, casting directors, and persons generally in positions of authority over memberships and positions.

From the organization's standpoint, the gatekeepers seek to obtain more valuable inducements from the individual without having to increase the standard offer of the organization. They will communicate, in some fashion, the lower relative value of the prospective recruit by pointing out his negative attributes, existing organizational resources, and the quality of alternative recruits believed to be available. Through such communications, they let the person know what sorts of additional contributions—either to the collectivity or to the special interests of the gatekeeper personally—might render the individual more attractive. For the collectivity, such additional contributions may include an unusually binding contract, acceptance of a lower than standard position, or even acceptance of an additional role as informant. Additional contributions to the personal interests of the gatekeeper may include help with pet projects, pay kickbacks, sexual favors, or membership in the gatekeeper's own power clique.

Since the bending or breaking of organizational rules and even the laws of the land may be involved, this bargaining between gatekeeper and applicant tends to be conducted diplomatically and through the more subtle interaction processes that we will be examining in Chapter 7. If recruitment is to occur under these circumstances, the individual must "catch on" to the real scene and then carry out some successful strategy—the usual one being compliance.

Negative Interests. The most seriously discrepant interest situations are those in which one party regards the other as undesirable. The party who so regards the other is then motivated to employ avoidance tactics by striving to make itself either unavailable or unattractive to the undesirable party. An organization, for instance, may simply tell an undesirable candidate that it has no positions available at this time for which he is qualified. "I'll call you when there's an opening" is a common refrain, from the largest organization on down to the disinterested potential love or friendship candidate. If such a tactic is not possible, the organization may conveniently lose part of the application papers, "find out" that the authorized decision maker is in a meeting or out of town, or declare a temporary freeze on admission of new members. And some organizations find such a large proportion of the populace undesirable as members that they deliberately conceal knowledge of their entry points from the public at large. Where does one go to join a survivalist group or the Trilateral Commission?

Within the organization itself, entry points to certain positions may be deliberately concealed or masked by behind-the-scene procedures unknown to the general membership. Anyone might apply and be easily accepted as an attendant on a Hollywood studio lot, but how does one apply to be a contracted scriptwriter or producer? Many a young organization man has suffered anxiety in trying to discover the real rules for entry into senior management positions. And many an individual has been left in permanent mystery over why some relationship never "clicked."

The culture of every organization includes certain patterns of rules of conduct and standards governing personal attributes and role performances. Some of these rules and standards apply to all members, while others apply only to occupants of certain positions. But for rank-and-file member or officer, there is a fair amount of leeway in these standards. A common avoidance tactic toward undesirables is to invoke such rules and standards in a highly stringent manner, as a means of demonstrating that the undesirable is not suitable for the position he seeks. For instance, during the 1960s, health and building inspectors would revoke licenses and close psychedelic shops and other hangouts unwanted by the community by applying regulations "to the letter." Management will often invoke some minor disqualification as a means of explaining why a candidate was turned down for a higher position. The important point is that these same rules and standards are bent or waived for desirable candidates. This tactic is easily used because few, if any, persons meet all the possible qualifications that could be applied to them.

Imposing application and membership "fees" is another tactic for making membership unavailable to candidates who cannot or will not pay the price demanded. These can be either legitimate fees or outright bribes, monetary or otherwise. A homeowners' association, for example, requires that candidates have purchased a house and thus effectively freezes out renters. An exclusive club may have high membership dues, and a clique may be open only to persons who own certain types of expensive cars or even airplanes. Again, desirable members may find some of these "entrance fees" waived, whereas they are stringently demanded of undesirables.

Rules, standards, and entrance fees lend themselves to use not only in unavailability tactics but also in an organization's attempts to appear unattractive to undesirable candidates. The high personal costs in meeting the various rules, standards, and fees may be heavily emphasized and even exaggerated in order to discourage persons whom the organization does not want.

Some organizations publicize and selectively exaggerate the existence of demanding, even frightening "rite of passage" rituals marking induction into the organization or into specific positions within it. The prospect of boot camp, with its harsh regimen, forced marches, and so forth, effectively deters many possible army recruits who dislike such rigors, while simultaneously attracting some who find it an exciting challenge. In the same way, motorcycle gang initiation rites repel the unlikely candidates and attract likely ones. Therefore, publicity can serve a dual function as a tactic for attraction and for making the organization appear unattractive, because the same publicity will be received differently by potential candidates with different plans and self-conceptions.

If the undesirable individual has no strong interest in the organizational position, he may apply, be subjected to unavailability tactics, and simply acquiesce in the organization's withholding of an acceptance. If, on the other hand, he views the position as highly desirable or a matter of his ascriptive rights, he is not so likely simply to give in to such unavailability tactics. He may be sufficiently motivated to undertake an active and persistent "campaign" for membership. Such a person might apply and reapply through all available channels, offering inducements of various sorts to many collective and individual interests, in hopes of winning sponsorship. And indeed it often happens that the person's persistence impresses organizational personnel to the point that he is reappraised into the acceptable or even desirable category. Many a contract or marriage proposal has been "renegotiated" into acceptance in just such a manner.

The person disqualified by stringent rules, standards, and entrance fees may adopt countertactics of taking actions to become more qualified—by taking special training, working out, dieting, getting into a better financial position, and so on. This is also a situation in which the person may offer inducements, such as gifts, favors, bribes, sex, and promised additional services, aimed at appealing to the personal interests of organization personnel. Either or both of these countertactics may, again, prove successful.

But if the person remains undesirable from the standpoint of the organization, it will reaffirm and strengthen its unavailabilty and unattractiveness tactics. The applicant is more actively discouraged in the hope that his interest might be reduced to the level where he will "get the message" and go away.

On the other side, the individual may find the organization undesirable and may undertake his own avoidance tactics. If the organization has only a standard interest in him, he may simply decline the offer and the whole process is terminated. However, in ascriptive recruitment or when the organization regards him as highly desirable, the matter is not so simple. Here the organization will stringently invoke its ascriptive rights or will make an exceptional offer of inducements. Sometimes these two tactics are combined into "an offer you can't refuse," as in *The Godfather*. The organization is motivated to campaign for the highly desirable person's participation actively and persistently.

Some "drafts" can be legitimately and effectively declined: "If nominated, I will not run; if elected, I will not serve." Other drafts, by an army or a street gang, for example, cannot be simply declined because of the real threat of substantial negative inducements—an arrest warrant, violence, or blacklisting.

Unavailability tactics may be employed by concealing knowledge of oneself or one's qualifications, for instance, by failing to register for Selective Service or by changing one's address and phone number and, sometimes, even one's name. More simply, a person may just fail to respond to letters and not be available for phone calls. An individual may also handle offers from undesirable organizations by joining some other organization, such as the ministry, the Peace Corps, prison, another firm, another marriage. In extreme cases, the person may simply desert his current social web. A distinctive unavailability tactic is to deliberately prepare oneself to fail the qualifications for the organizational position. One may deliberately do poorly on performance tests, be insulting, disfigure oneself, and otherwise create a presentation of self as unfit.

Such tactics, of course, make a person not only unavailable but also less attractive to the organization. Even if its rights to the individual are legitimate, it may not be worth the time and trouble to track him down. The person may also diminish his attractiveness by emphasizing his negative qualities or by demanding unreasonable inducements.

THE CONTRIBUTIONS OF RECRUITMENT

Our principal interest in the various basic social processes lies in what contributions each makes to the development of an individual's web of organizational roles. Basically, the process of recruitment determines whether the organizational participation of an individual is to be of the membership or nonmembership type. And if the individual does participate as a member, the process of recruitment also determines which organizational positions he or she is to occupy.

Recruitment is somewhat precarious for both the organization and the individual because both sides are dealing with only a few facts about the other and a lot of unknowns. A hope-it-works-out attitude is common, because the process can so easily go astray despite the best efforts of all concerned. Job turnover, divorce rates, and percentages of dropouts and washouts give some statistical clues to the sometimes hit-or-miss nature of recruiting. Attraction tactics may be stretched so far beyond the truth that the realities of membership are shattering. Selection may be based on faulty data or inappropriate qualifications, to the embarrassment and expense of all concerned. Social change may lead to altered requirements on either side. Either party may find itself committed, even legally bound, to a situation that turns out to be a bad bargain.

The recruitment process may be fraught with peril in discrepant situations as well. The person denied membership even after countertactics may not let the matter rest there. He may seek legal redress, through equal opportunity laws and the like; he may seek "reform" of the organization; he may turn on the organization and attack it; or he may join a revolution to overthrow it. Organizations are aware of these possibilities and so tend to be wary and diplomatic in their handling of rejections, attempting at the same time to maintain good public relations. The organization denied a desirable recruit may also take actions, such as blacklisting the person, using violence against him, and so on. Such retributive actions are particularly likely at the pair relationship and family levels, but they are also frequent in large organizations. Thus, the individual too is motivated to employ some public relations and diplomacy in his declining of offers. Thus, in both directions, the very real, sometimes stark, organizational process of recruitment tends to be covered with a veneer of good manners and etiquette.

Yet, for all these vagaries, recruitment can be considered perhaps the fundamental social process, because it determines the individual's participation in organizations at all levels, from the planetary to the encounter. Nor does recruitment merely set the stage for the operation of other organizational processes; it is inextricably intertwined with them, as we shall see in the next several chapters.

Throughout the remainder of this book we shall see that the recruitment process never terminates, either for the organization or the individual. For both parties, membership remains, at least potentially, an open question, and so does the subsidiary question of the individual's place in the social structure of the organization. Both selection and placement recur in continuing cycles of ongoing negotiations, always employing the tactics described above. As we will see in Chapter 10, recruitment processes continue to operate throughout the person's life career.

SUMMARY

Recruitment is the process through which individuals' organizational participation is determined. The aspect of selection concerns which individuals will act as members of a collectivity. The organization attempts to obtain desirable members while avoiding undesirable members; the individual strives to obtain desirable memberships and to avoid undesirable memberships. The aspect of placement concerns which positions in the social structures of an organization will be occupied by particular members of the collectivity. Organizations recruit not simply members but position occupants; individuals seek not merely memberships but positions and roles.

Recruitment, in both these aspects, is a never-ending process for both organization and individual. Members are continually being selected into and out of the organization and are continually being placed anew, through promotion, demotion, and transfer.

In ascriptive recruitment, the organization holds membership rights to an individual (and/or vice versa), based on his birth, developmental characteristics, behavior, and so on. In voluntary recruitment, neither organization nor individual has any special rights concerning membership. A third and prior aspect of voluntary recruitment is, then, attraction—organizations and individuals attempting to make their favorable features widely known in order to stimulate a set of applicants or offers from which to select. Voluntary recruitment can be thought of as an exchange of benefits between organization and individual. Through attraction tactics, each party communicates what benefits it could provide the other. Through selection tactics, each party communicates what benefits it wants from the other in return. Various attraction/selection dilemmas arise to plague voluntary recruitment.

In both voluntary and ascriptive recruitment, the exchange of benefits between organization and individual is quite important. Each party bases its selection decisions on the relative value of the other party—relative, that is, to the other's costly attributes, to its own existing resources, and to the potential value of other recruitment alternatives. The specifics of the recruitment process depend on the congruency or discrepancy of the recruitment interests of organization and individual.

When these interests are congruent, each party finds the other either (1) desirable, resulting in a "superior deal"; (2) acceptable, resulting in a "standard deal"; or (3) undesirable, resulting in "no deal."

When recruitment interests are discrepant, the more interested party strives to make itself more attractive to the other through a wide range of attraction tactics. These tactics vary according to how discrepant and how negative is the interest of the less interested party. If the less interested party regards the other as undesirable, it will counter with avoidance tactics, striving in various ways to make itself unavailable and/or unattractive to the other party.

SUGGESTIONS FOR ADDITIONAL READING

The individual's viewpoint in recruitment is considered in Victor R. Tom, "The Role of Personality and Organizational Images in the Recruiting Process," *Organizational Behavior and Human Performance,* 1971, 6: 573–592, and in Orlando Behling, George Labovitz, and Marion Gainer, "College Recruiting: A Theoretical Base," *Personnel*

Recruitment

Journal, 1968, 47: 13–19. The organization's viewpoint is represented in Benjamin Schneider, *Staffing Organizations* (Pacific Palisades, California: Goodyear, 1976).

The recruitment give-and-take between organization and individual is examined in John P. Wanous, *Organizational Entry: Recruitment, Selection, and Socialization of Newcomers* (Reading, Mass.: Addison-Wesley, 1980). An unusually readable and fascinating study along these lines is Theodore Caplow and Reece McGee's research on recruitment of college professors, reported in *The Academic Marketplace* (New York: Basic Books, 1958).

One of the most engaging studies of the effects of recruitment and selection is Erwin O. Smigel's article on "The Impact of Recruitment on the Organization of the Large Law Firm," *American Sociological Review,* 1960, 25: 56–66. The effects of placement are perhaps most easily seen in studies of replacement, or succession, reviewed by Oscar Grusky in "The Effects of Succession: A Comparative Study of Military and Business Organizations," pp. 439–461 in Oscar Grusky and George A. Miller, editors, *The Sociology of Organizations: Basic Studies,* New York: Free Press, 1970.

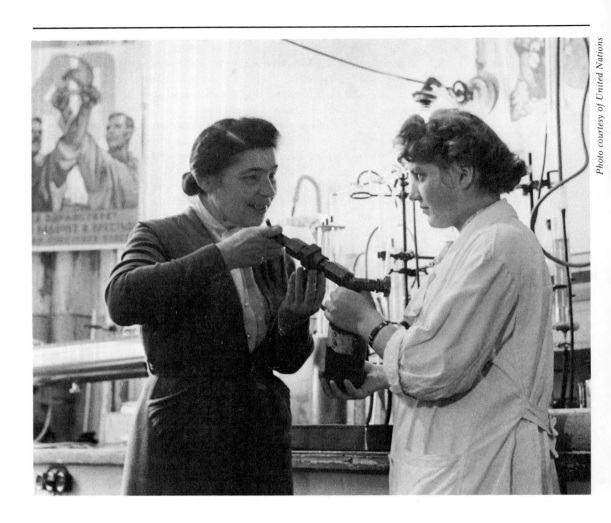

A beginning Moscow lab technician learns the requirements of her work role from the Head of the lab, while being reminded by a wall poster of the ideals and beliefs prescribed for her as a Soviet citizen.

CHAPTER 6

Socialization

How do recruited individuals become role-performing members of organizations? How does an infant become a Chinese citizen, Susan become a successful attorney, and Billy become a functioning electronics company vice president? The answer in each case is through *socialization*.

Socialization is the organizational process through which an individual's participation is *defined* and refined as he or she learns to be a functioning member. In any sort of social grouping the person and the organization must learn—and shape—what each may expect of the other. At the core of this defining process lie role expectations—both the expectations held for all members of an organization, and the more specific expectations held for the occupants of particular organizational positions. Through socialization processes, expected role enactments are "transmitted" from the organization to the individual. Such role expectations are typically wide-ranging, covering how members will look, dress, communicate, think, feel, believe, evaluate, and behave. Thus, through socialization, a recruited newcomer becomes an actual member.

In order for any person to enact a role expectation successfully, he or she must at the very minimum be (1) aware of that expectation and (2) able to comply with it. The more effective an organization's recruitment has been, the more able and aware members will be. But no organization is so fortunate in its selection tactics as to obtain members who are fully aware of or capable of complying with every organizational expectation. Some socialization is therefore always necessary. If nothing else, the individual must learn who's who and "where things are at" in the particular local scene. Socialization interlaces all aspects of social life. Even reading the newspaper or watching the evening news amounts to socialization regarding the current scene.

ASPECTS OF SOCIALIZATION

The socialization process accordingly involves *communication* to bring about awareness of expectations and *development* to build necessary personal capacities. For either of these aspects, socialization procedures may be explicit or implicit, as shown in Figure 6–1.

Communication of organizational expectations to the individual may take place through explicit procedures, such as written orientation materials for the newcomer, collective orientation sessions and briefings, indoctrination meetings, friendly advice, and direct admonition. Communication of expectations may also take place implicitly, through a subtle process of altercasting (see Chapter 2), in which the individual must strive to detect what was expected, from organizational responses to his own and others' actions. Unfavorable responses may indicate that a behavior is discouraged or proscribed, favorable responses that it is encouraged or prescribed, and an absence of response may be taken to mean that a behavior is permitted or tolerated. In every organization, such implicit communication procedures are employed; explicit procedures are used much less widely and less predictably. For example, extensive implicit socialization of children is found in all societies, while explicit socialization such

FIGURE 6-1. Selected Explicit and Implicit Procedures for Communicating Organizational Expectations and for Developing Individual Attributes

Aspects of Socialization

	Communication of Expectations	Development of Attributes
Explicit Procedures	Orientation materials, procedure manuals, rulebooks, memos, posters Orientation meetings, briefings, indoctrination sessions Advice, admonitions, supervision	Training manuals, self-study aids, programmed instruction, exercise plans Training courses or sessions, demonstrations, lectures, work-outs, pep talks Apprenticeship, coaching, supervision
Implicit Procedures	Observational learning Inference from organizational responses to behaviors	Learning from role-models Trial-and-error learning

as schooling is absent in some and quite varied as to length and content in others. "Learning the ropes" is a universal part of any new job, while only some jobs have training courses laid out to prepare the person for the post.

Development efforts may have as their target virtually any human capacity—not only such obvious features as knowledge, skills, and abilities, but also motivations, attitudes, beliefs, perceptions, and resources (such as body size or even style of nose in certain occupations and tribal cultures). If an individual is to be expected to speak the organization's language, to operate a particular machine, or to give up his life in battle, the organization must, as a collectivity, develop within him all the required capacities he may lack as a recruit. Even a pair relationship requires extensive socialization of each member, as we will see in Chapter 21. Much of this physical, emotional, and motivational capacity building is ordinarily called "training."

Explicit development procedures may include a wide variety of techniques: schools, special courses, written self-study materials, group training sessions, coaching, apprenticeships, and supervised on-the-job training. The kinds and extent of explicit socialization vary widely from organization to organization. At the extreme are those organizations that establish separate training centers under their own direct control, such as medical schools, boot camps, and convents.

Implicit development procedures are found universally and are, in fact, the fundamental human learning processes. These include observation of others who serve as role-models and trial-and-error experiences coupled with corrective feedback from self and others. Such procedures are virtually built into social interactions and underlie even the most explicit training programs. Indeed, children, recruits, and candidates for specific positions are judged in good part on how quickly they "catch on" through implicit procedures, and such organizational judgments often outweigh any test results of explicit procedures. The brilliant contributions of anthropologists to our understandings of these implicit socialization processes cannot be overstated. They have shown how an individual becomes a fully certified human only through the successful operation of these implicit procedures.

ORGANIZATIONAL TACTICS

The tactics used by an organization to communicate its role expectations depend on the judged difficulty of this task. If the individual is adjudged intelligent and reasonably motivated and needs only to be made aware of a few specific expectations, the usual tactic of choice is "orientation"—a relatively brief period of explicit communication procedures, followed by a somewhat longer period of implicit procedures. Throughout the orientation, the person is treated as a functioning (although perhaps probationary) member, not just an expected future member.

If, however, the individual is regarded as less able or less willing to learn the organizational expectations, and/or if the expectations to be communicated are numerous or difficult, the tactic to be employed is "education." Education is a relatively long period of intensive communication, through both explicit and implicit procedures, in which the individual is formally cast in the role of learner—not yet trusted to function as a true member. In our society, the high school student is the prototypic example of someone in the learner role.

The organization's tactics in the development of individual capacities also depend on the assessed difficulty of this task. If the individual's attributes nearly match those required for his position and if those few attributes needing development are not considered difficult to develop, the organization will employ a tactic of "supplementation and revision." The existing skills of a new typist, for example, may need supplementation through the addition of an ability to prepare statistical tables, and revision through adjusting typing habits developed on electric typewriters to those required for the use of electronic word processors. Supplementation and revision tactics involve both explicit and implicit development procedures, although the period of explicit development is relatively brief. The individual is placed in the role of a learner or trainee for only a short time and may be expected to make some membership contributions even during this period.

If a great many of the individual's attributes require modification or if any of these modifications is seen as difficult to bring about (for example, unlearning deep-seated habits or attitudes), the preferred organizational tactic is "stripping and substitution." The situation is not one of tinkering with the individual's attributes but rather one of major overhauling; revision is out of the question, and substitution is required. Deeply seated in most humans, for example, is the tendency to freeze, hide, or flee when shot at, but for the purposes of an army or a police force these tendencies must be eliminated and replaced by quite different automatic tendencies.

Such radical socialization demands a long and extremely intensive period of explicit development procedures. To strip away and replace deeply rooted individual attributes requires (1) suspension of all the environmental features on which such attributes rest and from which they derive support and (2) the imposition of an environment tailored to support and reinforce the attribute to be substituted. The organization must place the individual into a separate training center in which it has virtually complete environmental control—boot camp, service academy, convent, or alcohol rehabilitation center.

In such stripping and substitution facilities, the individual loses virtually all control of his life-round. His clothing, hair, possessions, social relationships, interests, mode of speech, and often his name are literally stripped away and replaced with new ones provided by the organization. His old self is mortified (Goffman, 1961a), and the new self proffered by the organization is exalted. Just as a plowshare must be melted down to be recast as a sword, so must the plowboy be melted down to be recast as a soldier. As Schein (1968) puts it, the self-structure must be unfrozen, changed, and then refrozen into the desired capabilities.

"Stripping and substitution" is far more common than is often realized because it is such a taken-for-granted part of social life. Kindergarten involves something of this process for many children, as does marriage for many young adults. Most cults and sects, a good many occupations, and even some lodges employ it to some extent. Anthropologists have documented its widespread use in most other societies. And it is, of course, the prime technique of total institutions, such as prisons and mental hospitals.

Figure 6–2 summarizes organizational tactics for the communication of role expectations and for the development of individual capacities and attributes, in relation to the expected difficulty of these two tasks. Orientation tactics tend to accompany supplementation and revision, while education tactics tend to accompany stripping and substitution. However, if the individual's capabilities are judged adequate but his or her awareness of a complex set of role expectations is poor, education tactics may accompany supplementation and revision as, for example, with Head Start programs for deprived children.

Of course, organizations are not necessarily correct in their estimates of the difficulty of producing the necessary awareness and capabilities in their members. Nor are their chosen tactics necessarily optimal or even very effective. If we use as a rough index of the effectiveness of socialization the percentage of members satisfactorily performing roles, we see that organizations vary greatly in the effectiveness of their socialization processes. Many organizations strive to increase their "success rates," since ably performing members are a vital resource. Some adopt a more fatalistic attitude which serves to justify their low success rate. Within some organizations, the basic collective position is that, through implicit socialization, the individual will either "make it" or not. Often individuals are judged for poor performance when the fault lies with the socialization tactics of the organization. For example, widespread testing suggests that in many areas there is actually a decline in IQ with number of years of schooling. As Jules Henry (1963) has shown in his provocative book, *Culture Against Man,* we cannot assume that an organization's socialization tactics actually implement collective goals or individual successes.

FIGURE 6-2. Organizational Tactics of Socialization Corresponding to Levels of Need to Socialize Individual Members

Aspects of Socialization

	Communication of Expectations	Development of Attributes	
Expectations Still To Be Communicated: Low in number and Low in difficulty	Orientation	Supplementation and Revision	**Attributes Still To Be Developed:** Low in number and Low in difficulty
High in number and/or High in difficulty	Education	Stripping and Substitution	**High in number and/or High in difficulty**

INDIVIDUAL TACTICS

The principal determinant of an individual's response to an organization's socialization efforts is his level of relative interest in the organizational position for which he is being socialized. As the reader should recall from Chapter 5, the individual may consider that position desirable, acceptable, or undesirable.

Cooperation with the organization's socialization efforts is the most likely response if the individual is highly interested in the position. He actively and positively strives to learn the expectations and to develop the desired attributes. He studies any materials, asks questions, solicits feedback, undertakes extra practice, seeks coaching, and goes out of his way to observe role-models. His peers are likely to view him as an overachiever, a "company man," or "teacher's pet." But the organization is likely to regard him as very promising, give him special attention, and perhaps bend the rules for him.

More neutral and more *passive participation* in socialization procedures is the most likely tactic for an individual who regards the position are merely acceptable. He does what is asked of him in socialization efforts—attending sessions, reading, listening, practicing, paying attention—but contributes no unexpected individual effort.

Resistance to the organization's socialization efforts is the most likely tactic if the individual views the position as undesirable. He does not want to become the sort of person the organization demands for that position, and he resents the expectations that the organization holds toward him. He strives to evade or violate many of these expectations and fails to attain many of the performance and attribute standards toward which development efforts are devoted. The point of these strivings is to try to teach the organization that its expectations are inappropriate and misguided—either in general or at least in specific relation to himself. In the general case, he will cite inconsistencies in expectations, absence of compelling rationales, and the existence of differing procedures in counterpart organizations; in other words, he attempts to teach the organization about its deficiencies and peculiarities. In relation to himself, he seeks to teach the organization about his own peculiarities—about special worthy attributes or about distinctive and irremedial deficiencies—which should exempt him from certain expectations. He does so, of course, through the process of "presentation of self" (*cf.* Chapter 2).

In undertaking resistance efforts, an individual will also strive to locate other persons (peers and/or superiors) who share some dissatisfaction with at least one of the same expectations and to ally with them in a sort of "resistance underground." Such a suborganization formed around this type of special interest constitutes a faction subverting the collective interest of the organization in uniform socialization. This is in fact a major source of factional suborganizations, particularly in ascriptive organizations such as public schools, the military, and total institutions.

Resistance and subversive factions are neither necessarily villainous nor heroic. The counterteachings of resisting individuals may be well-taken or ill-founded and self-serving. At this point, our interest is not in the right or the wrong but in the forms of individual tactics.

Socialization

In real-life social situations the response of most individuals to the socialization tactics of an organization is a blend of at least two of these tactics. Highly interested individuals will actively cooperate in many aspects of socialization efforts and passively participate in others. Resistance to certain specific expectations or development procedures is not out of the question, however, as when an otherwise exceptional student balks at learning statistics. Conversely, even disinterested individuals are not likely to offer resistance to every expectation and procedure; such uniform resistance is, at the least, tactically unwise and ineffective. Passive participation in numerous aspects can be expected, and even active cooperation (to acquire a particular skill) may be exhibited occasionally. Of course, those individuals who find the position merely acceptable are more likely than the highly interested or the disinterested to employ the entire range of individual tactics. A youth inducted into the navy, for instance, may resist the most strenuous exercises, passively conform to the schedules, and actively cooperate in learning to program computers or to fly airplanes.

Interest level is not the sole determinant, however. An individual's response to the organization's various socialization tactics is also, in part, a function of how much change is required of him and how personally costly he feels the procedures for attaining such changes will be. On these grounds alone, whatever the interest level, education tactics are more likely to be resisted than are orientation tactics, and stripping and substitution are more likely to be resisted than are supplementation and revision. This is so because the more extreme measures are more likely to shake up the person's role-identities and self-concept. Induction into prison or the armed services does more violence to a person's self-concept than does a briefing or a short training course. On the other hand, individual resistance tactics are less feasible and less effective where organizational control is high. Therefore, the individual may be more motivated but less able to resist the high-control tactics (education; stripping and substitution) than the lower-control organizational tactics (orientation; supplementation and revision).

Finally, it should be noted that the effectiveness of an individual's resistance efforts is affected by the organization's level of interest in him as an occupant of the position. The more favorable the organizational interest in a person, the more effectively he may resist organizational expectations and socialization efforts. The more an organization values a recruit—a new employee, a student, a soldier—the more it will "wink at" his efforts to bend the rules in certain areas.

STAGES OF SOCIALIZATION

Like recruitment, the process of socialization begins prior to any direct contact between the organization and the individual.

Anticipatory Socialization

A person almost always has some awareness about an organization and some membership capabilities before his or her arrival. How does this occur?

BASIC SOCIAL PROCESSES

"Anticipatory socialization" refers to an individual's prior *indirect* acquisition of beliefs about what life is like as a member of a given organization (or type of organization) or as an occupant of a certain type of organizational position and may also include the development of some beginning capabilities. Much of this learning takes place in the family, in school, and through the mass media. Thus, even small children may obtain highly detailed conceptions of such roles as breadwinner, housewife, policeman, senior citizen, teacher, and so on. These conceptions may cover the expected physical characteristics of position occupants, major activities and techniques, distinctive vocabulary items, central problems and concerns, and important norms and values. The child's conceptions are, of course, quite incomplete and often amusingly unrealistic, but often not altogether inaccurate.

Later in life, the things that schools, the media, and personal experiences teach about various roles becomes more explicit and somewhat more accurate. The individual comes to have direct contact with a great many more organizations and roles, as well as fairly serious conversations with other persons who have different information bases. Mass media exposure is no longer limited to television drama and situation comedy; newspapers, magazines, books, and movies provide variegated fictional and nonfictional accounts of various roles. For instance, a child growing up in contemporary America might learn a great deal about the duties, concerns, problems, and role strains of being a policeman, a teacher, a lawyer, or a working woman on her own. But there are biases in these indirect personal experiences and mass media presentations which favor the professions and the more dramatic occupations. The media, for example, skimp on sanitary engineers, draftsmen, building inspectors, and morticians, even though in reality these may be legitimate, interesting, and even highly lucrative occupations.

Anticipatory socialization of this diffuse kind plays an important part in the recruitment process, significantly influencing whether an individual might be attracted to a particular organization or type of position. It is for this reason that many organizations invest in career pamphlets, buy expensive advertisements, distribute films, host field trips, and otherwise propagandize. Such public relations tactics of attraction do at times significantly contribute to anticipatory socialization.

For those individuals who do become anticipatorily attracted to some type of organizational position, a not uncommon response is to prepare themselves to meet the relevant rules and standards—taking certain courses in school, practicing certain skills, and so on. Such responses—however well- or poorly grounded—represent attraction tactics by the individual and reveal that even anticipatory socialization can exhibit an aspect of developing individual capacities and attributes.

When, in the recruitment process, direct contact is made between organization and individual, pre-entry socialization becomes rather more specific. Through its direct tactics of attraction, selection, and placement, the organization communicates to the individual (explicitly and implicitly) some rather specific expectations that it holds concerning persons who occupy a given position in that organization. The employment agency circular may spell out a job description and job qualifications; the admissions officer or the football coach may make certain requirements and expectations quite clear.

No matter how extensive the indirect and direct pre-entry learning, no individual really knows what he is letting himself in for by entering an organizational position. Pre-entry beliefs, though sharpened through the recruitment process, are always incomplete and significantly unrealistic, if for no other reason than that the attraction/selection dilemmas inherently limit the realism of information exchange between the parties (see Chapter 5).

Initial-Entry Socialization

Upon entry into the organization, the individual is subjected to greatly broadened and intensified socialization efforts, implicit and/or explicit. Organizational efforts to communicate expectations to the newcomer typically prove confusing for a number of reasons. First, the person does not yet know the contextual framework for remarks and orders (what does ''take it downstairs'' mean?) Second, although some organizations devote substantial resources to socializing the newcomer, most do not—leaving the person largely on his own to do the best he can. Third, as anyone who has ever been handed an incomprehensible manual, flowchart, or briefing sheet can confirm, the expertise with which expectations are communicated to the newcomer varies greatly and is always less than perfect. Finally, various official and unofficial suborganizations tend to communicate somewhat different expectations. Unofficial suborganizations in particular may be threatened by the introduction of a newcomer and may more or less deliberately impart misleading expectations in order to test his commitment and adaptability. Such suborganizations may also be looking the newcomer over as a potential recruit into their own ranks.

Development efforts of any direct sort are usually delayed until initial entry. Rather suddenly, the new recruit is then required to learn the language, how to perform certain new tasks, the names and roles of many new faces, and the whereabouts of the bathrooms. Almost at once he is required to drop many of his old ways, conquer exhaustion by developing endurance and proper pacing, and avoid mistakes that might cause the loss of a major customer or blow up the entire building. Going through training of any kind is personally demanding, and the inevitable mistakes and failures are often humiliating.

How extensive and intensive these initial-entry socialization efforts are varies widely. Organizational tactics of education and of stripping and substitution are, of course, most encompassing and intensive and take the greatest toll on the new recruit. But whatever the tactics, initial-entry socialization effectively represents another step in the recruitment process. Many new members are ''recruited out'' at this stage. On a voluntary basis, individuals may drop out or resign, because the position is no longer attractive to them in view of the new and more realistic information concerning organizational expectations, or because they feel they cannot (or will not) develop the required capacities. Other individuals may be dropped or terminated by the organization on the basis of their inadequate performance in learning the expectations or developing the expected capacities. On an ascriptive basis, drafted individuals are not permitted to drop out or resign, in which case they may deliberately perform poorly in development procedures (''screwing up'') in order to be discharged by the organization as no longer attractive.

In most organizations, however, initial socialization proves more or less successful for the majority of new recruits. These individuals learn what is expected of them and develop the knowledge and skills needed to comply with these expectations. They become accepted members of the organization and true occupants of their positions—displaying a new self-image, accepting their altered personal attributes, social relationships, and behaviors. They have ''arrived.'' Their socialization does not cease, however, but only abates in intensity.

Continuing Socialization

During routine participation, an individual continues to receive explicit and implicit messages confirming and extending the organizational expectations of him. In periods of organizational change, these messages may redefine some aspects of the expectations, but such occasional redefinitions are seldom profound. Development similarly continues, but generally at a much lower level of intensity, amounting to a matter of brushing up old knowledge, practicing old skills, and keeping up with new developments.

Socialization efforts may reintensify, however, should either the individual or the organization begin to consider a possible change of position for him. Anticipatory socialization concerning the possible new position will already have gone on during his routine participation in the old position, possibly including some preparation to meet or to fail the standards for the new position. With any overt renewal of the placement process, the pre-entry socialization implications of attraction/selection dynamics are also renewed.

Should the individual indeed change positions, the whole gamut of organizational and individual tactics in socialization comes into full play once more, not unlike the situation he experienced upon entry into his initial position.

Socialization, like recruitment, is thus an on-going, never-ending process for both the organization and the individual.

THE CONTRIBUTIONS OF SOCIALIZATION

Socialization and recruitment jointly establish the individual's prescribed organizational role. A prescribed role, after all, consists of the expectations held toward the occupants of a social position. Recruitment determines what position (if any) the in-

Socialization

dividual will occupy within the organization. The socialization process determines what will be expected of him as an occupant of that position, that is, it *defines* his participation.

As these chapters have demonstrated and as Figure 6-3 shows, recruitment and socialization are not completely independent processes.

An organization's precontact attraction tactics may contribute to anticipatory socialization. Pre-entry selection and placement tactics also serve to communicate some of the organization's expectations. After entry, any reintensification in recruitment of the individual, such as a possible position change, triggers a reintensification of the socialization process.

Similarly, anticipatory socialization influences the attractiveness of an organizational position to the individual. The heavy wave of socialization efforts upon initial entry serves as a crucial test of the respective levels of interest—that is, attraction—of both the organization and the individual, frequently leading to recruitment back out of the organization.

The efficiency, the success, and sometimes even the survival of an organization depend in part on the effectiveness of its socialization processes. As we will see in detail in Part III, this holds true for the largest national and international organizations as well as for the simple pair relationship between friends. An organization whose members are well-socialized into their role performances simply does better, whatever other circumstances prevail. From the individual's standpoint, the crucial test of socialization is whether he or she can ''win''—or at least come out all right—at performing a member's role.

The experiencing of socialization processes may produce a wide variety of emotional responses, ranging from joy and enthusiasm through tedium to deep distress and even shock. Somewhat independent of how socialization is experienced, the result may range from the person's becoming capable and integrated in his role patterns to a shattered self-conception and inability to perform. The latter outcome may lead to recruitment and socialization into other organizations such as welfare agencies or mental institutions.

It should be noted that socialization is never completely a one-way process, as any

FIGURE 6-3. Contributions of Recruitment and Socialization to Development of Individual's Organizational Role

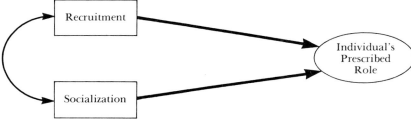

teacher, parent, or supervisor can attest. There are always some feedback channels through which the individual members also socialize their organization. Parents learn their parent roles in part from their children, executives learn more about management from handling their employees, statesmen are further socialized by their populaces, and so on. We shall see something of how this takes place as we take up an examination of interaction processes in the next chapter.

SUMMARY

Socialization is the organizational process through which an individual's participation is *defined*. Member and position role expectations are transmitted by the organization to the individual, regarding how he should look, dress, communicate, think, feel, believe, evaluate, and behave.

In order to enact any role expectation successfully, the individual must at least be aware of that expectation and able to comply with it. The two major aspects of socialization, accordingly, are the *communication of expectations* and the *development of necessary capacities*. In both of these aspects, socialization procedures may be either explicit or implicit (see Figure 6–1).

Organizational tactics in the communication of expectations range from the less intensive "orientation" of members to the more intensive and prolonged "education" of members. Organizational tactics in the development of individual capacities range from "supplementation and revision" of attributes to the more radical "stripping and substitution" of attributes. Choice of tactics is related to the perceived extent and difficulty of the socialization task, as summarized in Figure 6–2.

The individual's response may be one of cooperation with, passive participation in, and/or resistance to the socialization efforts of the organization. This response depends in part on his level of relative interest in the organizational position—whether he considers it desirable, acceptable, or undesirable. Other factors behind his response include how much change is required of him, how personally costly these change efforts would be, and how much control the organization has over him.

The process of socialization begins through anticipatory socialization, before any direct contact between the organization and the individual, as the person indirectly acquires certain conceptions of particular organizations and roles from family, schools, and the mass media. Initial-entry socialization is direct and greatly broadened and intensified. Even seasoned members receive continuing socialization—generally at a mere maintenance level, but reintensified if either the organization or the individual begins to consider a possible change of position for him. Socialization, like recruitment, is an ongoing, never-ending process for both parties.

As shown in Figure 6–3, socialization and recruitment are not completely independent processes, and together they suffice to establish the individual's prescribed organizational role. Socialization is never fully adequate, but without it organizations could not exist.

SUGGESTIONS FOR ADDITIONAL READING

Much of the widespread fascination with the television series *Shōgun* (based on the best-selling novel by James Clavell) lay in its detailed depiction of a most difficult and radical socialization process as medieval Japan attempted to assimilate its first Englishman. With no initial linguistic communication, implicit socialization procedures predominated for some time, after which the entire range of implicit and explicit procedures came into play.

On a more scholarly level, a solid and comprehensive review of socialization processes is to be found in John A. Clausen's edited volume *Socialization and Society* (Boston: Little, Brown, 1968). An invaluable and massive reference work is David A. Goslin, editor, *Handbook of Socialization Theory and Research* (Chicago: Rand McNally, 1969).

Of special importance to sociological social psychology is the topic of "adult socialization." A slim but informative treatment is Orville G. Brim, Jr., and Stanton Wheeler, *Socialization after Childhood: Two Essays* (New York: Wiley, 1966). A landmark study of adult socialization, emphasizing the emergent give-and-take of the process, is Howard S. Becker, Blanche Geer, Everett C. Hughes, and Anselm L. Strauss, *Boys in White: Student Culture in Medical School* (Chicago: University of Chicago Press, 1961). The socialization of nurses affords a useful comparison, in Virginia L. Oleson and Elvi W. Whittaker's *The Silent Dialogue: A Study in the Social Psychology of Professional Socialization* (San Francisco: Jossey-Bass, 1968).

For our own purposes, of course, "organizational socialization" is most central. Perhaps no reading on this topic has been more influential than Edgar H. Schein's article, "Organizational Socialization and the Profession of Management," *Industrial Management Review,* 1968, 9: 1–16. These ideas are developed further in John Van Maanen and Edgar H. Schein, "Toward a Theory of Organizational Socialization," *Research in Organizational Behavior,* 1979, 1: 209–264. The give-and-take of socialization, and its close connections with the recruitment process, are examined in William M. Evan, "Peer Group Interactions and Organizational Socialization: A Study of Employee Turnover," *American Sociological Review,* 1963, 28: 436–440.

One interesting conceptualization of the impact of socialization on the character of the individual, by Orville G. Brim, is that of "Personality Development as Role-Learning" (pp. 127–159 in I. Iscoe and H. W. Stevenson, editors, *Personality Development in Children,* Austin: University of Texas Press, 1960).

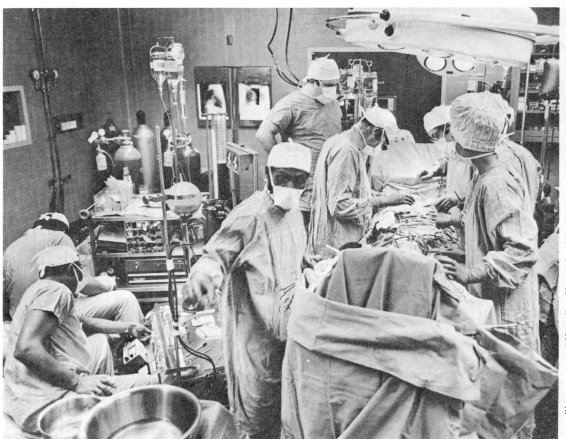

Photo courtesy of Montefiore Hospital and Medical Center, New York, Carl Samrock, photographer

During surgery, doctors, nurses, and technicians coordinate their individual activities according to hospital procedure, modified by personal inclination, hopefully for the benefit of the patient.

CHAPTER 7

Interaction

How do individuals—recruited and socialized into occupying various positions—coordinate to get the organization's work done? How are leadership's programs worked out and transmitted to those who will carry them out? How are conflicts, misunderstandings, and "bugs" worked out in organizations from the World Bank to a strolling couple? And how are the unofficial suborganizations able to function? The answer in each case is the basic organizational process of *interaction*.

Interaction is such a basic aspect of human social life that it tends to be taken for granted and is left unexamined, just as a fish might be the last creature to discover water because he is always immersed in it. Indeed, the interaction process is most noticeable (and most alarming) when interaction is temporarily absent. "She won't talk to me; I don't know what's going on with us." "Flight 407 hasn't reported in." "Waiting for orders," the shipping clerk and the soldier are immobilized. Those organizations that are successful in providing necessary interactions among occupants of various positions tend to do well while those which have interaction breakdowns tend to do poorly. Whether in a marriage, in a company, or in international relations, interaction is a process worthy of serious study.

In the two preceding chapters, we have seen how the processes of recruitment and socialization are closely linked, and how these processes jointly determine an individual's prescribed organizational role. If it is through recruitment and socialization that an individual's participation is determined and defined, it is through the organizational process of "interaction" that such participation is *implemented*. Through interactions an organization "comes alive."

FORMS OF INTERACTION

Organizations, particularly large ones, employ numerous forms of interaction to coordinate activities among their position occupants. The more elaborate the division of labor, the more elaborate these forms of interaction tend to become.

In our earlier discussions of social interaction, we tacitly assumed that the participants in an interaction process were in one another's physical presence, participating in direct, face-to-face communication. This prototypic form of interaction is certainly the richest and probably the most important type. But in this age of telephones and CB radios, direct interaction need not be face-to-face. *Direct interaction* requires only that a person be able to respond immediately to a message from another (indeed, to interrupt if necessary). Bargaining and negotiation tactics are much more powerful and responsive where these conditions obtain. Indeed, the greater richness of face-to-face interaction over other forms of direct interaction (for example, telephone conversations) stems from the availability of additional channels for immediate communication—vision, touch, smell—simultaneous with vocal messages.

In *indirect interaction,* messages can only be relayed, via some time-lagged transmission channel, detracting from the intensive give-and-take of the interaction process. The most obvious example is correspondence—an exchange of letters through the mails. But perhaps the most important such channel is other persons. That is, two persons may communicate only through some third party, in a two-way relay arrangement or "interaction chain." As the phrase implies, an interaction chain may have more than one intervening link. Most often, however, an interaction chain is not strictly linear but resembles a set of parallel and cross-linked chains, really an "interaction network." Indirect interaction through chains and networks is a notable phenomenon in the majority of organizations. The fabled "grapevine" is an unofficial manifestation, and the formal "chain of command" in which nonadjacent levels of personnel communicate only through intervening levels demonstrates the reliance that even highly structured organizations may place on indirect interaction.

Such indirect interactions are found everywhere in social life and have not received the attention they merit.

- They serve as a "backup system" for face-to-face interactions ("Tell Debbie we enjoyed the party," "Tell Anita to hurry up and get well").
- They serve as a means of extending one's interaction reach ("If you see Walter, tell him to call me right away," "Tell David it's suppertime").
- They can serve as a kind of interaction by proxy ("Did Nancy say anything about me?," "How's Lavonne doing these days?").
- They can be creatively used to get messages to other persons in the network in cases where direct interaction might be more problematic ("I think Donald's cute, I wouldn't mind going out with him," "You might let Jenkins know his sales quotas aren't high enough," "Let the Securities man know we'll need fifteen percent guarantees before we'll even talk").

Such indirect interaction networks interface with a person's or an organization's interpersonal network.

Relay channels may also be impersonal (such as the Postal Service, Western Union, or a telephone answering service), even when the messages are quite personal. Less personalized, more broadly applicable messages may be relayed through broadcast (or mass) media of communication, such as bulk mailings, general memos, newsletters, newpapers and magazines, and radio or television broadcasts. In such cases, the responding message might also be relayed through broadcast media or might instead use more personalized media, such a personal letter or an interaction chain. Beyond these, impersonal response channels do exist, such as Nielson ratings, surveys, buyer responses, and votes.

Thus, we find a wide variety of interaction forms employed both for internal interchanges and for interchanges with individuals and other organizations in the external environment. Through such interchanges any organization "does its business," whatever the content of that business may be.

Although both direct and indirect interaction clearly depend on communication, interaction is primarily a matter of individual position occupants influencing one another's lines of action.

INTERACTION PROCESS

In Chapter 2, the process of social interaction was analyzed as one of jointly negotiating (1) the identities, or personal characters, of the participants; and (2) the particulars of their individual lines of action. The negotiation of identities was viewed as proceeding through symbolic interchanges between persons, in which imputations of roles to others and improvisation of roles for self are communicated and reconciled through tactics of altercasting and presentation of self. Benefit/cost considerations were seen as the evaluation criteria employed by each individual in weighing the acceptability of any identities so communicated to him. Such a process of negotiating identities is clearly involved in the recruitment process, especially in its aspect of "placement."

In Chapter 2, the negotiation of individual lines of action was similarly viewed as a process in which an individual's actions are decided upon on the basis of anticipated benefits to be gained and costs to be incurred—where many of these benefits and costs could be conferred or withheld by fellow participants in joint ventures and exchange. What each interactant proposes to do is weighed, by himself and by the others, in terms of its "profitability"; the other persons communicate their judgments of these proposals through reactions, suggestions, demands, and offers. It is through such bargaining or conferring on the profitability of particular acts that the other persons involved derive significant ability to shape an individual's line of action. As was noted in Chapter 6, such negotiation of lines of action is clearly involved in the socialization process, through which others' expectations are communicated to the actor and the actor strives to accept or to redefine these expectations. Thus, a job foreman and a machinist come to a working agreement on what the latter is to do.

A major emphasis in the previous discussion of interaction was the thesis that "social acts generate social objects"—including characters, organizations, cultural artifacts, symbolic objects, and—most important—social roles. We have here reviewed how social interaction, through its contributions to recruitment and socialization, generates the individual's prescribed role—determining his organizational position and defining his organizational role.

But a prescribed role is only a prescription. Like a doctor's prescription, this collective prescription may influence and even constrain the person's activities, but it is seldom literally followed. What an individual actually does in his organizational position—that is, his *performed role*—is an emergent product of much further negotiation, a resultant of more extensive interpersonal bargaining or conferring with fellow participants. In constructing his actions, the individual will be influenced and even constrained by his prescribed role, but within these broad limits he will follow whichever course he appraises as being most beneficial for himself and his significant others.

Unless an observer has some notion of the individual's own priorities, plans, and dreams, it may often appear that the person is not acting optimally or even rationally. People tend to judge others as "dumb" or even "crazy" in their role performances, because they typically judge from the viewpoint of the observers' own plans and dreams. A lot of the interpersonal blindness that shows up in social interaction stems from this tendency. To put it another way, one usually has to get something of the person's own story to make sense out of some of his or her behaviors. Why a man passes up a lucrative but demanding promotion, for instance, makes sense when we discover the importance he places on his family and his hobbies. It is in this way that some understanding about the other person's position tends to reduce intolerance and social distance. In fact, increased mutual awareness is one of the basic contributions of interaction to social life.

The central concern of this chapter is to delineate the contributions of organization and individual in this negotiation of "performed roles," this compromising of the "officially" defined and transmitted "prescribed roles." Consequently, the aspect of interaction with which we shall be most concerned is the various patterns (involving organization members, and sometimes certain nonmembers as well) of who gets together for what activities when and where, and how these activities are performed.

THE ORGANIZATIONAL VIEWPOINT

To the organization, such patterns of interaction should (but may not always) constitute collective action in pursuit of its distinctive collective interests—the implementation of its division of labor.

The who and the what are by definition the primary features of any division of labor; the when, where, and how represent the fine-tuning of this orchestration of effort. The role structure will demand that certain persons get together at the same time that it may forbid or discourage other combinations of persons. Commissioned officers, for instance, are to remain in tight but ritualized communication with one another and are not to fraternize with the troops. Similarly, some activities will be demanded of members whereas other actions are prohibited. More important, activity prescriptions and proscriptions will be made specific to certain persons or combinations of persons. For example, children may joke with each other in ways that they are not permitted to use in joking with adults. Married couples are expected not to engage in sexual behaviors in the office. From the organization's viewpoint, any member's being in the wrong place, or at the wrong time, or with the wrong person, or doing the wrong things represents a breach of role structure.

Actual interactions frequently fail to exemplify the who/what specifications of the role structure and are viewed by the organization as mistakes or errors. Errors of omission include the absence or tardiness of a participant, as well as the failure of an assembled set of actors to perform the authorized activity—as when a committee doesn't get its work done or the children don't get the house picked up. Errors of commission include the participation of an unauthorized person in a specified activity as well as the performance of an unauthorized activity by a legitimate set of actors, as when the members of an athletic team get stoned instead of practice for their next contest.

As a secondary feature of the division of labor, the role structure may also specify when and where certain persons shall or shall not assemble and certain activities shall or shall not be performed. Here too, actual interactions may be viewed by the organization as errors of omission or commission. Otherwise legitimate who/what combinations may fail to occur at the authorized time or place or may actually occur under unauthorized circumstances. It is all right for the children to play, as long as they don't do it in the living room. Newsmen may interview military officials, but not during drill or in restricted areas.

Finally, the role structure may also specify how an activity is to be performed. Actual interactions, while correct in every other respect, may represent organizational errors by employing an unauthorized procedure or through failure to display the appropriate manner or spirit. Examples of such content discrepancies between role expectations and role performances abound and are, in fact, the crux of innumerable organizational squabbles at all levels. Parents are intermittently concerned over how their young children talk or play. A guard retaliates against a chain-gang prisoner on the basis of how he says "boss." A wife complains to her husband about how he makes love to her. A Senate committee investigates how an official got a foreign trade agreement. We will be examining later in this chapter and in the next chapters why these discrepancies are so widespread.

In numerous ways, then, actual interactions involving members may either reflect or contravene the organization's role structure—may represent, that is, either conformity or innovation. A second and somewhat independent concern of the organization regarding these interactions is whether they contribute to or interfere with satisfaction of the wider collective interests. The main posture of most organizations regarding this last point is one of wariness.

BASIC SOCIAL PROCESSES

Not all conforming interactions actually contribute to the pursuit of the collective interest. In some cases a rigid and "bureaucratic" conformity may actually detract from successful organizational functioning—a phenomenon usually referred to as "goal displacement" (Merton, 1940), where administration takes the place of production, the office becomes caught up in "paper chains" of circulating forms and memos, and these internal actions become ends in themselves. In following every role expectation "to the letter," perhaps to stay out of trouble with supervisors, the spirit and original aim of those expectations may be subverted. Emergency-room admissions clerks may painstakingly elicit every required bit of financial data while the patient's life-blood drains away. Conversely, interactions that may be viewed as errors from the standpoint of the role structure sometimes contribute greatly to achieving the collective interest and represent creative innovations. A foreman who ignores company policy against swearing at workers but gets the job done, a teacher who unceremoniously sits on the floor to talk to her pupils and so gets them to perform well, both serve the collective interest through performance innovations. Indeed, creative innovation may become a routine means of handling inept or rigidly bureaucratic seniors or fossilized role structures while still getting the job done. Other innovations, of course, do interfere with the satisfaction of the collective interest and constitute deviant behavior. Factor workers develop a means of defeating the time-clock, and bank tellers work out a clever system of cash transfers that auditors cannot trace.

Figure 7–1 depicts the relationships between the two concerns of the organization, and Chapter 8 provides a more detailed analysis of innovation.

Even in the most totalitarian organizations, not every aspect of interactions involving members is regulated by the role structure. A factory, for example, may stringently regulate who can speak to whom, when, and how often on the shop floor, but it is unlikely to specify whether they chat about bowling or about the weather. Nor is the factory likely to specify which workers may play cards together after work or may ride together to the plant in the mornings. Even in a prison, mental hospital, or slave camp, there is always some interpersonal and role performance leeway. Conversely, there is no social situation that does not have some organizational structuring.

Aspects of interaction patterns not falling under the scope of the division of labor may nonetheless prove quite important to the organization. Such officially nonrelevant aspects of interaction—not a part of the organization's primary (that is, role) structure—contribute greatly to the development of *secondary* social structures. Dimensional social structures (e.g., status, affect, or communication structures) are significantly influenced by unofficial aspects of interaction; the clerk-typist who brings a box of cookies on every co-worker's birthday becomes well liked. Unofficial suborganizations frequently emerge on the basis of special interests generated by or discovered through such nonofficial aspects of interaction. Through idle chatter, several factory workers discover their mutual interest in backgammon and become a regular lunch-hour clique. Such interaction spillovers into other areas of interest are virtually inevitable within every social structure that has any duration.

For the organization, then, the process of interaction is an important influence on

114

Interaction

Relation to Organizational Expectations

Relation to Satisfaction of Collective Interests	Conformity	Innovation
Contribution	Goal Attainment	Creativity
Interference	Goal Displacement	Deviance

FIGURE 7-1. Significance of Role Performance in Relation to Organizational Expectations and to Satisfaction of Collective Interests

its actual division of labor and organizational success, on the one hand, and on its social differentation and organizational cohesiveness on the other.

THE INDIVIDUAL VIEWPOINT

For the individual, interaction represents the pursuit of his own identities and goals within the arenas of the organization and its membership. These individual concerns may correspond to, overlap, or diverge from the collective interests of the organization.

Organizational Arena

Some of these personal identities and goals may, of course, be organizationally relevant, such as becoming a manager, obtaining a raise, acquiring some pertinent skill. Satisfaction of such wants could be obtained from the organization itself, through participation in the division of labor of collective action. The individual's prescribed role serves as both an opportunity for and a constraint on his striving to obtain satisfaction of these relevant personal interests. By authorizing him to perform certain activities and to develop relationships with certain persons, his prescribed role opens certain avenues for the pursuit of personal interests. At the same time, however, this prescribed role forbids or discourages other activities and other relationships that might prove strategic in these pursuits. The worker is encouraged to become skilled in converting the organization's raw materials into marketable products, but not in ''borrowing'' these materials and products to beautify his home. He is to be friendly with other employees, but not so friendly as to subvert official authority or develop an illicit sexual liaison. Yet, fixing up his own home, pushing his own ideas, and having an affair may be quite important in his pursuit of personal interests.

115

The individual thus is motivated to push the limits of tolerated behaviors by evading the proscriptions against activities and associations which seem to him potentially rewarding to his pursuits and by minimizing those prescribed involvements which do not seem particularly rewarding. Taking advantage of position, "making out" (Goffman, 1961a), and "getting by" are fabled tactics in schools, armies, prisons, mental hospitals, and factories. Within the arena of an organization, the individual seeks (1) to maximize those aspects of prescribed role that serve as personal opportunities to satisfy organizationally relevant interests; and (2) to minimize those aspects that serve as constraints on such pursuits.

Through its initial socialization tactics—and also through the encouragements and discouragements which are an inherent part of organizational interactions—every organization attempts to align the personal pursuits of individual members with the interests of the organization. That is to say, the organization tries to bring the member to the viewpoint that what is good for the collectivity is good for him or her. Often, this attempt is somewhat successful. But the organization always has some interests beyond the individual's, and the individual always has at least some latent plans of action beyond the organization's, so that there is never a "perfect fit" between the two.

Membership Arena

Many of the individual's identities and goals, however, have little to do with his role or with the interests of the organization. The American Medical Association, for example, would probably be quite disinterested in the fact that one of its many clerk-typists is a champion hog-caller or is sexually lonely. Yet, many of the other employees might be quite interested indeed and thus might constitute potential resources for the pursuit of this typist's personal interests.

Organizationally irrelevant interests of this kind are not provided for in a person's prescribed organizational role, and their pursuit must somehow be "worked in" to interaction patterns if the membership resources are to be tapped. Here again, the prescribed role acts as both an opportunity for and a constraint upon such pursuits by authorizing certain contacts and activities while discouraging others. The individual will be motivated to maximize the opportunity aspects and to minimize the constraints of prescribed role (even for such an irrelevant interest as selling Girl Scout cookies for his daughter) by taking advantage, making out, and getting by.

Whatever the arena, then, the individual strives to change, alter, distort, stretch, and shape his prescribed role, the better to pursue his personal interests. Who interacts with him, what activities he performs when, where, and how are matters of "role negotiation"—what better role fits he can work out through bargaining and through conferring on joint ventures. The successful individual often, through interactions, *redesigns* his organizational roles into integrated patterns which further both collective and personal interests. This greatly reduces role strain. The less successful person may simply work out a pattern of accommodation by "cutting corners" on both his own and the organization's plans, thus "getting by." The person who fails is one who is not able to work out a package of performances acceptable to self and/or others—that is, who cannot effectively interact with the organization, be it Xerox or his own family.

THE CONTRIBUTIONS OF INTERACTION

The contributions of the process of interaction to the development of an individual's organizational role are multiple.

Indirectly, through its effects on recruitment and on socialization, the interaction process contributes to the determination and definition of the individual's prescribed role. One aspect of interaction—the negotiation of identities—is involved in one aspect of recruitment—placement, the determination of the position to be occupied. A second aspect of interaction—the negotiation of lines of action—is involved in one aspect of socialization—the communication of role expectations. Essentially, there can be no recruitment or socialization without some (direct or indirect) interaction.

Most directly, however, the process of interaction mediates between the individual's prescribed role and his performed role; interaction is the process through which individuals' prescribed roles are implemented or performed. Although the organization's defined role structure significantly influences the interaction process, it is the ongoing negotiative interaction process that directly determines the character of the role actually performed by an individual. Consequently, it is generally to be expected that performed roles will differ substantially from prescribed roles—omitting some prescribed elements and/or including some proscribed elements. Therefore, no two position occupants—whether pilots, teachers, or mothers—will perform their common role exactly alike.

FIGURE 7-2. Contributions of Interaction to Development of Individual's Organizational Role

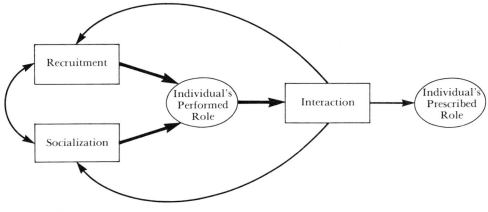

In interaction, an individual may not be *willing* to comply with his prescribed role in the situation. He may find the personal character implied by that role to be demeaning to his self-concept, in which case he may refuse to perform it or at least to perform it sincerely, exhibiting "role-distance" (Goffman, 1961a) from it in a disdainful mockery. He may consider that one of his significant others or reference groups would regard his performance of that role in the situation to be disloyal or inappropriate. His role in some other organization may seem to him to take precedence over the presently prescribed role. Often enough, he simply perceives some alternative situated action as being of greater expected "profitability" at the moment. Thus, no organization can automatically count upon members to perform their assigned roles.

In interaction, the individual may not be *able* to comply with the organizationally prescribed role in the situation. He may not know just what he should do there; the role expectations may not seem clear, compatible, or consensual. On the other hand, he may know what he is expected to do or to be, but may lack the knowledge of how to do it or may temporarily lack the necessary capabilities, equipment, or information. He may find it prohibitively costly to comply; for instance, the college student "cannot" take the exam because his mother has just died. Very often, the individual is not able to perform the prescribed role because other persons will not permit him to do so; they may fail to perform their own parts, may sabotage his efforts, may mislead, threaten, or coerce him, or may seduce him into some other course of action. For these reasons, the refrain "I couldn't do it" is a common occurrence at every organizational level.

Of course, an individual's unwillingness or inability to perform a prescribed role may be traced back to inadequacies in the organization's recruitment and socialization processes. In any case, it is generally to be expected that performed roles will differ from prescribed roles as a typical result of the interaction process.

In some dim recognition of its importance, organizations from time immemorial have bestowed and withheld interaction as a means of aligning memberships. A promising recruit is showered with additional interactions. Interaction is the first line of defense used with an errant member, through intensified guiding and admonishing messages. Withdrawal of interaction opportunities is an almost universal response of disapproval—"go to your room," exile, "I'm not speaking to him," and so on. Those who are particularly favored are given one's phone number, granted an audience, invited to lunch by the boss, and so forth.

On a grander scale, modern communication technologies have welded, first, nations, then the entire globe together into a web of at least potential interactions. If one can get into this international grid, one can almost literally "speak to the world."

Without interaction, an organization could not operate.

SUMMARY

Interaction is the process through which individuals' organizational participation is *implemented*. Interaction is not necessarily face-to-face or even direct, but may be indirect through some time-lagged transmission channel. These channels of communica-

Interaction

tion may be personal, in the form of interaction chains or networks, or impersonal, in the form of postal or telegraph services or of broadcast media.

Earlier in this book, interaction was analyzed as a process of jointly negotiating (1) the identities, or personal characters, of the participants; and (2) the particulars of their individual lines of action. Negotiation of identities, based on benefit/cost considerations, can now be seen as implicated in the recruitment process, especially in the aspect of placement. Negotiation of individual lines of action, similarly based on benefit/cost considerations, can be seen as involved in the socialization process, through which others' expectations are communicated to the person and he strives to accept or to redefine these expectations. Recruitment and socialization together generate his prescribed role. But while such a collective "prescription" may influence and even constrain his activities, it is seldom followed literally. His performed role—what he actually does in his organizational position—is an emergent product of much further and more situated negotiation through the process of interaction.

As an *organizational* process, the central aspect of interaction is its patterning—who (including members and nonmembers) gets together for what activities when and where, and how are these activities performed.

To the organization, such patterns of interaction should, but may not always, constitute collective action in pursuit of its collective interests—that is to say, they should constitute the implementation of its division of labor. That division of labor (or role structure) prescribes certain combinatorial patterns of these elements and proscribes certain other patterns. Actual interactions may (1) constitute "errors" of either omission or commission; (2) represent either conformity, reflecting the role structure, or innovation, contravening it; and (3) contribute to or interfere with satisfaction of the collective interests. Conformity does not always contribute to satisfaction of collective interests nor do "errors" and innovation necessarily interfere with such satisfaction, as summarized in Figure 7-1. The process of interaction thus greatly influences the actual division of labor and organizational performance.

Not all aspects of every interaction pattern are covered by the norms of the role structure. Such officially nonrelevant aspects of interactions contribute in an important way to the development of secondary social structures—suborganizations and dimensional structures. In this way, the interaction process influences social differentiation and organizational cohesiveness.

For the individual, interaction represents the pursuit of his own identities and goals within the arenas of the organization and its membership. His prescribed role serves as both an opportunity for and a constraint on his pursuit of personal interests, both the organizationally relevant (within the organizational arena) and the irrelevant (within the membership arena). In either arena, then, the individual strives to change, alter, and distort—to stretch and shape—his prescribed role, the better to pursue his personal interests.

Consequently, it is generally to be expected that performed roles will differ substantially from prescribed roles. For a variety of reasons, an individual may not be willing or may not be able to comply with his prescribed role in a particular situation. Although such unwillingness or inability may often be traced back to inadequacies in

119

recruitment and socialization, more often they stem directly from the situational give-and-take negotiations of the interaction process itself.

The several contributions of interaction process to the development of an individual's organizational role are summarized in Figure 7–2. Indirectly, through its effects on recruitment and socialization, the interaction process contributes to the determination and definition of his prescribed role. Most directly, the process of interaction mediates between his prescribed and his performed roles; it is the process through which prescribed roles are implemented or performed. Prescribed roles significantly influence the interaction process, but it is that process itself that directly determines performed roles.

SUGGESTIONS FOR ADDITIONAL READING

The organization's concern in the interaction process is for the functioning of its division of labor. "The Elements of Organizational Performance" are reviewed by Stanley E. Seashore and Ephraim Yuchtman (pp. 172–188 in Bernard P. Indik and F. Kenneth Berrien, editors, *People, Groups, and Organizations,* New York: Teachers College Press, 1968).

The individual's concern is for pursuit of personally "profitable" lines of action. The classic account of this perspective within organizational interaction is Erving Goffman's essay on "The Underlife of a Public Institution: A Study of Ways of Making Out in a Mental Hospital" (pp. 171–320 in Goffman, *Asylums,* Garden City, N.Y.: Doubleday Anchor, 1961).

The realities of interaction and communication patterns, as influenced by interpersonal relations, are reviewed in Robert C. Sedwick's *Interaction: Interpersonal Relations in Organizations* (Englewood Cliffs, N.J.: Prentice-Hall, 1974) and in Jerry C. Wofford's *Organizational Communications* (New York: McGraw-Hill, 1977).

Representative studies of the interaction process within organizations include: William Karracker, "Teamwork and Safety in Flight," *Human Organization,* 1958, 17: 3–8; Peter M. Blau, "Cooperation and Competition in a Bureaucracy," *American Journal of Sociology,* 1954, 59: 530–535; Melville Dalton, "Conflicts Between Staff and Line Managerial Officers," *American Sociological Review,* 1950, 15: 342–351; and Robert B. Faulkner, "Orchestra Interaction: Some Features of Communication and Authority in an Artistic Organization," *Sociological Quarterly,* 1973, 14: 147–157.

The impact of the interaction process on the character of organizations is most sharply expressed in the concept of "negotiated social order." An invaluable reading in any examination of interaction is Anselm L. Strauss's *Negotiations: Varieties, Contexts, Processes, and Social Order* (San Francisco: Jossey-Bass, 1978).

His Hyde Park performance will probably alter this speaker's participation in society, identifying him with a particular political, social, or religious position.

CHAPTER 8

Innovation

Few, if any, real-life situations are entirely covered by role prescriptions, as anyone can testify after his or her first day on the job, first combat experience, or first week of marriage. What happens when the actual situations encountered by the individual are not covered by the learned patterns or do not even seem to fit them? How does a person reconcile the conflicts and discrepancies between organizational and personal desires? And how does an organization adjust its patterns to meet external contingencies and internal failings? The answer is through *innovation*.

Innovation is that organizational process through which individual's participation is *altered*. These changes may range from minor, such as a shift in office arrangement or in laundry day, to radical, such as a thorough revamping of the division of labor or even a shift to production of a quite different collective good. In any case, organizational changes almost always have repercussions on the role structure and, conversely, innovations in role performances almost always have repercussions for the organization at large.

ROLE IMPROVISATION

No matter how extensive the socialization or how exactly specified the role, no prescribed role will cover all actions under all circumstances of actual role performance. And no matter how well worked out the organizational pattern and division of labor, these will never exactly meet or handle all of the external and internal events impinging on the organization. And no organization will exactly and continually meet the personal needs and plans of all its individual members, as we saw in Part I.

For these reasons, role improvisation is a necessary and universal part of social living. Almost by definition, any role improvisation involves innovation. The vast majority of these improvisations are trivial and do not engage the full innovation processes discussed in this chapter. They are simply viewed as a matter of "style" of role performance, with a category of "eccentric" at the borders of judgment. But *any* improvisation has the potential of being judged a full-blown innovation from the viewpoint of some others. An improvisation that seems trivial from one person's standpoint may be experienced as radical by another. A high school teacher may offhandedly assign a certain novel only to discover that her job is in jeopardy because a local censorship group objects to its "provocative content." An executive may carry out a minor tax writeoff contribution to charities that wins him the Community Achievement Award.

At what point do improvisations become defined and treated as full role innovations? Organizational roles vary a great deal in the latitude granted their performers; an executive has more autonomy and freedom to improvise than an assembly line worker. But any role has boundaries beyond which an innovation becomes more than a matter of mere style of performance.

Even when they are obviously necessary, organizations regard innovations with some wariness and suspicion because they go beyond the prescribed patterns and so are unknown in content and possible consequences. In this very real sense, any improvisation has at least the potential of being considered an innovation, and every innovation is "on trial." Even a mother's experimenting with a new recipe for a favorite family dish is likely to receive suspicious and quarrelsome comments until it "passes the test" at the dinner table.

TYPES OF INNOVATIONS

Some innovations are *externally imposed* on the organization by the actions of other organizations in its environment. Certain changes in role performances may be imposed on a business, for example, by the enforcement of a new federal regulation or by the loss of vital raw materials in the wake of distant international turmoil. Upheavals in the physical environment, such as hurricanes or floods, may necessitate altered role performances. But since the majority of any organization's environment is composed of other organizations, impingements from other organizations are the far more common source of imposed innovations. The economic upheavals of 1980 in the United States closed many more businesses and displaced far more persons than all of the year's natural disasters put together.

Some innovations are *internally planned* at the organizational level itself. A board of directors may adopt an equal opportunities program for the company's women employees or a family may decide to move to another city. In such cases, proposals for specific changes are usually developed and put forward by individuals or suborganizations for more general consideration. One of the interesting features of this type of innovation is that it may necessitate further innovations at the individual level because of unforeseen and unintended consequences. The board may discover that they now need a women's lounge built on the executive floor. When the family moves, the mother may discover that she now has to chauffeur the children around because there is no public transportation in their new town.

Finally, innovations may be neither externally imposed nor internally planned but *internally emergent* (or crescive), developing through apparently ordinary interactions among members as they strive to carry out their organizational and personal roles. In Chapter 7, we saw that, although an individual is influenced by his prescribed role, his performed role is directly worked out within the give-and-take of the interaction process. Thus, his or her performed role is virtually always somewhat discrepant from the prescribed role—what is expected by the organization. Role implementation almost always diverges from the designed role. These emergent discrepancies are *innovative* participations and comprise by far the largest category of innovations. Internally emergent innovations, whether trivial or radical, are thus widespread, involving most members of any populace and all organizational levels. Many of our greatest scientific and social inventions have stemmed from such emergent innovations. But managers down through the ages, from the early kings of England to modern parents fretting over their teenage children, have tended to regard this type of innovation as something of a social plague.

Whichever the source, innovations are always "sponsored" by some individual or some suborganization, at the very least in the sense that they enacted them. Indeed, the fate of any innovation (and perhaps its sponsor) is never determined simply on the basis of its correctness or value "under the circumstances." Its fate is determined also in large part by who sponsors it and by the tactics the sponsor employs in seeking to have it ratified—or at least not stigmatized—by the organization. Many an innovation which turned out to be appropriate has been simply overruled by more powerful elements within the organization. And many an inappropriate innovation has been visited upon the heads of members by executive fiat.

We might note in passing the special case of the person who attempts "ratification" of his or her innovations by concealing them from the organization. However, this is usually only a very temporary situation, because interactions and surveillances almost always eventually bring it to organizational light, where the processes described in this chapter come into full play.

Sponsorship of externally imposed innovations frequently falls on individuals who occupy positions of considerable authority who have boundary-keeping and boundary-spanning functions. Senior executives and heads of families usually have these functions, as do more specialized position occupants such as accountants, legal consultants, and liaison officers. These authorities evaluate the external impingements and formulate innovations to meet them. In the process, they may unwittingly create the necessity for many internal role performance innovations. For example, changes in regulations resulting from external impositions may force a foreman or church official to spend the majority of his time in record keeping. Internally planned innovations are likely to be more broadly sponsored, if not by some official suborganization charged with planning responsibilities, then at least by some coalition of persons in authority positions. Again, these innovations often produce unintended internal role changes, as when a merger of departments overloads a supervisor, forcing her to neglect on-the-floor inspections so that productivity suffers.

Any member is a potential sponsor of internally emergent innovations, simply by virtue of the discrepancies between prescribed and performed roles discussed above. A member may sponsor the innovation only to one superior, as a justification of his performance, or only to one or a few coworkers in order to gain a bit of support, but at the very least the innovation will have been "sponsored" through the very fact that he enacted it.

When some individuals or suborganizations serve as sponsors of organizational role innovations, at least some others (members or nonmembers) find themselves "targets" of the innovation because they stand to have this innovation or its consequences imposed on them, possibly altering their own organizational role performances and/or positions. For example, some male junior executives may feel their advancement opportunities threatened by a strong board resolution implementing equal opportunities for women employees. The teenage son of a family moving to another city might find his sports career, as well as the budding relationship with his girlfriend, interrupted. These targets attempt to anticipate the effects of the innovation upon themselves. On the basis of this evaluation, the anticipated effects may sometimes be welcomed, even eagerly supported. More often, targets are skeptical of or actively opposed to an innovation. If all the potential targets oppose the innovation, they will probably be able to muster sufficient power to block or at least subvert the change. Even a totalitarian organization can seldom carry out a universally unpopular measure. The most common situation, however, is a split response among targets—some supporting the innovation, some opposing, and perhaps many indifferent or apathetic.

At this point, the organizational or individual sponsor, from the Chrysler Corporation to the wife in a marital relationship, is faced with the "public relations" task of winning the potential targets' support and cooperation or at least of cooling off the opposition.

By potentially or actually altering the content of roles, innovations almost inevitably generate organizational tensions, whether the innovation is externally imposed, internally planned, or internally emergent. Within the organization, the intensity and scope of these tensions will vary greatly, depending on (1) the degree of change involved; (2) the balance of benefits and costs expected to be generated by the innovation for the organization and for its various members; and (3) the degree of organizational influence wielded by the sponsors. The parties involved may not be correct in their appraisals of the innovation or its eventual consequences. But whether correct or not, some tensions surrounding innovations are almost inevitable. And whatever their source, intensity, or scope, these internal tensions must somehow be handled by the organization.

ORGANIZATIONAL TACTICS

Fundamentally, an organization must deal with these tensions by somehow resolving the normative standing of the innovation for the collectivity as a whole. That is, some "official"—and ideally consensual—position must be reached regarding the innovation. The organization must either *ratify* the innovation as being a creative one (and therefore to be normatively prescribed or at least permitted) or *stigmatize* it as being deviant (to be normatively proscribed or at best tolerated). Since, as many wise men have noted, the dividing line between creative genius and mad deviance is often thin and blurry, the fate of any innovation hinges on fairly arbitrary processes of collective definition (Davis and Stivers, 1975). Whether the innovation eventually gets defined as genius or madness may depend on nothing more than who wins.

Procedures

One class of organizational procedures for ratifying or stigmatizing an innovation is essentially "proactive," on the model of the legislative process of enacting a norm. Some decision-making authority deliberates the pros and cons of some practice and eventually issues a prescription or a proscription of that practice. If that practice seems on balance to be a creative innovation *in the eyes of that body,* a ratifying norm is enacted requiring or favoring the practice. If it seems on balance to be a costly, harmful, or repugnant practice, a stigmatizing norm is enacted forbidding or discouraging the practice. Proactive procedures of this "legislative" variety are most commonly employed in dealing with externally imposed or internally planned innovations. For example, the United States Olympic Committee decided, after deliberation, to issue a sanction against American athletes' competing in the Moscow games. Two parents might decide, after discussion, that their children must be in the house by dark unless they have specific permission to be out later.

Internally emergent innovations—stemming from discrepant role performance—are most often dealt with after the fact. "Reactive" organizational procedures more closely resemble judicial proceedings, issuing "rulings" or "opinions" in response to complaints or appeals concerning some practice. Some decision-making authority considers and weighs the case made by the sponsors (for the practice) and the case made by the various targets (generally against the practice). In some instances, cost/benefit analysis may be an important part of the deliberations. In other instances, the relations of the practice to existing formal norms and customary rights, duties, and privileges are more central considerations. Through deliberation, the decision-making authority issues a ruling, either ratifying the practice as creative (or at least legitimate) or stigmatizing it as deviant. The results of such a deliberation process may not be "rational" in any absolute sense, and history may (and sometimes does) prove the judgment wrong. Such deliberations tend to display a cautious, even conservative bias, but they do tend to reflect the perceived best interests of the organization at the time of the judgment.

Organizational procedures through which an innovation is either ratified or stigmatized (hereafter more conveniently referred to simply as "ratification procedures") vary not only in form—proactive or reactive—but in at least two other major ways.

Ratification procedures vary in the degree of centralization of decision-making authority, from highly autocratic procedures at one extreme to completely democratic procedures at the other. The following range of possible procedures has been identified if the decision-making authority is an individual (Vroom and Yetton, 1973):

1. He may make the decision himself, using only information already available to him.
2. He may obtain the necessary information from subordinates and then make the decision himself. Other members are not involved in generating or evaluating alternative solutions.
3. He may share the problem with relevant other members on an individual basis, getting their ideas and suggestions without bringing them together as a group. He then makes the decision, which may or may not reflect the influence of the consulted members.
4. He may share the problem with relevant other members as a group, collectively obtaining their ideas and suggestions. He then makes the decision, which again may or may not reflect the influence of the group.
5. He may share the problem with relevant other members as a group, and together he and they generate and evaluate alternatives and attempt to reach agreement on a solution.

Of course, the decision-making authority may not be an individual but rather a designated subset of members, such as a council, committee, or cabinet. The above-listed alternative procedures are equally applicable to such a case. If the decision-making subset of members is elected or is in some other manner representative of the larger membership, we speak of "representative democracy." Finally, in "pure democracy," all interested members directly participate in decision making.

None of these alternative decision-making forms is necessarily better or more effective under all circumstances than the others. Blind tyranny, which does not consider the opinions of others and the realities of the situation in judging innovations, is both ineffective and often unjust. But so is the endless, bogged-down committee work where no decision can be reached. Whatever the degree of centralization, the crucial variable seems to be the degree to which an innovation is realistically appraised and judged with regard to the organization's overall situation.

The forms of ratification procedures employed within an organization are, of course, closely linked to the shape of its primary and secondary social structures (particularly those of authority and power). Flat structures—in which relatively few individuals have authority over relatively many members—are likely to employ fairly autocratic procedures. Wide (that is, decentralized) structures tend to employ more

Innovation

democratic procedures, ceding partial autonomy to parallel divisions. Figure 8-1 cross-classifies ratification procedures in terms of both the proactive/reactive and the democratic/autocratic dimensions, to suggest their diversity.

The examples shown in Figure 8-1 are all quite formal procedures. However, ratification procedures for handling innovations also vary in their degree of formality. Democratic procedures, for example, may not involve the formal mechanism of voting, as in a referendum or parliamentary proceeding, in order to explicitly determine consensus. Democratic decisions may sometimes be reached simply through discussion reflecting an apparent or implicit consensus, ''the sense of the meeting.'' Similarly, highly autocratic decisions need not be formal proclamations, such as a papal bull or royal proclamation, but may be more informally and implicitly rendered as apparent edicts—collective interpretations of the autocrat's casual remarks or reactions. An autocratic father may not have to announce to his intimidated children that they are no longer to play in the schoolyard after school; the message is clearly communicated through his informal reactions to a single incident. Informal ratification procedures, where both the deliberation and the ''verdict'' are carried out during interactions with the innovator, are the means employed for handling the large majority of innovations, whatever the shape of the structure. ''Let's talk it over'' is a response heard at all levels of organization.

Informal ratification procedures—often built into the interaction process itself—thus are a universal aspect of human social life. Seldom will a day pass that they are not applied several times by parents toward their children and by a senior toward his subordinates. It should be noted also that such procedures contribute heavily to the continuing informal socialization of members.

Whereas informal ratification procedures will be employed in every organization, formal procedures tend to be used only in organizations that have rather highly formalized structures. When informal procedures fail and the organization does not have a highly formalized structure (as in a relationship or family), it is likely to call in one of the more structured, larger organizations in which it is embedded. Help may be requested from school authorities, a community agency, or the police, for example.

FIGURE 8-1. Examples of Proactive and Reactive Ratification/Stigmatization Procedures, by Extremes of Democracy and Autocracy

	Democratic	Autocratic
Proactive	E.g., a ballot proposition	E.g., a dictator's proclamation
Reactive	E.g., trial by peers	E.g., a governor's pardon

process. According to Wilson (1966), the greater the structural differentiation within an organization, the higher the rate of innovation and the lower the rate of ratification of innovations will be. In highly elaborated role structures with complex role relationships, performed roles are especially likely to depart from prescribed roles—resulting in a high rate of innovation. But the greater diversity of individual perspectives that accompanies an elaborate role structure increases the difficulty of obtaining an acceptable degree of consensus for any new idea, resulting in a relatively low rate of ratification. Such elaborate organizations—sprawling structures, such as the federal government, a large university, or a multinational corporation, with a host of loosely coordinated departments and bureaus—tend to accommodate to this difficulty by operating on a "live and let live" basis as long as things go along fairly well.

Outcomes

Ratification of an innovation—certifying it as prescribed (or at least acceptable) practice—clearly tends toward resolving the collective tensions generated by and surrounding that innovation. The tension-resolution function of stigmatization may be less obvious, but a number of sociologists (Dentler and Erikson, 1959; K. Erikson, 1966; L. Coser, 1956) have shown that the process of collectively defining a practice as deviant (through reactive procedures) can itself be highly useful. Reactive stigmatization proceedings serve to (1) make organizational norms more explicit and clearly understood; and (2) help the collectivity to clarify its boundaries and to gain a better sense of what is distinctive about the organization and central to its identity. For example, the stigmatizing of a company's buyer for accepting gifts from suppliers reaffirms that this is not to be a part of purchasing raw materials and that company officials should not place personal aims above collective interests. It also indirectly validates all those who have been working steadfastly for the expansion of the firm.

Neither ratification nor stigmatization is likely to prove completely successful in resolving the tensions surrounding an innovation. Even though the normative standing of an innovation may have been settled as far as the organization and the majority of the membership are concerned, various suborganizations may seriously disagree with that settlement. Such an outcome is of course more likely where relatively autocratic procedures have been employed, but even in the case of completely democratic procedures (such as a vote by the entire membership) the decision is unlikely to have been unanimous. The losing parties in such contests may acknowledge that the organization has resolved the issue but may themselves consider that resolution to be troublesome. Not infrequently, some factions will feel that the resolution is an outright disaster or a gross injustice. No resolution is likely to be wholly acceptable to everyone involved, members and nonmembers. Therefore, even the harshest autocrat is likely to use some public relations to make a decision more palatable. In more democratic organizations, some compromise is usually sought through negotiations to further ease the tension and at least give some nod or promise to those who remain dissident.

Innovation

All ratification procedures are weighted heavily in terms of what is considered important to the collective interests and culture of the specific organization involved. An autocratic chairman of the board might be forgiven for virtually any actions (that would be regarded as deviant elsewhere, in other types of organizations) so long as he makes money for the company. At the same time, his family might stigmatize him on the grounds of personal neglect. Conversely, a minister might be stigmatized for making "excessive" amounts of money for his church.

INDIVIDUAL TACTICS

The innovation process is just as problematic for the individual as for the organization. One factor influencing the participation of an individual in the innovation process is his own evaluative judgment of the particular innovation in question—whether he thinks it is a good or a bad idea, creative or deviant. This has two aspects, the first of which is his own normative standards of right and wrong, "OK" and "not OK," even good and evil. Second, what does it mean for him personally, for his roles and plans? In his estimation, does he stand to win or lose from it in a benefit/cost balance?

A somewhat independent factor is his estimate of the likelihood that the organization will ratify the innovation. This estimate reflects not only his judgment of how other sectors of the organization would evaluate the innovation but also the relative organizational influence of those sectors he thinks would favor it and those he thinks would not. Of course, his own influence must be included in this reckoning. If he himself favors the innovation and is an individual of high authority, power, status, or leadership, he must conclude that the ratification potential of that innovation is high. Of course, the innovator can be wrong in such estimates of ratification potentials, to his relief or surprise. Many a leader—from pope to president to family head—has been surprised by membership opposition to an innovative measure.

Tactics in Proactive Ratification

In general, the individual who originally conceives of a potential organizational change evaluates that idea favorably. In the case of externally imposed change, a member must figure out a specific adaptation, which he may regard as a bad idea in itself but as the best of a set of bad alternatives. He may either carry through the idea in his role performances and keep it a secret from official organizational lines or he may seek ratification of his idea "through channels." The best of a set of bad alternatives is an interesting and fairly common case, most frequent when either the individual or the organization is "in trouble." Cutting losses and maintaining some semblance of order are the usual guidelines for choice under the circumstances of, for example, a marriage on the rocks or a company in financial crisis. The troubled couple might agree to wait to divorce "until the children are grown," meanwhile each pursuing their personal interests.

131

Even though the initiator may consider his idea to be a good one, he is unlikely to put it forward as a proposal unless he judges its ratification potential to be substantial (at least in comparison to available alternatives). By making an explicit proposal, the individual thereby initiates ratification/stigmatization proceedings and assumes the role of sponsor. This can be as formal as a proposal typed in triplicate and sent "up channels," or as informal as a conversational suggestion at the dinner table. In some cases the individual may judge that his sponsorship would diminish the ratification potential of his idea; he may then propose his idea more informally to other individuals or suborganizations that could more appropriately and effectively initiate proceedings by openly proposing and sponsoring the idea.

In the ratification/stigmatization proceedings themselves, both sponsors and targets engage in political deliberations around the proposal. In addition to more or less thoughtful, persuasive debate (in which opinions, testimony, and evidence are provided and considered), tactics of lobbying, bargaining, logrolling, and threats may be used. These processes may range from highly formalized—scheduled hearings, designated arbiters, and selected spokesmen—to highly informal—interaction in the shop, in the office, or at the family dinner table. In one form or another, they are to be found in every organization.

Again, proactive proposals for organizational change are commonly a major responsibility of members in positions of high authority or leadership; planning change is an important function of the executive. Indeed, the proactive ratification tactics of such high authorities amount to organizational management, the principles of which are codified in textbooks on management (for example, Drucker, 1974; Caplow, 1976). More specific management approaches to planned organizational change are the subject of an extensive literature (Burns and Stalker, 1961; Bennis, Benne, and Chin, 1969).

Tactics in Reactive Ratification

In reactive ratification, the innovations in question are not proposed changes but actual changes—unauthorized role performances which may have an impact on the roles of other members and thereby create tensions. Ratification/stigmatization proceedings are, however, usually initiated only when some party raises questions concerning the unauthorized role performance. It may be quite some time before anyone raises such questions, leading to an "organizational drift" of the organization's entire role structure in which it shifts position along some variable such as conservatism–liberalism, authoritarianism–permissiveness, or control–autonomy. But sooner or later, an official test case will arise, challenging the structural drift, and full ratification procedures will then come into play. A public school may drift toward more permissive education until a coalition of school-board members challenges the selection of textbooks and the abandonment of traditional grading.

Initiation. Occasionally, the perpetrator himself will initiate proceedings if he views his performance as deviant—upsetting to himself, perhaps generating shame or guilt concerning his performance. More often, however, the performer considers what he has done as quite justifiable and adaptive, perhaps even necessary. He will not then be motivated to initiate proceedings unless he judges the ratification potential of his innovation to be very high indeed, indicating some kind of creative breakthrough. Since few innovative performances are likely to be of such great ratification potential, the innovative performer is most often motivated to avoid proceedings. He will thus attempt to conceal from the organization the discrepant aspects of his performance. If he is otherwise doing well, the organization may cooperate by deliberately not inquiring very closely into his performances and may even bury attempts to initiate ratification procedures. A successful and productive member is a highly valuable resource for any organization and tends to be protected to some extent.

Targets—those members whose roles are affected by an innovative role performance—may cooperate in these concealment attempts if they share the initiator's evaluation of the innovation and his low estimate of its ratification potential. That is, both sponsor and selected targets may come to share a special interest in this altered role, an interest not shared by all members.

Often, however, at least some targets object to the innovation imposed on them by the altered role performance and are motivated to initiate proceedings by voicing a complaint, raising an issue, or filing an appeal. Such whistleblowing tactics are especially likely if an objecting target—a "busybody," a "bluenose," a "moral entrepreneur" (Becker, 1963)—estimates the ratification potential of that innovation to be quite low. Even if not, an objecting target can be expected to initiate proceedings in the hope of being able somehow to sabotage its ratification by contriving the failure of the innovative practice.

Contest. Once initiated, reactive proceedings closely resemble their proactive counterparts, centering on tactics of persuasive debate, with lobbying, bargaining, logrolling, and threats as frequent adjuncts. At the core of reactive proceedings—since these would not have been initiated unless at least one member considered an innovation to be deviant—is the collective consideration of the perpetrator's offered *account* for his performance (Scott and Lyman, 1968). The sponsor may offer an excuse (admitting that his action was wrong but arguing that he was not truly responsible for that action) or a justification (accepting responsibility for his action but arguing that it was not truly a wrong action under the circumstances). In seeking to have the organization honor his own account of the performance in question (Blumstein et al., 1974), the sponsor may employ the whole range of techniques of persuasive communication. Since in many cases his persuasive appeals rest finally on his personal credibility, the sponsor will also employ tactics designed to enhance that credibility (Shields, 1979).

Those targets who evaluate the innovation favorably and judge its ratification potential to be high may effectively join with the sponsor in promulgating that innovation, serving as cosponsors or supporters in ratification proceedings. Those targets who object to the innovation can usually be counted upon to articulate their objections in the course of these proceedings and to hold out for significant concessions in any lobbying or bargaining that may take place.

BASIC SOCIAL PROCESSES

Despite these essential similarities, reactive proceedings differ from proactive ratification proceedings in at least two major respects.

First, because the innovation has already taken place, there is some evidence (as opposed to mere speculation) about its effects. This evidence may well be preliminary, incomplete, weighted in favor of the most powerful factions, and suffering from "tunnel vision" in failing to take note of many of the overall and long-term consequences. But some notion of the relative benefits and costs may be directly and concretely documented.

Second, because the proceedings involve past actions rather than proposals, allegations regarding the character and motives of the actors are likely to be brought forth, so that the contest becomes less contemplative and more personalized. It is one thing to propose an equal opportunities rule or a move to another city and quite another to announce that one has hired women executives or has signed a binding contract for a job in another town. In the latter, personalities and character always become implicated. Deviance tends to be viewed as stemming from the character of the performer, as reflecting failure of the organization's recruitment and/or socialization processes. Creativity, too, tends to be seen as rooted in the character of the individual, as reflecting unusually successful functioning of the organization's recruitment and socialization processes.

Labeling theory (Becker, 1963; Schur, 1971; Lemert, 1951) emphasizes the self-fulfilling nature of inferences involved in reactive proceedings of ratification or stigmatization. When a person's performance is defined as deviant, the person himself tends to be defined (and subsequently treated) as being deviant. That is, he is thereafter organizationally *expected* to perform deviant acts and, consequently, is likely to do so. However, a person so stigmatized may refuse to accept the label of deviant and attempt to resist this organizational definition of his character (Rotenburg, 1974; Rogers and Buffalo, 1974; Prus, 1975). If the definition as deviant particularly jars the person's self-concept, he or she may embark on a long, sometimes bitter, campaign to lift the label and regain good standing.

Similarly, a person labeled as creative is likely to have heightened influence on the organization by virtue of his enhanced standing in the leadership structure. This "Pygmalion effect" has been the subject of studies in a variety of organizational settings (Rosenthal and Jacobson, 1968; Livingston, 1969).

The self-fulfilling power of these labels can be easily underestimated. Many a small-town person finds himself or herself somewhat "frozen" into the character—good or bad, spunky or shifty—imputed by the townspeople on the basis of a few early incidents. Subsequent behaviors are then selectively perceived and evaluated on the basis of this label, and future opportunities open or close as a result. To some extent, the labeled deviant can do no right and the labeled creative innovator can do no wrong. Often, the only real escape from such labelings is through a move to another organizational web.

Position changes and shifts in role-career opportunities often result from reactive, after-the-fact ratification procedures. The direction of the shift may be enhancement or decline, depending on the outcome. For instance, as a result of a hearing on his innovative methods of teaching, a school teacher may have enhanced prestige, a raised salary, and perhaps an offer to write a manual; or he may find it difficult to get another job and be forced to sell his house. Such outcomes tend to have self-fulfilling influences upon the person's subsequent organizational career, in line with the old adage "success breeds success, and failure breeds failure." Of course, being causative agents themselves within the individual/organization balance, persons can and often do break out of such self-fulfilling influences—by changing locations, redeeming themselves, switching to other organizational lines, and so forth.

THE CONTRIBUTIONS OF INNOVATION

As shown in Figure 8–2, the innovation process contributes to the development of an individual's organizational role in part through its feedback effect on socialization. For targets of an innovation, ratification of that innovation entails their resocialization by the organization in the form of altered role expectations. For sponsors, ratification of an innovation represent successful socialization of the organization, while stigmatization represents failure in the sponsors' tactics of resisting the organization's socialization efforts.

In a more forward direction in Figure 8–2, innovation also leads to the process of social control (discussed in Chapter 9). For sponsors of an innovation, ratification leads to rewards and stigmatization leads to punishments.

At a minor but universal level, innovations add "style" and "a personal touch" to interactions and role performances. They also provide a means for filling in the gaps that result from the always imperfect and incomplete transmission of expectations during socialization. Innovations also provide the individual with a chance to work out some creative compromises among his or her multitudinous role demands. This is a major tactic in reducing role strain, as we will see in Part IV.

FIGURE 8-2. Contributions of Innovation to Development of Individual's Organizational Role

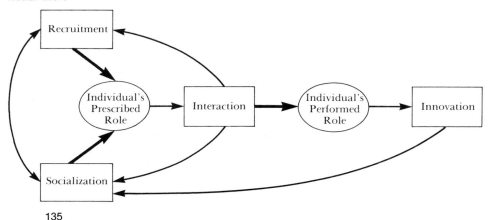

BASIC SOCIAL PROCESSES

At a major level, innovation is the social process employed in meeting the inevitable environmental shifts which impinge upon organizations and individual's alike. From one viewpoint, innovations provide much of the risk of social living; from another, much of the adventure and stimulating challenge.

SUMMARY

Innovation is that organizational process through which individuals' participation is altered. Innovations within any organization may be externally imposed (by the actions of other organizations in its environment), internally planned (through organizational actions on proposals developed by members or suborganizations), or internally emergent (developing, unplanned, through apparently ordinary interactions among members).

Whichever the type, innovations are always "sponsored" by some member or suborganization. The social position of the sponsor and the sponsor's tactics in seeking to have the innovation ratified (or at least not stigmatized as deviant), greatly affect the eventual fate of the innovation. Externally imposed and internally planned innovations tend to be sponsored by persons of considerable authority, but any member is a potential sponsor of internally emergent innovations, by virtue of the discrepancies between his prescribed and performed roles discussed in Chapter 7.

Other members (and/or nonmembers) find themselves to be targets of an innovation, in that they stand to have the innovation or its consequences imposed on them, possibly altering their roles or social positions. Based on their evaluation of its anticipated effects on them, targets may support, remain skeptical of, or oppose the innovation.

By potentially or actually altering roles, almost any innovation generates organizational tensions, the scope and intensity of which depend on (1) the degree of change involved; (2) various benefit/cost ratios; and (3) the organizational influence of its sponsors. The organization must deal with these tensions by somehow resolving the normative standing of the innovation—either ratifying it as creative or stigmatizing it as deviant.

"Proactive" procedures, on the model of the legislative process of enacting a norm, are most often employed in dealing with externally imposed or internally planned innovations. "Reactive" procedures, on the model of judicial proceedings, are typically resorted to in dealing with internally emergent innovations. Procedures also vary from the autocratic to the democratic, and from the highly formal to the highly informal. The forms of ratification/stigmatization procedures employed are related to several of the organizational attributes discussed in Chapter 3—particularly the shape, formalization, and elaboration of social structures.

Stigmatization, nearly as much as ratification, tends to reduce the organizational tensions induced by an innovation, but neither outcome is likely to eliminate such tensions completely.

An individual's tactics in ratification/stigmatization proceedings depend on his own evaluative judgment of the innovation and on his estimate of its ratification potential. The influence of these factors is most clearly seen in reactive proceedings, where both sponsors and targets may either seek or avoid initiation of proceedings. Reactive proceedings tend to be quite personal, with the result that not only the innovation but also its sponsor is labeled as creative or deviant.

The multiple contributions of the innovation process to the development of an individual's role are summarized in Figure 8–2. For targets of an innovation, ratification entails their resocialization through the imposition of altered role expectations. For sponsors, ratification represents successful socialization of the organization by those individuals, while stigmatization represents failure of their attempts to resist the organization's socialization efforts. Innovation also leads to the process of social control; for sponsors, ratification leads to rewards and stigmatization leads to punishments.

SUGGESTIONS FOR ADDITIONAL READING

The central contribution to an understanding of the innovation process itself remains James Q. Wilson's "Innovation in Organizations: Notes Toward a Theory" (pp. 193–218 in James D. Thompson, editor, *Organizational Design,* Pittsburgh: University of Pittsburgh Press, 1966). A more recent contribution of substantial importance is Thomas S. Robertson's *Innovative Behavior and Communications* (New York: Holt, Rinehart, and Winston, 1971).

An introductory general background to a consideration of ratification/stigmatization procedures is provided in R. J. Ebert and T. R. Mitchell, *Organizational Decision Processes* (New York: Crane, Russell and Co., 1975). These procedures receive more direct examination in Jack D. Douglas, editor, *Deviance and Respectability: The Social Construction of Moral Meanings* (New York: Basic Books, 1970).

Still the best account of the ratification of creativity is Gary A. Steiner's edited volume *The Creative Organization* (Chicago: University of Chicago Press, 1965).

Several fine treatments of the stigmatization of deviance are available. Three of these include: F. James Davis and Richard Stivers, *The Collective Definition of Deviance* (New York: Free Press, 1975); Richard Hawkins and Gary Tiedeman, *Creation of Deviance: Interpersonal and Organizational Determinants* (Columbus, Ohio: Merrill, 1975); and John Lofland, *Deviance and Identity* (Englewood Cliffs, N.J.: Prentice-Hall, 1969).

Although only the ticketed vendor must pay a fine, the policeman may constrain the onlookers too by reminding them of his presence, the law, and the consequences of breaking it.

CHAPTER 9

Social Control

How is the pattern of an organization maintained in the face of external and internal difficulties? How is it kept ''on the rails'' in producing collective goods? And why do individual members keep performing their designated roles? The answer is through *social control.*

Social control is that organizational process through which individuals' participation is *constrained.* Constraint has guiding, channeling, and deterring aspects to it, which together maintain the organization's structure by overseeing the role performances of the members. The U.S. Senate has its role-constraining traditions and its ethics committees. A group has its code of what it means to be a member, and its informal hazings. A pair relationship has its smiles and gifts, its frowns and angry disapprovals. Too often, perhaps, social control is thought of only in terms of its negative aspects of threat and duress toward transgressors. But most organizations actually emphasize *positive* social control to a far greater extent in seeking to establish and maintain their interests, values, and norms, and their social structures. Even in prisons and mental hospitals, the guiding and channeling aspects predominate, with deterrence serving as a ''back-up'' when these fail.

In the process of social control, the organization seeks both to develop and sustain creative or at least conforming participation, and to prevent and correct deviant participation. The various organizational processes are heavily relied upon to accomplish these two aims, and each process contributes to the maintenance of social control. In recruitment there is always a ''screening'' aspect which selects candidates predicted to be creative or conforming and rejects candidates judged to be high risks for deviance. A good deal of socialization guides the recruit toward desired performances and away from undesired actions. The encouragements and discouragements virtually built into interactions further channel and constrain the members' participation to mesh with organizational patterns. The arbitrations over ratification/stigmatization of innovations further guide members toward what is wanted and deter them from what is collectively unwanted.

There are, however, several factors unique to the social control process itself. Principal among these is the promise and provision of *rewards* for valued participation and the threat and provision of *punishments* for wayward and undesired participation. Rewards are either benefits bestowed or costs removed. Punishments, conversely, are either costs imposed or benefits removed. Both rewards and punishments are, in essence, adjustments in the selective sidepayments made to individual members to secure their participation in the organization's collective action. Such rewards and punishments range in degree from smiles and frowns to Nobel prizes and brutal executions, and they are constantly encountered at all levels of organization, from the dating couple to the United Nations.

Benefits most commonly manipulated in the social control process include personal invitations, inclusions and approvals, various material goods, desired services, social privileges, prestige, affection, and role support. Such individual benefits can be diminished or taken away by an organization as punishment, or can be enhanced or bestowed as reward. Organizational rewards and punishments most often involve the giving or taking away of benefits, with the manipulation of costs as a "back-up system." This is true even in more totalitarian institutions and societies, and it may well be the case that any organization which emphasizes manipulations of costs for members is not likely to long survive, as we shall see in Part III. For example, the brutal and unpredictable treatment of conquered peoples by the Nazis, with the resulting "what have we got to lose" resistance on the part of virtually entire populaces, contributed as much as any other factor to the downfall of the Third Reich.

Costs commonly manipulated are (1) members' expenditures of time, effort, and personal resources; (2) subordination and loss of personal autonomy; (3) participation in activities with an intrinsic aversive aspect, such as KP duty; and (4) social or physical pain, such as humiliation or spankings. Suspending or diminishing any of these costs can be highly rewarding, and organizations do fairly frequently provide such cost reductions as member rewards.

Punishment, particularly when positive approaches (coupled perhaps with admonitions and withholding of rewards) have failed, takes the form of imposing just these sorts of costs. The most extreme forms of member punishment, such as confinement, bodily injury, death, and eternal damnation of the soul, can be imposed only by an insignificant fraction of modern-day organizations, and then usually only after elaborate procedures. Even the extreme cost imposition of expulsion from the organization typically requires a good deal of "red tape." Since it is also likely to disrupt the solidarity of the collectivity, it is usually resorted to only after the milder measures discussed above have failed. Organizations which fall into the use of extreme punishments are usually regarded as aberrant by the surrounding social order; intervention from the larger organizations in which they are embedded is likely, as in the case of wife-beating or child abuse.

140

Social Control

Given that an organization views social control as a process of maintaining its organizational character, it is paradoxical that rewards and punishments so frequently take the form of *changes*—in the division of labor and in the primary and secondary social structures—that is, in the character of the organization. This apparent paradox is resolved when we realize that adjustments in role performances by manipulating the role prescriptions implement and reinforce the organization's character.

Rewards and punishments most often involve: (1) *changing the individual's position* through promotion, demotion, transfer, or expulsion; and/or (2) *redefining the individual's role,* by adding or subtracting rights, privileges, or duties. These adjustments may be temporary, as with a bouquet of flowers or "being in the dog house," or more permanent, as with a new title and office, or a nonrenewal of contract. These two types of changes are not independent of each other; even the manipulation of such sidepayments as prestige, affection, and salary often has the effect of altering the person's position in one or more of the secondary (dimensional) social structures. A change in the person's position in the primary role structure always has some effect upon his own roles and sidepayments.

Even in very informal social control situations there is likely to be a slight shift in the person's standing. For example, a recruit who is cooperative will have a slight rise in status, and a child who messes up the kitchen may experience a cooling off of affection from his parents for several hours or even days. Such minor shifts induced by the social control process are to be found everywhere in organizational life.

ORGANIZATIONAL TACTICS

Social control is, in part, a reactive response to the members' role performances. That is, distributive justice is to be rendered through a redistribution of benefits and costs on the basis of differential performance. Valued performances are rewarded, deviant performances are punished, and merely acceptable performances are accorded only the standard fare of benefits and constraints.

Reactive Social Control

The organization's first task is to detect and distinguish both valued and deviant performances. This is accomplished through *surveillance*—the monitoring and evaluation of performances. Surveillance rests primarily on observation of the individual's performance by superiors and by peers. In the vast majority of cases, the performance is lightly examined or "screened" to see that it fits within the acceptable range of expected style. This screening occurs in the ordinary flow of interaction and routine organizational communications. For example, patrolling policemen may glance at several hundred people along a street before checking out one person in detail. A supervisor may go through a dozen staff reports before chasing down some discrepant detail in one of them. A mother may glance at her child many times during a day before deciding to investigate his sticky hands.

On an ongoing basis, an organization screens performances to see (1) if they are really innovative; and (2) if innovative, whether they are worthy of more attention or are too minor to justify spending time and resources. A bit of extra work or a bit of boondoggling will, in most cases, be passed over with no more than a nod or a frown. But even here some "alert" has occurred, at least in the memory of the person adjudging. The fact that "Walter looks promising" or that "Sue took a long time on coffee break" may well be mentioned to others, and so the individual begins to accumulate a "reputation" and a "record," written or not, within the organization.

Observation by superiors may be direct, as in a site inspection or "walking the floor," or indirect, through intermediaries or closed-circuit scanners. It may be formal, with job reports and statistical data, or informal, through inquiring, prowling, or snooping. Peer observations may be acted upon directly or reported to superiors—formally, through "channels," or informally, through gossip, the grapevine, informing, and the like.

In highly formalized organizations, surveillance tends to be highly formalized also, as through time clocks, meters and charts, case files, and performance graphs, perhaps even computerized in the form of management information systems.

Finally, self-reports play a part in many surveillance systems. These may be quite formal, such as self-ratings or monthly statements of accomplishments, or highly informal, such as bragging, "leaks," requests for assistance, or an answer to the perennial questions "How are you doing?" and "How's it going?"

Information gathering (or monitoring of role performances) is but one facet of surveillance. The information must be evaluated as to whether the performance is creative, is within the acceptable boundaries of conforming, or is deviant. It is at this point that the process of innovation, discussed in Chapter 8, has an impact on the process of social control. Discrepant and therefore "newsworthy" aspects of role performances become the focus of ratification/stigmatization procedures. Essentially, a ruling is arrived at and the performance is pronounced creative, conforming, or deviant. It should be emphasized that these rulings and pronouncements vary greatly depending on the setting and the organizational level involved. They range from the rejection of an uncouth remark or the smile of a wife, to a resolution from the board of directors or a statewide referendum vote.

With such a verdict rendered, the distinctive tactic in social control is to decide on an appropriate adjustment of benefits and costs for the performer in question; what rewards should be conferred, what punishments imposed? Again, such decisions range in degree of formality from laboriously deliberative to utterly impulsive.

Those doing the adjudging often become quite creative in the use of the social control process. If the person is otherwise desirable or at least acceptable, resocialization processes tailored to the situation may be employed, ranging from "we need to talk about this" to some sort of training "retread." If the discrepant performance is creative, the member's valuation is further enhanced and he or she is possibly recruited and socialized for a higher position. If the person is otherwise undesirable or the discrepancy is a major deviance, extreme stigmatization may be employed to (1) terminate the person's membership; and (2) make a point with the other members. If the person has been considered generally undesirable but the discrepant performance is adjudged a creative contribution, a concerted effort to "salvage" the member through further socialization is likely to arise.

If the person is fairly new, either to the organization or to a particular position, creative performances will place him or her in some such category as "promising," "bright," or "bushy-tailed." If the fairly new member's performance is judged deviant, any benefit/cost adjustments are likely to be light, and the tactic of resocialization will probably be employed, but the person is now likely to have "a strike against him."

Selection of punishment is more often straightforward. Formalized norms, such as laws and regulations, often explicitly state a penalty or range of penalties for transgressions, and custom frequently provides clear guidelines for punishment of violators of important but less formal norms. Appropriate rewards for various types of creative performance are typically unaddressed within most formal statements of norms (with the major exception of pay-incentive systems, such as bonus plans) or within the body of custom. Usually, there is simply a more vague and generalized custom that "good works will be rewarded," which tends to prove true in that successful and productive members are likely to be considered highly desirable, in terms of both collective and special-interest aims. In either case, however, some organizational authority (boss, leader, judge, committee, jury) must decide what reward or punishment is warranted. This authority may or may not be the one that passed verdict, and this decision may or may not be made during the same proceeding in which the verdict was rendered.

Finally, some organizational authority (perhaps the same, perhaps different) must *administer* the decision. In the case of rewards, it is more likely to be the same authority that passed the verdict or decided on the sanction. In the case of punishments, the "sentencing" authority is likely to delegate administration of punishment to some separate authority. This is a curious but easily observed phenomenon. It might be speculated that it is so universal because it is a means of keeping the leadership's "hands clean." The more informal the social control process, the greater will be the likelihood that the same person does the evaluating, "judging," "sentencing," and administering of the rewards and punishments.

Although the reward and punishment of members is the central core of the social control process, such actions typically constitute a rather small part of an organization's total social control efforts.

Proactive Social Control

Too many discussions of social control overemphasize the matter of an organization's after-the-fact responses to individual performances—that is, punishing deviant performance and rewarding creative or conforming performance. Actually, the majority of the organization's efforts are not reactive but proactive, seeking to prevent deviance and to develop creative or at least conforming participation. Organizations at every level, from a pair relationship to a national polity, spend large amounts of resources, attention, and energies in such positive, proactive efforts; they engage in more pep talks than court martials, more celebrations than trials, more cozy talks than "chewings-out."

One distinctive tactic is *rituals of solidarity,* which serve to enhance members' sense of collectivity, of belonging to a social unit engaged in the production of a collective good in which members have a share. Through the performance of such rituals, the collective interests, values, and norms of the organization are symbolized, brought to mind once more, and perhaps exalted.

Such rituals of solidarity commonly include:

1. special terms of address and reference, such as father, mother, brother, sister, and other borrowed kinship terms; doctor, professor, governor, judge, master; buddy, pal, sweetheart, Mr. President, His Honor;
2. special handshakes, such as the thumbs-up handshake of the youth culture, the elaborately choreographed handshakes of the black street culture, the Boy Scouts, fraternities, lodges;
3. salutes, such as the conventional military salute, the Scout salute, the raised-fist salute, the Nazi salute;
4. uniforms and insignia, whether official or unofficial, elaborate or simple;
5. distinctive songs, chants, and ritual sayings; and
6. kissing of persons or adornments, bowing, kneeling, clapping, or cheering.

Occasions on which a number of rituals are performed together, perhaps in a patterned sequence, are known as *ceremonies.* Some ceremonies—the so-called *rites of intensification*—are intended primarily as expressions of solidarity; examples include club rallies, Veteran's Day parades, election victory parties, Fourth of July pageants, and wedding anniversary celebrations. But *all* organizational ceremonies—for example, *rites of passage* such as college commencement exercises, celebrating the transition of a member from one organizational position to another—function in part as rites of solidarity, exalting the sense of collectivity.

Two other basic tactics of proactive social control are *promises* of rewards and *threats* of punishment. The organization attempts to communicate to members that certain benefits and certain costs will be selectively administered, contingent on performance. These promises and threats are key aspects of the organizational expectations communicated to individuals in the ongoing socialization process. Accordingly, promises and threats may be communicated through explicit procedures, such as contracts, rulebooks, briefings, advice, admonitions, and/or through implicit procedures, such as observational learning and inference from organizational responses to behaviors (see Figure 6–1). The effectiveness of promises and threats depends in part on (1) the clarity and consistency with which they are communicated; (2) the rationality and fairness of the contingencies they present; and (3) the memberships' perception of the likelihood that they will be carried out. In general, explicit promises and threats are more effective than implicit ones.

Social Control

No promise or threat can be effective unless a member has reason to believe that the organization will know that his participation has fulfilled the conditions for reward or punishment. *Surveillance*—the monitoring and evaluation of individuals' role performances—is thus a vital organizational tactic of proactive (as well as reactive) social control. Various forms of surveillance have already been discussed in the preceding section. In most cases, recruits are informed about at least some of these surveillance procedures as a deliberate proactive tactic. The new bagboys and clerks are shown the store's video system, in part as a gentle reminder that there is a security system.

Whatever the forms of surveillance, the effectiveness of threats in deterring deviance and of promises in motivating valued performance depends in part on the perceived likelihood that the nature of any performance would in fact be reliably detected by organizational authorities. Given such detection, deterrence and motivation further depend on the perceived likelihood that the organization will in fact carry out its threat of punishment or its promise of reward. Ironically, members also run something of a reciprocal surveillance on the organization to see what it actually does in cases of breach and of creative contributions. Every new officer, new executive, and new babysitter is "tested" to see what they will actually put up with.

For both these reasons, it is important for an organization to dramatize incidents of reactive social control—of actual punishments and actual rewards—in order to increase deterrence and motivation proactively. The administration of punishments and rewards is thus often made a ceremonial occasion, in which the solidarity and effectiveness of the organization are ritually reaffirmed for the bystanders. Award ceremonies and public hangings are two examples.

Organizational Contributions

The benefits an organization can confer as rewards or withhold as punishments are greatly limited by the kinds and amounts of its collective resources. Without monetary resources, for example, salary manipulation is not a feasible tactic; without plentiful monetary resources, the magnitude of possible salary manipulation may be too small to motivate the desired performance.

The costs an organization can inflict as punishments or withhold as rewards are similarly limited by the nature of its collective interests, its values, and its costs of production. A bridge club, for example, can exact no blood whatsoever, very little sweat, and only a few tears (and then only from social rather than physical pain), in stark contrast to an army or a prisoner-of-war camp.

Manipulable costs are also limited by the degree of participation of members—the proportion of members' life-rounds and personal resources that are devoted to the organization. In segmental organizations (like a bridge club), no role is highly demanding. In more totalitarian organizations (such as an army), all roles are highly demanding, with role expectations extending into virtually every aspect of an individual's conduct. Such organizations control whether, when, where, and with whom an individual shall eat, sleep, or go to the bathroom—and sometimes even whether he shall live or die. The range of costs that can be manipulated in such organizations is vastly greater than in more segmental organizations. The greater the variety and amounts of manipulable costs or benefits, the more likely an organization's role structure will include specialized social control functionaries, analogous to police, judges, jailors, and executioners. Such specialized roles are common in the more totalitarian and role-encompassing organizations. Finally, surveillance of individuals' performances is both more intensive and more extensive in organizations that are relatively totalitarian and/or have specialized social control roles.

Etzioni (1961) has proposed a rough typology of organizations based on major strategies of social control. "Coercive organizations," such as prisons, armies, asylums, and certain gangs, rely on close surveillance and totalitarian manipulation of minor benefits and major costs—including physical force and violence—to control the behavior of low-ranking members. "Utilitarian organizations," such as bureaucracies, rely on manipulation of benefits, principally of the material varieties. "Normative organizations," such as voluntary associations, small groups, and relationships, rely more on shares in the collective good than on manipulation of their limited selective sidepayments of prestige, rank, and privilege; rituals of solidarity are a central tactic of social control in normative organizations.

INDIVIDUAL TACTICS

From the standpoint of the individual, the process of social control represents being constantly recycled through both the process of *recruitment* (in the form of promised, threatened, or actual promotion, demotion, transfer, or expulsion) and the process of *socialization* (in the form of promised, threatened, or actual changes in rights, privileges, or duties).

As in recruitment, then, the individual's tactics in the social control process depend on his level of relative interest in his organizational position. And as in socialization, his tactics are basically restricted to cooperation in or resistance to the organization's social control efforts.

Cooperation

If she is highly interested in her position, the individual may be expected to cooperate in the organization's surveillance of her by providing more or less honest reports and perhaps even by volunteering performance information that seems pertinent. She will be eager to make her successes known and may be motivated to confess her errors with an eye to getting organizational help in improving her role performance. The cooperative individual will generally believe and respect organizational promises and threats, will positively value organizational rewards, and will be disturbed by—but accept—organizational punishments. Often the organization will recognize this basic cooperativeness and soften the punishments to reprimands and some resocialization.

The cooperative individual will participate respectfully in organizational ceremonies and most lesser rituals of solidarity, and will perform whatever part he is assigned in the social control of other members. This part will at least include reasonably vigilant observation of others' performances and responsible reporting of at least the more serious infractions. If his organizational position is one of some authority, he will not normally avoid communicating organizational promises and threats or administering rewards. Even highly cooperative members, however, experience personal conflicts over conducting certain unpleasant surveillance duties and over administering punishments. There is a curious and important form of member cooperation which bears upon interorganizational relationships. Quite common is at least a mild resistance by an entire organization toward the "parent" organizations in which it is embedded. In this case, virtually the entire membership may be involved in the conspiratorial alliance. Examples include families and small businesses bending tax laws, field units ignoring central command dispatches, and franchises presenting a public relations "line" to the parent company. The members cooperate in evading full surveillance and in presenting a "front" that covers the actual goings-on. This seems to be an ingroup versus outgroup manifestation in which even warring members will close ranks against the outside organizational world.

Resistance

An individual who finds his organizational position undesirable can be expected to resist substantially the organization's social control efforts, at least in so far as they are directed toward himself. He can be expected to attempt to evade surveillance—by distorting objective records, by evading or misleading superiors' direct observation of his performance, by biasing any self-reports, and by interfering with peer observation and reporting of his activities. He becomes involved in an elaborate counterintelligence enterprise, attempting to figure out how and when the organization might be trying to learn about his activities and then feeding in misleading information. Secrecy, deception, and outright lies are commonplace, particularly if such an individual is able to form a conspiratorial alliance with others. Cajolings, "badmouthings," seductions, even intimidations, bribery, and blackmail are sometimes used to forge such an alliance. Organizational mistakes and injustices will be exaggerated and organizational successes devalued in the resisting individual's attempts to gain support from fellow members.

The resistant individual can be expected to discount, privately and publicly, the credibility of organizational promises and threats. Organizational rewards are devalued by the uninterested member, and he is undisturbed by most organizational punishments—although he will strive to evade them in many cases by pleading excuses and justifications. The uninterested individual will seek to point out distributive injustices in rewards and punishments—both among members within the organization and through invidious comparisons between that organization and its counterparts.

The resistant individual attempts to avoid participation in rituals and ceremonies of solidarity; if participation is unavoidable, he will mock and debase those rituals. His stance toward participation in the social control of other members may be more variable, particularly if he has entered a conspiratorial alliance to subvert the surveillance process. He will be motivated to report favorably on himself and his allies, and unfavorably on most others, particularly organizationally cooperative members and those who aid in surveillance. He is rather unlikely to occupy a position of substantial authority, but should he do so, he may either abstain from delivering promises, threats, rewards, and punishments, or—at the opposite extreme—delight in exercising these powers. He is also most likely to abuse his position in pursuit of his own private discrepant interests. He may also employ his position to mount some sort of mutiny to overthrow the current structure. At the very least, he is likely to shelter like-minded fellows.

Passive Participation

As in the socialization process, some members may adopt a tactic of more passive participation, midway between active cooperation and active resistance. In surveillance, for example, the individual neither volunteers any information that is not required of him nor schemes to manipulate reported information. Even though he is not entirely persuaded by organizational promises and threats or particularly impressed by organizational rewards and punishments, he does not cynically discount or devalue them. Ritual participation is an accepted part of the game, and he does what seems personally comfortable in the social control of others.

No individual, of course, is completely cooperative or completely resistant in the organization's tactics of social control. Mixed strategies are the general rule. A family member may be cooperative in finances and budgeting, passively accepting the ceremonial Sunday dinner with relatives, and actively resisting the division of house-cleaning chores, in conspiratorial alliance with his little brother.

THE CONTRIBUTIONS OF SOCIAL CONTROL

The social control process—serving to channel and constrain individuals' participation—contributes to the development of an organizational role in several respects, as shown in Figure 9-1.

Most centrally, social control vitally affects the interaction process. The organizational tactics of promises, threats, and surveillance represent important conditions or ground rules for the social negotiation process involved in interaction. Moreover, organizational rewards and punishments constitute major commodities within that

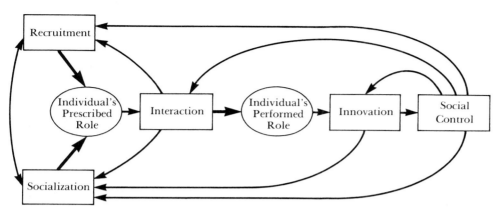

FIGURE 9-1. Contributions of Social Control to the Development of an Individual's Organizational Role

bargaining. Finally, of course, the rituals of solidarity provide occasions for members' interaction.

Organizationally, social control also affects the innovation process, in that surveillance tactics both call into play ratification/stigmatization procedures and influence sponsor/target dynamics within the innovation process. In turn, ratification is expected to lead to the administration of rewards, and stigmatization to the administration of punishments. Individually, social control feeds back into the recruitment process, through promised, threatened, or actual changes in a person's organizational position. Similarly, social control feeds back (both directly and indirectly, through links with innovation) into the socialization process by means of promised, threatened, or actual changes in the individual's rights, privileges, or duties and through providing proactive examples for others.

Social control also contributes to organizational life by curbing exploitation, either of the organization by individuals or of individuals by other members of the organization. There are rules guarding against extremes of exploitation at all levels of organization; even occupied peoples and slaves have some rights. Organizations which have embedded suborganizations within them often take a surveillance and social control hand in how these suborganizations are getting along. This is done to maintain boundaries of acceptable performances—to "keep the peace" within the terrain of the larger organization. Examples include a community overseeing the families within it, a parent corporation keeping tabs on the companies it holds, and the federal government acting as watchdog over state and city governments. The parent organization usually has more or less legal rights to do so, at least in cases that exceed certain bounds, such as child abuse or municipal fraud with federal funds. The embedded organizations tend to resist such incursions, but they are in a dilemma; they want support and services and protection from the parent organization, but not interference. This dilemma is usually handled through accommodation, whereby the embedded organization is granted autonomy at the same time that the parent organization retains the right to review ratification proceedings and to protect its own organizational interests. Such arrangements will receive further attention in the chapters of Part III.

Social control is inevitably imperfect, and perhaps this is just as well. Otherwise, organizations might come to dominate individuals totally. On the other hand, too little social control provides insufficient curbs on the unbridled pursuit of personal special interests and the more aberrant extremes of behavior; few would argue that axe murderers should be free to "do their thing." Historically, a breakdown in social control has generally entailed a breakdown in the social order. It might be speculated (1) that social control becomes excessive and oppressive when the other basic social processes have been far from successful; and (2) that social control works best for all participants when it is in balance with the other processes.

SUMMARY

Social control is that organizational process through which individuals' participation is *constrained.* In seeking to establish and maintain its character, an organization strives through social control (1) to develop and sustain creative or at least conforming participation; and (2) to prevent and correct deviant participation.

Principal mechanisms include the promise and provision of rewards and the threat and imposition of punishments. Rewards may be either benefits bestowed or costs removed; punishments may be either costs imposed or benefits removed. Both are essentially contingent adjustments in the selective sidepayments made to members. Paradoxically, rewards and punishments frequently take the form of changes in the division of labor and in the primary and secondary social structures, involving (1) a change in the person's position in such structures, through promotion, demotion, transfer, or expulsion, and/or (2) a redefinition of his role, by adding or subtracting rights, privileges, and duties.

Social control is in part a reactive response to members' role performances—an attempt to render distributive justice. Through surveillance, an organization seeks to detect and distinguish both valued and deviant performances. Surveillance involves not only monitoring but evaluation. Following the ratification or stigmatization of a performance, the organization must decide on an appropriate reward or punishment. Finally, some organizational authority must administer that sanction. Although the sanctioning of members is the core of the social control process, such actions ordinarily are but a small part of an organization's social control efforts. Proactive attempts to prevent deviance and to develop creative or conforming participation are normally much more prominent than reactive social control. One distinctively proactive tactic is a wide variety of rituals of solidarity and organizational ceremonies, undertaken to enhance members' sense of collectivity. Two other basic proactive tactics are promises of rewards and threats of punishments; communication of promises and threats may be either explicit or implicit. The effectiveness of threats in deterring deviance and of promises in motivating valued performance depend on members' beliefs that (1) performances will be noticed and properly evaluated; and (2) threats and promises will be carried out. Thus, surveillance and the ceremonialization of sanctioning serve as proactive as well as reactive tactics.

The nature of potential rewards, punishments, and surveillance procedures available for use by an organization varies characteristically. Coercive organizations rely on close surveillance and totalitarian manipulation of minor benefits and major costs. Utilitarian organizations rely on manipulation of benefits, principally of the material varieties. Normative organizations rely more on shares in the collective good than on manipulation of their limited sidepayments; they also emphasize rituals of solidarity.

For the individual, the process of social control essentially represents being constantly recycled through both the recruitment process (in the form of promised, threatened, or actual promotion, demotion, transfer, or expulsion) and the socialization process (in the form of promised, threatened, or actual changes in his rights, privileges, or duties). As in recruitment, then, his tactics depend on his level of relative interest in his organizational position. As in socialization, his tactics are basically restricted to cooperation with, passive participation in, or resistance to the organization's social control tactics of surveillance, promising/threatening, sanctioning, and rituals.

The social control process—serving to channel and constrain individuals' participation—contributes in several ways to the development of any organizational role, as summarized in Figure 9-1. Most centrally, an organization's social control tactics impose major conditions, commodities, and forms upon the social negotiation process that is interaction. There is also a reciprocal influence between social control and the innovation process. Finally, social control feeds back into the recruitment process and (both directly and indirectly) into the socialization process.

SUGGESTIONS FOR ADDITIONAL READING

Amitai Etzioni's typology of social control strategies ("Organizational Control Structure," pp. 650–677 in James G. March, editor, *Handbook of Organizations,* Chicago: Rand McNally, 1965) still has much to say to any interested reader. More detailed and contemporary analyses of formal control processes are to be found in Edward E. Lawler III's "Control Systems in Organizations" (pp. 1247–1291 in Marvin D. Dunnette, editor, *Handbook of Industrial and Organizational Psychology,* Chicago: Rand McNally, 1976) and in Arnold S. Tannenbaum's *Control in Organizations* (New York: McGraw-Hill, 1968).

Collusive manipulations of formal control systems are classically described in Donald Roy's "Efficiency and 'The Fix': Informal Intergroup Relations in a Piecework Machine Shop," *American Journal of Sociology,* 1954, 60: 255–266.

The role of nonmaterial rewards in social control is lucidly described in Orrin E.

Klapp's *Heroes, Villains, and Fools* (Englewood Cliffs, N.J.: Prentice-Hall, 1962) and in William J. Goode's *The Celebration of Heroes: Prestige as a Social Control System* (Berkeley: University of California Press, 1979).

Informal social controls are examined in Eliot Freidson and Buford Rhea, "Processes of Control i.. a Company of Equals," *Social Problems,* 1963, 11: 119–131; in Warren Breed, "Social Control in the Newsroom: A Functional Analysis," *Social Forces,* 1955, 33: 326–335; and in Edward Gross, "Some Functional Consequences of Primary Controls in Formal Work Organizations," *American Sociological Review,* 1953, 18: 368–373.

Surveillance tactics and individual responses to them are studied in Rose Laub Coser's "Insulation from Observability and Types of Social Conformity," *American Sociological Review,* 1961, 23: 56–63.

Photo courtesy of Marcia Due, Yale School of Organization and Management

An internship program allows business school students to actually practice the roles they have learned in school, and to gain experience under the guidance of professional brokers.

CHAPTER 10

Role-Making and Career Development

How do the five basic social processes examined in the preceding chapters come together to shape organizational life? How do they establish both an individual's roles and the social structures of the organizations in which he or she is involved? And how do their influences continue through the years to affect a person's organizational career? If we put these processes together, we can gain an enriched understanding of Keith's or Stephanie's social life and an increased understanding of organizations, from the Smuthers family and Jack and Jill's pair relationship to the United States government and General Motors.

In these chapters of Part II, we have shed some light on the character of social process. The nature and functions of five rather distinct but highly interrelated processes—recruitment, socialization, interaction, innovation, social control—have been examined at a quite general level; they are summarized in Figure 10-1. The purpose of this examination has been to set forth the basic model of social psychology employed in this book. The model is depicted in Figure 10-2.

In our examination of each of the processes, we have emphasized the contributions made by both the organization and the individual—through the attributes and tactics

FIGURE 10-1. **Functions of Basic Organizational Processes**

Recruitment
Socialization
Interaction   } is the process through which { determined
Innovation   individuals' participation is   defined
Social control   implemented
                                                         altered
                                                         constrained

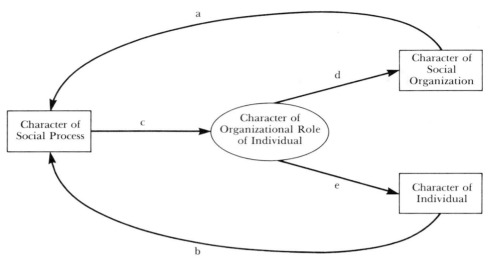

FIGURE 10-2. **Interconnections among Individual, Organization, Social Process, and Organizational Role**

of each—to the complex and dynamic interplay that constitutes the social process. These contributions are symbolized by arrows *a* and *b* in Figure 10–2. Thus, interactions among members of a health club influence both the character of the individuals involved and the character of the club. Similarly, the mutual socializations of parents and children have a shaping influence upon the character of each member and that of the family as a whole.

ROLE-MAKING

Our basic model further states that the character of social process determines the character of the individual's organizational role (arrow *c* in Figure 10–2). Through the chapters of Part II, we have developed the thesis that our five basic processes together suffice to determine the character of a role (see Figure 10–1), as long as we include the interplay among these five processes and the interplay between individual and organization *through* the processes, as in Figure 10–2. Taken together, these processes and the interplay among them suffice, for example, to determine the social role of "soldier" for a young man.

The joint action of these five processes implies that they are inextricably interconnected in real life. And indeed, the interconnections are quite dense and intricate. The core connections are exhibited in the left-to-right sequence of unlabeled arrows in Figure 10–3, where broad arrows signify "completely determines" and thinner arrows signify "contributes to or leads to."

To recapitulate that sequence, recruitment and socialization jointly determine the

156

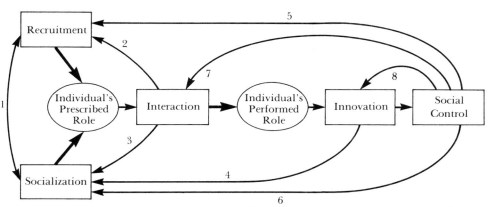

FIGURE 10-3. Interconnections among Basic Processes in the Development of an Individual's Organizational Role

individual's *prescribed* role—that is, the organizational position he occupies and the expectations held toward him by virtue of occupying that position. This prescribed role in turn influences the interaction process, which determines his *performed* role. Role performance always involves the individual in the innovation process, as a creative or deviant performer, and this process in turn involves him in the social control process, in which creativity is rewarded and deviance is punished.

As Figure 10-3 indicates, however, this sequential picture is far too simplified. The interconnections among the five processes include not only the left-to-right core sequence of unlabeled arrows but also the right-to-left feedback connections represented by the eight numbered arrows.

1. The mutual influence between recruitment and socialization must be acknowledged. The pre-entry recruitment tactics of attraction, selection, and placement contribute heavily to anticipatory socialization. In turn, anticipatory socialization influences the attractiveness of an organizational position to the individual. The heavy wave of socialization efforts upon initial entry serves as a crucial test of the respective levels of interest (attraction) of both the organization and the individual, frequently leading to recruitment out. Subsequently, any reintensification in recruitment of the individual (a possible position change) leads to a reintensification of the socialization process.

2. One aspect of the interaction process—the negotiation of identities—essentially represents a situational ''fine-tuning'' of the organizational identities determined through the placement aspect of recruitment.

3. A second aspect of interaction—the negotiation of lines of action—similarly amounts to a fine-tuning of role expectations communicated in socialization.

4. Innovation, too, exerts a feedback effect on socialization. For targets of an innovation, ratification of that innovation entails their resocialization by the organization in the form of altered role expectations. For sponsors of an innovation, ratification represents their successful socialization of the organization, while stigmatization of

their innovation represents failure in their efforts to resist the organization's socialization tactics.

5. The social control process feeds back into the recruitment process through promised, threatened, or actual changes in the individual's organizational position (or even in his organizational membership).

6. Similarly, social control feeds back into the socialization process through promised, threatened, or actual changes in the individual's rights, privileges, or duties.

7. Social control affects interaction in several ways. Promises, threats, and surveillance channel and set boundaries to the social negotiation process that is interaction. Organizational rewards and punishments constitute major commodities within that negotiation process. Rituals of solidarity provide occasional forms for members' interaction.

8. Social control affects the innovation process, in that surveillance tactics both call into play ratification/stigmatization procedures and influence sponsor/target dynamics within the innovation process.

These five processes, then, must not be thought of as linked in a distinct temporal (or even logical) sequence. Each of them is continuous, interlinked directly and indirectly with each of the others to form an endlessly cycling system which shapes and reshapes the individual's organizational role and through which the individual influences the shape of organizations.

CAREER DEVELOPMENT

If this system cycles long enough (without ejecting the individual), the continued recruitment process is almost certain to place the individual into some other organizational position, in which a different role must be shaped.

The sequence of positions occupied by an individual constitutes his *organizational career* and is determined by this same cycling system of five basic processes. The system of Figure 10–3 can be read, then, in two ways. Considered as operating over a short span of time, that system can be seen as generating an individual's organizational role; considered as operating over a longer span of time, it can be viewed as generating his organizational career. In a short-term perspective, individuals can be seen as recruited and socialized into roles. In a long-term perspective, they can be seen as recruited and socialized into organizational careers. Interaction can be viewed as either the performance of roles or the playing out of careers. Careers, like roles, can be influenced and altered through the innovation process. Actual or potential changes in organizational position, which figure so prominently in the social control process, are part and parcel of organizational careers. A college graduate may accept the position and perform the organizational role of high school teacher. As time goes on, he may occupy the further positions of student adviser, assistant principal, and principal at a different school. After retirement, he may serve part-time as a salaried youth-programs consultant for the city. Similarly, his family career would move through a sequence of specific roles—child, youth, lover, young married, father of infant, head of household with several growing children, retired widower involved in a pair relationship with a divorcee.

Just as both the organization and the individual have a stake in the individual's organizational role and strive to develop that role satisfactorily, so both have a stake in the individual's organizational career and strive to develop that career. In every organizational role structure, some positions require more valuable contributions from individuals than do others, and these positions also confer more valuable selective sidepayments to their occupants. An organization has a stake in restricting occupancy of these core positions to persons who can and will make the special contributions required; core positions should not be filled by an individual who no longer can (or is not yet able to) make these contributions. An individual, on the other hand, has a stake in obtaining the more valuable sidepayments accompanying a core position. Thus, both parties have an interest in the movement of persons from position to position, although these interests are not always congruent.

Core positions are those which rank high (in authority and status, for example) and/or are central to the division of labor and the communication structure. Schein (1971) has proposed a conical model of organizational structure, shown in Figure 10-4, to represent the fact that higher positions almost always are also more central positions.

In moving from one position to another, then, an individual may progress along one or more of the three dimensions depicted in Figure 10-4. He may move up or move down in the organization. He may move in on the organization—becoming more of an "insider," more central to organizational workings—or he may move out and become more peripheral. Finally, he may move around in the organization, circling it to enter some other division or official suborganization. Some organizations, such as a pair relationship, are quite simple in structure and would not have a full development of all three of these dimensions. Even in such simple structures, however, there is some "social distance" movement—inward or outward—and some movement "around" to other roles. There could also be up or down movement, in terms of dominance shifts.

Important to Schein's model is the concept of organizational boundaries, marking off the various positions and serving as barriers to movement between positions. Hierarchical boundaries separate the various vertical ranks, inclusion boundaries mark off inner from outer circles, and functional (or departmental) boundaries separate functionally distinct divisions, departments, or other official suborganizations. As examples, a person would have to penetrate a hierarchical boundary to be promoted to an executive position, an inclusion boundary to reach the inner circle of a religious group, and a functional boundary to transfer from medical school to law school.

Boundaries can vary in (a) *number,* (b) *degree of permeability,* and (c) type of *filtering properties* which they possess. For example, in the military there are a great many functional boundaries separating the different line and staff activities; but the overall policy of rotation and keeping all officers flexible makes these boundaries highly permeable in the sense that people move a great deal from function to function. On the other hand, a university would also have many functional

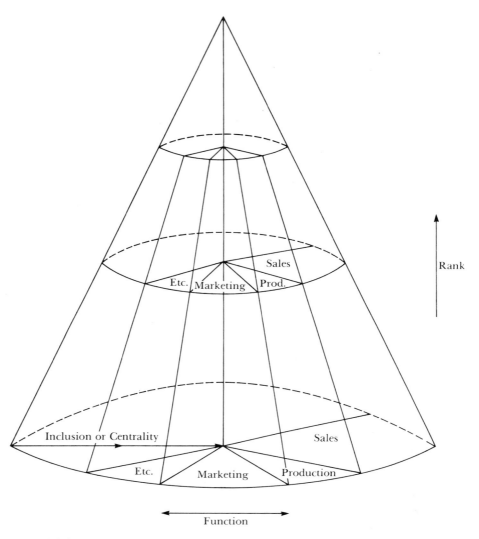

Source: Schein, 1971: 404.

FIGURE 10-4. Conical Model of Organizational Structure

boundaries corresponding to the different academic departments; but these would be highly impermeable in the sense that no one would seriously consider the movement of an English professor to a Chemistry department, or vice versa. A small family-run business, to take a third example, is an organization with very few functional boundaries in that any one manager may perform all of the various functions.

160

Role-Making and Career Development

Similarly, with respect to hierarchical or inclusion boundaries one can find examples of organizations in which there are many or few levels, many or few degrees of "being in," with the boundaries separating the levels or inner regions being more or less permeable. The external inclusion boundary is, of course of particular significance, in that its permeability defines the ease or difficulty of initial entry into the organization. Those companies or schools which take in virtually anyone but keep only a small percentage of high performers can be described as having a highly permeable external inclusion boundary but a relatively impermeable inclusion boundary fairly close to the exterior. On the other hand, the company or school which uses elaborate selection procedures to take in only very few candidates, expects those taken in to succeed, and supports them accordingly can be described as having a relatively impermeable external inclusion boundary but no other impermeable boundaries close to the exterior.

Further refinement can be achieved in this model if one considers the particular type of filters which characterize different boundaries, i.e., which specify the process or set of rules by which one passes through the boundary. Thus, hierarchical boundaries filter individuals in terms of attributes such as seniority, merit, personal characteristics, types of attitudes held, who is sponsoring them, and so on. Functional boundaries filter much more in terms of the specific competencies or his "needs" for broader experience. . . . Inclusion boundaries are probably the most difficult to characterize in terms of their filtering characteristics in that the criteria may change as one gets closer to the inner core of the organization. Competence may be critical in permeating the external boundary, but factors such as personality, seniority, and willingness to play a certain kind of political game may be critical in becoming a member of the "inner circle." Filter properties may be formally stated requirements for admission or may be highly informal norms shared by the group to be entered.

With reference to individual careers, organizations can be analyzed and described on the basis of (a) number of boundaries of each type, (b) the boundary permeability of the different boundaries, and (c) the filtering system which characterizes them. For example, most universities have two hierarchical boundaries (between the ranks of assistant, associate, and full professor), two inclusion boundaries (for initial entry and for tenure), and as many functional boundaries as there are departments and schools. Filters for promotion and tenure may or may not be the same depending on the university but will generally involve some combination of scholarly or research publication, teaching ability, and "service" to the institution [Schein, 1971: 405–407; emphasis in original].

Organizations also differ in the number and location of initial entry points. New members do not always start in low-ranking peripheral positions and work their way up and in. In many organizations, some new members may be recruited specifically to fill quite high-ranking and central positions. Some entry positions, whether high or low, are essentially dead ends, from which occupants cannot move up or in. And in some organizations—such as a taxi-dance hall (P. Cressey, 1932)—virtually all new members (young and good-looking) start at the top and move down and out (as age and long hours take their toll).

In any reasonably stable organization, given its structure of internal boundaries, various career patterns (or expected career trajectories) can be defined, depending on initial entry point. The direction, probable distance, and timing of an individual's career movement through the social structures of an organization are often the subject of rather clear organizational expectations (Becker and Strauss, 1956; Glaser, 1968;

Van Maanen, 1977). In extremely fixed societies, an individual's life career can be virtually inevitable, predetermined by ascriptive characteristics such as the hereditary occupation of the family he is born into. Most modern societies are much more open. But, as we will see in Chapter 11, no society remains all that fixed over a period of time and, conversely, no society is without persisting patterns. So we are speaking here of organizational influence upon individual careers, not determinism.

The expected trajectory defines which internal boundary is the next filtering system (set of standards) to be applied to the individual in the continuing recruitment process. Development efforts—training, coaching, sponsorship—are undertaken by the organization (through the socialization process) to prepare the individual to pass through this filter, whether this passage be up or down, in or out, or merely around (Glaser and Strauss, 1971). Individuals may cooperate in or resist these development efforts, may prepare themselves either to meet or to fail the standards posed by the next filter (D. T. Hall, 1976).

IMPACT ON THE CHARACTER OF THE ORGANIZATION

In Figure 10-3, arrow *d* indicates that the character of the individual's performed role (or career) in turn influences the character of the social organization. An organization is, after all, a structured collectivity—a set of persons undertaking differentiated but coordinated lines of action. An organization *is* a division of labor in collective action; thus, what roles are developed for and by individuals though the five basic processes is constitutive of the organization. The individuals who participate and the way in which they do so totally determine the character of that organization—its size, resources, interests, norms, values, culture, and internal social structures. Since recruitment, socialization, interaction, innovation, and social control are social organization *as process,* it is hardly surprising that the joint outcomes of these processes represent social organization *as product.* That is, the processes produce the organization.

In the longer view, an organization can be regarded as a system of interlocked careers:

Staffing an organization adequately is not simply a matter of having all jobs filled by people who presently are capable of doing them competently. The environment in which organizations exist is always changing, and the skills that are needed to carry out a job one day may not be the right skills at some point in the future. This means that the occupants of jobs either have to develop new skills to keep pace with the changing job demands, or the organization has to replace the person with someone who has the needed skills. Finally, most organizations have life spans that exceed the career of any individual; thus, prospective successors must be available to fill in when job holders retire, change organizations, or are promoted. It is obvious, therefore, that the long-term effectiveness of an organization depends on its developing an adequate supply of people who are prepared to fill the jobs that will exist in the future.

People are a unique kind of resource and often prove difficult to develop, maintain, and utilize. They have their own career objectives, and these may or may not fit the organization's short- and long-range plans. People can be developed through various kinds of training and other experiences, and once they are developed they increase in value both to the organization that has developed them and to other organizations. Unlike other assets, they rarely can be sold and they can decide to leave the organization at any time, thus forcing the organization to write off its investment in them. Efforts to develop them may fail either because the people are incapable of developing in a given way or because the development was poorly planned or administered. People also often develop and increase in value on their own. Sometimes this occurs as a result of job-related experiences, but often it results from other experiences. Most people want to utilize their skills and abilities, and if they cannot they may leave the organization. Unlike many physical assets, human assets cannot be easily stored or put on the shelf for future use. The organization that trains someone to be the next president may find that the person will leave if he has to wait too long to become president. In a sense, human resources are perishable resources that can be cultivated and that have to be used at the right time. . . . When there is a convergence between the individual's career goals and the organization's development plans, an effective integration of the individual and the organization can take place. . . . When there is a lack of convergence . . ., however, poor individual-organization integration develops, and the results are organizational ineffectiveness and [individual] dissatisfaction. [Porter et al., 1975: pp. 189–190].

Although history books often emphasize the profound effects of single individuals on the character of nations and other organizations of great scope, the impact of one individual's role (or career) on such large organizations is seldom substantial. In smaller organizations, of course, the impact may be very great indeed, as we shall see in the later chapters of Part III.

IMPACT ON THE CHARACTER OF THE INDIVIDUAL

In Figure 10–3, arrow *e* calls attention to the impact of the individual's role (or career) on her own individual character. This impact is very often quite pronounced, as organizations require of (and actively develop in) individuals a wide variety of personal attributes. An organizational role not only provides an individual with an identity (an answer to the question of who she is) but may quite specifically influence what she does, thinks, feels, and wants; how she looks and behaves; and what she knows, has, and can do. Identical twins raised in different environments with correspondingly different organizational roles, show the influence of such divergent role influences upon individual character traits. A twenty-year career involving a sequence of roles with the same organization is bound to influence many of the individual's attributes as compared with those of someone spending twenty years along some different line.

An organizational career, as an objective sequence of roles, entails for the individual recurrent transformations of identity and personal attributes (Strauss, 1959; Becker, 1964). "Subjectively, a career is the moving perspective in which the person sees his life as a whole and interprets the meaning of his various attributes, actions, and the things which happen to him" (Hughes, 1937: 409–410).

Various attributes of a person may either come to the fore or recede under various organizational or positional shifts. A scientist, for instance, promoted to head of a foundation, may find himself employing leadership skills which had been dormant since his high school class presidency. A woman might find her tendency toward orderliness a highly appreciated skill as a legal secretary. These skills would then be enhanced by the new positions, while others might fall into relative disuse.

The specific impact of a role or career depends, of course, on the nature of that role and of the organization in which it is lodged. In Part III, therefore, a major focus of each chapter will be a more specific examination of how roles in each type of organization affect the character of the individuals who perform them. But first, we must examine the workings of these processes with regard to individuals and organizations under the impact of social change.

SUMMARY

Individuals' organizational participation is determined through recruitment, defined through socialization, implemented through interaction, altered through innovation, and constrained through social control.

These five basic processes are dynamically interrelated (as summarized in Figure 10-3) and together suffice to determine the character of an individual's organizational role.

Recruitment and socialization jointly determine an individual's prescribed role. This in turn influences the interaction process, which determines his performed role. Role performance always involves the individual in the innovation process, as a creative or a deviant performer, which in turn involves him in the social control process through which creativity is rewarded and deviance is punished.

However, eight "feedback loops" enrich and complicate this basic story. First of all, recruitment and socialization are reciprocally linked in several ways. Second, the identity-negotiation aspect of the interaction process feeds into the placement aspect of recruitment. Third, the action-negotiation aspect of interaction feeds into the expectation-communication aspect of socialization. Fourth, innovation loops back into socialization, differently for sponsors and for targets. Fifth, social control feeds back into the recruitment process, through implied or actual changes in individuals' memberships or positions. Sixth, social control similarly feeds back into socialization, through implied or actual redefinitions of prescribed roles. Seventh, social control provides vital conditions, commodities, and forms for the negotiations of the interaction process. Eighth, the surveillance aspect of social control affects the innovation process in a variety of ways.

All these direct and feedback linkages form an endlessly cycling system of social process which shapes and reshapes the individual's organizational role. Viewed over a short span of time, it is a system of role making. Over a longer timespan, it is a system of career development. That is, if the system cycles long enough—without ejecting the individual—the continuing recruitment process is almost certain to place him into some other organizational position. The sequence of positions occupied by an individual constitute his organizational career.

In Schein's conical model of organizational structure, a person may move up or down, move inward or outward, or simply move "around" in an organization. Any change in position is likely to represent movement along two or more of these dimensions simultaneously. Movement requires penetration of organizational boundaries. Hierarchical boundaries separate the various vertical ranks, inclusion boundaries mark off inner from outer circles, and functional (or departmental) boundaries separate functionally distinct official suborganizations.

Organizations vary in the number, nature, and permeability of such boundaries and in the number and locations of initial entry points. Most organizational cultures define an expected career trajectory associated with each initial entry point, anticipating the probable direction, distance, and timing of a person's career movement. Just as both organization and individual have a stake in the person's organizational role and strive to develop that role satisfactorily, so each has a stake in his organizational career and strives to develop that career.

The impact of the role-making/career-development system on organizational character is direct indeed. An organization is, by definition, a structured collectivity—a set of persons undertaking differentiated but coordinated lines of action in a joint venture. The set of roles and careers developed for individuals through the operation of the five basic processes constitute the organization.

The impact of role-making and career development on the character of the individual is similarly quite pronounced. An organizational role not only provides him with an identity but may quite specifically influence any and all of his individual attributes. An organizational career, as an objective sequence of roles, entails for the individual recurrent transformations of identity and of personal attributes, and provides him with an evolving perspective from which to view and interpret his life as a whole.

SUGGESTIONS FOR ADDITIONAL READING

The concept of role-making was introduced by Ralph H. Turner in his article on "Role-Taking: Process Versus Conformity" (pp. 20–40 in Arnold M. Rose, editor, *Human Behavior and Social Processes,* Boston: Houghton Mifflin, 1962). The most comprehensive treatment of this topic, in our own more specific sense, is George Graen's "Role-Making Processes within Complex Organizations" (pp. 1201–1245 in Marvin D. Dunnette, editor, *Handbook of Industrial and Organizational Psychology,* Chicago: Rand McNally, 1976).

Many of the finest contributions to theory and research on organizational careers have been collected in two edited volumes: Barney G. Glaser, editor, *Organizational Careers: A Sourcebook for Theory* (Chicago: Aldine, 1968), and John Van Maanen, editor, *Organizational Careers: Some New Perspectives* (New York: Wiley, 1977). A basic contribution, as we have already seen, is Edgar H. Schein's "The Individual, the Organization, and the Career: A Conceptual Scheme," *Journal of Applied Behavioral Science,* 1971, 7: 401–426. An intriguing, though fairly mathematical, approach is developed in Harrison C. White's *Chains of Opportunity: Systems Models of Mobility in Organizations* (Cambridge, Mass.: Harvard University Press, 1970). A more practically oriented examination of career development, from the individual's perspective, is Douglas T. Hall's *Careers in Organizations* (Santa Monica, Calif.: Goodyear, 1976).

Surely the richest vein in modern sociological social psychology concerns the personal impacts of roles and careers. The effective beginnings of this vein are to be found in two early papers by Everett C. Hughes: "Institutional Office and the Person," and "Cycles, Turning Points, and Careers" (reprinted in his *The Sociological Eye: Selected Papers,* Chicago: Aldine-Atherton, 1971, pp. 132–140 and 124–131 respectively). These beginnings have been thoroughly developed by many of Hughes' students; only a few of the key works can be cited here: Howard S. Becker and Anselm L. Strauss, "Careers, Personality, and Adult Socialization," *American Journal of Sociology,* 1956, 62: 253–263; Becker, "Personal Change in Adult Life," *Sociometry,* 1964, 27: 40–53; Becker, "The Self and Adult Socialization" (in E. Norbeck, D. Price-Williams, and W. M. McCord, editors, *The Study of Personality: An Interdisciplinary Appraisal,* New York: Holt, Rinehart, and Winston, 1968); Strauss, *Mirrors and Masks* (New York: Free Press, 1959); and Barney G. Glaser and Strauss, *Status Passage* (Chicago: Aldine-Atherton, 1971). Further such works by these and other scholars will be discussed in subsequent chapters.

The sewing machine has changed women's lives by standardizing their work, reducing the time required for each job, and familiarizing them with technology.

CHAPTER 11

Social Change

How does it happen that so many organizational and individual plans of action go astray? How do today's storybook lovers become tomorrow's divorce court contestants? How did yesterday's giant industry become today's commercial hulk surviving precariously on federal handouts? Conversely, how does a bright young engineer puttering around in his workshop become a leader in the air freight or electronics industry? There is, of course, a story to each of these "twists of fate," but somewhere in the story is the variable of *social change.*

Social change is not an organizational process like recruitment or socialization. It is instead an independent variable—a contextual phenomenon—which interlaces through the processes we have examined thus far. The influences of social change occur along the dimension of time. Therefore, it also provides a historical perspective for viewing shifts in structure and process, in organizations and individuals.

Social organizations, too, have "careers"—beginnings and endings, ups and downs, periods of growth and decline, and changes of direction (Kimberly, Miles, and Associates, 1980). Although the causes of these turnings are various, such changes in the character of an organization are always reflected in—and sometimes even result from—the character of its recruitment, socialization, interaction, innovation, and social control processes. Changes in these basic organizational processes in turn effect the roles and careers of individuals. There are, then, always close ties between social change, organizations, and individuals which require examination.

STABILITY AND CHANGE

Organizations and individuals are often profoundly influenced by social change—the shift in social realities through time. Heraclitus, a maverick ancient Greek philospher, said that "you never step into the same river twice." To put this idea in more modern language, we may say that if a social scientist does not find significant changes in any social scene, it is because the time period of observation was too short to reveal the occurring shifts. It is a historical and social fact that social change is the rule and that stability is the local, temporary exception. The United States (as well as virtually all other countries) presents a quite different picture in the 1890s, the 1920s, the 1940s, the 1960s, and the 1980s.

A social organization, be it a nation, a blue-chip corporation, or a marriage, may appear quite stable—even set in its patterns—when viewed over a period of months or even years. But viewed from a slightly longer time perspective, such as a decade or a generation, sweeping social change becomes quite apparent, as shown in Figure 11–1.

However, timely detection and awareness of social changes are rather rare, and evaluation of these changes is generally provincial and self-serving. Because of the force of social habits, most organizations and individuals can be said to be walking backward into their own futures. In the mid-1970s, American automobile manufacturers, although alerted, failed to retool for production of smaller cars and so lost much of their market to foreign economy imports.

Why should this be the case? One factor is the very strength of the existing role prescriptions and routinized role performances. Similarly, individuals have vested interests in the continuation of their existing organizational positions and of their current sidepayments. Further, the culture of any organization is an internally maintained "reality" which ignores or explains away contrary perceptual clues. The more this internally maintained social reality departs from the actual changed social conditions, the more likely there is to be a rude awakening which, in the extreme, may shatter the organization. Examples include a family continuing to spend as though it were still affluent, a company planning and acting as though it still had clout in the industry, and parents performing their parental roles as though their grown children

FIGURE 11-1.   Stability and Social Change as a Function of Time-Perspective

No
Measurable
Change

1970   1971

Measurable Change

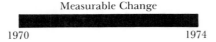

1970   1974

Sweeping Changes

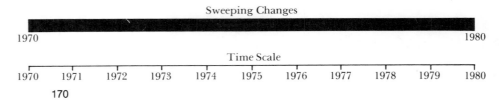

1970   1980

Time Scale

| 1970 | 1971 | 1972 | 1973 | 1974 | 1975 | 1976 | 1977 | 1978 | 1979 | 1980 |

were still toddlers. In such cases, the internally held reality is sufficiently disparate from actual conditions that plans of action and performances almost inevitably go astray.

Organizational fitness for social change varies widely, however. Some leading-edge organizations are able to ride the crest of a wave of rapid social change, while some of their counterparts are outdated dinosaurs unable to adapt to changing times. In the contemporary industrial realm, this comparison can be made between, say, electronics firms and the railroad companies.

But even in leading-edge organizations, in times of rapid change most organizational patterns are at least somewhat out-of-date and act as a brake on change. Always, however, there is beneath the crust of these patterns the surging dynamics of diffuse collectivities (as we shall see in Chapter 17) and of dissenting suborganizations supporting the new wave and facilitating change. These usually reveal themselves in factional disputes, which can be observed at all organizational levels, from relationships and families up to societal-level structures.

The fact of social change is everywhere demonstrable. *Rates* of social change at different times and in different areas, however, vary tremendously, ranging from slow organizational drift through the generations to massive disruptions and overturnings of the very social order. A pre-Columbian Indian might perceive little change throughout his entire lifetime, whereas a Vietnamese boat family might experience an utter scrambling of most of the rules for successful social living.

ORGANIZATIONAL RESPONSES IN SOCIAL CHANGE

A change in the career and character of an organization can arise in a multitude of ways, yet all these sources of change can be classified into three familiar categories:

1. Changes in the environment within which the organization exists. Frequently, but not always, this is a change in some larger organization within which it is embedded, such as the national economy, of which the firm or family is a suborganization. Both historically and currently, this is the most common—and usually the most dramatic—type of social change. This type stems essentially from the interlinkages of all the organizations on the planet. For example, a rise in the international price of silver leads to the reopening of an old mine and sudden prosperity for the populace of the nearby struggling western town.

2. Changes by the organization itself. Most commonly, social change at this level results from unintended and unforeseen consequences of planned actions. A nation may make an arms sale to an Arab state, only to have the Arab state raise oil prices to pay for the arms and subsequently increase inflation in the first country. Some changes resulting from unintended consequences of planned actions are frequent at all organizational levels. Of course, these changes can be either good or bad depending on the viewpoint of those involved.

3. Changes emerging from internal actions within the organization, most commonly through suborganization activities. Here the change spreads upward, and

usually outward, as with children introducing their parents to drugs or health foods, or a government take-over by young military officers.

The majority of these changes are minor—only adding to the flux of daily organizational and individual living. But a major social change at any one of these levels will reverberate widely and will induce some change, in turn, in each of the other two levels. To complete the loop, these induced changes are likely to feed back upon the level at which the original change occured to (1) reinforce that original change; (2) alter its course; or (3) resist its effects.

It should be noted that social change and innovation are often related but are not the same thing. A firm successfully performing its traditional role may bring ruin to a competitor and thus bring deteriorating social changes to the community or industry within which both firms exist. An individual may achieve planned-for wealth, only to find that the resulting changes create much stress and turmoil for his family. Conversely, innovations are frequently called for to minimize the impact of social change and to maintain some organizational and individual stability. Thus, the relationship between innovation and social change is extensive but quite variable.

Environment-Based Changes

An organizational change often originates in some aspect of the environment of the organization—the physical environment, through such "acts of God" as a tornado or a flood, or even the cultural environment, through the appearance of new technology. The environmental sector of most frequent impact, however, is the web of interorganizational relations. An organization may take a new turn as a result of distant political or economic events, of altered strategies by some other organization in its immediate set, or of the appearance or disappearance of an organizational partner, rival, competitor, or antagonist. For instance, a gas station might start doing well simply because the only other station in town closes down. Or a beach shop might suffer bankruptcy because of a drastic drop in tourist trade resulting from a "distant" large increase in OPEC oil prices.

Social change of a fairly explosive nature often follows contacts between organizations previously isolated from one another. Classic examples include Marco Polo's return from Asia and the impact upon tribal native life of the intrusion of Europeans onto the American continent. More recent examples include the reopening of relations between mainland China and the United States and the rapid spread of both Catholicism and Communism over the newly freed African continent. Consider, too, the mutual influence of a business firm and a scientific community—for example, electronics firms and space science, or the modular home industry and space engineering. These contacts often give birth to new industries and new role-careers. Such cross-effects can be creative or destructive, and there is usually the shadow of some ratification/stigmatization procedure, although its evaluations may be swept aside by events. In social change, the losers tend to be nameless and unrecorded.

Under the impact of imposed change, an organization may undergo any result

172

from rapid expansion, on the one hand, to shattering, on the other. This result will in turn affect the individuals within the organization (through alterations in the five basic processes) and also its organizational environment. Effects ripple both inward and outward from, say, an electric company's being forced by government inspectors to close one of its nuclear power plants. Workers in the local plant are let go, and middle managers at corporate headquarters have their duties and authorities rearranged; these workers and managers may attempt to resist or to alter these implications. Nearby industrial firms now receive less, but more expensive, electricity and may have to curtail their operations; these firms may reluctantly acquiesce or may take counteractions on the federal government in an attempt to reopen the plant. Or consider the inward and outward rippling effects of the British government's forced involvement in North Sea oil production—affluence to northeast Scotland, stabilization of the pound sterling against the dollar, and so forth. It is virtually impossible to count how many organizations and individual lives are touched by such major changes as the effects ripple in all directions through the social web.

Organization-Based Changes

At the level of the organization itself, its plans and goals regarding organizational conditions are also factors producing reverberating social changes through both intended and unintended consequences.

The most common profile is one of an organization trying to expand its resources and spheres of influence, under the motto of bigger is better. Particular attention will be paid to creative innovations, both within the organization and in related organizations. Considerable attention will also focus on the quantity and quality of role performance of individual members in order to reward and protect its high performers. Rather less concern will be manifested regarding the "correctness" of performances; productivity is seen as more vital than style of performance. Indeed, some of its original values and goals may be jettisoned, along with some previously influential but now obsolete members, as its dependence on external organizations grows and changes (Caplow, 1976).

This profile applies to the majority of young families and growing businesses. For example, a regional fast-food company may decide to expand nationwide. This move will place greater strain on the working relations between its purchasing and its sales departments; junior executives who see in this move enhanced opportunity for career advancement will actively support the move, whereas the directors of purchasing and sales may attempt to slow the pace of expansion. Restaurants and other competitors in the geographic areas affected by the expansion may feel the sting of a smaller market share and of increased wholesale prices, and may raise legal challenges or stoop to fomenting rumors of unpalatable ingredients in the company's products.

Some organizations attempt to remain as they are, although they would not object to having more resources. In this tradition-oriented profile, socialization is extensive and much attention is devoted to monitoring the way in which role prescriptions are

173

carried out. The organization emphasizes correctness and is wary of innovators, who will almost automatically be stigmatized. Turnover is low (Caplow, 1976), and the organization tends to become more inflexible as its members age. Organizations displaying this profile tend to shatter under the impact of even moderate social change, although they may linger on for a long time as "decayed" organizations. A private country club, for example, may strive to maintain its traditional services and exclusive membership, even in the face of major demographic shifts in its suburban area. Younger members who agitate for racketball facilities are firmly rebuked, and black applicants are declined, with the result that both categories go elsewhere. The vitality, and eventually the prestige, of the club suffers until, in the end, the club grounds are purchased for a shopping center or condominiums.

Finally, there are some organizations whose plans envision reduction of scope or even dissolution. The organization's strategy is one of "cutting its losses." Morale and productivity are low (Caplow, 1976), and the organizational costs of administrative overhead become disproportionate to direct operating costs. Innovations are largely confined to ingenious means of executing the necessary minimal functions—in a bankrupting company, getting the last shipments delivered somehow; in a dissolving marriage, getting the kids fed and off to school. There is a whole class of professional experts who help to handle such situations: divorce lawyers, corporate merger lawyers, and the like. The larger organizations within which such a declining organization is embedded want as little upset and catastrophe as possible, and usually claim some rights of surveillance, potential intervention, and ratification/stigmatization over the activities of the declining organization. In the dissolving marriage, for example, the standard of living of each partner falls substantially, and each becomes embittered; perhaps one of them becomes an alcoholic. The extended families of each partner are affected, and so perhaps is the husband's realty firm. The plan to divorce may be reinforced or resisted—by either of the spouses, by one or both of their families, or by the husband's business associates.

The general point is that each of these profiles of organizational plans has implications not only for the organization itself but also for many other organizations and numerous individuals, both members and nonmembers. And again, some will profit and some will lose from the standpoint of their own plans of action.

Internally Emergent Changes

At the internal level, social change usually stems from the actions of suborganizations or members pursuing interests and plans divergent from those of the organization. At the extreme is outright subversion; for example, one marital partner secretively working to destroy the marriage or a highly placed double-agent producing outcomes contrary to the organization's collective intentions, as by "fingering" members or selling patented industrial secrets to business competitors. In a milder but far more common situation, individuals simply pursue their own special interests and personal plans—a problem and a source of tension for every organization, as we have seen. If actions by members and suborganizations, based on these discrepant plans, overreach the organization's social control mechanisms, social change will follow in the form of a coup, reform, "troubled times," or dissolution.

Social unrest in Cuba and Haiti, for example, led to widespread individual defections of "boat people" to Florida. The Cuban government eventually responded by enacting a deportation program of selectively "permitting" troublemakers to "leave" the country. Effects then spread, ripple-fashion, to other organizations, as the refugees strained the resources of Florida municipalities and disrupted airline organizations through the skyjack attempts of disillusioned refugees seeking to return to Cuba. These affected organizations responded in turn, attempting to alter or resist these moves.

IMPACT ON ORGANIZATIONAL CHARACTER

In times of *extensive* social change, both organizations and individuals focus more attention on surviving the changes. Such previously taken-for-granted events as reorders from regular customers or the paying of routine monthly bills can shift from the category of standard procedures to the category of major executive concerns. There is heightened emphasis upon environmental data gathering and evaluation (Wilensky, 1969): "What's going on?" and "What does it mean?" There is re-examination of one's own and others' routine role performances in an atmosphere of question marks. Tensions and conflicts are heightened, and there is a marked hunger for more information than is available through standard channels (Shibutani, 1966). The change may provide opportunities or emergencies, but either way it will call into question routine procedures.

Major norms may come under test—not only conventions and customs, but even taboos and other vital mores. Role prescriptions may be called into question or, more often, stubbornly clung to even when they do not fit the current, changed social realities. Social positions themselves may come up for redefinition, frequently with a reshuffling, even within families. Existing role performances may now work better or worse, affecting organizational and individual plans—facilitating, bypassing, altering, impeding, or utterly negating them. These impacts are usually coupled with shifts in opportunities for "getting by" and "making out," resulting in newly emerging organizational patterns. Sometimes, brand-new positions and roles must be hammered out, but the ghosts of the old patterns usually linger. For example, most continental royal families still exist in some shadowy form.

Not surprisingly, then, the basic organizational processes become strained. In recruiting for an anchorman for the local news report, a television station may find that it needs a chic female rather than a Walter Cronkite. The adequacy of past socialization and of the current procedures for socialization may come under review. Debate may become more frequent, even within totalitarian organizations. More attention is paid to innovations, and greater emphasis may be placed on ratification/stigmatization proceedings. Standard social control actions may come under test and appeal and certainly will be swamped with heavier traffic.

Indeed, social control mechanisms tend to break down in the face of extensive social change. Organizational discipline, from the level of the polity to that of the family, becomes more chaotic, and ordinary procedures cannot be counted on to maintain order. Martial law may be imposed; innovators may be treated with similarly extreme reactive procedures. The rise of subversive suborganizations is typical, with a heavy emphasis on recruitment and quick socialization. A graphic portrayal of the breakdown of the polity, the front lines, and eventually the family is provided in Boris Pasternak's novel *Doctor Zhivago*.

In social change, there are always both winners and losers among both organizations and individuals. A basic impact of social change is that it alters opportunity structures. The economic upheavals of the 1970s in the United States made many individuals and organizations wealthy while it ruined many others.

Organizationally, there are five potential outcomes of social change:

1. *Explosive expansion,* with wide-open recruitment, rapid and truncated socialization, extensive innovation, and rapid career advancement (as in the military during major wars or in colleges during "baby boom" enrollment waves). Recruitment criteria are usually lowered in this situation and social controls are loosened except for the grossest violations. Personnel shortages tend to soften up the basic organizational processes, and competence standards therefore tend to suffer. Individual opportunities to pursue both collective and personal interests tend to be greatest in this situation. Both creative and deviant innovations tend to be rampant.

2. *Expansion,* with a somewhat lesser liberalization of the five basic organizational processes. In this case, more of the structure and stability of the organization is maintained, and the five basic processes (although relaxed) remain largely under official management planning and control. Recruitment standards may be lowered but in a planned and probationary manner; socialization procedures may be overhauled, with rational care; innovations are duly considered, with ratification/stigmatization procedures still in place; "wildcat" tendencies are constrained. Good examples of this situation are those banks that successfully expanded during the financial tumults of the late 1970s and early 1980s.

3. *Maintenance,* or successful accommodation to change, with the basic processes geared to maintain in stable form the social patterns of the organization. Wariness and defensiveness tend to pervade the processes in this situation. Recruits may be screened for "proper attitudes" as well as competencies; the organization's traditions (and justifications) may be fairly heavily incorporated into the socialization process; innovation and social control may become a bit ponderous in their deliberativeness. This is basically a mixed situation, with elements of the categories above and below held in some sort of balance. This balance tends to erode, and as time passes, the organization usually will move either upward or downward on the scale of outcomes.

4. *Decline,* during which the most prominent features of the five basic processes are

ritualization and decay. Recruitment criteria are stubbornly enforced; socialization tends to be tradition-oriented; interactions are ritualized; innovations and social controls are stultified. Emphasis is often on form, and member morale tends to be low. The pervading attitude toward the social changes might be characterized as one of "a stiff upper lip and closed eyes." Declined (or decayed) organizations often form interactions with other organizations in similar straits, creating a social world, as some of the ex-nobility of Europe or the remnants of the turn-of-the-century leisure class in the United States have done.

5. *Shattering,* with the structure of the organization being at least partially broken, as in the case of a defeated army, a bankrupted firm, or a broken home. Recruitment out is most common in this situation, but other individuals may be recruited in to cope with emergency situations for which they have little socialization. Any socialization is extremely brief and aimed at helping cope with the impacts of the change. Interactions tend toward desperate attempts to discover what is going on and making plans for handling the situation. There may also be exploitations of the crisis by individuals pursuing private aims, as in the forms of rape or looting. Innovations—both creative and deviant—are rampant, with heroisms and treacheries commonplace. Ordinary channels of social control usually break down, surveillance falters, and constraints are either absent or quick and rather savage, such as the shooting of deserters and looters or a court order that the husband can interact with the children on weekends only.

INDIVIDUAL RESPONSES IN SOCIAL CHANGE

An individual's priorities of concerns may be externally shifted by social change at any of the organizational levels. In times of easy jobs and extensive credit, for example, the person's work roles may be taken-for-granted "background" overshadowed by other role pursuits. Economic downturns, inflation, and tightened credit may reverse these priorities, so that job and finances become the person's main concerns, with other role pursuits becoming quite secondary. Indeed, this shifting of role priorities is the main impact of "history" upon daily life. The responses of multitudes of individuals toward such events, in turn, have enormous influence in the shaping of subsequent events.

The person who shifts role-careers may produce social change, particularly if he is eminent or especially skillful. Such people are often eagerly sought by organizations and social movements, as we will see in Chapter 17. Examples include Little Richard and Bob Dylan turning to charismatic Christianity, and Thomas Szasz becoming an outspoken critic of his fellow psychiatric practitioners. Understandably, they are regarded quite positively by those they join and somewhat negatively by those they leave. Such "defections" are notable events for both sides.

Also, large numbers of persons may switch careers because of social change and thereby help to bring about further change. The classic example, being replayed today in developing countries, is the migration of people from rural to urban areas. Within urban areas, we find the flight of the more affluent from the central city to the suburbs, which simultaneously creates mushrooming new communities and greatly increased inner-city financial problems.

Thus, shifts in role-careers (1) may be forced by social change; (2) may result in major role innovations; and (3) may lead to further social change, as when an out-of-work engineer becomes a successful inventor or a down-and-out becomes a revolutionary.

First-wave innovators are in a precarious position, as we will see in our detailed discussion of fashion and social movements (Chapter 17). Even if their innovations are creative, these are forged in the teeth of established role patterns, position stratifications, and perhaps vested interests in "the way things are." Many an innovator has been stigmatized, even martyred, only to have his innovation later become the accepted role prescription. For this reason, first-wave innovators tend to be clandestine about their innovations; they interact with others through tentative hints coupled with acute perception of interpersonal reactions. Of necessity, innovators tend to be personally hardy.

IMPACT ON INDIVIDUAL CHARACTER

For the individual, embedded in various levels of social organizations, the fundamental fact of social change is that his or her role prescriptions and role performances do not work out as they had worked before. In fact, this is how most individuals discover that social change has occurred.

To reach the individual, change must always filter through some organizational level in a two-step flow. Otherwise, the changes are simply events heard or read about. Changes in mortgage interest rates, for instance, reach the individual only through the organizations he becomes involved with in buying or selling a house. Wholesale food price index increases connect with the individual's budget through the chain grocery organizations where he or she buys food. A rise or decrease in unemployment rates directly influences the person as he or she looks for a job with various organizations. A medical breakthrough may become real to a person only when applied by a local health organization in saving the life of one of his significant others.

The feedback influence of individuals upon the course that change takes also filters up through the level of specific organizations in a two-step flow. Individual influence is thus reflected mainly, for instance, in the sales figures of stores on specific items (e.g., through consumer boycotts), in shifts in the positions taken by political parties or social movements, in changes in the number of building permits issued by municipalities, and so on. Individuals do influence the direction of social change, but this occurs through their influences upon organizations.

There are always individuals seeking to bring about change because of their personal plans (which can range from lofty beliefs to vindictive retribution), and individuals resisting change because of personal plans (which can range from similarly lofty beliefs to mere vested interests). Each or both may subsequently feel the effects of *unintended consequences*. Someone may do volunteer work for a liberal candidate who, when in office, changes the tax structure, which in turn reduces the resources of the volunteer's company available for sidepayments. The intellectuals in a country may support a radical movement which eventually sweeps them off the field after confiscating their properties. A husband may successfully push for a more active social life, but this may lead to his wife's finding an alternative partner and breaking up their marriage.

But often the individual is more or less correct in his evaluation of a particular social change. The new bonus system does lead to more profits, more flexible work schedules do make life easier and enhance opportunities without production loss, and an augmented social life does enhance the couple's relationship. The unintended consequences may also be rewarding as when, for example, a person failing in one career line finds a surprisingly rich and fulfilling alternative.

If nothing else, the ordinary individual will apply the socialization process to himself in an attempt to handle the changed outcomes of formerly routine role performances. The newly unemployed individual, for example, may busy himself in locating food co-ops and discount stores, learning about creative house financing, or finding some political or religious position which enables the person to cope with the changes. The latter example may include joining a radical movement or seeking the literature of despair, which reinforces and justifies the person's own cynical and despairing responses.

Social change may bring adventure to some individuals, but the majority finds it discomforting because of its disruptive effects upon established role patterns and ongoing careers. Those who yearn for major changes often get more than they bargained for when the changes comes.

Even those who "win" from social change will experience increased uncertainty and figure-ground reversals. Adventure can be traumatic. It is one thing to see a war movie but quite another to live through the incidents it is based on. It is one thing to read a book about a child-custody fight; quite another to actually go through one. Romanticisms about social change or naïve assertions about how it represents "progress" ignore the often tragic effects it has on individual lives.

However, social change can also bring organizational and personal enhancement: more freedom, raised living standards, cultural enrichments, and the fulfillment of dreams. Social change will sometimes release individuals from entrapment in the labeling process so that he or she is now able to rise in the primary and secondary structures of organizations, as has happened with the equal opportunities movement for minorities. Finally, social change sometimes opens up hitherto unavailable identities, as the opening of the professions to women has done over the last few decades.

In summary, social change is something of a "wild-card variable" which may augment either—or both—the creative and deviant aspects of the basic social processes we have examined in Part II. We will see further implications of its workings as we examine each of the organizational levels in Part III.

SUMMARY

Social change is not an organizational process (in the same sense that recruitment or socialization are) but rather is an independent variable or a contextual phenomenon that interlaces through all the basic processes examined in this book.

Organizations themselves have "careers"—beginnings and endings, ups and downs, periods of growth and decline, and changes of direction. Whatever the causes of these turnings, such changes in organizational character are always reflected in (and sometimes result from) the character of its five basic processes and thereby affect the roles and careers of individuals.

Social change is the rule, and stability is a local and temporary exception, when viewed over any appreciable timespan. Yet organizational and individual awarenesses of changes are generally deficient, owing to the force of existing social roles, vested interests, and self-serving organizational cultures.

The three broad sources of change in the career and character of an organization are (1) changes in its environment; (2) changes made by the organization itself, through strategies of expansion, stability, or reduction; and (3) changes emerging from internal actions within the organization, especially by its suborganizations. A major social change at any one of these levels will induce some change, in turn, at each of the other two levels. These induced changes are likely to feed back upon the original change, reinforcing it, altering its course, or resisting its effects.

Organizationally, there are five potential outcomes of social change: explosive expansion, expansion, maintenance, decline, and shattering. Each of these outcomes represents a characteristic pattern of effects upon the basic organizational processes.

Social change at any level of social organization may externally shift an individual's priorities of concerns. Shifts in the role-careers of individuals (1) may be forced by social change; (2) may result in major role innovations; and (3) may lead to further social change. To reach the individual, social change always filters through some organization, in a two-step flow. For the individual, the fundamental fact of social change is that his role prescriptions and role performances do not work out as they had before, for better or for worse. Although individual responses to social change vary widely, at the very least the individual reimmerses himself in a process of socialization in an attempt to handle the changed outcomes of his formerly routine role performances.

SUGGESTIONS FOR ADDITIONAL READING

The "career" turnings of social organizations are thoroughly examined in John R. Kimberly, Robert H. Miles, and Associates, *The Organizational Life Cycle: Issues in the Creation, Transformation, and Decline of Organizations* (San Francisco: Jossey-Bass, 1980). The distinctive managerial problems faced by expanding, stable, and declining organizations are reviewed in the final chapter of Theodore Caplow's *How To Run Any Organization* (New York: Holt, Rinehart, and Winston, 1976).

Social Change

Provocative and highly readable analyses of the nature and impact of social change are to be found in two recent popular books by Alvin Toffler: *Future Shock* (New York: Bantam Books, 1971) and *The Third Wave* (New York: Morrow, 1980).

More scholarly introductory accounts of general social change include Wilbert E. Moore's *Social Change,* 2nd edition (Englewood Cliffs, N.J.: Prentice-Hall, 1974), and George K. Zollschan and Walter Hirsch's *Social Change: Explorations, Diagnosis, and Conjectures* (New York: Halsted Press, 1975). The individual impact of social change is reviewed in Egbert De Vries, *Man in Rapid Social Change* (Garden City, N.Y.: Doubleday, 1961).

All these readings emphasize externally imposed, environmentally originated change. Changes emanating from the organizational environment will be covered extensively in Part III, when we examine the interrelationships among levels of social organizations. The management of organization-based change is examined usefully in Gerald Zaltman and Robert Duncan's *Strategies for Planned Change* (New York: Wiley-Interscience, 1977). Internally emergent change will be more closely examined in Chapter 17; meanwhile, the reader might wish to examine Ralph H. Turner and Lewis A. Killian's *Collective Behavior,* 2nd edition (Englewood Cliffs, N.J.: Prentice-Hall, 1972).

PART III

LEVELS OF ORGANIZATION

At this point the reader has become familiar with the full detail of our abstract model of social psychology. He or she should now appreciate all that is comprehended in the character of each of our four major elements—the individual, the organization, the individual's organizational role, social process. The reader should now grasp the operation of each of the guiding principles of the model, that is, how and why it is that:

1. The character of the individual's organizational role affects both the character of the individual and that of the organization;
2. The character of the organizational processes determines the nature of individuals' organizational roles; and
3. The character of the individuals and that of the organization jointly affect the character of organizational processes.

In Part III, the very heart of the book, this abstract model is rendered more concrete through application to a series of distinct varieties and levels of social organization in order to show how the workings of the model are conditioned fundamentally by the distinctive character of each general variety of social organization. Although the basic elements and guiding principles remain invariant, the details of their operation will be shown to vary strikingly and most informatively from one organizational variety to another. These chapters contain a good deal of fundamental organizational analysis as well as research findings from a wide range of sociological specializations relevant to social psychology.

Within Part III the chapters are sequenced in descending order of organizational scope so that the organizational environment of each variety can be understood most fully, with the result that those organizational levels generally thought most central to social psychology—groups, relationships, and encounters—are deferred to the end of that sequence.

The U.N. is our most "planetary" official organization, where most nations of the world meet to coordinate activities and mediate their conflicting goals and needs.

CHAPTER 12

The Planetary Level

Each of us belongs to a number of social organizations, at varying levels of organizational scope. Any person is quite aware of his or her membership in most of these organizations: a marriage or friendship, a family or gang, a company or church, a town, a nation.

But knowingly or not, we all belong to a worldwide network of interlacing relationships and interdependencies that is the *planetary level* of social organization. From some very distant point in this global web, events may arrive with our morning coffee that change our lives. For better or for worse, we are together what passes for the crew of "spaceship Earth."

The planetary level of social organization is that level or "field" within which national and international organizations are embedded. This level is vague and amorphous in structure and is not yet very well understood by social scientists, but its impact on organizations and individuals is as real as boom or bankruptcy, as enriched living or political enslavement. This global level is the field, the forum, and often the arena in which conflicts, accommodations, and alliances among nations and other giant organizations are hammered out. Just as any building exists within a surrounding field, so any national- or international-level organization exists in a planetary organizational environment, whether its aims are health, profit, or terrorism.

This is not a recent historical development. Throughout history, there has been such a planetary level, at least within the "known world." Researchers in the past two decades have found that far-ranging—even intercontinental—travel, commerce, and cultural exchanges were far more widespread, in all times and places, than had previously been thought. For example, Norse relics have been found as far away as Africa, North America, and the interior of Russia.

LEVELS OF ORGANIZATION

A number of leading-edge thinkers have begun to describe and research a worldwide organizational level:

- Certainly and inescapably, there is a single planetary-level ecological system. Agricultural pesticides are found in the snows of Greenland and in the fat cells of Antarctic penguins, and Ohio's industrial fumes fall to earth as "acid rain" to sterilize New York's mountain lakes.
- Ecology and economy share more than their common Greek root; the spatial differentiation of resources inherent in a planetary ecology entails a worldwide exchange of goods—a planetary economic system, in which tin, coffee, and diamonds are traded for transistor radios, blue jeans, and nuclear power plants (Wallerstein, 1974, 1980). There is an international monetary, banking, and trade system which determines in part how far our vacation dollars go in Europe and how much a loaf of bread costs at home.
- There is a world political order which constrains planetary travel, trade, and conduct. The fields of international law and even of space law are growing enterprises, and there is already a World Court.
- There is, therefore, also a global military order, with shifting coalitions and enmities. World wars and world peace are no longer empty concepts, particularly in this nuclear era.
- There is a worldwide communications system, employing futuristic computers, satellite transmissions, and supersonic airliners.
- Accordingly, there are international communities of science, arts, and sports, each with truly global audiences. It is now common parlance to speak of "world class" orchestras and "world champion" tennis players.

Much of the character of this planetary level of social organization stems from two somewhat incompatible facts about it. First, the level is very little structured, at least in terms of the attributes that matter most, such as power and authority. Second, the influence of that level of social organization upon even the most gigantic and powerful embedded organizations—such as the United States, OPEC, or the United Nations—is very real indeed.

In the absence of a centralized authority at the world level and with only an amorphous social structure, negotiation and arbitration are pre-eminent processes in planetary matters. In the absence of a formally recognized executive stratum which can say yes or no and "make it stick," decisions are reached and carried out through mediation and diplomacy. Titles abound at this level, but power and influence often lie elsewhere.

The main function of planetary-level organizations is to mediate between their sprawling suborganizations: national polities, national economies, ethnic groups, and so on. Such mediations take the place of a clear-cut formal structure, although they tend to reflect the biases and vested interests of dominant members. This bias gives rise to the persisting legends of international cartels, "illuminati," world conspiracies, and so forth, as depicted in Taylor Caldwell's best-selling novel *The Captains and the Kings*. It is difficult to establish the degrees of truth of these "legends" for any given historical period. Certainly, there have always been small groups of men with tremendous international influence who have had their own private plans not broadly publicized. However, the process models we examined in Part II would suggest that these groups do not often bring off control of world events, and that they are often themselves caught up in some of the unintended consequences of their own actions. It appears, for example, that the scheming of the Hunt brothers in 1980 to corner the world silver market collapsed of its own weight and threatened to bring down their entire financial empire. Certainly, OPEC oil price increases have spurred an inflationary spiral in the West, resulting in the diminished value of OPEC nations' stockpiled oil dollars, a matter of concerned discussion at recent meetings of that cartel.

MEMBERSHIP AND POSITION

There are two levels of membership in the planetary community: (1) those organizations and special-role individuals who have a recognized position in the world social structure; and (2) the rank-and-file population of the planet.

Whereas membership in the planetary community is very much ascriptive, position is not. By simply existing on earth, any organization or individual becomes a member, but its standing is uncertain, shifting, and rather temporary. In our own time we have seen the rise of Israel, OPEC, the PLO, and mainland China; the fall of the American steel and auto industries; the rise of U.S.-based international electronics corporations; and the virtual end of the British Empire.

Position in the world social structure is measured in terms of ability to influence the outcome of events at the world level. Although that structure is amorphous and shifting, members do vary, for example, in degree of centrality. That is, some nations or other large suborganizations may be under sanction, not recognized as legitimate, "shut out" from negotiations, and so forth. Also, some members rank higher than others; vertical mobility is through a member's rise and fall in power, influence, and reputation on the world stage. Reputation may, however, have little to do with power and influence. A suborganization may have a bad reputation but extensive power, as was the case with Hitler's Germany or the contemporary OPEC. Conversely, a member can have a good reputation but little real influence, as is the case with many small nations and international humanitarian organizations.

There are a number of *individuals* whose main role performances have a planetary base—executives of multinational corporations, diplomats and other government representatives, "jet-setters," members of international terrorist groups, and persons with an international reputation and influence in the sciences, the arts, or sports, to name a few examples. The loose term "world citizen" has real application to such men and women, in terms of their personal plans, performances, concerns, positions, and reputations.

Although these citizens of the world are usually "based" in some particular polity (that is, nation-state), they are almost always at least partially transcendent in their loyalties and in the basis of their power and position. Their role in some planetary-level organization is quite commonly more central to their life and their self-conception than is their legal national citizenship.

ORGANIZATIONAL PROCESSES

Again, recruitment to membership in a planetary-level organization is ascriptive; to exist is to become a member. The social position of any member, however, is not so simply ascriptive; the aspect of placement rests on a member's reputation and ability to influence world events. A rank-and-file nation like Pakistan might achieve greater rank and centrality if it succeeded in developing a nuclear capability. Most individual "world citizens," of course, owe their ability to influence world events almost entirely to their occupancy of executive positions within some powerful suborganization; if the "little old lady from Dubuque" were somehow to become president of the United States, she would suddenly become a world citizen.

Socialization of members is diffuse and informal, carried on mainly by or through the mass media in an incidental fashion. Currently, the majority of organizations and individuals are probably only dimly aware that they are members of planetary-level organizations. Socialization for specialized positions seems to be largely through apprenticeship: the courier becomes an aide and finally an ambassador; the special representative becomes chief of overseas operations and eventually chairman of an international bank. Although there are formal training courses in international trade, international law, and so on, the skills required for planetary-level positions seem to be acquired mostly through successful learning from role-models while occupying a succession of junior posts.

Interaction among members of planetary-level organizations is overwhelmingly indirect and impersonal. Direct interaction is episodic and sporadic, except in specialized professions such as international diplomacy and trade. When direct interaction among ordinary members does occur, it tends to take place in situations of crisis, for which prior socialization has ill-prepared the participants, as among the multinational hostages at Entebbe. Of course, interactions of a less stressful and more conventional type, such as Olympic Games and international conferences, also take place. But whatever the underlying circumstances, these direct interactions tend to be somewhat shallow and rudimentary because of the lack of a firm social structure at the planetary level and a corresponding absence of well-defined social roles. A Saudi, a Texas oil expert, a West Point-trained military attaché, and a Swiss banker, for example, meeting to confer on the development and protection of a Middle Eastern oil field, will almost inevitably suffer from differences in language, culture, and perhaps even age-sex role definitions. No one is likely to be firmly in command, and the possibilities for misunderstandings are multiple. Each may leave the conference with secret plans of his own.

Innovation is frequent and, within a few very broad constraints, is almost to be expected. Because roles are so scantily defined, members very much tend simply to pursue their own interests and plans of action. Ratification/stigmatization procedures tend to be reactive, informal, and decentralized; verdicts are usually rendered only in the court of world opinion.

Social control is mostly informal and reputational, although in certain arenas (such as the world military or political orders) surveillance is regularized, thorough, and precise. Proactive social controls are little developed, and the effectiveness of reactive control tactics of reward and punishment remains problematic, as witness attempts to boycott the Moscow Olympics in 1980 or to impose economic sanctions on Iran. Success in such tactics requires temporary coalitions which together have sufficient clout to carry them through. But even such coalitions are difficult to hold in force, as shown, for example, by the difficulties in maintaining the U.N. peace-keeping efforts in the Middle East or the embargoes on South Africa.

IMPACT ON MEMBERS

There is no really effective planetary-level organization. In any planetary arena, the dominant suborganizations tend to pursue their own ends successfully, although everywhere all suborganizations are becoming increasingly aware of their mutual interdependencies, engendering some constraints on the dominants. When situations arise, outcomes of some sort are usually worked out through negotiation and accommodation, but unintended consequences are rampant and there is real difficulty in holding suborganizations to their agreements. Interdependencies are sometimes recognized only after the fact; one suborganization can produce immense, often unintended, social changes for others.

Unintended consequences of action among planetary suborganizations are more the rule than the exception at this stage of planetary development. Ironically, unintended consequences are a major source of socialization through which suborganizations learn about their mutual interdependencies. India sells silver on the open world market, with the result that the value of its remaining silver holdings drops substantially. America made a large arms sale to Iran in the early 1970s, which caused Iran to double its oil prices in order to make the payments. A world health organization succeeds in drastically cutting the infant death rate in a poor country, only to produce a swell of jobless and starving young adults, politically desperate for any solution to their plight. The "bottom line" lesson being learned is that an action taken by one of the large suborganizations may reverberate in the markets and capitals around the world.

For individual persons, the main fact about planetary–level organization is that individuals are only dimly aware of its influences upon them, because these influences often are felt only after passing through a chain or sequence of steps through all the intervening organizational levels. The child knows only that there is no sugar for his cereal; the woman knows only that her fiancé has been drafted. Few Americans can comprehend why the dollar is no longer the world's index currency, but they do see that Japanese television sets and cars are better buys.

The planetary level of organization is barely perceived and ill-understood by the individuals within its web and by the organizations seeking to manipulate it or to survive in it. Its regularities and processes are obviously as yet but poorly researched and understood by social scientists. Question marks abound, but no one who has looked can doubt that that level of organization is real and influences our lives. It sets the stage for our examination of other organizational levels, from giant speech communities down to pair relationships and encounters, because it *is* the stage upon which these other levels are played out.

SUGGESTIONS FOR ADDITIONAL READING

The concept of *Spaceship Earth* (Barbara Ward, New York: Columbia University Press, 1966) is not the invention of California politicians. The global interdependence of human beings is, however, only slowly translating into anything remotely resembling *World Society* (John W. Burton, Cambridge: At the University Press, 1972) or a "world community" (Organization to Build a World Community, *World Citizens Assembly: Report of Proceedings,* San Francisco, World Citizens Assembly, 1976).

Nevertheless, significant world systems and social orders do already exist and have an impact on our daily lives. An introduction to actions in the planetary ecological system is David A. Kay and Eugene B. Skolnikoff, editors, *World Eco-Crisis: International Organizations in Response* (Madison: University of Wisconsin Press, 1972). An overview of the planetary economic system can be gained from W. W. Rostow's *World Economy: History and Prospects* (Austin: University of Texas Press, 1978). A much more incisively sociological account of the nature and emergence of the single division of labor that is the modern world economy is Immanuel Wallerstein's brilliant multivolume work, *The Modern World-System* (New York: Academic Press, 1974, 1980). If you are one of those Americans baffled by the decline of the dollar against the yen and the mark, read Martin Mayer's *The Fate of the Dollar* (New York: Times Books, 1980).

The world's political order is cogently reviewed in James S. Rosenau et al., *World Politics* (New York: Free Press, 1976) and in Andrew W. Axline and James A. Stegena, *Global Community: A Brief Introduction to International Relations* (New York: Harper & Row, 1972). World military order is examined in a book by that title by Mary Kaldor and Ashborn Eide (New York: Praeger, 1979).

Prominent and distinctive suborganizations within the planetary level are the wide variety of international organizations—voluntary associations, agencies, and firms. A good general introduction is to be found in Leroy A. Bennett's *International Organizations: Principles and Issues* (Englewood Cliffs, N.J.: Prentice-Hall, 1977).

More focused accounts of particular types of international or multinational organizations are also available. Regarding selected agencies, for example, see: Moshe Y. Sachs, editor, *United Nations: A Handbook on the United Nations, Its Structure, History, Purposes, Activities and Agencies* (New York: Wiley, 1977); Shabtain Rosenne, *World Court: What It Is, How It Works,* 3rd revised edition (Dobbs Ferry, N.J.: Oceana Publications, 1974); and *World Bank Operations: Sectoral Programs and Policies* (Baltimore:

The Planetary Level

Johns Hopkins University Press, 1973). Perhaps the most global and efficient of such worldwide agencies is described in *World Weather Watch: The Plan and Implementation Programme* (New York: Unipub, 1975).

Giant multinational business firms are also potent planetary actors. An excellent introductory account is Richard Eells, *Global Corporations: The Emerging System of World Economic Power,* revised edition (New York: Free Press, 1976).

The social psychological literature pertaining to this organizational level is reviewed in Amatai Etzioni, ''Social-Psychological Aspects of International Relations'' (pp. 538–601 in Gardner Lindzey and Elliot Aronson, eds., *The Handbook of Social Psychology,* revised edition, vol. 5, Reading, Mass.: Addison-Wesley, 1969).

Moslems in Upper Volta celebrate the end of Ramadan, expressing shared values in a common tongue.

CHAPTER 13

The Societal Level: Speech Community

The planetary level is the organizational level of greatest scope, but it is not well-structured and not very real to the majority of earth's populations. The next level down—the societal level—is quite real to almost everyone, because it is so extensively treated during childhood socialization and in daily communications from the mass media. Every nation that has schools teaches "The History of the United States," "The History of Ecuador," "The History of Uganda," or the like. Every nation-state has an intimate, mutually reinforcing relationship with its citizenry. But the very intensity of this awareness of country hides some ambiguities and lumps together a number of quite different structured collectivities at this level. Unless we separate these different collectivities, we will have a false picture of social life at the societal level.

SOCIETAL-LEVEL STRUCTURES

In Chapter 3, in our review of the varieties of social organizations, we distinguished four such societal-level structures important in modern life:

- *speech community,* the structured collectivity comprised of all those persons who speak a particular language;
- *age-sex structure,* a collectivity structured by a particular system of social positions and social roles based on the individual attributes of age and sex;
- *polity,* a relatively independent "political" organization for public safety and welfare; and

- *economy,* a bounded social organization for producing and distributing services and material goods.

Among less modernized peoples, *kinship structure*—a collectivity defined by a shared sense of interrelatedness through "blood ties" of descent from specific common ancestors and/or through the ties of intermarriage—must also be considered a societal-level structure, collectively organizing family life by means of rules and roles regulating marriage, parenthood, inheritance, succession, extramarital sex, domestic residence, and obligations of assistance.

Why must these several societal-level structures be separated in order to understand social life at this level of social organization? Don't we each simply live within some single *society*? The notion of "a society" is a slippery one. The rather romantic concept of a discrete, integral society is based heavily on stereotypes of primitive peoples and holds that all the speakers of a distinct (and probably isolated) language together comprise a distinct society. In other words, a society in this view is a people whose age-sex structure, kinship structure, economy, and polity all coincide with the boundaries of its speech community.

There are of course only a few isolated peoples left on the planet, and even those now live with the potential of being "reached" at any moment, as a result of decisions made in the larger organizations they are unknowingly embedded in. But indeed, among isolated primitive peoples, these societal-level structures often *are* fairly coincident—with the critical general exception of the polity. Let us briefly examine the major types of polity and their relations to the speech community.

The most primitive type of polity is the *band,* a local group of families engaging in some collective enterprises with episodic leadership. In the case of band peoples, a speech community will contain several polities (or bands); the Crow Indian speech community, for example, contained three bands, with no higher political structure. Any social integration and social control between bands was primarily a kinship function, since clans (that is, unilineal-descent kinship groups) did cut across the three bands.

The *tribe* polity most nearly resembles the concept of "a society." All the bands (or villages) of a speech community are united under an overarching tribal polity; however, this polity is episodic, narrowly focused, and fairly weak. Integration and social control are still primarily functions of the bands and of the cross-cutting clans. On sporadic occasions of tribalwide cooperative enterprises of great collective importance, a chief is designated, together with his helpers (messengers, police). The authority of the chief is limited to the specific occasion; at all other times, he can exert only leadership, through persuasion and personal influence.

A *confederacy,* such as the League of the Iroquois, is a polity linking several tribes. Representatives from each tribe comprise a council, operating under a decision rule of unanimity, meeting annually to coordinate the voluntary activities of the member tribes. As with tribal chiefs, these representatives are chosen by their tribes on the basis of personal qualities and achievements and govern by persuasion and influence. Unlike tribes or bands, however, a confederacy is a polity containing more than one speech community.

The Societal Level: Speech Community

Not all polities among primitive peoples are weak and episodic. *Nation-states,* such as the Mayan, Incan, and Ashanti empires, displayed strong and continuous central authority of a highly bureaucratized nature. Unlike the preceding polity types, in which warfare is merely a matter of incessant raiding, nation-states approach warfare as a matter of conquest of other polities. Conquered peoples are incorporated into the nation-state as a lower stratum (or caste), to be exploited economically. Consequently, even among "primitive" peoples, the nation-state includes multiple speech communities, one of which is politically and economically dominant over the others.

The notion of a discrete, integral society is therefore not a very useful one even in the study of primitive peoples because speech community and polity seldom coincide. As depicted in Figures 13-1 and 13-2, the five societal-level structures important among primitive peoples stand in highly variable relation to one another. For example, many who speak the same language do not have the same leaders and, conversely, many who have the same leaders neither speak the same language nor share the same definition of a woman's role.

Each of these structures is a collectivity organized to produce through collective action a profoundly fundamental collective good. The speech community is organized to produce communication. The age-sex structure is organized to produce social order, that is, orderly relations among individuals. Both the kinship structure and the polity are organized to produce public safety and welfare; the larger and stronger the polity, the less significant is the contribution of kinship structure to the production of these collective goods. Indeed, in nation-states—which dominate the political scene in modern times—kinship can no longer be regarded as a societal-level structure. Finally, the economy is a social organization to produce and distribute goods and services.

If these vital societal-level structures seldom coincide even among primitive peoples, the degree of coincidence is still less among modernized peoples. Accordingly,

FIGURE 13-1.   Typical Relations among Five Societal-level Structures for Band Peoples and for Tribal Peoples

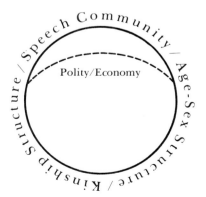

Band Peoples   Tribal Peoples

LEVELS OF ORGANIZATION

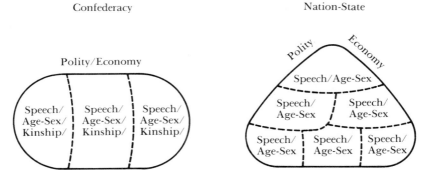

FIGURE 13-2. Typical Relations among Societal-level Structures in Confederacies and in Nation-states.

in this book we shall first discuss each of the four pertinent structures separately and then consider the mutual effects of their overlap.

In the remainder of this chapter, we examine the social organization of the speech community—as a collectivity, with interests, resources, and culture, and as a social structure, with a division of labor, suborganizations, and dimensional structures. In doing so, we shall come to see the specific impact of this organizational character on (1) the basic social processes underlying role-making and career development; and, thereby, (2) the character of the individual. In Chapters 14 through 16, each of the other modern societal-level structures is similarly examined. We then briefly consider the significance of various degrees of coincidence and overlap among all four structures.

SPEECH COMMUNITY

A speech community, the reader will recall, is a collectivity comprised of all those persons who speak and understand a particular language (L. Bloomfield, 1933). The central common interest of such a collectivity is sharing in the fundamental collective good of *communication.*

Most people take this good—and their speech community—so much for granted that it requires an experience such as being stranded in a foreign airport to bring home how important this good is in social (and sometimes even biological) life. In such circumstances, virtually any fellow member of one's speech community is a highly prized other.

Without the basis of common understanding provided by the speech community, interaction breaks down to the most rudimentary levels. The other basic organizational processes will also operate only at the crudest levels; chances of miscommunication are exceedingly high and interpersonal disasters are fairly frequent.

Milder forms of breakdowns across speech-community boundaries include attempting to understand a French, Chinese, or Mexican menu or to comprehend foreign films. One usually returns to the world of his or her own speech community with a sigh of relief.

Collectivity

Speech communities vary enormously in membership size, ranging from the estimated 800 million speakers of Chinese down to two or three dozen speakers of certain dying North American Indian languages. Similarly, some speech communities, such as English and Spanish, extend across several continents, while other speech communities are confined to one tiny Pacific Island or to one valley.

Aside from membership size, the human resources of speech communities vary most importantly in the percentages of members who can read and write. Material resources include the presence and type of writing system and postal system, as well as the numbers and distribution of publications, radio and television stations and receivers, telephones, and similar communications devices. That is, speech communities vary enormously in the extensiveness and efficiency of their communications systems, some possessing little more than the spoken word and others having virtually instantaneous intercontinental communications by satellite. An American executive of an international bank, for instance, could communicate more quickly with his agent eight thousand miles away than a primitive islander could go back up the hill and speak to his father.

The most critical feature of this type of collectivity, however, is an elaborate set of cultural *norms* (or rules) which constitute the language of that speech community. Through custom and convention, certain sequences of sounds are taken to signify certain ideas, while other sound sequences not conforming to these complex rules strike members as meaningless, confusing, or inappropriate.

Linguists consider the three major components of language to be the structure of expression (recurrent patterns of sounds), the structure of content (recurrent patterns of conceptual meaning), and vocabulary.

In linguistic terminology, the social norms comprising the *structure of expression* include:

1. Phonological rules, concerning "phonemes," those vocal sounds—out of the large variety of humanly possible sounds—which are common to all speakers of a given language and which can be repeated exactly by any speaker of that language. English, for example, has 46 phonemes, few of which are precisely identical to similar phonemes in other languages, as can be attested by anyone who has tried to learn another language or has listened to English spoken by a nonnative speaker. The /s/ phoneme in cultivated Spanish, for instance, sounds like an inappropriate lisp to English speakers.

2. Morphological rules, concerning the various classes of words (what schoolteachers refer to as "the parts of speech": nouns, verbs, adjectives, and the like)

and modifications of words, as by adding prefixes or suffixes. It is a perplexing morphological rule, for example, that the plural form of *duck* is *ducks,* but the plural of *goose* is *geese.*

3. Syntactical rules, concerning "word order" and larger constructions of words, such as phrases, clauses, and sentences. English syntax, for example, places the adjective before the noun it modifies: "the foolish man" or "the slender girl."

The social norms of a speech community comprising its *structure of content* are semantic rules, governing "concepts" and the relations among conceptual meanings that underlie the operations of logical inference itself (Leech, 1974). For example, even in the absence of any knowledge about Joe, the statement "Joe is an orphan" logically entails that "Joe has no father"; this logical inference rests entirely on the semantic relations between our concept of "orphan" and our concept of "having a father."

Vocabulary, the third major component of a language, constitutes the bridge between the structure of content and the structure of expression. Vocabulary (words and their meanings) is actually the least distinctive and the least stable of the three components of language. Social norms regarding vocabulary—that is to say, conventions regarding which word shall express a given meaning—change relatively easily and rapidly. In part, this occurs because people develop words to communicate about any changed conditions or new social objects.

In addition to these three classes of rules constituting a language, there are various rules regulating its use. Sociolinguists emphasize the existence within any speech community of two broad sets of regulative social norms:

1. Norms constraining the *situational selection of functional varieties* of speech (or writing) appropriate to the setting, participants, and topic of a communication occasion (Gregory and Carroll, 1978). In English, for example, there are five broad "styles" of speech (Joos, 1961): "frozen" or oratorical speech, used by preachers and lawyers in formal presentations; "formal" or deliberative speech, as in public addresses to medium or large groups; "consultative" speech, as in everyday conversations with acquaintances; "casual" speech, used in informal conversation within well-established personal relationships; and "intimate" speech, an almost completely private type of communication with family members and deepest friends in which wording and grammar nearly disappear and meaning is carried largely by intonations. As one descends this scale of styles, more background information and trust are taken for granted, so that all aspects of the structure of expression can be progressively simplified, and vocabulary descends through slang toward jargon. For example, the same individual might say "restroom," "toilet," "john," or "toity," depending on the company and the occasion.

2. Norms concerning gestures and other *nonverbal communications* accompanying speech. The languages of gesture map very neatly onto the boundaries of speech communities (Morris et al., 1979). In some speech communities, pointing with a finger is considered inappropriately aggressive, and pointing is to be done with the lips instead. Even posture and position during speech communication are normatively regulated; for example, speakers of Arabic feel comfortable at much closer speaking distances

than do speakers of English (E. Hall, 1966). In some speech communities, a speaker would feel insulted if his listener did not generally maintain eye contact, while in others he would feel insulted if the listener did not deferentially gaze at the ground.

Normative culture—the linguistic rules constituting a language and regulating its uses in communication—does not exhaust the customary cultural understandings among members of a speech community. Anthropological linguists emphasize that, through the medium of semantic rules, linguistic norms connect with a very elaborate culture, in the fullest sense of that term. Most directly, the members of a speech community share a distinctive belief system founded on those semantic rules, carving out a distinctive "world" of social objects in which they dwell (Frake, 1969; M. Harris, 1964). The categories of kinship (Lounsbury, 1964), of firewood (Metzger, 1966), and even of color (Berlin and Kay, 1969) rest on the distinctive semantic rules of a speech community. The dependence of culture on language has long been a major theme of cultural anthropology (Hoijer, 1954; Sapir, 1949).

Embroidering the cultural core of the semantic system, of course, is the full range of proverbs, legends, myths, rituals, values, customs, mores, conventions, cultural themes, and jokes understood only by members, that are the special province of folklore studies (Clarke and Clarke, 1963) and of cultural anthropology (Keesing, 1958).

Social Structure

The social structure of a speech community is far less elaborated than its culture. The primary social structure in particular is relatively undifferentiated, consisting of two interchangeable core roles: speaker and listener. In speech communities with a written as well as a spoken language, there are also the two analogous core roles of writer and reader. There is also a range of more specialized roles, such as author, editor, proofreader, grammarian, lexicographer, poet, censor.

Secondary social structures tend to be somewhat more elaborate. Suborganizations, for example, are unofficial, taking the form of *dialect groups*. A dialect group is a subset of speech community members who share a "dialect" of the language; that is, a distinctive pattern of accent, vocabulary, and grammar. Dialects may be:

1. *Geographical*—sometimes national, as in Australian English, Irish English, and American English; sometimes regional, as in Northern, Midland, and Southern dialects in the United States; and even local, as in the Brooklyn or Boston dialects (Allen and Underwood, 1971);
2. *Ethnic,* such as "Black English" (Dillard, 1972) or the polyglot English of Jewish, Italian, and Polish enclaves (Labov, 1966);
3. *Social,* based on the social stratification of the speech community (for example, the upper, middle, and working classes in England), taking the form of a "standard" (or preferred) level and one or more "substandard" levels of speech (Labov, 1966; Wolfram and Fasold, 1974).

LEVELS OF ORGANIZATION

If geographical and ethnic dialects are viewed as horizontal varieties, social dialects are vertical varieties, cross-cutting geographical and ethnic dialects. Horizontal varieties differ less sharply at higher vertical levels (especially at the standard level) than they do at lower, substandard levels.

In addition to such unofficial suborganizations, certain dimensional social structures are likely to be well developed within a speech community. The most pivotal of these is the *communication* structure, since the way in which any person speaks is a function of how often he listens to and speaks with each of the other members of his speech community (L. Bloomfield, 1933). In other words, the dialect one speaks is determined by the selective subset of speakers with whom one interacts most frequently.

Since linguistic norms are so central to the functioning of a speech community, the *conformity* structure tends to be well marked. Indeed, the very notion of standard and substandard reflects degrees of conformity to these norms, and certain dialects are likely to be regarded as more or less deviant. *Status,* in turn, is largely a function of position in the conformity structure; certain dialects are viewed as more prestigious than others, as everyone who has seen *My Fair Lady* can appreciate.

The control structures tend to be rather flat and decentralized. In terms of *authority,* for example, certain specialized positions rank fairly high, such as grammarians, lexicographers, editors, and schoolteachers. Within families, schools, and other organizations embedded in the speech community, leaders also serve command positions on what is correct speech under various circumstances and what is unacceptable, but there is no specialized "speech authority." In terms of *power* (the control of resources), in modernized speech communities editors, publishers, censors, and network executives tend to be fairly influential concerning who and what is heard. In the *leadership* structure, stylists—that is, speakers and writers exhibiting a distinctively creative or accomplished style—tend to rank highest, although persons of authority or power in the speech community tend to rank fairly high in leadership also.

Organizational Processes

Recruitment into a speech community is most often ascriptive. Parents decide which language(s) their child shall speak at home, although other organizations having an ascriptive right to the child, such as the local community or school, may make different demands. Similarly, through military conquest, economic domination, or immigration, some second speech community may effectively force even an adult to join it. Whenever one country is dominant over another militarily, politically, or economically, pressures develop for anyone in the subordinate group who wants to get ahead to learn the dominant group's language. Similar semiascriptive pressures may exist for anyone who wishes to rise in the status/class system when distinct social dialects exist within a speech community.

On the other hand, an adult may voluntarily join a new speech community, learning a new language so that he may enjoy a foreign literature, reside in another country, do business with foreign firms, or get along with his wife's immigrant family.

Socialization into a speech community is primarily a matter of language acquisition.

The Societal Level: Speech Community

The process through which linguistic norms are internalized is awesomely complex and differs significantly for a child's original language and an adult's second language (de Villiers and de Villiers, 1978).

Much of a speech community's primary socialization effort relies on implicit procedures, such as role-modeling. "Beyond providing children with some correct models for their utterances and encouraging them to talk, there may be little more that adults need to do (or can do) to facilitate language development" (Foss and Hakes, 1978: 276). However, a number of explicit socialization procedures do seem nearly universal. Perhaps the most important of these is "baby talk," the practice of using very brief and grammatically simplified utterances in talking to very young children (Snow and Ferguson, 1977) and thus providing them with more easily grasped models. Another explicit procedure is what Brown (1958) calls The Original Word Game; that is, naming objects in response to the question, "What is this?" A third explicit procedure is "expansions"—taking the child's grammatically incomplete utterances and expanding them into appropriate full sentences, thus providing him a particularly useful model that demonstrates the correct linguistic form for expressing the meaning he is trying to communicate.

Metalinguistic ability—that is, the ability to reflect upon one's language—tends to develop by the age of 4 or 5 years. After this point, explicit procedures for communicating linguistic norms become reasonably effective. The rules and customs governing "appropriate" speech within that community can be explained to the learner, and corrections of inappropriate usages become meaningful. At that point, in modernized societies, children are placed in schools for formal instruction in their language. Formalized linguistic norms are communicated through lectures, grammar books, spellers, and dictionaries. Linguistic capabilities are developed through formalized training, involving drills and graded exercises, particularly in the arts of reading and writing.

An adult tends to acquire a second language through the medium of his first language, in a process of supplementation and revision. Using his English/German dictionary, say, he learns that *wife* translates to *Frau,* and he attempts self-consciously to modify the phonological and grammatical principles of his original language to accommodate those of the second. The difficulties of this mode are well recognized by linguists, who instead recommend a radical immersion in the new speech community—stripping away the social supports for one's original speech habits and being forced to substitute the practices of the new language. For an English speaker learning German, even the formal metalinguistic instruction should preferably be given in German rather than English. The traditional recommendation from European men of letters was to learn the new language from a lover.

Interaction in the speech community revolves around the five functions of language: relaying information, expressing feelings and attitudes, influencing the behavior or attitudes of others, keeping lines of communication open, and elaborating linguistic usage for its own sake ("word play"). The range of speech acts implied by these functions is enormous. Indeed, it is principally through words that people negotiate, bargain, and confer, deliberate, argue, and debate. They offer, plead, coax, appeal, request, urge, and insist; they agree, concede, pledge, authorize, assign, decline, and refuse. It is principally through words that people, in recruitment, invite, draft, or welcome; in socialization, teach, advise, or correct; in innovation, complain, accuse, testify, excuse, or justify; in social control, promise, threaten, praise, congratulate, ridicule, condemn, or console.

Each full-fledged member of a speech community has under his or her control an impressive repertoire of speech varieties. Sociolinguists construe interaction as a matter of speakers' situationally adjusting their speech style in view of the setting, topic, and participants of a speech act (see Chapter 22). Interaction between speakers and listeners may be either direct or indirect in form, while writers and readers are necessarily linked only through indirect interaction. The interpersonal chains and networks of indirect interaction are believed by linguists to exert as great an effect on the speech style of an individual as do the sociolinguistic adjustments of direct interaction. Linguistic theory holds that an individual's speech style is essentially a (somewhat biased) statistical average of all the speech styles he hears. And since no two individuals can occupy precisely the same location in the communication structure of a speech community, each speaker's language is unique in detail—which linguists refer to as an "idiolect." An idiolect is to a language as a performed role is to a prescribed role. The fact that each person has his or her own idiolect may create some communication difficulties on occasion, but it also adds a good deal of sparkle to ordinary social interaction.

Innovation within a speech community, therefore, is obviously a high-rate occurrence. To preserve any common language at all, the speech community must react to these innovative usages, either ratifying them as creative forms, to be emulated, or stigmatizing them as deviant, to be discouraged. Reactive procedures of ratification/stigmatization in a speech community tend to be informal, democratic, and diffuse. In fact, they take the form of statistical drift, resulting from the cumulative individual (often unconscious) decisions of members to add or not to add the new usage to their own repertoires. Ratification is therefore a slow, gradual and uncertain process, even in the case of mere vocabulary innovations (C. Barber, 1964). Innovations sponsored by members high in the status structure of the speech community (however lowly their originator may have been) are much more likely to be ratified, as are those innovations which are consistent with some broader linguistic pattern (Gleason, 1961: pp. 394–398). Finally, if the innovation puts a name to some important new emergent social object or some widespread new awareness in the speech community, it is likely to be ratified simply by being widely adopted. Examples in our own times include such expressions as "détente," "black hole," "the Fed," and "DNA."

As a fringe subculture within a speech community gains new adherents and mass media exposure, its "dialect" will spread to some extent, and portions may even become standard usage a few years later. This has happened to some extent in our own time with the linguistic modes of the health food, science fiction, and occult subcultures. Two decades ago only a tiny fraction of the American populace had ever heard of "pH balance," "toxic wastes," "cholesterol," "hyperspace," or "space shuttle." It is interesting to speculate on which fringe idioms of today will be household words tomorrow.

Although internally emergent innovation of these kinds is far the most prevalent mode within speech communities, both the externally imposed and the internally planned modes of innovation have become quite important in the course of nation building. In many developing nations, a committee or agency of the polity may be charged with developing one common language to replace the diversity of languages or sharply differing dialects that may exist within that nation's bounds. Here, more pro-active, more formal, and less democratic ratification procedures are likely to be employed in choosing among the various expert proposals (Rubin and Jernudd, 1971).

In times of extensive population movements or extensive influences from other speech communities, linguistic innovations are likely to occur in reponse to these changes. The term ''gringo'' arose in response to the early Americans' impinging upon the Mexican-dominated Southwest; ''mantra'' and ''acupuncture'' have come from the Orient in our own time. Often, these are already existing but obscure words—found only in the larger dictionaries or known only by specialized scholars—which come into wider use because they now meet a general expressive need.

Social control, like emergent innovation, tends to be decentralized and diffuse. The speech community has few specialized functionaries engaged in surveillance or sanctioning of linguistic usage. (The major exceptions are to be found in schools and the mass media—places with stylesheets, editors, and censors.) In the general absence of a centralized authority structure, the burden of social control falls on each individual member. Each listener/reader monitors every usage he encounters, makes a judgment concerning its normative standing, and selects and administers rewards or punishments for its sponsor. The basic rewards for creative or conforming linguistic usage are, first of all, successful communication and, second, social support and prestige within the speech community. Punishments for deviant usages are seldom more than the situational loss of these expected benefits—communication, support, prestige—and take the form of puzzled looks, interruptions to seek clarification, or ridicule.

The fact that social control is diffuse does not, however, mean that either reward or stigmatization cannot have great influence upon individuals. Opportunities in many areas—from job to companionship, from invitation to isolation—may open or close on the basis of one's communication performance. The right words can make one famous; the wrong words can make one a social outcast.

Role-Making and Career Development

The manner in which these organizational processes jointly operate to determine the character of an individual's situational roles within the speech community will be examined in more detail in Chapter 22.

In highly modernized speech communities, the organizationally expected career sequence involves initial placement into the listener position, followed very quickly by placement into the speaker position and, somewhat later, into the reader and then the writer positions. Unlike most career sequences, this sequence is cumulative rather than progressive; that is to say, occupancy of any one of these positions does not involve relinquishing any of the earlier positions. The common career trajectory is rapid expansion of all linguistic abilities through the first two decades of life, followed by a much slower but continuing increase until the debilitation of extreme old age.

Advancement in this career sequence is based almost exclusively on performance criteria and not on length of tenure, "political" considerations, and so on. However, a career timetable is generally recognized among members of the speech community, based on expected rates of development of linguistic abilities (Foss and Hakes, 1978: 234–318). Rudimentary linguistic comprehension is expected to begin at around 6–9 months of age and rudimentary linguistic production by around 9–12 months. By 4–5 years, the individual is expected to be a basically competent performer of both the listener and speaker roles, displaying also some metalinguistic and sociolinguistic competence—that is, the ability to make some kinds of judgments regarding the linguistic correctness and the social appropriateness of his own speech. At about this time, he is also expected to exhibit rudimentary elements of reading and writing performance: alphabet recognition, alphabet printing, some word recognition. By the age of 8 years, the person is expected to display basic competence in both reading and writing.

Career sequence and timetable may also be defined for movement within the *secondary* social structure of a speech community, particularly its status structure. Labov (1964) proposes six stages in the acquisition of the standard social dialect. In the first stage, up through age 5, the child learns basic features of the language adequate for rudimentary communication with his own family. Second, from ages 5 to 12, he learns the use of local dialect to communicate with immediate friends and neighbors. Third, from ages 13 to 15, his wider contacts with the adult world confront him with many speech varieties; he becomes sensitive to different varieties and, perhaps, insecure about how his own speech sounds to others. Fourth, early in his high school years, he begins to modify his speech in the direction of the prestige standard, mainly in formal situations but even in some consultative speech. Fifth, he attains the ability to maintain standard speech with reasonable consistency for substantial lengths of time. Sixth, in the college years, he attains complete consistency in a range of standard styles appropriate for a wide range of occasions.

Of course, relatively few members of the speech community complete this full progressive sequence. Socially isolated persons may not even advance to the third stage, and perhaps the majority of members never advance beyond the fourth stage. The pace of advancement is also variable; some persons progress more rapidly than the conventional timetable prescribes, while others advance more slowly.

Impact on the Character of the Individual

Since a speech community tends to be more elaborately developed in its aspect of collectivity than in the aspect of social structure, it should not be surprising that the personal impact of participation in this type of social organization stems primarily from membership in it and only secondarily from position.

204

The Societal Level: Speech Community

The speech community to which an individual belongs effectively determines which other human beings on this earth he can directly relate to, which age-sex structure he belongs to, and which nation-states he could effectively reside in. In other words, membership in a particular speech community greatly limits his personal opportunity structure, that is, the choices easily available to him. More immediately, membership norms of a speech community provide the person with a set of concepts (and words) with which to view the world—beliefs about what kinds of things there are, what these things are like, and what they might mean to him or her. Although psycholinguists have generally rejected the Sapir-Whorf hypothesis that language totally *determines* thought, they remain persuaded that the semantic structure of an individual's language significantly influences his perceptions, emotions, memory, and thought processes (Foss and Hakes, 1978: 375–397).

Thinking involves both ideas (mental representations of features of the world) and inferences (reasoning and problem solving). Language is of course a most powerful representational system, and the rules of logic itself rest on semantic relations among concepts, as noted earlier. Not all thinking involves a literal process of "talking to oneself" in the privacy of the "inner forum," yet the syntax and semantics of a person's language have repeatedly been shown to affect the ease, speed, accuracy—and even the types of common mistakes made—in the whole range of cognitive tasks.

Even an individual's perceptions (G. A. Miller and Johnson-Laird, 1976) and his memory functions (J. R. Anderson, 1976) are conditioned by his system of concepts, words, and beliefs. Identification, recognition, recall, and reproduction of patterns, facts, and events are affected by the person's linguistically encoded categories and labels.

It is also through language that a person thinks about himself; the contours of self-conception reflect the "culturally constituted environment" of a speech community—its concepts and beliefs about the nature of persons and their relationships with other beings and objects. The shared language of a speech community thus provides a conceptualization of the nature of persons themselves—their powers, limitations, and ultimate situation. Hallowell (1954) showed how these concepts and beliefs among speakers of Ojibwa produce strong emotional restraint (particularly, repression of anger) and behavioral dependence on the perceived actions of certain supernatural helpers (the "dream visitors"). The field of "culture and personality"—now more often called "psychological anthropology"—has long endeavored (Barnouw, 1979) to show how in such ways a given culture facilitates the development not only of certain personal traits (such as warm versus cold, trusting versus suspicious, industrious versus easygoing, self-centered versus altruistic) but even of certain personality types (such as other-directed or anal-compulsive.)

Of course, the culture of a speech community encompasses more than a system of concepts and beliefs. Anthropologists have long known that the broader culture influences many attributes of its members as well. Most obvious, perhaps, is the extent to which cultural standards and practices shape the physical appearance of its members—not only modes of dress and hairstyling, but the likelihood of tattoos, body painting, rings through the nose, elongated necks, "Ubangi lips," flattened heads, tiny feet, and the like. Clearly, the culture of a speech community does determine many of the interests and attitudes of its members—for instance, their preferences regarding various possible foods and sexual objects—as well as feelings and emotions. What tends to evoke laughter, anger, guilt, shame, fear, and so on, can vary strikingly between different speech communitites. Psychological anthropologists have shown that even the technological culture of a speech community influences individual attributes—visual perception, for example. Peoples living in rounded dwellings are more affected by one type of standard optical illusion, while those living in an environment of rectangular buildings are more susceptible to a different type of optical illusion, owing to differences in their perceptual habits (Segall, Campbell, and Herskovits, 1966).

Although membership norms thus have an enormous influence on the character of the individual, position in the social structures of the speech community is not without impact. Performing the role of listener entails speech comprehension, which greatly increases the individual's capacity to receive help from other persons, for example, in receiving information about the world and in taking instructions, directions, and advice. Competence in the speaker role—being able to communicate to others and to oneself—sharply increases one's ability not only to seek help but also to influence others through persuasive communication. Speaker competence even increases the vital ability to regulate one's own behavior through verbally mediated processes. The 2-year-old may be heard telling himself: "You be careful. William get hurt. No, I won't get hurt" (Ames, 1952). A great deal of experimental research (Zivin, 1979) has shown how a child's private speech makes possible much more complicated physical acts than he was able to perform at lower levels of linguistic development.

Reading and writing roles allow the individual to enter the modern world of letters, memos, forms, instruction manuals, books, newspapers, and signboards—a world so foreign and uncongenial to illiterates. The impact of reading comprehension is similar to that of speech comprehension, but in relation to a vastly extended set of others through indirect interaction (extending perhaps over the centuries to share the thoughts of Plato or Aquinas). In a similar fashion, the impact of the role of writer is an extension of the effects of speaking; writing permits the exercise of influence over an enormously extended set of others (over time and space) through indirect interaction. It can enhance both the performance of verbally mediated cognitive tasks, such as by taking notes or working out a problem on paper, and the regulation of one's own conduct, such as by writing grocery lists or balancing one's checkbook.

Since in the modern speech community the individual is expected to perform all four of these core roles, the impact of *career* is most obvious in the case of failure to achieve the expected career sequence or timetable. The upward career mobility of an individual may be blocked at any point. Congenitally deaf children, for example, may fail to attain basic competence even in the listener role and therefore also in the more advanced positions. Deaf-mutes and autistic mutes fail to attain basic competence in the speaker role, even though they may be adequate listeners. Congenitally blind children, though competent listeners and speakers, may not learn to read or write, at least through normal visual signs. Physically normal but culturally deprived children may remain illiterate or may attain only semiliteracy. Such diminished development is likely to reduce significantly the person's opportunities at all other organizational levels.

Other persons may exhibit downward mobility through this structure of primary roles, as when literate adults become blind or deaf or through brain injury become "aphasic"—losing most or all of the four core linguistic abilities (Goodglass and Blumstein, 1973).

Even if an individual does come to play all four roles in the expected sequence, his career movement may lag behind the expected timetable (as in the cases of the mentally retarded and children with dyslexia) or may exhibit low levels of performance in one or more roles (for instance, stutterers, functional illiterates, those who can read only Braille or speak only in sign language).

Abnormal career patterns of any of these types not only deprive the individual of the personal benefits intrinsic in the various core roles but also consign him to relatively low positions in the dimensional social structures of the speech community—affecting not only his social opportunities but also his self-esteem. Stutterers, for example, or those who read below their grade level, have been shown to develop less favorable self-concepts than their more conventional age mates (Rieber, 1963; Quandt, 1972). On the other hand, unusual skills in these core roles open a host of opportunities within other social organizations, because such competence is likely to place the individual in the highly desirable category of potential recruit. At the very least, the person will reap the benefits of such unusual competence in, for example, his or her ability to understand and influence others.

No matter how he came to occupy it, the individual's position in the *secondary* social structures of the speech community—particularly its status structure—also significantly conditions the positions he may attain within other organizations embedded in that speech community. Literacy and a standard social dialect greatly enhance his chances for admission to college or obtaining an executive job. A severe aphasia renders him unfit for any organization other than a hospital or protective family, and even functional illiteracy virtually consigns him to the most menial of occupations. Even speaking a substandard social dialect may make a person unattractive as a potential recruit for any organizational position requiring direct interaction with middle-class coworkers, customers, or clients.

Career trajectory within the status structure—that is, degree and timing of advancement along the six-stage sequence in acquisition of competence in the standard social dialect (Labov, 1964)—thus affects not only the person's skills and opportunities but also his self-esteem. Blocked mobility (particularly at an early stage) or an unusually slow rate of advancement often engenders a sense of social insecurity and even shame. Conversely, persons who complete the entire sequence tend to feel socially secure and to exhibit high self-esteem, particularly if the completion is precocious.

Although language does not predetermine culture or thought, the influence of one's position and career within the status structure of the speech community is great, particularly in anticipatory socialization. Is the *Wall Street Journal* or *Scientific American* lying around the house, and are these talked about at the dinner table as the child is growing up? Is the television set tuned to public television or to commercial network sit-coms as a steady background? Who comes by for coffee, what do they talk about, and what concepts are used in talking about it? More broadly, is the speech community atmosphere of the home and the neighborhood professional, white-collar, blue-collar, or "poor trash"? There are examples of individuals who have risen (or fallen) from every status position in the speech community to every other, but the very fact that these are noteworthy points up the fact that they are exceptions, not the usual outcomes. The social psychological implications of speech community are thus many and varied indeed.

SUMMARY

Few human beings today live in "a society," yet everyone holds membership in several societal-level organizations: speech community, age-sex structure, polity, economy. The boundaries of societal-level structures generally overlap and cross-cut; even among primitive peoples they seldom coincide to mark a discrete, integral society. In order to grasp the realities of social life at this level of social organization, each societal-level structure must be examined separately first, and then their overlapping relations must be taken into account.

The societal-level structure examined in this chapter is the speech community, a collectivity comprised of all those persons who speak and understand a particular language, organized to produce the fundamental collective good of communication.

Speech communities vary enormously in their human resources (membership size, geographical coverage, literacy rates) and material resources (writing systems, communications technologies). However, culture is the most critical feature, especially that set of cultural norms or rules that constitute its language. These "constitutive rules" include (1) the structure of expression—phonological, morphological, and syntactical rules governing sequences of vocal sounds; (2) the structure of content—semantic rules governing concepts and relations among conceptual meanings; and (3) vocabulary—the bridge between content and expression. Normative culture also includes "regulative" rules governing the situational selection of language varieties and the use of gestures and other nonverbal communications accompanying speech. Apart from normative components, the culture of a speech community is highly elaborate in every other respect as well.

Its social structure is far less elaborate. The core primary roles are few and interchangeable: speaker and listener, writer and reader. Suborganizations are unofficial "dialect groups" (geographical, ethnic, or social), closely connected with the well-developed dimensional structures of communication rank, conformity, and status. Structures of authority, power, and leadership tend to be flat and decentralized.

Recruitment is most often ascriptive. Socialization—a matter of language acquisition—relies largely on implicit procedures (for example, modeling), but even with young children some explicit procedures are employed (baby talk, the word game, expansions). Formalized linguistic education and training must await the development of metalinguistic ability. Second-language learning by adults follows somewhat distinctive principles. Interaction revolves around the five functions of language: relaying information, expressing feelings and attitudes, influencing the behavior or attitudes of others, keeping lines of communication open, and word play. Interaction requires constant situational adjustment of speech style, with the result that each member's style becomes unique in detail (an "idiolect"). Innovation is thus a high-rate occurrence, and reactive procedures of ratification/stigmatization tend to be informal, democratic, and diffuse. Ratification is a slow, gradual, and uncertain process of statistical drift, except in the externally imposed and internally planned modes of innovation. Social control, like internally emergent innovation, tends to be decentralized and diffuse.

Career within the primary social structure is cumulative rather than progressive; both sequence and timetable are conventionalized. Career movement within the secondary social structures also follows a conventional sequence and timetable in the stages of acquiring the standard social dialect.

Membership in a given speech community greatly limits the individual's personal opportunities (whom he can directly interact with, which age-sex structure he belongs to, which polities he can effectively reside in). More immediately, membership norms provide him with fundamental concepts and beliefs that deeply influence all of his cognitive, perceptual, and memory processes and his fundamental self-concept—perhaps even his "personality type." Other aspects of the culture of the speech community also influence many individual attributes: physical appearance, interests, attitudes, feelings and emotions, perceptions.

The listener and reader roles deeply influence the person's capacity to receive help from other persons, directly and indirectly. The speaker and writer roles greatly increase his abilities to seek help from others, to influence others, and to regulate his own behaviors through verbally mediated processes. Impact of primary career is most obvious in the case of failure to achieve the expected career sequence (blocked mobility, downward mobility) or timetable (retarded, precocious, or uneven development), affecting receipt of the benefits intrinsic to primary roles, social opportunities, and self-esteem.

Position and career trajectory within the secondary social structures exert similar effects on opportunities and self-esteem.

SUGGESTIONS FOR ADDITIONAL READING

Despite the fundamental centrality of symbolic communication in all human affairs, universally acknowledged by social scientists of every variety, relatively few students of social science ever acquire a disciplined knowledge about language and meanings. Any student would certainly profit from exposure to one of the many fine textbooks in the rapidly advancing field of linguistics; one such is H. A. Gleason, *An Introduction to Descriptive Linguistics,* revised edition, (New York: Holt, Rinehart, and Winston,

1961). Readable treatments of meaning—particularly the components and contrasts of conceptual meanings—are far more scarce; we particularly recommend Geoffrey Leech's *Semantics* (Baltimore: Penguin Books, 1974).

Accounts of language that emphasize constitutive rules to the relative exclusion of regulatory rules tend to afford a socially unrealistic view of the speech community. To redress this imbalance is the aim of the interdisciplinary field of "sociolinguistics," which has done much to illuminate not only the internal differentiation and dynamics of speech communities but also the dynamic interplay of separate speech communities, through language contacts, conflicts, and accommodations. See, for example, Roger T. Bell, *Sociolinguistics: Goals, Approaches and Problems* (New York: St. Martin's Press, 1976).

At the micro level, sociolinguistics has made substantial contributions to the analysis of the interaction process within speech communities, emphasizing the uses of regulatory norms in situational adjustments of speech conduct and in the social-contextual interpretation of meaning. A readable account of this work is Michael Gregory and Susanne Carroll's *Language and Situation: Language Varieties and Their Social Contexts* (London: Routledge & Kegan Paul, 1978). An intimately related, but distinctively anthropological, strand is reviewed in Richard Bauman and Joel Sherzer, editors, *Explorations in the Ethnography of Speaking* (Cambridge: At the University Press, 1974).

The socialization process has in the past few years received renewed attention, revising many earlier unrealistic views. An excellent treatment of this work is Jill G. de Villiers and Peter A. de Villiers, *Language Acquisition* (Cambridge, Mass.: Harvard University Press, 1978). A particularly fascinating type of language socialization would, of course, be that applied to the "feral man" we alluded to in Chapter 2. As luck would have it, just such a case has recently been studied, as reported at length in Susan Curtis's *Genie: A Psycholinguistic Study of a Modern-Day "Wild Child"* (New York: Academic Press, 1977). Genie was an unwanted American child, of a sadistic father and a blind mother, who was confined to a small bedroom—harnessed, naked, to an infant's potty chair—until age 13, when she and her mother finally fled the home. Genie was turned over to a rehabilitation center, where intensive socialization procedures were applied and studied.

In the study of the recruitment process, most of the attention has been directed toward those persons claimed at once by two speech communities—the bilingual individuals. The social psychological consequences of this recruitment situation are reviewed in Peter A. Hornby, editor, *Bilingualism: Psychological, Social, and Educational Implications* (New York: Academic Press, 1977).

The innovation process—particularly language change through internally emergent modes—tends to be slow and gradual, requiring a historical viewpoint. Of substantial interest along these lines is Morton W. Bloomfield and Leonard Newmark, *A Linguistic Introduction to the History of English* (New York: Knopf, 1963).

An excellent critical summary of the vast research on the cognitive impact of language is to be found in Donald J. Foss and Davis T. Hakes, *Psycholinguistics: An In-*

troduction to the Psychology of Language (Englewood Cliffs, N.J.: Prentice-Hall, 1978). A review of the personal impacts of the broader culture of speech communities is Erika Bourguignon, *Psychological Anthropology: An Introduction to Human Nature and Cultural Differences* (New York: Holt, Rinehart, and Winston, 1979). Victor Barnouw's *Culture and Personality,* 3rd edition (Homewood, Ill.: Dorsey, 1979) is an able review of the research on cultural impact on personality traits and personality types.

Today a woman can graduate from West Point, but sex roles, like age roles, continue to influence social interactions here and around the world.

CHAPTER 14

The Societal Level: Age-Sex Structure

The age-sex structure, like the speech community, tends to be taken for granted because it is so thoroughly socialized into the participants. It becomes for them literally part of "the way things are." A great many people are not even aware of the fact that they are members of a particular and historically distinctive age-sex structure.

Differences between the sexes and between individuals of different chronological ages are biologically based; a 2-year-old child cannot perform as a combat sergeant, a male cannot nurse babies, and an 80-year-old woman is not likely to be found in high school. But the *meanings* assigned to these age-sex differences, the role performances expected of these persons, and the structure of relationships among them are not biological but *social,* comprising a major societal-level structure.

Age and sex differentiation is a fundamental structural feature of social organization among both nonhuman and human species, reflecting biologically based statistical differences in size, strength, appearance, experience, and many other personal attributes (van den Berghe, 1973). In humans, such differences are quite pronounced among babies, toddlers, children, and adolescents as stages of development. After about age 30, size, strength, energy, elasticity, and adaptability decline once more, leading to notable differences among young adults, the middle-aged, and old people. Similarly, on the average, males tend to be taller, heavier, stronger, more aggressive, and less verbal than females. Females, on the other hand, tend to pass through the developmental stages toward adulthood more rapidly than males. What meanings are assigned to these differences, however, is a "societal" matter.

As primordially important to social differentiation as these age and sex differences may be, they are not in nature sharply categorical. On almost any personal attribute, such as height, the statistical distributions for almost any pair of age or sex categories would be found to overlap significantly. That is, there are tall women and short men; some old men are stronger than some young men. We are speaking of biological averages here.

Among peoples everywhere, nonetheless, some system of categorical age-sex differentiation is elaborated from these average biological differences. Such social definitions then tend to become self-fulfilling; for instance, if women are defined as weak and unable to do heavy work, they predictably will tend to remain weak from lack of body-building muscular exertion and so "demonstrate the truth" of the social definition. Age-sex classificatory systems vary widely in the number of categories recognized, but all include at least two categories of sex and at least four categories of age. Distinctive age-sex classificatory systems tend to be associated with distinct speech communities.

SOCIAL STRUCTURE

Linton (1940, 1942) found that all age-sex structures distinguish at least the age categories of infancy, childhood, adulthood, and old age, and that sexual differentiation is most sharply marked in adulthood and least in infancy. In most age-sex structures, more age categories are marked for males than for females, and females are categorized as adult at an earlier chronological age than males. One representation of the age-sex categories distinguished among the American people is depicted in Figure 14–1.

Whatever system of age-sex categories is recognized, the most distinctive aspect of any age-sex structure is the *expectations* held toward the occupants of a category concerning their appearance, beliefs, interests, capabilities, responsibilities, privileges, and habitual actions. These expectations comprise a system of *age-sex roles,* with each role deriving its significance through contrasts and complementarities to each of the other roles. These roles tend to be central both to the character of the individual and to the character of organizations (such as family and school) embedded within the societal-level age-sex structure.

In the United States, for example, males are expected to be massive, solid, angular, hairy, aggressive, action-oriented, conflictive, competitive. Complementarily, females are expected to be delicate, soft, curvy, smooth, conciliatory, feeling-oriented, accommodative, cooperative. In an analogous fashion, the very young are expected to be naïve, energetic, and egocentric, while the old are expected to be wise, tired, and altruistic; the intervening age categories—nearer to the prime of life—represent some sort of synthesis or golden mean between the characteristics of the young and the old.

In the construction of specific age-sex roles, virtually every personal attribute—as well as almost every cultural element—is sex-typed, age-graded, or both. Take the human nose, for example. Within a given age-sex structure, certain shapes of nose will be defined as being masculine and others as being feminine, some as being "babyish"

Male Age Categories	Ages	Life-Phases	Ages	Female Age Categories
		Old Age		
Old Man	80	-----------------------	80	Old Woman
		Final Transition		
	75		75	
		Late Adulthood		
Elderly Man	65	-----------------------	65	Elderly Woman
		Late Adult Transition		
	60		60	
		Middle Adulthood Culmination		
	55	-----------------------	55	
		Age 50 Transition		
Middle-Aged Man	50	-----------------------	50	Middle-Aged Woman
		Entering Middle Adulthood		
	45		45	
		Mid-Life Transition		
	40		40	
		Settling Down		
	33	-----------------------	32	
		Age 30 Transition		
Young Man	28	-----------------------	25	Young Woman
		Entering Adult World		
	22		20	
		Early Adult Transition		
	17		16	
		Adolescence		
Adolescent Boy	13	-----------------------	12	Adolescent Girl
		Adolescent Transition		
	11		10	
		Schoolchild Years		
Boy	6	-----------------------	5	Girl
		Preschool Years		
	3		2	
		Early Childhood Transition		
Baby Boy	0		0	Baby Girl

FIGURE 14-1. U.S. Age-Sex Categories, with Typical Chronological Ages and Life-phases Adapted from Levinson (1978)

and others as being adult. Cultural elements are even more sharply sex-typed and age-graded.

Dress is an obvious example. Despite unisex trends toward jeans and T-shirts, almost any item of clothing one sees in a laundromat can instantly be categorized as masculine or feminine, and—even apart from size—a female's shoes would seldom be taken to be a male's shoes. Clothing is also age-graded; bibs, bras, girdles, and support stockings each have their place in the life cycle. Short pants are considered highly inappropriate to certain age-sex roles, and no self-respecting teenage girl would be caught dead wearing old-lady shoes or dresses. Shorter, simpler hairstyles are masculine, while longer or more elaborate styles are feminine. Even for females, some styles such as hanging braids and long straight hair are considered appropriate only for the young. Unlike body adornment in some other age-sex structures, in the United States paints, powders, and dyes are considered feminine while scars and tattoos are considered masculine. The use of any of these is generally forbidden to the very young.

Just as there are dialects within a speech community, so too there may be variant systems of age-sex roles within an age-sex structure. These variant systems usually correspond to other substructures such as region, ethnic background, or fringe-group membership. For instance, New York City women are supposed to be more self-sufficient than the national norm, and long hair is part of the male role in several cultural enclaves. But again, these tend to be variations on a basic societal-level theme; differences between variant role systems within any one age-sex structure are almost always less pronounced than differences between two age-sex structures. The "hip" and the "square" American male have more in common than either has with a Kurdistani male.

Even language is sex-typed and age-graded. Although male and female language is marked less distinctly in the United States than among certain other peoples (for example, the Zulu or the Carib, where male and female dialects are linguistically distinct), several studies have indicated fairly noticeable differences, apart from pitch. Female English (Lakoff, 1975; M. R. Key, 1975) tends to employ hypercorrect grammar, superpolite forms, more differentiated forms of emphasis and intonation, frequent verbal hedges, question intonations where declaratives might be expected, "empty" adjectives (such as "divine" or "charming"), few jokes, and many vocabulary items related to female interests (precise color names, sewing terms). Similarly, age grading in language is apparent not only in the linguistically simplified speech of the very young child but especially in the creative slang of adolescent speech (Sebald, 1968: 248–255).

Age-sex differentiation is notable, too, in the so-called body language of gestures and postures. Males and females in the United States conventionally differ in the manner in which they fold their arms, cross their legs, and sit on a chair (Nierenberg and Calero, 1971; Goffman, 1979). Similarly, infants, children, adolescents, adults, and old people exhibit characteristically different modes of sitting on a chair. Before leaving the area of expressive behavior, we should note that the masculine/feminine contrast in expressive style carries through even to the level of handwriting style (Eisenberg, 1938).

Many elements of culture are essentially avocational diversions, and these too are strongly tied to the contours of the age-sex structure. Toys and games, music and songs, literature and movies, even jokes all are sharply age-graded and sex-typed. Bridge is for grownups and "Go Fish" is for kids; poker is mostly played by men, while needlework and macramé are mostly done by women; Gothic romances are read mostly by women and war novels by men; few teenagers buy Lawrence Welk records and few senior citizens "dig" the Eagles or Pink Floyd. Many commercially produced toys, games, and books come prelabeled as appropriate for certain age categories, and much popular music is implicitly labeled as "for youths only." Many books, magazines, and movies explicitly offer "adult entertainment" and are, further, often clearly aimed toward either a male or a female audience. The sex-typing of children's toys and games (guns for boys, dolls for girls), while contested, still persists widely.

Age-sex differentiation in the vocational arena is perhaps even more significant. Within the household, domestic chores are still strongly sex-typed in the United States. Males are expected to perform heavy duties, such as carpentry, moving furniture, and maintenance of heavy machinery, while females retain dominion over cooking, cleaning, and sewing. Children are likely to do little more than take out the trash, dry the dishes, or mow the lawn. Outside the household, too, occupations are strongly sex-typed, as we shall see in Chapter 16. Females are most likely to be secretaries, schoolteachers, or nurses; truck-driving, police work, and construction are considered examples of highly masculine occupations. Children's occupations are largely confined to newspaper delivery and babysitting. As a result, the range of tools familiar to an individual is also largely determined by his age and sex.

Even outside the occupational sphere, organizational memberships and roles within organizations are age-graded and sex-typed to a great extent. Grade schools and scout troops are for kids, while Golden Age clubs are for old people; fraternities are for males, and sororities are for females. Children cannot be wives or husbands, and adolescents cannot be scout leaders, let alone senators.

In modern societies, the stringency of these age-sex role prescriptions has broken down to some extent, and individuals are now freer to pursue vocations and activities that were once within the strict domain of other age-sex categories. There are female policemen and male nurses, middle-aged athletes and teenage business tycoons. Men sometimes do the grocery shopping and women sometimes assemble furniture. But in the 1980s women still do most of the shopping and men still do most of the carpentry; most nurses still are women and most cops still are men. *No society ever has seen the complete disappearance of age-sex roles.* Whatever changes a new age may bring us, men will continue to be the overwhelming consumers of aftershave lotion and women the overwhelming consumers of moisturizers.

For each position in an age-sex structure, then, a limited range of interests, skills, responsibilities, behaviors, modes of appearance, and opportunities is marked out as normatively appropriate, constituting the corresponding age-sex role. When persons do manifest attributes from another age-sex role, the fact is often remarked upon by others in terms of the specific deviation: "he's young for his age," "she comes on like a man," "the child was a perfect little lady."

Role relationships are also fairly clearly marked between the occupants of any pair of age-sex categories—particularly with regard to authority, deference, and sexual behavior. In general, males tend to have greater authority than females, and older persons tend to have greater authority than younger persons. Authority figures generally have a paternalistic obligation to aid and assist those below them, and these persons in turn are obliged to reciprocate by showing deference. This may open the way to exploitation because of power and authority differentials, but social control tends to hold such potential exploitations within bounds. These sociable obligations of aid and deference serve to soften somewhat the major structural conflicts between persons with differential authority in the age-sex structure, but the "battle between the

217

sexes'' and the conflict between generations are inevitable aspects of every age-sex structure (van den Berghe, 1973; Eisenstadt, 1956).

Authority relations between age-sex categories are further constrained by relationship-specific norms which govern what behaviors are deemed ''appropriate'' between occupants of specific categories. Sexual interactions, for example, are differentially defined depending on the respective categories of the two participants. Depending on the female's age, a 50-year-old man having sex with her may be seen as a child molester, a statutory rapist, a ''dirty old man,'' or a reputable and healthy specimen. In other age-sex structures, different relationship-specific norms exist; for instance, France virtually institutionalized the role of mistress.

Even strictly verbal interactions across age-sex categories must be adjusted to take into account proprieties of role relationships. Males and females speak differently cross-sex than within-sex, and all speakers must adjust their speech style when addressing persons much older or much younger than themselves. Even small children know to speak ''baby talk'' when addressing an infant, using short and grammatically simplified sentences, speaking in a higher pitch with heavily marked intonation patterns and maintaining direct eye contact throughout (Schatz and Gelman, 1973).

Indeed, conventional proprieties regarding age-sex role relationships make up the bulk of the contents of those ever popular etiquette books. For any two persons, the proper forms of address, modes of approach, greeting, leave taking, visiting, corresponding, joint entertainment, gift giving, and even the circumstances under which they may properly be seen together, all hinge most directly on their respective age-sex categories.

Secondary social structure tends to be most highly developed in the aspect of dimensional social structures. The authority structure, already discussed, rests greatly on power—not only the coercive power of superior size and muscular strength, but also the expert power of greater knowledge and the economic power of controlling material resources. As implied by the previously discussed reciprocity between authority and deference, age-sex categories ranking high in authority also rank high in status. Such differences in authority and status between age-sex categories are often backed up by law. In ancient Rome, for example, parents literally had the power of life and death over their children, and in certain male-dominant societies women have been barred from owning property. Conversely, in some female-dominated societies (matriarchies), men have had no say in the upbringing of the children they fathered. Needless to say, such differentials in authority and status have social psychological implications for the individual.

The status structure among members is, however, somewhat more complex. The status of an individual in an age-sex structure does not rest solely on the status of his category but is significantly modified by his position in the conformity structure as well—that is, by his degree of conformity to the corresponding age-sex role. If a person acts ''out of character'' with age-sex expectations, he or she is likely to be denied the full status of that category or at least given only probationary accreditation by others. The person will be told: ''if you want to be treated like a woman, act like one,'' ''act your age,'' and so on. The person will, further, be suspected of having the character of the age-sex category his or her actions most resemble. A "boyish" middle-aged man might be admired by some but is likely to be passed over as a candidate for a senior executive post.

The leadership structure among members tends to be poorly developed. Whatever age-sex leadership there is tends to occur within rather than across age-sex categories; that is, a person's age-sex peers may emulate his stylistic choices, may become followers to his leads. This is often a matter of emulating winners within the category, and the eminent individual may then serve as a reference other for many members of his or her age-sex category. With this following, the person may then become something of a "champion" who speaks out for that category.

Suborganizations are fairly visible. A substantial degree of sex segregation is practiced among all peoples, and age segregation is significant in industrialized societies, frequently giving rise to various "age groups," such as youth gangs (Eisenstadt, 1956), "adults only" condominiums, and senior citizen communities. Furthermore, persons playing deviant age-sex roles may form deviant communities, for example, the homosexual community (C. A. B. Warren, 1974).

COLLECTIVITY

As a societal-level social organization, an age-sex structure has not only a structural aspect but also an aspect of collectivity—a membership with collective interests, resources, and culture. The defining common interest of any age-sex structure is in the collective production of that collective good we have termed *social order*—an orderliness and predictability of relations among persons based simply on outwardly visible attributes. Paramount among the material resources of such a collectivity is its domestic (household) technology—the basic tools, props, objects, and toys members employ in routine daily life, conditioning the basic interests and skills of the collectivity. Where domestic technology centers on fires, tents, and horses rather than on electricity, houses, and automobiles, it may be expected that age-sex roles will differ significantly.

The human resources of this type of organization—aside from these interests and skills—include membership size and age-sex composition. In very large age-sex structures, age-sex roles become less confounded with kinship roles, and age and sex segregation become more pronounced (Eisenstadt, 1956). The effects of age-sex composition are manifold. Where there are relatively few young men (through the devastations of warfare, for example), sex-typing of occupations tends to be less sharply defined. Where there are relatively many old people (predominantly females, owing to greater female longevity), the authority and status of old people tends to be lowered. The importance of age-sex composition is dramatically underlined by the practice among some primitive peoples of selective male or female infanticide to regulate sex ratios (M. Harris, 1977).

Much has already been said here regarding the culture of this type of social organization. The content elements of culture tend to be segregated into a series of overlapping subcultures: the distinctive cultural world of children, featuring fairy tales, rhyming games, riddles, songs, and so on (Opie and Opie, 1959); the less tradition-bound youth culture (Blixt and Provost, 1971); the subculture of the aging (Rose and Peterson, 1965); and the somewhat distinct subcultures of males and females.

The central features of the culture of an age-sex structure, however, are to be found in its classificatory system of age-sex categories and its set of sex-typing and age-grading norms. Norms concerning age-sex roles and role relationships carry the force of custom and include major mores as well as conventions of propriety. Violations of mores (for example, concerning sexual relations) generally lead to guilt, shame, and punishment, and even violations of mere sex-role conventions usually cause deep social and personal embarrassment. A woman can be mortified by accidentally spilling a drink on her dress at a party and a man who "can't hold his liquor" and displays drunken comportment is likely to be socially shunned and derogated.

ORGANIZATIONAL PROCESSES

Recruitment is almost exclusively ascriptive. Selection into a particular age-sex structure is primarily based on the membership of the individual's mother. Placement into a position within such a structure is, obviously, based on the age and sex of the individual. Medically speaking, biological gender reveals itself in three ways: chromosomally, hormonally, and anatomically. Almost always, these three aspects of gender are consistent, but for some individuals one of these aspects proves discrepant; even more rarely, an individual is born with sex organs of both genders. In either type of biological ambiguity, the individual's placement into a sex category must be decided *socially,* most often by the child's physicians and parents (Garfinkel, 1967). Similarly, some individuals manifest precocious maturation (a physical age much greater than chronological age) or growth deficiencies (midgets and dwarfs, in whom physical age lags behind chronological age), requiring a more social definition of age category. In any case, age-category placement is often rather loosely related to an individual's precise chronological age. One type of *voluntary* placement should be noted. Since the mid-twentieth century, some individuals unhappy with their sex role have elected to undergo so-called sex-change surgical operations.

Socialization into any age-sex role involves both communication of expectations and development of personal attributes. The growing literature on sex-role socialization (Maccoby, 1966) and on age-role socialization (for instance, Rosow, 1975) most heavily emphasizes the aspect of communicating role expectations. In the anticipatory socialization phase, the very young child is taught by its parents the rudiments of the age-sex classificatory system and of the accompanying age-sex role system. Throughout life, the individual elaborates on his conception of these systems through role-models and through observation of reactions to his own and others' behaviors in various age-sex role relationships. These conceptions are further developed through exposure to depictions of age-sex roles and relationships in oral and printed lore and literature, in movies, drama, and television.

More explicit organizational tactics come into play whenever an individual approaches the transition to his next age-sex position. Direct peer coaching by members of that category is a highly significant influence, particularly among children and adolescents. In his new role relationships with the other age-sex categories, the individual may be instructed through direct admonitions or advice from the other parties to these relationships. Part of "growing up" successfully is actually learning and adequately performing the graduated sequence of role expectations as one moves along from one age-sex category to the next. Successfully getting through the transition phases from one to the next is often the most difficult part, social psychologically, for the individual. Examples include a young girl's transition into puberty, an adolescent boy's transition into "manhood," and an older person's transition into retirement. The travails of such transitions have been extensively depicted in story and song.

But the aspect of developing personal attributes and capabilities also warrants further examination. The young adult, newly independent, may at last have to learn to cook, launder his clothes, and fill out income tax forms; the adolescent may now have to learn how to drive a car, shave, and ask for dates. Even the expected physical attributes may require explicit development, directly (through weightlifting or bust-building exercises) or indirectly (through wigs, padded bras, and the like). A great deal of the socialization efforts by parents and by schools are devoted to developing skills and other personal attributes of their charges. Explicit training is also provided by a wide range of specialized schools, courses, and teachers—in driving, dancing, singing, "charm," cooking, consumerism, childbirth, parenting, retirement, and many other areas for persons of all ages. Textbooks, manuals, "how to" books, and specialized magazines afford explicit instruction in life skills of all sorts through a more impersonal medium. Every society expends a great deal of effort socializing its members into "proper" age-sex role performances.

Interaction among human beings everywhere is primordially based on and constrained by age-sex role relationships. More than any others, age-sex role relationships between persons are directly apparent, rather than having to be either inferred or announced—hence the centrality of age-sex roles in producing orderly relations among persons. Yet even age-sex roles are subject to occasional misidentifications. Under imperfect observational conditions (a hasty glance, over the telephone, or in an exchange of correspondence), inaccurate sex identifications may be made in interpersonal interaction. Very young children are fairly often subjects of incorrect sex identification by strangers, and even adolescents (long-haired males or short-haired females) may be wrongly categorized. Given the even looser nature of age categories, as well as the motivating consequences of age differentials in privileges, inappropriate attributions of age roles are somewhat more common, as when a sailor takes a girl to be of legal age or a diminutive teenager is able to enter a theater for the children's price. As with sex-category mistakes, age misidentifications may be highly embarrassing and deeply resented. Thus, within an age-sex structure, the first task in interaction—that of negotiating identities—remains a vital though greatly simplified one. It is an interesting fact that many societies have very distinctive patterns of dress, hair style, and other body adornment for each age-sex category, reducing to a minimum the possibility of misidentification and also serving as a constant reminder to the individual of the age-sex role he or she is expected to enact.

Even though age-sex roles and role relationships tend to be culturally well defined, the second task in interaction—the negotiation of lines of action—is more problematic. As in all roles, performers tend to attempt to enlarge upon the rights and privileges of an age-sex role and to evade or minimize its costly duties and obligations. Again, adolescents provide the most fabled instances of these tendencies.

From the organizational viewpoint of the age-sex structure itself, patterns of interaction—who gets together, when and where, to do what—are a major concern, reflected in the mores and proprieties of age-sex role relationships. Again, the patterned segregations of sexes and ages tend to give rise to sex and age solidarity, as manifested in the battle of the sexes and the conflict of generations. Other forms of suborganization, such as the homosexual community, similarly arise through the patterned interaction of the age-sex structure.

Each age-sex category thus tends to develop something of a subculture of its own, with it own media, its own problems and worldviews based upon a shared position in the larger structure, a degree of easy mutual understanding among its occupants, and a degree of "us against them" mutual support against the other categories. The bonds of male/female and parent/child relationships tend to cut across these category subcultures and prevent them from becoming full-fledged groups. Yet, they seem an inevitable appendage to the age-sex structure. For example, male office workers will tend to support a fellow in some sexual adventure, and youth groups tend to close ranks and keep most adults "out of the picture." Category occupants also tend to take sides with fellow occupants in any cross-category dispute, unless the person has deviated grossly from category role expectations.

Innovation within an age-sex structure is largely internally emergent, spurred principally by changes in domestic technology. The wide availability of cars, telephones, and electrical appliances has triggered major changes in the American age-sex structure, and the dissemination of oral contraceptives is largely responsible for the recent "sexual revolution." As in the speech community, ratification/stigmatization procedures are largely reactive, informal, democratic, and diffuse. Age-sex role innovations are generally sponsored by individuals, and it is up to each individual to adopt or to scorn each new practice. On occasion, emergent change takes the form of social movements (see Chapter 17), as in the case of women's liberation or the Gray Panthers, which lobby for formal, proactive changes in the laws of relevant polities. Of course, these laws very often formalize fundamental mores of some age-sex structure, particularly concerning sexual relations. Accordingly, formal court proceedings may be invoked to adjudicate the normative standing of certain discrepant age-sex role performances. The legal challenge to mandatory retirement at age 65 or of the right of two consenting adults to enter into a homosexual marriage are formal proactive attempts to alter age-sex role expectations.

Social control, similarly, is generally informal and diffuse in surveillance, determination of sanctions, and administration of rewards and punishments. Surveillance is largely a matter of observation and gossip, except for police surveillance regarding those age-sex norms formalized by some polity. Old men loitering around schoolyards are likely to be questioned by patrolling police, and in our larger cities police also cruise looking for underage runaways. The fundamental rewards are the differential privileges of the various sexes and ages—precedence in seating on a bus, access to sex, drinking, smoking, and so on. Punishments are largely social: loss of privileges, loss of status, ridicule, scorn, condemnation. Violent punishments are not unknown for violation of mores; a male who "takes advantage" of a girl may be roughed up by her family or friends. Polities formalizing age-sex norms may use fines and imprisonment as punishments of a more formal nature. Implicit promises of reward are a vital tactic in this type of organization, and tacit threats of punishment are a major consideration in every member's framing of personal conduct.

Rituals of solidarity—in the form of rites of passage—are a notable feature in many age-sex structures. Elaborate ceremonies are conducted to signal the transition of an individual (or group of individuals) from one age-sex category to another, particularly from a preadult to an adult category, as in puberty rites, manhood initiations, and the like. In our own structure, such rites of passage have almost disappeared, leaving only subcultural remnants such as the Bar Mitzvah and debutante or "coming out" parties, aside from the universal ceremonialization of birth and death. The relentless centrality of chronological precision—atomic clocks and astronomical calendars—in our culture instead dictates that every passing year be ceremonialized in the ubiquitous birthday celebration. The marking of age-category transitions tends to take the form of "special" birthdays (1, 5, 10, 13, 20, 21, 25, and all subsequent ages ending in 0 or 5) and of milestone events—a girl's first formal dance, getting one's driver's license, high school graduation, retirement banquets, and so on.

ROLE-MAKING AND CAREER DEVELOPMENT

Powerful though they may be, the sex-typing and age-grading norms merely mark off a limited range of appropriate attributes and behaviors for the individual. Significant latitude exists within this limited range for personal style. Indeed, individuals frequently attempt to resist the placement efforts of the collectivity, particularly with respect to age-category placement but less often with respect to sex-category. Similarly, individuals often attempt to resist socialization efforts by disputing the legitimacy of certain age-sex role expectations, by arguing for exceptions on the grounds of individual peculiarities, and by fighting the development of expected skills or personal features.

Through such individual negotiation, some variant age-sex role may be defined for the person. In the sex-role area, these include the variant roles of sissy, tomboy, transvestite, homosexual, slut, spinster, and ugly duckling (on the deviant side) and those of All-American sweetheart, beauty queen, muscleman, and "brain" (on the creative side). In the age-role area, variant roles include those of the immature, the precocious, and the retarded person. Some individuals find such variant roles quite acceptable while others greatly resent the imputation of roles of this type.

Whether the age-sex role prescribed for an individual is a variant or a standard one, the role actually performed by that person through the interaction process is certain to diverge in various ways from the prescriptions as he strives to exploit the benefits and avoid the costs of the prescribed role. These discrepancies, as individually sponsored innovations, create significant tensions in the age-sex structure and frequently precipitate informal or even highly formal proceedings to ratify or stigmatize the novel practices (Plummer, 1975). The individual, as sponsor, seeks at least to avoid stigmatization (imputation of an undesired variant role) and perhaps even to attain recognition for creative performance. Every personal style of performing any (standard or variant) age-sex role bears some similarities to several variant roles. The aim of the individual is to steer a course near enough to creative variants to derive some benefits, yet far enough from deviant varieties to minimize the ridicule or the condemnation that accompany them (Klapp, 1962).

Career development in an age-sex structure is as inescapable as aging, since the continuous process of placement is based (somewhat loosely) on chronological age. The sequence of career movements is inevitable (except for reasons of early death), but the timetable for such movements is not. Whether through biological, psychological, or social contingencies, some individuals find themselves out of phase with their age cohort in their progression through the sequence of age-sex categories. Some individuals are very slow in reaching adolescence, and others become old prematurely. Such "age incongruents" have received much attention in the aging literature (for instance, Riley et al., 1972; Neugarten et al., 1965).

Socially, the age-sex structure provides incentives for career movements in the form of age-graded privileges, such as being allowed to cross the street alone, to drink, to vote, to have sex, and—in the case of old people—to be freed from certain onerous duties. Such increases in privileges are necessary to offset the increased duties (domestic, military, economic, political, familial) that accompany movement through the sequence.

As noted earlier, however, some individuals actively resist the recurrent placement process (and the accompanying resocialization efforts) involved in career development. Such resistance generally involves devaluation of the age-graded privileges of the next category, as well as preparing themselves to fail the rules and standards for occupancy of that next position. Other individuals, of course, actively cooperate in the recruitment and socialization processes, preparing themselves at an early point to meet the rules and standards for the new position in hopes of early promotion. Children, for instance, frequently work and scheme to acquire the attributes and increased privileges of teenagers—learning the dress, the dance steps, and the slang in hopes of early passage into this category. It is not uncommon for one individual to cooperate in the first few movements but to resist the later ones—a pattern we might call "the Peter Pan syndrome" of wanting always to remain a youth. This pattern is especially likely when the later categories embody lowered status and privileges—for example, old age among the Eskimos.

IMPACT ON THE CHARACTER OF THE INDIVIDUAL

The personal impact of an individual's age-sex role can scarcely be exaggerated. Relatively clear and quite compelling role expectations bear on literally every attribute of the individual. The age-sex structure to which he belongs and, especially, the position he occupies within that structure condition every thread of his personal fabric: how he looks, how he crosses his legs, what common objects he can manipulate, what he does around the house, whether he can leave the house, what he finds to be fun or funny, what he finds embarrassing about himself. Age-sex role largely determines the individual's interests, skills, and beliefs, which in turn critically shape his perceptions, memory, attitudes, and behaviors.

An individual's age-sex role provides a model pattern (or template) for his personal identity, that is, for his self-concept of what kind of person he is or should be, his sense of how he is a normal and competent human being. The flat-chested adolescent girl, the youth who has nothing to shave, and the gray-haired young mother all fear that something is wrong with them. Sex-role or gender identity (Money and Ehrhardt, 1972) and age-role identity (Mutran and Burke, 1979) are core aspects of personal identity. For example, Rosenkrantz et al. (1968) have shown that divergence of one's self-concept from the relevant sex-role stereotype has important consequences for self-esteem, and even senior citizens derogate and pity those whom they consider to be "old" (McTavish, 1971).

Objectively, a person's career within the age-sex structure reflects and affects the changing nature of his personal attributes. Across the life span there is ordinarily an increase and then a decline in activity level, sex drive, acuity of visual and auditory perception, speed of learning, accuracy of recall and recognition, strength, agility, coordination, intellectual abilities, social participation, and the like (Pressey and Kuhlen, 1957). An individual's appearance, interests, values, attitudes, dreams, and activities shift rather predictably across life's seasons (Neugarten et al., 1965). Subjectively, his age-sex career provides him with a moving perspective on himself—a framework for interpreting personal change as a normal process of developmental self-transformation, with some continuity of identity.

The social psychological importance of one's subjective career is attested to by the popularity of recent works—by Erik Erikson (1959), Daniel Levinson (1978), Roger Gould (1978), and Gail Sheehy (1976, a number one best-seller at the time)—concerning the crises and identity implications of the various transitions between the age categories of the life cycle. The midlife transition, for example, poses a serious life crisis for most men and women. Every aspect of life is questioned, personal attachments to significant others loosen greatly, and recriminations against self and

225

others abound. Depression and anger are common reactions, and the incidence of alcoholism, divorce, illness, and even suicide greatly increases. Interestingly, men tend to respond with redoubled efforts in their occupational careers, sensing that time is running out and the world is closing in, whereas women in a midlife crisis more frequently see time lengthening out interminably and life opening up. Research further suggests (Foner, 1975) that these career impacts may be even greater for "age incongruents" with atypical career timetables.

As individuals move along from category to category in the age-sex structure, there are often major shifts in perspective and position on a host of issues. For instance, "have-not" youth tend to be liberal while their "have" elders tend to be conservative on economic issues, and persons often shift from one position to another as they move across age categories. Most of those who, in the 1960s, said "don't trust anyone over thirty" are now over thirty themselves.

The partial "emancipation" of a particular age-sex category, such as women or senior citizens, does not necessarily lead to any diminishing of their distinctive attributes and may, in fact, facilitate expansion of certain role aspects. For example, the sale of provocative feminine underclothing is now at an all-time high, and a full-blown senior-citizen culture is beginning to emerge.

Age-sex structures manifest a good deal of change through time, usually as a result of the impact of other social changes such as technological shifts or the impact of cross-cultural influences. The lengthening of the life span will, no doubt, affect age-sex roles in the coming years. But whatever the changes, the age-sex structure never disappears and, as we will see in the coming chapters, always permeates many other organizational levels.

SUMMARY

Age and sex differentiation is a fundamental structural feature of social organization among both nonhuman and human species, reflecting biologically based differences in many individual attributes. Biologically, age and sex differences are not sharply categorical but are statistical averages. Socially, however, all peoples develop some system of categorical age-sex classification. Different speech communities tend to employ different age-sex classificatory systems, varying in the number of categories of sex and age. In most of these systems, (1) sexual differentiation is most sharply marked in adulthood and least in infancy; (2) more age categories are distinguished for males than for females; and (3) females are categorized as adult at an earlier age than males. Figure 14–1 depicts the American age-sex categories.

The most distinctive aspect of any age-sex structure is the expectations held toward the occupants of a category concerning the whole range of personal attributes. These expectations comprise a system of age-sex roles, with each role deriving its significance through contrasts and complementarities to each of the other roles. Both personal attributes and cultural elements (dress, grooming, language, occupation,

The Societal Level: Age-Sex Structure

avocations) are sex-typed, age-graded, or both. Role relationships are rather clearly prescribed between the occupants of any pair of age-sex categories, particularly with regard to authority, deference and demeanor, and sexual behavior. These serve to perpetuate and to regulate the "battle between the sexes" and the conflict of generations.

Dimensional social structures of power, authority, and status are well developed. However, an individual's status is modified by his position in the conformity structure. Leadership structure is poorly developed and fragmented. Suborganizations are fairly visible, in the form of sex segregation, age segregation (particularly in industrialized societies), and deviant communities (such as the homosexual community).

As collectivity, an age-sex structure is a membership undertaking collective action to produce social order, an orderliness and predictability of relations among persons based simply on outwardly visible attributes. Material resources take the form of a domestic (or household) technology, conditioning interests and skills of the membership. Other human resources include membership size and age-sex composition. The nature of age-sex roles varies characteristically with the domestic technology, membership size, and age-sex composition of the collectivity. The content elements of its culture tend to be segregated into a series of age-graded or sex-typed subcultures. The overarching cultural elements are (1) a classificatory system of age-sex categories and (2) a set of sex-typing and age-grading norms which are customary and which include both mores and conventions of propriety.

Recruitment is largely ascriptive, with selection based mainly on membership of the individual's mother and placement based on his age and sex (socially defined if biologically ambiguous). Socialization is extensive, involving both communication of expectations and development of personal attributes. Interaction is everywhere primordially based on and constrained by age-sex role relationships, since these are directly apparent rather than inferred or announced. Yet, misidentifications do occur, and performers do seek to reshape such role relationships in pursuit of their personal plans of action. Innovation tends to be internally emergent, spurred largely by changes in domestic technology; ratification procedures are mainly reactive, informal, democratic, and diffuse. Social control is generally informal and diffuse, with the fundamental rewards being differential privileges and punishments being largely social; rituals of solidarity, in the form of rites of passage, are a notable proactive tactic, along with implicit promises and tacit threats.

In the role-making process, significant latitude exists for personal style. Through individual resistance to placement and socialization, some variant sex role or age role of either a deviant or a creative type may be defined for a person. In career development, the sequence of career movements is inevitable but the timetable is not. Although incentives are provided for career movements in the form of age-graded privileges, individuals sometimes attempt to resist timely movement along the sequence of positions.

An individual's age-sex role influences literally his every personal attribute—most centrally his appearance, interests, skills, and beliefs, which in turn shape his perceptions, memory, attitudes, emotions, and behaviors. This role also provides a template for his personal identity—for his self-concept and for his sense of how he is a normal and competent human being.

His career within the age-sex structure (1) reflects and affects the changing nature of his personal attributes; and (2) affords him a framework for interpreting personal change as a normal process of developmental transformation with some continuity of identity. The various transitions between categories within the life cycle tend to be fraught with social stress and identity crises, particularly for age incongruents with atypical career timetables.

SUGGESTIONS FOR ADDITIONAL READING

The importance of the age-sex structure as a distinctive societal-level organization was first brought home to sociologists by the renowned anthropologist Ralph Linton in a pair of articles some forty years ago: "A Neglected Aspect of Social Organization" (*American Journal of Sociology*, 1940, 45: 870–886) and "Age and Sex Categories" (*American Sociological Review*, 1942, 7: 589–603). A more current examination of this topic is Pierre van den Berghe's little volume *Age and Sex in Human Societies: A Biosocial Perspective* (Belmont, California: Wadsworth, 1973). Relevant, too, is Jesse Bernard, *The Female World* (New York: Free Press, 1981).

Such works clearly establish that any separate consideration of either sex roles or age roles runs a clear danger of oversimplification and even distortion, since sex roles vary importantly over the life cycle and since most age roles differ greatly between the sexes. We recommend, therefore, that the reader seek out instead discussions of *age-sex roles* and of the transitions between age-sex roles.

Along such lines, Leonard Cain's "Life Course and Social Structure" (pp. 272–309 in R. E. L. Faris, editor, *Handbook of Modern Sociology*, Chicago: Rand McNally, 1964) rests solidly and explicitly on Linton's formulations. A more recent treatment is Bernice L. Neugarten and Nancy Datan, "Sociological Perspectives on the Life Cycle" (pp. 53–69 in Paul B. Baltes and K. Warner Schaie, editors, *Life-Span Developmental Psychology: Personality and Socialization*, New York: Academic Press, 1973).

Among the popularly available empirical studies of age-sex careers, Daniel Levinson's *The Seasons of a Man's Life* (New York: Knopf, 1978) is easily the most soundly based and informative. Many students will be interested in Erik H. Erikson's "Identity and the Life Cycle" (*Psychological Issues*, 1 (1), 1959).

Incidentally, the study of the feral child Genie, recommended in the previous chapter (Susan Curtis, *Genie: A Psycholinguistic Study of a Modern-Day "Wild Child,"* New York: Academic Press, 1977), contains much fascinating material regarding the child's necessarily radical socialization into an appropriate age-sex role. When first observed at age 13, Genie was almost completely uncivilized. She was violent and unrestrained, totally unused to clothing or grooming, and incontinent; she spit constantly and masturbated in every situation. Within a couple of years of socialization, however, she had become a reasonably normal adolescent girl.

Ronald Reagan addresses the citizenry after being officially sworn in as President of the United States and vowing to uphold its laws and Constitution.

CHAPTER 15

The Societal Level: Polity

Although not much aware of their speech community or their age-sex structure, most individuals have a keen awareness of the polity they belong to—and of other polities which impinge upon their own. The polity is less taken for granted than any other societal-level structure. And from time immemorial it has been the arena for personal adventures in gaining or manipulating privilege, power, and influence. Even those barred from direct participation in the political arena, such as the lower classes or others lacking necessary resources to play, have been keen observers and armchair commentators. No doubt even the slaves of every society have gossiped about the doings of those at the top.

But there is much more to a polity than exhaustively covered presidential elections or intrigues over the succession to a kingly throne. This is the societal-level structure where the laws (written and unwritten) are formulated and administered, the citizenry is channeled along "appropriate" paths, and the "ship of state" is navigated through its often troubled history, be it a primitive tribe or modern supernation. When the name of some country is mentioned on the evening news, it is almost always in the context of a *polity*.

A polity is a collectivity organized to promote the public safety and welfare of its membership. Unlike the other societal-level structures reviewed thus far, the polity is both formalized and explicitly territorial. That is to say, the polity has a written constitution spelling out in a formalized manner its basic purposes, structure, and fundamental operating principles. Furthermore, this collectivity claims the right to employ force (if necessary) to produce public order and safety among all persons found within a certain geographical territory.

The nation-state, in particular, claims the sole right to exercise legitimate force within its territorial bounds, to enforce its own norms concerning social relationships and conduct among individuals and lesser social organizations (Weber, 1947). The right to use force may be delegated to certain embedded organizations such as local police or private security agencies, and even to ordinary citizens under certain circumstances (such as the protection of one's home), but the ultimate authority remains with the polity. More than any other organization, the polity formally and explicitly regulates aspects of individual lives and all embedded lower-level organizations within its domain. Polities vary in their regulation of their populaces in a great many respects: degree of consent of the populace, effectiveness/ineffectiveness, degree of justice/injustice, amount of freedom left to the individual and lesser organizations, and so on.

It might be asserted that a desirable polity provides "the good life" for its individuals and organizations, that an acceptable polity leaves its individuals and organizations sufficiently alone to pursue their own aims, and that an undesirable polity produces an unpleasant social life and/or individual and organizational disasters.

There is an intimate partnership between a populace and its polity—however that partnership fares in the short and the long run—because neither can exist without the other.

COLLECTIVITY

Formalized enacted norms—that is, *laws*—are at the heart of the normative culture of a polity (Weber, 1954). Civil laws are enacted to regulate conduct in such a way as to prevent certain harms to the special interests of individuals and organizations. Criminal laws are enacted to prevent certain harms to the collective interests of the entire membership. Law, then, can be said to reflect the values, attitudes, and customs of the polity (Hart, 1976).

The culture of a polity is fully developed in every respect (Kavanagh, 1972; Almond and Verba, 1963). A specialized vocabulary includes not only distinctive titles for administrative positions but also political terms (for example, in the United States, "McCarthyism," "New Deal," "hawks") and legal-bureaucratic terms and styles (Edelman, 1977). Nation-states are generally quite prolific in generating cultural objects (such as flags, seals, uniforms) and social objects (such as positions, departments, bureaus). A substantial body of cultural lore arises concerning the characteristics of these social and cultural objects and how they may be successfully manipulated.

Myths, such as the social-contract doctrine in the United States or Aryanism in Nazi Germany, play a significant part in explaining and justifying the sovereignty of a nation-state. Legends, such as George Washington's cherry tree, embellish the shared sense of social history of the nation-state. This sense of social history not incidentally provides a salient time frame, or calendar, within which members locate themselves and their actions. For example, the Bicentennial, the various wars, and the Great Depression provide common historical reference points.

Political rituals are quite abundant. Examples are the wearing of military and police uniforms, salutes, the pledge of allegiance to the flag, and the playing of the national anthem and of "Hail to the Chief." On many occasions, a number of rituals are combined to constitute ceremonies, such as inaugurations, state funerals, or Independence Day celebrations.

This richly elaborate culture of the polity plays an important part in the development of a rather strong sense of collectivity among the membership. Patriotism, civic mindedness, and even nationalism typically are important values, engendering social mores concerning loyalty. Rituals of solidarity are more frequently and more seriously engaged in during times of national crisis, such as war, to increase the sense of collectivity by promoting *esprit de corps* and morale.

Chief among the human resources of a polity are (1) membership size, ranging among contemporary nation-states from a few thousand to hundreds of millions; (2) the age-sex composition of that membership, particularly the number of young men of military age; and (3) the skills distribution, best indexed by average educational level. Of these three, the skills distribution has come to be dominant over the last few centuries because it most closely measures what a populace can accomplish, relative to other polities. For instance, the relatively small but highly skilled populations of Europe dominated the rest of the globe for several centuries.

Material resources include, first of all, the natural resources—mineral deposits, soil, vegetation, water supply, climate, terrain—of the territory controlled by the polity. Territories range in size from the 109 acres of the Vatican to the nearly nine million square miles of the Soviet Union. Almost equally important are the economic, military, and communications technologies available to the polity (largely dependent on the skills distribution among its membership). The monetary resources of a polity are derived from members—through various devices of taxation—and from other polities—through sale of materials and services or through various forms of exploitation such as military domination and restrictive trade agreements. Trade with other polities has been, and remains, the most common solution to the problem of locally scant resources.

SOCIAL STRUCTURE

The fundamental positions in the primary social structure of a polity are alien, citizen, and official. Citizenship is equivalent to membership; an individual can be a full member of only one nation-state at any time. He can, however, be an alien within any nation-state whose territory he can gain entry to—legally (that is, with the permission of that polity) or illegally. As an alien, he is subject to the authority and laws of that polity while within its territory, as well as to further and distinctive legal restrictions imposed only on aliens (Konvitz, 1946).

Citizens, entitled to all the protections of the polity, may yet vary in their privileges. For example, in many polities, some citizens are "enfranchised," that is, they have the privilege of participating in the political process through voting, while others are not, either having lost the privilege of voting or having never gained it.

LEVELS OF ORGANIZATION

There are sometimes further distinctions among citizens, such as the right to own property, the right to hold official positions above a certain level, even the right to travel, as in ancient Egypt and medieval Japan. But any citizen—as "one of us"—has more rights than the alien.

The more specialized positions in the primary structure of a polity—such as judge, legislator, mayor, FBI agent—may be grouped together as "officials," and are filled almost exclusively from the rank-and-file of the citizenry. Some of these positions are appointive while others are elective (H. Y. Bernard, 1969). In either case, an official has formalized authority over certain other officials and over ordinary citizens and aliens in specified matters.

Three broad classes of roles cut across these three classes of positions (Greenstein, 1968). Aliens, citizens, and officials all play the role of *subject* of the state, complying to the legitimate authority of the polity. Citizens and officials sometimes play the role of *citizen,* actively striving to influence the decisions of the polity through political participation (D. F. Thompson, 1970). Only officials, of course, can play the more specialized role of *official,* serving as a formalized agent of the polity to make and carry out those decisions.

The scope of demands placed upon performers of these political roles varies significantly. In so-called authoritarian or totalitarian polities, the aggregate authority of officialdom is virtually total, extending to almost every aspect of a subject's life. In so-called libertarian polities, such authority is more clearly circumscribed, for example, by the Bill of Rights, due process of law, and the legal requirement of warrants for many types of searches and arrests.

Secondary social structure is also well developed in polities. Official suborganizations within the polity of a nation-state are formally developed along both geographical and functional lines. In the United States, for example, official geographical suborganizations take the form of regional authorities, states, counties, and local governments. Official functional suborganizations take the form, first of all, of the three branches of government—the legislative, the executive, and the judicial. Each of these in turn is divided into specialized departments, bureaus, and agencies. To complicate matters, each of the geographical suborganizations is also functionally suborganized; each state for example, has its own legislature, courts, and executive branch. Indeed, polities are notorious for developing a bewildering welter of official suborganizations, and these in turn often have a maze of their own suborganizations. As one city worker put it, "sometimes the person gets lost in the hallways."

In some polities, castes or parties are recognized as official suborganizations. In other polities, such castes or political parties function instead as unofficial suborganizations (Duverger, 1962). As we shall see in Chapter 17, publics are vital official or unofficial suborganizations within any polity, and social movements are a vital type of embedded unofficial organization within every polity.

In terms of dimensional social structures, the *authority* structure among members is of greatest importance. In the polity, the authority structure is highly elaborate, formalized, centralized, and strongly hierarchical. The position of an individual in the authority structure is a function of his position in the primary role structure (and thus

234

is most clearly differentiated within the ranks of officials). Political *power* and political *leadership* are much less formalized but often very real in their influence. Those individuals who control large volumes of money, mass media coverage, or the votes (or lobbying pressures) of other citizens rank high in the power structure of a polity (Rose, 1967). Those whose actions have contributed heavily to the shaping of political or governmental decisions—in the provision of collective goods—rank high in the leadership structure (Frohlich et al., 1971). The power structure, particularly, may heavily influence what actually happens within a polity.

An individual's rankings in authority, power, and leadership may be congruent, as with an acclaimed president or a successful revolutionary. But these three can also vary widely; a person such as Walter Cronkite may rank high in political leadership and power but have no official political authority. Some official may rank rather low in leadership yet have the authority radically to influence organizational and individual careers; examples would include government inspectors and income tax officials.

Political *conformity* is primarily a matter of obedience to law and lawful authority. Whether through ''civil disobedience'' as a political act (Bay, 1968) or through less principled noncompliance, serious violators—particularly of criminal laws—rank low in the conformity structure. The ordinary citizen tends to maintain something of a minimally acceptable obedience as a balance between collective and personal aims.

Position in the *status* structure of the polity is, for officials, first, a function of position in the authority structure and, second, a function of position in the power and leadership structures. For ordinary citizens, status in the polity is, first of all, a matter of position decreed by age-sex and perhaps caste structures—old enough to vote, of an enfranchised caste, and so on. Beyond this, a citizen's status rests heavily upon his or her positions in the power and leadership structures. Men and women with no official position can wield tremendous political influence because of their power and leadership. Widely read newspaper columnists and writers, famous ex-officials, and individuals of fame in other fields such as science or entertainment, cannot be ignored in understanding the polity—and usually are not ignored by polities themselves. Even at the local level, some citizens are ''opinion leaders'' to whom others come for interpretations and decisions about political events. Citizens may or may not have equal rights, but citizens are never equal in their influences upon their polities.

ORGANIZATIONAL PROCESSES

Recruitment into citizenship is most often ascriptive, based on the citizenship of the individual's parents or on the territorial bounds within which he was born. Similarly, enfranchisement is generally ascriptive, based on age, and perhaps sex, race, or economic status.

However, voluntary recruitment into alien or citizen positions is not uncommon. A foreigner may seek such a position in order to accompany his citizen spouse, to escape military duty or political oppression in his own country, or to pursue greater economic opportunity. Indeed, most polities have an interest in recruiting some im-

235

migrants (those falling in the ''desirable'' category) and may actively engage in organizational tactics of attraction through their foreign embassies, such as offering land, jobs, or tax havens. But immigration is always selective; elaborate rules and standards are imposed even to select persons for legal alien status, and these rules are still more demanding for becoming a naturalized citizen.

In every polity, the more specialized positions of officials tend to be filled from among a political elite, that is, those citizens ranking high in the dimensional social structures of political power, leadership, status, and/or authority. In some cases, membership in the political elite is ascriptive (based on parents' position), while in others it is based on individual achievement (Bachrach, 1971). In the case of military and police positions, however, only the higher offices tend to draw on the political elite.

Placement into a particular office of the polity may be accomplished through a variety of devices, including hereditary succession, seizure of office, and purchase of office. Military offices, particularly the lower positions, may be filled through conscription—an ascriptive draft. Most commonly, however, officials are either appointed (on the basis of an examination or of an apprenticeship) or elected (whether through voting, drawing of lots, or rotation). The various offices differ, of course, in who is authorized to appoint or elect the occupants. A wide range of selective sidepayments serve as incentives: salaries, material perquisites, social privileges, political status, power, and authority. In virtually every polity, differences in selective sidepayments are quite marked, corresponding to the hierarchical structure of offices, whatever the ideology (capitalism, socialism, communism) prevailing in the realm.

Finally, some mention should be made of recruitment into certain suborganizations. Where castes function as official or unofficial suborganizations of the polity, individual placement into a caste is, of course, hereditary. Recruitment into a particular political party is generally voluntary, although in the United States it is somewhat ascriptive, in that party preference has been shown to be heavily influenced through childhood socialization and closely reflects parental preferences (Greenstein, 1965).

Within the polity, recruitment *out* of a position is often more critical than recruitment into a position. An alien may be declared *persona non grata* and deported; a citizen may be disenfranchised or even have his citizenship revoked; an official may be impeached (if not assassinated or executed) or may fail to be reappointed or re-elected at the end of his term of office.

Political *socialization* involves teaching all participants what it is to be a subject of the polity, teaching many participants what it is to be a citizen, and teaching a few what it is to be an official. Subjects must learn the rudiments of the polity's culture: something of its constitution and its basic laws, its social and cultural objects, its lore and folklore, its rituals and ceremonies. Subjects are expected to develop a profound loyalty and commitment to the polity and a sense of the legitimacy of its authority. Such socialization into the basics of the polity is more or less mandatory in all nation-states; even tyrannical polities tend to rely more upon socialization than force to indoctrinate their subjects with proper role prescriptions.

The Societal Level: Polity

Polities vary widely in their modes of subject socialization (Langton, 1969; Dennis, 1973). Totalitarian nation-states, as well as those swelled by great numbers of immigrants or facing major instability, place great emphasis on explicit "civic training" and political inculcation. Their schools, youth organizations, and mass media devote disproportionate efforts to formal instruction, training, and testing on political topics, seeking to develop national unity and a cooperating populace which shares approved and desired "definitions of the situation."

In more libertarian and stable polities, where the subject role is less problematic, political socialization tends to be less partisan, concerned more centrally with the citizen role than the subject role, less formal, and less explicit. In the United States, for example, much of it is left to the family, with only a modest offering of school instruction in the dynamics of government and in national and state history. The mass media—through their adult-directed, "nonpartisan" news coverage of government and politics, as well as through the paid political announcements of parties and candidates—have an extraordinary implicit impact on the political knowledge and attitudes of children and adolescents.

As citizens, members are expected (Almond and Verba, 1963) to develop an interest in political participation—some party affiliation and some political ideology, tempered by a dedication to due process and the public good—as well as some ability to exert political influence through informed discussion, communication with officials, and voting. Citizen socialization is largely through implicit means and generally amounts only to orientation and supplementation/revision. Enfranchised citizens often receive further political socialization from parties, not only concerning ideologies and issues, but even concerning how to become a registered voter, how to obtain an absentee ballot, and so forth.

Those few citizens who become officials are expected to have excelled in internalizing these values, mastering this culture, and developing these interests and skills. Since officials are paid to perform their specialized (full- or part-time) roles in the polity, their further socialization is essentially that encountered in an occupational community (Chapter 18) and in a bureaucracy (Chapter 19). Depending on the person's level of preparation for a particular position, this socialization may be merely orientation and supplementation/revision. Professional as well as military and police positions require explicit education and perhaps even stripping and substitution, as in military boot camps or police academies. During such socialization, the recruit official is examined for display of more than the usual citizen attributes and may be recruited out if too wide a divergence from the citizen role is found, even in the face of excellent promise on other counts. This tactic helps to produce a solidarity with the polity on the part of its officialdom.

Interaction in the polity can be viewed at three levels. At the level of officials, it is largely a matter of doing the business of government—drafting legislation, conducting hearings, drilling military troops, policing the streets, handing out food stamps, and so on. All these are work interactions within bureaucratic settings and are carried out under an "official rhetoric" affirming the ideals of the polity. As in any organization, unofficial interactions may occur among officials or between officials and subjects in pursuit of organizational aims or individual purposes. No polity conducts all of its business entirely openly, and every polity has its scandals.

In citizen roles, members' interactions take the form of political participation—political discussions, party meetings and committee work, pressuring officials, making speeches, campaigning, voting (Milbrath and Goel, 1977; Lane, 1959). Such interactions generate, and largely take place within, embedded voluntary associations, publics, and social movements. In the more libertarian polities, these interactions take place more or less openly; in the more totalitarian polities, they become more clandestine or underground. Participation is then more likely to take such forms as anonymous leaflets, cabals, covert communications, and perhaps violence. All citizens seem to have a keen interest in their polities, and so it may be that a polity that curtails open participation will inevitably spawn underground participation and unofficial suborganizations.

In subject roles, interactions can scarcely be characterized on the basis of content or context. Rather, they are a matter of observing or violating the law. Virtually every sphere of everyday life is penetrated by the prescriptions and proscriptions of the polity—family law, commercial law, tax law, and so forth. Factional suborganizations generated through subject interaction include, for example, the criminal community. These factional suborganizations provide interactional supports for their members and, interestingly enough, often form shadowy "polities" of their own, with their own structures and enforcements of unwritten "laws."

Innovation is a central process within any polity. Innovations may be externally imposed, as in the imposition of policies on its satellite nations by the Soviet Union, or the multilateral embargo against South Africa. Innovations may be internally planned, such as President Carter's energy plan or the famous five-year plans of socialist countries. In either case, officials of the executive branch are primary sponsors, responsive to political pressures from citizens, special-interest pressure groups, and other officials (Mayer, 1972).

However, internally emergent change always remains a major force. A notable characteristic of the polity is its impressive range of formal procedures for ratification or stigmatization of emergent innovations. Proactive procedures—enacting new norms to resolve the legitimacy of some practice—are centrally the province of officials of the legislative branch (responsive to political participation) and take the fairly democratic form of parliamentary debate and voting on proposed laws (Keefe and Ogul, 1964). In much less democratic form, however, executive officials may proclaim certain administrative regulations which, while not laws, have the force of law (Lorch, 1969). Similarly, a single judge may issue a ruling which, as a legal precedent in the context of case law, essentially has the force of law. Somewhat more democratically, of course, a supreme court may modify or overthrow any of these types of enacted norms as being inconsistent with the polity's basic constitution. Much more democratically, and therefore much less often, the question may be put to a referendum, a vote by all enfranchised citizens. Whatever the form, proactive procedures always have the effect of defining some type of action as deviant (Taylor and Taylor, 1973).

238

The Societal Level: Polity

Reactive procedures, on the other hand, are primarily conducted by judicial officials, in the form of civil and criminal court trials (Cole, 1973; Eisenstein and Jacob, 1977). Such proceedings may be quite autocratic, with the ruling made by a single judge, or somewhat more democratic, with the ruling made by a jury of ordinary citizens or by a panel of several judges. Somewhat similar proceedings may be conducted by executive officials—in the form of administrative hearings, to determine compliance with regulations—or by legislative officials, in the form of legislative hearings. In any case, the purpose is to adjudge whether a subject's innovative role performance is to be considered conforming or deviant (in this context, illegal, and perhaps criminal).

Of all social organizations, the polity has the most to do with formal *social control*, both proactive and reactive. It monitors disparities between prescribed and performed roles of its members in virtually every sphere of social life. The polity is also usually the final arbiter in disputes between individuals, between individuals and organizations, and between organizations.

The central tactic of polities in social control is to set up surveillance and enforcement of boundaries beyond which role performances of subjects are not to stray. For example, it is acceptable for a man to argue with his wife—even bitterly recriminate—but not to beat her; it is acceptable to spank children but not to abuse them physically; it is acceptable for a business to engage in competitiveness—even in sharp practices—but not in fraud. There is a gray zone of semilegitimacy in most spheres of life in which officials have much leeway in administering the polity's rules, and it is in this gray area that the majority of disputes in ratification/stigmatization occur.

What does a polity have to work with in social control? The basic benefits of polity membership, of course, are a share in the collective good—protection, public services, individual welfare. Selective sidepayments, including salaries, perquisites of office, political status, power, leadership, and perhaps authority, constitute the primary rewards for creative performance. Mild punishments for deviant performance may take the form of loss of primary position—through, for instance, deportation, disenfranchisement, or impeachment—or of loss of rewards, such as parental rights or perquisites of office. More severe punishments may involve some loss of share in the collective good; these punishments include imprisonment, material loss through civil judgment or criminal fine, floggings, disfigurement, and even execution.

Promises of basic benefits and possible rewards—as well as threats of punishment—play a major part in a polity's social control efforts. Rituals of solidarity, glorifying the polity, serve to enhance perception of the benefits and rewards promised, as well as the awesome power and authority of the polity over its subjects. Those proceedings in which rewards or punishments are determined or administered are often made public ceremonies for ritual effect; inaugurations, bestowal of medals, court proceedings, and public hangings are just a few examples.

Specialized functionaries of social control are an invariant feature of polities. Soldiers, police, prosecutors, judges, jailors, and public executioners are to be found in every nation-state.

Surveillance and law enforcement are relatively elaborate. Patrol, wiretapping,

239

mail opening, required submission of records, and undercover infiltration are common tactics of surveillance, yet every system rests ultimately on the cooperation of informers (Blum, 1972). If such cooperation is not forthcoming, it may be coerced through police harrassment and even torture. Specialized surveillance personnel are not confined to the ranks of police and also include government inspectors, program monitors, intelligence agents, and censors.

A polity usually attempts to have its subjects serve as informers in case of deviant role performances, and indeed the majority of known infractions will have been reported by citizens. However, there is always some reluctance on the part of the populace to serve in the informer role. First, this role can entail a good deal of effort without reward. Second, there is the possibility of retribution from those informed on or from their associates. Third, the person may have committed infractions of his or her own and may therefore be avoiding any official notice, since a cursory check on any informer is routine. Most citizens resolve these dilemmas by reporting only the most serious types of discrepant performances, such as murders or grand thefts.

Although specialized surveillance officials may informally decide upon and administer punishments, formal procedures always exist as well. Upon a court verdict against an individual, a separate decision regarding the appropriate civil or criminal punishment is made, sometimes by a jury and sometimes by a judge (through a sentence hearing—Dawson, 1969). In many cases, the enacted norm (law or regulation) itself explicitly prescribes an appropriate range of punishments. Formal administration of punishments is the province of other specialized functionaries: court clerks (in the case of monetary punishments), jail and prison officials, probation and parole officers, hospital authorities, and hangmen.

Although police may confer rewards upon informers and judges may make compensatory awards to victims, the conferral of rewards within a polity is generally much more diffuse. Appointments, promotions, medals, grants, government limousines, Secret Service protection, and the like are formally or informally determined by officials responding to individual performance and political pressures. Access to the rewards of elective offices is determined by the votes of citizens.

ROLE-MAKING AND CAREER DEVELOPMENT

Even in the face of the centralized authority and power of the nation-state, an individual exerts considerable influence on the development of his role in the polity. Membership, even when ascribed, can be evaded; citizenship can be renounced, and thousands have fled even totalitarian nation-states through illegal emigration. Similarly, countless aliens obtain effective membership through illegal immigration, evading the restrictions of selection. Even more make legal application for admission, arduously striving to make themselves attractive candidates through selective presentation of self and development of desired personal features.

Placement within the primary social structure of the polity can also be influenced by the individual. On the one hand, government appointments and party drafts can be declined, and many thousands have discovered ingenious means of avoiding drafts for military service (Tax, 1967) or jury duty. On the other hand, many aliens apply for citizenship and work very hard to prepare themselves to pass the required tests. Similarly, many young citizens actively prepare themselves to meet the requirements for Civil Service positions and even for the military. But it is candidates for elective office who display the fullest range of individual tactics of placement (Schwartzman, 1973), doing everything they can to make themselves attractive to their party and to the voters: contributing money and effort to the party, seeking sponsorship, engaging in elaborately devised presentations of self, and campaigning for the position.

One can resist or comply with socialization efforts, too. One may sleep through a boring civics lesson or laugh off the lectures and advice of the police juvenile officer in favor of the cynically defiant bravado of the corner gang. Alternatively, aliens may voluntarily attend special classes on the American constitution or on reading English, and aspiring politicians may take courses in public speaking or law and stuff envelopes for some political hack in order to obtain an apprenticeship. Variant defined roles may thus be negotiated, even within the class of subject roles (the rebellious revolutionary, the defiant scoff-law, the draft dodger). Similar socialization failures in organizational role-definition efforts may produce apathetic citizens and incompetent officials.

Even when an individual does not embrace a variant defined role, his performed role in interaction is likely to depart from the prescribed role. As a law-respecting subject, he is nevertheless almost certain to be tempted or entrapped into violating some traffic ordinance or tax regulation, if not some criminal statute. The confusions of political campaigns and the pressures of other interests are likely to cause a civic-minded citizen to neglect to register for, or vote in, some election or another; a citizen with strongly held convictions may even find himself taking part in civil disobedience as a political gesture. As a qualified public official, he will almost certainly find that the political pressures of maintaining office or seeking higher office involve him in some awkward indiscretions, suggesting corruption, misuse of office, or partisan injustice.

Such individual innovation in the polity may be a prelude to stigmatization and punishment. Labeling theorists in criminology have emphasized the criminogenic consequences of official stigmatization, effectively forcing stigmatized individuals to embrace variant subject roles (Becker, 1963; Schur, 1971). On the other hand, a creative performance in the citizen role can lead to membership in the political elite, and perhaps from there to the rewards of an official position.

Studies of political *careers* (Marvick, 1961; J. D. Barber, 1965) have focused entirely on the ranks of officials and particularly on their recruitment and socialization. These studies have emphasized the organizational importance of sponsorship, apprenticeship, and coaching as modes of socialization. Except perhaps in the bureaucratized arena of the Civil Service, no clear sequence of career movements is conventionally defined; even candidates for very high office may have had little or no previous public service. Neither, accordingly, is there in the United States any conventional career

241

timetable for officials. The career problem of the mobile official is, therefore, one of deciding which office to seek and when. Given the polity's concern to remove unpopular officials, downward mobility (perhaps even to the rank of ordinary citizen) is a constant threat and a major career contingency. Frequently, of course, the removed or demoted official is able to move laterally to another societal-level structure—in modern nations, usually the economy. Ex-officials of high rank usually retain a high cultural status which enables them to fare quite well in large and powerful economic associations, for example.

Within the less specialized classes of positions, some career movement is also evident and important. Aliens may move up to the position of naturalized citizen (although with some attendant restrictions on further upward mobility), and born citizens generally move up to the rank of enfranchised citizen. Less conventional but more striking career movements within these ranks involve downward and outward mobility. Through formal punishments, a citizen may be disenfranchised, a naturalized citizen may be brought back to the rank of alien through revocation of citizenship, and any subject may become a convicted criminal with attendant loss of civil liberties. In outward mobility, an alien or a naturalized citizen may be deported, and any subject of the polity might emigrate.

Within the primary social structure of the polity, then, very few members experience extended trajectories of career movements, and these are primarily officials. Even for officials, career trajectories tend to be little conventionalized in the culture of the polity. Career movements are much more clearly visible within the *secondary* social structure, as many individuals rise and fall in the dimensional structures of political power, leadership, status, and conformity.

IMPACT ON THE CHARACTER OF THE INDIVIDUAL

One's position in the primary and secondary social structures of the polity clearly conditions one's rights, opportunities, and personal resources. Contrast, for example, a convicted criminal with a high public official and political leader. With respect to rights, the criminal lacks even the right to vote, whereas the official may be entitled to public funds to finance his campaign. With respect to opportunities, the official is besieged with invitations and offers of all kinds, while the convicted criminal is shunned and may find it almost impossible to obtain even the most menial job. Imprisonment is itself a most direct and serious restriction on opportunity, and execution is of course the extreme in this regard. With respect to personal resources, the criminal may be permanently bankrupted by having to pay off a huge fine, while the public official is awarded a handsome salary and many expensive perquisites. A criminal may be physically crippled through torture, while the official develops not only political skills but an attractive "political personality" (Di Renzo, 1974) and many potentially useful interpersonal connections.

One's roles in the polity affect many other personal attributes. The subject role, for example, brings to bear on the person an enormous range of demands and limitations—backed up by the potential of legitimate force—regarding his conduct in many spheres of everyday life. More implicitly, the subject role carries strong expectations regarding the development of certain knowledge (of the law and of governmental procedures) and of certain beliefs, attitudes, and values (concerning the sovereign authority and national pride of the polity). The citizen role brings to bear strong expectations for the development of some level of political interest, knowledge, ability, and participation. The specialized political roles of public officials constrain a wide range of personal attributes, from personal appearance and demeanor to very specific types of knowledge, interest, skill, habits, and actions, depending on the particular role.

Career mobility within the primary and (more commonly) the secondary social structures of the polity entails patterned alterations in the person's rights, opportunities, and personal resources. Such alterations often require some transformation of the person's self-concept, particularly when the change in social position is inconsistent with either his aspirations or his expectations. Becoming a convicted criminal, for example, has been shown to be a very serious blow to self-esteem, unless the individual had had a prior commitment to the criminal life (A. R. Harris, 1976). We may suppose, too, that a long-term incumbent of a presumed "safe seat" who unexpectedly fails re-election suffers more in diminished self-esteem than an aspiring political long-shot who loses an election.

The major impact of the polity on individual character, however, has been thought to derive not from position, role, or career but from *membership*. Certainly the chances of murder, execution, military service, or starvation vary from polity to polity, as do taxes and the specific legal prescriptions and proscriptions conditioning every aspect of private life: whom one may marry, what substances one may ingest, what side of the road one may drive on, what books and theories are forbidden, and so on.

Empirical research (for instance, Almond and Verba, 1963) has demonstrated cross-national differences in political values, attitudes, and practices even between relatively similar polities. Some social scientists have conceptualized such findings as reflecting differences in *national character*—the modal constellation of values, attitudes toward various authorities, and personality traits—that is said to prevail among the members of a particular nation-state (Inkeles and Levinson, 1969). European scholars in particular have been impressed by the differences in character between, say, Germans and Italians, Belgians and Dutch, or Swedes and Danes. During World War II, explicit studies of the Japanese, German, and Russian national characters were commissioned for strategic purposes; Ruth Benedict's (1946) analysis of the Japanese self and sense of social obligation remains influential today. Subsequent and more carefully controlled studies of various nationalities have recently lent renewed interest to the concept of national character, particularly among political scientists (for example, Needler, 1971).

But lest we too simplistically imply a "polity molds the subjects" perspective, it must be pointed out that the polity is made up from the actions of individual citizens and officials. No polity, in the final analysis, can rule without the consent of its people, because every polity—whatever its form—must employ significant numbers of these very same people. To understand a polity is to understand much about its people and, conversely, to understand a people is to understand much about what type of polity they will create and what they will tolerate from it.

SUMMARY

A polity is a collectivity organized to produce the public safety and welfare of its membership. Distinctively, it is both formalized and territorial. The nation-state, the dominant modern type of polity, claims the sole right to exercise legitimate force within its territory, to enforce its own norms (laws).

Civil and criminal laws are formalized enacted norms, reflecting the values, attitudes, and customs of the collectivity. Laws are at the core of a richly developed culture, which tends to engender a strong sense of collectivity among members of a polity. Key aspects of its human resources include membership size, age-sex composition, and skills distribution. Material resources include territorial size, natural resources, wealth of membership, and economic, military, and communications technologies.

The fundamental positions in the primary social structure include those of aliens, citizens, and officials. Three broad classes of political roles cut across these fundamental position types. Occupants of all positions play the role of subject of the authority of the state; occupants of both the citizen and the official positions also play, at times, the role of citizen striving, through political participation, to influence decisions of the polity; only occupants of positions of official can play the more specialized role of official, a formally designated agent of the state in making and executing those decisions.

Official suborganizations of the polity are formally elaborated along both geographical and functional lines. Castes and political parties are official suborganizations in some polities and unofficial ones in others. Some publics are official suborganizations, while other publics within the same polity are unofficial. Social movements are a vital type of embedded unofficial organization in every polity.

The authority structure is most important in any polity and is highly elaborate, formalized, centralized, and hierarchical. Structures of power, leadership, and conformity are much less formalized. Position in the status structure is largely influenced by authority, qualified by rank in power, leadership, and conformity.

Selection to membership is most often ascriptive, although voluntary recruitment into alien or citizen positions is not uncommon. Placement is generally voluntary, through appointment or election, although some positions may be hereditary or filled through an ascriptive draft. In the polity, recruitment out of a position is often more critical than recruitment into it.

In socialization, all must learn the role of subject, many must learn the role of citizen, and a few must learn some specialized official role. Polities vary widely in their modes of subject and citizen socialization. In the United States, for example, political socialization is less formal, less explicit, and more concerned with the citizen role than in totalitarian or unstable polities.

Official interactions are essentially work interactions in bureaucratic settings. Citizen interactions take the form of political participation. Subject interaction is a matter of observing or violating the law.

In externally imposed or internally planned innovation, executive officials are the primary sponsors. Internally emergent innovation is the province of legislative officials (if proactive) or of judicial officials (if reactive). Any type of innovation within a polity encounters highly formalized procedures for ratification or stigmatization; degree of centralization varies significantly between polities.

Social control is a very visible process; every polity has a substantial range of specialized social control officials. Surveillance and law enforcement are quite elaborate, and administration of rewards and punishments is highly formalized, using the full range of human benefits and costs. Promises, threats, and rituals of solidarity are salient tactics.

Despite the authority and power of the state, individuals play a considerable part in developing their roles and careers through their contributions to the five basic processes. Career mobility is rather poorly defined, even within the specialized ranks of public officials.

Position in the primary and secondary structures of the polity greatly affects the opportunities, personal resources, and skills of the individual. Through attendant changes in these attributes, career mobility exerts a direct effect on self-esteem as well. However, the major individual impact of the polity seems to stem from membership itself, affecting the person's life chances, legal constraints, attitudes, and values. Many social scientists regard cross-national differences in such attributes as reflecting differences in national character: the typical pattern of values, attitudes toward authorities, and personality traits that is said to prevail among the members of a particular national polity.

SUGGESTIONS FOR ADDITIONAL READING

Our reasons for distinguishing between society and the state—that is, for regarding the polity as merely one among several societal-level structures—are rooted in the eloquent arguments of Robert M. MacIver, particularly in his influential book *The Web of Government* (New York: Macmillan, 1947). A more detailed organizational analysis of the polity, from a sociological viewpoint, can be found in Robert E. Dowse and John A. Hughes, *Political Sociology* (New York: Wiley, 1972).

The aspect of collectivity is most clearly seen in analyses of the cultures of polities. A general review is provided in Dennis Kavenagh, *Political Culture* (New York: Macmillan, 1972). The classic study on this topic remains Gabriel A. Almond and Sidney Verba's *The Civic Culture: Political Attitudes and Democracy in Five Nations* (Princeton, N.J.: Princeton University Press, 1963).

LEVELS OF ORGANIZATION

Of the five basic processes, socialization and interaction have received the greatest attention in the context of the polity. See, for example, Barrie Stacey, *Political Socialization in Western Society: An Analysis from a Life-Span Perspective* (New York: St. Martin's, 1978) and Lester W. Milbrath and M. Lal Goel, *Political Participation: How and Why Do People Get Involved in Politics,* 2nd edition (Chicago: Rand McNally, 1977).

The bulk of the social psychological research concerning the individual and his polity has emphasized personality traits, as cause and consequence of political membership and role. A good critical examination of these studies is to be found in Fred I. Greenstein, *Personality and Politics: Problems of Evidence, Inference, and Conceptualizaton,* revised edition (New York: Norton, 1975). A somewhat more germane line of research concerns *Political Identity* (W. J. M. Mackenzie, Manchester: Manchester University Press, 1978).

The buying and selling on the stock exchange floor both reflect and shape economic activity around the world.

CHAPTER 16

The Societal Level: Economy

Even the most primitive human groupings engage in exchanges of goods and services with one another, and such basic cooperative exchanges necessarily underlie any human endeavors. Even Robinson Crusoe brought tools, implements, and weapons—acquired through previous exchanges—to his lonely exile, and he and Friday had to work out a "you do for me, I'll do for you" division of labor.

In any modern nation-state, the economy has been expanded layer upon layer into a complex structure in which the individual's productions ripple outward through many points in the system in which the goods he or she consumes will have emanated from a multitude of distant points. The contents of any ordinary household, for example, represent an incredible nexus of chains of multiply exchanged items. And a great many individuals and organizations measure their successes by their standings in the societal-level structure called the *economy*.

An economy is a collectivity organized to produce and distribute goods and services. Owing in good part to the regulatory activities of nation-states, distinctive economies tend to coincide with the boundaries of polities.

In subsistence economies—generally based on gathering and hunting, on horticulture, or on pastoralism—little surplus of food or other goods is produced beyond the immediate needs of members (Herskovits, 1952). In such economies, families are relatively self-sufficient, serving as the basic units of production, distribution, and consumption. Little internal exchange takes place within the economy, and the levels of consumption of the various family units are quite similar. The division of labor is based largely on age-sex roles—the so-called natural division of labor. Trade with outside groups is sporadic and minimal.

In other economies (Pryor, 1977), a favorable environment and/or a more advanced technology leads to the production of surplus goods. The existence of such surplus production in turn makes possible occupational specialization—the so-called true division of labor. It becomes feasible, for example, for a person skilled in iron-working to devote all his efforts to that work without facing starvation, since he can exchange his iron products for food. Occupational specialization and internal exchange develop hand in hand. With fairly developed specialization, for example, not only an exchange market for goods but also a labor market develops, as production shifts from the family unit to more specialized work organizations that hire workers. Finally, in surplus economies, differential patterns of consumption develop, with some members enjoying greater wealth than others. That is, as differentiation occurs within the economic structure, accompanied by differential valuation of various positions, selective sidepayments come into play. The leaders get more than the widows, and the skilled artisan gets more than his apprentice.

Whereas economists devote most of their attention to the dynamic complexities of exchange markets (that is, to factors of supply, demand, prices, and the like), sociologists' interests in the economy have focused primarily on occupational specialization and on the resultant differentials in wealth. Accordingly, we shall here consider an economy mainly in its aspect of an *occupational structure* (Caplow, 1954; R. Hall, 1975). Of any economy, we would ask: How many occupations are there? What is the nature of those various occupations? What is the numerical distribution of workers across that set of occupations? How are various benefits distributed across that set of occupations? What are the social psychological consequences of various occupational positions and careers?

In the "agrarian/craft" type of occupational structure, for example, there are relatively few distinct occupations, and the great majority of workers is engaged in either agriculture or the crafts (smiths, weavers, carpenters, millers). Even specialized occupations are carried out in or around the worker's home. Of course, differing degrees of competence in these occupations lead to different social standings and wealth levels, and thus to differing quality of life. The person's position in this rudimentary structure thus influences his or her opportunities and self-conception.

In the "industrial" type of occupational structure, on the other hand, the number of occupations is greater and the majority of workers is engaged in some aspect of manufacture—generally performing unskilled or semiskilled labor as wage employees in a factory or similarly specialized work organization separated from their homes.

Sociologists now speak of the "postindustrial" type of economy, in which the majority of workers are "white-collar"—that is, working in offices rather than in factories or on farms—and engaged in providing services rather than in producing material goods.

The type of economy of which the individual is a part—subsistence, agrarian/craft, industrial, postindustrial—will obviously have numerous social psychological implications for many other aspects of his life, from expected life span itself, to degree of interdependence between himself and others, to amount of time and resources for pursuit of other interests.

SOCIAL STRUCTURE

The primary social structure of an economy, then, is its occupational structure, and the basic positions comprising this structure are occupations. "An occupation is the social role performed by adult members of society that directly and/or indirectly yields social and financial consequences and that constitutes a major focus in the life of an adult" (R. Hall, 1975: 6). In this sense, then, even such "nonemployment" roles as housewife, student, or welfare recipient may be occupations. In the U.S. economy, currently some 20,000 distinct occupations are officially recognized, ranging alphabetically from artificial-eye maker through mud-analysis well-logging captain to zyglo inspector (one who examines metal parts for defects by dipping them in a reflective solution and viewing them under black light). More than 300 different types of clerks are distinguished. The nature of each of these thousands of occupations is briefly but precisely described in the U.S. Department of Labor's *Dictionary of Occupational Titles*.

The obvious complexity of such a highly elaborate occupational structure dictates reliance on some simplifying device in order to comprehend the major outlines of that structure. Numerous classificatory schemas for occupations have been put forward, and most reflect the collectivity's belief that the type and level of skill required in an occupation are its most central features. The classificatory schema devised by Alba Edwards for the U.S. Census Bureau has been the most widely adopted. Table 16-1 adopts that schema to depict the U.S. occupational structure on the basis of 1976 data.

Turning from primary to secondary structures, we find that the dimensional social

TABLE 16-1.   Major Occupational Groups as Percentages of 1976 U.S. Employed Labor Force

Major Occupational Group	Percent Distribution	
White-collar workers	49.9	
Professional and technical workers		15.2
Managers, officials, and proprietors (nonfarm)		10.6
Sales workers		6.3
Clerical workers		17.8
Blue-collar workers	33.1	
Craftsmen, foremen, and kindred workers		12.9
Operatives (except transport)		11.5
Transport equipment operatives		3.7
Nonfarm laborers		4.9
Service workers	13.7	
Private household workers		1.3
Other service workers		12.4
Farm workers	3.2	
Farmers and farm managers		1.7
Farm laborers and supervisors		1.5

SOURCE: Bureau of Labor Statistics, U.S. Department of Labor

structure of occupational *status* has received a great deal of attention. Through a nationwide sample survey in 1947, the National Opinion Research Center obtained ratings of the prestige of selected occupations. Using these ratings and census data, O. D. Duncan (Reiss, 1961) devised a socioeconomic status (SES) index that makes it possible to assign status scores to each of the detailed occupational categories recognized by the Census Bureau. Collapsing these categories into the major groups distinguished in the Edwards classificatory schema, we arrive at the average status scores shown in Table 16–2. It should be noted that the status of an occupation and its monetary rewards may not coincide. There are many occupations—such as teacher or minister—with high status and relatively low salaries. Conversely, many garbage collectors, undertakers, and skilled mechanics earn more than most white-collar workers and many professionals. It should also be noted that different status rankings would hold in different economies; in many European countries, professors have a higher relative status than in the United States.

The *power* structure of an economy is a matter of control of economic resources by certain occupations. Karl Marx, of course, emphasized control of capital (the means of production). Proprietors, as well as executives and officials—the proxy counterparts to proprietors in this era of the modern corporation and government bureaucracy—tend to control capital. The other major resource—labor—tends to be controlled by those occupations that are either highly unionized or highly professionalized. Such occupations have the ability to withhold certain types of work temporarily and to control the number of available workers within a given occupation over a longer run. In a sense, the economic power structure extends both above and below the occupational structure. At the top are individuals with such economic power—the Rockefellers or

TABLE 16–2.   Mean Socioeconomic Status Index Scores of Major Occupational Groups, United States, 1950

Major Occupational Group	Mean SES Index Score
White-collar workers	
Professional and technical workers	75
Managers, officials, proprietors (nonfarm)	57
Sales workers	49
Clerical workers	45
Blue-collar workers	
Craftsmen, foremen, and kindred workers	31
Operatives and kindred workers	18
Nonfarm laborers	7
Service workers	
Private household workers	8
Other service workers	17
Farm workers	
Farmers and farm managers	14
Farm laborers and supervisors	9

SOURCE: A.J. Reiss, 1961: 155.

the Gettys, for example—that any job they pursue cannot match their power positions. At the bottom are those who have no occupation, little individual power, and are essentially wards of the state—the unemployed, and those on welfare.

The *authority* structure varies a great deal from economy to economy, both in form and in degree of elaboration. In socialistically organized and totalitarian states, the economy is often essentially administered by the polity. Even here, however, there is usually a relatively free middle and lower occupational stratum. In less centralized regimes, the economy's authority structure is more fragmentary and diffuse, with a smattering of centralized controls, usually over job competence standards in the specialized professions. Although each occupation, however lowly, has a license (the right to carry out certain activities which others may not perform, and to receive compensation for it) and a mandate (the right to define the proper conduct of others toward matters concerning its work), license and mandate tend to be rather weakly developed except in the cases of craft occupations and of professions (Hughes, 1958: 78–87). In relatively few cases is one occupation clearly subordinated to and supervised by another occupation; examples of these exceptional cases include nurses (supervised by physicians) and clerks (supervised by executives). Only a few occupations necessarily include supervisory duties. Interestingly enough, these tend to be male-dominated occupations, with their authority most clearly defined over female-typed occupations; for instance, dentists (over dental hygienists), school superintendents (over teachers), and airline pilots (over stewardesses).

Leadership within an economy tends to come most centrally from government economists and economic planners. However, entrepreneurs, executives, officials, and management consultants also frequently make distinctively significant contributions to the functioning of an economy. Within occupations, leadership tends to be diffuse and reputational, often based on a rough consensus among members on who are opinion leaders and trend-setters in their field.

Suborganizations are always prominent in any economy. Perhaps the most salient official suborganizations are business firms and public agencies, as work organizations comprised of interrelated occupations producing some good or service. Much looser and more unofficial suborganizations include "industries"—clusters of firms or agencies producing similar goods or services, such as the electronics or the airline industries—and "situses," clusters of related industries, such as manufacturing or transportation. Occupational associations such as unions, guilds, and professional associations (see Chapter 19) constitute another important type of official suborganizations. Occupational communities, as we shall see in Chapter 18, represent important but unofficial suborganizations of the economy. In most modern nation-states, there is also a fringe of unofficial suborganizations dealing in illicit and semilegal goods and services—blackmarket weaponry, gambling, influence-peddling, and so on.

A final type of suborganization requiring mention here is the "market." In fact, economists sometimes analyze an economy as a set of markets—for labor, for various specific goods, and for various particular services. Oversimply, the market is the entire web of institutions within which take place all commercial exchanges—buying and selling, employing and paid work, borrowing and lending, trading and contracting, and shopping around for bargains. The market mechanism, with its associated market behavior, is a distinctively important organizational model of social exchange (Schelling, 1978). What goods and services organizations and individuals are able to procure depends heavily upon their relative positions in this market structure.

COLLECTIVITY

The shape of an economy's occupational structure is necessarily influenced by the interests, resources, and culture of that collectivity. After all, interests determine the demand for goods and services. Where enough members are sufficiently interested in whale meat, overseas travel, and baseball, some workers will specialize to satisfy the economic demand for these things. The occupational structure will then include whalers, airline captains, and professional baseball players. A whole advertising industry exists to stimulate interest in various potential goods and services.

The material resources of an economy—particularly its natural resources and its economic technology—greatly constrain which economic interests can be satisfied, to what degree, and at what price. Similarly, its human resources—the number of workers and the skills distribution among them, as roughly indexed by educational level—are a constraint on the distribution of workers across actual and potential occupations. It is difficult for an economy dogged by semiliteracy and little cultural familiarity with machinery to develop an engineering class or to field an air force.

The normative culture of an economy is expressed in the conservative force of custom, which socially defines the acceptability and respectability of various technologies and of the work patterns involved in various occupations (Braibanti and Spengler, 1961). Lores concerning the nature of certain occupations (Caplow, 1954: 134–137) and of how economic forces operate in the universe tend to be highly developed. After all, occupations are themselves important social objects, and the goods and services produced by an economy constitute almost the entire range of cultural objects. An economy, accordingly, exhibits a distinctive vocabulary, as a quick glance at *Business Week* or *Fortune* magazines—let alone an economics textbook—will demonstrate.

The culture of an economy thus embodies a whole range of "definitions of the situation" which a person is likely to encounter in his or her economic life. Through extensive socialization, these shared conceptions become deeply embedded in organizational and individual thinking and behavior.

Economies display something of the force of social habit; their cultures often are weighted with some intertia from the attitudes and the adages of yesterday. For all its investments in "research and development," an economy's deeply ingrained values and standards about work, money, the good life, and so on act both as a stabilizing influence and as a brake on excessive innovation.

254

ORGANIZATIONAL PROCESSES

Recruitment

Selection into an economy is generally ascriptive. An economy recruits its members primarily from the membership of the corresponding polity, although foreigners may be specifically recruited through tactics of attraction to fill manpower needs in certain occupational categories (and thus become aliens in the corresponding polity). Selection is also ascriptively based on age, as occupations are restricted to adults and youths, as defined by the locally prevailing age-sex structure. Finally, one is usually ascriptively recruited into an economic culture of attitudes toward work, measures of success, notions of what is worth striving for, and so on. For instance, those ascriptively recruited into the American middle class have fairly specific standards on what young marrieds should have in the way of lodgings, furniture, and food that differ markedly from Egyptian or Chinese standards.

Placement within the occupational structure is largely voluntary. Only a few occupations, such as soldier or professional football player, are commonly filled through ascriptive drafts. Occupations that require special capital investments or very early socialization—farmer, business proprietor, private professional practitioner, skilled craftsman—display very strong tendencies toward intergenerational occupational inheritance (Blau and Duncan, 1978). For the most part, however, modern economies rely on individual occupational choice and capabilities.

Occupations vary widely in the particular types of knowledge, skills, and physical abilities required for their performance. These requirements are often indexed by formal education, special training, and/or previous experience. In addition to such functional requirements, more strictly social requirements, including age, sex, race, social dialect, family connections, or lifestyle, may be applied to candidates.

Occupational incentives typically include some mix of both intrinsic and extrinsic benefits (Vroom, 1964). Intrinsic benefits include the satisfactions of sheer activity, the exercise of skill (leading to a sense of mastery or productive accomplishment), and social interaction. Central among extrinsic benefits, of course, are financial compensations: wages, salaries, or fees (in ascending order of prestige), fringe benefits, and other material perquisites. Also important as extrinsic benefits are social status, authority over others, security, and prospects for advancement.

Tactics of attraction to an occupation are frequently employed by occupational associations, firms and agencies, industries, or branches of the polity, such as Manpower Planning and the Department of Labor. Promotional advertisements, brochures, and films prominently feature the distinctive incentives associated with a particular occupation.

Vocational guidance programs, particularly in high schools, play a key part in the placement process, providing individualized vocational counseling, based on testing of aptitudes and interests (Peters and Hansen, 1971). Brokerage agencies, such as employment bureaus and job-finding services, also facilitate placement, and licensing boards or committees are key gatekeepers for certain occupations. But in the end, it is the employing firms and agencies themselves that directly enforce occupational requirements and directly administer occupational incentives.

The way in which people find jobs and firms find employees is, however, a "live" social psychological process. Both the individual and the organization employ promotion or advertising, at least at the informal level of letting some people know that a job or an employee is wanted. A great many jobs get filled through already existing interpersonal, family, or friendship networks. Want ads play a part in this process, but here also each side is likely to gather additional data from their interpersonal webs: "What's it like working at the 7-Eleven?" and "How do UCLA grads work out in our production department?"

The majority of a populace tends to be somewhat passive in job selection in that they are not thorough in their search. Frequently, economic pressures, such as the rent coming due, force a person to choose from among the first few alternatives available.

Socialization

Long before entering the world of work, the individual acquires some conception of the occupational structure through anticipatory socialization (Moore, 1969). Children and young people get the idea that they will be expected to work when they become adults and begin to learn the range of accepted social attitudes that go with work in that society. From parents, mass media, and the schools, children learn something of the work nature of at least the major occupational groupings, as well as their requirements and incentives, including the place of these occupational types in the status structure. During the high school years, more explicit communication of expectations occurs through vocational guidance testing, counseling, and materials. Parents and schools greatly develop the individual's capacities, in the form of a work ethic, work motivations, work habits, and an accommodation to impersonal bureaucratic modes of discipline. In modern economies, formal education is vital in developing generally useful knowledge and skills, including the skill of learning itself (B. R. Clark, 1964).

In anticipatory socialization, the child observes firsthand some "facts of life" about work, and is also told or overhears informative remarks: "Sure don't feel like it, but I gotta go to work now." "I haven't missed a day in three years." "Think I'll call in and say I'm sick." "Herman lost his job? Well, it's not surprising. He never showed up for work on time." "I can't tonight, I've got to go see a client."

The child sees father come home sighing with tiredness or cheerful because he made the sale. He or she sees that the parents must prepare meals whether they feel well or not and are exempt only when really "sick in bed." On the farm, the chores get done every day—family fight or harmony, rain or shine, company or Sabbath.

If the child's parents are not successful, relatives, neighbors, or teachers will informally step in with admonitions for the child and will point out more successful models.

Therefore, the child, whatever its background, knows a great deal about the working world long before it draws the first paycheck.

Direct socialization for a specific occupation is somewhat less diffuse (L. Taylor, 1968: 220–234). Tactics for communicating expectations may take the form of job orientation for unskilled occupations; vocational training for skilled and semiskilled occupations; and advanced formal education for technical and professional occupations. One major aim of a medical school, for example, is simply to teach what it is to be a physician. For other than unskilled occupations, development of individual capacities requires specific formal training, through trade schools, apprenticeship, technical schools, or professional schools. The medical school, for example, also aims to teach how to do the work of a physician—it strives to develop the requisite attitudes, technical knowledge, and practical skills. For unskilled occupations, the necessary capacities are generally developed through minimal on-the-job training and probationary employment. There is, then, a rough correlation between the rewards and status of an occupation and the amount of formal and informal training required for it.

Resocialization efforts, too, are quite visible within an occupational structure. Many workers change occupations and must therefore be retrained (Hoos, 1967), and increasingly even workers who are firmly established within an occupation require updating of their knowledge and skills in order to keep up with advances or changes in their chosen line of work (Hall and Miller, 1975).

Interaction

Within an occupational structure, the interaction process is a matter of occupational performance. Various aspects of work-related interactions will be discussed in Chapters 18 through 22. Here we would wish to point out only that since work is such a central part of most adult individuals' lives, on-the-job interactions tend to form a very important part of one's interpersonal life. Fellow workers are often core significant others, and a large proportion of adults find their friendships, role-models—and even mates—in the workplace.

Innovation

Innovations may be externally imposed on an economy, as through war mobilization, or internally planned, as through manpower planning by executive agencies of the polity. Many changes in an occupational structure are, however, internally emergent, through the diffuse dynamics of the labor market. In response to changing markets for goods and services, to technological change, and to demographic shifts in the population, the demand for specific types of work may shift markedly. Some occupations disappear and new occupations emerge. Moreover, the nature of any particular occupation may change significantly in response to technological innovation or to the modern trend toward professionalization of occupations (Scoville, 1969). Such emergent changes, reflecting the informal and democratic diffuse ratification process of the market mechanism, receive more formal and autocratic ratification through explicit recognition by personnel officers of employing firms and the job analysis officials of the Department of Labor (Fryklund, 1970).

Not all occupations receive such official ratification, of course. A sizable number of well-established deviant occupations (such as prostitute, thief, gambler) remain officially stigmatized by omission from the *Dictionary of Occupational Titles* and are thus "odd jobs" indeed (G. Miller, 1978; Letkemann, 1973). These too, however, must often change with changing conditions. For example, the thief must gain new skills in order to surmount advances in security systems.

The inertia of established culture within an occupation, sometimes coupled with large investments in its existing procedures and techniques, acts as something of a brake on innovations. For example, the American automotive industry, despite data-based warnings from expert economists, was slow to retool for production of small cars in the 1970s and as a result lost a great deal of its domestic market. Even scientific research can become somewhat plodding and conventionalized under such inertia, and acceptance of leading-edge research can suffer from the same cultural lag, as with slow acceptance over the last decade of research findings on nutrition and immunological systems. Thus, even professionals sometimes walk backward into their own futures, as history has repeatedly demonstrated.

Social Control

Within an occupational structure, social control is centrally accomplished by making receipt of occupational incentives contingent upon satisfying occupational requirements. That is, the individual whose vocational performance is judged to be in conformity with occupational requirements will receive its basic intrinsic and extrinsic benefits. Creative performance is typically rewarded by promotion to a higher-ranking occupation with correspondingly greater benefits. (The Peter Principle points out, however, that this mechanism of reward frequently leads to occupational mismatches, since the skills so clearly demonstrated in the first occupation do not necessarily entail possession of the somewhat different skills required for the higher occupation [Peter and Hull, 1969]. A good shop foreman, for example, may make a lousy junior executive, and a good medical diagnostician may prove to be a terrible hospital administrator.) Deviant performance is typically punished by loss of basic benefits, through unemployment within that occupation. This in turn frequently leads to effective demotion by having to accept employment in a lower occupation with correspondingly lower benefits. Fellow members of an occupation, sharing a common culture, are often reluctant to target one of their own for stigmatization. Often, they will do so only if the performance deviation is gross. Doctors, lawyers, policemen, and ministers have proven very reluctant to testify against one of their fellows in malpractice or incompetence hearings. Within the occupation itself, the erring individual more often simply loses status, referrals, and any advancements, which not infrequently lead to the person's eventually being recruited out of the occupation.

At the aggregate level, surveillance within the occupational structure takes the form of some agency of the polity gathering labor statistics (based on personnel records of firms) to monitor occupational trends of the labor market. Differential benefits of the various occupations are essentially determined by demand factors in the labor market, but they are also conditioned by skill requirements, status, organizational strength of occupational associations, and sex composition (Bielby and Kalleburg, 1975). For instance, a strongly organized profession controlling a service vital to the public can increase members' rewards and can perhaps even maintain an artificial scarcity by limiting the number of its members through its control of schools and licensing agencies.

At the individual level, both surveillance and the determination of rewards and punishments are basically functions of the diffuse response of the labor market to the person's own vocational credentials. In some occupations, peer review of those credentials may influence market response. Entry into and continued practice in the occupation may depend on formal peer-review processes by organizational associations, such as the bar association (for lawyers) or the union (for plumbers). More informally, similar processes of peer review may be conducted by occupational communities, as for instance among scientists.

ROLE-MAKING AND CAREER DEVELOPMENT

As Kohn and Schooler (1973) have shown, the individual shapes his occupation as surely as he is shaped by it.

Because the placement process within an occupational structure is primarily voluntary, the individual has a great deal of influence on his position within that structure. In fact, numerous theories of occupational choice have been developed to illuminate that influence. Blau et al. (1956) emphasize the sociological determinants not only of the individual's abilities and characteristics but more directly of his knowledge about various occupations (the nature of the work, requirements, incentives) and of the values he places on various occupational incentives. Sewell et al. (1970) give direct weight to the heavy influence of significant others on the individual's occupational and educational aspirations. Ginzberg et al. (1951) and Tiedeman and O'Hara (1963) more explicitly analyze the dynamic process through which an individual, often tentatively, chooses his occupation and frequently revises that choice at some later point.

One factor, of course, in the individual's choosing of an occupation is his own assessment of his vocational credentials relative to his knowledge of the requirements for various attractive occupations. In many cases, he may undertake great efforts to prepare himself to meet the rules and standards of a desired occupation—often by actively cooperating in his own socialization. For instance, realizing that specialized education is necessary, he may spend hundreds of hours in specific preparation to score well on the standardized aptitude tests for admission to professional school and then devote several years of very hard work within the curriculum of that school. At various points in the application process, a carefully selective presentation of self (through formal credentials and through personal interviews) can often enhance the candidate's attractiveness, as many popular "how-to-get-your-job" books emphasize (for example, Greco, 1975).

Career, like position, is significantly influenced by individual tactics. A person's career within a single occupation will be treated in Chapter 18. Here, our interest is in his career within the occupational structure as a whole. Career in this sense is essentially a matter of occupational mobility, of movement from one occupation to another (Slocum, 1966). Occupational mobility may be vertical, to an occupation higher or lower in the status structure, or horizontal, to an occupation on the same level of status. Research has shown such mobility to be almost universal, with most workers changing occupations several times. The height an individual eventually reaches within the occupational structure has been shown to be greatly influenced by the level of his initial entry, that is, his first occupation. In turn, initial entry point is affected most significantly by educational level, and secondarily by social background, as indexed by father's education and occupation (Blau and Duncan, 1978).

A conventional career sequence and a timetable have been put forward by D. Miller and Form (1964). The first, or preparatory, phase (from birth through about age 15) is devoted to largely informal anticipatory socialization. The second phase is the initial work period of part-time and full-time employment concurrent with high school and college education (and more formal vocational guidance). Third, a trial work period ensues, with rather frequent job changes until the individual secures a more or less permanent occupation. By at least his mid-thirties, he is expected to have settled down into a fourth, or stable, work phase, characterized by development of strong ties to one occupation (see, for example, Becker and Carper, 1956a, 1956b, concerning the process of identification with an occupation). Fifth, there is a retirement phase, typically around age 65.

Several less conventional career patterns are fairly common, however (Miller and Form, 1964; Super, 1957). The stable career pattern is one in which the individual moves directly and permanently from his schooling into the stable work period, omitting the trial work phase. The unstable career pattern, on the other hand, exhibits high horizontal mobility, with the person going from trial jobs to stable work, then back to trial jobs, on to stable work in a different occupation, and so on. Even more pronounced in horizontal mobility is the multiple-trial career pattern, in which the individual never remains in one occupation long enough to achieve stable employment but instead moves from one trial job to another. There is another pattern in which the person displays upward mobility, with each occupation serving something of a training ground and steppingstone for the next, for example, from practicing lawyer, to politician's staff, to official, to consulting elder statesman. There are also those individuals who gain success in a field and then move on to other challenges, and those who work at an occupation while pursuing some hobby such as writing, ceramics, or coin collecting, and eventually leave the occupation to pursue the former hobby full-time when it has become lucrative enough to make them a living. Finally, we might mention the unconventional pattern of the individual who has fallen out of favor, has been disgraced, or has simply left a prestigious occupation to turn to a less notable (but perhaps more intrinsically rewarding) occupation such as running a sports shop or being a housewife.

It should also be pointed out that events external to the occupation or to the person's own competence and intentions may intervene to produce an unconventional career. Examples would include failures within an industry, the ''ripple effect'' of failures in related industries, major technological advances, and so on. For example, the advent of the automobile virtually did away with the blacksmithing craft. Such career shocks can have a drastic and continuing social psychological effect upon the individual. With diminished income, the individual is often prone to further career shocks, such as the loss of his home and a lowered stardard of living. The healthiest outcome is a new career, and many achieve this. For those who do not, one often finds such a career shock to have been a negative turning point in their personal lives.

Individual strategies for career management within the occupational structure are a recurrent subject of many popular books (Souerwine, 1978) and some scholarly works (Thompson, Avery, and Carlson, 1962) and appear to be a significant factor in the process of career development.

IMPACT ON THE CHARACTER OF THE INDIVIDUAL

The particular economy in which an individual participates is quite significant. Economies vary not only in their average standards of living but also in their occupational structures—the types of occupations available to a member as well as their respective requirements and incentives. The nature of an occupational structure directly affects the occupational aspirations of individuals. In the postindustrial type, more persons aspire to service occupations, such as social worker or travel agent, than in an industrial type. Labor markets may be relatively free or quite ascriptive; they may have either high demand for labor or a surplus of workers. Ascriptive labor markets greatly constrain occupational aspirations, and labor demand influences occupational expectations; where demand is slack because of extensive unemployment, individuals' expectations tend to be lower than their aspirations.

The individual's position and role in an economy—that is, his occupation—by definition dictate what behaviors he engages in during the majority of his waking hours. In many cases, occupation constitutes a central life interest (Orzack, 1959). Accordingly, occupation greatly determines many of his habits, skills, perceptions, interests, and attitudes, as shown by numerous studies in vocational psychology (Super and Bohn, 1970). Work as an accountant, for example, develops a person's tendency to check and recheck his own and others' work, the speed and accuracy of his computations, his ability to quickly spot arithmetic errors, his interest in tax-law changes, and his social/political position (conservatism). In fact, one's role in the occupational structure is a major source of personal identity: ''A man's work is as good a clue as

261

any to the course of his life, and to his social being and identity'' (Hughes, 1958: 7). The life and character of any farmer, for example, differ sharply and consistently from those of a dentist, a cab driver, or a prostitute.

One's corollary position within the *secondary* social structures of the economy exercises independent effects on the individual. For example, work satisfaction has been shown repeatedly to correlate positively with status of occupation, and work dissatisfactions—particularly, alienation and stress—occur most among lower-ranking occupations (R. Hall, 1975: 41–64).

More broadly, the lifestyle of an individual—his area of residence, type of housing and other material possessions, family size and structure, child-rearing practices, type of leisure activities and cultural possessions, travel, social participation, values and attitudes—depend primarily on his socioeconomic status, i.e., the prestige level of his occupation (Rothman, 1978).

The fundamental ''life chances'' of the individual depend directly on his social class—the level of wealth associated with, or derived from, his occupation. Life chances include not only life expectancy itself but also level of physical and mental health, educational attainment, mobility prospects, and marital stability. The greater one's wealth, the greater are one's life chances in each of these respects (Hurst, 1979).

The individual's *career* within the occupational structure also has its personal effects. No matter what his specific career pattern, movement into the world of work profoundly alters his personal situation, and movement into the retirement phase always entails major readjustments. Becoming a worker requires subordination of self to the demands of one's job, a lessening of freedom in scheduling personal pursuits of daily life (N. Anderson, 1961). Retirement involves diminished income and a loss of routine, of purpose, and of familiar associates, as well as an adjustment of family roles within the household (Streib and Schneider, 1971). Between these two endpoints, conventional occupational mobility generally carries with it increasing material benefits, prestige, responsibility, and authority. When occupational expectations do not fall too short of aspirations, or career movements do not lag too far behind expectations, the person's self-esteem tends to remain positive. Deviant career sequences and/or timetables—particularly common among women and minority groups—affect not only life chances and lifestyle but also self-esteem. A woman's occupational career, interrupted or delayed by child-rearing, may not rise as far or as fast as her childless peers. Delayed, blocked, or downward mobility—especially if unexpected—generally fosters a sense of frustration, resentment, or despair, and always dictates some redefinition of self and personal priorities (Wilensky and Edwards, 1959; Wilensky, 1960).

Finally, the impact of social change upon an economy can have a great many implications for the individual. Most people experience one or more major economic social changes during their life career. Extreme examples include runaway inflation, as in Brazil and Israel in the late 1970s; major depressions, as in the Western world during the 1930s; and wartime economy, as most of the world experienced in varying degrees in the 1940s. Less extreme, but more frequent, are recessions, easing or tightening of credit, fluctuations in interest rates, unemployment, and shortages of basic goods. There are winners and losers in such social changes, but all entail increased uncertainty for the majority of individuals and organizations. It is in a sense a tribute to individuals and organizations that so many of them come through massive social changes in the economy more or less intact and doing well.

INTERORGANIZATIONAL RELATIONS AMONG SOCIETAL-LEVEL STRUCTURES

One of the most important facts influencing any societal-level structure—speech community, age-sex structure, polity, economy—is that it never exists in isolation. First, each is embedded in a poorly structured but powerful planetary organization of which it is a member. At least in some shadowy sense, each of the five basic processes can be applied to it as such a member. For example, no polity can entirely ignore global opinion without being on the receiving end of some inconvenient social control sanctions.

Second, any societal-level structure may find itself influenced by, and influencing, any other societal-level structure. Moves by a Middle East economy may impinge upon the American age-sex structure by curtailing travel for senior citizens because of increased fuel costs. Conversely, the American polity may influence another Middle Eastern speech community—and perhaps age-sex structure and eventually polity—by training large numbers of their young people in our universities. Such influences are very complex but ubiquitous chains which require a historian's craft to trace.

Third, each type of societal-level structure has relationships with its fellows, as in Olympic competitions among polities and the fluctuating economic standings of various national currencies.

Fourth, within any geographical area, the four types of structures have intimate, overlapping relationships one to the other—sometimes in conflict, often in alliance, most commonly in some balance of accommodations. Hitler, as head of the polity, was continually working out mutually acceptable accommodations with the German economy.

Fifth, the structures overlap in terms of the smaller organizations which are embedded within them, such as the community and the family. Indeed, they must often compete for the loyalty, support, and resources of this multitude of embedded smaller organizations, a competition which sometimes translates into role strain for the individuals. For example, does a young man want be "be with the guys," support and help his newly pregnant wife, or answer the call of his country's mobilization in the Vietnam conflict?

Thus, interorganizational relationships among the four societal-level structures are important for all organizations and individuals involved, and they are very much the prevailing scene.

Within a particular geographical domain, the overlapping societal-level structures usually develop a number of organizational positions to handle these relationships: political, economic, and cultural delegates to various United Nations organizations, for instance, or diplomats, trade commissioners, and lobbyists for particular age-sex categories. The president has economic advisers, and the corporations have attorneys and public relations personnel to deal with impingements from the polity.

The individual may also become embroiled in relations between societal-level structures. Particularly, he or she must balance the demands and expectations of each and achieve some sort of accommodation through which an acceptable standing is maintained in each of them. This might be difficult if it were not for the fact that the structures do overlap to such an extent that success within one sphere facilitates successes within the others. For example, a girl who achieves well in her age-sex category and speech community is likely also to do well economically and politically, through enhanced opportunities.

To grasp a further understanding of the social psychological impacts of relationships among societal-level structures, let us turn to some of the specifics. Each of the four structures exhibits a fairly full range of relationships with organizations of the *same type*. Speech communities, age-sex structures, polities, and economies all compete with their counterparts for human and material resources, and all engage their counterparts in rivalry for recognition of the distinctive qualities of their products—a higher literature, a more just age-sex division of labor, a more responsive or more disciplined citizenry, a higher standard of living. Such competition and rivalry can often result in conflict (even violent conflict), although conflict is more common and visible between polities than between the other types of structures. Cooperation is sometimes seen between polities, in the form of alliances or joint projects, but is somewhat more frequently observed between economies. Exchange relations, in the form of external trading, are of course the bread and butter of economies.

But more pertinent here are relations between different types of societal-level structures. We have already noted that in modern times a speech community tends to be paired with an age-sex structure, and a polity with an economy. What remains to be explored are the relations between these two pair types.

One such relation emerges where one large speech community, such as that of the Spanish or the English language, and its associated age-sex structure are in effect cross-cut by political/economic boundaries. The English-speaking world, for example, exhibits national subdivisions: Great Britain, the United States, Australia, and so on. The organizational character of the polity and the economy of each of these nation-states modify the cultures of the speech community and the age-sex structure, resulting in fairly distinctive geographical variants and, quite often, fully developed subcultures. It is for this reason that "societies" are so often equated with nation-states; "mostly, when we look for a society, we find a political unit, and when speaking of the former we mean in effect the latter" (Nadel, 1951: 187). Thus, when a speech community contains a number of polities, we can expect that influences from the polity will produce distinctive subcultures, so that members of each polity will inhabit somewhat distinctive social worlds.

On the other hand, since there are some three or four thousand distinct languages but only somewhat more than 150 nation-states, it follows that most national polities and economies must be cross-cut by several speech communities (and their associated age-sex structures). Indeed, most nations *are* multilingual, although many of these have designated only one language as the official medium of political and economic discourse (Katzner, 1975; Fishman, Cooper, and Conrad, 1977). But even if two or three languages are formally recognized as official, all the incorporated speech communities are engaged in competition, rivalry, and sometimes even violent conflict (Stewart, 1968; Kloss, 1967). In this process, the various speech communities become key suborganizations of both the polity and the economy, arrayed along dimensions of power and status in the phenomenon of "ethnic stratification" (Shibutani and Kwan, 1965). Each of these embedded speech community/age-sex structures will have its own culture and hence a unique social psychological world which its members inhabit. The standing of each ethnic subculture, compared with the others, will influence the members' opportunities and color their daily lives. Those in the dominant subcultures may almost automatically "have it made," at least in terms of minimum survival, while those in the lowest-ranking subcultures may be more or less automatically condemned to a bleak existence.

The United States, for example, constitutes both a geographical variant of the English speech community (and its age-sex structure) and a multilingual nation, with dozens of languages spoken by significant numbers of citizens, even though only English is an official language. Various ethnic groups, through speech-community loyalties, seek to maintain their languages and to obtain greater official recognition for them—for instance, in the form of bilingual instruction in the public schools. Many of these groups—including speakers of Spanish, Chinese, and Vietnamese—strive to obtain institutional concessions to the distinctive features of their age-sex role systems, where these differ from the age-sex structure of Anglo-Americans. In multilingual nations, a number of members are necessarily bilingual. Their speech repertoires include two languages, and perhaps more than one social dialect of each. An important topic in sociolinguistics, then, is the factors that determine which social dialect of which language is employed in various social domains and situations (Fishman, 1972).

SIGNIFICANCE OF OVERLAPPING SOCIETAL-LEVEL STRUCTURES

Each societal-level structure by itself has a tremendous impact on the character of any member. Perhaps no social phenomenon has been so thoroughly documented as the pervasiveness and persistence of the impact of membership norms, roles, and careers within the four types of societal-level structures on the whole range of individual attributes. Over the past few decades, a vast portion of the literature of all the social sciences has been devoted to demonstrations of language differences, age differences, sex differences, national differences, occupational differences, and social class differences on nearly every conceivable individual-level variable (see, for example, Willerman, 1979). Societal-level structures do influence individuals.

Since the interrelationships of societal-level structures are so complex, an individual's positions in all of them tend to be highly correlated. Consider, for example, position in the status structure of each societal-level structure. Within any nation-state, the political elite—dominated by occupants of the most prestigious age-sex categories—corresponds quite closely to the economic elite, the occupational elite, and the linguistic elite (Bottomore, 1964).

The sociological concept of social stratification of a "national society" implicitly regards socioeconomic status (social classes, socioeconomic status levels, status communities, and so on) as the fundamental suborganizations, effectively cross-cutting all societal-level structures. Each stratum is considered to have its own characteristic social dialect, political role, and so forth. Indeed, the notion of "class culture" (Rodman, 1968) asserts that each stratum has its own distinctive values, attitudes, beliefs, customs, and practices—its own way of life, cutting across the polity, the occupational structure, the age-sex structure, and the speech communities. Beginning with Kahl's (1957) work, much has been written concerning the lower-class culture (W. B. Miller, 1958), the working-class culture (S. Miller and Riesmann, 1961), the middle-class culture (Gans, 1962a), and the upper-class culture (Baltzell, 1958).

What is the social psychological significance of such correlated positions, of social strata cross-cutting the four societal-level structures of a national society? To grasp the full significance, we must understand a major issue in the study of the impact of social organization on the individual.

The field of "culture and personality," or psychological anthropology, has long sought to analyze the influences of national society on the individual member. Fundamentally, research in this field has attempted to show how immersion in a common societal culture produces in each of its members a "typical personality," character type, or social self, distinctively different from that of other societies. Around 1950, such research came under serious criticism as (1) being logically circular in its conceptualization of culture and of personality; (2) relying too heavily on projective tests and other culturally biased measures; and (3) most important, ignoring or explaining away substantial variability in individual character within the membership of any single society.

Indeed, much of this criticism was leveled by sociological social psychologists (for example, Lindesmith and Strauss, 1950). Sociologists have generally favored the alternative approach of "social structure and personality," rejecting the uniformity assumption of a one-to-one relation between the culture of a "national society" and a typical personality or character type. Instead, they emphasize the crucial importance of structural position in shaping personal characteristics. For example, extremely wealthy Arabs and Americans would have more in common with each other than they would with the poor of their own country. Bock (1980) distinguishes three broad versions of this alternative approach. The *materialist* (or Marxist) version holds that, ultimately, all social psychology is "class psychology"; a person's social class (irrespective of societal membership) largely determines his beliefs, actions, and characteristics. The *positionalist* version considers that social class is but one of a number of social positions that influence belief, action, and other personal characteristics; for example, that position in the age-sex structure, in the ethnic stratification system, and even birth-order position within the family exert comparable influences on the individual. The *interactionist* version is more concerned with effects of the person's immediate situation, contending that one's self or sense of identity is continually constructed from ongoing interactions. According to Bock, these three versions of the "social structure and personality" approach "are united by the fact that they all address the [social] psychological characteristics of groups or roles within a society or across several societies rather than characteristics alleged to be typical of entire societies" (1980: 185).

Each of these approaches has contributed its insights, yet when taken alone each seems inadequate to depict the full scope of the individual in organized society. That is to say, *both* culture and social structure seem necessary in examining the relation of the individual to his or her society. After all, any social organization exhibits both an aspect of collectivity and an aspect of social structure. The aspect of collectivity involves a sharing of collective interests, collective resources, and a common culture; such sharing implies, in turn, the likelihood of *some* common effects on its members. The aspect of social structure, on the other hand, involves differentiated social positions and social roles, with differential sidepayments and special interests; such social differentiation implies, in turn, the likelihood of *some* differential effects on its members by position. Some effects would be uniform, while other effects would be variable.

Accordingly, in each of the chapters of Part III, we have addressed the impact on the character of the individual of his membership in the collectivity and of his position and role within its social structure. At the societal level of social organization, these two classes of effects are summarized in Table 16–3. A "national society," as a

TABLE 16–3. Personal Impacts of Membership, Position/Role, and Career within Societal-Level Structures

Societal-Level Structures	Impact of Membership	Impact of Position/Role	Impact of Career
Speech Community	Provides share in collective good of *communication* Limits with whom he can communicate directly Dictates membership in a particular age-sex structure Constrains which nation-states one could effectively reside in Provides system of concepts words, and beliefs—"culturally constituted environment"—which channels one's cognition, perception, memory, fundamental self-concept Provides cultural values, mores, conventions, and	Primary roles limit one's capacities to receive help from others, to influence others, to regulate one's own behaviors, to form conceptions of self and others Primary roles bound extent of one's direct and indirect interaction within the speech community Both primary roles and position in secondary social structures limit one's personal opportunities in most other organizations	Conventional career pattern provides increasing communication and interpersonal skills and increasing personal opportunities in all other organizations Unconventional career pattern deprives one of intrinsic role benefits, limits personal opportunities in all other organizations, favors development of low self-esteem

(continued)

TABLE 16–3.   (CONT.)

Societal-Level Structures	Impact of Membership	Impact of Position/Role	Impact of Career
Speech Community (*Cont.*)	habits, which in turn influence one's physical appearance, interests, feelings, emotions, skills, perceptions, traits, preferred personality type		
Age-sex Structure	Provides share in collective good of *social order* Provides differentiated concepts of and expectations toward persons, based simply on outwardly visible clues of age and sex Provides primordial yet differentiated standards— mores, conventions of propriety—for evaluating own and others' interpersonal conduct	Position in both primary and secondary structures limits and channels one's personal opportunities in most other organizations Role provides fundamental social expectations regarding virtually all of one's individual attributes Role provides fundamental template for assessing developmental normality and competence of one's personal identity	Career movements reflect and affect changes in nearly every individual attribute Career movements tend to engender life crisis and to threaten personal identity Conventionalized career trajectory provides a conceptual framework for interpreting one's personal changes as a normal developmental process of self-transformation Unconventional career pattern heightens the impacts of career movements and favors development of low self-esteem
Polity	Provides share in collective good of *public safety and welfare* Enforces sharing in collective costs of production (through taxation of various sorts), affecting personal resources Dictates membership in a particular economy Imposes legal prescriptions and proscriptions regulating many aspects of personal life Favors development of characteristic pattern of political values, attitudes toward authorities, and personality traits	Position in both primary and secondary structures limits one's rights, personal opportunities, and personal resources Role provides strong social expectations regarding one's development of certain political knowledge, beliefs, values, interests, attitudes, skills, participation Role often provides a source of personal identity	Career mobility (typically within secondary structures) dictates patterned alterations in one's rights, personal opportunities, and personal resources Career mobility engenders changes in one's self-concept and political identity Career movements inconsistent with one's aspirations and/or expectations tend to diminish self-esteem

(continued)

TABLE 16–3.   (CONT.)

Societal-Level Structures	Impact of Membership	Impact of Position/Role	Impact of Career
Economy	Provides share in collective good of *average standard of living* Limits the types of occupations and associated benefits available, thus influencing one's aspirations and expectations Determines level of demand for labor, again influencing one's aspirations and expectations	Role dictates one's principal activities during majority of waking hours, thus favoring development of particular habits, skills, perceptions, beliefs, interests, and attitudes Role often provides a central life interest and always provides a major source of personal identity Role is primary source of one's material resources Position in secondary structures limits one's fundamental life chances, influences one's work satisfaction, and channels one's fundamental lifestyle	Entry into and exit from the occupational structure always affect one's personal resources, opportunities, habits, interests, associates, and personal identity Conventional career pattern provides (until point of retirement) generally increasing material benefits, prestige, responsibility, and authority Unconventional career pattern tends adversely to affect life chances, lifestyle, and self-esteem

polity/economy producing a distinctively variant speech-community/age-sex structure, might indeed induce among its members some common tendencies befitting the term "national character." The effects of position with the social structures of such a "national society"—particularly, position within the ethnic stratification system of incorporated speech communities and the social stratification system of socioeconomic strata—might or might not overshadow the membership effects of national character. Methodologically speaking, the effects of membership and the effects of position confound and obscure one another. Research on their relative importance is, therefore, particularly difficult, and we take no a priori position on that issue. Where the collectivity of a "national society" is especially strong, we would expect a "national character" to predominate in influence. Where stratification is pronounced, as in a caste system, we would expect stratum to predominate in influence. But we would expect to find *no* societal organization where both the common culture and internal social differentiation do not have some influence.

Finally, we note yet a third approach which might be called "career and personality," concerned with the influence of career movement on change and continuity in the character of individuals. After all, career movement always involves changes (with greater or lesser continuity) in the person's life situation: in his associates (including reference groups and significant others), in role expectations, in opportunities, in benefits and costs, and in activities. A person's objective career trajectory thus reflects and affects changes in his individual attributes—particularly his opportunities, personal resources, skills, interests, attitudes, and standards—through a process of transformation of character. On the subjective side, career movement produces a transformation of self-concept and personal identity. The culturally expected career trajectory provides the individual with aspirations and expectations for personal change—where he might be going and where he has been, how far he has come and how far he has to go, whether he is moving quickly or slowly. Against this background, then, career movement engenders a wide range of feelings and emotions. As with any voyage, setting out from one position to another engenders (1) a sense of excitement, anticipation, opportunity, and challenge; (2) a sense of risk, danger, and fear of mistakes; and (3) the pain of relinquishing the old and familiar. Upon completion of the transition, the person may feel some mixture of satisfaction, gratification, achievement, relief, nostalgia, anger, or resentment about his move. Most important, however, are his feelings about himself; the move may lead the person to regard himself with pride or with shame, as a success or a failure, as normal or abnormal. At the societal level of social organization, the effects on the individual of his careers within the various structures are also summarized in Table 16–3.

As Table 16–3 indicates and as we have emphasized in the last four chapters, these structures do not *determine* the character of the individual so much as set up recipes, boundaries, and predispositions toward certain outlooks and behaviors. They do not tell the whole story of any life. Jack and Jill still give the live performance.

SUMMARY

An economy is a collectivity organized to produce and distribute goods and services. Owing largely to the regulatory activities of nation-states, each polity tends to spawn an accompanying distinct economy.

In subsistence economies, families are the basic economic units, internal exchange and wealth differentials are minimal, and division of labor is based largely on age-sex roles. In surplus economies, division of labor is based on occupational specialization, a labor market, and internal exchange, with resulting wealth differentials among families.

Unlike economists, sociologists tend to focus on the occupational structure of any economy: the number, nature, prevalence, and associated benefits of its occupations. The principal broad types of occupational structures include the agrarian/craft, the industrial, and the postindustrial.

The primary role structure of any economy is its occupational structure. Occupations can also be located in dimensional social structures of status, power (based on occupations' control of capital or labor), authority, and leadership. Important suborganizations include business firms and public agencies; industries, or clusters of related firms; situses, or clusters of related industries; occupational associations; and occupational communities. The "market" is both an important type of suborganization and a vital mechanism of social exchange.

An economy's occupational structure is shaped by the collectivity's interests (determining the demands for various goods and services), its material resources (including economic technology), its human resources (numbers and skills of workers), and its normative culture (regarding work and occupations).

Selection of individuals into an economy is generally ascriptive, while placement within the occupational structure is, in modern economies, largely voluntary, shaped by the differential incentives and requirements of the various occupations. Such incentives include a wide range of both extrinsic and intrinsic benefits.

Anticipatory socialization, beginning in childhood, is typically diffuse. Direct socialization for a particular occupation tends to be more explicit and more formal, the extent and duration varying with the skill requirements of the occupation. Resocialization is common, as workers change their lines of work and as occupations themselves undergo change.

Interaction is a matter of occupational performance, dealt with in several later chapters. Innovations may be externally imposed on an occupational structure, may be internally planned, or (most often) may be internally emergent through the diffuse dynamics of the labor market and technological innovations with subsequent formal ratification by official agencies.

Social control of occupational performance is largely diffuse, through the dynamics of the labor market, although some occupations exert formal internal reviews. Centrally, the social control process relies on making receipt of occupational incentives contingent upon satisfying occupational requirements.

Because the placement process is primarily voluntary, the individual has a great deal of influence on his role within the occupational structure, as explained by various theories of occupational choice and works on individual tactics in occupational placement. Career within the occupational structure (as distinguished from career within any occupation) is a matter of occupational mobility—movement from one occupation to another. The conventional career sequence involves a preparatory phase, an initial work period, a trial work period, a stable work phase, and a retirement phase. However, a number of less conventional career patterns and timetables can also be identified. Individual strategies of career management appear to be a significant influence on career trajectory.

The economy in which an individual participates affects his average standard of living, occupational aspirations, and occupational expectations. His position and role in the economy—that is, his occupation—dictates his behaviors during most of each day and thus influences many of his habits, skills, perceptions, interests, and attitudes. Occupation may or may not be a central life interest of the individual, but it is always a major source of personal identity. Position within the dimensional social structures of the economy is a vital influence in several respects: satisfaction and lifestyle depend heavily on the status level of his occupation, and his very life chances (life expectancy, health, educational attainment, mobility prospects, marital stability) depend on his social class or level of wealth. Significant social changes within the economy, such as depressions or wartime mobilizations, also greatly affect the subsequent life course of the individual. Career trajectory affects life chances, lifestyle, and self-esteem of the individual, and career movements—particularly entry into and exit from the world of work—entail major readjustments in personal life.

271

LEVELS OF ORGANIZATION

This chapter concludes the four-chapter examination of societal-level structures. Such structures engage their counterparts in other societies in relations of competition, rivalry, conflict, cooperation, and exchange. More pertinent, each type of societal-level structure relates to every other type. In modern times, for example, one speech community tends to be paired with one age-sex structure, and each polity tends to be paired with some economy. Typically, such pairs tend to cross-cut one another. A large speech community/age-sex structure pair may be cross-cut by political/economic boundaries, with each subdivision resulting in variant geographical subcultures or "national societies." Most polity/economy pairs are multilingual—cross-cut by several speech communities, with resultant ethnic stratification. Since societal-level structures overlap in these ways, a person's positions within each of them tend to be closely related. Any "national society" is socially stratified, with socioeconomic strata cross-cutting all four societal-level structures.

The social psychological significance of such overlapping and cross-cutting has been a subject of some controversy. The *culture and personality* approach, favored by anthropologists and political scientists, attempts to show how the culture of a "national society" produces in its members a "typical personality" or a "national character." The alternative approach of *social structure and personality* rejects the uniformity assumption and addresses social psychological characteristics of positions, roles, and situations rather than characteristics alleged to be typical of entire societies. But since any social organization is both a collectivity and a social structure, it seems likely that membership would induce some common effects and that position/role would engender differential effects. The two types of effects confound and obscure one another, so that is very difficult to decide their relative importance and thus to choose between the two approaches. An obvious answer seems to be that both have impact. A third approach—*career and personality*—is concerned with the influence of changes in position on change and continuity in the character of individuals. In Table 16–3, all three types of effects—the influences of membership, position and role, and career—are summarized for each of the four societal-level structures.

SUGGESTIONS FOR ADDITIONAL READING

Too few students of sociology or social psychology have any real background in economics. Only one textbook in any field has ever won its author a Nobel Prize; that textbook is Paul A. Samuelson's *Economics,* now in its tenth edition (New York: McGraw-Hill, 1976).

A general sociological introduction to the economy is Neil J. Smelser's little volume *The Sociology of Economic Life,* 2nd edition (Englewood Cliffs, N.J.: Prentice-Hall, 1976). But the primary role structure of an economy is its occupational structure. An excellent textbook of occupational sociology is Richard H. Hall's *Occupations and the Social Structure,* 2nd edition (Englewood Cliffs, N.J.: Prentice-Hall, 1975). Peter M. Blau and Otis Dudley Duncan provide a more detailed and technical analysis of *The American Occupational Structure* (New York: Free Press, 1978).

The Societal Level: Economy

The process of recruitment into the occupational structure has been widely ana-
lyzed as one of occupational choices and decisions; see, for example, William H.
Sewell, Archibald G. Haller, and George W. Ohlendorf, "The Educational and Early
Occupational Attainment Process: Replication and Revision" (*American Sociological
Review,* 1970, 35: 1014–1027). Extensive research on "Occupational Socialization" is
reviewed by Wilbert E. Moore (pp. 861–883 in David A. Goslin, editor, *Handbook of
Socialization Theory and Research,* Chicago: Rand McNally, 1969). Perhaps the best
overall account of the five basic organizational processes in the occupational structure
is to be found in Lee Taylor's *Occupational Sociology* (New York: Oxford University
Press, 1968).

A useful treatment of careers within the occupational structure is Walter L.
Slocum's *Occupational Careers: A Sociological Perspective* (Chicago: Aldine, 1966).

The intimate connections between work and the self are cogently examined in
Everett C. Hughes's collection of his classic articles, *Men and Their Work* (New York:
Free Press, 1958), and in Lee Braude's *Work and Workers: A Sociological Analysis* (New
York: Praeger, 1975, Chapter 7). The reciprocal influences between individual
character and occupational career are thoughtfully examined in Melvin L. Kohn and
Carmi Schooler, "Occupational Experience and Psychological Functioning: An
Assessment of Reciprocal Effects" (*American Sociological Review,* 1973, 38: 97–118).

Turning now to the social psychological significance of overlapping and cross-
cutting societal-level structures, the classic reading is Tamotsu Shibutani and Kian M.
Kwan, *Ethnic Stratification: A Comparative Approach* (New York: Macmillan, 1965). A
very readable introduction to social stratification, with considerable emphasis on
lifestyles and life chances, is Robert A. Rothman's *Inequality and Stratification in the
United States* (Englewood Cliffs, N.J.: Prentice-Hall, 1978). An excellent and informative analysis of the varying approaches to the influence of the societal level of social
organization on the character of the individual is Philip K. Bock's *Continuities in
Psychological Anthropology: A Historical Introduction* (San Francisco: W. H. Freeman,
1980).

Hospital workers and community members temporarily unite to protest a common grievance.

CHAPTER 17

The Diffuse Collectivity Level

On almost any subject an opinion poll or survey will reveal a variety of responses within a given population. Some percentage of people are "in favor of the equal rights amendment," some are "opposed to legalized abortion," some are "against the building of nuclear power plants in our state." It is seldom indeed that a populace is wholly unanimous on any question of fashion, taste, attitude, preference, opinion, or ideology. No doubt, a poll would reveal some Palestinians who favor the Israelis, some Russians who hope the Americans win the space race, some blacks who oppose the civil rights movement, and some women who believe men should be chattel. This sometimes astonishing variety of positions on any issue has been well-documented by several decades of pollsters.

But responses to a survey question are only statistical items which are then tabulated into a series of categories for analysis. When instead an individual steps out from such a response category to become actively involved in some position, he or she has become a member of a *diffuse collectivity*. This involvement may be as minor as the occasional, informal voicing of that position by word or deed, or as extensive as making it a "ruling passion" in one's social life.

Diffuse collectivities—mass, public, social movement—rank in scope below the societal-level structures and are embedded within them. Their structures are often amorphous, makeshift, and temporary, but diffuse collectivities can exert crucial influences upon the organizations above and below them. They are also powerful social channels through which individuals have influence and are influenced.

Membership in a diffuse collectivity is defined by a common focus of attention, whether this shared focus be Elvis, the preppy look, a Voyager mission to the outer planets, an earthquake in Italy, a SALT treaty proposal, or the consequences of forced

275

busing of school children. Because membership is a matter of sharing actively in such a focus, the membership of such a collectivity tends to be geographically dispersed, indeterminate in number, and continually shifting. What makes such a fuzzily bounded set of persons a collectivity rather than a mere social category is the fact that when a member responds to the common focus of attention, he does so with an awareness that a large (though indeterminate) number of other persons are also responding to it. When a homeowner speaks out against rising property taxes or a woman emulates the Brooke Shields look, the person does so with an awareness that such actions are part of some moving social current.

Members of a diffuse collectivity interact by participating in interaction chains and networks that are closely geared into one or more of the mass media of communication. Indeed, we shall see that persuasive communication and propaganda are central activities within all types of diffuse collectivities.

The real significance of diffuse collectivities lies in the part they play in the innovation process within large organizations of all types, particularly (but not exclusively) societal-level structures. Many masses, publics, and social movements are indeed national if not international in scope, with millions of members. Some may be much smaller and more localized, embedded within a community or even a large association (Zald and Berger, 1978). Whatever the embedding organization, masses, publics, and social movements are distinctive vehicles for individual expression and organizational change. Diffuse collectivities form an important part of the social psychology of modern life.

MASS

A *mass* is a diffuse collectivity in which the defining focus of attention is some matter of personal taste—typically, some cultural item, event, or person which some (but not all) members of the embedding organization find to be of compelling interest, such as the American Bicentennial, the Star Wars phenomenon, the rise of home computers as an alternative form of recreation, or the furor over "designer" jeans in the early 1980s. Such interest is greatly stimulated and sustained through mass media coverage (Freidson, 1953). But the members of a mass are not content merely to consume media coverage of their focus of attention; rather, they are motivated to actively talk about or otherwise indulge in that collective focus. They actively *seek* communications concerning the focus; for example, they will buy a magazine or tune into a television show which features that focal item. Thus, the mass media serve to stimulate, link, and cater to widely dispersed interaction chains sharing a common focus.

Whatever the focus, a mass is organized to produce *fashion,* that is, to establish new norms regulating matters of taste. It should be emphasized that such tastes are not confined to fashion in dress or brand-name preferences, but can apply to any aspect of human living.

Fashion is a basic phenomenon in social life, from child-raising practices to sexual preferences and views on the afterlife. Yet, fashion is not a new phenomenon; a close

The Diffuse Collectivity Level

study of history shows fashion at work in ancient Rome, medieval England, and among American Indians after the arrival of Europeans on the continent. Blumer (1969: 286–287) has specified six conditions necessary for the emergence of the fashion mechanism:

1. The content area must be one in which people are ready to revise old practices, beliefs, and attachments and are poised to adopt new forms, responding to changes taking place in a surrounding world.
2. The area must be open to the recurrent presentation of models or proposals of new forms.
3. There must be a relatively free opportunity for choice between these models (that is, the models must be open to observation, and facilities and means must be available for their adoption).
4. The pretended merit or value of the competing models cannot be demonstrated through open and decisive tests.
5. Prestige figures must be present to espouse one or another of the competing models.
6. The area must be open to the emergence of new interests and dispositions in response to (a) the impact of outside events; (b) the introduction of new participants into the area; and (c) changes in inner social interaction.

And indeed, tastes in a fairly wide variety of cultural items, persons, and events within each of the four societal-level structures do seem to fulfill these conditions, as the selected examples in Figure 17-1 would suggest. Each of these examples would also, of course, have some spillover into the other structures.

The fashion mechanism is a process of "collective selection" from among competing models or proposals. Around each of the competing models a mass forms—a set of persons who are, in common, paying attention to one model and thus serving as its fans, adherents, advocates, or following. For example, those interested in science fiction movies as opposed to other types of films comprise a mass, as do the followers of one rather than another politician or comedian. Each of these rival masses competes for members and other resources until one becomes clearly predominant for a time—that is, until its model becomes epidemic within the area (Wills and Christopher, 1973) and is no longer newsworthy.

> The convergence of choice occurs not because of the intrinsic merit or demonstrated validity of the selected models but because of the appearance of high standing which the chosen models carry. Unquestionably, such high standing is given in major measure by the endorsement and espousal of models of prestigeful persons. But it must be stressed again that it is not prestige, *per se,* which imparts this sanction; a prestigeful person, despite his eminence, may be easily felt to be "out of date." To carry weight, the person of prestige must be believed or sensed to be voicing the proper perspective that is called for by developments in the area . . . what is collectively judged to be up-to-date practice. The formation of this collective judgment takes place through an interesting but ill-understood interaction between prestige and incipient taste, between eminent endorsement and congenial interest [Blumer, 1969: 287].

277

LEVELS OF ORGANIZATION

Speech Community	Age-Sex Structure	Polity	Economy
Cultural Items Words and idioms, pronunciations, spellings, etc.; Literary forms, styles	*Cultural Items* Clothing, hair-styles, games, songs, dances, recreations, etc.	*Cultural Items* Campaign tactics, political stances, "planks," etc.	*Cultural Items* Investment oppor-tunities, occupa-tions, theories, technologies, etc.
Events Linguistic events (e.g., publica-tion of new dictionary); Literary events (e.g., announce-ment of Pulitzer Prizes)	*Events* Entertainment events (e.g., sports, show business); Social events (e.g., charity ball)	*Events* "Current events" (i.e., world, national, local news); Political events (e.g., elections)	*Events* Business events (e.g., market transactions, corporate mergers)
Persons Literary figures, stylists	*Persons* "High society" leaders; Entertainment "stars" (music, sports, etc.); Designers	*Persons* Political celebrities, political parties	*Persons* Entrepreneurs, labor leaders; Academic or scientific celebrities

FIGURE 17-1. **Some Areas of Fashion within Societal-level Structures**

The fashion mechanism is one of the clearest examples of the basic principles we examined in Parts I and II, that is, an outcome emerges from mutual influences of in-dividuals and organizations, with the outcome subsequently influencing both. New York fashion media, for example, may push a certain dress style in opposition to the prevailing style. This new model may come to be accepted through the fashion mechanism, producing something of a nationwide change in women's appearance. That outcome in turn heightens the prestige of the eminent dressers and the media which pushed it and diminishes the standing of those individuals and organizations which resisted it, thus resulting in some stratification shifts regarding who is "in."

A related yet somewhat distinct mechanism for the diffusion of changes in tastes is the *fad,* which arises under similar conditions and relies similarly on competition be-tween masses (Meyerson and Katz, 1957). The term fad, though certainly more derogatory than the term fashion, is not simply a put-down but refers to those changes in taste which are in some sense relatively isolated changes, socially and/or culturally. Two senses of *socially isolated* changes may be distinguished: that of being confined to a single segment or category of the population (for instance, to one age category), and that of taking place on the fringes of society rather than within the mainstream of social life. Similarly, two senses of *culturally isolated* changes may be noted: that of abrupt rather than gradual change (being either very rapid in its spread or radically different from prevailing proprieties), and that of piecemeal rather than patterned change (for instance, cowboy hats alone seem faddish, while the total western look might be fashionable).

From the larger perspective of the embedding organization, diffusion of changes in taste may be relatively widespread, central, gradual, and continuous—"fashion"—or may be rather confined, marginal, abrupt, and/or piecemeal—"fad." These defining contrasts lead to several differences in the mechanisms and consequences of fashions and fads. First, unlike fashion leaders, who rank high in the status structures of societal-level structures (Katz and Lazarsfeld, 1955), the fad leaders who lend their weight to a potential fad item may come from any social position, and they derive their socially bounded prestige mainly from their reputation of being early to identify the latest craze. In this way, the spread of fashion both reflects and reinforces the secondary social structures of the embedding organization (Barber and Lobel, 1952), whereas the spread of fads typically does neither. Second, whereas the succession of fashions tends to display some continuity or trend, the succession of fads does not; the hallmark of fashion is "modern but respectable," while the essence of fad is simply "the latest thing sweeping the nation." Finally, in the case of fashion but not of fad, "it is important to note that behavior is not all that changes. No matter what initial opposition to a fashion change may develop, even the tastes of its opponents usually change once the style has become established" (Turner and Killian, 1957: 215). For example, a good many of those who in the late 1960s railed against men wearing long hair now display expensively styled longer hair themselves. And even shopping centers now provide soft versions of rock music hits as piped-in background music for their solidly middle-class customers.

Social Structure

The social structure of a mass is depicted in Figure 17-2. The three classes of positions in the primary social structure are the producers of the competitive model, its distributors, and its consumers (Hirsch, 1972). The specialized roles of producers include (for popular songs) writers and performers, (for clothes) fashion designers, (for an event such as the World Series) the participating teams, the two leagues, and major league baseball as a whole. The corresponding specialized roles of distributors include (for popular songs) the record companies, disc jockeys, radio stations, and record retailers; (for clothes) store buyers, retailers and advertisers, fashion writers, newspapers and magazines; (for the World Series) TV and radio networks, stations, sponsors, sportswriters, and newspapers. In the case of a personal following, the producer is the celebrity himself, and the distributors include his press agents, columnists and talk-show hosts, and the mass media.

Within the consumer segment, the secondary social structure exhibits two dimensions: centrality (degree of participation) and status. The degrees of participation (Rogers, 1962) include:

279

LEVELS OF ORGANIZATION

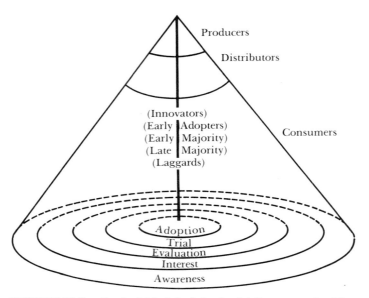

FIGURE 17-2. **Conical Model of the Social Structure of a Mass**

1. awareness: the individual has heard of the innovation but lacks information about it;
2. interest: the individual is interested enough to seek further information about the innovation;
3. evaluation: the individual deliberates whether it would make sense for him to try the innovation;
4. trial: he tries the innovation on a small scale or in a tentative manner to improve his estimate of its utility for himself; and
5. adoption: he decides to make full and regular use of the innovation.

The status dimension within the consumer segment reflects seniority within the mass as well as prestige position within the embedding organization (Rogers, 1962):

1. innovators: venturesome and cosmopolitan, they like to try new ideas even at some risk to their social standing;
2. early adopters: respected in the surrounding organization, they are opinion leaders or influentials who adopt new ideas early but with discretion;
3. early majority: aware but deliberate, these persons like to adopt new ideas before the average member but they are not risk takers;
4. late majority: skeptical in nature, they do not adopt an innovation until the weight of majority opinion seems to have legitimated it; and
5. laggards: traditional in nature, they are suspicious of any change, associate primarily with other tradition-bound people, and adopt an innovation only when it has come to acquire a measure of tradition itself.

The Diffuse Collectivity Level

The first two categories—innovators and early adopters—do incur some actual risks, at least in terms of status, power, and leadership standings and perhaps even in career opportunities. For instance, many a music group has made the wrong bet in terms of upcoming musical fashions, losing their ratings on the charts and sometimes their very careers. However, groups that "catch the pulse," as the Bee Gees did with disco in *Saturday Night Fever* or as George Lucas's film group did with *Star Wars,* may rise to new heights in the secondary social structures.

Although not depicted in Figure 17–2, the conical social structure of any mass would also show wedgelike slices from the periphery to the core, corresponding to the various suborganizations (geographical or functional) of the embedding organization. Looking down from the top of the cone, one would see these suborganizational wedges as so many slices of a pie; and indeed, the top producers at the pinnacle often speak of "market segments" and of distributing various "pieces of the pie." A national magazine, for example, ordinarily (though quietly) divides its mass following into regional segments and produces a modified edition for each segment—taking out certain advertisements, adding others, and switching the social and racial characteristics of the models featured in the photographs in various common advertisements. A regional pie-wedge segment of the social structure of this mass would encompass the magazine's regional production staff, regional advertisers, regional and local magazine distributors, and the region's consumers.

As a diffuse collectivity, the mass exhibits no sharply outlined authority structure. Distributors, rather than producers, tend to exert the most visible power (Hirsch, 1972). Often operating in terms of strict mercantile cost/benefit calculations, distributors frequently tip the balance between competing models by deciding, for example, to push a certain book or record, featuring it over others in terms of promotion expenditures. However, there are many examples, such as *Jonathan Livingston Seagull* or the television show *Saturday Night Live,* where distributors are overruled by the consumers. Actually, leadership is the characteristic influence structure within a mass, and such leadership rests solely on the reponse of other members. Within a totalitarian polity, the government sometimes attempts to "dictate fashion," but even governments have extreme difficulty in doing so; such dictates tend to be evaded where these jar with popular consent.

Careers within the social structures of a mass consist primarily of movements along the centrality dimension of Figure 17–2. Many persons will reach awareness (thus entering the structure) but progress no further; some will penetrate further before turning back; and some, of course, will go all the way to become full adopters.

Collectivity

As a result of competition between masses, each mass tends to develop some in-group feeling, with central members congratulating one another concerning their superior tastes and belittling those models around which rival masses are formed. This sense of collectivity is particularly sharp in the case of fads and of personal followings (Turner and Killian, 1972: 129–136, 388–389). "Factual" information, "buzz words," and testimonials about the model constitute a little culture within a mass.

Resources, however, are the central issue within any mass. Human resources are a matter of the number—and the societal prestige—of its relatively central members. Material resources are mainly a matter of the monies members make available to the mass for purposes of acquiring access to the mass media of communication. Obviously, the magnitude of both human and material resources vitally affects the competitive success of any mass within the fashion mechanism.

PUBLIC

The common focus of attention that defines a public is an *issue,* some matter of shared concern pertaining to some organizational decision to be made, about which members feel they have the right to disagree. A nation-state, for example, may be considering declaration of war, imposition of some new tax, or prohibition of alcohol; a community may be considering a new swimming pool or elimination of parking meters; a giant labor union may be considering a national strike. If affected individuals feel they have the right to disagree about such matters, these matters become social issues among those who care about them.

A *public,* then, is a dispersed set of people "interested in and divided about an issue, engaged in discussion of the issue, with a view to [diffusely] registering a collective opinion which is expected to affect the course of action" of some organization or individual (Turner and Killian, 1972: 179). *Public opinion* "need not be either majority opinion nor any sum of individual opinions, unless the mode of expression available to the particular public at the moment is the ballot box. Public opinion becomes that which is communicated [in some manner] to the effective decision-makers as a consequence of the functioning of a public" (Turner and Killian, 1957: 219).

By definition, then, a public (as well as the resultant public opinion) can arise only within larger organizations with fairly centralized authority structures; indeed, we usually think of a public as being embedded within the polity. In fact, the phenomena of publics and public opinion can arise within an economy, an age-sex structure, or any large collectivity with a discernible structure where organizational decisions are not utterly dictatorial. The character of a public is greatly shaped by the modes of expression permitted by the embedding organization. In terms of the typology of ratification procedures set forth in Chapter 8, relatively authoritarian decision making requires a public to target informal expressions toward a small and coherent set of decision makers; highly democratic procedures, on the other hand, call for a public to express itself formally but diffusely through a balloting mechanism. Intermediate between these two modes are a wide range of means for expressing collective opinion—from letters to the editor and public opinion polls to marches, demonstrations, boycotts, and picket lines.

The functioning of any public includes three overlapping phases: (1) the definition and redefinition of the germane issues; (2) efforts toward selection of an effective program to meet those issues; and (3) the effective registration of the pattern of opinion.

Social Structure

The acting units of a public are not necessarily or simply individuals (C. D. Clark, 1933); "in any realistic sense the diversified interaction which gives rise to public opinion is in large measure between [social organizations] and not merely between disparate individuals" (Blumer, 1948: 545). This late-won insight has been elaborated in the form of the "group-theory of politics" (V. O. Key, 1961; Truman, 1951), which emphasizes the role of corporations, unions, and other associations in the political process.

Such "interest groups" tend to view all matters nearly exclusively in terms of their implications for some strong collective interest around which the association is formed. When an issue arises within the polity, association spokesmen examine its significance for the association's interest and translate the issue into interest-group terms. In so doing, interest groups effectively redefine the issue—that is, those points which are considered relevant and about which the members of a public agree to disagree. For example, minority group spokesmen will examine a presidential candidate's promises and redefine their "meaning" in terms of that group's special interests and concerns.

> Through discussion, the initially varied points of view concerning the issues are consolidated into a limited number of alternatives. Once this takes place it is difficult for an individual within the public to communicate any view other than one of those predefined. Each participant is assigned to one of the accepted divisions, and those who resist such classification are said to be confused and inconsistent [Turner and Killian, 1972: 192].

In other words, as a restricted set of viewpoints and programs emerges within a public, an "opinion mass" forms around each of these viewpoints. Such an opinion mass displays the same sort of social structure described above and exhibited in Figure 17–2. The producer roles within such an opinion mass are generally played by those interest-group spokesmen who reformulate issues into interest-group terms in the form of a coherent viewpoint and program. The distributor roles are played by lesser functionaries within those same interest-group associations, working conjointly. That is, the distributor's role is to promote and disseminate the viewpoints and programs of the producers, perhaps tailoring them to the local social climate.

> The diverse interest groups within each faction are unified by alliances, *ad hoc* committees, or new integrating associations. As organizational problems within the interest groups attain solution, more attention is given to the uncommitted outsiders [that is, potential consumers] whose support is needed to achieve dominance in the controversy, and they are subjected to persuasion by means of propaganda and personal influence [Baur, 1960: 210].

The contributions of reference groups and of primary groups in this process of persuasion have been shown to be paramount (Baur, 1960; Turner and Killian, 1972: 199–214; Katz and Lazarsfeld, 1955). The clamorous clash of opinions, "facts," and arguments provoked by a social issue proves confusing to many individuals, who turn to their families, peer groups, and key reference groups for clarification, guidance, and relief from the cross-pressures of the competing factions within the public.

The secondary social structure within the consumer ranks is the same as pictured in Figure 17-2 with respect to both the centrality and the status dimensions, except that high-status consumers are here spoken of as opinion leaders (E. Katz, 1957) rather than as fashion leaders.

A public's efforts toward choosing an effective program to meet the defined issues is essentially a matter of "collective selection" through competition between rival opinion masses. In this case, however, the decision-making structure toward which the public is directed effectively renders judgment of the fashionableness and respectability of the rival viewpoints, based on the number and the societal prestige of the memberships of the competing opinion masses.

The effectiveness with which the pattern of opinion is registered upon these decision makers rests centrally on their judgment of the significance of the public as a whole—again, the number and the societal prestige of individuals and interest-groups centrally engaged in the public as a whole. The extent and distribution of voting or other less official modes of opinion communication are always taken into account in interpreting public opinion.

These twin judgments by decision makers pose a strategic problem for any opinion mass. A grass-roots strategy seeks to obtain the largest possible numbers of members, while an elite strategy seeks selectively to recruit members of high societal prestige. Although both numbers and prestige are desirable, the common incompatibility of these two strategies usually dictates that one be accorded priority over the other. The strategic choice made by the leadership of an opinion mass regarding the direction of its persuasive efforts may be shaped by the leadership's position within the communication structure of the embedding organization, as well as by the available modes of registering opinion (for example, an election public generally favors a grass-roots strategy).

It should be pointed out that strategic choice, the means of registering opinion, and the decision maker's response are not necessarily "rational" or optimal for those concerned. As a careful reading of any large daily newspaper will show, all factions involved in a public frequently make mistakes in their calculations and choice of tactics. Diffuse collectivity phenomena are often emotional and occasionally hysterical, but whatever the wisdom of the choices made, such collectivities do provide the members of large-scale organizations a means of expression and more of a voice in the shaping of social life than would probably otherwise be the case.

Collectivity

Being organized around an issue, a public usually does not have a long life. It generally disappears when the decision makers have acted, although it may leave various residual associations and groups in its wake. Even during its existence, the membership of a public expands and contracts fairly markedly in competition with other publics formed around other issues. At any point in time, however, the resources of a public are the sum of the resources of all the participating opinion masses.

The Diffuse Collectivity Level

The distinctive culture of a public centers on the eventual definition of the issue and the recognized alternative viewpoints. These collective formulations exert major normative constraints on the character of individual participation in a public; failure to conform leads to being characterized as uninformed, confused, irrelevant, and so on.

The culture of a public is most fully and clearly developed in the case of a conventionalized public, such as an election public. A public of this type arises

> because a predetermined interval has passed rather than because of heightened mass preoccupation with a problem; the main issue is largely organized and arranged; a set of interest groups known as political parties presides over the deliberations; the manner in which public opinion is to be identified is formally established as the ballot; and the secret ballot and the one-person–one-vote principle diminish the unequal social pressures on individuals at the crucial point of voting [Turner and Killian; 1972: 221].

The linkages between specific interest groups and the various political parties are generally traditional and well-established, the symbolic trappings and campaign tactics of the parties are almost ritualized through traditional practice, and the party preferences of individual members of the public are largely predetermined (Lazarsfeld, Berelson, and Gaudet, 1948). Of course, as we saw in examining social change, the routinized circumstances on which such conventionalization of publics depends are but temporary calm periods in the stream of history. As these phases of temporary local stability pass, the occasions and dynamics of publics become much less ritualized. For example, the 1980 United States presidential election saw the breakdown of such conventionalized publics on the heels of widespread economic and cultural upheavals.

The underlying normative agreements upon which publics operate may vary from societal structure to societal structure, and from period to period in history. In stable democracies, publics rest on certain normative foundations—trust that the decision makers will receive public opinion and take it into account, trust that every opinion mass and interest group will confine itself to discussion rather than undertake direct action, and trust that participants will not be penalized for the opinions expressed (Turner and Killian, 1972: 196–198). Within other polities, a gradient range of more violent actions—ranging from strikes and angry demonstrations to coups and assassinations—may be generally considered appropriate. According to legend, the warlords of ancient China succeeded one another through an elaborately ritualized ''bloodless revolution,'' while a confrontation between Cossacks and populace was a virtually expected aspect of registering diffuse collective opinion in Czarist Russia.

SOCIAL MOVEMENT

Social movements are a particularly interesting form of diffuse collectivity, in that many of our own now hallowed institutions began as social movements. Christianity, the principle of representation in government, the right to vote for all who are of legal age, public education, playgrounds, and so on, were all, once upon a time, struggling social movements.

A *social movement* is a diffuse collectivity in which the defining focus of attention is a particular "demand for change in some aspect of the social order" (Gusfield, 1970: 2). Turner and Killian (1972: 246) define a social movement as a diffuse collectivity "acting with some continuity to promote or resist a change" in the embedding organization. In comparison with the other types of diffuse collectivity, a social movement exhibits more sustained activity (with some continuity in strategy), greater stability of role structure, and substantial continuity of membership.

Among the necessary aspects of any social movement are, "first, a program for the reform of society; second, the establishment of power relations favorable to the movement; and third, the promotion of membership gratifications" (Turner and Killian, 1972: 256). The balance among these value orientations, power orientations, and participation orientations is always a delicate one for a movement to maintain. In most cases, one of these aspects will therefore eventually predominate, although the others will never be entirely absent.

Value-oriented social movements subordinate tactics and gratifications to the promotion of the social program and ideology, which may point to changing individuals—personal transformation—or to changing social institutions—"societal manipulation." For example, most of the world's great religions developed as value-oriented movements.

Power-oriented movements subordinate program, ideology, and membership gratifications to tactics of external power relations. The communist movement in various countries subordinated both value orientation and membership gratifications to the goal of achieving power: the end justifies the means. Control movements seek to dominate the embedding organization, while separatist movements seek to reduce their own subordination by achieving some degree of separation from the embedding organization.

Participation-oriented movements subordinate both program and power relations to membership gratifications. A contemporary example might be the widespread movement in the United States to prepare to survive member-predicted collapse of the economic system through such actions as buying silver and gold, storing nonperishable foods, and otherwise preparing to survive a possible breakdown in the economy. Both values and power aspects are subordinated to such participatory actions, although certainly neither is absent.

Quite often, a social movement will come to emphasize either power, values, or participation while particular suborganizations within the movement will emphasize one or another of the neglected aspects. The various monastic orders in the Roman Catholic church during the Middle Ages tended to emphasize differing aspects. Of course, individual members of any movement may emphasize any of the three aspects (or even some unconventional goal) because of their own personal plans of action and definitions of the situation. A person may be seeking a fuller social life or personal security within a value-oriented religious movement. An individual may be promoting idealistic values within a highly power-oriented political movement.

Social Structure

Although it is a diffuse collectivity, a social movement essentially functions as an interest group, promoting issues and striving to influence the resulting publics in line with the movement's program for social change, as worked out and issued by those occupying the producer positions.

The typical developmental sequence of a social movement exhibits four stages (Hopper, 1950). The preliminary stage of diffuse social unrest is followed by a popular stage in which unrest becomes open and focused and a topic of collective discussion. It is only in the formal stage that a movement attains sufficient social organization to effectively promulgate and redefine issues and to propagandize the accompanying publics. To function effectively as an interest group in this manner requires formation of some formal organization to lend stability and continuity to the movement across issues and publics. This organization (technically a voluntary association, in our terms) at the core of a movement is referred to as a *movement organization* (Zald and Ash, 1966). In the final or institutional stage of a movement, this movement organization has beome an accepted and more or less permanent fixture in the society, that is, it is viewed more as another influential voluntary association than as the core of an active social movement (for example, the National Association for the Advancement of Colored People and the American Federation of Labor). Once maverick, these have now become an accepted part of the American social landscape.

As a fairly diffuse interest group persisting with some continuity across a number of publics, a social movement closely resembles an opinion mass in primary social structure. The *producer* roles are essentially the various leadership roles within the movement. In the preliminary stage, the most visible leaders are agitators, fomenting social unrest. In the popular stage, prophets (providing ideologies) and reformers (providing broad programs of social change) are predominant. In the formal stage, leadership shifts increasingly to statesmen as masters of strategy who have attained positions of authority in the movement organization. In the institutional stage, administrators (of the movement organization) achieve greatest prominence (Hopper, 1950). *Distributor* roles, on the other hand, are played by propagandists, by more or less sympathetic agents in the mass media, and (in the more mature stages) by the formal rank-and-file members of the movement organization. As—and if—the movement reaches the later developmental stages, the producer and distributor roles, such as public relations man, committee chairman, founder, and so on, tend to become more standardized and conventional. Hand in hand with this conventionalization of positions, charisma and a crusading spirit sometimes become secondary to rational organizational planning and production. *Consumer* roles display a secondary social structure very much like that in any other opinion mass (see Figure 17–2), with centrality a function of degree of commitment to the movement's program and ideology, and status a joint function of seniority and societal prestige.

The structure of a social movement is seldom so neatly unitary, however. Often enough a social movement contains organized factions and even splinter groups—competing movement organizations—serving as suborganizations within the general social movement (Zald and Ash, 1966). Although they seek rather similar ends, each of these competing movement organizations offers a somewhat different program for attaining those ends—perhaps based on differing ideologies. Compare, for example, the different factions in the black community during the civil rights movement of the 1960s or the moderate and militant Iranian factions during the American hostage crisis of 1980. Factional suborganizations within a larger movement may also not be truly seeking the same ends, as was the case in the labor movement of the past century. Some movement organizations merely sought better conditions, some wanted ''a piece of the pie,'' and some wanted the pie itself. If the factions differ in overall goals as well as programs, strong conflicts between them are virtually inevitable. At the extreme, such factional conflicts may spark mass violence, as in the religious wars of the Middle Ages or the radicalization of the Russian Revolution during the early decades of this century.

Finally, some movements generate focused opposition in the form of a ''countermovement''—a reactionary social movement persistently opposing the original movement across all pertinent publics (for example, Phyllis Schlafly's countermovement to the Equal Rights Amendment movement), thus factionalizing each of these publics. It can be expected that any movement of large scope will spawn something of an oppositional countermovement because almost inevitably there will be some members of the populace who will feel their positions or values threatened by changes.

Every movement necessarily encounters some opposition, ranging from passive disinterest to violent suppression. The form and strength of this opposition heavily influence the range of tactics available to a social movement and are in turn determined by each public's definition of the movement's consistency with the fundamental interests and values of the embedding organization (Turner, 1964). If consistent, the movement is regarded as a respectable reform movement; if inconsistent, it is viewed either as a dangerous and revolutionary movement to be suppressed or as a harmlessly peculiar movement to be ridiculed. It should come as no surprise that the kind and the degree of opposition have a major influence upon the character of the movement and on the social life of the individual members. All of the basic processes we examined in Part II—recruitment, interaction, etcetera—would have a very different character in a mild reform movement than in an outlawed underground.

Collectivity

The shared interest in promoting or resisting a particular change in the social order is the defining feature of any social movement considered as a collectivity. The sense of collectivity is manifest in the sharp ingroup–outgroup distinction and in the shared sense of righteousness. Such *esprit de corps* fluctuates somewhat with variations in morale (the collective sense of success or failure) in response to the ebb and flow of victories and defeats, but it is generally enhanced by the recognition of shared risks incurred through participation in the movement. The more unconventional the movement and the more risks involved for individual members, the sharper this in-group–outgroup distinction and the stronger the sense of righteousness are likely to be.

Every social movement develops an organizational culture, most fully elaborated in the belief-system aspect of ideology and program. These elements in turn generally entail the development of a somewhat distinctive vocabulary and of rituals (slogans, songs, gestures, logos, emblems, and sometimes even uniforms) to heighten *esprit de corps* (Killian, 1964). Researchers have found that each social movement, whatever its orientation, develops a world of richly elaborated culture, usually spilling over far beyond the central focus to touch upon most aspects of social living. Core members particularly may come to virtually inhabit this world, with a corresponding attenuation of their conventional ties.

The success of a social movement is greatly influenced, of course, by its human and material resources. As with all diffuse collectivities, the numbers and societal prestige of its members are vital determinants of public influence. Material resources are needed not only to obtain access to the mass media (as with other diffuse collectivities) but also to finance ''propaganda of the deed'' (through demonstrations, marches, sit-ins, and so on) and to make possible the continuous full-time activities of officials in the movement organizations. The overall resources of a movement may have at least as much to do with its success as the ''rightness'' or value of its programs.

ORGANIZATIONAL PROCESSES IN DIFFUSE COLLECTIVITIES

All three types of diffuse collectivity—mass, public, and social movement—emerge within some larger social organization as vital mechanisms in its innovation process. Any diffuse collectivity involves some type of interplay among two or more factional suborganizations within the embedding organization, all competing to establish the popularity and respectability of their respective foci. Whatever the form of a diffuse collectivity, the normative outcome of this competition is largely determined by the human resources (numbers, societal prestige, and skills of members) and the material resources of the various factions. Thus, it is not necessarily or automatically the case that the ''best'' faction eventually wins out, just as the polity in the most ''honorable'' position does not necessarily win a war. The most rational program will not prevail unless it is also the program or model which acquires the most resources and the most effective strategies. Nor does every needful area within an organization somehow automatically have a public or social movement focusing upon it. History has shown that the issues on which diffuse collectivities focus and the solutions to which they lead may be quite arbitrary compared to what might prove optimal for the organizations and individuals involved. The witch-hunt movements certainly did not enhance the social life of England or New England, and few would argue that McCarthyism in the early 1950s enhanced the quality of American life. The emergence of the Stalinist group among the competing factions in postrevolutionary Russia led to a very bleak and uncertain social life in that nation for several decades.

LEVELS OF ORGANIZATION

In an important sense, the fashion mechanism underlies the operation not only of masses but also of publics and social movements, identifying what opinions, ideologies, and programs of social change are "fashionable."

> Fashion should be recognized as a central mechanism in forming social order in a modern type of world, a mechanism whose operation will increase. . . . As I have sought to explain, the key to the understanding of fashion is given in the simple words, "being in fashion." These words signify an area of life which is caught in movement—movement from an outmoded past toward a dim, uncertain, but exploitable future. . . .
>
> [First,] fashion introduces order in a potentially anarchic and moving present. By establishing suitable models which carry the stamp of propriety and compel adherence, fashion narrowly limits the range of variability and so fosters uniformity and order, even though it be passing uniformity and order. In this respect fashion performs in a moving society a function which custom performs in a settled society.
>
> Second, fashion serves to detach the grip of the past in a moving world. By placing a premium on being in the mode and derogating what developments have left behind, it frees actions for new movement. . . . In this sense there is virtue in applying the derogatory accusations of being "old-fashioned," "outmoded," "backward," and "out-of-date."
>
> Third, fashion operates as an orderly preparation for the immediate future. By allowing the presentation of new models but by forcing them through the gauntlet of competition and collective selection the fashion mechanism offers a continuous means of adjusting to what is on the horizon [Blumer, 1969: 289–290].

As we have seen, this fashion mechanism is operative in a great deal more than dress styles; in fact, it can apply to any aspect of organizational or individual life, from premarital sexual patterns to styles in family living and favored procedures for selecting senior executives of church and state. The social force of the fashion mechanism—in forming tastes, public opinion, and ideology—is a powerful process, displacing the force of outmoded customs and often leading to the emergence of new formal norms and behaviors.

Against this background of the common significance of diffuse collectivities, let us examine the core organizational processes as they operate within diffuse collectivities.

Recruitment is, of course, the most critical of the five processes within this type of organization because of the strategic importance of human resources. Participation in a mass, a public, or a social movement is necessarily venturesome and somewhat risky, since it involves taking a stand concerning some innovation within the embedding organization. If one's chosen faction should happen to lose in the competitive struggle, the individual will be derogated as out of step or even labeled an outright deviant. And even if his faction should ultimately prevail, the outcome is certainly in doubt for a period of time. To align oneself with the faction during this doubtful period is to risk punishment by one's unaligned or differently aligned associates—incurring their dismay, anger, even retaliation. Factional recruitment of members is, therefore, impeded by individual reluctance to undertake such risks.

This is probably a major reason why only a relative minority of the members of the embedding organization are actively involved in any particular diffuse collectivity, even though a majority may be sympathetic with one faction or another. For example,

The Diffuse Collectivity Level

during the German occupation, the vast majority of Frenchmen were sympathetic toward the cause of the resistance underground, but only a small fraction was actively involved. For the individual potential recruit, the benefits and costs of joining must be weighed against other personal alternatives and considerations, in a complex and ill-understood social psychological process taking place at all levels of consciousness. If the person does join, however, he is generally swept up into the culture of the collectivity, which is often sufficient to sustain his participation.

In the cases of publics and social movements, the "theory of mobilization" (Oberschall, 1973) suggests that it is not so much individuals who join but, rather, interest groups. The impediment of risk is somewhat muted thereby, since

> in group recruitment, members of the group provide each other with social support and negatively sanction those who would hesitate to join. The premovement group leaders take the initiative in mobilization, and the movement builds up rapidly through a merger of such groups. Thus, a heterogeneous leadership and membership, loosely held together in their pursuit of some common goals, comes into being, joined by others who are attracted by the initial successes of the movement. Yet, the movement will have little central organization, and the primary loyalties of the members may be to the component groups, leaders, and associations, and not to the overarching movement itself. Each group seeks to have its leaders recognized as the top leaders of the entire movement. There are no preestablished norms for choosing or establishing the top leaders, and their authority does not rest on institutional positions. There are no agreed upon, legitimized procedures for reaching collective decisions. The movement presents the picture of heterogeneity and confusion. . . . Each group seeks to orient the entire movement to the pursuit of its goals and may not be strongly committed to achieving the goals of other component parts of the movement that it does not share. Thus, as the movement succeeds in some of its goals, the interest and commitment of some groups may be waning and entire groups drop out of active participation in the movement [Oberschall, 1973: 143].

This view of recruitment through the mobilization of interest groups, while a powerful contribution, does not readily apply to the case of recruitment into a mass. Moreover, the mobilization of an interest group within a public or social movement is itself a difficult and uncertain business:

> We cannot assume that people will automatically form opinions or even define issues according to the self-interest they share as members of interest groups. This is so partly because most people belong to several interest groups, some of whose relationships to the issue are contradictory. Individuals have ideological commitments that are not easily abandoned merely because they run contrary to perceived group interest. Also, the more personal and particularistic influences in primary groups dilute whatever consistent effect interest-group membership might have. Furthermore, the relationship of an issue to group interest is not always noticed, and when noticed is not always in an obvious direction [Turner and Killian, 1972: 204].

For these reasons, recruitment into diffuse collectivities must ultimately focus on individuals. The basis of this process remains the tactics of attraction and selection examined in Chapter 5, since the ascriptive call of interest-group mobilization will always fall short of full effectiveness. Just because a particular labor union endorses a

LEVELS OF ORGANIZATION

Democratic candidate for political office, it does not follow that the individual union members will vote for him in the election booth or promote him when they stop for a beer after work. The individual's gun-club circle or church fellowship may already have successfully recruited him to the Republican cause or he may have simply decided on his own that he does not like the Democratic candidate.

The central tactic in such individual recruitment is that of attraction. Proselytizing of potential members—seeking to lead them through the stages of awareness, interest, evaluation, trial, and adoption—is a ubiquitous feature of every organizational action of the diffuse collectivity. Such promotional efforts rely on persuasive communication (Bettinghaus, 1973), conveyed through mass media propaganda and through personal influence.

Propaganda takes the form not only of paid advertisements and promotional announcements in print and electronic media but also of manipulating "straight news coverage" of speeches, demonstrations, and press releases. Promotional bumper stickers, billboards, posters, brochures, and leaflets are additional tools of propaganda. Studies of the effects of the mass media (for example, Klapper, 1961) have indicated that propaganda is more effective in building awareness and interest than in persuading the uncommitted, and more effective in reinforcing individual predispositions than in altering them. More subtly, the mass media serve to authenticate events, validate preferences, legitimate taboo preferences, symbolize and focus both discontents and preferences, and signal the relative importance and prestige of competing models (Turner and Killian, 1972: 215–216).

In the actual recruitment of individuals, personal influence on a one-to-one small-group basis remains overwhelmingly the major source of memberships (Snow, Zurcher, and Ekland-Olson, 1980). A most important sociological contribution has been the repeated demonstration that the persuasive functions of mass media propaganda are vitally mediated by personal contacts. The "two-step flow of communication" (E. Katz, 1957) depends on information passing through the mass media to "influentials" (fashion leaders, opinion leaders), who in turn selectively relay some of this digested information to those associates who respect their specialized competences and judgments. Thus, the character of an individual's interaction network is an important determinant of both the messages that come to his attention and the meanings and credibilities he attaches to those messages. In shops and offices and homes around the nation, small groups gather to hammer out what a presidential speech or a news bulletin "really means."

Not only an individual's significant others but also his reference groups condition his exposure and receptiveness to persuasive communications. Communications consistent with the position of a relevant reference group are more likely to be both received and accepted. Again, however, an individual will often identify with more than one relevant reference group. If the positions of these reference groups are contradictory, the individual finds no consistent social support for his reactions and indeed feels cross-pressured (Kriesberg, 1949). Baur (1960) suggests that such cross-pressures are especially likely to be brought into the individual's primary groups to be clarified and

The Diffuse Collectivity Level

resolved. Far from being unusual, such cross-pressures and their resolutions within the person's primary groups may well be the most common situation.

Rogers (1962) found that individuals at the stage of interest are especially likely to consult the mass media for further information, and that personal influence is especially sought out and used by individuals in the evaluation stage.

Since membership in a diffuse collectivity is defined by attention, such an organization is relatively powerless to exclude any individual; organizational tactics of selection in or selection out are seldom very prominent in the collective actions of most diffuse collectivities. Perhaps the clearest cases of such organizational tactics of selection are an opinion mass that seeks selectively to attract influential persons through an elite strategy or a social movement that almost exclusively relies on one interest group for its social base in recruitment through mobilization. It is, however, fairly common for specific movement organizations within a general social movement to be highly selective and exclusive in their memberships, imposing rigorous rules and standards for admission. The early Black Muslims had strict requirements for membership and stringent rules of conduct to be followed if one wished to remain within the organization.

The aspect of placement in a diffuse collectivity, though entirely informal, tends to be somewhat ascriptively based on the individual's position in the secondary social structures of the embedding organization. Particularly in publics and social movements, producer roles tend to be filled by the officials of interest group associations, and distributor roles by the rank-and-file of those associations as well as by fashion/opinion leaders. Consumer roles in a diffuse collectivity tend to reflect the individuals' societal prestige, as Rogers (1962) has shown; early adopters, for example, tend to have had a higher than average education.

Socialization in diffuse collectivities is primarily a matter of learning the organizational culture and membership norms. However, some development of skills may be necessary for activist roles in social movements and even in certain masses (for example, the recent craze for rollerskating or hang-gliding). In virtually all cases, much of this is accomplished through anticipatory socialization (principally through mass media); direct socialization is relatively modest and is conducted mainly through implicit procedures. (Again, however, a movement organization may impose a very demanding socialization based on formalized education and on stripping and substitution tactics.)

At a minimum, the individual is expected to become familiar with the collectivity's culture, jargon, catch-phrases, and stands on a variety of issues, usually extending far beyond the focal item itself. Those who do not yet display such savvy are regarded as not having fully arrived and are pressured to get their "homework" done. A diffuse collectivity of any size and duration almost inevitably produces its own literature—its "bible" and subsidiary works—with which a true insider must show that he is thoroughly acquainted. Because of the recognized value of recruits, however, the inside members are usually quick to help, guide, and encourage the newcomer through his socialization.

LEVELS OF ORGANIZATION

With regard to degree of socialization, there are four generally distinguishable classes of members: the newcomer, the regular member, the veteran, and the originator, who has reached a level where his productions feed back into the system as material for further socialization. In certain movements, such as some religious orders, these classes may take on some of the quality of a highly structured grading of members.

Interaction in a diffuse collectivity consists largely of persuasive communication, propagandizing both friend and foe, with the aim of proselytizing nonmembers and maintaining the ingroup solidarity of the membership. Of course, a crude division of labor among producers, distributors, and consumers is evident within these communication activities.

The attention focus of the collectivity tends to serve as a rallying point for interactions, but, as with all social life, these interactions spill over into other areas in two major ways. First, the focus itself tends to generalize into positions on other areas of life. For instance, a far-right stand may touch upon family and child-rearing attitudes, modes of dress, responses to foreigners, and even preferred hobbies. Second, individual members bring to the collectivity their personal aims and plans of action, which may find opportunities for enactment through available interactions with other members. For instance, several members may find additional interactions through a discovered common interest in coin collecting, or a young man may find a girlfriend while working to get out the movement's newspaper.

Innovation is a highly significant process, even within these organizations, which themselves exist only as parties in the innovation process of the embedding organization. As emergent organizations, diffuse collectivities lack established norms and regularized procedures. The conduct of any member—and especially of leaders—is quite likely to be challenged by other members as inappropriate. Leadership in a diffuse collectivity rests not on established authority but wholly on the responsiveness of members. Tactical moves of a leader that are inconsistent with the ideology or program of a social movement, for example, are likely to be met with indignation, a sense of betrayal, and a loss of faith or confidence. But given the pressures, temptations, and dilemmas continually faced by a leader in such a loosely structured organization, a correct line of conduct is difficult to discern.

Innovations among rank-and-file members are likely to be evaluated by comparison with the "party line." If creative, the person rises in status, perhaps being recruited into a specialized position in the primary role structure. If judged deviant, resocialization will be applied; if this measure is unsuccessful, the person is likely to be recruited out, at least in the informal sense of other members avoiding interaction. Shunning is probably the oldest and most widespread informal tactic for expelling someone from a group.

Social control within a diffuse collectivity is heavily reactive. Creative performance is rewarded by promotion (within the secondary and sometimes the primary social structure) and deviance is punished by demotion, diminished centrality, and sometimes even by expulsion (in the sense of being redefined as a member of the outgroup).

The more risk involved in membership, the more stringent the social control efforts will be. In revolutionary political movements, for example, deviance is curbed by frequent threats of death, sometimes backed up by an occasional execution. In milder diffuse collectivities under less harsh social and political climes, social control may still invoke substantial hardships in terms of reduced career and interpersonal opportunities. Sometimes, the ousted deviant will, however, be successful in forming a rival faction within the diffuse collectivity.

Only within the more durable movement organizations are the standard organizational proactive tactics likely to be found to any extent, although the publicizing of successful reactive-control incidents serves as a kind of shadow proactive tactic. More implicit proactive tactics aimed at the diffuse collectivity level are quite prominent. Proactive measures provide some offsetting degree of stability. Incentive benefits (in the form of membership gratifications or participation orientations) and, especially, promises (of the benefits of the expected eventual competitive success of the factional suborganization) weigh heavily in this regard. Similarly, threats of demotion or excommunication coupled with obvious and continual surveillance greatly constrain and discipline participation. In all diffuse collectivities, rituals of solidarity to promote *esprit de corps* (and, thereby, member commitment) are prominently visible.

ROLE-MAKING AND CAREER DEVELOPMENT

In any diffuse collectivity, the overwhelming majority of members play consumer roles. The individual can exert a great deal of control over the nature of his consumer role, since such a role is based mainly on degree of interest and participation; recruitment to consumer roles can seldom be highly restrictive, and the implicit socialization procedures of the collectivity can readily be resisted. However, the strong social control emphasis of diffuse collectivities places vague but significant limitations on the range of acceptable performed roles.

In many diffuse collectivities, access to producer and distributor roles is much more restricted and rests significantly on special skills and/or societal prestige. Moreover, social control more sharply restricts the freedom of the individual to redefine the nature of his prescribed role.

Actual career mobility within the primary social structure tends to be limited; many fans want to become a movie star, but very few even make it into the business as an extra. However, in publics and social movements, significant numbers of consumers attain distributor roles by obtaining membership in some interest-group voluntary association (for instance, a movement organization). Further, a small proportion of distributors (for example, association members) manage to attain producer roles by working their way up through the association ranks to become association spokesmen or officials. Finally, in certain masses, a consumer may be able to move directly to a producer role, as when a popular-music consumer becomes a recognized songwriter or performer. Indeed, part of the exciting appeal of diffuse collectivities is the perception that rapid promotion to dizzying heights is more likely than elsewhere, since these organizations tend to lack established channels of placement. For the lucky few, for the quick and the daring, diffuse collectivities can in fact offer accelerated career opportunities in the primary role structure. For example, during the diffuse social and political "hip" movement of the 1960s, many individuals found careers as head-shop owners, issue promoters, drug suppliers, commune leaders, writers, pamphleteers, and gurus. Such facilitated careers have a somewhat precarious basis, however, resting as they do on the strength of the social movement.

Within the secondary social structure, very definitely, career mobility is quite easy and rapid with respect to degree of centrality, being based largely on interest and participation. Similarly, to the extent that consumer status structure is based on seniority, the individual's position in the status structure is primarily a matter of timing. For example, to become an innovator or an early adopter requires only an early receptiveness to the focal object. However, as noted by Oberschall (1973: 163), the timing of entry into active participation tends to reflect the situation of the individual in that only those who perceive the benefits of participation to outweigh the personal risks can afford to join early. Partly for such reasons, status is not merely a matter of seniority in the diffuse collectivity but is frequently also a function of the individual's societal prestige.

Of course, not all consumers progress uniformly through all five stages of the adoption process. Some have arrested careers, progressing only so far and remaining permanently in one of the less central stages (for instance, the stage of interest). Others progress to some point and then turn back; for example, having reached the trial stage, an individual may totally reject the focal object and recruit himself out of the mass or, less radically, retreat to the stage of mere interest. Although such arrested or reversing career trajectories are very common indeed in diffuse collectivities, they are considered deviant career patterns by the ingroup of committed members, who are almost always a hard-core minority of those involved. Nevertheless, hopping from one diffuse collectivity to another and then to yet another is actually the prevalent individual pattern.

IMPACT ON THE CHARACTER OF THE INDIVIDUAL

The principal aim of participation in a diffuse collectivity is to exert some influence on the innovation process within the embedding organization in order to shape the changing character of that organization and, thereby, the nature of one's role in it. Therefore, the primary impact of diffuse collectivity participation is the same as the impact of one's prescribed role in the embedding organization.

If the individual's chosen faction ultimately prevails through the fashion mechanism, not only is his prescribed role more nearly shaped to his liking but his position in the secondary social structures of the embedding organization (especially the leadership and status structures) is also enhanced. The downtrodden peasant joins a revolutionary movement believing that the promised land reforms will make him a successful independent farmer with political influence and social respect. If, on the other hand, his faction ultimately fails, he may be punished for his deviance. Losers in revolutionary struggles, for example, may find themselves stripped of possessions, humiliated, imprisoned, exiled, or even executed. Even in much less radical, almost trivial diffuse collectivities, backers of the winning and losing factions experience milder but parallel effects on their positions and roles in the embedding organizations.

Even during the perhaps lengthy period when the eventual outcome is still in doubt, participation in a diffuse collectivity subjects the individual to various social tensions and antagonisms within the embedding organization. College students from the North taking part in civil rights sit-ins during the 1960s were taunted as ''nigger-loving'' outside agitators, and feminist invaders of previously all-male occupations are still subjected to extensive sexual harassment on the job. Being the first in one's community to try out the miniskirt or hot-pants fashions subjects the individual to considerable tension and hostility within the age-sex structure. Participation in controversial religious or political movements in particular can affect one's opportunities in a wide range of other organizations, as ''Moonies'' and communists can confirm.

Faction aside, participation in any diffuse collectivity tends to influence various personal attributes. By sustaining a diffusely shared focus of attention—event, person, cultural item, social issue, or demand for social change—the individual is subjected to membership norms constraining certain interests, beliefs, perceptions, activities, and even facets of appearance. Although these influences may be most visible in the case of a Hare Krishna adherent—standing with shaved head and saffron robes on a street corner, soliciting funds and chanting scripture—one need only enter the living space of an ecology freak or Star Wars buff to begin to appreciate the impact of diffuse collectivity participation.

Such membership influences on the character of the individual may be enhanced or diminished by one's position, role, or career within the diffuse collectivity. For members of high centrality within its social structure, the diffuse collectivity becomes a significant reference group from which compensating or substitute benefits may be derived as a hedge against the risked benefits from the embedding organization. For its central members, a diffuse collectivity thus helps them not only to find meaning in their lives but also to satisfy their need for social security, unmet in the larger social scene. Particularly for members located high in its status structure, an exalted position within the diffuse collectivity may in fact provide more gratification than the individual's ordinary role in the surrounding organization does. The lonely and frustrated ne'er-do-well may find considerable self-respect and social esteem by developing a distinctive familiarity with foreign stamps, with the life of John Lennon or of V. I. Lenin, or with the political subtleties of the Middle East oil sheikdoms. Indeed, it is on just such bases that radical social movements, such as Hare Krishna, are so often able to require members to renounce and repudiate their prior conventional patterns of speech, dress, domestic arrangements, and occupation (Cohn, 1957).

Apart from such eccentric alterations of lifestyle, the individual impact of occupying a core position in a diffuse collectivity is most often registered on one's self-conception or personal identity. To the extent that one becomes more aware of oneself as a Beatles fan, a hang-glider, a pro-abortionist, or a feminist than as a man, a husband, a citizen, or a salesman, one's self-conception is anchored to the diffuse collectivity, with important consequences for one's habits, attitudes, and activities.

All of these membership influences are modified by role as well as by position. In any social movement, for example, the agitator, the prophet, and the statesman tend to be easily distinguishable. Producers, and to a lesser extent distributors, may successfully resist many membership norms and are sometimes privately appalled by the innocent fanaticism of their followers; Marx proclaimed that he was not a Marxist, and Freud that he was not a Freudian. The "true believer" is most likely to be found in the ranks of the high-status consumers.

Membership influences are also affected by one's career pattern, not only in terms of mobility within the primary role structure but more commonly of that within the secondary social structures. Arrested and reversing career trajectories, so frequent within all diffuse collectivities, clearly limit or even undo many of the influences of membership norms (Toch, 1965). As noted, the majority of participants hop from one diffuse collectivity to another, adopting an often bewildering series of belief systems (Hoffer, 1951). Although these highly mobile individuals represent only a small fraction of the populace, Klapp (1969) contends that this fraction is increasing and that the increasing American participation in diffuse collectivities of all sorts represents "a collective search for identity" in the face of a societal loss of identity supports. The type of diffuse collectivity joined by any such identity seeker is said to depend primarily on the momentary dimensions of his search.

> A person's identity search may be: (1) stylistic (modifying appearance, looks; pose, role to audience) versus inner self-exploration and realization; (2) square versus offbeat or radical directions requiring a break with old identity; (3) activities on one's own, or supported by a peer group; (4) real action versus vicariously living in the roles of dramas and heroes; and (5) practical achievement versus ritual or cultic symbolism aiming at emotional intensification and rebirth [Klapp, 1969: 45–46].

Diffuse collectivities also have social psychological influences on those individuals who do not join them. Those who remain uninvolved in a particular diffuse collectivity may yet find their social lives changed by its contributions to changing customs and norms in the embedding organization, to changes in their own organizational role prescriptions, and to the redefinition of many situations as time goes on. Thus, the nonmember role is still a role involved in the workings of diffuse collectivities. Those who don't vote are still affected by the outcome of an election public; those who join no faction in a public, mass, or movement will yet be influenced by the actions of the winners upon the embedding organization. It happens sometimes that some individuals so dislike the shifts in social realities resulting from diffuse collectivity actions that they form a countermovement to resist and to return things to the way they were.

Whatever history we experience over the next few decades will be shaped in part by diffuse collectivities.

SUMMARY

Membership in a diffuse collectivity is defined by a common focus of attention—a cultural item, event, or person, in the case of masses; a social issue, in the case of publics; and a particular demand for change in some aspect of the social order, in the case of social movements. The membership of any diffuse collectivity tends to be geographically dispersed, indeterminate in number, and continually shifting; yet when a member responds to the common focus, he does so with the awareness than many others are similarly responding. This awareness stems from participation in interaction networks closely geared into the mass media of communication. Diffuse collectivities arise in the innovation process within large organizations of all types, but particularly within societal-level structures.

A mass is organized to produce fashion—to establish new norms regulating matters of personal taste. Six specific social conditions are necessary for the emergence of the fashion mechanism, which is a process of "collective selection" from among competing models or proposals, around each of which a mass forms. The social structure of a mass is depicted in Figure 17–2; primary roles include producers, distributors, and consumers. Within the consumer segment, the secondary social structure exhibits two dimensions: centrality (based on degree of participation) and status (based on seniority and societal prestige). Geographical or functional suborganizations are common. Power and authority are limited, and leadership is the characteristic influence structure.

A public is a dispersed set of people interested in and divided about an issue (pertaining to some organizational decision to be made about which members feel they have the right to disagree), and engaged in discussion of that issue with a view to register some collective opinion which is expected to influence that decision. Public opinion is simply whatever is communicated to decision makers through the functioning of a public. Interest groups serve to narrow and redefine the issue as one between a restricted set of viewpoints and programs, around each of which an "opinion mass" is formed. The functioning of a public is essentially a matter of collective selection of viewpoint and program through competition between opinion masses through the fashion mechanism.

A social movement, focused upon some particular demand for social change, acts with more continuity than other diffuse collectivities, exhibiting more sustained activity, greater stability of role structure, and substantial continuity of membership. Although it is very much a diffuse collectivity, a social movement essentially functions as a rather fuzzy interest group, promoting issues and striving to influence the resulting publics in line with its program regarding social change. At the core of a movement arises a voluntary association or "movement organization" to provide necessary stability and leadership. Formed around this core, the social structures of a movement closely resemble those of an opinion mass. However, many movements are splintered and factionalized, containing as suborganizations rival movement organizations differing in goals, ideologies, and programs. Many movements generate focused opposition in the form of a countermovement. The nature and the degree of opposition greatly influence the strategy, tactics, and character of any social movement.

Although the structure of any diffuse collectivity tends to be somewhat vaguely defined, its culture tends to be rather highly developed and sustains a vital sense of collectivity. The competitive success of a diffuse collectivity depends centrally on its human and material resources.

Through common reliance on the fashion mechanism, diffuse collectivities resemble one another in their contributions to innovation within the embedding organization, detaching the grip of past customs, preparing in an orderly way for the future, and introducing order in the moving present of organizational change.

Because of the strategic importance of human resources, recruitment is the most critical organizational process in diffuse organizations. Membership is always somewhat risky, so recruitment in publics and social movements often targets groups and associations rather than individuals. This strategy is not fully dependable, and considerable effort must be devoted to individual attraction through propaganda and interpersonal influence. Organizational tactics of selection, on the other hand, are surprisingly minor. Placement is entirely informal (except within embedded associations) but is significantly ascriptive.

Socialization is mainly a matter of learning the culture and membership norms, especially through mass media in anticipatory socialization; direct socialization is mainly implicit, except within some embedded movement organizations. Interaction consists largely of propagandizing to attract new members and maintain ingroup solidarity. Since diffuse collectivities tend to lack established norms and regularized procedures, innovation is frequent among both leaders and followers. Social control tends to be highly reactive, although implicit promises and threats, as well as rituals of solidarity, are usually quite prominent.

One of the common attractions of diffuse collectivities is the relatively high degree of individual control over the nature of one's role and the prospect of more rapid and extensive career mobility. Actual mobility within the primary role structure may be rather limited, but within the secondary structures it is quite extensive, being based largely on interest and participation. Although arrested or even reversing career trajectories are viewed as deviant, these are actually the most common patterns.

The principal impact of diffuse collectivities on members and nonmembers is revision of one's role in the embedding organization; such impact is most marked for members of the winning and the losing factions, but they are notable even while the outcome is still in doubt. Participation also affects one's opportunities in many other organizations and, through membership norms, directly affects a wide range of personal attributes. These effects on lifestyle and personal identity are sharpest for members of high centrality or status; the diffuse collectivity becomes a major reference group, helping them to find meaning in their lives and satisfying their need for social security. Effects of participation are modified not only by one's position but also by role (type of producer, distributor, or consumer) and by career pattern (particularly the arrested or reversing trajectories).

SUGGESTIONS FOR ADDITIONAL READING

Diffuse collectivities are a principal topic within that branch of sociological social psychology known as "collective behavior." An excellent comprehensive introduction to that branch is Ralph H. Turner and Lewis A. Killian, *Collective Behavior,* 2nd edition (Englewood Cliffs, N.J.: Prentice-Hall, 1972). A more specialized review of that branch may be found in Stanley Milgram and Hans Toch's "Collective Behavior: Crowds and Social Movements" (pp. 507–610 in Gardner Lindzey and Elliot Aronson, editors, *Handbook of Social Psychology,* 2nd edition, vol. 4. Reading, Mass.: Addison-Wesley, 1969).

The diffuse nature of masses, publics, and social movements dictates their considerable reliance on mass media of communication. A useful introduction to the structure, process, and effects of mass media is William L. Rivers, Theodore Peterson, and Jay W. Jensen, *The Mass Media and Modern Society,* 2nd edition (San Francisco: Rinehart Press, 1971). Early studies of mass communication heavily emphasized its role in propagandizing and intentful persuasion; this role is examined broadly in George N. Gordon, *Persuasion: The Theory and Practice of Manipulative Communication* (New York: Hastings House, 1971) and more psychologically in Erwin P. Bettinghaus, *Persuasive Communication,* 2nd edition (New York: Holt, Rinehart, and Winston, 1973). Currently, greater emphasis is being placed on the functions of mass communication in informing individuals and conveying images of social reality. See, for example, Lewis A. Dexter and David Manning White, editors, *People, Society, and Mass Communication* (New York: Free Press, 1964).

A provocative but somewhat challenging analysis of the mass is Jean Lohisse's *Anonymous Communication: Mass Media in the Modern World* (London: Allen & Unwin, 1973). An excellent compilation of research on the structure and dynamics of masses is Gordon Wills and David Midgley, editors, *Fashion Marketing: An Anthology of Viewpoints and Perspectives* (London: Allen & Unwin, 1973).

Similarly, many of the basic writings on publics and public opinion have been compiled into two fine anthologies: Bernard Berelson and Morris Janowitz, editors, *Reader in Public Opinion and Communication,* 2nd edition (New York: Free Press, 1966), and Daniel Katz, Dorwin Cartwright, Samuel Eldersveld, and Alfred McClung Lee, editors, *Public Opinion and Propaganda* (New York: Holt, Rinehart, and Winston, 1954). Both of these rather timeless volumes treat the social dynamics of public opinion, squarely confronting the hazards of attempting to ascertain developing public opinion through even sophisticated techniques of public opinion polling. A fascinating view of individual factors in opinion is afforded in M. Brewster Smith, Jerome S. Bruner, and Robert W. White, *Opinion and Personality* (New York: Wiley, 1956).

The literature on social movements is a sprawling one indeed. John Wilson provides a solid *Introduction to Social Movements* (New York: Basic Books, 1973). *The Dynamics of Social Movements* are examined in an edited volume by Mayer N. Zald and John D. McCarthy (Cambridge, Mass.: Winthrop, 1979). From the social psychological viewpoint, a useful basic anthology is Barry McLaughlin, editor, *Studies in Social*

Movements: A Social Psychological Perspective (New York: Free Press, 1969). A more unified treatment is to be found in Hans Toch, *The Social Psychology of Social Movements* (Indianapolis: Bobbs-Merrill, 1965), which devotes particular attention to recruitment, socialization, careers, and impacts on individual character.

Finally, Orrin E. Klapp's *Collective Search for Identity* (New York: Holt, Rinehart, and Winston, 1969) is a useful attempt to describe and understand the personal uses of all types of diffuse collectivities.

Chinese immigrants to several American cities created Chinatowns, where their languages, food, and festival celebrations predominate.

CHAPTER 18

The Community Level

In most historical times and places, the community has been the setting in which most daily life went on. It is the background for most of an individual's life activities; it is where one lives. One grows up in a home, a neighborhood, and a community. Other organizational levels seem less real for most people because they are simply not viewed and penetrated many times every day, as the community is. Here is where one goes to school, buys one's commodities, has one's small adventures and tragedies. And here is the circle of persons one is most acquainted with outside the home itself.

Even in modern times, with widespread geographical mobility, individuals still display a relatively strong sense of community. When strangers meet, they almost inevitably tell one another the community they hail from. "Where are you from?" is one of the most common questions in conversation—and rightfully so, since it often gives some first clues about who the person is and what he or she is like.

The majority of a person's daily life, from basic necessities to recreation, takes place within a community and a majority of persons one knows personally reside there. Even when one moves away, the move is most often made in search of a "better" community. A large number of people manipulate events so as to return to a favored community—one they grew up in or visited and found rewarding as a location for living.

In an important sense, the field of sociology emerged along with the notion of the decline of community—in Tönnies's terms, the transition from *Gemeinschaft* to *Gesellschaft,* that is, from close primary solidarity to impersonal secondary interdependence. This rather romantic concept of the lost community envisioned an ascriptively based and rather homogeneous collectivity characterized by a profound sense of belongingness and moral order, by strong social bonds, and by primary (personal) rather than secondary (role) relations among its members (Nisbet, 1962).

Rather early in the development of sociology, it appeared somewhat doubtful that communities in this romantic or utopian sense had ever been historically prevalent. Closely knit small communities were indeed the common mode of living during many eras, but these proved upon closer study to be less stable and far less idyllic than had been supposed. It turned out that life in such communities was bleak and brutal for many who dwelled in them. Accordingly, the concept of community underwent some revision in order to maintain any substantial empirical value. In this revision, the concept of community was more broadly defined as a reasonably self-sufficient (but subsocietal level) true collectivity in which "the individual can have most of the experiences and conduct most of the activities that are important to him" (Broom and Selznick, 1963: 31).

> Wherever any group, small or large, live together in such a way that they share, not this or that particular interest, but the basic conditions of a common life, we call that group a community. The mark of a community is that one's life *may* be lived wholly within it, that all one's social relationships *may* be found within it [MacIver, 1937: 8-9; emphasis in original].

> Theoretically, the member of a community lives his whole life within it; he feels a sense of kinship with others who belong to it; and he accepts the community much as he accepts his own name and family membership.
>
> Communities are usually based on locality. . . . The geographical area and a sense of place set the boundaries of common living and provide a basis for solidarity. However, without respect to geography, one may speak of the "Catholic community," in the sense that there is a unique set of Catholic activities and institutions which, taken together, permit many Catholics to live out much of their lives within boundaries set by religious affiliation. They can be educated as Catholics, live in a Catholic neighborhood, work for a Catholic organization, belong to a Catholic professional society, and read a Catholic newspaper. Similarly, one may speak of a Japanese-American community, a Jewish community, and even an academic community [Broom and Selznick, 1963: 31-32].

In a sense, then, segregation (or differential association) is the indicator that a community exists. The primary index of community in empirical research has been the degree to which a person's neighbors, friends, workmates, and spouse are found within the set of persons marked off by the social or geographic boundaries in question. Most of the person's roles can be enacted within a community. We have in the concept of community, therefore, not only a fairly self-sufficient collectivity but also a sufficient web for the individual to conduct most of his or her social living. One can live out one's entire life in, say, Plains, Nebraska, leaving town only a few times a decade. One can travel one's daily rounds within, say, Jewish circles, only impersonally brushing against strangers from other social worlds—other communities. Why is there a scientific community, for example, but not really a cigar-smokers community?

SOCIAL COMMUNITIES

Virtually any socially defined characteristic of individuals could serve to bound a community—age, sex, language, race or ethnicity, religious affiliation, socioeconomic status, occupation, and so on. Not every such characteristic does in fact produce a community, however. One important sociological problem has been to identify the conditions under which a socially defined characteristic does give rise to a community.

Here, we shall maintain that a community is likely to emerge among the occupants of some position within a societal-level structure when that position is marginal in status and when the corresponding social role is pervasive in its demands and restrictive of the occupant's social contacts (Salaman, 1974). "Marginal" here means that the position is simply not central and conventional; it could be "above," "to the side," or "below" the normal mainstream of a societal-level structure. "Marginal" thus could include the power elite and those who work night shifts, as well as the hobo community which existed in the 1930s. For far different reasons, each of these social positions is marginal (or unconventional), pervasive, and restrictive as to available contacts. And each has given rise to a social community.

A position will especially be considered *marginal* when its occupants identify, and wish to associate, with occupants of a high-status category but these associational ambitions are unsuccessful, for whatever reason. The corresponding social role will be considered *pervasive* when its role expectations pertain to a wide range of the life activities and situations of its performers. For example, performing the role of doctor will usually touch upon more aspects of a person's life than performing the role of sales clerk. A role will be considered *restrictive* when it substantially limits the range of social contacts, situations, and activities of its performers (Salaman, 1974: 30–37). For instance, the role of scientist is more restrictive—in terms of the number of other persons potentially available for extensive communication and shared understandings—than those of the salesman or the secretary.

As we have seen in Chapters 13 to 16, most roles within societal-level structures are quite pervasive, and many are fairly restrictive. Accordingly, marginality of status is most often the differentiating determinant of community. If all three factors are present, a social community is likely to emerge.

All age-sex roles, for example, are highly pervasive and rather restrictive. Only those age categories that are marginal in status seem to give rise to age communities: the youth community (Eisenstadt, 1956) and the old-age community (Hochschild, 1973). Similarly, only marginal sex categories give rise to communities, for example, the homosexual community (C. A. B. Warren, 1974).

Within the economy, socioeconomic status is highly pervasive and restrictive in its impacts on individuals' lifestyles. The so-called status community (Weber, 1946: 186–187; Martindale, 1960: 452–456) appears to be more clearly developed within those SES levels that experience greater marginality or unconventionality in the present sense (Stub, 1972).

Occupations, on the other hand, vary more significantly in both pervasiveness and restrictiveness. Unskilled occupations, in particular, tend to be rather sharply separated from the rest of their performers' lives (Dubin, 1956). Some occupations involve long periods of spatial isolation or unconventional hours and are thus more restrictive (Cottrell, 1940). Moreover, many occupations are marginal in status in that their performers accord them more prestige than do outsiders. Salaman (1974) and Gerstl (1961) have attempted to account for the differential emergence of "occupational communities" in terms of just these factors. Pervasiveness seems to be the first factor in the case of professional occupations—for example, the medical community (O. Hall, 1946), the legal community (Carlin, 1962), the military community (Janowitz, 1960)—and of similar creative occupations—the academic community (Millett, 1962), the scientific community (Hagstrom, 1975), the artistic community (Becker, 1974), the business community, and even the student community. Marginality is an additional factor in the case of craft occupations (Caplow, 1954), such as printers (Lipset, Trow, and Coleman, 1956). Restrictiveness is a major factor in the case of such widely diverse occupations as fishermen (Tunstall, 1969), policemen (Banton, 1964), and jazz musicians (Mack and Merriam, 1960; Becker, 1965).

Within the framework of the polity, certain highly restrictive and very marginal roles give rise to "deviant communities." Some of these are intrinsically political, such as the revolutionary underground. Others are only indirectly political, formed around deviant age-sex roles (the homosexual community) or deviant occupations (the criminal community). Important studies of deviant occupational communities include Maurer (1940), Polsky (1969), Milner and Milner (1972), Letkemann (1973), and G. Miller (1978).

Finally, racial or ethnic communities and religious communities arise in relation to the speech community. As discussed in Chapter 16, a nation-state typically includes within its bounds several speech communities, representing a system of ethnic stratification. Speakers of any one of these languages, together with their genealogical descendants, comprise an ethnic category, sharing not only the cultural traditions of that speech community but also a somewhat distinctive range of physical characteristics.

In virtually all national societies, race and/or ethnicity is a major basis of stratification. Membership in a racial or ethnic minority category is well known to exert pervasive and restrictive effects. Marginality of status, in the sense employed here, is then quite likely to give rise to a racial or ethnic community (Lyman, 1974; Gans, 1962a).

A distinctive core of the fundamental belief system of any speech community can be characterized as religious beliefs. Differences in religion have often been considered socially diagnostic because of the pervasiveness and restrictiveness of religious beliefs and norms. Again, those religions that are marginal in status—not mainstream—are more likely to give rise to religious communities (Herberg, 1960; Greeley, 1972).

These social groupings can be termed communities because the individuals involved tend toward living the full round of their social lives within them. They buy goods and services from fellow members whenever possible (seek a fellow dentist and lawyer if they can), often work with fellow members, pursue leisure activities together (some of which may be unique to that community), and so on. Frequently such groupings have their own schools, colleges, directories, sections of town, clubs, hangouts, sometimes even cemeteries. The pervasiveness, restrictiveness, and marginality of a social category may be somewhat self-fulfilling and self-perpetuating, in that members are pressured to stay, to buy, to companion, and to marry within that social category.

There are objective and subjective aspects of the degree to which a social community exists within a social category. Objectively, a community exists to the degree that its members carry out their social lives within it as opposed to outside of it. For example, do most Quakers trade, visit, and marry with other Quakers? Applying such an index would show, for example, that there is more of a homosexual community than a Methodist community. If members do not associate in all ways far more often with other members than with nonmembers, we have only a social category, or at best a "shadow community" which might perhaps blossom into a full social community in the future under the impact of social change.

Subjectively, a community would exist to the extent that members feel a "sense of community." A sense of community is a variable thing, ranging from virtual indifference to one's social category up to fierce identification, alignment, and attachment. The fact that a man is a printer or a Presbyterian might be either incidental or utterly basic to his self-concept. The "bonds of community" have no doubt loosened in modern times for the planet's populace, but they are still very strong for a great many.

GEOGRAPHIC COMMUNITIES

When people see the word "community," they usually think first of a geographic setting where the dwellers interact extensively with one another—our town. We have examined social communities first, so that some of the basic social psychological aspects of communities of any type could be set forth. As with social communities, the degree to which a geographic setting develops a community, and the degree to which the individuals who live there experience it as a community, are highly variable.

Human beings live in an environment that is neither geologically nor socially uniform. In different locales, there are sharp differences not only in the availability of natural resources but also in the availability of various goods, services, and activities. For example, there are only certain places on the entire planet that feature orchestral symphonies, open-heart surgery, and major-league ball games. One must usually go to at least a medium-sized town to find hospitals, a savings and loan office, a large discount store, and specialty shops. The structure of this geosocial environment is the subject of human ecology (Berry and Kasarda, 1977)—an important subfield of sociology—and of human geography (Murphy, 1974).

The habitations and other architectural constructions of human beings are arranged in *settlement patterns*. The basic unit is a building (or single-owner group of buildings) and its surrounding grounds (a homestead or farmstead). In rural areas, these basic units are organized into distinctive settlement patterns (Bertrand et al., 1958: 78–81). In the nucleated-village pattern, the homes of a number of farmers are clustered together, with the farmlands of each located away from the cluster. In the line-village pattern, homes are arranged in a double row (generally on both sides of a stream or road), with the farmland of each farmer extending in a long narrow strip behind his home and perpendicular to the rows of homes. In the trade-center pattern, farmsteads are scattered across open country and depend on a nearby cluster of non-farm homes and service establishments (a village or town).

Urban settlements include the large villages and towns but range up through cities and metropolitan areas (clusters of adjoining cities, towns and villages) and even to the megalopolis (a cluster of adjoining metropolitan areas). These urban settlements too display a wide diversity of spatial patterns (Murphy, 1974). A city, for example, may segregate its several land uses into concentric zones, into pie-shaped sectors radiating out along major lines of transportation, or into multiple nuclei. A smaller settlement may serve a larger one as a suburb or as a satellite. The type of settlement a person lives in has an important bearing upon his or her social life.

Settlements are arranged in an urban hierarchy, a gradient scale based on the range of human services they provide (Berry, 1967). Every settlement affords some basic set of services, such as retail sale of groceries and gasoline, postal facilities, elementary education, and at least one church. Only in settlements higher up the gradient scale can establishments be found for secondary education, basic medical care, banking, and a more comprehensive line of retail goods. The even more specialized services of higher education, specialized medical care, art museums, daily newspapers, and radio and television stations, are afforded by still higher-grade settlements. The higher the grade of a settlement, the larger the area for which it provides some services. The highest-grade settlements may provide unique services for the entire planet, such as the movies of the Los Angeles megalopolis or the financial exchange institutions of New York City. One could then speak of the "reach" of each grade of settlement, ranging from a few miles, to an entire state, to the globe. The spatial distances between settlements of various grades therefore display rather striking regularities; rural villages might occur every five miles, for example, while market towns might be found twenty miles apart.

Even among settlements of the same grade within the urban hierarchy, however, functional specialization may be observed (Duncan and Reiss, 1956). A given city, for example, may serve as a center for manufacturing, industry, wholesaling, retailing, mining, transportation, education, public administration, military, or entertainment and recreation. In this way, settlements serve as specialized suborganizations of the national economy. Many cities have become famous through such specialization: Las Vegas, Washington, Berkeley, Dresden, Nashville, and so on.

Furthermore, a settlement may choose to incorporate, to become chartered by the state as a municipality—a functional subdivision of the polity. However, the boundaries of a municipality frequently fail to coincide with the boundaries of the corresponding settlement; the "legal city" may be either larger or smaller than the "built city."

Settlements are ecological (or economic) units, and municipalities are political units. While both are of great sociological significance, neither should be confused with communities. "Community" is thus a social psychological phenomenon, not a geographical or political one.

The Community Level

Territoriality plays a large part in the lives of human beings (Hediger, 1961), as it does in the lives of most animals. The human individual displays a "home range," a bounded geographic area with which he is familiar and relatively comfortable, and within which he circulates in the pursuit of his needs and his ordinary affairs. The bounds of his home range, while anchored by his place of residence, need not coincide with those of a single settlement but may encompass or cut across several smaller settlements and/or municipalities or may encompass only a small proportion of the area of some large settlement and/or municipality.

A geographic community, in the classic sense, emerges when a number of individuals become aware that their respective home ranges are substantially similar, that they share the basic conditions of a common life. Such individuals necessarily encounter and re-encounter one another in a variety of role relationships and in a variety of establishments and institutions, thus developing a base of acquaintanceship and local intimacy. Since their home ranges center on their habitations, residential proximity emerges as a common characteristic. Indeed, the geographic or local community is often referred to as the residential community.

Communities, in this sense, are most easily noted in villages, towns, and small cities, as evidenced by the overwhelming preponderance of such settlement types in the literature of "community studies" (Bell and Newby, 1973). Ever since the early work of Galpin (1915) on determining community boundaries, rural communities too have received frequent (though less well publicized) study. Finally, much attention has been devoted to identifying and describing residential communities nested and embedded within the sprawling settlement patterns of giant cities and polynucleated metropolises (Burgess 1925; Hunter, 1974).

In view of the relentless urbanization of America and most of the rest of the world, this last-mentioned theme perhaps warrants special attention. Community areas within a metropolis do not exist as physically or officially bounded local areas but are *socially constructed* (Suttles, 1972). Neither the boundaries nor the social character of adjacent residential areas are physically given or legally fixed. Through communications of residents and outsiders, shared images of character emerge, based on the currently characteristic lifestyles of the two residential areas; some convenient physical feature—street, railroad, fence—arbitrarily comes to symbolize the dividing line between them. Convenience then becomes convention; people and activities sort themselves out onto one or the other side of this symbolic boundary, in keeping with the presumed character of the two areas. This amounts to a "cooperative defense" of the characters of adjacent areas—against outsiders of differing lifestyles and against the vagaries of external political and economic forces.

> The quest for a good community is, among other things, a quest for a neighborhood where one does not fear standing an arm's length from his neighbor, where one can divine the intent of someone heading down the sidewalk, or where one can share expressions of affect by the way adjacent residences dress up for mutual impression management.
> Decisions like this about an area require us to draw distinctions among areas and ultimately boundaries between them. . . . Naturally, this need not mean that there will be much consensus on such boundaries, although the reasonable tendency to consult other residents on

this matter is a powerful move in that direction. Often, however, the new resident will have only an ill-formed notion of the boundaries of the area he is moving into and the character of his fellow residents beyond what is conveyed by the appearance of their houses. For such a new resident there seem to be two separable strategies, not mutually exclusive, but likely to receive greater or lesser emphasis depending on his capacity for residential mobility. One emphasis may be on selecting a residential area where the character of fellow residents is assured by the costs of living there and the presumed respectability of people so heavily rewarded by society. Another emphasis is to cultivate one's neighbors once one is in an area to the point that they come to share a personal convenant, look out for one another, and exempt each other from the general suspicions and defensive provocations which are so productive of the violence, insult, or damage that neighbors fear in the first place. The first type of strategy is most available to people with high incomes and transferable skills. Where this first strategy is pursued to the exclusion of the second, it is apt to produce what Morris Janowitz (1967) has called the community of limited liability: a community where the resident invests neither himself nor his capital so deeply that he cannot pull out when housing values and the character of his neighbors begin to decline. The practice of cultivating one's neighbors is apt to be more common among people who are disbarred by color or who cannot afford to live in a wide range of neighborhoods or are less mobile because of their jobs, local investments, or family traditions which give them a large place in a small pool [Suttles, 1972: pp. 234–236].

Examination of the growth of entirely new settlements—''new towns''—after World War II demonstrates that a geographic settlement can develop into a true community in a very short time through a collective creative process. The data suggest that if a group of people are thrown together, there to pursue in common the majority of their activities, a community will develop within a matter of months.

SUPERIMPOSED COMMUNITIES

The various types of social communities need not be mutually independent. Two or more types may overlap or intersect. An ethnic community (for instance, German-American) and a religious community (Lutheran) may overlap, as may an ethnic community (Irish-American) and an occupational community (policemen).

More radically, one type may be nested within another type. By definition, an occupational community will be nested within a particular status community. Similarly, an ethnic community (Italian-American) might be virtually nested within a larger religious community (Catholic). Or conversely, a religious community (Black Muslims) might be nested within a larger racial community (black).

Most dramatically, two or more social community types may be coincident in their boundaries. For example, an ethnic community and a religious community may coincide, as in the case of the Jews. When an ethnic, an occupational, and a status community are all mutually coincident—as is not infrequent, say, in India— a ''caste'' is defined.

A far more frequent phenomenon is the superimposition of a social community on a geographic community. First of all, the social composition of the residents of any local area is greatly determined by that area's place within the urban hierarchy and by its specialized niche within the national economy. In some cases, then, a local community may take on the character of an occupational community or, more commonly, a status community—becoming a mining, a railroad, or a fishing community (Horobin, 1957) on the one hand, or a white-collar or a blue-collar community (Kornblum, 1974) on the other. As a consequence of such specialization, even the age and sex composition of a local area may be sharply affected, so that some local communities are almost exclusive male (a sex community) or are peopled almost entirely by the elderly (an age community). These are some of the social factors which lend virtually every settlement a distinctive social flavor.

A second point regarding the superimposition of community types is that the segregating tendencies of any social community lead its members to seek greater spatial proximity with "their own kind." Within a great metropolitan settlement, for example, each of the local community areas tends to be dominated by and identified with some social community—racial, ethnic, religious, occupational, or status (Hunter, 1974). Indeed, some local community areas (for instance, the commercialized vice district) are dominated by deviant social communities, and others (the "bohemian" areas, the district of inner-city luxury apartments, the bedroom suburbs) are dominated by specific age-sex categories and their associated family life-cycle stages and lifestyles (Gans, 1962b).

The character of a local community is most affected, of course, when it is dominated by two or more superimposed social communities. Certain rural communities, for example, are almost exclusively German-American, Amish, blue-collar, farming communities (Hostetler, 1980).

The continuing force of communities is well documented, not only by studies of residential segregation (Lieberson, 1963; Kantrowitz, 1973), but also by studies of mate selection. Even in contemporary America, choice of spouse is heavily endogamous within the bounds of race, ethnicity, religion, socioeconomic status, and locality (Eckland, 1968).

COMMUNITY AS SOCIAL ORGANIZATION

A community (whether social, geographic, or both) is a highly informal, emergent, but rather determinately bounded collectivity. Membership is open only to those individuals who display the defining social characteristic(s), and is manifested through differential association with others who share the criterial characteristic(s). Thus, if one lives in a Quaker or an academic community, one must either become a Quaker or an academician, or remain a relative outsider.

Collectivity

The aspect of collectivity is paramount in viewing any community. Sharing the basic conditions for a common life, individuals organize to produce a rather distinctive collective good: a setting where members can conduct their daily rounds within a more or less congenial social atmosphere and the suspension or relaxation of certain demands, pressures, and (especially) status anxieties attendant upon their common position within one or more of the societal-level structures. All communities are subcultural lumps within these largest social organizations.

Each type of community, for example, sponsors its own linguistic variant. Within any official national language, geographic dialects are sponsored by geographic communities, social dialects by status communities, ethnic dialects by ethnic communities; each occupational community and each religious community employs a distinctive jargon of special technical terms (Hudson, 1978; Wright, 1974), and each deviant community employs a distinctive argot, a defiantly sinister special vocabulary (Maurer, 1940). An ethnic community may rely on its own native language, alongside or in place of the official national language.

The folk beliefs, myths, legends, narrative and literary forms, jokes, et cetera, that accompany a language similarly vary among communities that differ in linguistic usages. The folklore of various ethnic, occupational, and local communities is a subject of boundless interest (Clarke and Clarke, 1963). Each of these is a *sub*culture—a world of its own, to some extent.

Moreover, any social or geographic community will embrace some variant conception of age-sex roles, of law and politics, and of the occupational structure. Community mores, conventions, traditions, and values are not uniformly those of the societal-level structures. Usually these are elaborations of the folkways of the societal-level structures, but they may also be quite at variance—even oppositional—so that such communities represent factional suborganizations within the larger structures. For example, an Italian-American enclave may oppose the sexual emancipation and more permissive patterns of the larger age-sex structure, regarding them as grossly immoral, and an urban campus community may stand in violent opposition to the policies of the embedding polity.

The resources of a community are, therefore, those commodities controlled by members which may contribute to the social life of the members and to the collective defense of the distinctive community culture against the forces of societal structures. Community newspapers (Janowitz, 1967), community schools, community associations, and similar specialized institutions are particularly vital resources (Suttles, 1972). Such community organs simultaneously serve the positive function of affirming the group's collective definitions and interpretations of situations, and the defensive function of disparaging and countering outside impingements. These institutions in turn depend on an adequate base of human and material resources (the numbers, skills, and wealth of its members).

Social Structure

The primary role structure of any community, even when pronounced and highly consensual, tends to be both derivative and diffuse. That is, individual roles within the common life of the community mainly reflect persons' roles within societal structures and associations. Relatively little distinctive and stable division of labor tends to occur within the community's own dynamics—except in those occupational communities organized to produce abstract cultural commodities such as science (Hagstrom, 1975; T. S. Kuhn, 1970) or art (Becker, 1974). Moreover, particularly in local communities, members encounter one another in a multiplicity of such derivative roles. The butcher may be encountered on different occasions by the same person as a neighbor, as a church elder, and as a volunteer fireman. Role relationships are thus multiple rather than segmental.

It is the secondary social structures that are most significant within a community. In terms of dimensional social structures, it must be noted that no coherent authority structure is to be found. Any fragmentary authority relations within a community rest on the authority structure of the municipality (in the case of a local community) or of a voluntary association (in the case of a social community). But this does not mean that communities are amorphous or lack leadership and direction.

Influence within a community is more aptly considered as a matter of power, status, and leadership. The community power structure, based on control of resources, has been a major focus of sociological research (Hawley and Wirt, 1974). Community status, as differentiated from socioeconomic status (B. Barber, 1961), is thought to reflect contributions made to the collective social life and to the defense of the community. Thus, community status is reputational (based on actions) rather than attributional (based on role and personal attributes). Since both leadership and community status reflect the worth of an individual's contributions to the collective action, it is scarcely surprising that the community structures of leadership and status are highly correlated. The relationship of these two structures to that of community power is, however, much less clear. The power elite theory of community influentials holds that all three are highly correlated, while the pluralist theory maintains that power and leadership are poorly correlated. Bonjean and Olson (1964) suggest that various communities may differ in the degree of correlation between power and leadership. T. N. Clark (1968) attempted to relate differences in the shape of the community power structure to differences in community decision making, finding that the flatter the power structure, the greater the differentiation between potential elites and the lesser the emphasis on provision of public goods.

As is heavily emphasized in many works on community, conformity to community standards of conduct is a matter of considerable importance. Because community status is reputational rather than attributional, one's position in the conformity structure of a community exerts substantial influence on one's position in the status structure as well and hence on the character of the social life one experiences.

Finally, in many localized communities (where interaction networks are quite extensive and are not based on segmental role relationships), something approaching a coherent affect structure can be discovered. Liking, as well as status, becomes a relevant basis for preferential association, and thus affects the communication structure of the smaller community and the individual's personal life.

Many students of community have called attention to yet another aspect of secondary social structure, namely, its suborganizations. An ethnic, racial, religious, or

315

status community is often densely populated by a variety of factional or special-interest voluntary associations. An occupational community, such as the academic community, is comprised of numerous scholarly societies and professional associations. A local community often teems with assorted civic associations, fraternal and service organizations, and neighborhood associations. In the absence of any substantial primary role structure, there is an important sense in which the collective action of a community is carried out through interaction among these voluntary associations rather than among individual members. In a very influential analysis, R. L. Warren (1978) considers the structure of a community (its horizontal pattern) to be found in the relations among its associations, and the community's connections to higher-level social organizations (its vertical pattern) to be found in the relations of these localized associations to state- and national-level associations. For example, the interactions among these associations will have a great deal to do with who is nominated and elected mayor. Associations are incessant lobbyists representing special interests to community officials.

Finally, in the case of geographic communities, one traditional conception takes a community to be an organization of *neighborhoods*. "The neighborhood . . . is an area within which borrowing occurs, where mutual aid is common, where first names are used, and where gossip takes place. The community, on the other hand, encompasses too large an area for these patterns to hold" (Bertrand et al., 1958: 78). Although some have argued that urbanism has made both neighboring and neighborhoods obsolete, numerous studies indicate that both remain fairly prominent even in large metropolitan settlements (Fava, 1958; Suttles, 1972; Keller, 1968).

Interorganizational Relations

The vital relations of community to the various societal-level structures have already received some attention above, so we now turn to supracommunity diffuse collectivities. Despite the relative social insulation provided by a community, the mass media and masses significantly penetrate and infiltrate any community, fostering awareness of life outside. National publics enlist communities in the opinion process, and supracommunity social movements sometimes focus upon specific local or social communities, as Birmingham and Selma, Alabama, during the civil rights movement of the 1960s.

The local community depends on settlements for its resources and on municipalities for the special resource of political authority, but must continually attempt to manipulate both types of unit in defense of its lifeways.

Principally, however, a community is engaged in relations with other communities of the same type. Communities of the same type (for example, ethnic) often seek to define and publicize their differences in order to maintain distinctive identities. They may compete for opportunities and scarce resources (as well as recognition), which sometimes leads to open conflict and power struggles. But often there is an exchange of commodities across community lines (as when Jews run grocery stores in black areas or Anglos patronize taco stands) and substantial mutual accommodation (R. M. Williams, 1977).

Communities diverge from one another and from their larger embedding organizations, but despite episodic dramatic incidents, there is usually little will or few resources to pursue these divergences into open conflicts. Conflict is most frequent in cases of encroachment; otherwise a "live and let live" accommodation, with perhaps a few disparaging remarks, predominates in interorganizational relations.

ORGANIZATIONAL PROCESSES

Recruitment into a community is ascriptive, in the sense that membership is limited to those individuals who exhibit the relevant defining social characteristic(s)—race, ethnicity, religion, occupation, local residence; other individuals are not free to apply. On the other hand, recruitment is voluntary in that qualified individuals need not accept membership in the community—that is, they need not identify with or differentially associate with other persons exhibiting the criterial characteristic(s). Consequently, a community does undertake tactics of attraction by seeking to contrast itself favorably with rival communities and to dramatize the dangers and risks of insult faced in the outside world by any person on account of the criterial characteristic(s). Stories and fables expressing these themes are a notable feature of any community's culture. Through such mechanisms, communities tend to be self-perpetuating and to perpetuate their divergences and conflicts with other communities and the larger societal-level structures. It is not simply the majority who perpetuates, say, the marginal status of a racial, ethnic, or religious minority.

The aspect of placement is not highly developed, since a community lacks an elaborate primary social structure. Position is defined mainly within the dimensional social structures, particularly that of community status, and is to a large extent developed by the individual through his or her own behaviors.

Socialization efforts are quite extensive and pervasive, although they are mainly implicit and informal. Since the culture of a community includes variations of the cultures of all societal-level structures, the types of expectations to be communicated and of personal features to be developed through socialization are very similar to (though discrepant from) those involved in societal-level socialization. It is not surprising, therefore, that the socialization procedures of a community closely resemble those described in Chapters 13–16. A community, however, must place less reliance on the mass media and on the public schools, since the supracommunity origins of the contents relayed through these channels suggest that the perspective and standards of the community may go unreflected or may even be contravened. Hence, communities struggle to control the public schools—often instituting alternative schools—and endeavor to censor or restrict the availability of mass media (magazines displayed in drugstores and books circulated in the libraries). Particularly in localized communities, not every member will have been born into the community, and some may therefore need to be resocialized, to strip away previously acquired features and expectations and substitute those of the new community.

Whether born there or recently moved, the individual is usually desirous of fitting in and getting along in his or her community, so that implicit socialization procedures—encouraging collectively desired role performances and discouraging undesired ones—are usually sufficient to produce a full-fledged integrated member.

An individual may resist the socialization efforts of a community by telling the community that its expectations of him are inappropriate or that the culture of some other community (or of the societal structures) is superior or otherwise preferable. It will never be the case that all members are fully aligned with the community; degree of alignment is a variable thing, and some people will always seek or promote alternative alignments. This is one of the major reasons why impingements from outside the community are regarded warily by aligned community members.

Interaction within a community exhibits a higher ratio of direct to indirect interaction than is characteristic of the larger organizations reviewed thus far. Nevertheless, even in small communities, any member will directly interact with only a fraction of the membership, and roles are poorly defined. At an individual level, interaction is basically a matter of members separately carrying out their daily rounds of routine life affairs (except, again, in occupational communities organized for collective production of abstract cultural commodities such as science or art).

More distinctively, perhaps, community interaction can be construed (Kaufman, 1959) as taking place among the numerous associations that comprise the suborganizations of a community. "Community action" (R. L. Warren, 1978) takes the form of episodic collective actions by temporary alliances and coalitions of associations to deal with some fairly specific community problem or external threats. The process of "community organization" arises during such episodes of community action as a deliberate attempt to foster these alliances and coalitions. The process of "community development," on the other hand, is a longer-range effort to stimulate the formation of—and individuals' participation in—a suitable diversity of viable associations, in other words, to foster the elaboration of community suborganization.

Individuals are encouraged to become active in the community, which in practice usually means becoming active in various associations within the community, such as the Parent-Teachers Association, the Cleanup Committee, Neighborhood Watch, Citizens for Yanksville, and so on. Coalitions among such associations are usually quite temporary and shift from issue to issue. Community organization strives for greater "united front" consensus, while community development is an attempt to expand the collective good by enhancing participation, a sense of community, and successful strategies for expanding resources. All of these involve an increase in community-focused interactions. It is an interesting fact that, for some persons, these community activities also serve as a training ground for careers in the societal-level structures, particularly the polity.

Innovation is a frequent but troublesome process within any community, at least from some viewpoints among the membership. Given the absence of a clear-cut primary role structure, almost any performance could be considered discrepant. By the nature of a community, surveillance (while quite informal) is both extensive and rather efficient, so that awareness of a possibly discrepant performance tends to be fairly widespread. Given the strong sense of collectivity that characterizes a community, "whistleblowers," "busybodies," and "moral entrepreneurs" (Becker, 1963) tend to be abundant. Community tensions concerning the normative standing of performances are endemic, in the forms of gossip about individuals' performances (Blumenthal, 1937; Hannerz, 1967) and rumor about performances of associations (Peterson and Gist, 1951).

A good deal of the informal conversation among members is directed toward reaching some consensus on the evaluation of others' behaviors and attitudes. In small towns, this process may reach the level of self-fulfilling labelings—"Suzie is shy and backward," "Morris is smart but not to be trusted"—which is why the person is hard put to escape the label.

Since a community lacks any coherent authority structure of its own, it also lacks any formal procedures for ratification or stigmatization of innovations, although the informal procedures of gossip and rumor can be powerful. Most often, then, the standing of an innovative performance must be resolved by reaching some apparent consensus through the very processes of gossip and rumor (Turner and Killian, 1972: 30–56; Shibutani, 1966; Rosnow and Fine, 1976). To phrase this point more analytically, the normative standing of innovations within a community is established or resolved through the operation of *diffuse collectivities* arising within the bounds of the community. We saw in Chapter 17 that masses, publics, and social movements are primary mechanisms of change within societal-level structures. Since the cultural concerns of a community parallel those of societal structures, it should not be surprising that similar mechanisms serve this function within a community. Indeed, many would maintain that the forces of fashion, public opinion, or ideology are nowhere more powerful than in the community context.

At the level of individuals' performances, the stigmatization procedure of gossip (using the mechanisms of fashion and public opinion) eventuates in "scandal" (Gluckman, 1963). At the level of suborganizational performances of associations, the stigmatization procedure of rumor (using the mechanisms of publics and, sometimes, social movements) eventuates in "community controversy" (Coleman, 1957; Crain et al., 1969). The more highly developed the community, the more likely a controversy is to spawn a social movement and an opposing countermovement polarizing the community in a process of rancorous "community conflict." Such conflicts can arise over virtually any conceivable issue, from plans for a nuclear plant to teenage morals, from fluoridation of the drinking water to impeachment of city councilmen. Wider societal-level issues, such as school busing or farm subsidies, are often reinterpreted and translated into the local scene and thus made into more strictly local community conflicts.

Social control within a community rests fundamentally on the fact that status is reputational. In the relative absence of a primary role structure, an individual's position within a community is most centrally his position within the community status structure. Creative performance is rewarded by an increase in reputational status, and deviance is punished by decreased status; a conforming performance allows the individual to maintain his status position. These rewards and punishments are determined and administered in the very conduct of the ratification/stigmatization procedures of gossip (Rosnow and Fine, 1976; Gluckman, 1963). Other sanctions are subsequently determined and administered inasmuch as the communication structure tends to reflect the status structure. A decrease in status typically leads to a decrease in communications received, as the deviant is shunned and ostracized, while the person moving up in the status structure is eagerly sought out for conversation, invited to sociable gatherings, and so on. More drastically—lacking any formal procedures for punishment—a localized community may respond to violators of its mores by informal harassment, vandalism, forcible excommunication, physical punishment, or even lynching. In some parts of the world, such as sections of the Middle East and India, the ritualized murder of those who have grossly violated community mores still occurs.

A community may also turn its more seriously deviant performers over to official municipalities for handling or call in help from the embedding organizations, such as county or state police officers. The fact that such options exist for a community, although they are perhaps seldom used, lends some additional weight to more informal reputational social control mechanisms.

In the more proactive aspect of social control, rituals of solidarity tend to be fairly abundant within any community, particularly a localized social community. Conventions regarding forms of address, terms of reference, conversational form, modes of dress and grooming, and vocabulary, signal common membership. Many events and gatherings—picnics, meetings, contests, parades, festivals, carnivals, dances—serve to celebrate the character of the community and to dramatize the magnitude of promised benefits and threatened punishments. Community members are continually exhorted to participate and become more active in all these collective affairs.

ROLE-MAKING AND CAREER DEVELOPMENT

Despite the partially ascriptive basis of community, the individual is fairly influential in determining his membership in any community. In the first place, he is often successful in influencing whether the criterial social characteristic(s) are attributed to him. Studies of "passing" (Goffman, 1963b) indicate that members of even racial or sex categories may be able to pass themselves off as belonging to another race or sex. A less abrupt maneuver is the "cross-over," in which an individual gradually transfers from one ethnic (or status) community to another (Fishman, 1977). And since some criterial characteristics (such as religion, residence, occupation, socioeconomic status) are to some degree voluntarily achieved, an individual can simply "switch" between rival religious (Newport, 1979), geographic (Rossi, 1955), occupational (Slocum, 1966), or status communities by altering his position on the underlying characteristic. Indeed, this is the classic portrait of upward social mobility depicted in novels, biographies, and advice to the aspiring—get into the "right" circles, join the "right" clubs and congregations, move to the "right" section of town, and so forth. For years, Hollywood aspirants would be groomed through conventionalization of everything from their hair color to their speech and their very name.

Second, even with a fixed social definition of his social category, the individual's degree of involvement in the corresponding community (his degree of identification with and participation in the community) is discretionary, limited only by his ability to find his significant personal relationships (neighbors, friends, workmates, spouse) outside the bounds of that social category. Of course, the rivalry between communities is often such that this associational freedom is sharply restricted.

Position within a community is largely a matter of reputational status. Thus, the individual is able to influence his placement within a community through his own choices regarding his degrees of (1) participation, particularly in the rituals of solidarity and in various associations; (2) contribution to those associations and, thereby, to community actions; and (3) conformity, through cooperation or resistance in community efforts toward his own socialization and surveillance.

Careers within a community are largely defined in terms of two dimensions of movement: centrality (or inclusion) and status. Every community distinguishes several degrees of centrality: newcomer, provisionally accepted member, categorically accepted member, personally accepted member, and imminent migrant (Janes, 1961). The degrees of community status recognized within a community vary more sharply. In most communities, nevertheless, the expected career pattern is inward and upward. Career timetables are most clearly defined in the cases of occupational communities (O. Hall, 1948, 1949; Janowitz, 1960; Caplow and McGee, 1958; Becker, 1952) and in religious communities. Among the types of deviant careers, arrested mobility is perhaps more common within communities than is downward mobility, although a scandal may result in a sharp drop in status and not infrequently motivate the individual to leave.

IMPACT ON THE CHARACTER OF THE INDIVIDUAL

By interposing its own variant culture between the individual and his societal-level structures, a community effectively modifies aspects of his role within each of these larger structures. The specific nature of these role modifications is, of course, determined by the community to which the individual belongs. Such subcultural modifications of his role in the speech community, in the age-sex structure, in the polity, and in the economy result, in turn, in modifications of those individual attributes determined by societal-level roles (see Chapters 13–16). Thus, the community is an active agent, not a passive transmitter of societal-level norms, and affects how the person talks, views men and women, perceives the government, and makes his or her living, along with a host of other attitudes and behaviors.

By modifying these basic individual attributes, the community affects both a person's attributional standing and his or her prospects for mobility within the societal-level structures. For example, full involvement in the Puerto Rican community would lead the person to speak and read Spanish to the detriment of developing greater competence in standard English; to associate heavily with other Puerto Ricans to the neglect of developing a wider network of occupationally influential contacts and sponsors; and to form deeply rooted attitudes toward men and women that may be at variance with the norms of the larger age-sex structure. For members of many social and even geographic communities, the variance between the culture of their community and that of societal-level structures poses a serious dilemma or "mobility trap" (Wiley, 1967): upward mobility within the community has the effect of handicapping one's upward mobility at the societal level and vice versa.

In partial compensation, however, the community offers the individual member some measure of insulation against the pressures, insults, and status anxieties of societal structures.

First, the solidarity of the community in its overvaluation of the characteristic around which its is formed helps to sustain the individual in his self-conception and his views of the world. This collective support may even enable him to take some measure of pride in a characteristic that has rendered him marginal within some societal-level structure. Because his involvement in the community gives that characteristic a more prominent position in his self-conception it constitutes a more important basis of his identity in comparison to similar individuals not involved in that community (Salaman, 1974). Community-based characteristics are collectively deemed "good" while outside characteristics are derogated and belittled, which supports the individual in his or her self-concept and reinforces the idea that he or she is "in the right place."

Second, while the community may have harmed the societal-level (attributional) status of the individual through modification of his personal attributes, the community offers its own compensatory status structure based on reputation. Reputational status is not only more socially immediate than attributional status but it is also more nearly controllable by individual efforts. Since the individual has the majority of his personal interactions within the community, his local reputational status is likely to have far more social psychological meaning for him than a much more abstract societal-level status does. Even in deviant communities, this in-group recognition can sustain the individual through many trials and tribulations in the larger society. The vital human impact of reputation on both conduct and self-image has been examined in Chapter 2.

> The lower animals . . . are natural and naive, and not concerned, as human beings are, about their reputations and their conduct [Park, 1927: 737].

> Thus man turns out to be a sophisticated animal, keenly conscious of himself . . . concerned at once about his reputation and his soul. Behavior of this sort is what we ordinarily call conduct, when that word is given an ethical connotation. Conduct is that form of behavior we expect in man when he is conscious of the comment that other men are making, or are likely to make, upon his actions [Park, 1931: 36].

Suttles suggests that the reputational status dynamics provided by residential community are essential for a child's development of an integrated self-system.

The Community Level

Full access to all areas of the city permits a highly segmentalized style of life where role playing need not go beyond impression management. To avoid this sort of chameleonlike behavior and personal development, individuals must be encompassed in a smaller and more nearly closed framework of social relations where they have to "keep their stories straight." Presumably, this type of closed informational system is especially crucial to the development of children who are still in the process of acquiring a wholistic personality [Suttles, 1972: 39].

Turning now from consideration of the impact of membership to that of position, we must bear in mind that social position within a community is largely a matter of reputational status. The impact of community position on the individual is most sharply defined in terms of self-esteem. As compared to attributional status, reputational status provides the individual with a much more socially anchored self-esteem.

The impact of a normal community career, then, is to produce continual enhancement of such socially anchored self-esteem. Deviant career trajectories, on the other hand, tend to diminish this benefit. Not only does a decline in community status diminish this type of self-esteem, but diminished centrality diminishes the social anchoring of that self-esteem and lessens the person's opportunities within the community.

We should note (with Fischer, 1975) that many discussions of the social psychology of community have failed to differentiate the geographic community from that ecological unit we have called a settlement. Accordingly, some attention should be allotted here to what might be called the social psychology of settlements. Park (1926) clearly pointed to such a distinction, and the classical statements (Simmel, 1950; Wirth, 1938) rather closely observed it.

This "social psychology of settlements" generally attempts to sort out, by grade within the urban hierarchy, the impact on the individual of his or her residence. What, for example, are the social psychological differences between living in a small town and living in a megalopolis?

One general feature of settlements varying over the urban hierarchy is the "built environment" of streets, parking lots, buildings, and the like. As a rule, higher-grade settlements exhibit greater population size, larger geographic area, higher population density, wider range of building sizes, more land-use specialization, higher traffic volume, more noise, and so on. Careful sociological investigation reveals, however, that any direct effects of such aspects of the physical environment are seriously blurred and muted by the social order of a settlement (Michelson, 1970). An area dominated by grand brownstone townhouses may easily become a crime-ridden slum, whereas an area of tiny bungalows may remain a safe and harmonious neighborhood.

A second general feature of settlements varying by grade within the urban hierarchy is the availability of specialized services. The higher the grade of a settlement, the greater the variety of specialized establishments, institutions, associations, occupations, and residential communities. The opportunity structures of the individual are therefore directly affected by the type of settlement in which he is located. Higher-grade settlements provide a far greater range of specialized opportunities, but comparative rates of divorce, crime, and even accidents suggest that such settlements may provide a less coherent and supportive framework for living. Persons in higher-grade settlements tend to be more "on their own"—more free and, simultaneously, more adrift.

This effect comes closer to the thrust of the classical contributors; namely, that each grade of settlement within the urban hierarchy affords a somewhat distinctive "way of life" (Redfield, 1955; Wirth, 1938; Gans, 1962b). Only in settlements of the lowest grades does the basis for conduct and social interaction generally resemble that of a community. Within settlements of the higher grades, the prevalent basis for framing conduct and interaction is essentially that provided by societal-level structures. In other words, in greater urban settlements interaction becomes more differentiated, specialized, segmentalized, depersonalized, anonymous, superficial, transitory, and calculating (Wirth, 1938), at least whenever the individual ventures out of his local community area into the settlement at large—into the world of strangers (L. Lofland, 1973). The distinctive social psychological tactics necessary for management of self and others in such a world of strangers have been thoroughly elaborated in a series of sociological studies (Goffman, 1963a, 1971; L. Lofland, 1973; Milgram, 1970). The individual must learn where and when he may safely go in the city, how to coordinate silently with others to avoid physical contact on crowded sidewalks and subways, how to answer the telephone without inviting a burglary or assault, how to erect "involvement shields"—by confining one's visual attention to safe stimuli, by placing one's possessions on the adjacent library chair, by traveling with known companions—to protect unacquainted individuals from accessibility to each other.

The impact on the individual of this distinctive way of life was considered by Simmel (1950) to include mental stimulation and intellectuality, an attitude of "indifferent sophistication," personal reserve, freedom, and a deep striving for personal individuality. Milgram's (1970) studies of urban "noninvolvement" norms provide some limited support for these hypothesized effects; city dwellers were shown, for example, to be far less willing to help a stranger—by letting him into the home to use the telephone—than were town dwellers, and were actually embarrassed to give up a seat on the bus or subway to an infirm old woman. Karp, Stone, and Yoels (1977) subsume the wide variety of research findings in these areas under the general proposition that, in the face of the overstimulation of urban life, urbanites must minimize attention and involvement while maximizing social order. They must strike a delicate balance between involvement, indifference, and cooperation with one another.

In modern times, an individual has a "cafeteria of communities" from which to choose. Most persons come to a community that is already well-formed, so that it is only a matter of gaining entrance, "learning the ropes," and fitting in to have a circle within which one's life can be largely conducted. Without such a circle, the person starkly faces the giant structures of the society at large.

However, since no community is entirely self-sufficient, such a circle is never complete. Throughout the planetary web, a host of other organizations can reach through the community's boundaries to touch the individuals there. Sometimes, the commu-

nity can intercede for the individual, but often not. The community itself can be erod-
ed or even shattered by outside forces, as we saw in the chapter on social change.

A breakdown in community—social or geographic—to which one has belonged
can be something of a life crisis. School authorities have often traced a child's troubles
to his family's move from one community to another. Displaced persons tend to
display similar anxieties and uncertainties.

On his own, an individual may also become alienated from his community—a
state which goes beyond mere indifference into active rejection and dysphoria, a
generalized distaste for things related to the community. This dissonance becomes a
part of the person's self-concept: "I'm no longer Catholic," "I left that town just as
soon as I could," "As an ex-serviceman I can tell you—stay out of the Army," and so
on. In the majority of cases, such tensions are resolved by the person's successfully
joining a different community more congenial to his present character. If not, the person is to some extent adrift in life.

SUMMARY

A community is a subsocietal-level collectivity providing the basic conditions and institutions of a common life, within which a member may conduct virtually all his life
activities and social relationships. Membership may be based on some social
characteristic or on place of residence. The primary empirical index of community is
the degree to which members' neighbors, friends, workmates, and spouses are found
within the set of persons marked off by the defining social or geographic boundary.

Virtually any social characteristic of individuals may serve to bound a community—age, sex, language, race or ethnicity, religious affiliation, socioeconomic
status, occupation. Most often, these do not produce a community. The occupants of
any such position within a societal-level structure are likely to constitute a community
only when (1) that position is marginal in status or unconventional; (2) the
corresponding role is pervasive in its demands; and (3) the role is restrictive of the occupant's social contacts.

Geographic residence may also provide the basic conditions of a common life and
bound a community. Human settlements vary widely and systematically in the range
of goods, services, and activities locally available. Even among settlements of the same
grade within this urban hierarchy, functional specialization occurs—mining towns, industrial towns, college towns. Legally, a settlement (or any part of one) may incorporate as a municipality, a political unit. A geographic community does not necessarily coincide with the boundaries of a settlement or of a municipality and may arise
within any grade of the urban hierarchy. Community areas within a great metropolis
are socially constructed through assortative segregation and cooperative defense.

One type of social community may overlap, intersect, or be nested within some
other type of social community or even a geographic community. Such superimposed
communities tend to produce a distinct community life.

LEVELS OF ORGANIZATION

As a collectivity, any community tends to be highly informal, emergent, but rather determinately bounded. As subcultural lumps within national society, communities produce the collective good of a congenial social setting for daily life-rounds and the suspension or relaxation of certain demands, pressures, and status anxieties imposed by societal-level structures. Community culture is quite elaborate in language, folk knowledge, and norms. Key resources include all those member-controlled institutions and commodities which may contribute to the social life of members and the collective defense of the distinctive community culture against the forces of societal-level structures.

The primary structure of a community tends to be diffuse and derivative in that a member's roles within the common life of the community mainly reflect his various roles within societal structures and within associations. Most important, role relationships within a community tend to be multiple rather than segmental. Secondary structures, particularly power, leadership, and status, are more significant. One's status within a community is reputational, based on actions and conduct, rather than attributional, based on role and personal attributes. Leadership correlates highly with status but more variably with power; status correlates highly with the conformity structure. Many communities also generate a fairly coherent affect structure. Key suborganizations within any community are a variety of voluntary associations; in localized communities, neighborhoods serve as important suborganizations.

Any community strives to insulate its members from societal-level structures, yet large-scale diffuse collectivities significantly penetrate community boundaries. Intercommunity competition and rivalry are inevitable, and local communities seek to manipulate the impinging settlements and municipalities.

Recruitment is ascriptive in that membership is limited to persons exhibiting the defining social characteristic, but voluntary in that qualified persons need not identify with or associate with their fellows. Community tactics of attraction are therefore necessary. The aspect of placement centers largely on position in secondary structures, such as status.

Socialization efforts are extensive, pervasive, yet mainly implicit. Direct interaction is very extensive, and indirect interaction is largely through personal networks rather than impersonal media. Community interaction centers on interactions between its voluntary associations—in the forms of community action, community organization, and community development processes. Given the diffuse role structure and the strong sense of collectivity, innovation is both frequent and stressful. Lacking any formal procedures for ratification or stigmatization, a community relies on gossip, rumor, fashion, and public opinion. Scandal, community controversy, and community conflict are not infrequent. Reactive social control rests on the fact that status is reputational. Proactive social control relies heavily on extensive surveillance (gossip and rumor) and on major and minor rituals of solidarity.

Membership, position, role, and career are quite significantly influenced by individual tactics. Membership leads to subcultural modifications of the person's societal-level roles, which in many cases diminish his attributional status and his prospects for mobility within societal-level structures. On the other hand, membership partially insulates the person against the pressures, insults, and status anxieties of societal structures, enhancing self-esteem through community overvaluation of the defining social characteristic and offering reputational status as compensation for diminished societal status. Reputation is vital to the framing of conduct and to self-esteem. Position (particularly in status structure) and career pattern exert their effects on the individual mainly through the critical leverage of reputational status on socially anchored self-esteem.

Different from but germane to the social psychology of community is the "social psychology of settlements," the effects of differences between settlement types in physical environmental features, opportunities, and ways of life.

SUGGESTIONS FOR ADDITIONAL READING

An exasperated critic once remarked that whereas most people read novels, sociologists read community studies. Case studies of community life do indeed make fascinating reading and are endlessly abundant. Some focus simply on a good example of some settlement type: rural community, small town, small city, suburb, or community area within a metropolis. Many are case studies of superimposed communities—an urban Polish enclave, a rural Hutterite community, a blue-collar suburb, an upper-class neighborhood near the heart of a central city, and so on. An orderly and thoughtful overview of this sprawling literature is provided by Colin Bell and Howard Newby, *Community Studies: An Introduction to the Sociology of the Local Community* (New York: Praeger, 1972). A representative example of such a case study, with more than ordinary consideration of the social psychological implications of community life, is Arthur J. Vidich and Joseph Bensman's *Small Town in a Mass Society,* revised edition (Princeton, N.J.: Princeton University Press, 1968).

Apart from case studies, a useful introduction to the community as social organization—not necessarily localized—is the collection of readings edited by David W. Minar and Scott Greer, *The Concept of Community* (Chicago: Aldine, 1969).

The most insightful analysis of social communities in general, with special focus on occupational community, is Graeme Salaman's slim volume, *Community and Occupation* (Cambridge: At the University Press, 1974). Of the many colorful studies that have been made on a variety of blue-collar and professional occupational communities (localized and otherwise) we recommend Morris Janowitz's study of the military community, *The Professional Soldier: A Social and Political Portrait* (New York: Free Press, 1960).

The nature of religious communities is best examined in J. Alan Winter, *Continuities in the Sociology of Religion: Creed, Congregation, and Community* (New York: Harper & Row, 1977). The distinctive characteristics of America's 1,200 religions are briefly surveyed in J. Gordon Melton's two-volume *The Encyclopedia of American Religions* (Wilmington, N.C.: McGrath, 1978).

With respect to racial and ethnic communities, a similar broadening of awareness may be obtained from an inspection of Stephan Thernstrom, editor, *Harvard En-*

cyclopedia of American Ethnic Groups (Cambridge, Mass.: Harvard University Press, 1980).

Still the fundamental introduction to an understanding of the geographic community is Roland L. Warren's *The Community in America,* 3rd edition (Chicago: Rand McNally, 1978). Of course, the geographic community must be viewed within the context of the urban hierarchy; a very readable introduction to urban geography and human ecology is Raymond E. Murphy, *The American City,* 2nd edition (New York: McGraw-Hill, 1974). Within the metropolitan context, the concrete dynamics of the social construction of community areas are best depicted in Gerald D. Suttles, *The Social Order of the Slum* (Chicago: University of Chicago Press, 1968). An interesting theoretical analysis, centered on the role of providing collective goods, is David J. O'Brien, *Neighborhood Organization and Interest-Group Processes* (Princeton, N.J.: Princeton University Press, 1976).

More social psychological is Erving Goffman's analysis of the role of reputation in social interaction, *Interaction Ritual: Essays on Face-to-Face Behavior* (Garden City, N.Y.: Doubleday, 1967). The social psychology of settlements is cogently integrated in David A. Karp, Gregory P. Stone, and William C. Yoels, *Being Urban: A Social Psychological View of City Life* (Lexington, Mass.: D. C. Heath, 1977).

Photo courtesy of James Heffernan, The Tablet

The Knights of Columbus, whose members are seen here in full regalia, is a voluntary organization with formal procedures regulating group activities.

CHAPTER 19

The Association Level

Below the level of community lies a group of organizations that occupies a great deal of interest, attention, and time of many individuals. We come now to the level of the workplace, of the structures within which many outside interests are pursued, and of the institutions to which the troubled and the troublesome are referred. Here also are the organizations which impinge upward upon the community and upon societal-level structures. What the prisoner, the white-collar worker, and the Save the Whales partisan have in common is that they all belong to *associations*.

When the average layman speaks of "an organization," he usually is thinking of an association—a business firm, a service agency, a club, a church, a union, or the like. The key feature that such social organizations display is that they have all been specifically constructed for some specifically delimited purpose. Associations are *designed* organizations—deliberately and formally designed to facilitate the rational efficiency of collective action in pursuit of the designated purpose (J. D. Thompson, 1966). Because they are so designed, associations tend to be the best laid-out, most formally structured and rationally patterned organizations of any level. They represent organization at its highest development.

Like a polity, an association has a formal constitution—spelling out not only its purpose but also at least the rudiments of its role structure and operating procedures—and is governed on the basis of formal authority deriving from the constitution itself. Positions within an association are, in this sense, "offices," and the occupants of those positions are "office holders," authorized and responsible for undertaking specified "official" actions on behalf of the organization. It is for these reasons that many social scientists refer to associations as *formal organizations*.

In many cases, the organizational design of an association involves a highly differentiated division of labor, distinguishing a great many specialized positions linked together through an intricate web of interdependencies, coordination, rules, and regulations to function as a single system. It is for this reason that some social scientists refer to associations as *complex organizations*.

Some associations (for example, multinational corporations) have hundreds of thousands of members and literally span the globe in the scope of their operations. Accordingly, some social scientists prefer to speak of associations as *large-scale organizations*.

As we shall see, associations vary widely on all these dimensions. The Abilene, Kansas, Garden Club, while undeniably an association, is far from large-scale and is probably neither highly formalized nor very complex. We prefer, therefore, to retain the term "association" and to recognize the potential importance of formalization, elaboration, size, and scope, as dimensions of organizational variation. Indeed, variations in these factors produce a striking range of different types of associations with quite different social psychological influences upon their members.

As a collectivity, an association is at root a set of individuals coming together to pursue a like interest of some kind (birdwatching, electing some particular political candidate, making money through the production and sale of automobiles, taking care of the mentally disturbed, and so on). It is, so to speak, a "company of shareholders" pooling some of their energies and resources in collective pursuit of a like interest. If the number of "shareholders" becomes too large for efficient decision making by the "company" as a whole, it may designate a smaller governing board to make routine policy decisions. Execution of those policy decisions is the function of the association's "officers" through some prescribed structure of social roles (or offices), as represented in Figure 19–1. For example, the dues-paying members of a national gun club are its shareholders, while the elected officials and full-time employees are its officers; its governing board handles routine policy decisions, such as maintaining legislation on the right to bear arms, scheduling conventions, and maintaining public relations. These officers and board members are in turn, ultimately responsible to the shareholders for the conduct of their official duties as laid out in the club's constitution and amended resolutions. The lone rifleman, joining the club for some good shooting and like-minded companionship, may of course not be aware of this structure. In the fullest sense, the collectivity includes not only the officers but also the board and the shareholders. However, many analyses of associations essentially confine their attention to the officers, a somewhat paradoxical practice in view of the centrality of the shareholders.

Generally speaking, the degree of participation and of contribution by any member of the collectivity tends to be quite limited. Accordingly, the relationships between members tend to be segmental and fairly impersonal, reflecting the impersonal basis for interaction provided by a formal division of labor. Cooperation tends to be indirect rather than direct; members tend not to share the same experience in the collective action but share primarily an interest in the product of that action (a collective good). As emphasized in Chapter 3, every social organization resting on a like or complementary interest endeavors to cultivate a common interest in the welfare of the

The Association Level

FIGURE 19-1. **Typical Organizational Structure of Associations**

organization as well. Within the framework of the association, members may of course find opportunities for pursuing more strictly personal interests as a spillover into association roles. But even such spillovers happen less frequently at this level than at other organizational levels because of the designed nature of associations.

A major factor contributing to such cultivation is the development of an organizational culture. Every association

> has a collective identity; a roster of members, friends, and antagonists; a program of activity and a time schedule to go with it; a table of organization; a set of formal rules partly undermined by informal rules; procedures for adding and removing members; utilitarian objects used in the organizational program; symbolic objects used in the organizational program; symbolic objects used in ceremonies and rituals; a history; a special vocabulary; some elements of folklore; a territory; and a method of placing members within that territory according to their relative importance. Every [association] has a division of labor that allocates specialized tasks to its members and a status order that awards them unequal shares of authority, honor, and influence [Caplow, 1976: 5].

When we look at social structure, an association may present a fairly elaborate face. The division of labor is often represented as differentiated along three dimensions: horizontal differentiation (substantive specialization, as in mining, refining, and machining); vertical differentiation (degrees of administrative responsibility); and spatial differentiation (localized operation). In any organizational chart, such as Figure 3–1, each of these dimensions of differentiation will be depicted.

When horizontal differentiation predominates, the shape of the primary social structure is that of a short, wide pyramid. Predominantly vertical differentiation produces a tall and thin pyramid. Short, wide structures tend to be more informal, at least at the rank-and-file level, even if they are autocratically run at the top. Tall, thin structures tend to be elaborated in terms of rules and rituals, often with complex procedures for passing from one rank to another; interrank relations will be stipulated and somewhat stringent.

What is not depicted in such a representation is the nature of the vertical differentiation—that is, the character of administrative responsibility in that association. Administrative responsibilities generally include coordinating, facilitating, supporting, and supervising the activities of the organization. In corporate-type associations (Sills, 1957), the supervisory function is emphasized; authority is vested in the top reaches of the pyramid, commands are sent down, and each vertical rank supervises the compliance of the rank below. In federative-type associations, the coordinative-facilitative functions of administration are emphasized; authority is vested in the lower reaches of the pyramid, information is sent up, and each vertical rank coordinates the messages from the rank below. Any actual association represents some compromise between these two ideal types but will tend to resemble one more than the other. The structural dimension of *centralization* reflects these differences; that is to say, centralization is measured by the degree to which decision-making authority is confined to the higher levels of the organizational hierarchy. Spatial differentiation tends to favor the federative model of decentralization.

It is interesting that there is almost inevitably a tension between these corporate (centralizing) and federative (decentralizing) tendencies within any association. Within Congress, for example, there is continuing conflict between centralization of power in Washington and movements to return powers to the state and local levels. During World War II, a similar conflict between the German general staff and the field commanders dragged on until the Allies intervened by winning the war. It seems to be in the very nature of these two opposing social forces that neither can reign supreme, that some kind of fluid balance between the two must be struck in every existing association.

The role expectations comprising the division of labor include both operative rules and procedures, governing horizontal differentiation, and regulative rules and procedures, governing vertical differentiation. That is, operative rules deal with the workflow and output of the association, while regulative rules deal with communication and supervision. For instance, operative rules in an army might specify handling of equipment in the field, and regulative rules would set forth the protocol for handling and communicating with a two-star general on inspection. Several structural dimensions of the division of labor reflect the nature of these rules and procedures.

The first of these dimensions is the degree of *specification* of roles—that is, the degree to which the actions of a position occupant are prescribed and proscribed clearly, consensually, and in detail. In highly centralized associations, operative rules tend to be more highly specified than regulative rules, while in decentralized associations the reverse is true. In either case, the degree of such specification is sometimes astonishing. In some armies, for instance, rules on the exact equipment and number of rounds of ammunition for each rank under each set of conditions, the exact content of meals under various circumstances, the bars and brothels to be patronized by soldiers on leave, all are spelled out and enforced by a shadow army of clerks and inspectors.

The Association Level

Somewhat independent of specification, roles may be more or less *formalized* (written down in some frequently consulted manual of rules and procedures or in job descriptions). For instance, the expected role performance of Internal Revenue Service personnel for a wide variety of circumstances is specifically set forth in the service manual. On the other hand, the role of president of the United States, although highly specified in some areas, is actually not very formalized.

Finally, roles vary in the *pervasiveness* or scope of expectations, measured in the proportion of the performer's life activities which are encompassed by the role. A factory worker's job may be minutely specified but very narrow in scope, whereas a manager's job may be only loosely specified but highly pervasive. It should be noted that most associations strain toward being pervasive in their role expectations. Most lodges and clubs—from Elks to Boy Scouts—have codes of conduct that are supposed to govern the members' attitudes and behaviors in the general business of living. Most associations also specify ''conduct unbecoming an officer''—sometimes in elaborate detail.

Before leaving the topic of the role structure of associations, we should note that many investigations lend support to the proposition that as an association increases in size, its role structure tends to become more differentiated, more specified, and more formalized. Again, it is for this reason that many social scientists speak of associations as large-scale, complex, or formal organizations.

The *secondary* social structures of associations tend to be rather fully developed. The dimensional social structures tend to be highly interrelated and tend to reflect the vertical differentiation of the primary (role) structure. Even in decentralized role structures, higher administrative ranks tend to place high up in the authority and communication structures, and by virtue of their control over decisions regarding allocation of resources, tend also to rank high in the power structure. In any association, occupants of high administrative positions necessarily rank high in status (though not necessarily in conformity or liking). An interesting aspect of associations is that, because the structures are so formally laid out, the occupant of a high administrative position almost automatically ranks high in the secondary structures such as power, whatever his own personal inclinations and dispositions. The head of a bureau— whatever his own personal characteristics may be—has informal ''clout,'' and his offhand remarks may be given the weight of commands and policy statements.

The *suborganizations* of an association are generally numerous and are interrelated in a complex way. As Figure 3-1 shows, an association can be regarded as an organization of official suborganizations; indeed, any pyramidal subdivision (a department, a regional sector, a local branch) could be analyzed as an association in its own right, a very common practice in organizational research. In fact, some federative associations on a national scale (the Federated Garden Clubs of America) are explicitly formed as an association of associations. Sprawling national corporations are also a pyramid of suborganizations within suborganizations—an individual outlet, a local, a district, a regional and a national, sometimes even international office.

Furthermore, no table of organization displays all of the official suborganizations of an association, such as committees and task forces. Such units, by cutting across segments of both the vertical and the horizontal dimensions of the association, do not lend themselves well to depiction in the traditional tables of organization. Figure 19–2 presents an attempt to depict such cross-cutting or "matrix" organizational designs.

Also, the existence of a good many unofficial suborganizations (comprising the much discussed "informal organization" of an association) must be recognized. For the most part, these unofficial suborganizations take the form of groups (see Chapter 20). "Task groups" are sets of individuals called upon to work together on official tasks of the association who develop patterns of interaction undesignated by the association in their execution of these tasks. "Communication groups" are sets of individuals (who may or may not be friends) who have voluntarily developed certain interaction patterns for the purpose of passing along certain types of information;

FIGURE 19-2.   An Example of a Matrix-type Structure.

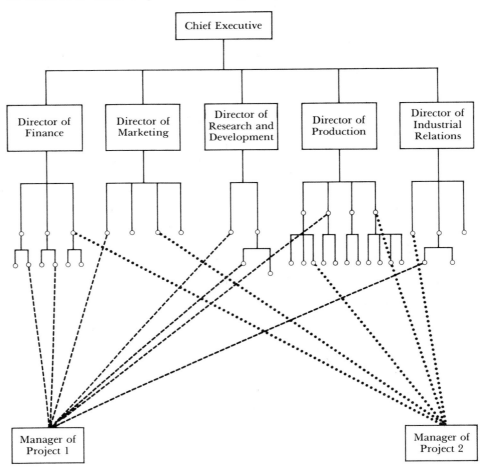

Source: Porter, Lawler and Hackman, 1975: 256. Reproduced with permission.

The Association Level

linkages among such communication groups constitute the organizational grapevine. "Friendship groups" or cliques are sets of individuals (who may or may not be officially called on to interact with one another) who decide voluntarily to interact either during work situations and/or during nonwork periods on or off the premises of the association (Porter et al, 1975: 75–77). There will also be factions within any large association that pursue their own special interests and partisan positions on organizational issues.

Finally, within any association there will be a large number of unofficial dyads, with a wide-ranging basis for the role partnerships: executive/right-hand-man, master/apprentice, mentor/beginner, buddy/buddy, lover/lover, exploiter/victim, and so on, through the whole range of human interaction pairings. These interaction pairings comprise a great deal of the actual social life that goes on within an association—not part of the official chart of organization, but part of the lives of its members.

In view of such elaborate suborganizations, the interorganizational relations of associations are often quite complex. To begin with, any association tends to be deeply embedded within one or more of the societal-level structures. Many analysts, influenced by American legal doctrine, consider that all associations are creatures of the state, (that is, chartered by the polity). And of course, many associations are in fact either direct agencies of the state or formally incorporated under law; on the other hand, a great many perfectly respectable associations have never bothered to seek incorporation or other legal recognition. Nevertheless, as a special-purpose organization, virtually every association sooner or later has dealings with some agency of the polity and finds itself functioning as a special-interest influence group in political decision making. Some associations (business firms, unions, professional associations) are deeply embedded in the economy, some (associations for women or senior citizens) are embedded in the age-sex structure, and others (ethnic associations) are embedded in the ethnic stratification system of the speech community.

By virtue of such relations to societal-level structures, associations are frequently major actors within diffuse collectivities (particularly publics and social movements) and thus have a hand in the innovation processes of societal-level structures. This influence runs both ways. A major topic in organizational sociology today is the impact of societal-level structures on the character of embedded organizations (Lammers and Hickson, 1979). Characteristic organizational differences can be noted, for example, between industrial firms in Japan and those in the United States, between the prisons of Sweden and of Turkey, between the political parties of totalitarian and of libertarian polities.

Similarly, associations are very often embedded in one or more communities. Occupational associations are embedded in occupational communities, ethnic associations in ethnic communities, civic associations and local business firms in local geographic communities. As discussed in Chapter 18, community action can itself be largely defined in terms of the actions and interactions of embedded associations. That is, individuals usually act upon communities through the medium of associations.

It is partly for these reasons that the increasingly significant topic of interorganizational relations has focused so heavily on the competition, conflict, cooperation, exchange, and power-dependency relations among associations (Aldrich, 1979), and particularly among associations formed to promote similar purposes. Other associations, in fact, turn out to be the major features in the external environment of any specific association; even such "hard" goods as raw materials, supplies, and money are all mediated through other organizations. The more stable—and the more simple—the environment of an association, the more likely that association is to become highly differentiated, centralized, specified, and formalized (Lawrence and Lorsch, 1967; Aldrich, 1979).

As we have seen, associations actually vary a great deal in size, shape, and features. Within this wide variation, three basic types are very important in social life and quite familiar in our environment: voluntary associations, bureaucracies, and total institutions.

VOLUNTARY ASSOCIATIONS

The voluntary association is as old as the tribal men's smoke lodge. A voluntary association provides a setting in which a person can pursue special interests and concerns, although there is usually a spillover into other congenial activities. Voluntary associations come to loom large in many people's lives, not so much on account of the time spent in them as by degree of interest and involvement in what the associations represent.

Collectivity

In some associations, almost all offices are filled from within the ranks of the shareholders, generally through some electoral mechanism; few offices—usually only those requiring full-time service and/or special expertise not readily available among the shareholders—are filled by employees. Most of the collective resources, both human and material, are donated by the shareholders, although some of the material resources may be expended to hire a few staff employees (Perrow, 1970). Because of their distinctive relation to the collective resources of the association, paid employees always constitute a special-interest group within the collectivity.

The like-interests around which a voluntary association may form are practically innumerable. Various typologies of purposes have been proposed; perhaps the most widely employed is that of Hausknecht (1962) shown in Table 9-1.

These eight categories necessarily obscure tremendous differences in the detailed interests of voluntary associations within any one category. But such a broad typology of interests should serve to suggest that the organizational culture of a voluntary association is distinctively linked to the nature of its collective interest. The folklore, customs, and special vocabulary of, say, a labor union may be expected to differ rather sharply from those of a church or the Audubon Society, no matter how similar they may be in formal social structure.

338

TABLE 19-1.   Types of Voluntary Associations

1. Civic and service associations
   (Examples: Rotary; Kiwanis; United Way)
2. Lodges and fraternal associations
   (Examples: Odd Fellows; Shriners; Elks; Moose)
3. Church and religious associations
   (Examples: Lutheran Church of America; Methodist Fellowship; Rosicrucian Society)
4. Social and recreational associations
   (Examples: Sertoma; Golden Age Club; country clubs)
5. Veterans, military, and patriotic associations
   (Examples: Veterans of Foreign Wars; American Legion)
6. Economic, occupational, and professional associations
   (Examples: AFL-CIO; National Association of Manufacturers;
   American Sociological Association)
7. Cultural, educational, and alumni associations
   (Examples: literary societies; PTA; Adult Education
   Association; Harvard Club of Chicago)
8. Political and pressure associations
   (Examples: Common Cause; John Birch Society;
   Planned Parenthood Federation; NAACP)

Social Structure

Voluntary associations, more than any other type of association, are likely to exhibit a federative-type primary social structure; local associations spring up and agree to federate in order to obtain greater resources or greater lobbying power, but they retain great local autonomy. However, corporate-type structures are far from uncommon, as is best illustrated in the category of church and religious associations. For sociologists of religion (for example, Nottingham, 1971), the fundamental structural dimension of contrast among denominations has been a continuum ranging from "congregational" denominations, where basic authority resides in the local congregation; through "presbyterian" denomination, where basic authority resides in the body of preachers; to "episcopal" denominations, where basic authority resides in the highest offices of the organizational hierarchy.

Within religious organizations, at the local level only the minister and perhaps a staff person or two are likely to be paid employees. In congregational denominations, the minister is chosen and paid by the local congregation; in episcopal denominations, he is appointed by and responsible to higher-ranking nonlocal officials. Accordingly, these structures differ signficantly in the role performed by the minister, not only in the nature of his administrative responsibilities but also in the degree of specification and formalization of his role prescriptions and proscriptions (Harrison, 1959; Fichter, 1961). In the more centralized type, for example, he is not to extemporize his own views on scripture, morals, or social issues but must adhere more closely to doctrines produced at senior levels. In the congregational type, on the other hand, there is great freedom of doctrine and interpretation of social events, as long as membership support can be garnered.

Organizational Processes

In voluntary associations, *recruitment* is largely a matter of obtaining members (''shareholders'') rather than filling offices. That is to say, the aspects of attraction and selection figure more prominently than the aspect of placement. Attraction and selection are based more on interest and social background than on skills, abilities, or knowledge (Minnis, 1953). Some voluntary associations are highly selective (exclusive) in recruitment of members while others are highly inclusive, basing their selection decisions almost wholly on interest and enforcing very few social requirements (Babchuck and Gordon, 1962). In either case, few candidates apply for admission without having been previously invited or even urged to do so (Sills, 1957). Exclusive voluntary associations may be more successful than inclusive associations in obtaining such applications, in that the status benefits they can confer are more valuable (Babchuk and Gordon, 1962). Whether exclusive or inclusive, it is a characteristic of all voluntary associations that they seek better qualified members, as this is a major resource. Frequently, there is also a collective urge to carry the association's viewpoints to the populace in general through some credo, such as ''gardening beautifies the land and freshens the air,'' ''our lodge strengthens the family everywhere,'' or ''an armed populace is a populace free from tyranny.''

The process of placement into a specific office (beyond that of rank-and-file member) is typically time-lagged, inasmuch as officers are generally filled through election from and by the members. In those cases where paid staff are recruited, of course, selection and placment are tightly coupled, selection is more heavily based on skills or abilities, and the incentives offered include material as well as social benefits.

The *socialization* process within voluntary associations varies widely in nature, depending on the degrees of differentiation, specification, formalization, and pervasiveness of the membership role. Toward the lower ends of these dimensions, socialization tactics tend to be of the implicit variety and tend to emphasize the communication of expectations. For membership roles ranking fairly high on these same dimensions, socialization efforts may be quite explicit (involving extensive self-study materials, formal classes, and even examinations) and may emphasize not only the communication of expectations but also the development of certain individual attributes. Again, the contrasts among socialization efforts of differing religious denominations afford a good illustration. The Roman Catholic church, for example, relies heavily on authoritative formal training and education through catechism classes and parochial schools, while a storefront charismatic sect relies on implicit communications shaping individual inspiration. Socialization of an individual into a more specialized office (treasurer or Sunday school teacher) within any voluntary association may require more explicit and more demanding procedures (including development of individual attributes) than socialization into the ordinary membership role.

The Association Level

Many voluntary associations spend time and resources in anticipatory socialization efforts, through public relations, appearance of their celebrities on television talk shows, lecture tours, and even paid advertising. The evidence is scanty, but from comments of association workers it appears that such tactics do furnish recruits who are already partially socialized.

The *interaction* process within voluntary associations is much like that within the polity, displaying a double aspect not unlike that of citizen and subject. As a shareholder, the member is expected to play some role in policy formation and in the election of officers. As the occupant of a position within the primary social structure, he is expected to carry out a direct role within the division of labor of collective action, and to honor and abide by the membership and positional norms of the association. A major theme of research on voluntary associations is the consistent finding of heavily unequal participation in either aspect; a minority of the membership both dominates the decision making and carries out most of the work of the association (Sills, 1968). The famous "iron law of oligarchy" (Michels, 1949) holds that the leaders of an association (including, often, any paid staff) will always assume working control of its affairs over the shareholders in whom ultimate authority is supposed to reside. On occasion, however, a disgruntled membership will reassert its ultimate authority by throwing its officials out.

In virtually all voluntary associations we find a gradient of involvement which could be envisioned as a series of circles within circles: (1) nonmembers who are interested, supportive, and friendly—the outermost and usually by far the largest circle; (2) nominal members—"on the roll-books" but inactive; (3) sporadically active members; (4) highly active and aligned members; and (5) insiders, who are privy to the "real" scene and who usually have some voice in the affairs of the organization. The ratio of members in the first three categories to those in the two inner categories may be as high as ten or twenty to one, yet for promotional reasons associations will almost invariably publicize their memberships as inclusive of all five categories.

Innovation is often proactive, given the designed nature of all associations. Externally imposed changes are quite frequent, as a consequence of the dense network of interorganizational relations typical of associations. Yet, the major focus of studies of social change in associations has fallen on the often tortuous process of internally planned change (Zaltman and Duncan, 1977; Hage and Aiken, 1970). This perhaps too narrow focus can miss the point that the reasons for internally planned innovations often stem from impingements by other organizations or from environmental social change, as we saw in Chapter 12. The fact that associations are designed organizations can lead to the misconception that they are more orderly and rational than they actually are.

Reactive innovation in a voluntary association varies with the degree to which the role structure is differentiated, centralized, specified, formalized, and pervasive. The more sharply and the more pervasively roles are prescribed, the more likely it is that some member will judge a performance to be discrepant. The more tightly coupled the division of labor, the more likely that a discrepant performance will be judged by some member to be deviant. The more centralized the organizational structure (the more that higher officials emphasize their supervisory responsibilities), the greater the surveillance and, hence, the more likely a discrepant performance will invoke some ratification/stigmatization procedure. In highly formalized associations (particularly where regulative as well as operative procedures are formalized), ratification/stigmatization procedures are likely be formal rather than informal. In corporate more than in federative associations, these procedures are likely to be authoritarian rather than democratic.

Similarly, the *social control* process varies between these two broad structural types. Proactively, both surveillance and rituals of solidarity tend to be more formally elaborated in corporate type associations. Reactively, the determination and administration of both rewards and punishments also tend to be more formally elaborated in corporate than in federative associations. In either type of voluntary association, promises and threats (as well as rewards and punishments) tend to emphasize social rather than material or physical benefits and costs. Reward and punishment tend to take the form of redefinition of the individual's position and role.

The fact that these are voluntary associations does not mean that ratification/stigmatization procedures and their consequent rewards or punishments do not have a strong impact on the individuals involved. To be cast out of one's chosen club or church can be a tragic event, and the rewards—even if only a parchment scroll—can be a treasured success. The fact that the voluntary association can confer such influences enables it to exert a measure of social control over its members that is sometimes astonishing to outsiders.

BUREAUCRACIES

Most laymen, and even many scholars, have come to regard bureaucracies as a dull and plodding subject. It is almost as if some of the stereotyped notions about bureaucracy have crept into the subject itself. The word bureaucrat has become a derogatory term which has produced its own folklore of humorous and angry anecdotes. Max Weber, the pioneer sociologist, was wistfully ambivalent about the rise of bureaucracy, and modern writers such as William H. Whyte and Alan Harrington are not enthusiastic.

What is the stereotype? Red tape, impersonality, robotic application of rules and regulations, inefficiency, faceless men, or as Bob Seeger put it in a popular song, "feel like a number."

Yet any organization of any size seems inevitably to develop a bureaucracy, which it then alternately curses and depends on. We find bureaucracies in ancient China and modern Russia, in the public education system, even within fringe social and religious movements. Bureaucracies run things and hold things together. They certainly seem to be an intrinsic part of social life beyond the level of the native hut and therefore are very much worth understanding.

The essential feature of a bureaucracy is that it is a work organization, an association in which most if not all of the positions (or offices) are filled by paid employees rather than by volunteer members. In bureaucracies, then, offices tend to be viewed as *jobs,* in the fullest sense of that term.

In its original usage, the term bureaucracy was applied only to bureaus, or associations that are functional suborganizations of the polity—governmental agencies staffed through civil service procedures. We shall certainly want to include under the rubric of bureaucracy not only such public agencies (police, military, Social Security Administration) but also any private social agencies in which paid staff outnumber volunteer staff members. Included in this category are such agencies as hospitals, private schools, and social work agencies.

In the modern world, business firms have joined the polity in developing bureaucracies to such extent that personnel so frequently interchange between the two that it is often difficult to tell where polity leaves off and business begins; examples are the diplomatic service and international trade or finance firms, and the Federal Reserve Bank and the private banking institutions. People move easily from firm to foundation to government agency, proving the basic similarities among them. All of us are directly and indirectly involved with such bureaucracies in many aspects of our social living, from getting educated to earning our incomes.

Collectivity

Public or private agencies are associations formed to provide some specified type of service (education, health care, custodial care) to the citizenry of the polity or some segment thereof. Yet, the one like interest shared by all members of a bureaucratic agency is that of deriving income (and possible economic advancement) through participation in that type of association. All too often, members' interests in providing service prove to be secondary.

A firm, on the other hand, is organized for the explicit purpose of making money through some particular type of collective action. The like interest of its members in deriving income through such participation is more nearly constitutive of the organization. Here, a member's interest in the work itself, while perhaps welcomed, more openly constitutes a special interest.

In either case, the like interest of deriving income through participation tends to engender a common interest in the continued vitality of the association itself. It has been noted that bureaus die hard, even when their purpose or usefulness has evaporated. Because the bureaucratic positions are jobs, there is a fairly concerted interest in perpetuating them for their own sakes, as livelihoods.

The material resources of a public agency derive from tax receipts of the polity allocated to the agency. In private agencies, material resources are primarily obtained through donations from nonmembers, often from businesses or voluntary associations. Firms obtain their material resources through a variety of channels: stock purchases by shareholders, sale of goods and services to customers, development of processes and technologies that yield patent or copyright royalties, discovery of salable resources on sites where they hold options, bond issues, and government and foundation contracts and research grants.

In all bureaucracies, most of the human resources of the association are purchased through expenditure of a sizable fraction of its material resources. Except in the smallest of firms, very few of a bureaucracy's offices are filled from among the ranks of its shareholders. (And as a consequence, office holders tend to develop special interests that may diverge somewhat from the interests of the shareholders.)

Whereas firms tend to serve customers, agencies tend to provide services to clients. Few analysts are inclined to consider customers as any part of the firm itself, but clients are sometimes regarded as members of an agency as a part of its human resources (Rosengren and Lefton, 1970). Particularly when large numbers of clients spend substantial and continuing periods of time on the agency's premises (and especially if this entails clients' receiving food, clothing, and/or lodging from the agency), it may be quite useful to regard clients as comprising a fourth stratum in the organizational pyramid, directly below rank-and-file workers.

The culture of a bureaucracy is often even more highly developed than that of a voluntary association, if for no other reason than that its office holders tend to participate for at least forty hours per week in contrast to the part-time efforts of most members of a voluntary association. Formal rules and regulations tend to be much more developed, in part because of the substantial monetary investments made in the productive efforts of its office holders. (Appropriately enough, in one sense of the term, a bureaucracy is an organization in which activities and relations are impersonal and governed by formal rules and regulations.) Bureaucratic language—with its ponderous formality and its obscurantist references to regulations, procedures, printed forms, and parts by their numbers (Section 243.5, Form 117, machine screw 22X)—is far from unheard of in many other formalized organizations but doubtless reaches it pinnacle within the cultures of bureaucracies. The elaborate formalization of rules and terms in a bureaucracy leads to a substantial emphasis on ritualism (Merton, 1940) and even on ceremony (Hamilton, 1956). Finally, the culture almost inevitably contains some mystique about the value and importance of the particular bureaucracy in the scheme of things, including a defense against the fact that this adjudged importance may not be recognized by others. Typically, the office holders are presented as unsung heroes of societal-level structures. This mystique also serves the function of elevating the sometimes routine and humdrum work to the level of a Cause. Individual members, of course, vary in the degree to which they are enthusiastic or cynical about such a mystique.

Social Structure

The primary social structure of a firm is very much as displayed in Figure 19–1, with the pyramid of office holders responsible to a board, which in turn is responsible to the company of shareholders. A private agency, on the other hand, often lacks shareholders but does have a board of directors (usually volunteers). A public agency may or may not have a board; if not, it is directly responsible to some specific officer in the organizational hierarchy of the polity. In any case, a public agency lacks any true company of shareholders but is instead ultimately responsible to the polity itself, which in turn is theoretically responsible to "the people."

In terms of the division of labor, bureaucracies are more likely to exhibit a corporate rather than a federative, decentralized structure. Major exceptions are to be found in those work organizations that operate in a highly complex or unstable environment (a firm in the rapidly evolving electronics industry) and/or with a nonroutinized technology or nonuniform materials (a scientific research laboratory), requiring that their rank-and-file workers are drawn from professional and technical occupations.

Larger, technologically complex bureaucracies tend to be more differentiated in their structures. The degree to which the structure is specified and formalized is, in turn, related to the degree of differentiation and centralization, at least among corporate bureaucracies. In corporate-type structures, pervasiveness of expectations tends to be most pronounced in management-stratum roles.

All of these features—differentiation, formalization, specification, size, and centralization—often thought to be inherent characteristics of all bureaucracies, are actually variables rather than constants. Furthermore, they tend to vary together; that is, as some of them increase in degree, so do the rest. At their extreme height, the situation would probably begin to approach the popular stereotype of bureaucracy, where six forms are required to requisition a box of paper clips and several dollars are administratively spent to get one dollar's worth of food into the mouths of refugees. At the opposite extreme of no organization, of course, there would probably be no paper clips to requisition or no dollars to spend for food.

It is worth re-emphasizing that in a bureaucracy roles amount to "jobs"—specified patterns of activity for which the performer is financially compensated by the association. Jobs must be distinguished from occupations, which are distinct *types* of work. An individual may have an occupation but no job, or may take a job which falls outside his occupation. A bureaucracy may hire representatives of various occupations, but a bureaucracy is made up of jobs, not of occupations.

Organizational Processes

A bureaucracy, then, differs from voluntary associations in that *recruitment* is a matter of filling jobs, primarily on the basis of skills, abilities, or knowledge and only secondarily on social background criteria. The aspect of placement cannot be separated from the aspects of attraction and selection. The nature of the job to be filled dictates the general characteristics of individuals whom the association must try to attract and select. Again, unlike the case in voluntary associations, individuals unknown to a bureaucracy frequently make application without previous personalized solicitation by that organization. In agencies that service individual clients, the recruitment of clients often takes place through somewhat different means—such as referrals from other agencies—but similarly emphasizes job-related criteria, such as degree of need for or ability to gain from the agency's services, although social-background criteria (such as religion or place of residence) may first be used to screen for eligibility.

The nature of *socialization* efforts in a bureaucracy greatly depends on the degree to which the individual already fits the job requirements. His occupational training and experience may have adequately developed the requisite capacities in him, in which case only minimal and implicit socialization procedures may be necessary to communicate local expectations and the local scene. At the other extreme, his occupation may have developed in him attitudes and habits which are in conflict with the expectations and desired capacities of the job into which he is to be placed, in which case radical procedures of resocialization (stripping and substitution) may be employed. More commonly, the individual's occupational background may be quite minimal, in which case the full range of implicit and explicit procedures (observational learning, self-study materials, formal in-service training, coaching) may be employed to make him aware of job expectations and to develop the desired knowledge and skills. (Agency procedures for the socialization of clients similarly vary depending on the client's degree of fit with the client role into which he is recruited.)

Regarding the *interaction* process, a bureaucracy's concerns in the patterns of interaction involving its members center on the efficacy of job performance and on preserving the horizontal and vertical differentiation of its role structure (see Chapter 7). Given the intricacy of official and unofficial suborganizations typical of most bureaucracies, an association of this type tends to view unprescribed aspects of interactions somewhat nervously as perhaps setting the stage for collusive violations of the carefully regulated relationships on which the organizational design rests. At the same time, individual members tend to find this thick blanket of rules and regulations to be restrictive of initiative (if not offensively impugning of personal integrity) and are motivated to devise more personally satisfactory patterns of activity.

As in voluntary associations, the reactive *innovation* process within a bureaucracy necessarily generates a high rate of discrepant performances, of allegations of deviance, and of supervisory surveillance. As in all associations, much innovation is distinctively proactive, whether externally imposed or internally planned (Brager and Holloway, 1978). Particularly since bureaucracies are likely to be of the corporate or centralized type, procedures for the ratification or stigmatization of innovations tend to be relatively formal and relatively authoritarian. Successful ratifications are most often sponsored by higher-ranking officials, but the suborganizational complexity of bureaucracies is such that even the carefully planned proactive proposals of executives charged with responsibility for planned change are seldom effectively ratified. Planned innovations are often imposed from above, particularly by agencies of the polity, but although ratified at this higher level they are still frequently "unofficially" stigmatized, resisted, and evaded at the level of the embedded bureaucracy, as a large number of congressional hearings have shown over the last decade.

The character of the *social control* process within a bureaucracy closely resembles that described for voluntary associations of the corporate type. One major difference stems from the characteristic incentives for membership in bureaucracies—namely, the interests in deriving income and economic advancement through participation. Given this cash nexus between a bureaucracy and its office holders, the benefits and costs most centrally manipulated in the social control process are financial in nature. Social benefits and costs are secondary in importance, and only in quite atypical bureaucracies (such as the army) are physical punishments administered to office holders (though somewhat more commonly to clients, as in public schools).

All of the organizational processes tend to reach their peak in rational design and conscious execution within the bureaucracy. Perhaps this is why bureaucracies are so ubiquitous in human history; they are attempts to impose order, stability, and predictability upon the more chaotic, uncertain, and changing flux of human events. Theirs is the technology of the "standard operating procedure." As one bureaucrat put it in conversation, "Maybe they don't win us all we want, but they keep the show going."

TOTAL INSTITUTIONS

In certain associations, the pervasiveness of the client role is so extreme that clients are more appropriately described as "inmates" and the association as a "total institution." The majority of total institutions are bureaucratic agencies, such as prisons, concentration camps, boot camps, mental hospitals, leper colonies, and nursing homes. A few are essentially voluntary associations, such as monasteries, convents, separatist sects, and ideological or cult communes. In either case, total institutions frequently are established as distinct facilities for radical resocialization on behalf of some larger social organization, such as the polity, the army, the church, or the like.

> A basic social arrangement in modern society is that the individual tends to sleep, play, and work in different places, with different co-participants, under different authorities, and without an over-all rational plan. The central feature of total institutions can be described as a breakdown of the barriers ordinarily separating these three spheres of life. First, all aspects of life are conducted in the same place and under the same single authority. Second, each phase of the member's daily activity is carried on in the immediate company of a large batch of others, all of whom are treated alike and required to do the same thing together. Third, all phases of the day's activities are tightly scheduled, with one activity leading at a prearranged time into the next, the whole sequence of activities being imposed from above by a system of explicit formal rulings and a body of officials. Finally, the various enforced activities are brought together into a single rational plan purportedly designed to fulfill the official aims of the institution [Goffman, 1961b: 5-6].

Total institutions find themselves in an ironic position in that most people are more than happy to stay away from them but are pleased that they exist to handle the troubled and troubling individuals in the populace. They find them a distressing but necessary part of the social order, and therefore, these institutions and their office holders tend to be shunned but supported. As a common characteristic, total institutions are "off the beaten path"—semi-isolated from mainstream society, both physically and socially.

Social Structure

In virtually all total institutions, the primary social structure features an extremely impermeable boundary between the rank-and-file staff stratum (conveniently called "guards") and the client or inmate stratum. Little social mobility and great social distance occur across this boundary, and the differences in power, authority, status, and pervasiveness are extremely pronounced. The starkness of this differentiation is such that in virtually any total institution the lowest-ranking guard holds immediate and tremendous power over even the highest-ranking inmate. A great many of the features of inmate life and the social psychological impact of being in a total institution arise from this one fact.

Horizontal differentiation within the staff sector of the structure is sometimes fairly extensive, but within the inmate stratum it is minimal. Vertical differentiation, overall, is much more prominent. The degree of centralization is typically very great; total institutions tend to represent the authoritarian extreme of the corporate-type structure.

The degrees of specification and formalization of roles are also great, as is the pervasiveness of at least the inmate role. In most total institutions, the paid staff is able to leave the premises at the conclusion of their shifts. When this is not the case (such as in monasteries or in naval ships at sea), the pervasiveness of staff roles may approach that of inmate roles, although even here the lowliest staff will have far more privileges than the inmates.

Turning now to secondary social structures of total institutions, it should be stated that dimensional structures of power, authority, status, leadership, and communication (initiation of messages) directly reflect the vertical differentiation of the primary structure. In the total institution more than in any other type of organization, all attributes of both the primary and secondary structures are highly correlated with one another; a leader usually has the power, the position, the status, the authority, and the communication lines. In terms of conformity, those at the top and the bottom of the institution conform the least, among both staff and inmates.

Given the rigid formality of the primary structure, it should not prove surprising that unofficial suborganizations loom large in the life of a total institution, particularly within the formally undifferentiated inmate stratum. A secondary structure of informal social roles among inmates is almost inevitable and often quite elaborate. Perhaps the most widely known of the inmate social structures is that of the prison, which Sykes (1958) describes as being comprised of "rats," "center men," "gorillas," "merchants," "wolves," "punks," "fags," "ball-busters," "real men," "toughs," and "hipsters." It should be noted that, like the primary structure of the institution, a secondary structure of this type displays both horizontal and vertical differentiation and largely determines the rankings of inmates on such informal dimensions as status, leadership, power, authority, and communication.

Collectivity

The collective interests of the staff are essentially those of any bureaucracy. The like interests of inmates, on the other hand, are typically at variance with the official purposes of the institution and center instead on avoiding trouble while minimizing the oppressive effects of the institutional climate and maximizing whatever gratifications can be mustered from the sharply reduced opportunity structure. The other main inmate interest is, of course, getting out.

Accordingly, two contrasting organizational cultures tend to develop, one among staff and one among inmates.

> The staff is charged with meeting the hostility and demands of the inmates, and what it has to meet the inmates with, in general, is the rational perspective espoused by the institution . . . a language of explanation that the staff . . . can bring to every crevice of action in the institution. Thus, a medical frame of reference is not merely a perspective through which a decision concerning dosage can be determined and made meaningful; it is a perspective ready to account for all manner of decisions, such as the hours when hospital meals are served or the manner in which hospital linen is folded. . . . The interpretative scheme of the total institution automatically begins to operate as soon as the inmate enters, the staff having the notion that entrance is *prima facie* evidence that one must be the kind of person the institution was set up to handle. A man in a political prison must be traitorous; a man in a prison must be a lawbreaker; a man in a mental hospital must be sick. If not traitorous, criminal, or sick, why else would he be there? . . .
>
> Given the inmates of whom they have charge, and the processing that must be done to them, the staff tend to evolve what may be thought of as a theory of human nature. As an implicit part of institutional perspective, this theory rationalizes activity, provides a subtle means of maintaining social distance from inmates and a stereotyped view of them, and justifies the treatment accorded them. Typically, the theory covers the "good" and "bad" possibilities of inmate conduct, the forms that messing up takes, the instructional value of privileges and punishments, and the "essential" difference between staff and inmates [Goffman, 1961b: 83–87].

Inmate culture, on the other hand, more centrally reflects the like interest of doing "smooth time," as indicated by the nature of the informal inmate roles previously described. The normative core of inmate culture is the "inmate code," again best described in the case of prisons. According to D. Cressey (1973), the inmate code of the prison centers on five normative ideas: (1) no inmate should do anything to jeopardize another's privileges; (2) inmates should avoid quarrels with other inmates; (3) no inmate should take advantage of another; (4) inmates should be strong and self-respecting; and (5) no inmate should accord respect to prison officials or the world they represent. Though often violated, of course, this code promotes inmate control of other inmates and thus greatly facilitates guards' custodial and order-maintenance efforts. The distinctive beliefs and meanings shared by inmates are often reflected in a special vocabulary or argot (Hargen, 1935).

At least for the inmates (and often for staff whose roles are highly pervasive), the regimented pattern of activity constitutes a shared home range, with the consequence that the total institution serves as a local community. Although the mutual loyalty of inmates may not be highly developed, their sense of collectivity is essentially that of a local—rather than a social—community (see Clemmer, 1958, and related works on "the prison community").

Along these lines, an interesting phenomenon is encountered in total institutions: the person who comes to feel security and comfort in regimented life and in fact feels bereft without it. Such "institutional personalities" will often manipulate events to remain under the protective umbrella of total institutions throughout their lives, sometimes moving back and forth between staff and inmate roles, and going perhaps from one total institution setting to another.

Organizational Processes

Regarding staff members, the organizational processes within a total institution scarcely differ from those of the typical bureaucracy. Accordingly, we shall here focus only on inmate roles.

Most often, *inmate recruitment* is ascriptively based and proceeds through some type of draft (involuntary commitment, sentencing, conscription). It must not be overlooked, however, that in certain total institutions (convents, military academies, and even mental hospitals and boot camps) all or many of the inmates make voluntary applications for selective admission.

To the extent that recruitment is ascriptive, the inmate ranks may be filled with more or less unwilling members. This fact has a strong impact on the character of the organization—bars on the windows, guards, provisions for handling those who leave illegally, and so on.

Whatever the type of recruitment process, *inmate socialization* invariably takes the radical form of stripping and substitution. On admission, almost all existing identity supports (name, clothes, hairstyle, eating and sleeping practices, leisure activities, external social roles) are stripped from the inmate and replaced by standardized, institutional substitutes. Even one's self-concept is stripped away, to be replaced only slowly through the explicit and implicit communication of new expectations and the development of new individual capacities. The distinctive socialization practices of total institutions have been the subject of considerable sociological research (Dornbusch, 1955; Wheeler, 1966). Since every total institution by its very nature calls for radical redefinition of a great many situations and social objects, including the person himself, socialization tactics must be radical to stand any chance of success.

To aid in this massive resocialization, every total institution has the common characteristic of isolating its inmates from the world outside. In addition, tight controls

The Association Level

are placed on communications and other impingements which might come in from mainstream society to reinforce previous behaviors and attitudes and thus to impede the resocialization. Some anticipatory socialization does occur, through the mass media and the circulation of tales through the populace. The new recruit is usually aware that stripping and substitution will occur and knows it is best to keep out of trouble.

The *interaction* patterns of inmates are, for the most part, rigidly prescribed and administratively coerced; inmates mainly do as they are told, striving to avoid punishments for noncompliance. Interactions with staff members are always fraught with tension and hostility—although inmates are usually compliant and deferent—and seldom involve unguarded communication. Interactions among inmates, within the narrow discretion permitted, tend to be colored by distrust and governed by the strictures of the inmate code. The overall pattern of an inmate's participation is quite similar to that within a community, framed to glean from the resources of his home range as best he can the necessities and the niceties of life. As Goffman (1961c) puts it, the framing principle is one of "making out" for oneself in a restricted environment through "secondary adjustments"—practices that do not directly challenge staff but allow inmates to obtain forbidden satisfactions or to obtain permitted ones by forbidden means.

Such secondary adjustments, by virtue of not challenging staff, represent *inmate innovations* that are at best tacitly and informally ratified by the institution. Most discrepant performances are stigmatized as deviant, often on the spot by the nearest guard. For major discrepancies, the ruling tends to be formally communicated upward; for lesser offenses, such as responding in a sullen tone of voice to a guard's question, the stigmatization is more likely to be informal.

In any total institution, the supervisory responsibility of guards in *inmate social control* is almost exclusively one of surveillance. Owing to the almost complete lack of privacy for inmates, the efficiency of staff surveillance of inmates is exceedingly great despite minimal cooperation from other inmates. The efficiency of surveillance, coupled with the extreme specificity of the formal inmate role, leads to very high rates of judgments of discrepant performances provoking organizational reactions. The distaste and hostility guards feel toward inmates leads to a high proportion of ratification/stigmatization proceedings eventuating in a verdict of deviance. Since regulations are so numerous and specific, an inmate can hardly help but break some of them in his routine actions. For instance, a newcomer may fail to carry his cup over to the designated disposal place after breakfast, or may fail to have all his belongings stowed in his foot locker before going out to muster.

Being almost entirely dependent on the institution for satisfaction of every need, inmates experience promises and rewards as "privileges"—trivial increments in benefits that are held out to inmates in exchange for obedience to staff in action and in spirit. Against a stark background of deprivation, the privilege of a phone call, a cigarette, or cream in one's coffee can loom very large. Threats and punishments concern, in the first instance, the withdrawal or withholding of just such privileges. An inmate may quite readily consent to kneel down and beg in the face of a threatened withholding of privilege. But more serious deviance is often punished through very severe means indeed, including solitary confinement or physical assault. Despite the sharp centralization of authority in such associations, the determination and administration of rewards and punishments are often informal, through usurpation of authority by the guards when these functionaries doubt that "justice" will be done through officially established formal procedures. Similarly, guards are often reluctant to intervene in inmates' punishment of violators of the inmate code, even though those punishments may be illegal or even brutal.

Official proactive social control of inmates does not rest solely on surveillance, promises, and threats but almost always includes substantial reliance on rituals of solidarity. In a lengthy discussion of institutional ceremonies in such organizations, Goffman (1961b) points to the ritual functions of institutional newspapers ("house organs"), annual parties and Christmas celebrations, theatrical and sporting events, open houses, and Sunday services in which staff and inmates participate together to blur the sharp social boundary.

Total institutions can be survived; millions of the planet's current population have certainly done so. But total institutions do represent bleak and stringent conditions for enacting a personal social life, and they are perhaps the extreme case of the impact of organization on the character of the individual.

ROLE-MAKING AND CAREER DEVELOPMENT

The character of the role of an individual in relation to any particular association is very much influenced by his own tactics within the organizational processes of that association. To a great extent, people create the situations which lead to their subsequent experiences within associations.

Whether or not the individual's role is of the membership variety is very much up to him; in no association is membership inevitable. Recruitment is generally voluntary, although the social pressures applied to the candidate can sometimes be powerful. Even in those total institutions that ascriptively draft inmates, the individual's line of action in commitment hearings, sentencing hearings, or conscription proceedings has been shown to exert substantial impact on their outcomes (Miller and Schwartz, 1966; Mileski, 1971). Indeed, a very small proportion of the population has ever been institutionalized, and at least one-quarter of that population belongs to no voluntary association whatsoever (Sills, 1968). At any time, less than half of the population holds any position within any bureaucracy.

Once a member of an association, an individual can—if he so desires—relinquish membership, usually by simply dropping out or resigning. For inmates of a total institution, such unilateral action may not prove so simple or uncostly, but there have been escapes even from Devil's Island and Alcatraz. Less risky, but still quite costly, is conduct calculated to cause the inmate to be expelled from the institution—whether sent home in disgrace or merely transferred to an alternative institution.

Conversely, determined and skilled efforts will generally suffice to gain some type of membership role in virtually any association, if the individual so desires. Even the most exclusive and highly selective associations have been infiltrated by spies, imposters, and frauds through skillful manipulation of credentials, through bribery and blackmail, and through invocation of powerful sponsorship.

The placement process is similarly malleable, even when the job requirements call for quite specific personal attributes. Through diligent efforts, an individual quite frequently can prepare himself to meet the requirements or, through careful attraction techniques, prepare himself to appear to meet them. Given the generally low levels of members' participation in and contributions to associations of all types, a dedicated individual willing to make sufficient personal sacrifice can so ingratiate himself as to obtain a position of great influence. (In the case of inmates, position within the structure of informal roles is informally conferred on the basis of apparent characteristics and style of conduct.)

Just as the individual can significantly influence his fate within the recruitment process, so can his tactics of resistance or cooperation influence his progress through the processes of socialization, interaction, innovation, and social control even as an inmate within a total institution. Even the intensive socialization efforts of "brainwashing" camps can be successfully resisted (Schein, 1956), despite the extreme surveillance tactics, arbitrary and intentionally unpredictable ratification/stigmatization procedures, carefully calculated privilege systems, and brutally severe punishments employed in support of these extreme socialization efforts.

In the context of the total institution, Goffman identifies four individual modes or strategies of adaptation.

> First, there is the tack of "situational withdrawal." The inmate withdraws apparent attention from everything except events immediately around his body and sees these in a perspective not employed by others present ["regression," "stir crazy"]. . . . Secondly, there is the "intransigent line": the inmate intentionally challenges the institution by flagrantly refusing to co-operate with staff. . . . A third . . . is "colonization": the sampling of the outside world provided by the establishment is taken by the inmate as the whole, and a stable, relatively contented existence is built up out of the maximum satisfactions procurable within the institution. Experience of the outside world is used as a point of reference to demonstrate the desirability of life on the inside, and the usual tension between the two worlds is markedly reduced. . . . A fourth mode . . . is that of "conversion": the inmate appears to take over the official or staff view of himself and tries to act out the role of the perfect inmate. . . .
>
> The alignments that have been mentioned represent coherent courses to pursue, but few inmates seem to pursue any one of them too far. In most total institutions, most inmates take the tack of what some of them call "playing it cool." This involves a somewhat opportunistic combination of secondary adjustments, conversion, and loyalty to the inmate group, so that the inmate will have a maximum chance, in the particular cirumstances, of eventually getting out physically and psychologically undamaged [Goffman, 1961b: 61–66].

Associations represent the most natural and native arena for the development of individual *careers*. Most associations are intended to be enduring organizations outlasting the lives of any members. Positions are definitely and formally marked (and are related along clearly defined dimensions of rank, centrality, and function), and procedures for filling these positions are formally defined. Staff positions are more often than not filled from among the membership—not only in voluntary associations, by election, but also in most bureaucracies, where organizational loyalty (as evidenced by seniority) is considered an attribute to be rewarded, generally through promotion. Indeed, the classical Weberian bureaucracy embodies a model of a "career escalator" succession in which openings are filled from below on the basis of seniority within a certain career line (Kaplan, 1959). Individuals are considered to be "in line" for a specific promotion and are deeply hurt if passed over for that position.

In contemporary bureaucracies, expected career trajectories tend to be rather more complex than this simple model suggests (see Chapter 10). Mobility across major boundaries of vertical rank is generally quite limited; few rank-and-file workers become managers, and few managers become executives, despite the myth of the mailroom clerk rising to become company president. Certain managerial and executive positions are often regarded as better filled from the outside (with "new blood") than through promotion from within. Promotion, then, tends to be within strata until the ceiling of a major boundary is reached and the career peaks out. Many individuals manage their careers by movement from one bureaucracy to another, so that someone who has reached a ceiling in one association may be the "new blood" at a higher stratum in another. Because association positions tend to involve similar skills, this is a fairly frequent pattern. Others simply work out a more or less comfortable niche for themselves, accumulating seniority and retirement funds, and building up house equity and community relationships.

Because work constitutes the tie between the individual and a bureaucracy, his career within a bureaucracy bears important relations to his careers within the occupational structure of the economy and within his occupational community. Even though a job is different from an occupation and from one's standing in an occupational community, all of these are dynamically linked.

With these facts in mind, Thompson, Avery, and Carlson (1962) describe four career strategies in the world of work: (1) in the *occupational* strategy, the individual's commitment to advancement within his chosen occupation is far greater than his commitment to any particular employing bureaucracy; (2) in the *organizational* strategy, conversely, his primary commitment is to advancement within a particular bureaucracy, whatever changes in occupation may be required in the course of such advancement; (3) in the *heuristic* strategy, the individual is simply oriented to personal advancement, without strong commitment to either an occupation or a bureaucracy, changing either or both as opportunity dictates; and (4) the *stability* strategy is one in which alternative job possibilities are disregarded, reflecting either satisfaction with or resignation to the individual's present position.

Of course, these strategies are not necessarily adopted consciously nor is one's choice of strategy fixed; over the course of a person's work career, strategy may be expected to shift, for example, from a heuristic to either an occupational or an organizational strategy until some ceiling to advancement is reached, after which a stability strategy might be adopted. A substantial body of sociological research has emerged to illuminate the complex interrelations of bureaucratic and occupational careers (Glaser, 1968; Van Maanen, 1977) that flow from these varying strategies of work careers. In most professions, for example, only the occupational strategy is regarded as appropriate; all other career strategies tend to be viewed as deviant choices resulting in lowered status within the occupational community of that profession. Among managerial workers, on the other hand, the organizational strategy tends to be regarded as most appropriate. D. T. Hall (1976) and Porter et al (1975: 188–218) provide detailed analyses of both individual and bureaucratic contributions to career development within the specific context of bureaucracy.

Client careers are examined in Rosengren and Lefton (1970), while the careers of those special clients here referred to as inmates are discussed by Goffman (1959a) and by Irwin (1970). One feature of inmate careers is that even upon successfully leaving the institution, subsequent career opportunities may be altered. If the total institution was one for the custody of stigmatized individuals, the person is likely to experience reduced opportunities.

IMPACT ON THE CHARACTER OF THE INDIVIDUAL

Without a doubt, the impact of role within an association is most dramatically pronounced in the case of the inmate role within a total institution. As Goffman (1961b: 12) puts it, associations of this type are "the forcing houses for changing persons; each is a natural experiment on what can be done to the self." The radical stripping and substitution procedures—even when fairly successfully resisted by the individual—effectively produce alterations not only in identity and self-concept but also in virtually every category of individual attributes set forth in Chapter 2.

Even staff roles within an ordinary bureaucracy have been shown to affect the character of the individual. Merton's (1940) description of the "bureaucratic personality" depicts a pattern of excessive aloofness, insistence on the rights of office over and above any regard for competence or new ideas, extreme attachment to ritualized procedures, resistance to change, and an extreme distaste for controversy. W. H. Whyte's (1956) account of "the organization man" explores the extensive ramifications of this pattern into the wider life of the individual on and off the job.

It is widely conceded, however, that this pattern of impact is far from universal. Howton (1969) maintains that only middle managers develop bureaucratic personality and become organization men, owing to the supervisory character and the high pervasiveness of the managerial role (F. E. Katz, 1968). However, Presthus (1978) links this development not so much to structural position as to career strategy, suggesting that "upward-mobiles" (individuals committed to an organization career strategy) of whatever rank develop characteristics of the bureaucratic personality. Perhaps some staff members, as well as inmates, adopt the tack of "conversion," fully identifying themselves with their formally prescribed roles and becoming organization men.

The impact of the individual's bureaucratic career may, then, lie partially in the likelihood of developing bureaucratic personality. In the famous "Peter Principle,"

LEVELS OF ORGANIZATION

Peter and Hull (1969) suggest that the promotion policy of bureaucracy generally results in the eventual promotion of the organizationally committed individual to some rank just above his competence, at which point bureaucratic personality may be expected to bloom. Perhaps the most common instance is the pattern in which a rank-and-file worker is promoted to foreman, entailing a rather sharp and generally unsatisfactory shift in attitudes, interests, perceptions, and so on (Gardner and Whyte, 1945).

As always, deviant career patterns—particularly demotions (More, 1962) or failure to keep pace with reference others (Jackson, 1959)—exert a substantial impact on the self-concept and the self-esteem of individuals. These individuals will, not infrequently, drop out of that bureaucracy with sour remarks about the "rat race" and seek a more congenial channel of livelihood.

The impact of role or career within voluntary associations has proved less evident. In some cases, of course, job or occupational advancement may be facilitated by membership in a particular union, church, political party, or country club (Dalton, 1951). But because membership is generally quite voluntary indeed, the principal effects of roles in voluntary associations seem to be to reinforce the relevant personal interest of the individual. Several scholars have suggested that, in addition, participation in voluntary associations provides the individual with valuable training in organizational skills, which enhances his level of functioning within the polity and within bureaucracies.

SUMMARY

Associations are designed, special-purpose organizations: bureaucracies, total institutions, voluntary associations. Although often referred to as "formal organizations," "complex organizations," or "large-scale organizations," associations actually vary rather widely on such organizational dimensions.

As a collectivity, an association is a "company of shareholders" pooling some of their energies and resources in collective pursuit of some like interest (and consequently cultivating, through organizational culture, a common interest in the welfare of the association as well). Individual participation tends to be limited, and cooperation is largely indirect, based on an impersonally designed division of labor; member relations are thus generally segmental and fairly impersonal.

The "company of shareholders" often delegates routine decision making to a smaller governing board; policy decisions of all types are executed and implemented by the association's "officers" through an elaborately designed division of labor among offices. The primary structure exhibits three dimensions of differentiation: horizontal, or substantive specialization; vertical, or degrees of administrative responsibility; and spatial, or localized fields of operation. Centralization reflects the degree to which authority is confined to the highest vertical ranks (as in the "corporate" type of association) rather than in the lower ranks (as in the "federative" type). Primary structures also vary in the degrees of specification, formalization, and pervasiveness of role prescriptions.

The Association Level

All the dimensional structures of secondary social structure tend to be rather fully elaborated and highly intercorrelated. Official suborganizations (departments, branches, committees) are generally numerous and interrelated in a complex way. Unofficial suborganizations abound in the forms of emergent informal groups and interpersonal relationships.

The organizational character of an association is clearly influenced by its environment—not only its network of related associations but also its community and societal-level contexts. In voluntary associations (clubs, churches, unions, lodges, political parties, and similar special-interest organizations), almost all offices are filled from within the ranks of the "shareholders" themselves; employees are few. The federative type of social structure is relatively common. Recruitment is voluntary, and is more a matter of obtaining members than of filling offices; it is based more on interest and social background than on placement. The socialization process varies widely. Sharply unequal participation colors the interaction process; a minority of members dominates decision making and does most of the work. Proactive innovation, both externally imposed and internally planned, is relatively common. Reactive innovation and the social control process vary sharply between corporate and federative voluntary associations.

In bureaucracies, at least the great majority of offices are filled by paid employees; offices are thus truly jobs. This category includes not only public agencies but also business firms and most private social agencies (hospitals, schools); members share an interest in deriving income through their participation. The social structure of bureaucracy is more commonly corporate than federative. Recruitment is almost always voluntary and is a matter of filling jobs on the basis of job-related skills; placement cannot be separated from attraction and selection. Socialization varies widely depending on how the individual already fits the job requirements. The interaction process is ponderously dominated by the designed division of labor. Reactive innovation abounds, yet proactive innovation is a central feature of bureaucracies; despite generally formal and authoritarian ratification procedures, ratification rates are low for both types of innovations. Given the cash nexus between a bureaucracy and its office holders, social control relies most heavily on manipulating financial benefits and costs.

Most total institutions are bureaucratic agencies (prisons, asylums) in which the client role is so extremely pervasive that clients become "inmates," their lives being totally administered by one agency. Total institutions generally represent the authoritarian, centralized extreme of the corporate social structure; vertical differentiation is remarkable, with extremely pronounced differentials in power, authority, and status between inmates and staff. The inmate role is extreme not only in its pervasiveness but also in its specification and formalization. Given this rigidity, a secondary structure of informal social roles among inmates is almost inevitable and often quite elaborate, determining the rankings of inmates on the informal dimensions of status, leadership, power, and communication. The like interests of inmates typically diverge from the official purposes of the institution, so that contrasting staff and inmate cultures develop.

For staff members, the organizational processes are essentially those typical of bureaucracies. Inmate recruitment, however, tends to be through some type of ascriptive draft. Inmate socialization invariably takes the radical form of stripping and substitution. Inmate interaction patterns are rigidly prescribed and administratively coerced. "Secondary adjustments" represent tacitly ratified inmate innovations; stigmatization procedures tend to be informal and very frequent. Surveillance is virtually total; promises and rewards center on minor privileges; and threats and punishments tend to be physical, even brutal. However, rituals of solidarity are frequent and significant.

In no association is membership truly inevitable; selection and placement are significantly influenced by individual tactics. Various individual modes of role-making are noted even within total institutions, so that even the intensive socialization and social control efforts of such institutions can be successfully resisted. Given the elaborately designed structures of associations, these represent the clearest arena for the development of individual careers. Career strategies in the bureaucratic world of work are demonstrably influential in shaping career trajectories.

Membership in any association at the very least reinforces (and to some extent satisfies) the like interest of its members and their common interest in the organization itself. The impact of position and role is most dramatically pronounced for inmates of total institutions (changing their self-concepts, appearance, habits, interests, skills, opportunities, even names), but is often notable even for staff roles within any quite ordinary bureaucracy—for example, in the phenomena of "bureaucratic personality" and "the organißzation man." The likelihood of such effects seems linked not only to position but to career trajectory. Of course, deviant career patterns within an association of any kind tend to have a negative impact on the self-concept, self-esteem, and opportunities of individuals.

SUGGESTIONS FOR ADDITIONAL READING

By far the greatest number of writings on organizations deals exclusively with associations, particularly bureaucracies. The most convenient analytic summary of and bibliographic guide to this vast literature on associations is James G. March, editor, *Handbook of Organizations* (Chicago: Rand McNally, 1965).

It should not be surprising that much of the best material of sociological social psychology has focused on the associations level of social organization. Much of the explicit theory and research regarding the nature of organizations, recruitment, socialization, interaction, innovation, social control, role-making and career development, interorganizational relations, and social change have been developed around the case of associations. Many of these excellent writings have already been suggested in Chapter 3 and in the various chapters of Part III and need not be relisted here.

Bureaucracies in particular have inspired much influential work in the social psychology of organizations. Two of these works which employ models much like that of this book are Lyman W. Porter, Edward E. Lawler III, and J. Richard Hackman, *Behavior in Organizations* (New York: McGraw-Hill, 1975), and Daniel Katz and

The Association Level

Robert L. Kahn, *The Social Psychology of Organizations,* 2nd edition (New York: Wiley, 1978). Of related interest is Chris Argyris, *Integrating the Individual and the Organization* (New York: Wiley, 1964). Two classic examinations of the impact of bureaucracy on the individual member are William H. Whyte, Jr., *The Organization Man* (New York: Simon & Schuster, 1956) and Robert Presthus, *The Organizational Society,* revised edition (New York: St. Martins, 1978).

The landmark volume on total institutions is itself thoroughly social psychological in nature: Erving Goffman's *Asylums: Essays on the Social Situation of Mental Patients and Other Inmates* (New York: Doubleday, 1961). Further detail regarding patient careers can be found in Stephan P. Spitzer and Norman K. Denzin, editors, *The Mental Patient* (New York: McGraw-Hill, 1968). The situation of prison inmates is examined with great insight by John Irwin, "Adaptation to Being Corrected: Corrections from the Convict's Perspectives" (pp. 971–994 in Daniel Glaser, editor, *Handbook of Criminology,* Chicago: Rand McNally, 1974). See also Stanton Wheeler, "Socialization in Correctional Communities," *American Sociological Review,* 1961, 16: 699–712.

Voluntary associations are abundant and socially vital. In Denise Akey's massive *Encyclopedia of Associations,* 15th edition (Detroit: Gale, 1980), some 15,000 nationally important voluntary associations of all types are briefly described; in Constant H. Jacquet, Jr.'s *Yearbook of American and Canadian Churches, 1980* (Nashville: Abingdon Press, 1980), comparable detail is provided regarding more than a thousand churches of national significance.

The study of voluntary associations of all sorts has played a prominent part in both classical and modern sociological theories. A convenient introduction to this literature is William A. Glaser and David L. Sills, editors, *The Government of Associations* (Totowa, N.J.: Bedminster, 1966). A solid portrait of individuals' relations to voluntary associations is Murray Hausknecht, *The Joiners: A Sociological Description of Voluntary Association Membership in the United States* (Totowa, N.J.: Bedminster, 1962). A critical overview of theory and research is presented in David L. Sills, "Voluntary Associations: Sociological Aspects" (pp. 362–379 in Sills, editor, *International Encyclopedia of the Social Sciences,* vol. 15, New York: Macmillan and Free Press, 1968). An annotated bibliographic guide is Constance Smith and Anne Freedman, *Voluntary Associations: Perspectives on the Literature* (Cambridge, Mass.: Harvard University Press, 1972). The personal impacts of voluntary association membership have been most extensively explored in the case of religious associations; this research literature is reviewed in James E. Dittes, "Psychology of Religion" (pp. 602–659 in Gardner Lindzey and Elliot Aronson, eds., *The Handbook of Social Psychology,* revised edition, vol. 5, Reading, Mass.: Addison-Wesley, 1969).

Even the work concerning the impact on organizations of variations in environmental context and interorganizational relations is most fully developed in the case of associations. See, for example, Howard E. Aldrich, *Organizations and Environments* (Englewood Cliffs, N.J.: Prentice-Hall, 1979), and Cornelis J. Lammers and David J. Hickson, editors, *Organizations Alike and Unlike: International and Interinstitutional Studies in the Sociology of Organizations* (London: Routledge & Kegan Paul, 1979).

359

Photo courtesy of United Nations

Both collective and individual interests can be pursued through a group activity.

CHAPTER 20

The Group Level

Groups are a level of social organization with which almost everyone is very familiar from his or her personal history of growing up and making one's way in the social order. This very familiarity, however, breeds a blindness through which many subtle and surprising features of groups may be missed. For example, the sheer size of a group—three, four, five, twenty—has far-reaching implications for its internal dynamics and its members. Another interesting point is that biologists, psychologists, sociologists, and philosophers all tend to agree that groups are an important factor in their respective fields, although their treatment of the group factor may differ significantly. We have already seen the importance of groups in forming public opinion and as suborganizations in the internal workings of larger-scale social structures. We are now ready to look at the group itself and its implications for its individual members.

A fundamental contrast in sociology is that between groups and associations. The ends or purposes toward which an association is organized tend to be quite limited and specific; the ends toward which a group is organized tend to be far more general and encompassing. For example, the family is usually far more multipurpose than a work association, and the individual shares more plans of action with his buddies than with his school. Within an association, the aspect of social structure is more prominent than the aspect of collectivity; within a group, the aspect of collectivity tends to be more developed than the aspect of structure. Whereas in a neighborhood play group, for example, the personal characteristics of the members tend to predominate, in a successful musical group the worked-out positions, roles, and division of labor generally prevail; in fact, the musical group is not likely to be successful until it develops many of the characteristics of an association.

LEVELS OF ORGANIZATION

Relations among members of an association tend to be formal and impersonal, sharply subordinating personal attitudes to the cause of like and common interests. Roles are more salient than persons, and cooperative interaction among members is largely indirect, through a highly differentiated and administratively coordinated division of labor.

In contrast, relations among members of a group tend to be informal and personal, with personal attitudes often overriding concern for the collective interest. Direct interaction in execution of the collective action is quite characteristic of groups.

> The face-to-face group, though it admits of subsidiary and preparatory division of labor, is essentially a mode of sharing a common experience. . . . The members of a study group may undertake separate tasks in preparation for the activity of the group, but they must bring their results into a common process at the point where the group activity begins. . . . The members of a group discussing the same problem make different contributions, but they do not have separate functions; all participate in the same process [MacIver, 1937: 240].

Thus, persons are more salient than roles in the functioning of a group.

This characteristically informal and personal mode of collective action virtually determines various organizational attributes of the group. Direct and person-based interaction dictates that a group be fairly small in membership size and that it also be geographically localized. Reliance on indirect, impersonal, and role-based interaction—as in associations—permits membership to be very large and geographically dispersed. As noted in Chapter 19, large size generally fosters greater differentiation and formalization of roles. Characteristically, then, groups tend to be smaller than associations, and their primary role structures tend to be less sharply, less stably, and less formally differentiated. On the other hand, the character of the individual—as opposed to his position—can more directly influence the group and its course.

Of course, this multidimensional contrast between group and association amounts to a theoretical idealization of two organizational types. Many actual organizations fall somewhere between these polar types and are labeled "secondary groups" as distinguished from the idealized or "primary" group. According to Cooley (1909), the central distinguishing feature between primary and secondary groups is the relative strength of the sense of collectivity. A primary group is one in which the members strongly identify themselves with the group, developing an emphatic "we-feeling" and a sharp ingroup–outgroup distinction. A secondary group is one in which the aspect of social structure is not sharply subordinated to the aspect of collectivity, more nearly resembling a voluntary association.

A work group, for example, might be either a primary or a secondary group. In Chapter 19, we distinguished between official and unofficial groups as a major aspect of the suborganization of an association such as a bureaucracy. On the basis of closely linked formal roles within the organizational hierarchy, certain individuals may be designated to work together face-to-face in a common process, that is, as a group in our sense. These individuals constitute an official group—a team, squad, committee, task force, or the like. So long as their interactions remain governed by their official roles, the aspect of structure outweighs the aspect of collectivity; official groups are thus secondary groups. Should such an officially designated group develop a sense of "we-ness" sufficient to permit spontaneous and emergent adjustments in the execution of the common process, the group becomes an *unofficial* task group (as defined in Chapter 19). Unofficial groups, whether their members have been assigned or self-selected, tend to be primary groups. Small secondary groups quite frequently develop into primary groups—in the factory, in the office, on the battlefield, or in the neighborhood. This is most likely to occur if (1) members are thrown together for some duration; (2) members face common situations and experiences; and (3) membership remains fairly constant.

Unofficial groups are a ubiquitous feature of the suborganization of all larger organizations. Social cliques emerge in the student body of every high school (Coleman, 1971), play groups emerge in every neighborhood (Z. Rubin, 1980), youth gangs in every defended neighborhood (Suttles, 1968), and work groups in every bureaucracy (W. F. Whyte, 1951; Sayles, 1958).

Somewhat intermediate between the official and the unofficial types of group is the *institutionalized* group—the prime example being the nuclear family. As in an unofficial group, members are not assigned (although membership may be officially regulated or certified, as in the case of the family). As in an official group, organizational positions within the group may be formally defined and allocated (although the corresponding roles are largely unofficial and informally differentiated through interaction of the members). In any case, the aspect of collectivity rather clearly outweighs the aspect of structure in such institutionalized groups, with the consequence that these too must be considered to represent primary groups.

ORGANIZATIONAL CHARACTER OF THE PRIMARY GROUP

Collectivity

A primary group, unlike a secondary group or a voluntary association, does not ordinarily cohere around some single like interest of its members but instead answers some overlapping ranges of like and complementary interests. A high school clique, for instance, involves a far wider sharing of interests and engages a greater range of its members' roles than does a committee of department heads. For members of a primary group, the nature of *any* interest becomes both focused and enriched—objectified, in Mead's (1938) sense—through the group process.

> We see it through the eyes of others and thus it is in some measure freed from irrelevant personal implications. It is defined more closely for each of us, for being now both mine and yours it must have a common meaning. Before we can effectively pursue it together we must learn to perceive it together. Each seeing it from his own viewpoint seeks to convey that aspect to his associates. Thus the character of the interest is enlarged and enriched, as each

contributes something different to the understanding of it . . . as the play of different minds is directed upon it. . . .

Not only does the presence of others contribute directly to the interpretation of the common interest which each acquires, it contributes also indirectly [through] a heightening of the emotional significance of the interest. . . . Each is spurred on in his pursuit by the fact that others are pursuing with him. When his own energy and devotion flag, for there is ebb and flow in all human endeavor, he is sustained by the energy and devotion of his fellows. It is partly the evocation of the competitive spirit, but it goes deeper than that. The interest, by being shared, acquires a new significance, a new emphasis, a new valuation. It has a breadth of support which it formerly lacked. The interest is thus maintained for the group more nearly at one level of intensity that would be possible for the isolated individual. That it is generally a higher level is seen in the fact that people are ready to pursue interests in [groups] which they would find too arduous or too uninspiring to pursue in isolation. . . . It may be said that this is because another interest, that of companionship, is added, but the latter is reflected in the enhanced value of the pursuit itself.

The sustaining power of companionship witnesses to the inherently social nature of man . . . men can endure in company hardships and privations and perils that would be utterly insufferable in isolation. Side by side, sustained by the sense of a common lot and a common cause, they will face the horrors of the trenches in warfare, they will live cheerfully through the winter darkness of the Arctic wastes, they will engage in unremitting and drearily monotonous toils. The primary group does more than sustain this interest or that; it sustains the interest of living itself [MacIver, 1937: 237–239].

Thus, many features of a group are emergent from the group process itself: definitions of situations, definitions of social objects, plans of action, and experience itself. In other words, whatever the constellation of like and complementary interests within a group, its members develop a common interest in the group process and in the group itself. Indeed, Cooley (1909) saw in the primary group "a certain fusion of individualities in a common whole," and Burgess (1926) characterized the family as "a unity of interacting personalities." However,

it is not to be supposed that the unity of the primary group is one of mere harmony and love. It is always a differentiated and usually a competitive unity, admitting of self-assertion and various appropriative passions; but these passions are socialized by sympathy, and come, or tend to come, under the discipline of a common spirit. The individual will be ambitious, but the chief object of his ambition will be some desired place in the thought of others, and he will feel allegiance to common standards of service and fair play [Cooley, 1909: 23–24].

But necessarily, effective participation in the characteristic group process is possible only for quite limited numbers. Most primary groups are therefore *small groups,* of not more than twenty members. Only where interest in the group itself somewhat outweighs interest in the group process—for example, the kinship group (Bott, 1971; Adams, 1968)—can a large group (of perhaps forty members) retain the character of a primary group. The significance of numbers in group life was brilliantly explored by Simmel (1950), who pointed not only to differences between large and small groups but also to the distinctive dynamics of three-person and two-person "groups" (triads and dyads).

In the smaller ranges, groups of each size tend to have distinctive characteristics.

The Group Level

The dyad (pair relationship) will be explored extensively in the next chapter. The triad (group of three) may have more flexibility than the dyad but is more unstable, because there is always the potential of its breaking down into a situation of "two against one" (Caplow, 1968). Groups of slightly larger size tend to have more differentiation of functions performed by the individual members and tend to display more durability, in that their continuance is less dependent upon any single member. The larger the group size, the more likely it is that there will be role differentiation and specialization. The smaller the group size, the greater influence a single member can exert and the more the group is affected by the addition or deletion of one member (for example, the birth of a child to a childless couple).

A group, like a voluntary association, depends on its membership for the entirety of its collective resources, both human and material. Owing to its smaller size, the resources of a group are usually quite meager in comparison with those of larger organizations. In fact, this is precisely why higher organizational levels are often able to predominate over a group for social control and other purposes. However, the ingenuity and brashness of group members in unofficially appropriating material resources through their memberships in other organizations are legendary. A factory work group "borrows" a company truck for its weekend outing, a group of teenagers "borrows" the home of a temporarily absent parent for a drinking party, and a neighborhood gang sets up a *sub rosa* clubhouse in the basement of a nearby shoestore.

Perhaps because groups tend to be much less enduring than many larger social organizations, comparatively little attention has been paid to the cultures of primary groups, even though these prove to be quite rich indeed (McFeat, 1974). Thrasher (1927) described the significance within youth gangs of gang name, songs, yells, argot, nicknames, games, and traditions. Bossard and Boll (1956) documented the proliferation of ritual in family living, and family folklore—including family sagas, stories, sayings, songs, and traditions—has been the subject of considerable research (Baldwin, 1975). Fine (1979) analyzed the processes through which group culture is created, suggesting that cultural items will be adopted to the extent that they are known to the members, usable in the course of group interaction, functional in supporting group goals and individual needs, appropriate in supporting the status hierarchy of the group, and triggered by events that occur in group interaction.

Often, items from the mainstream culture are adapted into the existing group culture by slightly redefining their meanings. For instance, a macho touch may be added to the roller skating fashion; currently fashionable clothing might be given a local twist to serve virtually as a group uniform; or mass media slogans may be picked up and given a special meaning to stand as in-group jokes.

It is, however, the *normative* culture of groups that has received the greatest attention—the output norms of factory work groups, the codes of gangs, the rules of families. In general, norms emerge in those areas of behavior, opinion, and belief where members have become dependent upon the group for gratification (Secord and Backman, 1974).

Every gang, family, and work group seems to develop rather quickly its own somewhat unique culture of norms, shared meanings, and distinctive traditions.

Social Structure

As previously noted, the primary social structure (role structure or division of labor) tends to be a somewhat troublesome matter in the case of a group.

Only in an official (and therefore secondary) group is the concept of role structure at all straightforward. Here, both the membership and the role structure are officially designated by the larger association of which the group is a functional unit. Since it is a relatively small unit, the extent of horizontal and vertical differentiation is usually quite limited but definite. Even in the case of an ad hoc committee or task force, one member will ordinarily have been designated to serve as chairman. The degree to which roles are specified and pervasive may vary widely among official groups, but formalization is ordinarily extensive.

In an institutionalized group (such as a nuclear family) and in informal work groups, the organizational positions into which the members have been placed are official and formalized, but the roles they play are unofficial and rather informally differentiated. In the nuclear family, for example, the titles of—and allocations of persons to—positions will be quite clear: John is father, Marcia is mother, Dick is oldest son, Jane is youngest daughter, and so on. Moreover, the horizontal and vertical differentiation among these positions is roughly institutionalized or formalized. Yet, the detailed differentiation of the accompanying roles is developed quite informally through interaction among the members of that unique group. Who shall carry out the garbage or feed the baby? Which parent shall discipline the children? Each family tends to answer such questions differently.

> The unique system of roles determines the way the essential business of family life is carried on. In one family the roles are interrelated, so that decisions are made and activities carried out with a minimum of sentiment. In another the process of decision making requires expressions of affection for each to play his role. In still another, roles are so organized that expressions of anger are a necessary way of indicating that a decision is seriously desired, so that chronic confict is built in as a phase of group decision making. The organization of roles can make explicit bargaining a necessary step in each transaction. It can place each member constantly on guard lest the other encroach on his prerogatives. Such differences in the manner in which the day-to-day interaction is carried out have sometimes been called differences in texture [Hess and Handel, 1959], some textures being smooth and some rough, some interesting and some uninteresting [Turner, 1970: 198].

Such informally differentiated role structures may sometimes be fairly centralized and/or highly specified and may often be quite pervasive, but they are never substantially formalized. Institutionalized groups like the family have a large degree of freedom in working out their own "live" role structures, role prescriptions, and role performances. If one visits a dozen families, one will find a dozen distinct and diverse primary groups.

In purely unofficial groups, where members are not assigned but are self-selected, both positions *and* roles are informally differentiated. According to Benne and Sheats (1948), the nearly infinite variety of informal roles may be grouped into three major categories: group task roles (initiator-contributor, elaborator, opinion giver, evaluator-critic); group building and maintenance roles (encourager, harmonizer, compromiser); and "individual" roles (aggressor, blocker, playboy, recognition-seeker). Again, the informal division of labor may vary in differentiation, centralization, specification, and pervasiveness, but it will never be substantially formalized.

In all types of primary groups, then, role differentiation tends to rest on an implicit, often almost accidental division of labor which comes to have the force of a group tradition. One member makes an especially good joke or brings a distinctively good batch of cookies to a group get-together and may thereby come to play the role of group wit or group provisioner in a ritualized division of labor, no matter how funny or how adept in the kitchen other group members may be. Such a traditionalized division of labor is likely to persist unexamined until someone becomes disgruntled or there is a change in membership, at which point it may be explicitly renegotiated through conferral on the shape of the joint venture.

In all primary groups, secondary social structure tends to be more influential than primary structure. Indeed, to the extent that a group relies on informal means of role differentiation, the operative social positions of its members are most meaningfully conceived in terms of the familiar dimensional social structures of power, status, communication, liking, and leadership. Thus, it is hardly coincidental that these dimensional social structures have been more closely and more thoroughly studied in small-group researches than in any other area of sociological investigation.

In the typical primary group, a rough ranking of members along the dimensions of status and power is readily discernible. An authority structure, on the other hand, is not to be found within what we have called a purely unofficial group. Authority is a function of officially designated positions, which (among *primary* groups) occur only within institutionalized groups such as the family and within those unofficial groups whose membership has been officially assigned, such as standing committees. Within primary groups, the actual exercise of one's power or authority tends to be counter-productive, placing grave strains on the predominating "we-feeling" sense of collectivity and solidarity (Safilios-Rothschild, 1970).

Leadership is the prevailing mode of influence and has received the most constant emphasis in studies of both primary and secondary groups. The reason, of course, is that this type of influence is most directly reflected in and based upon differential participation in the group process. Leadership (defined as the significance of contributions to the collective action) is essentially tantamount to the process of informal role differentiation discussed above.

The dimensional social structures of communication and conformity rankings can be more readily studied in groups than in most other social organizations, owing to their small size and to the characteristic emphasis of group process on face-to-face interaction. The *affect structure* is fully developed only within groups, owing not only to their smaller size but also to the fact that within any group persons are more important than roles. Indeed, virtually all studies of the affect structure have been conducted within secondary and primary groups; the "sociometric method" of asking individuals whom they like or dislike is itself often regarded as essentially a method of small group research (Lindzey and Byrne, 1968).

LEVELS OF ORGANIZATION

Studies of small groups indicate that, with the general exception of the affect structure, the dimensional social structures tend to be highly intercorrelated and mutually reinforcing (Secord and Backman, 1974: 204–363). For example, a member ranking high in, say, status is also likely to rank high in power, leadership, communications initiated and received, and conformity, but he may or may not be well-liked. The reason for this general convergence is that common factors underlie the various dimensions. The first common factor is differential interest among members in the collective good produced through the group action. According to Olson (1971), those members with greater interest tend to make greater contributions to the collective action (thus rising in both leadership and communication) and to receive greater sidepayments for these contributions (thus rising in status). The second underlying common factor is power: control over some resource relevant to collective production of the collective good. Members with great power necessarily exert substantial leadership (at the very least, leadership of the dissuasive, veto variety). Great status tends to be offered to them as an incentive to contribute their scarce resources.

The underpinnings of group structure are, then, individual differences in interests and in resources. Because the dimensional social structures are so highly intercorrelated, they permit some rough delineation of social positions within even a purely unofficial group. Those members ranking high on the dimensions of status, power, leadership, and communication are generally referred to as "leaders." Some groups appear to have more than one leader, each specializing in a particular type of contribution. "Instrumental leaders" (Zelditch, 1955) are "task specialists" (Bales and Slater, 1955), whereas "expressive leaders" are "social-emotional specialists." In a family, for instance, one parent may largely handle the family finances, travel arrangements, and the like, while the other parent does most of the counseling of the growing children. The conditions under which such specialization among leaders is likely to occur have been explored in a number of works (Verba, 1961; Burke, 1967, 1968).

Members ranking rather lower on the dimensions of status, power, leadership, and communication—but relatively high on the dimension of conformity—are referred to as "followers." Although specialization is seldom extensive within any group, such horizontal differentiation does tend to be greater within the rank of followers than within the rank of leaders.

Members ranking very low on conformity are "deviants" and tend to rank quite low on the other dimensions as well. Some common deviant roles are the group mascot, the group clown, and the group scapegoat (Heap, 1977). Burke (1969) suggests that groups which evolve the scapegoat role tend not to develop specialization of leadership into distinct instrumental and expressive roles. Dentler and Erikson (1959) maintain that deviants are necessary to the clarification of both group norms and group culture, particularly in view of the informal process through which these components develop. The supposition is that in reacting to the deviating member, the group simultaneously rediscovers and reaffirms its normative patterns and culture.

One final role commonly observed in groups is the "isolate," a member who ranks low on all dimensions but particularly on communication and affect (Jennings, 1950).

The Group Level

The structure of liking, or affection, is a somewhat peculiar one. A leader is not necessarily more widely liked than a follower or even a deviant (Jennings, 1950). The affect structure seems to rest not on collective interests and resources but on special interests and special resources (see Chapter 3). Member A's affection for member B depends not on how B relates to the functioning of the group but on how B relates to the functioning of member A. That is, A's affection depends not on B's resources pertaining to the group's interests but on B's resources pertaining to A's personal and special interests (Secord and Backman, 1974: 284–285). The isolate, then, may be an acceptable member of the group but may simply fail to answer to the personal interests of very many of the other members. A member of a high school clique might be quite acceptable as a tag-along and a source of rides but not share fully in the lives of any of the other members. The characteristics and career of the isolate are a promising area for further research on social groups.

Sociometric studies of the affect structure of groups disclose not only a continuum of liking, from "stars" down to "isolates," but also the frequent occurrence of cliques—fairly distinct clusters of members who particularly like one another. Even primary groups often display substantial unofficial suborganizations, in the form not only of cliques but of factions and temporary coalitions. Indeed, the varying potential patterns of coalitional factions lend distinctive characteristics to groups of various sizes—dyads, triads, tetrads, pentads, and so on (Caplow, 1968; Hare, 1976). Of course, even a primary group may generate at least temporary official suborganizations in the form of task forces or special teams.

One of the most common and important suborganizations within any group is the dyad or pair relationship. Sometimes fleeting, sometimes permanent, dyads abound in small groups and may either reinforce or cut across the dimensional structures. Potentially, there are as many dyads within a group as there are mathematically possible pairings of the members, and in reality at least traces of each of these possible relationships can be found to exist. It might even be said that one of the resources a group provides its members is the opportunity for a variety of relationships under intimate but "safe" circumstances.

The interorganizational relations of primary groups also have some interesting features. As previously noted, every primary group is embedded within some larger organization—an association, a neighborhood, a community, or a diffuse collectivity—and serves as an official or unofficial suborganization of it. The character of the group will be greatly influenced by this embedding context. Families, for example, are embedded in communities, geographic and/or social; suburban families differ from innercity families, blue-collar from white-collar, Catholic from Jewish, Italian-American from Finnish-American (Adams, 1971). Play groups in middle-class neighborhoods differ from those in the slums, and work groups in the corporate type of bureaucracy differ from those in the federative type. The organizational character of a high school affects the nature and culture of its embedded student cliques.

Conversely, one major thrust of small group research has been to document and explain the tendency for an embedded group either to facilitate or to subvert the collective action of the larger organization (Shils, 1951). Subversion now appears to be essentially a defensive effort in the face of imposed or threatened innovations within the larger organization. A work group, for example, may engage in restriction of output when it fears that management plans to raise the expected rate of production (Collins, Dalton, and Roy, 1946). A play group of neighborhood boys may become an aggressive gang when it fears that the neighborhood will undergo change in ethnic composition. Groups are more effectively harnessed into the collective action of the larger organization when group input into the innovation process is substantial and fair (Lewin, 1948)—that is, when the group is not shut out from the five basic processes operating within the larger embedding organization.

A group may also come into conflict with the embedding larger organization because of its own innovations, a very common circumstance for youth groups of various kinds. The potential of disapproval or a backlash from the higher organizational levels tends both to make such groups covert, edgy, and combative and to strengthen in-group feelings. Societal leaders (such as musicians or media stars) who seem to resonate with group members' innovative behaviors are likely to become significant others over and above local role-models. In general, a group is likely to form when individuals holding attitudes and behaviors contrary to their organizational environment have some chance to get together.

Relations among comparable groups are significantly influenced by the extent of defensiveness. Under any circumstances, a sharp ingroup–outgroup distinction is a central feature of the primary group. When the interests of the group facilitate the action of the embedding organization, its relations with parallel groups tend to assume the character of a marked but friendly rivalry. When the group is placed in a defensive and subversive posture, its relations with parallel groups tend to be relations of conflict, suspicion, and even enmity. Under either circumstance, groups will sometimes form coalitions and alliances with comparable groups to facilitate similar interests. For instance, families in a neighborhood will often develop patterns of joint activities. If these are at all stable, a new larger group—or even an association—can result.

ORGANIZATIONAL PROCESSES

The basis of *recruitment* in groups is, perhaps surprisingly, often ascriptive. In most secondary and many primary groups, as we have seen, members are officially designated (certified, if not assigned) by the embedding organization. Even in the nuclear family, the parents' ascriptive claim to birthright is officially honored (or, in some cases, not honored) by the state. Also, a person's placement in a geographic area, a particular station in an institution, an assigned seating arrangement—resulting from outside circumstances—may essentially place him or her ascriptively into the available group.

Yet, even some secondary, official groups obtain their members through voluntary recruitment; a committee or a task force, for example, may be formed by soliciting volunteers rather than through administrative assignment. In purely unofficial groups, new members are most often obtained through highly selective invitations and urgings, quite like those of an exclusive voluntary association. But even here, one minimal criterion of selection will ordinarily be prior membership in the embedding organization.

The aspect of attraction has received the greatest share of attention in the analysis of group recruitment process, often under the heading of "group cohesiveness" (Cartwright and Zander, 1968). The greater the attraction of its members to the group, the more likely it is that those members remain in the group and the greater its cohesiveness will be. The aspect of selection has been much less studied, although some note has been made of the possibility that severity of initiation rites is positively related to group cohesiveness (Lott and Lott, 1965).

Since many primary groups essentially lack any true primary social structure, the aspect of placement is virtually reduced to the process of informal role differentiation. Placement thus takes place after selection; a member is not recruited for and into a particular position but is instead recruited into membership, with his position being settled only gradually. In fact, the introduction of a newcomer or the loss of a member often precipitates a renewed round of placement in which the social positions and roles of all members are somewhat redefined (Mills, 1957; Perry, Silber, and Bloch, 1956).

Whether the group is a gang or a family, the loss or addition of a member can have such a profound effect on the informal role structure that it changes the very character of the group. In many cases, this amounts to a situation of crisis, as when the leader of a gang is jailed, a couple has its first child, or one of the parents dies. But even when the addition or loss is less critical—the birth of the sixth child, the eldest daughter getting married, or D'Artagnan joining up with the three musketeers—shifts in the division of labor and innovations in role performances are almost inevitable. Role structure in a primary group is exceedingly dependent upon membership size and the member's personal characteristics.

Socialization is, in some ways, the central process of a primary group. As MacIver pointed out above, any and all shared interests of group members become defined, concentrated, enriched, and objectified through the group process itself. In this sense, the continual mutual socialization of members is the heart of group participation. The newcomer, however, is at a disadvantage. Group culture, as we have seen, is often quite elaborate but is essentially unformalized. No self-study materials are available, and there are no classes to be taken. The primary group must communicate its expectations and develop the desired capacities in the individual largely through implicit procedures, supplemented by some explicit advice and coaching. Of course, among all primary groups, the socialization procedures of the nuclear family are both the most significant and the most thoroughly studied (Clausen, 1968; T. R. Williams, 1975).

Despite the essential centrality of socialization, it is the *interaction* process of groups that has received the most thorough and careful empirical investigation. The distinctive reliance of groups on face-to-face interaction of persons not only constitutes the chief attractive benefit of groups to their members but also facilitates direct sociological examination of their social structures as these unfold through informal role differentiation. Indeed, the now vast array of methods and techniques for observational study of the interaction process (Weick, 1968) was originally developed with the

371

almost exclusive purpose of facilitating the study of group dynamics (Cartwright and Zander, 1968; Bales, 1950; Carter, 1954). Beginning in the laboratory, an enormous empirical literature has accumulated concerning the determinants, patterns, and consequences of group interaction (Hare, 1976; McGrath and Altman, 1966). To some extent, such procedures were extended to the study of highly controlled groups outside the laboratory setting (Sherif et al., 1961). Finally, they were applied to naturally occurring groups in natural settings such as gangs (Short and Strodtbeck, 1965) and families (Winter and Ferreira, 1969).

A few key findings include the following. As group size increases, the group interaction process tends to favor contributions of information and suggestions at the expense of resolving differences of opinion. Productivity is greater under instrumental leadership, whereas morale is greater under expressive styles of leadership. Cohesive groups perform more adequately; if newcomers join a group, there tends to be a short-run decline in performance while the group reorganizes itself.

Regarding the *innovation* process, mention has already been made of the significance of imposed change by the embedding organization as frequently provoking embedded groups into defensive hostility and intergroup conflict. Planned change within a primary group tends to be informal in nature and a relatively rare occurrence. Within a group, the innovation is largely reactive. Because roles are not formalized and are typically not even highly specified, relatively few performances are viewed by any member as actionably discrepant. On the other hand, the emphasis on face-to-face participation leads to a high level of organizational surveillance; relatively few questionable performances escape the attention of the group. Proceedings for the ratification or stigmatization of innovations are quite informal and tend to be rather highly democratic. However, the fact that primary groups tend to be so significant in the social lives of the members means that such informal ratification/stigmatization procedures may carry tremendous weight with the individuals involved. A few remarks of praise or scorn may have a tremendous social psychological impact.

Social control is similarly diffuse, even in the reactive aspect. The benefits and costs manipulated as rewards and punishments are primarily social in nature: affect, communication, status. As befits an organization in which the aspect of collectivity is most prominent, rewards and punishments revolve around manipulation of the benefits of companionship and sentiment. Punishments are often ritualized, particularly the limited indulgence of groups in corporal punishment, such as the spanking of children in a nuclear family or the "binging" of the arm of an errant member of a factory work group (Homans, 1950). The determination of appropriate rewards or punishments is normally a very informal and somewhat democratic proceeding, except in the case of ritualized punishments, where the appropriate level may be normatively prescribed. The administration of rewards and punishments is generally democratic (although in families, the father may specialize in administering punishments and the mother in administering rewards). Such administration of sanctions also tends to be informal, except insofar as these sanctions are ritualized for dramatic effect.

Given the prominence of the aspect of collectivity, it should not prove surprising that various rituals of solidarity are ubiquitous and feature prominently in proactive tactics of group social control. These rituals of solidarity are seldom so formal and extensive as to constitute organizational ceremonies, yet their sheer frequency is such as to provide almost continual reminders of the strength of the collectivity. Rituals may be daily, as with the family dinner-table chatter or the evening meet at a particular bar and grill. These recurring ritualized events abound in every group: a big dinner every Sunday, Monday is "wash day," Saturday night at the disco, a stopover every payday for a couple of beers, the garbage hauled out late Sunday night for pickup. Such routines have a two-way influence: the group develops them as rituals, and the rituals comprise a good deal of the pattern of the group. In a gang, for example, even punching and cursing tend to become so ritualized.

Promises and threats within a primary group are mainly tacit (although, within a family, a parent may explicitly state them in view of the lesser social awareness of children). Given the members' acute recognition of the high level of effective surveillance, even tacit promises and threats are typically sufficient to maintain cooperative participation. So long as an individual is strongly bound or attached to a group, the group's channeling and guiding social control tactics are likely to be extremely effective.

ROLE-MAKING AND CAREER DEVELOPMENT

For the first time in our review of varieties of social organization, we can safely state that here the impact of the individual tactics of even the average member is quite great. In the primary group, persons are more salient than roles, and no member is greatly outnumbered. The personal characteristics and interpersonal styles of members have been shown to exert a substantial impact not only on the individual's role but also on the character of group process and group structure (Mann et al., 1967).

In conventional analyses of most types of social organization, the role-making process receives little or no systematic attention. In the case of the group, the role-making process (the informal differentiation of roles) has long been the very center of analysis.

We have already touched upon the tendency of even official secondary groups to develop primary characteristics—the assigned squad becomes a gang of buddies, the designated office workmates develop a "we-feeling." Even the most structured bureaucracies seem to develop some group character in which the individual may pursue his role-making over and above the officially designated table of positions. Such "informal organization," functioning as a quasi-primary group, may have more to do with the person's official roles and social life than his official actions.

On the other hand, when role-making within the primary group fails or falters, some secondary characteristics are likely to be invoked. In a family, the parents might remind an errant teenager that he or she is not yet of legal age or a wife might call the state marriage laws to the attention of her husband. In the workplace, official regulations might be called into play by one's group mates, and in the high school clique, school regulations might be invoked. When primary joint action bogs down, there is usually some reversion to role bargaining: "I'm earning a paycheck and doing all the housework too," or "I've been providing all the transportation for this group." Such negotiations are essentially over the division of labor or over adjustments in distribution of gratifications.

If such bargainings fail, the next step is usually an appeal to some agency of the larger embedding organizations, such as the police, a counselor, school authorities, a senior officer of the company. However, at that stage the group is in deep organizational trouble and the likelihood of its continuance and success, at least in its present form, is rather slim.

The process of career development has not been so widely recognized within the study of groups, perhaps because most groups are not intended to be long enduring in relation to the life span of the individual. Some longitudinal studies of laboratory groups have examined changes in the position and role of individual members (Slater, 1966), and students of the nuclear family have not overlooked the role changes of family members (Aldous, 1978), as when the mother must readjust to the "empty nest" or the father to his unemployment or retirement.

In a more generic and fundamental sense, the basic career pattern within a group involves movement from the position of newcomer to that of regular member, to that of "old hand." Deviant careers would, of course, be any departure from this trajectory, such as a newcomer who becomes disgruntled and leaves the group.

Also, the fact of biological and socially defined age-sex maturation produces something of a typical life-sequence trajectory from group to group within each societal-level structure: from family of origin to neighborhood play group, to school groups, to a "singles" group, to job-centered groups, to marriage and family group, and so on. Any deviation from this career pattern is itself likely to involve affiliation with marginal groups.

IMPACT ON THE CHARACTER OF THE INDIVIDUAL

In some ways, the impact of the primary group is more fundamental and more enduring than that of any other type of social organization. Indeed, according to Cooley (to whom we owe the concept of primary group), it is through such groups that the individual acquires human nature itself.

> By human nature, I suppose, we may understand those sentiments and impulses that are human in being superior to those of lower animals, and also in the sense that they belong to mankind at large, and not to any particular race or time. It means, particularly, sympathy and the innumerable sentiments into which sympathy enters, such as love, resentment, ambition, vanity, hero-worship, and the feeling of social right and wrong. . . .
>
> What else can human nature be than a trait of primary groups? Surely not an attribute of the separate individual—supposing there were any such thing—since its typical characteristics, such as affection, ambition, vanity, and resentment, are inconceivable apart from society. If it belongs, then, to man in association, what kind or degree of association is required to develop it? Evidently nothing elaborate, because elaborate phases of society are

The Group Level

transient and diverse, while human nature is comparatively stable and universal. . . . It is the nature which is developed and expressed in those simple, face-to-face groups that are somewhat alike in all societies; groups of the family, the playground, and the neighborhood. In the essential similarity of these is to be found the basis, in experience, for similar ideas and sentiments in the human mind. In these, everywhere, human nature comes into existence. Man does not have it at birth; he cannot acquire it except through fellowship, and it decays in isolation [Cooley, 1909: 30].

Apart from such fundamental and universal effects on the character of the individual common to all primary groups and all individuals, each primary group also imparts a distinctive "shape" to each person. A child's family of origin and his peer groups greatly shape his basic character (Youniss, 1980), yet—as we have seen—no two families are truly alike, and some youth groups are positive forces while others are delinquency-oriented. Since every primary group is a unity of interacting personalities, each of these participating personalities undergoes certain adaptations—in virtually every category of individual attributes—through the give-and-take of the distinctive group process.

One absolutely fundamental theme in social psychological research, in either sociology or psychology, has been the range and extent of this person-changing capacity of groups. Through both laboratory and field studies, groups have been shown to modify individual members' perceptions, judgments, beliefs, attitudes, opinions, motivations, behaviors, habits, and self-concepts (McGrath and Altman, 1966). Such effects should not prove surprising, since primary groups figure prominently among any individual's most important reference groups.

Some of these changes can be attributed to the *informational* influence of the defining and objectifying character of the group process itself (Klapper, 1961). Group process not only shows the individual how to think intelligently and how to see creative solutions he would never have found himself (Taylor and McNemar, 1955), but it also provides him with seemingly credible group interpretations of ambiguous or contradictory situations and social support or "consensual validation" for its social realities. Other personal changes can be attributed to the powerful *normative* influence of the group, to members' desires to adhere to and live up to the norms of the group (Deutsch and Gerard, 1955). Loss of primary group support can be a serious, sometimes even life-threatening, crisis, so that group pressures for conformity are often highly effective. Even the leaders of a group may find themselves trapped in an attitude or course of action about which they harbor serious doubts. The dangers of "groupthink" are very real indeed (Janis, 1973).

Indeed, group-induced changes are found to be both more feasible and more enduring than personal changes produced through other means (Lewin, 1948). Accordingly, in recent decades we have witnessed the rise to prominence of various group-based technologies for person-changing: group therapies, self-help groups, T-groups, encounter groups (see, for example, Schein and Bennis, 1965). The relative ease and permanence of group-induced changes is due not only to the informational and normative influences of group participation, but also to the facilitating and sustaining influence of group support in members' efforts to alter deeply entrenched attitudes and behaviors. In primary groups, people are ready to pursue interests which they would find too arduous or too uninspiring to pursue on their own, and to endure hardships that would be insufferable alone. This influence can be seen not only in such self-help groups as Alcoholics Anonymous and weight-loss groups, but also in rifle squads under enemy fire, in the crews of spaceships and submarines, and in scientific teams wintering in the Antarctic.

Primary groups are a place to which an individual can take a wide range of personal problems in search of insight, assistance, and support. He can rely on his primary group to support, sharpen, and focus many of his personal interests; as a consequence, groups tend to be "fun." And, feeling "at home" in the group, one can display and receive some affirmation for most if not all of one's personal identities. The family, in particular, fulfills an "archival function" of retaining and affirming members' various external roles and identities—even "lost" identities such as the student-council presidency of a now middle-aged son (Weigert and Hastings, 1977).

Finally, the individual derives some gratification from being able to exert some social influence on the nature and course of the group in a direction congenial to his own interests. His influence in this way is seldom nearly so significant or frequent in larger organizations.

Primary group participation also has consequences for the individual's external roles and careers. One's family or work group, for example, may sacrifice to further a career in a bureaucracy, the economy, the polity, or the educational system. Even belonging to the right clique may enhance a manager's chances for promotion, while, on the other hand, membership in a delinquent gang may diminish a youth's opportunities to enter college, get a respectable job, or marry the girl of his dreams. Failure to join groups appropriate to one's life-cycle stage—a mature woman who declines to marry and start a family—may diminish one's attractiveness to other organizations and perhaps also one's self-esteem.

Position and role within a primary group are not without their own effects on the individual. A classic example (W. F. Whyte, 1955) is the really excellent bowler who, given his somewhat low status within the peer group, consistently loses at bowling to the group leaders despite his very best efforts. A person who plays the role of clown or scapegoat in some primary group is likely to incorporate this role into his self-concept, thus perhaps reducing his attractiveness to other organizations.

Career passage within a primary group, from newcomer to regular member, is likely to prove difficult and frustrating. Such career movement is, however, likely to enhance all the above-noted effects of participation as one becomes a more central and respected member. An arrested or reversing career trajectory, conversely, diminishes participation effects and may engender a sense of personal failure as well as group scorn.

A group is an emergent level of social reality in and of itself; its character and course cannot be predicted simply as the sum of the characteristics and interests of its individual members. It is instead a collaborative creation. The individual member as "co-author" and "co-producer" contributes to the shaping of the group experience and is himself influenced by participation in that experience as it unfolds.

SUMMARY

Groups contrast fairly sharply with associations. Group purposes are general rather than limited; collectivity is more developed than structure; relations tend to be informal and personal; cooperative interaction is direct, with personal characteristics more important than roles. Groups tend to be fairly small and localized.

Those groups strongly displaying all these features are primary groups, in which members strongly identify themselves with the group, developing an emphatic we-feeling and a sharp ingroup–outgroup distinction. Secondary groups more nearly resemble voluntary associations, in that their social structures are not sharply subordinated to the sense of collectivity. Groups that are official suborganizations of larger organizations are generally secondary groups, although these may sometimes develop into primary groups. Unofficial groups (cliques, gangs) and "institutionalized" groups (such as the nuclear family) tend to be primary groups.

As a collectivity, a primary group answers some overlapping ranges of like and complementary interests, focusing and objectifying any interest of its members. Members develop a strong common interest in the group itself, as noted. Primary groups are generally small groups of not more than twenty; not only do small groups differ from large groups, but even a one-member difference in size significantly alters various group features. The cultures of primary groups tend to be richly elaborated, although researchers have mainly emphasized the normative components.

In most groups, positions and roles are differentiated only informally; division of labor is generally implicit, ritualized through group traditions. Secondary social structure is often more influential than primary structure; all the dimensional structures (except authority) tend to be clearly developed, intercorrelated, and mutually reinforcing. These structures define four strata of members—leaders, followers, deviants, isolates—within which horizontal differentiation may occur; a group may have an "instrumental leader" and an "expressive leader." Suborganizations, in the forms of cliques, factions, and coalitions, greatly influence the dynamics of a group; in many cases, these suborganizations are essentially dyadic pair relationships.

The character of any group is vitally affected by the nature of the embedding organization, and the group may significantly facilitate or subvert the functioning of the larger organization. Given the sharp ingroup–outgroup distinction made by all primary groups, intergroup relations are typically problematic.

Recruitment to groups is often ascriptive, yet most groups take seriously both attraction and selection tactics; placement is separate from selection. Mutual socialization of members is the heart of group participation, yet it is the interaction process that has received greatest research attention. The innovation process tends to be informal and rather democratic; externally imposed innovations tend to produce the greatest group tensions. Social control is similarly diffuse; rewards and punishments center on the benefits of companionship and sentiment. Punishments are often ritualized, and rituals of solidarity are abundant.

Individual characteristics and tactics exert a great impact not only on one's own role but also on the character of group process and group structure. Given the reliance of groups on informal role differentiation, the role-making process is very much an open matter of interpersonal give-and-take. In enduring groups, career development takes the form of changes in one's informal roles as the group adjusts to imposed innovations and to membership changes. In all groups, there is an expected career trajectory of movement from newcomer to regular member to "old hand."

According to Cooley, it is through primary groups that the individual acquires human nature itself. The character of one's particular primary groups also imparts a distinctive personal character beyond the common features of human nature. The person-changing capacity of groups to modify virtually any individual attribute has been thoroughly documented and harnessed to various social technologies: group therapies, self-help groups, T-groups. This capacity hinges in part on the fact that primary groups are important reference groups, exerting powerful informational and normative influences. But the comparative ease and permanence of group-induced changes are also partly due to the facilitating and sustaining influence of group support in members' efforts to alter deeply entrenched attitudes and behaviors.

Individual members generally enjoy and feel at home in their primary groups. A person can turn to his primary groups with his various personal concerns and problems, and within such groups he can safely exercise many of his personal interests and personal identities. One's comparatively substantial influence on the course and character of the group is itself a source of gratification. Membership in primary groups also has a variety of consequences for one's external roles, careers, and organizational opportunities.

Position and role within a primary group may influence individual characteristics, self-concept, and external opportunities. Such effects of membership, position, and role are generally enhanced through the conventional career trajectory and are diminished through deviant careers.

SUGGESTIONS FOR ADDITIONAL READING

Still the most engaging and hard-hitting introduction to this area is George C. Homans's *The Human Group* (New York: Harcourt, Brace, 1950). Among the textbooks on groups, three merit special note. Howard L. Nixon II's *The Small Group* (Englewood Cliffs, N.J.: Prentice-Hall, 1979) emphasizes the structures and organizational processes of small groups. Michael S. Olmsted and A. Paul Hare's *The Small Group,* 2nd edition (New York: Random House, 1978) affords greater attention to group culture and to the functions and effects of small groups for individuals and society. Dexter Dunphy focuses more specifically on *The Primary Group* (New York: Appleton-Century-Crofts, 1972).

No case study of a group has been so widely read as William F. Whyte's *Street Corner Society,* 2nd edition (Chicago: University of Chicago Press, 1955). Of related interest is Frederic M. Thrasher's classic analysis of *The Gang: A Study of 1,313 Gangs in Chicago* (Chicago: University of Chicago Press, 1927). A modern classic, illuminating not only the internal structure of gangs but their intergroup relations and dependence on neighborhood organization, is Gerald D. Suttles, *The Social Order of the Slum* (Chicago: University of Chicago Press, 1968).

Children's play and friendship groups are examined in Hugh C. Foot, Antony J. Chapman, and Jean R. Smith, editors, *Friendship and Social Relations in Children* (New York: Wiley, 1980). High school cliques are characterized in James S. Coleman, *The Adolescent Society* (New York: Free Press, 1971).

Work groups are the subject of many fine and readable studies. In the white-collar ranks, Melville Dalton's *Men Who Manage* (New York: Wiley, 1959) is an unusual account of managerial cliques and factions. Leonard R. Sayles examines *Behavior of Industrial Work Groups* (New York: Wiley, 1958). For a case study of industrial work groups, we especially recommend Abraham Zaleznik, C. R. Christensen, and F. J. Roethlisberger, *The Motivation, Productivity, and Satisfaction of Workers* (Boston: Harvard Business School, 1958). These may be compared with "Primary Groups in the American Army" by Edward A. Shils (pp. 16–39 in Robert K. Merton and Paul F. Lazarsfeld, editors, *Continuities in Social Research: Studies in the Scope and Method of "The American Soldier,"* New York: Free Press, 1950).

The nuclear family remains foremost among primary groups, however. Perhaps the most useful treatment of the family as group is Ralph H. Turner, *Family Interaction* (New York: Wiley, 1970), with special emphasis on the role-making process. The ritual character of much small-group interaction is most thoroughly revealed in James S. Bossard and Eleanor S. Boll, *Ritual in Family Living,* 2nd edition (Philadelphia: University of Pennsylvania Press, 1956). Family role-making and career development processes are examined in fuller detail in Joan Aldous, *Family Careers: Developmental Change in Families* (New York: Wiley, 1978). Since the forms of kinship and family vary rather sharply across national societies, the reader may wish to broaden his perspective through any of the many family textbooks or through the *Handbook of Marriage and the Family* (Harold C. Christensen, editor, Chicago: Rand McNally, 1964).

Two very useful examinations of the influence on groups of their embedding contexts are William F. Whyte's "Small Groups and Large Organizations" (pp. 297–312 in John H. Rohrer and Muzafer Sherif, editors, *Social Psychology at the Crossroads,* New York: Harper, 1951), and Tom Burns's "The Reference of Conduct in Small Groups: Cliques and Cabals in Occupational Milieux (*Human Relations,* 1955, 8: 467–486).

The individual and organizational impacts of group process are reviewed critically in Edgar H. Schein and Warren G. Bennis, *Personal and Organizational Change through Group Methods* (New York: Wiley, 1965) and in Alfred Jacobs and Wilford Spradlin, eds., *Group as Agent of Change* (New York: Human Sciences Press, 1974).

A very useful analytic summary and bibliographic guide is A. Paul Hare, *Handbook of Small Group Research,* 2nd edition (New York: Free Press, 1976).

Photo courtesy of United Nations/L. Barns

Father and son share a moment of discovery.

CHAPTER 21

Relationships

For most individuals, the deepest, most troubling, yet most meaningful and fulfilling aspects of their social lives revolve around dyadic or pair relationships. Such relationships are often the key to successful experiences within larger organizations, as we have seen; a strong argument can be made that pair relationships are the building blocks of the social order.

A relationship is much more than two people reckoning benefits and costs with a speculative eye upon each other, although such calculations may enter into the story. Relationships are a creative force in and of themselves, with some very special properties. The range of relationships is phenomenal, including the familiar ones of parent/child, friend/friend, teacher/pupil, lover/lover, doctor/patient. But there are a host of others: helper/helped, minister/parishioner, agent/artist, mugger/victim, pilot/controller, sponsor/recruit, interrogator/prisoner, supervisor/worker, policeman/violator, performer/listener, and so on. Even in the more fleeting and impersonal relationships such as teller/customer, activity is seldom confined to a single role pair. Some spillover into other aspects of the participants' lives is the common occurrence if there is any duration or recurrence at all in the pairing.

In most respects, a social or interpersonal relationship is essentially a two-person group or dyad. Why, aside from the semantic oddness of the notion of a group of two, should the relationship be given separate treatment in this book? The answer is that Simmel (1950) convincingly demonstrated that such an absolutely minimal "group" exhibits sharply distinctive features both as a collectivity and as a social structure. The organization and dynamics of a friendship are not the same as those of a clique or play group, nor are those of a marriage the same as those of a family.

Before undertaking to examine these distinctive differences, let us extend to social

NOTE: Portions of this chapter are based on McCall and Simmons (1978: 165–199) and on McCall et al. (1970: 3–34).

relationships some of the basic concepts developed regarding groups. A primary relationship, like a primary group, is one in which the aspect of collectivity outweighs the aspect of structure; central examples include various family and kin relationships, friends and lovers, neighbors and roommates. A secondary relationship is one in which the aspect of structure outweighs the aspect of collectivity. At the extreme is the relationship between personal enemies or adversaries (Burns, 1953); more typical secondary relationships are the wide range of contractual, instrumental, commercial, and professional relationships organized for a specific limited purpose with little personal involvement, such as cashier/customer or flight attendant/passenger. To the extent that these endure, they tend to take on some primary qualities; one's accountant becomes something of a friend as the years roll by. Yet, although a person may like and admire her dentist or accountant, their pair solidarity rarely subordinates their respective roles of client and professional.

Similarly, as with groups, a relationship may be either official, institutionalized, or unofficial. Within a state hospital, for example, neither doctor nor patient choose each other; their relationship is administratively assigned, as are their respective positions and roles. In contrast to such an official relationship stands the purely unofficial relationship of two playmates; neither their membership nor their positions and roles are officially designated. An institutionalized relationship, such as a marriage, is one in which membership is not officially assigned (though it may be officially certified) but in which social positions (though not roles) are officially allocated. Official relationships, then, are secondary in character. Only those relationships in which considerable informal role differentiation occurs can be regarded as primary relationships.

There are several interesting social psychological features involving the primary/secondary dimension of relationships. For example, a good many organizations, such as hospitals and armies, have regulations designed to keep certain relationships (doctor/patient, officer/enlisted man) official and secondary, as a curb against any primary involvements. Another feature is that many secondary relationships are traditionally carried out with some of the dressings of a primary relationship; the bank teller smiles warmly as she takes your deposit, and the dentist asks about your school work. In fact, a host of books and special courses are aimed at teaching individuals the skills of presenting a primary "front" in their secondary dealings. Yet another feature becomes evident when the primary aspects of an institutionalized relationship falter. At that time, its more official and secondary aspects are called into play: the proprietor and long-time customer refer to their sales contract and the troubled marriage partners each seek a lawyer.

ORGANIZATIONAL CHARACTER OF PRIMARY RELATIONSHIPS

Collectivity

Unlike any other type of social organization, relationships do not vary in membership size; all include only two members. All the material and human resources of a relationship are thus limited to those contributed by two persons, which generally reduces the potential range and effectiveness of collective actions. If neither roommate can cook or sew on a button or if neither of two elderly friends has access to or can drive a car, their collective actions are constrained and the relationship must make trades with its external environment. Marital couples vary in interpersonal skills such as communication, which greatly affects the ability of a marriage to survive the inevitable conflicts and external jolts of joint living (Gottman, 1979). Otherwise, with respect to both resources and culture, a relationship is essentially just a minimal group.

A relationship of any significant duration exhibits a unique, emergent culture—typically more fully elaborated in primary than in secondary relationships. Normative expectations arise regarding appropriate activities; the division of labor; the amount, distribution, and priority of time and effort to be contributed; relations to external persons and organizations; patterns of communication and revelation; and so on. Private understandings of a less normative, more cognitive and emotional sort are also elaborated. Private terms, or neologisms, bearing on its organizational concerns are frequently invented by the members of a relationship, and almost universally some private meanings are attached to common terms. These private terms and meanings often stem from or give rise to private jokes. Yet another important type of private understanding is the unique calendar provided by the historical development of the relationship. Members frequently date events in relation to significant incidents in the history of the relationship (''it was right after our trip to Yellowstone''). In these and many other ways, standard items from the culture of societal-level structures are distinctly ''personalized'' in the culture of a primary relationship.

Rituals take on key importance in relationships, both as an expression of the dyadic culture and as a manifestation of the social structure. Virtually any recurring event or behavior is likely to become ritualized to some degree—morning coffee at the kitchen table, flipping a coin to see who buys the beer, repetitive catch-phrase greetings, sex after the Saturday dance, an ostentatious yawning stretch to let the other party know one is too tired to do any more work, and so on. Such rituals are virtually endless in variety from relationship to relationship. They also often serve as shorthand signals to the other member as to one's mood and as to what activities one is willing or unwilling to engage in at that time. Symbols from the dyadic culture become incorporated into these rituals as settings, ''props,'' and cues: the table in the back at the rendezvous restaurant, the colored scarves for the bicycle ride, a particular nightgown, and any other words or objects which have taken on special meanings. Although every organizational level has such rituals, nowhere do they have such significant personal meanings as in a relationship. Such rituals arise from the routinization of any recurring activity and form the basis for much of the interaction within the relationship.

Like a primary group, a primary relationship does not ordinarily cohere around some single like interest of the two participants but instead answers some overlapping ranges of like and complementary interests. Brothers share a like interest in winning favorable supervisory terms from their parents, friends tend to have similar recreational tastes, and grandfather and grandchild may hold complementary interests in the telling and the hearing of tall tales about days gone by. All primary relationships provide for the fulfillment of a range of recurring individual and joint plans of action, and one essential complementary interest in any primary relationship is a distinctive exchange of role support (see Chapter 2) for a specifically designated set of role-identities, as we shall see shortly. Of course, the members must develop a common interest in the relationship itself.

These various types of collective interests effectively constitute or give rise to several sorts of interpersonal ties, or social bonds, between the members of a relationship.

First, a relationship may be *ascriptive* in its formation and perhaps some of its structure. Family and kinship relationships are perhaps the most common examples but there are many others, such as teacher/pupil, supervisor/worker, and colleague or peer relationships. One important feature of such ascriptive dyads is that they exist independently of the individual characteristics of the members. A child and mother or a kindergarten teacher and a pupil do not personally choose each other. The subsequent content of their relationship is, however, mutually worked out. In addition to such passive ascriptions, many people actively strive to achieve "ascribed" (officially certified) statuses which, by their nature, generate ascribed relationships with others. Such ascriptions are typically conferred by officials of the embedding organizations, as in a marriage ceremony. Again, the content of the subsequent relationships, as opposed to their ascription, is interpersonally generated by the participants.

Second, in a good many relationships there is the element of *commitment*. Such commitments to a relationship may be official, as in the case of public marriage vows, or unofficial, such as an understanding between friends; they may be either explicit or tacit. The strength and content of such commitments vary a great deal but they essentially involve the intention to honor some agreement within the relationship—for example, that one will pursue sexual behavior only within the dyad or that each can trust the other to keep personal secrets. Such commitments are usually a mix of semi-exclusive joint activities and "restrictive covenants" or "exclusive trade agreements" regarding negotiated behaviors and role supports. In addition to joint actions and exchanges, there is often something of a "for better or for worse" commitment to the relationship itself.

Commitments are a means of increasing and insuring the dependability of a source of joint action and exchange benefits—a way of handling recurring human situations (Becker, 1960). But they are much more. They are frequently entered into because of moral convictions, as well as or even instead of opportunism or desire. If, however, there are no elements of commitment beyond those of moral conviction, the relationship is literally only a duty. Examples might include a woman undertaking the care of an aged relative or a teacher helping a student in which she has no personal interest or involvement. Even if the commitment is not made on moral grounds, the person is usually under some moral obligation to fulfill it. To have made a commitment is to have bound oneself, and it requires a very good excuse to withdraw without losing face and perhaps receiving other negative sanctions. Even personal relationships are thus at least partly public affairs.

Although ascriptions and commitments often blend, we must be careful to distinguish between them. Persons often enter into what they think are commitments, such as going steady, only to discover later that they have effectively recruited themselves into "ascribed" relationships (marriage) that they cannot dissolve without the formal consent of other social organizations.

Third, the members of a relationship may be bound by the factor of *attachment* (McCall, 1974). Attachments to others are formed as the individual's identities evolve and change. One's dreams of oneself, the idealized picture one has of oneself in certain social positions, are seldom constant over long periods of time. As a person faces new tasks and new others, these tasks and others become incorporated into one's daydreaming about oneself in these social roles. Consequently, *specific persons and their behaviors get built into the contents of role-identities* and become crucial to the legitimation and enactment of those identities. This building of specific others into the very contents of role-identities is what we mean by becoming "attached" to particular others. Thus, mother and the math teacher become woven into the fabric of one's subjective life.

Such attachments make the individual vulnerable to the decisions, reactions, and whims of these others and to all the physical and social vicissitudes that may befall these others. As the Buddhists put it, to become involved with another is to surrender a hostage to the fates. When one becomes attached to a particular other, the resulting relationship tends to become nontransferable. Any competent clerk or repairman will do, but one cannot so easily go looking for another mother, another brother, another child. The less transferable a relationship, the more vulnerable the members are.

Fourth, *investment* is a ubiquitous and powerful bond between persons. When someone has expended such scarce resources as money, time, and life chances in establishing and maintaining a relationship, he cannot afford to throw them away without realizing substantial losses. The normative standards involved in most relationships—sometimes termed the "norm of reciprocity" (Gouldner, 1960)—demand that one show some consideration for the other's investments as well, for the tie is, after all, a joint venture. If a woman worked to put her husband through medical school, it would be socially and legally actionable for him to simply abandon her upon his graduation.

Fifth, *dependability of benefits* is a major reason for the existence and continuation of many relationships. As a consequence of their recurring needs for joint activities, role supports, and the commodities of social exchange, people are disposed to seek dependably recurring sources of these benefits. When one locates or is thrown together with individuals or groups that for whatever reason are able, willing, and ready to afford one the supplies of such goods, one is disposed to "corner the market" by establishing further and more durable bonds with those others—bonds of ascription, commitment, attachment, and investment.

These bonds usually blend and run together in most continuing relationships. Nevertheless, they are distinct factors; they are present in different proportions in different relationships and they often vary independently of one another. For example, a person sometimes has commitments that differ from those ascribed to him; individuals frequently forgo the potential benefits of joint ventures and exchanges because of "prior commitments," or fret over interpersonal investments that have not yielded dependable benefits; one seeks to secure one's attachments through mutual commitments and formal ascriptions and, conversely, may grudgingly fulfill commitments that no longer reflect one's attachments.

Individuals are usually most concerned about their attachments, but the various organizational levels are most concerned with a person's ascriptions and commitments. At the very least, these embedding levels seek to produce in the person commitments which correspond to his or her ascriptions—for example, commitments to nurture one's child, to "cleave unto" one's marriage partner, and to treat one's assigned patients competently and ethically. If ascriptions, commitments, and attachments are all aligned, conventional social opinion regards this consistency as even better. But the person is not simply left on his honor in these matters. Such ascriptions and commitments, once made, are enforced by a host of informal social pressures and formal social controls. Ordinarily, the individual cannot seriously violate them without incurring social control tactics.

A wide divergence between one's commitments and one's attachments is likely to create a good deal of personal discontent, and the person will be motivated to reduce the divergence, either by giving up his attachments or by changing his commitments—his job, his spouse, his style of life. Neither of these strategies is easily brought off, and most persons carry around some freight of discontent and restlessness because the two sets of factors are not mutually aligned. Most frequently, the individual attempts compromise solutions of moderate divergences by negotiating redefinitions of the contents of the commitments and by reshuffling the intensities of his or her attachments.

How "close" one member of a relationship feels to the other depends on the strength and the degree of alignment of these various bonds. Yet, this felt closeness may or may not be reciprocated; one member may be strongly bonded to the other, while the second member may be only weakly or partially bonded to the first. Because relationships vary in the symmetry of interpersonal bonding, they also vary in the mutuality of members' behavioral involvement, intimacy of disclosure, and warmth of feeling.

Awareness of the relationship as an organization in its own right is heightened for the members by impingements from the environment in which the dyad is embedded (McCall and Simmons, 1978: 173–174). Married people are invited to events not as persons but as couples; social considerations extended to one person are often extended to his or her close friend in recognition of their relationship. The members themselves, recognizing their shared interests and shared fate in dealing with the larger social world, tend to act in concert rather than as individuals. Married couples, friends, and colleagues typically act toward outsiders as *teams,* cooperating to maintain proper fronts of solidarity and to further their joint ventures. (Waller [1938: 383–389] has discussed these phenomena of dual participation and pair-centered interaction with considerable insight.) In other words, awareness of the relationship depends significantly upon external impingements that evoke a we-feeling.

When dealing with matters more internal than external to the relationship, this awareness diminishes and often disappears. This fact, its causes, and its consequences were brilliantly analyzed by Simmel who recognized that under most circumstances,

> each of the two feels himself confronted only by the other, not by a collectivity above him. The social structure here rests immediately on the one and on the other of the two, and the secession of either would destroy the whole. The dyad, therefore, does not attain that superpersonal life which the individual feels to be independent of himself. . . . This dependence of the dyad upon its two individual members causes the thought of its existence to be accompanied by the thought of its termination much more closely and impressively than in [a social group], where every member knows that even after his retirement or death, the group can continue to exist. . . . A dyad, however, depends on each of its two elements alone—in its death, though not in its life: for its life, it needs *both,* but for its death, only one. This fact is bound to influence the inner attitude of the individual toward the dyad, even though not always consciously nor in the same way. It makes the dyad into a [social organization] that feels itself both endangered and irreplaceable, and thus into the real locus not only of authentic sociological tragedy, but also of sentimentalism [Simmel, 1950: 123–124. Emphasis in original.].

Thus, even though rivalry and conflict may seriously embitter brother and sister, parent and child, husband and wife, the very real prospect of losing the other evokes at some level a compensating sentimentality of attachment and closeness. No ''significant other'' (see Chapter 2) could ever truly be replaced.

Social Structure

The fundamental structural fact regarding any relationship is that differentiation of any kind is absolutely minimal; along any dimension of contrast or comparison among members, only two positions can be defined. Here is social structure at its absolute simplest.

The concept of the primary social structure (role structure or division of labor) is itself as troublesome in the case of the relationship as in the case of the group. Only in secondary relationships is the notion of primary structure at all straightforward; between the dean and the student, the lawyer and his client, the prostitute and her john, their respective social positions and organizational roles are rather formally clear-cut. In primary relationships, on the other hand, major reliance is placed on informally differentiated roles. Indeed, any primary relationship between two persons is not at heart a role relationship, even though its interactions take place through performances of informally differentiated roles.

In Chapter 2, we defined the structure of each individual as a more or less organized set of role-identities—each a conception of self as an occupant of some social position. We saw also that these role-identities are not necessarily compatible, giving rise to role strain and role conflicts within the individual. We can further assume that no one is fully acquainted with the entire set of another's role-identities, and that for reasons of economy, security, and ''public relations,'' each individual displays a somewhat different subset of his role-identities to different others. In this very real sense, Connie is a somewhat different person with George, with her chums, with her mother, with her baby sister, and with her broker. We will refer to any one of these subsets of identities revealed to another person as a *persona* (see McCall and Simmons, 1978: 84–85).

The primary social structure of a primary relationship, then, is the fit between the personas that the members present to one another. There are several interesting points regarding such a primary structure. First, although social roles and social positions are involved, they are only the raw materials from which role performances for the relationship are fashioned. That is, the conventional roles are idiosyncratically adapted and reworked by the individual in the light of his or her other positions and personal characteristics. Role-identities are idiosyncratic rather than cultural objects, even though they may be fashioned from cultural "blueprints."

Second, the degree of functional fit between organized sets of such idiosyncratic conceptions is considerably more problematic than that between conventionally paired social roles. For example, even though the social roles of husband and wife fit relatively smoothly, two individuals' self-conceptions as husband and as wife may greatly clash. If he has something of a *Playboy* conception of himself while her self-conception is built upon Gothic romances, one can easily foresee trouble ahead for the couple. Any pair of role-identities that fits smoothly is likely to be retained and become more prominent in the relationship between two persons, whereas a pair that does not fit is likely to be dropped or to fade out. In this manner, the contours of the relationship are altered by the functional fit between personas.

Third, this fit between personas shapes the form of interaction between the members of the relationship in two ways: (1) it effectively requires them to avoid certain actions that are prescribed by their cultural role relationships but that happen to be inconsistent with a member's role-identity; and (2) it allows them to perform actions that deviate from cultural role relationships but that happen to be consistent with the role-identities of the members. That is, they will drop certain conventional interactions and will creatively add and elaborate interactions that enhance the fit between their personas. For such reasons, it may happen that neither member of a marital couple will do any cooking or that in the privacy of their own apartment they speak to each other largely in baby talk. Through such tailoring and elaboration of culturally prescribed roles, every relationship develops unique interaction patterns.

Even in an institutionalized primary relationship such as marriage, where the official positions of "husband" and "wife" are allocated to members, knowledge of these positions tells us little about the divison of labor (Aldous, 1978). As the man and the woman informally differentiate their respective roles, each is guided by his or her own role-identities and by the presented persona of the other. From the interplay between the two subsets of role-identities an emergent structure and culture are developed. The richness, variety, and natural history of such resulting pair organizations have been a major theme in world literature.

Secondary social structure is similarly sharply limited. Indeed, the aspect of *suborganization* is necessarily absent, strictly speaking. That is to say, from within a

Relationships

total membership of two persons, no subset could comprise a social organization—faction, coalition, or clique—although in situations of conflict each member may constitute a "faction of one" and seek supporters from outside the relationship.

Dimensional social structures permit only two possible positions: higher and lower. Nevertheless, such distinctions are often quite apparent and socially significant. Here, these dimensional rankings must first be examined for each distinct pair of roles or role-identities that is included in the primary structure of the relationship. A husband, for example, may be older than his wife; he may be a mentor in scuba diving to his wife who is eager to learn these skills; but he may be an undergraduate student while the wife is a professor in the same field. Their rankings on status, power, and the like may differ sharply for each of these role pairs, and only through a weighted pooling of their rankings on each of the role pairs can the overall dimensional structures be discerned.

The status structure of a relationship, for example, is revealed by determining which member respects the other more than he or she is respected, over the range of included role (identity) pairs. The status structure tends to be more clear-cut in ascriptive relationships than in purely voluntary ones, and in secondary relationships more than in primary ones.

Authority differentials similarly vary across role pairs and, again, the authority structure is more clearly developed in secondary relationships than in primary, in ascriptive relationships more than in the purely voluntary ones. However, even ascriptive rights to compliance in a strictly secondary relationship are often modified by the development of some primary elements, for example, where a senior and a junior officer become friends.

If power is viewed as the ability (rather than the right) to exact compliance to one's wishes, both members of a relationship typically have considerable power over the other. The power structure is then depicted in terms of power differentials: over the range of included role pairs, which member has relatively more power than the other? Many ascriptive relationships have a power differential built into their role prescriptions—for instance, doctor over patient, or policeman over violator. Yet, power rests centrally on the control of resources that another person needs or desires, in line with Waller's "principle of least interest," which holds that the person who is less dependent on the other for resources maintains a power differential over that other (Waller, 1938; Emerson, 1962). The power structure of a relationship is thus likely to reflect differences in the bonds of overall investment, commitment, and attachment to the relationship. These bonds, in turn, would at least partly reflect each member's alternatives available as sources of joint actions and exchange benefits. When power differentials in a relationship are great, there is always the possibility of exploitation and abuse, as in the case of sexual abuse of a child by a parent or in the charging of exorbitant fees by professionals. Higher-level embedding organizations attempt to maintain social control over such exploitations.

Leadership represents contributions to determining an organization's line of action, for example, by posing problems, structuring alternative courses of action, proposing solutions, or persuading members to accept or reject alternatives. The leader-

389

ship dimension of a relationship is structured in terms of which member makes greater contributions of these sorts, over the included role pairs, to the functioning of the relationship. Leadership does not appear to reflect clearly any differences in the social bonds but rests more on the personal characteristics of the members. However, in some secondary relationships—manager/worker, for instance—leadership is more or less ascribed.

In most organizations, conformity to the norms and decisions of the organization is not uniform among the members. In relationships, the degree to which members conform probably reflects differences in the bonds of commitment, attachment, and investment, as well as any subordination inherent in the ascriptive relations; that is, a subordinate member will be more constrained to conform to the relationship's norms and to the will of the higher-positioned member.

In a relationship, unlike larger organizations, it is logically impossible for one member to rank higher than the other on both the rate of initiating communications and the rate of receiving them. One member must largely initiate and one must largely receive.

The affect structure in a relationship has little to do with its role pairs and is essentially a matter of whether one member likes the other more than he or she is liked. If the degrees of liking are roughly equivalent, there is probably a stable balance of influence; but if liking is clearly asymmetrical, the member who is liked more than he or she likes is in an advantageous negotiating position—through the principle of least interest discussed above. Degree of liking is intimately bound up with the bond of attachment, so that the doting mother, for example, is prey to the whims of the uncaring son. A somewhat similar principle may operate in secondary relationships. In a town with only one doctor, for example, the doctor may operate on a principle of least interest, but in a town with many doctors the situation is reversed, and potential clients can employ this principle.

One might expect that in a relationship, because of the inherent limitations on structural differentiation imposed by the small number of members, the correlation among these dimensional structures might be even greater than in groups. Particularly in primary relationships, the member who is liked more will probably be the more powerful and more respected, exert greater authority and leadership, and receive more communications. He or she will have more leeway to deviate (Hollander, 1958) but be more likely to structure some norms of the relationship to suit his or her own preferences in the first place—and therefore be less likely to deviate from them (Secord and Backman, 1974: 312-313).

On the other hand, especially in primary relationships involving a wide range of role (identity) pairs, position in these dimensional structures (with the possible exception of affect) is likely to vary between content areas or role pairs. For example, a wife may be dominant in the areas of the children, the household, and emotional matters, while the husband is dominant in the areas of finance, education, and external social situations. The proportion and centrality of content areas in which a member is superordinate determine his position in the overall structure of the relationship. Because one member is seldom superordinate in all content areas (thus giving his partner counterpower over him), broad primary relationships achieve a close, peerlike quality.

Interorganizational Relations

Social relationships may, of course, be embedded in any of the larger organizations, including groups, and function as official or unofficial suborganizations within the larger organization. A marriage, for example, serves as an official suborganization within both a group (the nuclear family) and a community. A "buddy-relationship" (Little, 1964) serves as a vital but unofficial suborganization within an army platoon.

Indeed, such pair relationships abound within all higher organizational levels, as we have seen. How significant and visible such embedded relationships are depends on the character and functioning of the larger organization. So long as the larger organization's actions are acceptable to the embedded individuals, relationships tend to support these actions and do not stand out sharply from their context. When such larger collective actions are not so acceptable, individuals tend to turn to their pair relationships for assistance and support in resisting the actions and influences of the larger organization. Thus, much as groups do, embedded relationships either facilitate or subvert the collective action of the larger organization. Subversion is typically a defensive reaction to imposed or threatened social changes within the embedding organization.

Because relationships are at least potentially subversive, higher-level organizations employ social controls to ensure that embedded relationships are "proper" in terms of the embedding organization's norms and purposes. This is done through a host of formal and informal regulations, and higher-level organizations will often cooperate with one another in carrying out such controls. The state, the community, and the parental families might all constrain a couple living together to become legally married. The members of relationships may of course, on their side, seek to evade or neutralize such constraining influences. Marital and sibling relationships are colored by the dynamics of the nuclear family (Turner, 1970; Aldous, 1978), while friendship, romantic, and marital relationships all vary characteristically between middle-class and working-class communities (L. B. Rubin, 1976; Allan, 1979).

Owing in good part to the intrinsic sentimentalism of the primary relationship, its relations with other organizations (and particularly with other primary relationships and groups) generally assume the character of a rather tense and jealous rivalry. When reacting defensively to imposed or threatened external social influences, a primary relationship tends to slip beyond competitive rivalry into a conflict mode of its interorganizational relations. However, the relationship may form coalitions with other relationships and groups on the basis of complementary interests, larger joint activities, exchanges, and mutual support against external pressures, sometimes forming a group of pairs, such as a high school clique and their steadies, or a group of young mothers who trade off baby-sitting.

More generally, relationships tend to interconnect to form networks of interpersonal relationships—friends of friends (Boissevain, 1974), extended kinship networks (Bott, 1971), and the like. Indeed, the entangled cross-connections between the social networks of any two related individuals constitute yet another force holding them together in their dyadic relationship. Third parties in such networks frequently serve as ''surrogate factions'' siding with one or another member in relationship disputes and conflicts.

ORGANIZATIONAL PROCESSES

To a degree unmatched in any other variety of social organization, the process of recruitment actually gives rise to the entire organization of a primary relationship. Accordingly, an extended treatment of recruitment is necessary here.

Recruitment

Many relationships are officially ascriptive—brother/sister, nurse/patient, neighbor/neighbor. More problematic are the many voluntary relationships, such as friends, lovers, and spouses, where ascriptive components amount to little more than similar social backgrounds and common organizational memberships.

Since a voluntary relationship can have only two members, it follows that basic recruitment is not conducted by the organization. Unless basic recruitment has been completed and the full complement of two members is on board, no collective action of any kind (including recruitment) could take place. Therefore, voluntary recruitment is conducted by individuals; a relationship emerges when two individuals have successfully recruited each other.

The aspect of attraction logically comes first. An individual seeking friendship or marriage, for example, seeks to generate through tactics of attraction a sizable number of qualified potential partners. An extensive research literature has accumulated regarding individual tactics and causal determinants of personal attraction (McCall, 1974; Murstein, 1971; Byrne, 1971; Z. Rubin, 1973). At the same time that a person is striving to attract others, many of those same others are likewise engaging in tactics of attraction. The first prerequisite in the recruitment process, then, is the establishment of mutual or *interpersonal attraction* (Huston, 1974; Berscheid and Walster, 1969; Levinger and Snoek, 1972).

In their first encounter, unacquainted people face the problem of identification in its purest and most agonizing form. Who is the other person? Who am I in this situation? Who could I be? What do I want to be? Who does he want me to be? The processes of interaction discussed in Chapter 2 reach their peak of difficulty and importance in first encounters. Each party must read the person with extra care for any clues to identity that he or she may give off. If either party has any reputational knowledge of the other, it serves to guide the process of reading cues. In either case, however, each party is sensitized to a much wider range of possible identities than in more ordinary interactions, for neither has much idea who the other may turn out to be nor is either acquainted with the idiosyncracies of the other's particular dramaturgical idiom—that is, the other's style in presentation of self.

While trying to read the other, each must also present a self, lay claim to a character. Being unable—and unwilling—to claim all one's identities in a first encounter with a stranger, each must select from his identity set a subset that represents his "opening bid," so to speak. Typically, each selects a subset that, on the basis of a tentative reading of the other, are "safe" identities—ones that will be acceptable to the other and for which the person can fairly easily validate his claims. Yet, this subset, or persona, must not be too safe, or else one will not seem interesting to the other or authentic to oneself. Each must cautiously hint at some of the less commonplace aspects of their identities while anchoring the performance on safe identities.

From clues given (or given off) in this manner, the person may sense that the other shares one of his or her less conventional identities. Yet, ordinarily neither dares to come right out and openly claim that identity, for fear that he may have misread the signs and will spoil the interaction.

> The paradox is resolved when the innovation is broached in such a manner as to elicit from others reactions suggesting their receptivity; and when at the same time, the innovation occurs by increments so small, tentative and ambiguous as to permit the actor to retreat, if the signs be unfavorable, without having become identified with an unpopular position. Perhaps all social actions have, in addition to their instrumental, communicative and expressive functions, this quality of being *exploratory gestures*. . . . By a casual, semi-serious, non-committal or tangential remark I may stick my neck out just a little way, but I will quickly withdraw it unless you, by some sign of affirmation, stick *yours* out. I will permit myself to become progressively committed but only as others, by some visible sign, become likewise committed. . . . We may think of this process as one of mutual conversion. The important thing to remember is that we do not first convert ourselves and then others. The acceptability [of claiming an identity] to oneself depends upon its acceptability to others. Converting the other is part of the process of converting oneself [Cohen, 1955: 60–61. Emphasis in original.].

This process of cautious mutual exploration and conversion in search of an opportunity to enact one's less conventional identities takes a good deal of time, ordinarily spread over a series of encounters. On the basis of tentative early readings of the other, the individual may detect enough promise to want to continue the exploration process. On the other hand, he or she may become alienated from the tentative, potential relationship at any point in this process of mutual recruitment and thus bring the process to an end before a primary relationship has been fully formed. It should also be noted that such mutual recruitments vary from being deliberate and even calculating to being utterly spontaneous and impulsive.

In selection, the individual chooses, from his pool of attracted candidates, someone who is, from his perspective, adequately qualified. Such a selection may be formal or informal, official or unofficial, deliberate or impulsive, depending on the nature of the relationship and the style of the individual. The selection criteria employed in choosing a friend (Chambliss, 1965) seem significantly different from those used in selecting a mate (Marcus, 1977). In selecting a friend, one need not consider the other person's dietary or sexual quirks, housekeeping and grooming habits, fiscal responsibility, genetic characteristics, child-rearing aspirations and theories, and the like. And both friendship and mating criteria are quite different from those used in selecting one's dentist or hair stylist.

As is true of attraction, selection does not generate a relationship unless that selection is mutual. Each party therefore redoubles his efforts to make himself attractive to the candidate he has tentatively chosen. A person is most motivated to impress when he is attracted to the other, has a reasonable chance of success in impressing that other, yet cannot take his success for granted (Blau, 1964). All of the standard tactics of attraction may be used, including formal or informal application, campaigning, preparing self to meet the rules and standards for the relationship, and offering inducements to the other party. The tentative and progressive nature of selection must be clearly recognized; the selection decision is seldom made abruptly, decisively, or formally. It involves a steadily deeper and broader examination and comparison of leading candidates, accompanied by augmented efforts to attract those same persons.

Where early impressions are favorable enough to encourage further encounters, continued exploration tends to set in motion an important process in relationships, which Simmel recognized as a strain toward "totality." The persona presented by each party, having been warmly received by the other, tends to take on a life of its own in the context of this nascent relationship. But they are only personas, after all, and not the whole and only truth about the parties involved; they are only subsets of their respective identity hierarchies. Consequently, each person comes to feel a bit uncomfortable with his persona.

First of all, some of the person's other valued role-identities, which the other person could support, are not being performed within the relationship because they were not included in the initial subset, which is all that the other knows of him. Second, and perhaps more important, the person fears that the other will discover that his persona is not the whole story—that he has other identities which may not be so compatible with those comprising his persona. And since this persona has been warmly received by the other, the person is understandably reluctant to have it perhaps embarrassed or discredited by other aspects of his self-structure. He is, in a sense, "passing."

The individual, then, grows uneasy with his persona and experiences a strain toward broadening the view of himself that he allows the other to see. Tentatively and cautiously, each party attempts to incorporate more and more of his self-structure into the relationship without introducing anything that might spoil it. The greater the number of role-identities that become involved in a relationship and the more deeply they become involved, the more rewarding and more durable the relationship becomes by reason of being less vulnerable to personal unmasking. As a result, there is a very strong tendency for the relationship to extend its claims infinitely, to encompass all of each participant's self. This is essentially what is meant by the growth and deepening of a relationship. Thus, two attracted strangers may become acquaintances, then casual lovers, then live-togethers, then life companions.

This strain toward totality in relationships operates not only to include larger segments of one's self-structure but also to include ever greater proportions of one's time and other resources. If a particular relationship is a rewarding one, the members may be tempted to exploit it further. If working with Millard is pleasant, why not invite him over for dinner, and if that proves enjoyable, why not go to a movie with him. In this way, the strain to spend more time with the other gives rise to a strain to include more activities—and thus more role-identities—in the relationship. Conversely, the more identities involved, the greater the number of activities in which the other person can legitimately request one to join him, thereby making further demands upon one's time, energy, money, and other resources.

As Bolton (1961) has argued, mate selection must be conceptualized as just such a process of developing a relationship. Newcomb (1961) and Lazarsfeld and Merton (1954) would extend a similar conclusion regarding the selection of friends.

But the social process of selection generally encompasses selection out of, as well as selection into, a social organization. In the case of a primary relationship, with its intrinsic sentimentalism, expulsion or secession of a member signals the demise of the organization. It cannot survive with merely one member, nor can any member be literally replaced. On the other hand, particularly in secondary relationships, essentially the same structure of relationship may be quickly established with another. Even if the relationship had been rather exclusive, as when a man patronized only one barber or had only one wife, he may well establish a (structurally) virtually identical relationship with another barber or another wife. Thus, we may speak of virtual, but not literal, replacement of members in a relationship. The unique aspects of any particular relationship are of course lost in such replacements, but the new relationship will develop unique aspects of its own.

One interesting phenomenon of selection-out is the "phantom relationship" in which—by preserving its culture, communicating about its history, and perhaps subjectively living to some extent wihin its bounds—one member keeps the relationship in some sense alive after the other member has departed. In this way, a treasured relationship with a lost sweetheart, a lost child, or a deceased partner may linger in the subjective life of the individual.

The aspect of placement is, of course, greatly restricted in any relationship, given the minimal differentiation of structural positions and the general reliance on informal means of role differentiation. More than in other organizational varieties, one individual's subsequent advancement within such dimensional structures as power, authority, or status does not necessarily entail a loss for the other member. As a relationship expands, through the strain toward totality, the total amounts of power and other factors also expand, so that both members may gain more of these quantities. Even leadership may increase for both, in that each becomes more and more of a leader for the other in specific added role pairs.

Other Basic Processes

In a primary relationship, just as each member must recruit both himself and the other, so each member must *socialize* both himself and the other. The process of socialization is effectively one of collaboratively creating the organization's unique culture rather than simply communicating existing expectations and understandings. In a marriage, for example, each member brings to it or develops conceptions of the goals, division of labor, and norms, that should characterize their relationship. Each recognizes that marriage will require some change in their own habits, beliefs, and skills, and each tends to cooperate in revising some of these and in developing new ones. Each will also attempt to resist certain other expected changes by attempting to teach the relationship about his or her own peculiarities (special abilities, experience, or defects) or about the distinctive peculiarities of the relationship itself.

The *interaction* process in a primary relationship largely amounts to the management of events in such a way as to preserve and cultivate the relationship. Preservation is a common interest of the two members; cultivation is a like interest—the pursuit of joint activities and personal ends within the arena of the organization and its tiny membership.

Members seek to preserve a relationship, first of all, by striving to manage events so as to maintain or even increase the interactions upon which it is based. The person will, for example, manage his schedule to make room for pursuit of the relationship and will seek environmental factors conducive to the relationship—fun things to do, material items useful to the relationship, and so on. A mother will seek interesting toys for her child, and a young man will arrange free time and seek an interesting place to go with his girlfriend for the weekend.

Second, members strive to manage threatening events that might interrupt, upset, or possibly terminate the relationship. A member will certainly attempt to neutralize or evade any negative influences from the embedding organizational levels. This may be as simple as not telling one's parents that one is going out with a motorcycle rider; for more deviant roles, this may require moving to another milieu. It may involve legitimation of the relationship, as in marriage or a work contract; it may involve public relations tactics, as when a youth persuades his parents that his new friend is "all right."

There are also potential internal threats to a relationship. Since it does not involve all the role-identities of either member—unless the relationship is a totally engulfing one—the members will have an existence outside of and in addition to it. In extreme cases, where one member is engaged in criminality, adultery, or espionage, the other must be kept unaware of these outside activities. More commonly, some of a members' identities are of little interest to the other and so must be pursued in some other way. Rare is the youth or spouse who tells everything to parent or mate, but also rare is the parent or mate who wants to hear everything that might be told.

This concern to manage events in such a way as to prevent disruption of a satisfactory relationship between personas is a common interest of its members. Each also has a like, but differing, interest in cultivation of the relationship—pursuit of joint activities and personal ends within the arena of the pair organization and its membership. Joint ventures for the collective benefit are generally a far more common mode of transaction than behavior exchanges in these pursuits. Temptations to use or exploit one's power or status differentials are tempered not only by the other member's counterpower in other areas but more directly by the strong sense of collectivity and attachment. As the relationship succeeds, there is, as we have seen, a strain toward broadening it—further involving its members and expanding its stores of available power, status, and so on, for each of its members. But as a dyadic organization emerges, it takes on a life of its own; in a sense, it cultivates its members by reshaping their role-identities and performances. Two people can make a marriage, but the ongoing social fact of the marriage influences the characters of its members.

In a primary relationship, *innovation* tends to be both unusually frequent and unusually fraught with tension. Externally imposed change is fairly common, if for no other reason than that such a tiny organization is easily influenced by larger organizations (the huge business firm decides that the husband will be transferred to an office on the opposite coast). Internally planned change is also quite common; one member decides to suggest or propose some addition or reallocation of activity (they should take up dancing; the husband should take over the cooking chores on weekends). Internally emergent change is perhaps most frequent of all; in seeking to pursue personal ends, one member's performance diverges from his or her established role within the relationship. One member might start to use some of the joint resources to pursue a hobby or one spouse might want to have a child. Since each member has identities beyond the relationship, such innovations are fairly frequent and are always a potential source of tension within the dyad. If the relationship is enduring, some accommodations are usually worked out to cover these divergences—each cedes the other the rights to some singular activities, and agendas are adjusted accordingly.

Internal innovations of either type generate an unusual degree of organizational tension, because in a relationship no coalitions are available for ratification or stigmatization. It is always a matter of one on one. The sponsor of an innovation can never be outnumbered, a situation that encourages him to innovate. On the other hand, he can have no internal backing in trying to persuade a reluctant or hostile member to accept his innovation. Without the strength of numbers, the deciding feature in the process of ratification or stigmatization must lie in the sponsor's power, authority, or leadership alone. In most relationships, however, no sharp differences in position within these influence structures are to be found; it is a fairly even contest between sponsor and opponent and may drag on for years, often with each being driven to uncivil and even violent tactics of persuasion (Steinmetz and Straus, 1974).

Some reluctance toward internal innovation is almost inevitable. If nothing else, there is an upset of the established rituals and routines. Also, the innovation may contribute nothing to the other's plans of action and may even be an impediment, as when the other has different plans for the weekend or for the extra money. Resolving tensions over innovations usually involves negotiation, further socialization efforts, and often a public relations campaign.

Social control is largely affective and sentimental, in the coin of interpersonal warmth or coldness, support or attack. Again, it is a matter of each member's controlling both himself and the other. Rewards and punishments are determined and administered informally, therefore; indeed, they can scarcely be distinguished from personal mood or whim. The severity of punishments is peculiarly constrained by the perils of pushing too far; if one member is expelled or decides to withdraw, the relationship itself would be terminated. (Nevertheless, the existence of strong interpersonal bonds often permits substantial punishment even in the forms of physical coercion and violence without leading to such organizational termination.) Degrees of withdrawal or increase of those role performances particularly valued by the other are a mainstay control mechanism in relationships, since such valued performances involve those joint activities, exchanges, and supports that are the heart of the relationship itself.

Proactive social control often seems similarly personal. Promises and threats tend to be seen as emanating from the other individual rather than from the relationship itself. Even organizational surveillance may be interpreted as suspicious prying rather than an expression of collective interest. A great deal of weight in the process of social control therefore falls on rituals of solidarity, which closely resemble those typical of primary groups in general.

ROLE-MAKING AND CAREER DEVELOPMENT

Given the minimal membership size of a relationship, the impact of the individual tactics is even more pronounced than within the primary group. No internal coalitions could hinder or assist the individual in his efforts to shape his own organizational role.

Individual tactics in the role-making processes of a relationship have been amply described in the preceding pages. The concept of career development in a social organization so structurally limited as a dyadic relationship requires further illumination here.

Career development rests heavily upon the career of the relationship itself. Internally the members may rise and fall relative to each other on the dimensional structures such as power, status, and liking. But they may also rise or fall together, for instance, as each comes to communicate with the other more or as the influence of each over the other diminishes when they are geographically separated for an extended period.

For the most part, then, any change in the individual's place within the relationship is a matter of how well he fares in the continual evolution of the relationship itself. As Woody Allen once put it, a relationship is like a shark: if it stops moving forward it dies. Career within any relationship is thus bound up with the career of the relationship itself. There are, for example, four levels of friendship (La Gaipa, 1977): social acquaintance, good friend, close friend, and best friend. Any friend relationship might pass through each of these levels as stages of its development through progressively deepening involvements of its members (Altman and Taylor, 1973; Huesmann and Levinger, 1976). Similar levels or developmental stages may be defined for romantic relationships (Bolton, 1961).

Actual career trajectories of (and within) relationships are quite variable, but there are a few common patterns. A person may form a relationship and experience its deepening and broadening—with perhaps a few minor setbacks—until it is terminated by the death or removal of one of its members. In arrested or reversing career trajectories, the relationship fails to develop through all the progressive stages, and the members may even fall back to the level of an acquaintanceship. A common pattern in secondary relationships is the development of a stable exchange of services which takes on a few primary aspects and continues in this form perhaps for many years until terminated by the removal of a member. Long-term doctor/patient, barber/customer, accountant/client, or senior colleague/junior colleague relationships are typical examples.

External environmental impacts may intervene to alter the course of any relationship and thus the career development of its members. An accident may terminate a promising affair, job movement may attenuate a friendship, or parents may forbid their son to play with the boy next door.

But the essential factor affecting relationship careers is that each member has a reality—a self-structure and an ''I''—above and beyond the personas brought to the relationship itself. In this sense, each member can become a special-interest faction within the dyad. At his level, the personal interests of members in addition to their collective interests come into play.

When we treat the self-structure of each member as a suborganization of the relationship, we immediately come upon the fact that such structures change over time in response to changing experience, skills, and opportunities. As a schoolgirl becomes a woman of forty, for instance, there will be significant shifts in both the contents and the hierarchical arrangement of her role-identities, which will have an important influence upon the personas and the relationships she maintains.

Changes in the contents of role-identities may, of course, result from many causes. Drastic social change may, as we have seen, cause a shift in the focus of roles. Impingements from higher organizational levels may dictate similar changes. The arrival of attractive alternative potential partners might provide the opportunity for pursuing different relationships. Changes in the relative costs and benefits of interacting with the other member may also affect the career of a relationship, as when one member moves—geographically or socially.

Such shifts are, at the least, disruptive of a relationship. If a successful redefinition of the relationship situation is not worked out, some degree of withdrawal on the part of one or both members is likely to commence. The outcome of this progressive withdrawal is variable, however, for the relationship does not lie entirely in the hands of its members. If the ties of ascription, commitment, and investment are not overwhelming, the parties to a progressively less rewarding relationship are allowed simply to give it correspondingly less priority. The two parties thus begin to fade out of each other's lives; they may still consider themselves friends, for example, but they simply see less of each other, ordinarily without much awareness of the fact. The relationship simply becomes attenuated, in keeping with the decline in its profitability.

Some relationships, on the other hand, in which the bonds of ascription, commitment, or investment are very strong, are not allowed to attenuate, no matter how unrewarding they may be. Husbands and wives, parents and small children, the affianced, lifelong business partners, creditors and debtors, are not allowed simply to fade out of each other's lives, to stop seeing each other. Beyond some point attenuation is not permitted. These persons are required to interact and exchange with each other at some specified minimal level, no matter how mutually painful or unprofitable it may be for them. Such relationships may end only through confrontations and unpleasant scenes in which the members overtly sever the remaining ties at considerable social and personal cost (Waller, 1938).

Not all changes in the self-structure of participants bring about the eventual death or decay of a relationship, however. Many relationships persist for decades, in the face of considerable changes in the personal features of their members. The relationship, defined in terms of the constituent personas, persists in a different form. A lasting relationship of any degree of intimacy must change many times as the couple progresses, for example, from young lovers, to fiances, to young marrieds, to young parents, to grandparents, and to life companions. The relationship must undergo metamorphosis at each major turning point in the personal career of each participant. If it does not or cannot, it will fade away or be destroyed. Relationships are nothing if they are not the projections and expressions of the selves of their members.

Finally, we should note that the culture of the age-sex structure anticipates a conventional life-cycle sequence of appropriate types of relationships, including certain family, friendship, and romantic varieties appropriate to some age-sex positions and not to others.

IMPACT ON THE CHARACTER OF THE INDIVIDUAL

Since a primary relationship is in most ways essentially a two-person primary group, some of its impacts on the individual are those of any other primary group (see Chapter 20).

In a primary relationship one may share many personal concerns and interests, find engaging companionship and fun, and develop shared interpretations of personal experiences through direct exchanges of information and ideas. Just as a primary group is likely to serve the individual as an important reference group, one's partner in a primary relationship is apt to serve as a reference other—indeed, in Mead's phrase, as a "significant other"—with similar person-changing capacities in the form of major informational, normative, and facilitative-supportive functions.

In fact, it is principally within just such primary relationships that persons grow and evolve. Most of the new identities that we acquire, as well as the changes in those we already hold, arise from intimate associations with others, who hold these changes up before us and let us try them on before we have to wear them in public view. Through such intimate associations, a desired or imagined role important to the individual is often first "energized" and first enacted. An obvious example is sexual activity, but there are a host of others; a child first sings for his mother, a youth first tries hang-gliding with his good buddy, a junior executive first tries out his new idea with his sponsoring senior.

In addition to such role trials and role rehearsals, a primary relationship also provides a comfortable and congenial setting in which the individual may display or receive affirmation and support for a variety of already established role-identities. Like larger primary groups, intimate relationships perform an archival function, serving as museums or at least warehouses of members' many social identities. In some cases, a person's informal role within the relationship may compensate for one or more roles he could not successfully establish in the outside world.

Again like primary groups, relationships are a ready source of assistance in dealing with a variety of mundane problems—borrowing a cup of flour, getting a ride to the auto repair shop, watching the children for a moment—as well as such emergencies as quickly getting to the hospital or doctor's office. Such assistance may be extensive—for example, putting one's spouse through college or long months of political campaigning for her husband's election to high office.

In addition to these functions of social integration, reassurance of identity and worth, and assistance, relationships serve more distinctive functions for the individual (Weiss, 1968): emotional integration, provided by relationships in which deep personal emotions may be expressed and reacted to in a way that is stabilizing for the participants, and opportunity for nurturance, an opportunity to care for and take responsibility for another human being and thus develop a distinctive sense of being needed.

No single relationship necessarily serves all these functions for a given individual. Some persons obtain these benefits through very intensive involvement in one or two relationships, while others obtain them through less intense interactions within a substantial number of primary and secondary relationships. Neighbor relationships tend to specialize in assistance of the more immediate and routine varieties; kinship relationships specialize in more extended assistance and in identity maintenance; and friendships are well-suited to social integration (Litwak and Szelenyi, 1969). Romantic, marital, and family relationships are likely to provide the fullest range of relationship functions for the individual.

The effects of one's position or role within a relationship tend to be fairly minimal, since social differentiation is not very clearly developed.

Effects of career trajectory, on the other hand, tend to be quite significant. A conventional career trajectory—for instance, a stable marriage or passage from social acquaintance to close friend—is almost certain to have wrought definite personal changes in the character of the individual, as the relationship between the two personas will have undergone repeated metamorphoses over its duration. These changes will be fewer in arrested or reversing career trajectories, but self-esteem may be significantly diminished for these individuals. The hurt, disorientation, and relative helplessness of individuals from terminated relationships are familiar and well-documented (Weiss, 1975).

Unconventional life-cycle sequences of relationship types may adversely affect one's attractiveness to other organizations at every level. A maturing young man who still plays ball every day with the little children of the neighborhood but has never had a serious romantic relationship will find many organizations leary of him and may come to suffer self-doubts.

The influence between relationships and the individual is a reciprocal one. The individual must continue to maintain a relationship so that it will continue to maintain his or her valued joint activities, exchange benefits, and role-identity supports. A spouse cannot depend upon honeymoon romance and intimacy to hold his or her mate, and a person cannot keep his friends without continuing to be a friend himself. The benefits available from relationships are not cheaply bought or easily earned nor are they everywhere available. Anyone who has found himself alone in a new locale, with all his ordinary relationship partners several thousand miles away, has experienced the reality of these truths.

In every human society, the fundamental problems of social living, of obtaining a more or less dependable and fruitful series of interactions, are partly resolved because individuals establish a web of primary and secondary relationships. Entering into relationships is a necessarily hazardous gamble, but social life would be "solitary, poor, nasty, brutish, and short" if millions of human beings did not routinely make such gambles. The individual develops and grows and lives within a nurturing web of such relationships.

SUMMARY

A relationship is, in most respects, essentially a two-person group or dyad. A relationship may be either primary or secondary, either official, unofficial, or institutionalized. Yet, Simmel has shown that a dyad has quite distinctive features as an organization.

Unlike any other type of organization, relationships never vary in membership size. With only two members, the collective resources (both human and material) of any relationship are sharply limited. Although secondary relationships may form around a single like interest of two individuals, primary relationships evolve around overlapping ranges of like and complementary interests, and all enduring relationships must develop a common interest in the organization itself. These collective interests give rise to social bonds, or interpersonal ties, between the two members: ascriptions, commitments, attachments, investments, and dependability of benefits. These bonds are distinct factors and do not necessarily converge, nor are the bonds of one member necessarily reciprocated by or symmetrical with those of the other. Thus, mutuality of closeness—behavioral involvement, intimacy of disclosure, warmth of feeling—varies from relationship to relationship. Members' awareness of the relationship as a social unit is greater when dealing with the external world than with internal matters. Yet, the realization that the loss of any single member terminates the organization and that no member can literally be replaced lends a unique sentimentalism to the sense of collectivity. The culture of a relationship is dominated by numerous rituals which have particularly personal meanings for the participants.

Social structure is at its absolute simplest in relationships, since along any dimension of social differentiation only two positions can be defined. Except in purely secondary relationships, the role structure is only informally differentiated. Roles are less important than persons; in primary relationships, the primary social structure is the fit between the "personas" (revealed subsets of one's role-identities) that the members present to one another. The secondary social structure of any relationship is also sharply limited. With only two members, no suborganizations can arise, and in any of the dimensional social structures only two positions are logically possible: higher and lower. The affect structure is particularly significant in the dynamics of relationships, through the operation of Waller's "principle of least interest." Yet, the fact that one member is seldom superordinate in all content areas—thus giving his partner counterpower over him—lends a close, peerlike quality to broad primary relationships.

Embedded relationships abound in any higher-level organization, are heavily influenced by its character, and either facilitate or subvert its collective action. Jealous rivalry tends to dominate relations between primary relationships, although relationships may themselves form temporary alliances and vital networks of interpersonal relationships.

More than in any other organization, the process of recruitment directly creates a relationship. Although many relationships are officially ascriptive, a voluntary relationship can emerge only when two persons have succeeded in recruiting each other. Interpersonal attraction and interpersonal selection occur through mutual exploration and elaboration of personas in response to a "strain toward totality." Interpersonal selection amounts to a process of progressive development of a relationship. With only two positions, the aspect of placement is greatly restricted; more than in other organizations, as a relationship develops and expands, both members may advance within any dimensional structure.

As a relationship develops, each member must socialize not only the other but also himself. Socialization is a matter not of communicating existing expectations and understandings but of jointly creating them. The interaction process centers on the management of internal and external events in such a way as to preserve and cultivate the relationship. Joint ventures are more significant than behavior exchanges, and the exploitation of position in dimensional structures is tempered by the distinctive sense of collectivity and bonds of attachment. Innovation is highly frequent and unusually tense, since no internal coalitions can be formed in ratification/stigmatization proceedings. Social control is largely affective and sentimental and apparently personal; each member must control both himself and the other.

Within this smallest of organizations, the impact of individual tactics in role-making is most sharply pronounced, since no hindering coalitions can emerge. Career development rests heavily upon the career of the relationship itself; as an acquaintanceship develops into a close friendship, the individual advances from an acquaintance to a close friend. Not every relationship fully progresses through such levels or developmental stages; in such cases the individual's career trajectory may be arrested or may reverse.

Some of the impacts of a relationship on the individual are those of any other group. First, it may provide social integration—fun and companionship, sharing of concerns and interests, shared interpretations of experiences; a primary relationship often serves as a reference group, with significant person-changing capacity through its informational, normative, and facilitative-supportive influences. Second, it may provide reassurance of identity and personal worth—constituting a safe setting for trials, rehearsals, and displays of external roles and identities, as well as directly affirming and supporting one's role-identities. Third, it may provide a ready source of assistance to the individual in dealing with a variety of his emergencies and mundane problems. A relationship may also serve the more distinctive functions of providing emotional integration and opportunity for nurturance. No single relationship necessarily serves all of these functions for a given individual; indeed, different types of relationships are better suited for some functions than for others.

Except in some secondary relationships, effects of position or role tend to be minimal. Effects of career trajectory are generally more significant. Changes in most individual attributes tend to be more striking in the case of a conventional career trajectory, with each metamorphosis in the developing relationship having altered the constituent personas. Self-esteem tends to be significantly diminished by arrested or reversing career trajectories; individuals in relationships which have been terminated but not replaced often suffer personal hurt, disorientation, and a sense of helplessness.

Unconventional life sequences of relationship types may adversely affect one's attractiveness to other organizations at every level.

SUGGESTIONS FOR ADDITIONAL READING

A useful overview of relationships in general, emphasizing matters of social organization, is the slim volume by George J. McCall, Michal M. McCall, Norman K. Denzin, Gerald D. Suttles, and Suzanne B. Kurth, *Social Relationships* (Chicago: Aldine, 1970).

A variety of primary relationships receive special attention in George Levinger and H. L. Raush, eds., *Close Relationships: Perspectives on the Meaning of Intimacy* (Amherst: University of Massachusetts Press, 1977), and in Murray S. Davis, *Intimate Relations* (New York: Free Press, 1973).

The character of friendship varies characteristically over one's life span. Friendship at the younger ages is examined in Zick Rubin, *Children's Friendships* (Cambridge, Mass.: Harvard University Press, 1980), and more deeply in Hugh C. Foot, Antony J. Chapman, and Jean R. Smith, editors, *Friendship and Social Relations in Children* (New York: Wiley, 1980). Interesting findings on adult friendships are presented by C. Ann Stueve and Kathleen Gerson in their chapter on "Personal Relations Across the Life-Cycle" (pp. 79–98 in Claude S. Fischer et al., *Networks and Places: Social Relations in the Urban Setting,* New York: Free Press, 1977). Zena Blau's study of "Sructural Constraints on Friendships in Old Age" (*American Sociological Review,* 1961, 26: 429–439) is a classic contribution.

Still the most insightful analysis of romantic relationships is Charles D. Bolton's "Mate Selection as the Development of a Relationship" (*Marriage and Family Living,* 1961, 23: 234–240). Also of interest is Zick Rubin, *Liking and Loving* (New York: Holt, Rinehart, and Winston, 1973).

A now somewhat dated—yet unsurpassed—analysis of marital relationships is to be found in Willard Waller's classic textbook on *The Family: A Dynamic Interpretation* (New York: Dryden Press, 1938). Another influential account is that by Robert O. Blood, Jr., and Donald M. Wolfe, *Husbands and Wives: The Dynamics of Married Living* (New York: Free Press, 1960).

Other family relationships are, of course, significant as well. In fact, the person's first relationship is typically with his mother. A useful account of how infant/mother interactions eventually give rise to a relationship is provided in Daniel Stern, *The First Relationship: Infant and Mother* (Cambridge, Mass.: Harvard University Press, 1977). Strangely enough, sibling relationships have received comparatively little attention. A cogent overview of such relationships is provided by Brian Sutton-Smith and B. G. Rosenberg, *The Sibling* (New York: Holt, Rinehart, and Winston, 1970).

The considerable variety of kin relationships beyond the immediate family is examined in Bert Adams, *Kinship in an Urban Setting* (Chicago: Markham, 1966).

The relative importance and differing functions of these and other primary relationships are considered in Graham A. Allan, *A Sociology of Friendship and Kinship* (London: Allen and Unwin, 1979) and in Eugene Litwak and Ivan Szelenyi, "Primary Group Structures and Their Functions: Kin, Neighbors, and Friends" (*American Sociological Review,* 1969, 34: 465–481).

Secondary relationships comprise an immense variety of social organizations. The most thoroughly examined of these is surely the doctor/patient relationship. A thoughtful and contemporary review of theories and research on that relationship may be found in Frederic D. Wolinsky's chapter on "The Patient–Practitioner Relationship" (pp. 160–185 in his *The Sociology of Health: Principles, Professions, and Issues,* Boston: Little, Brown, 1980).

Finally, it should be noted that not all relationships are progressive and enduring. An interesting case in point is Fred Davis's study of "The Cabdriver and His Fare: Facets of a Fleeting Relationship" (*American Journal of Sociology,* 1959, 65: 158–165).

Nonetheless, much of the best recent work on the development of relationships takes the form of models of progressive mutual involvement. Progressively deeper self-disclosures are emphasized in Irwin Altman and Dalmas A. Taylor, *Social Penetration: The Development of Interpersonal Relationships* (New York: Holt, Rinehart, and Winston, 1973). Progressively greater exchanges of all kinds are considered in L. Rowell Huessman and George Levinger, "Incremental Exchange Theory: A Formal Model for Progression in Dyadic Social Interaction" (pp. 191–229 in Leonard Berkowitz and Elaine Walster, editors, *Advances in Experimental Social Psychology,* vol. 9, New York: Academic Press, 1976). More closely compatible with the views of this chapter is the work by Steven W. Duck, *Personal Relationships and Personal Constructs: A Study of Friendship Formation* (New York: Wiley, 1973).

Soldier and young civilian focus intently on each other, neither entirely certain of the outcome of this unforeseen encounter.

CHAPTER 22

Encounters

In the encounter we can see social processes in their purest form because this organizational level has the least structure in the sense of pre-existing patterns of positions, roles, norms, and culture. It is the most extemporaneous of organizational levels; there is always an element of uncertainty and adventure in encounters.

Social encounters range widely in content, from a cocktail-party conversation or some shared banter around the pool, to a mugging or a policeman at the door with a warrant. Their moods vary from joyous to humdrum to grim; their courses and outcomes vary from fulfillment to disaster. Their formats range from utterly spontaneous to totally ritualized, but encounters of every sort contain enormous potential for surprise.

Yet, encounters do not take place in a vacuum but are deeply embedded within each of the higher organizational levels we have examined, and they take place within a welter of organizational constraints and rules.

A social encounter is a bounded and focused episode of direct interaction within a face-to-face gathering of persons. Such an episode occurs "when people effectively agree to sustain for a time a single focus of cognitive and visual attention, as in a conversation, a board game, or a joint task sustained by a close face-to-face circle of contributors" (Goffman, 1961a: 7).

Such an encounter may or may not coincide with the gathering as a whole. If it does, we may speak of a fully focused gathering; if some of the persons present are not participating in the encounter, we may speak of a partly focused gathering. An unfocused gathering is one in which no encounter is taking place; a multifocused gathering, on the other hand, is one in which two or more encounters occur simultaneously.

NOTE: Portions of this chapter are based on McCall and Simmons, 1978: 121–164.

Official gatherings, such as board meetings or conferences, tend to be more fully focused. Informal gatherings, such as a party or open house, tend to be partly focused or multifocused, with several overlapping and shifting encounters occurring. Wholly spontaneous gatherings, such as a crowd waiting for the next showing at a movie theater, tend to be unfocused, although a few small encounters will develop along the lines as time passes.

Gatherings, along with any included encounters, are sometimes *occasioned* by a more enduring social organization as an integral event within the collective action of its division of labor. Committee meetings, community festivals, family reunions, weddings, funerals, and college football games are examples of officially occasioned gatherings. Gatherings may also be unofficially occasioned, such as coffee-break card games. Some gatherings are completely unoccasioned, resulting from the fortuitous convergence of individuals in one setting at the same time, as when people are thrown together on a journey or during some crisis. This incidental and accidental bringing together of people is far more common and significant than is sometimes realized. For instance, the mechanics of alphabetical seating arrangements in high school classes may generate encounters which lead to friendships or romances.

An unoccasioned gathering is normally an unfocused gathering. Any social act—that is to say, any encounter—that might develop within an unoccasioned and unfocused gathering would first require the negotiation of some collective "definition of the situation" (as described in Chapter 2). For the members of an officially occasioned gathering, however, the social situation is essentially predefined by the nature of the occasion itself, although some of the attending individuals may have different or additional aims.

It is the existence of a shared definition of the situation that provides an encounter with both its focus and its bounds. In Chapter 2, we noted that the attentional focus of an encounter is some joint involvement in a social act or task—building canoes, making love, idle chatter, the purchase of a pair of jeans, doing psychotherapy, or the negotiation of a military surrender. Any such task focus rests upon some working agreement regarding the identities of the participants. Goffman (1961a) argues that such a definition of the situation (the working agreement on identities, together with the negotiated task focus) effectively serves as a set of *boundary rules* governing the actions and personal attributes that can be admitted to that particular encounter. Such boundary rules set broad limits to what should "legitimately" go on within the encounter and influence the performances of the members.

ORGANIZATIONAL CHARACTER OF ENCOUNTERS

Collectivity

The fundamental collective good for which an encounter is organized is a single common focus of cognitive and visual attention, in pursuit of the interests of the prevailing social occasion—that is, the like or complementary interests that have brought these persons together. All members therefore also share a common interest in the collective sustaining of that attentional focus.

The human resources of an encounter include the number of participants and the range of personal attributes they manifest. The larger the number of participants, the more difficult it is to sustain a common focus of attention (but the smaller the proportion of responsibility for task accomplishment each member must bear). Similarly, when the personal attributes of the various participants differ most widely, the difficulties of sustaining a common focus of attention are greatest.

The material resources of an encounter are limited to whatever "things" are present in the environmental setting of that gathering, including whatever things the members happen to have brought with them into that setting. These may be carefully planned, as when a manager brings sales charts to an executive conference or a man brings a bottle of wine to his girlfriend's apartment. They might be utterly fortuitous, as when a woman is holding an umbrella when accosted by a would-be assailant. One interesting aspect of many encounters is the creative use of things present and brought.

The culture of an encounter is essentially entailed in the definition of the situation. As noted in Chapter 2, the definition of a situation generates "social objects"; it converts the material resources of the encounter into social objects. Through a shared understanding of the situation, consensual meanings arise concerning the significance of immediately present persons, things, and events. In addition, quite ordinary words or phrases may acquire certain unique senses or shades of meaning as shared interpretations of experience develop within the encounter. Also, much use is made of pronouns ("this," "him,") and other situationally specific terms of reference ("over there," "the thingamajig," "the old bastard," "what happened before," "what Joe said"), the meanings of which depend entirely on the context of that particular conversation and would have to be explained to any nonparticipant.

The normative culture of an encounter, including its boundary rules, is closely intertwined with such understandings and meanings. One class of boundary rules is "rules of irrelevance," specifying what properties of things and events may be paid attention to and which properties must be overlooked. In conversations between strangers or mere acquaintances, for example, a crippled participant's shriveled legs are supposed to be overlooked and certainly not referred to. In a bit of office horseplay, a wad of paper may become a "baseball" and a ruler become a "bat" by focusing on those properties that these things share with the real items, while ignoring their divergent properties. A second class of boundary rules is "rules of transformation," specifying how some property of a person, thing, or event must be modified in its expression within the encounter. For example, among intimates there may be a tacit understanding that the cripple's legs can only be mentioned in a joking manner, but never seriously. Major status differentials may be expressed only in an inverted fashion, as when in the opening round of personal introductions at a working conference, the host takes care that the highest-ranking persons are introduced last.

Finally, the definition of the situation implies certain norms of conduct or "situational proprieties." A funeral, for example, enjoins the participants to adopt a certain appropriate facial expression, posture, costume, tone of voice, vocabulary, and pace of movement, and also to forgo such habitual actions as chewing gum, spitting, cursing, and smoking.

The culture of an encounter is more fleeting and ephemeral than are those of higher-level organizations, but it is nevertheless an observable reality. In fact, a culture of shared meanings must be established if an encounter is to occur.

Sharing in the definition of the situation therefore tends to generate both a social order and a sense of collectivity.

> For the participants, this involves: a single visual and cognitive focus of attention; a mutual and preferential openness to verbal communication; a heightened mutual relevance of acts; an eye-to-eye ecological huddle that maximizes each participant's opportunity to perceive the other participants' monitoring of him. Given these communication arrangements, their presence tends to be acknowledged or ratified through expressive signs, and a "we rationale" is likely to emerge, that is, a sense of the single thing that *we* are doing together at the time. Ceremonies of entrance and departure are also likely to be employed, as are signs acknowledging the initiation and termination of the encounter or focused gathering as a unit. Whether bracketed by ritual or not, encounters provide the communication base for a circular flow of feeling among the participants as well as corrective compensations for deviant acts [Goffman, 1961a: 18].

Social Structure

The role structure of an encounter is dictated by whatever definition of the situation is formulated. This may be predetermined, as in the case of an officially called conference, or it may be worked out through interaction, as in an informal gathering at the swimming pool. This definition of the situation in turn generates the social objects of the encounter, which include both the cast of roles and the relevant possible events. The available roles, objects, and possible events imposed by an impromptu game of "office baseball" with paper wads and rulers are not as elegant but they are just as apparent as those imposed by a church wedding.

The vertical and horizontal differentiation of the role structure of an encounter may sometimes be fairly sharp. In such cases, the dimensional ranks of secondary social structures (authority, status, communication, leadership) tend to reflect closely the vertical differentiation of the role structure. But in direct interaction, the extent and the nature of one's communicative contributions effectively determine leadership rank—and thereby influence one's ranking in status as well—as we have seen in other chapters. These contributions to the encounter sometimes rest on ephemeral power differences, on control over quite transitory resources such as isolated and atypical pieces of information, momentary determination, transient advantages in energy level, and the like. Thus, a generally high-ranking individual may find himself temporarily dominated by an inferior in a particular encounter if he is ill or tired or bored while his inferior is operating at normal efficiency.

An interesting and common aspect of encounters is that their structures—resting as they do on momentary resources and abilities—are so flexible compared with the far greater predetermination of structures at all higher organizational levels. An individual who happens to have the right information or a zestful mood may carry the day within the structure of an encounter.

Suborganizations are very common within encounters. A subset of the participants may band together, tacitly or explicitly, as a coalition to influence the bargaining process within the encounter. They may do so in an attempt to coerce others into granting certain concessions in return for the particular resources controlled by that coalition; at an elementary level, this behavior can be seen in gatherings with unequal sex ratios, which place the scarcer sex in a favorable bargaining position. Coalitions may also form to protect individuals' common investments in an identity that they legitimately share but that is now claimed by an unproven outsider. If a cocktail party includes a number of political scientists, for example, and some other person begins to hold forth on the political crisis of the day, the political scientists are quite likely to cooperate tacitly in putting him in his place. Whatever the particular purpose, coalitions more easily acquire power than do individuals through such "restrictions of free trade" (Blau, 1964: 187–194). In many cases, then, exchange in encounters can more profitably be viewed as taking place between rival coalitions than among disparate individuals. Goffman (1959b) has taken some tentative steps toward analyzing such coalitional strategies in his discussions of dramaturgical "teamwork."

More readily visible subencounters are the "collusive by-plays," such as a whispered side conversation between two members during a committee meeting while they ostensibly continue to share in the focus of attention of the whole. In such by-plays, members are pursuing either a special-interest position on the focus of the encounter or private interests of their own which lie outside the focus. Unless there is virtually total consensus on the focus, the definition of the situation, and the meanings of all the social objects present, such by-plays are likely to occur within any encounter. If nothing else, some of the participants will pursue "solo" by-plays, such as cleaning their nails, working on a separate problem, or daydreaming. Where such by-plays are clearly unofficial, they may be viewed as expressions of disloyalty to the encounter.

Interorganizational Relations

Encounters have a crucial place in the carrying out of organized social life. Much of the collective action necessary for the functioning of all the higher-level organizations we have examined takes place through them—from the international conference to the dyadic rendezvous. Conversely, any encounter which takes place is necessarily embedded within a host of larger social structures.

Yet, encounters are not simply passive enactments of higher-level organizational scripts—they are an organizational reality in their own right. They may facilitate, subvert, or simply be irrelevant to the purposes of higher-level organizations. Viewed as official or unofficial suborganizations, encounters may be the source of special-interest or innovation influences for the embedding organizations. When diplomats or cronies meet, they cannot be simply counted on to carry out the prescriptions and expectations of their embedding social structures.

In order to grasp these subtle interorganizational relations, care must be taken to distinguish encounters from other small and geographically compact organizations, such as groups or relationships; their organizational character differs sharply. This distinction is readily grasped in general but has not always been clearly recognized, no doubt because groups and relationships share with encounters a similar membership size and a reliance on direct face-to-face interaction. One must recognize the differing organizational character of groups and encounters in order to grasp their subtle interorganizational relations.

Some of the properties that are important to focused gatherings or encounters, taken as a class, seem less important to little groups, taken as a class. Examples of such properties include embarrassment, maintenance of poise, capacity for nondistractive verbal communication, adherence to a code regarding giving up and taking over the speaker role, and allocation of spatial position. Furthermore, a crucial attribute of focused gatherings—the participants' maintenance of continuous engrossment in the official focus of activity—is not a property of social groups in general, for most groups, unlike encounters, continue to exist apart from the occasions when members are physically together. A coming-together can be merely a phase of group life; a falling-away, on the other hand, is the end of a particular encounter, even when the same pattern of interaction and the same participants appear at a future meeting. Finally, there are many gatherings—for example, a set of strangers playing poker in a casino—where an extremely full array of interaction processes occurs with only the slightest development of a sense of group. All these qualifications can be made even though data for the study of little groups and for the study of focused gatherings are likely to be drawn from the same social occasion.

In the life of many little groups, occasions regularly arise when all the members and only the members come together and jointly sustain a situated activity system or encounter: they hold a meeting, play a game, or take a cigarette break together. To call these gatherings "meetings of the group" can easily entrap one into thinking that one is studying the group directly. Actually, these are meetings of persons who are members of a group, and, even though the meeting may have been called because of issues faced by the group, the initial data concern participants in a meeting, not members of a group.

It is true that on such occasions there is likely to be a correspondence between the realm of group life and the realm of face-to-face interaction process. For example, leadership of a little group may be expressed during gatherings of members by the question of who is chairman, or who talks the most, or who is most frequently addressed. It is also likely that the leadership demonstrated in the gathering will both influence, and be influenced by, the leadership in the group. But group leadership is not made up exclusively of an "averaging" of positions assumed during various gatherings. In fact, the group may face circumstances in which its leader is careful to let others take leadership during a meeting, his capacity to lead the group resting upon the tactful way in which he plays a minor role during gatherings of group members. The group leader can do this because "taking the chair" is intrinsically a possibility of gatherings, not groups. . . .

When all and only the members of a little group come together in a gathering, the effect of the gathering, depending on the outcome of its activity, will be to strengthen or weaken somewhat the little group. The potentiality of the encounter for generating its own group seems to be expended in what it does for and to the long-standing group. Often, there seems to be no chance for the fleeting circle of solidarity to develop much solidity of its own, for it fits too well in a pattern already established. However, when individuals come into a gathering who are not also members of the same little group, and especially if they are strangers possessing no prior relationships to one another, then the group formation that is fostered by the encounter will stand out as a contrast to all other groups of which the encounter's participants are members. It is under these circumstances—when the participants in a gathering have not been together in a group before and are not likely to be so again—that the locally generated group seems to cast its strongest shadow. It is under these circumstances, too, that the fate of these two units of organization seems most closely tied together, the effectiveness of the gathering rather directly affecting the solidarity of the group.

Paradoxically, then, if a gathering, on its own, is to generate a group and have group-formation mark the gathering as a memorable event, then a stranger or two may have to be invited—and this is sometimes carefully done on sociable occasions. These persons anchor the group-formation that occurs, preventing it from drifting back into the relationships and groups that existed previously among the participants [Goffman, 1961a: 11-14].

Similarly, encounters involving all and only the members of a dyadic relationship are embedded in but distinguishable from the collective action of that relationship. Such encounters may, however, either facilitate or subvert the collective action of that relationship. Particularly distinctive are those encounters that Goffman (1971: 62-94) analyzes as "supportive interchanges"—interpersonal rituals serving to ratify and maintain the relationship, such as morning coffee together or the ritualized friendly greeting of "How's by you?"

Relations of one encounter with another, in the same gathering or setting, are variable. At a party, for example, more than one focused conversational huddle may develop, and each essentially competes for membership. Within this competitive framework, relations between encounters may be cooperative—displaying mutual respect, as each seeks to communicate its awareness of (but civil inattention to the contents of) the other. The relation may be one of conflict, in which each encounter raises its conversational loudness and perhaps even seeks to distract the attention of members of its rival encounter.

ORGANIZATIONAL PROCESSES

For illustrative purposes, let us examine the basic organizational processes as these operate within that fundamental and ubiquitous type of encounter, the conversation.

Recruitment into an occasioned gathering is often somewhat ascriptive in that the sponsoring organization essentially brings it about that certain persons are co-present. But unless that occasioned gathering is a fully focused one, recruitment to the gathering does not entail recruitment to an encounter within it. Ordinarily, participation in an encounter is selective. The membership of an ongoing encounter may invite a bystander to participate or the bystander may apply for admission. Such application is ritualized in form and minimally involves seeking to "catch the eye" of an influential member. The organizations's selection decision is signaled by avoiding or overlooking

the application ritual, in the negative case, or through some return signal of acceptance, in the positive case, ratifying the candidate as an official member of the encounter. The aspect of placement is a matter of informal role allocation, of consensual
identification of the newcomer. In many cases this process is facilitated by the almost
mandatory ceremony of greeting, a brief period of "phatic communication"—relatively empty sociable chitchat—in which previously acquainted members reaffirm
their respective relationships and any strangers are ritually introduced (Laver, 1975).

In other types of encounters, one individual may essentially "draft" other participants through his actions toward them—a policeman may stop a motorist or a
parent may call a child forward for a "talk." Often, such enforced encounters present
a social psychological problem for the erstwhile recruit: how best to negotiate one's
way through the encounter (best, that is, on cost/benefit criteria). Those in a generally
superordinate position, within any organizational level, usually have some ability to
recruit other members of that level for desired encounters.

Recruitment out of the encounter is similarly selective and ritualized, involving
both some sort of leave-taking signal by the individual—perhaps clearing his throat,
looking around, or shuffling his feet—and a departure ceremony by the remaining
membership, in which most if not all give verbal or nonverbal acknowledgment of the
fact of his leaving. If the departure is voluntary, the leave-taking signal serves as an
application for retirement and is generally ratified by the departure ceremony. In unwanted encounters, the unwilling member will manipulate the leave-taking signal to
get out of further interaction by looking at his watch or remarking that is has been nice
to chat, since the other participants are under some constraints of etiquette to honor
such signals and say goodbye. If, on the other hand, the member's departure amounts
to an expulsion, that temporal order is reversed; the collective staging of the departure
ceremony occurs first ("We'll see you later, OK?") and is then ratified by the individual's leave-taking signal ("Oh. All right, catch you later.").

An important special case of entering and leaving is the matter of initiating and
terminating an encounter. Within any gathering, each encounter must somehow be
initiated and terminated. Some member of the gathering must make application to
another, who in turn must accede to the request for focused interaction, and together
they must collectively define the situation. This beginning will be marked by greeting
ceremonies and a period of phatic communication. Other members of the gathering
may subsequently enter and/or depart as described. But eventually the encounter
must be terminated through some individual proposal and collective ratification,
similarly marked by departure ceremonies in a brief period of fairly empty remarks.

The *socialization* process is largely subsumed in the foregoing. The initiation of an
encounter essentially carries with it the creation of its core culture through the negotiation of some definition of the situation and some consensual identification of the
characters of the participants. Any subsequently admitted members must be apprised
of the prevailing definition of the situation, be briefed on what has happened thus
far, and have their roles communicated to them through altercasting tactics. Such
newcomers may also periodically require clarification of certain conversation-specific
expressions. Occasionally, a member will not fully understand how to perform his

414

assigned role and must be advised or coached on the spot. Similarly, a member may resist some of these communicated expectations or overlook them in the press of interaction; some influential member must then exert leadership by reminding all of the prevailing definition of the situation (and thus of their respective roles). Such rapid socialization of members is greatly facilitated and possible only through extensive generalized anticipatory socialization and through previous direct socializations within the embedding structures. A manager knows more or less how to behave at a board meeting and an experienced college student knows how to act on a date. The depth of such previous socialization training for encounters is brought home when one participates in encounters with foreigners or even with members of distinctly different ethnic groups. There, it may be difficult to get past the most rudimentary meetings, and the ordinary fast-flow interactions of encounters falter. A major aspect of social competence at all organizational levels is to catch on quickly to the situation in an encounter so as to perform one's allocated role.

It can be said more generally that part of an individual's survival and success depends upon managing one's encounters. The newcomer to New York or Los Angeles or the army is often "taken" one way or another, whereas the experienced hand moves easily from encounter to encounter through the social order.

From the organizational standpoint of the encounter itself, the process of *interaction* amounts to the coordination of members' behaviors so as to sustain a single focus of cognitive and visual attention. In recent years, a great deal of research in various disciplines has illuminated the extent, the difficulties, and some of the mechanisms of such coordination of behavior (see, for example, Kendon et al., 1975).

First of all, the bodies of the members must be coordinated in spatial location and orientation. The norms specifying a comfortable speaking distance have been shown to vary widely among speech communities (E. Hall, 1966). The degree to which members of an encounter locate themselves closer or farther than this normative distance may be socially interpreted as accepting, intrusive, or rejecting (Watson, 1970), and actual physical touching is always socially interpretable (Scheflen, 1972). Similarly, the allocation of available spatial locations among the various members of the encounter (Sommer, 1965) is considered to facilitate certain types of action and to express certain aspects of the relationships among those members (Henley, 1977). A position at the head of a table, for example, has been shown to facilitate leadership and to express higher status. Finally, the body angles of orientation (the degree to which members face one another) affects how efficiently each may monitor the others' behaviors (Goffman, 1971) and also expresses some aspects of the social relationships among these members (Scheflen, 1964). For example, sitting with one leg emphatically crossed over the other, so that one's lower body (but not one's head) turns away from the conversational partner, may indicate a rejecting attitude of withdrawal. Looking and watching are most important; coordination of actions often depends on a "conversation of the eyes," and declining to meet the gaze of another generally signals a less than candid relationship. The significance and functions of gaze direction and of mutual gaze in social interaction are now rather widely appreciated (Kendon, 1967; Exline, 1971; Argyle and Cook, 1976; see also Simmel, 1921).

LEVELS OF ORGANIZATION

Bodily movements, too—postures (Scheflen, 1972), gestures (Birdwhistell, 1970), and facial expressions (Ekman et al., 1972)—are carefully coordinated. In fact, all these visible bodily adjustments among the participants of an encounter strongly resemble an expressive and well-choreographed dance (Kendon, 1973) with a marked rhythm of movements (Kendon, 1970).

Such "body language" in interactions is part of the definition of what is proper in a particular encounter. It is learned as a general part of socialization (particularly within one's speech community and age-sex structure) and tends to become a ritualized aspect of the communication process. In certain types of encounter, leaning forward may, for example, convey an accosting attitude, while leaning back may signal something of a disengagement, at least from the seriousness of the focus.

Coordinations among the participants in an encounter can be heard as well as seen. Indeed, coordination of vocal gestures may be even more obvious than that of visible ones. The sequential coordination of conversational talking—that is, the taking of "turns" in speaking—is a striking and complex accomplishment and depends on a variety of linguistic, paralinguistic, and gestural signals (S. D. Duncan, 1972; Schegloff, 1968). Such sequencing reflects not only formal or grammatical relations between consecutive speech acts, such as questions and answers (S. D. Duncan, 1973), but also their content relations; one speech turn is ordinarily a continuation of the topic expressed in preceding turns, and shifts in topic normally require some justificatory transition which may or may not be ratified by the membership.

An even more fundamental coordination of speech within encounters is to be found in the situational adjustments of speech style prescribed by the speech community, as discussed in Chapter 13. Linguistic features of speech are always adjusted to social features of the situation. Such relevant situational factors always include: the setting of the encounter, its occasion, characteristics of the participants (age, sex, native language, geographical and social dialects), relationships with these participants (degree of acquaintance, social distance, subordination), topic (religion, politics), and role (requesting, commanding, suggesting). Such sociolinguistic adjustments modify each speaker's choice of language, dialects, key, and vocabulary (Hymes, 1962; Ervin-Tripp, 1964), as well as intonation and inflection patterns.

Overall, then, the audible features of face-to-face interaction have also been shown to exhibit marked "rhythms of dialogue" (Jaffe and Feldstein, 1970). The participants in an encounter can be said to have "gotten in tune" with one another, and these shared auditory rhythms have been shown to pace the visible "dance" of coordinated body movements (Kendon, 1972; Duncan and Fiske, 1977).

Again, this apparently smooth coordination characterizing most encounters (despite whatever personal tumult may lie beneath their surface) rests upon the elaborate socialization process involved in learning the generalized rules for encounters within a given social order, rules that are mostly taken for granted by the socialized participants. The "awkwardness" often displayed by people in new situations or in a new organizational setting is seldom anything more than inexperience with the locally prevailing rules of conduct in different types of encounters. The rules for a lunch encounter with senior management will differ slightly from those for lunch with the other young executives, while the rules for the lunch "dance" with an evasive client may be quite different indeed. The troubles a newcomer has in mastering even the most rudimentary encounters when thrust into an entirely different culture are brilliantly depicted in the first half of James Clavell's *Shōgun*.

Even though the adequately socialized participant wants to "get in step" and "keep in tune" with the others, he also has an interest in pursuing his personal ends within the arena of the encounter and of its membership. It is within encounters that he is able, through joint actions and social exchange, to obtain many of the intrinsic and extrinsic gratifications for which he strives, as well as direct expressions of role support. He is often motivated, then, to drive a hard bargain within an encounter and to strive to manipulate its role structure in pursuit of his own special interests (McCall and Simmons, 1978: 121–164; Blumstein, 1973).

Innovation within an encounter is frequently a result of such self-strivings causing a break or a change in the boundary rules of the encounter, that is, in the working agreement concerning the identities of the participants. This working agreement is easily upset, because it is a precarious balance (see Figure 2–1) between the expressive processes of each participant and the cognitive processes of all the others. These complementary processes—presentation of self and role imputation, altercasting and role improvisation—do not cease when an agreement is attained but go on as long as the participants remain in contact. Each member must continually monitor the expressive implications of his behaviors so as not to contradict the others' images of him and of themselves. If any participant's act should contradict one of these images, it must be successfully explained away. If not, the working agreement will at once collapse.

Yet, there is every pressure to continue the struggle over one's character and role, to bring them more in line with one's role-identities. As a natural consequence, some member will occasionally push too hard in this struggle and upset the working agreement, spoiling the encounter and embarrassing the character of everyone present. If the working agreement cannot somehow be repaired or restored, the encounter does not necessarily terminate. Very often a new agreement is negotiated, perhaps itself to be upset and superseded. A single encounter, then, often presents the appearance of successive *phases* of interaction, each marked by the negotiation of a new working agreement (Strauss, 1959: 44–88). In real-life social situations, this is probably the most frequent occurrence.

Because roles within an encounter are often informally defined, discrepant performances are frequent. Organizational surveillance is virtually complete under the face-to-face circumstances of an encounter, yet relatively few of these discrepant performances provoke organizational reactions—owing in part to the inherent time limitations on any encounter. Most violations of the situational proprieties are tactfully overlooked by the membership, thus tacitly ratifying them through an informal and democratic procedure of "saving face." If a participant's performance is so discrepant as to be disruptive, a common tactic by the other members is simply to terminate the encounter, perhaps reconvening it elsewhere.

Some violations, however, are too threatening to be overlooked and provoke a formal corrective interchange (Goffman, 1955): the discrepant performer is challenged

417

("Hey! Watch it!"); he offers an excuse, a justification, an apology, or a request ("Sorry!"); the membership considers and accepts his offering ("Well, that's OK"); and he expresses his gratitude ("Thanks!"). Through such a corrective (or remedial) interchange, the discrepant performance is stigmatized as a violation but is also redressed, restoring the ritual order.

Reactive *social control* in an encounter is thus more concerned with remedies and reliefs than with compensations or sanctions. It is less concerned with punishing the violator than with rehabilitating him from a state of disgrace and an uncertain character (Goffman, 1955, 1971: 95–187). However, under certain circumstances, encounters are themselves employed as informal punishments, as when a student is called before the principal, an errant worker is summoned before a union board, or some group member is called into line by the rest of the members. In these cases informal negative sanctions are themselves the focus of the encounter. But here, too, the major aim is usually rehabilitation of the discrepant member's performances.

Proactive social control in encounters relies most heavily on ceremonies and rituals of solidarity, backed by a universal awareness of the thoroughness of surveillance.

ROLE-MAKING AND CAREER DEVELOPMENT

Each member of a gathering exerts considerable influence on his role in relation to any contained encounter. As emphasized in Chapter 2, the collective definition of the situation must often be negotiated by the participating individuals. Each individual's cognitive processes (imputation of roles to others and improvisation of a role for himself) and expressive processes (altercasting and presentation of self) are fundamental constituents of any working agreement that may develop. Of course, it cannot be denied that individuals are seldom equal in influence within such negotiations.

In view of the transient nature of an encounter, to speak of a member as having a "career" within such a passing organization may seem to strain the concept. Still, individuals do move up and down within the secondary social structures of an encounter (particularly of a multiphased encounter). For the most part, however, an individual's course through the social structure of an encounter is most clearly marked in terms of when and how he enters and departs the encounter. Initiators, "founding members," newcomers, deserters, and the expelled all experience rather distinctively different modes of participation.

In general, the individual is more free to determine his or her own role and career within encounters than at any other organizational level. Indeed, some persons specialize in encounters as a tactic in managing their careers within higher-level organizations or even make something of a career out of encounters themselves, sometimes as a substitute for more enduring relationships or for memberships in groups or associations. The "social butterfly" and the "swinging single" are examples.

The career outcomes of many encounters—job interviews, hearings, dates, play episodes, and so on—influence the subjective social psychological career of the individual and also influence his or her careers within all the other organizational levels.

IMPACT ON THE CHARACTER OF THE INDIVIDUAL

The most direct effects of participation in an encounter are fairly transitory. The focus of the encounter effectively controls what it is that the individual pays attention to, and the boundary rules determine how he perceptually encodes or interprets current stimuli (bottle caps may be temporarily viewed as "checkers" on the "checkerboard" of a tile floor). His allocated role within the encounter temporarily dictates his interests (dropping clothespins into a bottle) and his behaviors (what he says, where he sits, and so on). His role may also affect his appearance and his personal style.

Perhaps central among such transient effects on personal attributes are the effects of participation on the feelings of the individual. His assigned role may lead to varying degrees of bodily engagement, ranging from utter boredom up to total involvement (Goffman, 1961a). More significant, perhaps, are the effects of performed role on the individual's self-feelings. An adequate performance leads to a sense of competence, and a superlative performance may lead to a sense of pride. A poor performance almost invariably results in the disturbing emotions of embarrassment or shame, thoroughly analyzed in a number of studies (Goffman, 1956a; Gross and Stone, 1964; Archibald and Cohen, 1971).

The special linkage between conduct and self-feelings was enunciated by Cooley in his notion of the "looking-glass self": the reactions of other persons are a mirror held up to the individual, reflecting an image of self which he might appraise in much the same fashion as he would appraise another person seen directly.

> A self-idea of this sort seems to have three principal elements: the imagination of our appearance to the other person; the imagination of his judgment of that appearance; and some sort of self-feeling, such as pride or mortification. The comparison with a looking-glass hardly suggests the second element, the imagined judgment, which is quite essential. The thing that moves us to pride or shame is not the mere mechanical reflection of ourselves, but an imputed sentiment, the imagined effect of this imagination upon another's mind. . . . We always imagine, and in imagining share, the judgments of the other mind [Cooley, 1902: 184–185].

Interestingly, the indirect effects of participation in an encounter tend to be more enduring. One's role and one's role-performance within an encounter often affects one's standing within relationships, groups, and larger social organizations. A superlative performance within a single encounter may lead the larger organizations to recognize within the individual previously unsuspected talents and thus may eventuate in a promotion. An embarrassingly deficient or discrepant performance, on the other hand, may seriously diminish the respect, affection, or trust with which one had been regarded and may eventuate in some type of demotion or even expulsion. Indeed, a flagrant violation of situational proprieties may land the individual in jail or in a mental hospital (Goffman, 1963a: 216–241).

Our longer-run social fortunes rest to a very large degree on the course and outcomes of our fleeting encounters.

SUMMARY

An encounter is a bounded and focused episode of direct interaction within a face-to-face gathering of persons in which the participants sustain for a time a single common focus of cognitive and visual attention. An encounter may or may not coincide with the gathering as a whole; gatherings may be unfocused, partly focused, multifocused, or fully focused. Some gatherings (and any included encounters) are officially or unofficially "occasioned" by a higher-level organization, predefining the social situation. Encounters arise in unoccasioned gatherings only through collective negotiation of a "definition of the situation."

In either case, the shared definition of the situation provides the encounter with its focus, its boundaries, and its social objects—defining the nature not only of its setting and props but also of the available social roles and possible events.

By sharing such understandings and interpretations and by sustaining a common focus, participants develop some sense of collectivity and become members of a fleeting social unit. Its human and material resources are restricted to those present in the situation. Its culture is largely created through the definition of the situation, as its "boundary rules" (of irrelevance and of transformation) convert available things and happenings into meaningful objects and events. Encounter-specific meanings of words also evolve, and "situational proprieties" follow from the definition of the situation itself.

The role structure of an encounter is likewise dictated by the definition of the situation. Where the primary social structure is sharply differentiated, dimensional social structures tend to reflect this. Otherwise, the extent and nature of an individual's communication contributions tend to determine his ranking in all the other dimensional structures. Suborganizations in the form of coalitions and "collusive by-plays" are common.

Although an organization in its own right, any encounter is also embedded in a host of higher-level organizations, coloring its character. Encounters are also vital suborganizations within all higher levels, directly though often subversively carrying out much of the collective action of larger organizations. Where encounters are embedded within a group or a relationship, particular care must be taken to distinguish them from the embedding organization. Relations among encounters within the same or adjacent gatherings may take the forms of cooperation, competition, or conflict.

Only in fully focused and occasioned gatherings is recruitment to an encounter truly ascriptive, although in certain circumstances an individual might be effectively

420

"drafted" or expelled. Recruitment into and out of encounters is generally voluntary and almost always selective. Although encounters depend heavily upon higher organizations to provide substantial anticipatory socialization, some direct socialization must often be provided by the encounter itself.

The process of interaction in encounters centers on coordination of members' behaviors so as to sustain the single focus of cognitive and visual attention. The positioning, orientations, and movements of members' bodies mutually adjust, resembling a dance, and numerous features of their vocalizations similarly exhibit rhythmic mutual adjustments. In addition, however, members have special interests in pursuing their personal ends within the arena of the encounter. Innovations often result because such self-strivings upset the boundary rules, that is, the working agreement concerning the identities of the participants. The negotiation of new working agreements marks off successive phases in the collective action of an encounter. Surveillance is virtually complete, yet many discrepant performances are implicitly ratified through procedures for "saving face." Corrective or remedial interchanges are often relied upon both to stigmatize serious violations of situational proprieties and to remedy the affront. Social control tends to be more concerned with remedies, reliefs, and rehabilitation than with punishments or compensations.

The influence of individual tactics in the role-making process is often considerable even in officially occasioned encounters and tends to be very great in unoccasioned encounters, as the participants jointly negotiate a definition of the situation. Individuals do move up and down within the secondary social structures of an encounter—a career of sorts—and initiators, founding members, newcomers, deserters, and the expelled all experience rather different modes of participation.

The most direct effects on the individual are fairly transitory. For a while, membership largely controls the individual's attention, perceptions, interpretations, interests, behaviors, style, and sometimes appearance. The individual's position and role within an encounter particularly influence his feelings of bodily engagement (from boredom to total involvement) and his self-feelings, such as competence, pride, embarrassment, or shame. The special linkage between encounter performance and self-feelings is articulated in Cooley's "looking-glass self." The more enduring effects tend to be indirect, as one's role and role performance within an encounter affect one's standing within a host of higher-level organizations.

SUGGESTIONS FOR ADDITIONAL READING

The foremost student of gatherings and encounters is surely Erving Goffman—a sociological social psychologist of distinctive interests as well as a unique stylist. His analysis of the relations between gatherings and encounters is best presented in *Behavior in Public Places: Notes on the Social Organization of Gatherings* (New York: Free Press, 1963). More detailed accounts of the social organization of encounters are developed in *Encounters: Two Studies in the Sociology of Interaction* (Indianapolis: Bobbs-

Merrill, 1961). The centrality of rituals to encounters is argued at length in *Interaction Ritual: Essays on Face-to-Face Behavior* (Garden City, N.Y.: Doubleday Anchor, 1967) and in *Relations in Public: Microstudies of the Public Order* (New York: Basic Books, 1971).

Less sociological in orientation are those analyses of encounters that focus on the coordination among participants in attempting to keep in step and in tune. Among such works, we particularly recommend Starkey Duncan, Jr., and Donald W. Fiske, *Face-to-Face Interaction* (Hillsdale, N.J.: Lawrence Erlbaum Associates, 1977), and Adam Kendon, Richard M. Harris, and Mary Ritchie Key, eds., *Organization of Behavior in Face-to-Face Interaction* (The Hague: Mouton, 1975). Mark L. Knapp provides a simple but solid review of research on *Nonverbal Communication in Human Interaction,* second edition (New York: Holt, Rinehart, and Winston, 1978).

Conversational encounters have received far more attention than other types and are well represented in the works suggested above. A masterful synthesis of these studies is provided by Erving Goffman, *Forms of Talk* (Philadelphia: University of Pennsylvania Press, 1981). The sociable party as an encounter type has been investigated by David Riesman, Robert Potter, and Jeanne Watson in ''The Vanishing Host'' (*Human Organization,* 1960, 19: 17–27). At the opposite extreme are various work encounters and highly stressful encounters. The gynecological examination represents a combination of both of these and is thoughtfully analyzed in James M. Henslin and Mae A. Biggs, ''Dramaturgical Desexualization: The Sociology of the Vaginal Examination'' (pp. 243–272 in Henslin, editor, *Studies in the Sociology of Sex.* New York: Appleton-Century-Crofts, 1971). A useful point of comparison, similarly emphasizing sustainment of defined realities through rules of irrelevance and transformation, is Fred Davis, ''Deviance Disavowal: The Management of Strained Interaction by the Visibly Handicapped'' (*Social Problems,* 1961, 9: 120–132).

Very large gatherings in public places—''crowds,'' in other words—hold a particularly interesting potential for generating encounters of all sorts, as examined in Stanley Milgram and Hans Toch, ''Collective Behavior: Crowds and Social Movements'' (pp. 507–610 in Gardner Lindzey and Elliot Aronson, editors, *The Handbook of Social Psychology*, 2nd edition, vol. 4, Reading, Mass.: Addison-Wesley, 1969). How a crowd may itself develop a shared definition of the situation—and the sometimes frightening consequences of such development—is brilliantly analyzed in Part Two of Ralph H. Turner and Lewis M. Killian, *Collective Behavior,* 2nd edition (Englewood Cliffs, N.J.: Prentice-Hall, 1972).

PART IV

THE WEB

Photo courtesy of United Nations M. Tzovaras

The modern individual must schedule his or her life to handle many and varied organizational involvements.

CHAPTER 23

The Individual and Organizational Society

The individual person is not a loner, standing at bay against a ring of sullen and opposing social forces—although almost everyone may have a few moments when he or she feels that way. Nor is the individual merely a puppet, dancing to the tune of this or that organizational orchestra—although at one time or another we all have felt the pull of strings held by others. When all the biochemical compounds and social influences have been added together in some grand summation, we have not yet fully accounted for the elusive person—the ''I'' who is the Knower and the Doer. Whatever its full nature may be, the ''I'' demonstrably does not float free. It does its knowing and doing and living within a web of human interdependencies that at once supports and enriches the ''I'' but that also gives rise to its problems. We have plumbed the nature of this web and its social psychological consequences for the individual in the preceding sections of this book. Now we turn to how the person copes with the web of oganized social life—how he manages his roles to reap its benefits without becoming hopelessly entangled in the strands.

The globe is thickly blanketed by a crazy-quilt of millions of densely intersecting, concentric, and coincident social circles, each circle representing the collectivity underlying one of the virtually endless variety of social organizations. Apart from their overlapping memberships, these millions of organizations are also interconnected through webs of functional interorganizational relations of joint actions and cooperation, exchange and dependency, competition and rivalry, conflict and accommodation. Each organization is, after all, the focus of an ''organization set''—those organizations with which it is directly linked in action. Even a small firm or a family is linked, as we have seen, to dozens upon dozens of other organizations, and indirectly with thousands more at all levels. In Chapter 1, we defined Society (in the capital-S sense) as the organized web of social life. At this point, we can refine this concept and regard Society as the loosely coupled and mildly hierarchical organizational network of the planet's millions of social organizations.

In Chapter 4 we set forth the position that each individual plays some kind of role with respect to each of these countless organizations. In the overwhelming majority of cases, these are nonmembership roles, and generally latent roles at that, such as indirect beneficiary or indirect victim. In chained linkages of such indirect organizational influences, recent decades have provided many instances of songs, speeches, and shots that were heard around the world. In a more direct fashion, each individual also performs manifest nonmembership roles—supporter, beneficiary, critic, opponent, or the like—in relation to a very large number of organizations. Finally, at any point in time, the individual performs some sort of membership role within a substantial number and variety of organizations. Quite commonly, an individual is a member of several political jurisdictions, of several social communities and at least one geographic community, of one or more work organizations and occupational associations, of one or more religious, fraternal, or civic associations, of several work, family, and social groups, of numerous social relationships, and of countless encounters. Virtually all of us participate simultaneously in several masses and publics, and many of us in more than one social movement. It is not even uncommon for a person to participate in more than one nation-state, speech community, age-sex structure, or economy.

The essential points here are that (1) each individual plays some type of role relative to every organization; (2) the pattern of roles is unique to the individual; and (3) this pattern of roles evolves continually over time. The manifold implications of these three points and how the individual manages them comprise the subject of this concluding chapter.

Before seeking to develop these implications, we must acknowledge that the countless roles of the individual are not and cannot be entirely independent, since the various organizations comprising Society are not independent but are loosely and hierarchically coupled. This fact sets some limits to the otherwise virtually infinite diversity of roles a person would be involved in.

In the first place, some roles are dependent on other roles of the individual (Banton, 1965). *Basic roles* (age-sex role) determine the individual's eligibility for a great many other roles, such as family and occupational roles; a child cannot be a mother. *General roles,* such as wife or policeman, restrict the individual from entering into certain specifically proscribed roles open to others who share the same basic roles. A cop is not supposed to be a drug pusher or a communist, and a wife is expected not to play the young single looking for a husband. *Independent roles,* such as science-fiction enthusiast or golfer, have few implications for entry into other roles.

Second, many roles neither require nor prohibit, but simply anticipate, that the performer will also be performing another role. For instance, the wife role normally anticipates that the individual will have some cooking role, and the professor role anticipates that the performer will also have some role in a professional association.

Third, in either of these general cases, the expectations comprising such a role will commonly include some restrictions on—or will provide for circumstantial priorities among—certain other roles. The role of federal employee, for example, places restrictions on the extent of one's involvement in certain outside roles, and most work roles contain provisions for temporary leaves of absence under the circumstance of a death in the immediate family.

Fourth, many roles involve the development of personal attributes which are highly transferable to other roles the individual may have, so that managing a multitude of role involvements becomes less difficult. The skills of shopper are fairly easily extended to the role of household finance manager, and an office manager can perform the duties of an association official with relative ease.

However, such routinized accommodative mechanisms only go so far as to set a few limits on what would otherwise be an overwhelming diversity of organizational involvements. They do not go far toward alleviating the widespread competition and conflict among the individual's various remaining role demands. *Competition* between roles occurs when the individual cannot adequately perform both roles because of limitations of time or other individual resources. It is difficult to be a full-time student and mother of a newborn at the same time, or a budding musician and the supporter of a large family. *Conflict* between roles occurs when one role requires behavior that in some degree is incompatible—physically, socially, and/or psychologically—with the behavior required by another role. One cannot be both a thief and a friend toward the same other, nor a priest hearing confessions and a lover. *Role strain*—the experience of competing and conflicting roles—is widespread in modernized societies and has been shown (Kahn et al. 1964) to have a variety of costly consequences for both individuals and organizations. For the individual, role strain leads to intensified internal conflicts, increased tension, reduced satisfaction, and decreased confidence in the organizations involved. For the organizations, this weakening of the bonds of trust, respect, and attraction leads to less effective collective action. Almost by definition, a person caught up in role strain cannot wholeheartedly pursue any course of action and cannot be wholly aligned with any organization.

LOGISTICS: THE SIXTH ORGANIZATIONAL PROCESS

How does any individual or any organization cope with the inescapable fact that every individual performs such a tremendous number and variety of competing and often conflicting roles? The joint process through which individuals and organizations strategically and tactically accommodate the multiple roles of living individuals is one of *logistics*—the balancing and creative managing of the interests and capacities of both individuals and organizations (McCall and Simmons, 1978: 226–251).

By belonging to many organizations, the individual belongs fully to none. This fact virtually guarantees some organizational cross-pressures upon any person but it also puts him or her in a position to play each organization against the others. In Part II, to simplify the analysis of the joint processes through which an individual's organizational role and organizational career are developed, we examined the give-

427

and-take between a single individual and a single organization. More realistically, in Part III, we noted that the nature of an organization is influenced by its interorganizational relations and that the individual is not isolated and naked but rather is socially anchored, simultaneously belonging to a variety of organizations at many different levels constraining him in various directions. Thus, both the individual and the organization have recourse to organizational allies in the role-making and career-development processes of recruitment, socialization, interaction, innovation, and social control.

Logistics is, however, most fundamentally related to the process of interaction, as described in Chapter 7. The reader will recall that, for the individual, interaction is a matter of the pursuit of valued identities and activities within an organizational arena. In reality, no single organizational arena can encompass all of the individual's pursuits; he will perform in numerous such arenas, and in moving from one to another he will bring with him some of his other social roles. Indeed, this intrusion of external roles is one significant factor leading to the inevitable divergence between the role prescribed for him within one arena and his actual pattern of performance there.

From the viewpoint of the individual, then, logistics is a matter of using the whole set of organizational arenas in whatever manner seems best suited to "satisficing" his obligations and his wants. As he looks out upon the incredibly complex organizational mosaic of Society, he may view it as a fabulously rich structure of opportunities; how shall he allocate his scarce resources to maximize (or optimize) the joint activities he might pursue and the personal benefits he may reap? Alternatively, he may view Society as an overwhelming structure of organizational demands; how should he spend his scant resources to avert being sucked dry or being catastrophically bankrupted?

The view of Society as demanding is common even among sociologists. L. A. Coser (1974) speaks of "greedy institutions" and Goode (1960) warns of "role overloads" and widespread role strain. The individual is seen as having scarce resources of time, energy, and sociability, which are in danger of being gobbled up by the incessant demands placed upon him by his many competing and conflicting social organizations at every level.

A contrary view, dating back to Durkheim at the turn of the century, holds that social participation does not so much drain as *expand* one's vital resources. True involvement in a social role may be highly energizing (Goffman, 1961a; Marks, 1977); dog-tired after a long day at work, one may become strikingly revitalized by getting caught up in a totally engaging conversation, game, or argument, for example. Whether a role adds to or subtracts from one's energies largely depends on whether one fully embraces the role or distances oneself from it. More broadly, Sieber (1974) contends that the more roles an individual accumulates, the greater will be his privileges, connections, information, favors receivable, status security, ego gratifications, and enrichment of personality functioning.

Where one's set of roles represents a net drain or a net source of personal vital resources seems to depend upon how well the individual can manage, balance, and integrate those roles (Marks, 1977). The basic life task of the individual is, then, to juggle and adjudicate the various demands placed upon him by his multitudinous organizational roles, through allocating his "capital resources" among alternative opportunities in a way that seems, on balance, most profitable.

From the viewpoint of an organization, the interaction process should constitute collective action producing collective good. The patterns of interaction that do occur, however, may either reflect or contravene the organization's division of labor and therefore facilitate or impede production of the collective good. Given the role accumulations of all its members, the maintenance of some patterned division of labor within its own arena of action becomes problematic. On the other hand, members' external roles may sometimes actually prove useful to the organization's own purposes; a member may develop useful business contacts at the country club or organizationally useful skills through his pursuit of an outside hobby. To the organization, then, logistics is a matter of juggling and adjudicating the demands it places on its individual members in light of their differing external roles. If mother takes on a job outside the home, the family group may need to reduce its domestic demands on her, with other members revamping their family roles to take over some of her chores. Typically, some redistribution of selective sidepayments will be necessary to make such induced role changes stick.

Time—the ultimately limited individual resource—is a fundamental framework for any consideration of logistics. That is, the process assumes a different aspect depending on the span of time over which the process is considered. Logistics for this coming weekend differs markedly from logistics for the next two or three years.

Within the framework of a span measured in years, logistics becomes a matter of *managing individual careers*. The individual's concern is with an orderly and coordinated evolution of his unique pattern of roles in relation to the entire set of organizations so as to come out all right from his own perspective. The location and the timing of his organizational entries and exits, of his organizational ups and downs, must preserve a certain balance if his life course is to be an interpretable and satisfying one (McCall and Simmons, 1978: 200–225; Gordon, 1971). An organization's concern, on this time scale, is with the orderly replacement of its personnel—demoting and moving out those members who are no longer effective and recruiting, developing, and promoting adequate replacements in a process of organized succession (Levenson, 1961). In this flow-through of members, the organization seeks to come out favorably while maintaining a viable exchange and sharing of personnel with a variety of other social organizations.

Within the framework of a span measured, say, in months or weeks, logistics becomes a matter of *managing performed roles*. On this time scale, the concern of the individual is to do the best he can for each of the organizations to which he belongs, to preserve some sense of personal integrity and satisfaction while minimizing the disappointment and unhappiness of those organizations concerning his contributions and performances. An organization's concern here is to extract from within its membership some distribution of performances and contributions sufficient for effective collective action. A satisfactory division of labor must somehow be contrived and sustained in the face of the role overload of all its members, hence, the emphasis on maintaining discrete patterns of interaction that facilitate collective action as described in Chapter 7.

Within the framework of a day or a specific occasion, logistics becomes a matter of the *situational resolution of role-conflict*. Here, the divided loyalties of the individual and the divergent interests of his organizations are revealed most acutely. The individual stands to lose in some way no matter what he does, and at least one organization is also bound to lose. Perhaps because of the heightened drama of logistics within this time frame, much of the sociological literature on role conflict has focused on just this scale.

Extensive Time Spans

Let us first, however, consider the process of logistics as it operates over relatively extensive time spans. Here, the classical tactic for managing strains of competition or conflict between roles is that of *role compartmentalization* or segregation. Often, two incompatible roles may be rather clearly confined to quite separate social arenas, with the result that the inevitable cross-pressures may be more readily overlooked by all concerned. The homosexual schoolteacher, for example, may carefully segregate his sexual role from his occupational role. Efforts will be made to separate these incompatible performances not only temporally and spatially but also interpersonally. Audience segregation is perhaps the most critical dimension of compartmentalization in evading cross-pressures, but a sharp segregation of settings and times also helps the individual to manage or overlook the contradictions in his behaviors. Role segregation is most easily practiced with independent roles since, by definition, they touch least upon other role involvements. Playing with model trains needs never intrude upon a senior executive's "official" role performances.

With or without segregation, *role scheduling* is a major logistical tactic. On no single occasion could all of an individual's roles be performed; she must construct an "agenda" or schedule of performances to provide for the satisfaction of her roles within some appropriate span of time. Long-term agendas may represent life plans or career strategies; a woman may plan, for example, to get married this year, complete her college degree in another two years, then work for three or four years before having a child, and return to the labor force as soon as the child enters school. Nested within these relatively long-term agendas are various shorter-term agendas, covering particular months, weeks, or perhaps only an afternoon or a lunch hour. Of course, an agenda is not entirely an individual matter but must be negotiated with one's various organizations. The demands of highly pervasive roles do not lend themselves to temporal scheduling, and some role demands are very rigidly specified as to the time and place of performance. Nevertheless, many organizational demands can be delayed, stalled, worked around, or worked in largely at the convenience of the individual. Duly established agendas impart some social order in the patterning of interactions, but they are always subject to disruption by various personal and organizational crises (McCall and Simmons, 1978: 244–248). Nevertheless, role scheduling is perhaps the

430

most common means of managing multiple organizational role demands employed by conventional adults in modern societies, and the various organizational levels tend to cooperate with individuals in this as a workable solution. Work shifts, school hours, store hours, family time, and the scheduling of entertainment events, for example, dovetail to facilitate role scheduling for the majority of the populace. (For some provocative discussions of role scheduling in preindustrial, industrial, and postindustrial societies, see Toffler, 1980.)

Role bargaining (Goode, 1960) is a more radical tactic than either of the preceding two in that it does not seek to maintain full performance of all the roles involved but rather seeks to negotiate some compromises in their performances. Any organizational role requires of the individual certain contributions (or costs), to be compensated for by organizationally conferred benefits. Norms of adequacy ("the going role price") define what levels of contributions constitute an adequate performance. Ordinarily, the organization confers rewards for surpassing (and imposes punishments for failing) the going role price. The individual's actual level of performance depends on both his own desire to carry out the performance and his judgment as to how much the organization is likely to punish or reward him for his performance. "It is to the individual's interest in attempting to reduce his role strain to demand as much as he can and perform as little, but since this is also true for others, there are limits on how advantageous a role bargain he can make" (Goode, 1960: 495).

The fact that members belong to a collectivity and manifest at least some commitment, attachment, and interest in its continued welfare also sets some limits on the rapaciousness of role bargaining. For example, most family members will hold themselves back from exploiting the family resources to the point where the family's working social order is destroyed. On the other hand, most organizations contain within their culture some concern for the well-being of their constituent members, which puts some kind of brake on the degree of exploitation. But these constraints set only extreme limits. As we have seen, organizations—from the polity down to the pair relationship—tend toward striving for total commitment, attachment, and involvement from members. Therefore, in order to avoid being engulfed by such pressures, the individual almost inevitably must resort to role bargaining to balance somehow his involvements (and his own desires) with his sweetheart, children, career, hobby interests, and friends.

Both the individual and the organization are to varying degrees dependent on each other; whichever party is more dependent is therefore at a disadvantage in the role-bargaining process and is at risk of exploitation. Other organizations in the network ("third parties" to the transaction) serve an important role in limiting the advantage of any role bargain struck.

> If either [party] is able to exploit the other by driving an especially hard role bargain, such third parties may try to influence either or both to change the relationship back toward the "going role price." Not only do they feel this to be their duty, but they have an interest in the matter as well, since (a) the exploiting [party] may begin to demand that much, or pay that little, in [its] role relations with them; and (b) because the exploiting [party] may thereby perform less well in [its] relations with them. . . .

> For adult or child, the family is the main center of role allocation, and thus assumes a key position in solutions of role strain. Most individuals must account to their families for what they spend in time, energy, and money outside the family . . . family members are often the only persons who are likely to know how an individual is allocating his *total* role energies, managing his whole role system; or that he is spending "too much" time in one role obligation and retiring from others. . . . Consequently, other family members can and do give advice as to how to allocate energies from a "secure center." Thus it is from this center that one learns the basic procedures for balancing role strains [Goode, 1960: 489–490, 493; emphasis in original].

Mention of the parts played by family and other third parties in role bargaining should serve to remind the reader that *collusion*—intermediate organizations "conspiring" with the individual over against the larger organization in question—is a fundamental aspect of the process of logistics. The interests of an individual's many organizations are not identical or even very harmonious. One organization may therefore side with the individual to conceal or to legitimate his performance of his role in some other organization—"covering for" or "speaking up for" the individual. His community colludes with him against societal-level structures, his family colludes with him against his work organization, and his friendship group colludes with him against the demands of his marital relationship. Colluding organizations perform this function for a valued member because the discrepant character of an external role performance is tolerated (if not sponsored) by the intermediate organizations. Such collusion constitutes one of the clearest ways in which an individual can play one organization against another in his logistical struggles. All too often, however, a colluding organization withdraws its support of the individual in a particular struggle—as when the family finally tires of concealing and making excuses for his bizarre behavior and commits him to a mental hospital—leading to a sense of betrayal on the part of the individual (Goffman, 1959a).

This withdrawal of support occurs essentially because the intermediate organization has its own multiplicity of involvements which must be balanced. The family has other members which must be protected, the circle of friends has some concerns for neighborhood or association stability. Some of the most poignant social psychological situations occur when an individual or intermediate organization must choose between spouse and family, career and friend, company and long-term employee, child and country.

Momentary Occasions

Much of the sociological literature on role strain has presumed the narrowest possible time span, namely, a specific occasion. Within such a compressed time span, the more extended tactics of segregation, scheduling, and role bargaining are necessarily inapplicable. Given the highly restricted resources available for a single occasion, very few of an individual's multitudinous roles can be enacted. Logistics here comes down virtually to a matter of *role choice.* But role choice is problematic to the individual in a large percentage of situations.

432

The Individual and Organizational Society

To most sociologists, an individual's choices of which role(s), within a set of competing or conflicting roles, shall be performed on a single occasion is considered to be determined by his reference groups (see Chapter 2). A military chaplain, for example, must at times decide whether to perform the role of a military officer or the role of a man of the cloth (Burchard, 1954). His choice may be expected to reflect his differential identification with army and with church (Ehrlich, Rinehart, and Howell, 1962).

Such differential identification is likely to be mirrored in the very structure of the self. As noted in Chapter 2, an individual's role-identities are arranged in a rather stable hierarchy of prominence and in a more fluid hierarchy of salience. In a situational conflict of roles, the role identity of greater prominence is more likely to be performed. In a situational competition of roles, the role-identity of greater salience is more likely to be performed. On specific occasions, the individual will often simply make a role choice on the basis of expediency. He or she may, for example, perform a role which is neither very salient nor prominent in order to be sociable with a spouse's parents.

The necessity of situational role choice is perhaps overestimated. The conduct of an individual in any single situation always involves the performance of more than one organizational role; that is, actual performances are always relevent to, if not motivated by, several of the individual's many prescribed roles. Logistics here becomes a matter of how best to blend and compromise these several roles in one performance. But again, this decision is not strictly individual, for both identities and lines of action must be negotiated with the other persons present in the situation (see Chapter 2). Such negotiations are particularly delicate when the performer's audience includes persons calling for quite divergent roles (McCall and Simmons, 1978: 159–160).

However, millions of individuals across the planetary field daily manage such interwoven performances as a kind of living tribute to the capabilities of a well-socialized human being. A running sequence of such performances is essentially the individual's responsive management of his multiple role involvements in the social web.

IMPACT OF LOGISTICS

The joint process of personal and organizational logistics shapes the individual's pattern of roles. In Part III, we examined the separate impact of particular types of roles on the character of the individual. We saw there that each role calls for him or her to become a specific kind of person, to manifest some characteristic profile of individual attributes expected of any person performing that role. Here, we strive to discern the impact of the uniquely patterned *set* of roles.

One such impact on individual character has already been mentioned. The degree to which a person is characteristically zestful and energetic, on the one hand, or harried and drained, on the other, depends in good part upon the logistical success he has in integrating his multiple roles (Marks, 1977). If well-integrated, his uniquely patterned set of roles should prove socially energizing without excessive demands upon his time and commitments; if conflicting and compartmentalized, his set of role demands of time and commitment may drain his fund of energy, spontaneity, and sociability.

But what might we expect regarding his other specific personal attributes? If each of his roles and identities calls for him to be some particular kind of person, what kind shall he actually be?

Some of his roles may compete or even conflict. The characteristic profiles of individual attributes associated with his various roles are, then, not entirely consistent and may sometimes be violently contradictory. We may expect, therefore, that the pattern of individual attributes manifested by any person over a series of occasions is unlikely to prove altogether consistent or stable. However, we can expect that the frequency with which the person displays various attributes (and sets of attributes) over any span of time is not utterly random and haphazard but instead reflects the individual's pattern of roles, as shaped through the process of logistics. That is to say, we do expect an individual to reveal some genuine character—some distinctive statistical regularity in individual attributes—stemming from the unique patterning of his multitudinous roles.

One aspect of a role pattern is its degree of cohesiveness or integration. Some roles, for example, may be tightly compartmentalized from others. If so, on those occasions when he performs the compartmentalized role, we may expect the individual's profile of attributes to vary sharply from his usual profile. In extreme cases of compartmentalization or dissociation of roles, the individual seems like two different persons—Dr. Jekyll and Mr. Hyde or the psychiatric phenomenon of "multiple personality."

Of course, some attributes or patterns of attributes are more persistent or stable than others. In some cases, this effect is due to the respective natures of the various roles themselves. For example, an attribute expected in a basic role is likely to be manifested more frequently than one expected in a general role or in an independent role. Similarly, an attribute expected in a highly pervasive role should be manifested more frequently than one expected in some less pervasive role.

Yet, beyond these structural factors pertaining to particular roles, the unique role pattern of an individual exerts its own effects on the frequency distribution of his various personal attributes by way of his prominence hierarchy of role-identities (see Chapter 2). The relative prominence of a given role-identity within the self-structure of an individual is a weighted function of the average past levels of its degrees of social support, of self-support, of commitment to it, of investment in it, of extrinsic gratifications received through it, and of intrinsic gratifications received through its performance (McCall and Simmons, 1978: 74–79; see also Turner, 1978 and Stryker, 1980). The more prominent a role-identity (that is, the more important it is to the individual's self-conception), the more likely it is to be performed *on any occasion*.

Certain roles, of course, by their very nature, are of relatively great prominence for any performer (Turner, 1978). The prominence-generating factors of commitment and investment, for example, are for most individuals virtually built into the nature of certain roles—basic roles such as wife or Moslem, and pervasive roles such as doctor or professional artist. Similarly, certain roles by their nature tend to imply relatively

The Individual and Organizational Society

high levels of support and/or of gratifications. For example, any role that ranks high within the dimensional social structures of an organization (organizational centrality, status, authority, power, leadership, affect) could be expected to carry with it relatively high levels of social and self-support for its performance and of extrinsic and intrinsic gratifications.

Nevertheless, none of the factors underlying the prominence of role-identities in the individual's hierarchy is wholly determined by structural features of the roles alone. Individuals have been shown (Rohrer and Edmonson, 1960; Stryker, 1980) to vary widely, for instance, in their degrees of commitment even to roles that are basic, pervasive, and highly restrictive, such as their age-sex roles. Investments, too, vary widely; some individuals put much more of themselves into the same basic role, such as father. Social support is very much a matter of perception, and self-support rests heavily on self-confidence and level of aspiration; many acclaimed performers consider themselves to be dismal failures. As for extrinsic and intrinsic gratifications, the reward value of any received benefit is both notoriously subjective and very relative—relative, that is, to costs, to alternative benefits, to desires and expectations, and to present holdings. To make a long story short, the prominence of a given role-identity for a particular individual cannot be safely inferred from knowledge of the structural features of that role. Prominence is instead an individual matter, resting on that person's own subjective reckoning of the six underlying factors. Thus, we are not surprised that the role-identity of father is highly prominent for one individual but not for another. The prominence of a role-identity reflects not the nature of the role but rather the logistical role pattern of the individual—the pattern of role bargains he has struck.

The frequency with which a person displays a given attribute is also affected by the contents of his corresponding role-identity. In an important sense, a person performs not a social role but a role-identity. A role-identity, again, is the way the individual has come to think of himself as an occupant of a given organizational position. Each such ''mask'' is ''bent'' a bit to achieve a better fit among them as a set adapted to his own performer characteristics and his own set of audiences. Role-identities are rather idiosyncratic and somewhat idealized conceptions of self that almost inevitably diverge somewhat from the kind of person called for by the social role itself. Through the juggling and adjudicating process of logistics, the contents of the individual's many roles become somewhat altered as a result of compromises and mutual accommodations. Accordingly, the contents of one's many role-identities are adaptively modified in a sort of contextual effect. The role-identity of Sunday-school teacher, for example, might be expected to differ between two performers, one of whom doubles as hockey coach while the other doubles as counselor. Even when performing the role of Sunday-school teacher, the coach might be expected to use language more action-oriented than that of the counselor.

Finally, the attributes an individual displays on any specific occasion depend significantly on situational factors. One of these is salience hierarchy of role-identities (see Chapter 2). Aside from the influence of prominence, the relative salience of various role-identities depends on their momentary need for support, on the person's

435

momentary needs or desires for the kinds and amounts of intrinsic and extrinsic gratifications usually obtained through their respective performances, and on the person's perceived degrees of opportunity for their respective profitable enactments in the present circumstances (McCall and Simmons, 1978: 79–84). However, even a role-identity that is temporarily salient may not be performed, since the identities and the lines of action of all persons present in the situation must be collectively negotiated through the process of interaction. It remains worth noting, though, that the various factors underlying the salience hierarchy of role-identities—momentary needs and momentary opportunities—are the very stuff of logistical allocations.

The character of the individual (that is, the relative frequency with which he or she displays various individual attributes) greatly reflects his or her unique pattern of roles, as shaped by the logistics process. Career-scale logistics alters not only the roles one performs—adding, dropping, and changing roles—but also the prominence hierarchy of one's role-identities (McCall and Simmons, 1978: 200–225; Gordon, 1976). Role-scale logistics are most closely relevant to empirical studies of individual character (Fiske, 1971), for here the role pattern and the prominence hierarchy of role-identities are reasonably constant. Situation-scale logistics are commonly viewed as nuisance factors contributing error variance to studies of character, since the salience hierarchy and the interactional structure of encounters are more fluid and unpredictable.

THE INDIVIDUAL IN RELATION TO SOCIETY

We return now to the basic question defining sociological social psychology: what is the nature of the relation between the individual and Society? With respect to the *content* of this relation, we have seen here that each individual stands in a different relation to Society, in that his or her pattern of roles is unique. In terms of the *form* of the relation, however, the relation of all individuals to Society is essentially similar.

In Chapter 1, we argued the utility of a twofold strategy of (1) analyzing Society—the web of organized social life in general—into its variety of component social organizations; and (2) examining the relation between the individual and each of these component social organizations. In Chapter 4, we stated three general principles which, taken together, express the form of that relation:

1. The character of the individual's organizational role affects both the character of the individual and the character of the organization.
2. The character of social process (the basic organizational processes of recruitment, socialization, interaction, innovation, and social control) determines the nature of individuals' organizational roles.
3. The character of the individuals and the character of the organization jointly affect the character of social process.

The conjoint operation of these principles was displayed in Figure 4–1, elaborated in Part II, and applied in Part III to a variety of discrete organizational levels.

The Individual and Organizational Society

If, now, we were to replace in the diagrammatic sketch of Figure 4–1 the term "social organization" with the term "Society," what other revisions would be required in order for that sketch to depict the nature of the relation between the individual and Society?

First, we should have to redefine those elements that were displayed in the rectangular boxes: Society, Individual, Social Process. Society, of course, would be taken to mean the loosely coupled, mildly hierarchical network of all the social organizations operating at that point in history. The individual would be construed as socially anchored in a variety of social organizations at that point, not as an isolated human being facing his fellows in some Hobbesian state of nature. Social process would now be taken to mean the joint process of logistics—the give-and-take between individuals and the multitude of structurally and operationally cross-linked social organizations—through which role demands are juggled and adjudicated. (This process of logistics does not so much replace as incorporate the five basic organizational processes, since logistics is a matter of balancing the recruitment, socialization, interaction, innovation, and social control processes of one organization against the similar processes of other organizations.)

Second, we should have to redefine that element which in Figure 4–1 was displayed within the elliptical box as the immediate product of social process. That is, the term "organizational role" must be replaced with the term "pattern of roles." All of these revisions are displayed in Figure 23–1.

Finally, the three basic principles of Chapter 4 would have to be restated to reflect the various sets of causal arrows shown in Figure 23–1.

1. The character of the individual's unique pattern of roles affects both the character of the individual and the character of Society.

FIGURE 23-1. Role Pattern as Key Linkage among Individual, Society, and Social Process

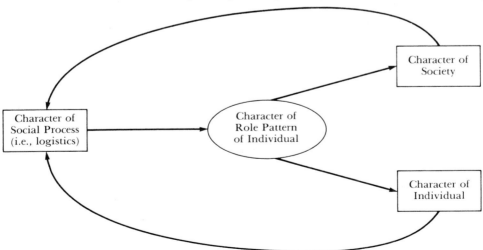

437

2. The character of social process (logistics) determines the unique nature of individuals' patterns of roles.

3. The character of the individuals and the character of Society jointly affect the character of social process (logistics).

As emphasized throughout Parts II and III, a diagram of this type depicts an endlessly looping system. As the system continues to cycle through time, the character of each of the four elements changes; their characters *evolve* jointly. For example, as any one of the four elements becomes more or less complex (or hierarchical, or integrated), so do all the others.

Such reciprocity between self and society is a fundamental sociological tenet. As Cooley noted long ago, the individual and Society are twin-born, two sides of the coin of social process. Simmel maintained that social process eventuates in a unique pattern of organizational affiliations for every person (and thus confers individuality). Mead attempted to show that social process is shaped through the give-and-take between individual impulse and Society. Park held that the individual's conception of his role in Society provided the key to the individual's participation in that social process.

What we have attempted in this book is, first, to clarify and further specify the meaning of these rough concepts. We have sought to illuminate the social organizational character of Society, the dramaturgical character of the individual, the multiplex and multilevel character of social process, and the negotiated character of social roles and role patterns. Second, we have tried to spell out more precisely and more explicitly the manner in which these classical principles combine systematically to depict the nature of the relation between individual and Society. Third, we have drawn on the results of an awesome variety of empirical sociological studies in an attempt to demonstrate the scientific soundness and utility of such a distinctively sociological social psychology. During an era in which psychological social psychologists have been evincing a heightened interest in the methods and insights of sociology, a renewed statement of the underlying sociological tradition may prove timely and useful to both scientific communities.

Our endorsement of Cooley's statement that the individual and Society are two sides of the same coin is not, of course, a naïve assertion that individuals are somehow "meant to be" reflected bits of the web, nor that Society is simply an idea and only persons are real. The important point is that *both* the self and Society are a bona fide reality. To posit selves without Society would be impossible—this would be the extreme case of feral man. To posit society without selves is equally impossible. To posit that self and Society are simply the same is never to have walked through the streets of the world. And to posit selves separated from or inevitably against Society is to deny the demonstrable overlappings and intertwinings of these two realities. Even those who live most outside the social mainstream display this heritage (Simmons, 1969). Developed individuals come about only in developed societies, and fulfillment does not go to those who shrink from the social process. Through taking on any role, the individual acquires character and identity and becomes a person—a social self. By accumulating roles, the person gains increased resources, privileges, security, and enrichment of character.

The Individual and Organizational Society

Selves exist *with* Society, and this relationship is simply variable. We have seen that the individual and each of the organizational levels represents an emergent reality of its own, and that any of these levels may be in mutual action or conflict with any of the others under given circumstances. There is a kind of "check and balance" among these levels that sets limits upon the encroachments of any level onto the others. A societal-level structure will intervene with suborganizations that are grossly out of alignment, and individuals will gather—through a diffuse collectivity—to "readjust," say, a polity that has become too onerous in their eyes. This balancing is not an automatic process and it does not prevent some tragedies from occurring, yet such mutual constraints discernibly serve to keep selves and societies *with* one another.

Social reality is thus multilayered. Only feral men confront the physical world directly; no developed self ever confronts only another human being—or any other type of "thing"—but always also the various social objects and social realities there sponsored by at least several organizational levels. If one's organizational loyalties are divided, these sponsored realities will be experienced as conflicting; it will seem unclear what kind of person one is. But to the well-integrated self—a person who has successfully managed the logistics of multiple roles—the multilayering of social reality lends a deep richness of meaning to experience and an expanded range of possibilities in plotting his course of actions.

In our examination of the individual's social character and his or her relationship with the organizational web, we have not presumed to tell the full story of a human being. There is still the "I"—the active creative agent operating behind the screen of social presentations, impingements, and appointments. Two "I's" wrote this book and an "I" is reading it.

There might be still other things involved in the human story. In *Star Wars*, the computer weaponry had failed to destroy the Imperial base, and time was running out. As doom approached, the disembodied voice of Kenobi tells young Luke to use the Force, and audiences around the globe came to their feet and cheered as he succeeded. It might well be that Mead and Cooley would also have cheered had they been there. However that may be, a responsive chord was struck with a multitude of moviegoers who made the film the number one box-office hit of all time.

Without becoming mystical, however, an important point stands out from this fictional scene: a feral man would never have been able to handle the Force. Within the movie, we find our six basic organizational processes in full play, a vast organizational web—encompassing a number of well-established cultures, polities, economies, speech communities, age-sex structures, social movements, bureaucracies, groups, a wealth of pair relationships and encounters—and logistics problems aplenty. Without all these threads, the final occasion could never have occurred. At most, there might instead have been a nature film about brutes in the forests. For now, perhaps, we can know about the "I" only by its traces, much as we perceive the passage of a rocket by the trail it leaves behind. The exploration of this question lies above and beyond the scope of the present book. Perhaps the reader will have his or her own adventures in this realm—but he or she will certainly do so as a social being, one fully caught up in The Web.

439

SUMMARY

Society, in the sense of the organized web of social life in general, is the loosely coupled and mildly hierarchical network of the planet's millions of social organizations of various levels of scope. Each individual plays some role—membership or nonmembership, manifest or latent—in relation to each of these many organizations. Some of his roles will themselves be interrelated in one or more ways, yet the pattern of roles is unique to the individual and evolves continually over time.

Competition between roles occurs when the individual, because of limitations of time or other personal resources, cannot adequately perform both roles. Conflict between roles occurs when one role requires behavior incompatible with the behavior required by another role. Role strain—the experience of competing and conflicting roles—has adverse consequences for both the individual and the organizations.

Through the joint process of logistics—the balancing and creative management of the interests and capacities of both individuals and organizations—persons and their organizations each make some accommodations to the multiple roles of individuals. To an organization, concerned to maintain some effective division of labor in its collective action, logistics involves adjusting the demands it places on its members in view of their differing external roles. To the individual, concerned with pursuing personal interests, logistics is a matter of using the whole set of organizational arenas in some manner best suited to "satisficing" both his obligations and his wants, by juggling and adjudicating the various role demands placed upon him. He may view Society as a rich structure of opportunities to be maximized or as an overwhelming structure of demands to be minimized. Whether one's set of roles represents a net source or a net drain of personal resources depends on how well one can manage, balance, and integrate one's many roles.

The logistics process presents three faces, depending on the span of time over which it is viewed. Over years, logistics is a process of managing individual careers. Over months or weeks, it is a process of managing performed roles. Within a day or an occasion, logistics is a matter of the situational resolution of role conflict.

The major logistical tactics over relatively extensive time spans include role compartmentalization, role scheduling, role bargaining, and collusion. Within the very narrow time span of a specific occasion, the principal logistical tactic is role choice, as influenced by the individual's reference groups and hierarchies of role-identities—both prominence hierarchy (in situations of role conflict) and salience hierarchy (in situations of role competition). Role choice can often be avoided through the blending and compromising of plural roles into a single performance.

Over and above the separate influences of each of the individual's roles upon one's character, there are distinct influences of the unique patterning of one's set of roles. For example, the degree of integration of those roles affects how zestful or how harried and drained one characteristically is and how stable one's character is—the consistency with which one displays various individual attributes and sets of attributes over a series of occasions. Some attributes of character are more persistent or stable than others, owing both to the structural features of certain roles themselves and to the contents and prominence of one's various role-identities. By shaping the individual's unique pattern of roles, the logistics process shapes one's character.

The basic question defining sociological social psychology concerns the nature of the relation between the individual and Society. In content, each individual stands in a different relation to Society, in that his pattern of roles is unique. In form, however, the relation of all individuals to Society is essentially similar, as depicted in Figure 23-1. The character of the individual's unique pattern of roles affects both his own character and that of Society. The character of social process (logistics) determines the unique nature of individuals' patterns of roles. The character of the individuals and that of Society jointly affect the character of social process (logistics). The system of Figure 23-1 is an endlessly looping one, so that over time the character of social process, of unique role patterns, of individuals, and of Society evolve jointly—reflecting the fundamental sociological tenet of reciprocity between self and society.

SUGGESTIONS FOR ADDITIONAL READING

The logistics of personal identity are explored in Chapter 9 of our earlier book, *Identities and Interactions: An Examination of Human Associations in Everyday Life,* revised edition (New York: Free Press, 1978), from which we have drawn substantially in the present chapter.

The "scarcity of resources" viewpoint in logistics is classically developed in William J. Goode, "A Theory of Role Strain" (*American Sociological Review,* 1960, 25: 483–496) and in Lewis Coser's *Greedy Institutions* (New York: Free Press, 1974). The concept of a "limited fund of sociability" is advanced in Joel I. Nelson, "Clique Contacts and Family Orientations" (*American Sociological Review,* 1966, 31: 663–672).

Such a "scarcity" viewpoint is vigorously criticized and qualified in Stephen R. Marks, "Multiple Roles and Role Strain: Some Notes on Human Energy, Time and Commitment" (*American Sociological Review,* 1977, 42: 921–936), and in Sam D. Sieber, "Toward a Theory of Role Accumulation" (*American Sociological Review,* 1974, 39: 567–578). The idea of a limited fund of sociability is critically evaluated in Robert S. Weiss, "Materials for a Theory of Social Relationships" (pp. 154–163 in Warren G. Bennis, Edgar H. Schein, Fred I. Steele, and David E. Berlew, eds., *Interpersonal Dynamics,* revised edition, Homewood, Ill.: Dorsey Press, 1968).

Time-budgets, or how people actually make use of the resource of time in their logistical tactics, are extensively studied in Alexander Szalai, editor, *The Use of Time* (The Hague: Mouton, 1973). More prescriptive analyses of individual tactics in the logistics process are fairly abundant in the popular self-help literature; a representative example is Alan Lakein's *How to Get Control of Your Time and Your Life* (New York: Wyden, 1973).

The management of multiple careers of the individual is usefully examined in Rhona and Robert Rapaport, *Dual-Career Families* (London: Penguin Books, 1971). Role strain and its management are cogently analyzed in Chapter 13 and 14 of Paul F. Secord and Carl W. Backman's *Social Psychology,* 2nd edition (New York: McGraw-

Hill, 1974). A case study in point is one of male students slinging hash in sorority kitchens: Louis P. Zurcher, David W. Sonenschein, and Eric L. Metzner, "The Hasher: A Study of Role Conflict" (*Social Forces*, 1966, 44: 505–514).

The classic analysis of individual character as influenced by multiple roles is, of course, Georg Simmel's essay on the web of group affiliations, to be found in his book *Conflict and the Web of Group Affiliations* (New York: Free Press, 1955). Virtually all of our own *Identities and Interactions*, mentioned above, is devoted to understanding the implications for self of multiple roles. Similar views of the self as hierarchical arrangements of multiple role-identities are developed in Ralph H. Turner, "The Role and the Person" (*American Journal of Sociology*, 1978, 84: 1–23) and in Sheldon Stryker, *Symbolic Interactionism: A Social Structural Version* (Menlo Park, Calif.: Benjamin/Cummings, 1980).

Finally, an excellent empirical study of the nature and effects of individuals' differential identification with their various social roles—over a twenty-year span from childhood—is John H. Rohrer and Munro S. Edmonson, *The Eighth Generation: Cultures and Personalities of New Orleans Negroes* (New York: Harper & Row, 1960).

Glossary

Prepared by Nola Simmons

accommodation Actions to reduce conflicts and promote mutual easing of tensions; a mutually acceptable compromise.

affect The degree to which one is liked or disliked, based on the perceived extent to which one's attributes and/or actions contribute to the individual, special interests of the members of an organization.

age-sex role Role conventionally performed by occupants of a given category in an age-sex structure. These roles tend to be basic and pervasive.

age-sex structure A collectivity structured by a particular system of social positions and social roles based on the individual attributes of age and sex, and organized to produce that collective good termed social order.

altercasting An individual's performance that not only expresses an image of who he is, but also expresses an image of who he takes others to be.

anticipatory socialization An individual's indirect acquisition of beliefs about what life is like as a member of a given organization or as an occupant of a certain type of organizational position, before one actually becomes a member of that organization or attains that position.

argot Special vocabulary employed by a deviant community reflecting its particular culture.

ascriptive recruitment Membership "rights" to an individual held by an organization (and/or vice versa), which may be backed by "legitimate" force or threats.

association A designed, special-purpose organization: bureaucracies, total institutions, voluntary associations. Although often referred to as "formal organizations," "complex organizations," or "large-scale organizations," associations actually vary widely on such organizational dimensions.

association, voluntary An association that may have a few salaried functionaries but is numerically dominated by unpaid voluntary members: local churches, charitable service organizations, and lodges.

443

GLOSSARY

attachment   Building of specific others into the very contents of a person's role-identities.

attraction   The process of generating a set of membership alternatives. Essentially, each party seeks to make its favorable features widely known so as to stimulate an appreciable number of applicants or offers.

audience   Relevant others viewing a role performance and evaluating it.

authority   The ability to influence others through the rights normatively invested in one's position in the organization structure.

band   Local group of families engaging in some collective enterprises with episodic leadership.

bargaining   Negotiation of mutual exchanges based upon the cost/benefit calculations of each participant.

basic role   Role determining the individual's eligibility for a great many other roles.

behavior coordination   Joint venture in which each performer chooses on the basis of the joint consequences of their respective actions, conferring (rather than bargaining) on joint alternatives.

boundary rules   Working agreement concerning the identities of the participants in an encounter.

bureaucracies   Those associations in which a significant proportion of the membership receives a salary or wages for organizational participation. Such organizations display rigorous authority structures and elaborate rules and regulations, and are job-oriented.

by-plays   Actions by members who pursue either a special-interest position on the focus of an encounter or private interests of their own outside the focus.

career   The sequence of organizational positions and corresponding roles held by an individual.

centrality   The degree of participation and the extent to which a member is an "insider" in an organization.

centralization   The degree to which authority is confined to the highest vertical ranks (as in the "corporate" type of association) rather than in the lower ranks (as in the "federative" type).

ceremonies   Occasions on which a number of rituals are performed that function in part as rites of solidarity, exalting the sense of collectivity.

character of the individual   The consensually arrived-at identity and meaning of the individual in any given situation and the relative frequency with which he displays various individual attributes.

character of a social organization   The pattern of basic attributes of an organization such as size, degree of internal differentiation, culture, resources, and aims.

character of social process   The nature of the recruitment, socialization, interaction, innovation, and social control processes as they form a pattern in any given social situation.

clan   Unilineal-descent kinship group.

coalitions   Factions temporarily joining together in pursuit of a shared interest or aim.

cognitive processes   The individual's imputation of roles to others and improvisation of a role for himself, having to do with judging the meaning of those key "things" in a situation that are the participants themselves.

collective action   A joint or social act required in order to produce a collective good; a sharing in the costs of production proportional to one's share in the collective good. To bring about collective action, selective sidepayments are ordinarily necessary.

collective effort   Joint action in the pursuit of a collective good.

444

Glossary

collective good Any good that, if any one person benefits from it, cannot feasibly be withheld from at least some other persons. A pure collective good is one from which all of its consumers receive exactly equal benefits.

collective interest An interest that can be enjoyed by one person without necessarily diminishing the enjoyment of that interest by others.

collectivity A set of persons sharing the sense of participating in a joint venture.

commitment Obligation to perform one's agreed-upon role in a relationship.

community A subsocietal-level collectivity providing the basic conditions and institutions of a common life, within which a member may conduct virtually all his life activities and social relationships.

competing interest Interest held by several members in the same limited good.

complementary interests Unlike but reciprocal and thus mutually beneficial interests.

confederacy A polity linking several tribes and thus containing more than one speech community.

conflicting interests Those interests that are such that if the interest of one member is satisfied, the interest of another member cannot be satisfied in any large degree.

conformity The extent to which individuals conform to the norms of the organizations.

congruent interests Interests in which each party finds the other either (1) desirable, resulting in a "superior deal"; (2) acceptable, resulting in a "standard deal"; or (3) undesirable, resulting in "no deal."

consensual meaning Meaning agreed upon by the participants in a particular situation.

continuing socialization The process of socialization that occurs during the course of an individual's continued participation in any organization.

countermovement A social movement springing up to oppose the aims and programs of another social movement. Any major social movement will create some countermovement sentiments within the larger embedding organization.

crescive norms Norms that emerge through members' interactions and come to be discovered only collectively. The category includes internally emergent customs, mores, and conventions.

cultural objects Objects central to the culture of any organization and used in rituals and ceremonies (flags, seals, uniforms).

culture The aggregate of shared meanings, norms, rituals, and traditions among the membership of an organization.

culture and personality approach Attempts to show how the culture of a "national society" produces in its members a "typical personality" or a "national character."

custom Any norm coming down from the past that regulates fairly fundamental forms of behavior, such as the sexual or racial division of labor, the timing of life rhythms, and the use of ceremony or ritual.

definition of the situation The meaning or significance of a given situation arrived at through negotiation and conferral among the participants; a working agreement in which the expressive processes of one party are in rough agreement with the cognitive processes of the other and vice versa.

GLOSSARY

diffuse collectivities   The organizations of greatest scope within societal-level structures, large in both membership size and geographical extent but of variable duration and characterized by mostly indirect interaction among members: masses, publics, social movements.

dimensional social structure   Evaluative rank-ordering of individuals along interpersonal social dimensions: power structure, status structure, communication structure, authority structure, leadership structure, affect structure, and conformity structure.

division of labor   The pattern of interdependent positions within an organization; the structure of internal positions coordinated for collective action to produce collective goods.

dyad   An interpersonal relationship or two-person group, formal or informal, primary or secondary, displaying many of the characteristics of a larger group but necessarily ending by the departure of a single member.

economic rationality   The optimization of a set of wants in the face of finite resources.

economy   A societal-level collectivity organized to produce and distribute goods and services.

elite strategy   The tactic by which an organization seeks to recruit members of high societal prestige.

embedded organization   Organization that is nested within (and may be structurally part of) a higher-level organization.

enacted norms   Norms that are deliberately created by explicit collective decision (a law or regulation).

encounter   A bounded and focused episode of direct interaction within a face-to-face gathering of persons in which the participants sustain for a time a single common focus of attention; the fundamental unit of collective action and, therefore, the basic building block for organizations of larger scope; the organization inherent in a direct face-to-face engagement between persons.

expressive processes   The communication of identities through selective presentation of self and altercasting.

externally imposed innovation   An innovation imposed on the organization by the actions of other organizations in its environment.

extrinsic gratification   Gratifications outside of benefits inherent in the role performance itself; pay for a job completed.

faction   Set of individuals pursuing their own special interests and partisan positions within an organization.

fad   Change in taste in some sense relatively isolated, socially and/or culturally.

fashion   The mechanism for establishing new norms regulating matters of taste.

feral   Having had little or no ordinary human socialization.

formalization   The degree to which organizational features are recognized, referred to, and understood by the membership in a standard and uniform manner.

formalized roles   Expectations written down in a manual of procedures or in job descriptions.

functional boundaries   Demarcations between functionally distinct divisions, departments, or other official suborganizations within an organization.

gathering   All those persons who are present together in a single social situation.

general role   Role restricting the individual from entering into certain roles open to others sharing the same ''basic'' roles.

Glossary

geographic community   A community that emerges when a number of individuals become aware that their respective home ranges (territory) are substantially similar, that they share "the basic conditions of a common life."

grass-roots strategy   The tactic by which an organization seeks to obtain the largest possible number of members.

group   A small organization (having from three or four members up to around forty) with rather generalized purposes and functions.

group cohesiveness   Tendency of members to remain in a group.

group tradition   Degree to which role differentiation rests on customary, implicit, and often almost historically accidental division of labor.

hierarchical boundaries   Boundaries separating the various vertical organization ranks and filtering individuals in terms of attributes such as seniority, merit, personal characteristics, and types of attitudes held.

hierarchy of prominence   The ranking of role-identities in terms of personal importance to the individual.

hierarchy of salience   The ranking of role-identities on the basis of situational factors.

human nature   "Sentiments and traits acquired through interaction with significant others" (Cooley). Human nature is not inherent in the individual specimen of *Homo sapiens* but is somehow brought about in him through social processes within social organizations.

human resources   The number, capabilities, and degree of participation of an organization's members.

"I"   The self as subject; the essentially unknowable active agent of the personality which does the thinking, the knowing, the planning, the acting; the active creative agent operating behind the screen of social presentations, impingements, and appointments.

idiolect   Each speaker's language, unique in detail.

impulse   Plan of action constructed out of bits and pieces of plans left lying around by the culture, fitted together in endless combinations of the larger patterns and motifs which the culture presents as models.

inclusion boundaries   Boundaries marking off the inner from the outer circles. Filtering criteria may change as one gets closer to the inner core of the organization.

independent roles   Roles having few implications for entry into other roles.

individual   A human being who is socially anchored in a web of social organizations.

individual good   Any good that when consumed by one person cannot be consumed by another.

inducements   Extra benefits offered to persuade a person to participate in an organization or offered to persuade an organization to permit a person's participation in it.

influentials   Fashion leaders, opinion leaders, etcetera, who selectively relay some of the digested information from the mass media to those associates who respect their specialized competencies and judgments.

initial-entry socialization   Intensive socialization, implicit or explicit, upon entry of an organization.

innovation   That organizational process through which individuals' participation in an organization is altered. Innovations are always "sponsored" by some member or suborganization.

institutional personality   Personality adopted when a person comes to feel security and comfort in regimented life (total institutions) and in fact feels bereft without it.

447

GLOSSARY

institutionalized group A group in which membership is not assigned (although it may be officially regulated or certified) and in which the aspect of collectivity outweighs the aspect of structure. Organizational positions within the group may be formally defined and allocated, although the corresponding roles are largely unofficial and informally worked out through interaction of the members. The family is the foremost such group.

institutionalized relationship A relationship in which membership is not officially assigned (though it may be officially certified) and in which positions are officially allocated but roles are worked out in interaction. Marriage is an example.

interaction The organizational process through which an individual's organizational participation is implemented; the process of jointly negotiating the identities, or personal characters, of the interactants and the particulars of their individual lines of action, and of carrying out the activity.

interactive role In a joint act, the role and the actual conduct of each party depends on the role and conduct of the other party.

interest group An association formed around a strong collective interest, promoting issues and striving to influence the resulting publics in line with the group's program for social change.

internally emergent innovations Innovations that develop, unplanned, through apparently ordinary interactions among members as they strive to carry out their organizational and personal roles.

internally planned innovations Those innovations planned internally at the organization level itself.

intrinsic gratifications Gratifications inherent in a role performance itself.

investment Resource expenditures put into a relationship.

issue A matter of shared concern to a public pertaining to an organizational decision to be made about which members feel they have the right to disagree.

jobs The roles in a bureaucracy; specified patterns of activity for which the performer is financially compensated by the association.

kinship structure A collectivity defined by a shared sense of interrelatedness through blood ties of descent from specific common ancestors and/or through the ties of intermarriage.

latent social roles Potential but not yet energized or enacted roles of an individual.

laws Formalized enacted norms central to the culture of a polity. Civil laws are enacted to regulate conduct in such a way as to prevent certain harms to the special interests of individuals and organizations. Criminal laws are enacted to prevent certain harms to the collective interests of the entire membership. Law can be said to reflect the values, attitudes, and customs of the polity.

leadership The prevailing mode of influence in an organization; the performance of key acts that advance collective action or enhance the sense of collectivity.

like interests Essentially parallel personal interests, the cooperative pursuit of which may prove mutually beneficial in varying degree to the members.

logistics The balancing and creative management of the interests and capacities of both individuals and organizations, as well as of the recruitment, socialization, interaction, innovation, and social control processes of an individual or organization.

looking-glass self A metaphor for the reactions of other persons as a mirror held up to the individual, reflecting an image of self which he might appraise in much the same fashion as he would appraise another person seen directly.

Glossary

marginal   Unconventional; relating to the position of the individual in a societal-level structure away from the center.

market   The entire web of institutions within which all commercial exchanges take place.

mass   A diffuse collectivity in which the defining focus of attention is a matter of personal taste. Recent examples are the Star Wars phenomenon, the interest in home computers, and the furor over fashion jeans.

''me''   All those perspectives on oneself that one has learned from others; the attitudes that the ''I'' assumes toward its own person when it is taking the role of the other toward itself. The ''me'' is the accumulated frames of reference in terms of which the ''I'' appraises, evaluates, and monitors the ongoing thought and action of its own person.

meaning   Implications for the plans of action of individuals.

membership norms   Norms applying to every member of the organization whatever their positions.

membership roles   Roles played only by a member of a structured collectivity.

metalinguistic ability   The ability to reflect upon one's own language.

mobilization   The theory of mobilization suggests that it is not so much individuals who join publics and social movements but, rather, interest groups—who then influence their members.

mores   A custom that has strong sanctions behind it, with a great deal of emotion associated with it.

movement organization   The formal organization formed by an interest group to lend stability and continuity to a social movement across issues and publics.

nation-state   The dominant modern type of polity which claims the sole right to exercise legitimate force within its territory to enforce its own laws.

natural division of labor   Economic division of labor based largely on age-sex capabilities and shared role definitions.

negative sanctions   Diminished benefits and increased costs as punishments applied to a role performer.

negotiation   The attainment of a definition of a situation through joint interaction and the establishment of identities and a working agreement on lines of actions within social interaction.

neighborhood   A small area of a larger community within which borrowing and mutual aid occur, where first names are used, and where gossip takes place among its members.

neologism   Private term invented by the members of a relationship, bearing on its organizational concerns, or private meaning attached to a common term.

nonmembership roles   Roles played by persons outside an organization. Manifest roles include: admirer, supporter, beneficiary (on the positive side), and detractor, opponent, victim (on the negative side). Latent roles include indirect beneficiary, indirect victim.

normative expectations   Expectations regarding how others ought to perform their roles.

norms   Conceptions of right and wrong, proper and improper, acceptable and unacceptable, moral and immoral, legal and illegal, legitimate and illegitimate, conventional and unconventional, tolerable and intolerable, suitable and unsuitable.

norms of adequacy   Norms that define what levels of contribution constitute an adequate performance (the ''going role price'').

GLOSSARY

occupation A distinct type of work; the social role performed by members of society that yields social and financial consequences and that constitutes a major focus in the life of an adult.

occupational communities Communities bounded by a shared occupation; important but unofficial suborganizations of the economy.

occupational structure The number and nature of occupations in an economy; the numerical distribution of workers and the various benefits distributed across that set of occupations.

official group A secondary group of certain individuals who are designated to work together face-to-face in a common process.

opinion leaders Members of an organization to whom others come for interpretations and decisions about organizational events.

opinion mass A subset of members of a diffuse collectivity, formed around and adhering to a particular position or fashion model.

organization A structured collectivity; a set of persons undertaking differentiated but coordinated lines of action in a joint venture.

organizational career The individual's movement through a series of organizational positions; the sequence of positions occupied by an individual.

organizational environment The external web of other organizations and physical features within which an organization operates, especially the larger organizations within which an organization is embedded.

organizational process One of five processes—recruitment, socialization, interaction, innovation, and social control—that comprise organizational functioning.

organizational role The expectations held toward an individual occupying a given position within an organization.

organizational structure The pattern of differentiated but interdependent positions in an organization.

organizational tactics Procedures employed by an organization in managing the basic processes of recruitment, socialization, interaction, innovation, and social control.

orientation A relatively brief period of explicit socialization procedures, followed by a somewhat longer period of implicit procedures, throughout which the individual is treated as a functioning (although perhaps probationary) member of the organization.

pair relationship Any mutual involvement, deep or fleeting, pervasive or incidental, between two individuals; dyad.

passive participation An individual tactic in the socialization process in which the individual does what is asked of him but contributes no unexpected individual effort.

performance The aggregate of an actor's actions that can be construed as relevant to an organizational role.

performed role Role as acts carried out rather than expectations held by others.

perks See perquisites

perquisites Something advantageous; anything received for work besides the agreed-upon pay; *See also* sidepayments.

persona A subset of role-identities revealed to another person.

personal resources The resources an individual can mobilize for action (knowledge, beauty, wealth, possessions, opportunities).

Glossary

personal style The demeanor, mannerisms, communicative idiom, and expressive manner of the individual in the actual performance of an organizational role.

pervasiveness of roles The scope of expectations, measured by the proportion of the performer's life activities encompassed by the role.

phantom relationship Relationship kept alive in some sense by one member after the other member has departed.

phatic communication Relatively empty sociable chit-chat.

placement An aspect of recruitment concerned with positions in the various social structures of an organization.

planetary level (of social organizations) That level or "field" within which national and international organizations are embedded.

plan of action An individual's role impulses and intentions in acting out a role.

polity A relatively independent "political" collectivity organized to produce the public safety and welfare of its membership. In modernized areas of the world polities tend to take the form of a nation-state.

position One's placement in the division-of-labor structure of an organization.

positional norms Norms that apply only to those persons who occupy a particular social position within an organization.

postindustrial economy A type of economy in which the majority of workers are "white-collar"—that is, working in offices rather than in factories or on farms—and engaged in producing services rather than material goods.

power The ability to influence others through control of human and/or material collective resources; control over a resource relevant to collective production of the collective good.

prescribed roles The expectations held toward the occupants of a social position or members of an organization.

primary group Group, generally of no more than twenty, in which the members strongly identify themselves with the collectivity, developing an emphatic "we-feeling" and a sharp "ingroup–outgroup" distinction; group on which an individual depends heavily for satisfaction of a wide variety of important interpersonal roles.

primary relationship Relationship in which the aspect of collectivity outweighs the aspect of structure—in which persons are more important than roles or positions.

primary social structure The pattern of positions corresponding to the division of labor of an organization.

principle of least interest Principle stating that the person who is least interested in or dependent on an other for resources maintains a power differential over that other.

proactive Anticipatory, as of planning and acting, as opposed to reactive.

public A mass or dispersed set of people interested in and divided about an issue, engaged in discussion of the issue with a view to registering a collective opinion which is expected to affect the course of action of some organization or individual.

public opinion Message(s) communicated in some manner to the effective decision makers as a consequence of the functioning of a public.

ratification/stigmatization procedures Organizational procedures through which an innovation (role improvisation) is either ratified (condoned) or stigmatized (rejected). They vary in:

(1) form—proactive or reactive; and (2) degree of centralization of decision-making authority—from highly autocratic to completely democratic.

ratify To collectively label an innovation as creative (and therefore to be normatively prescribed or at least permitted).

reactive After-the-fact, as of a responsive action, as opposed to proactive.

recruitment The organizational process through which individuals' participation in an organization is determined, involving both membership and differential placement. Recruitment may be ascriptive or voluntary, and may involve attraction, selection, and placement aspects.

recruitment interests, individual Interests on the part of the individual in the attributes of an organizational position as they relate to his personal interests, resources, and plans of actions.

recruitment interests, organizational Interests on the part of an organization in the attributes of a potential member as they relate to the organization's perception of its relative needs.

reference group, reference other An organization or person that has in some fashion impressed the individual in either a positive or a negative manner to the degree that he or she employs that group or other as a basis for self-evaluation and attitude formation.

regulations Official decisions that have the force of "laws" within an organization.

relationship *See* dyad, pair relationship.

relative value (of individual) A criterion for selection relative to potentially costly consequences, to existing resources, and to the potential value of other potential recruits.

reputational status Status in a community based on contributive actions.

restrictive role Role whose performance substantially limits the range of social contacts, situations, and activities of its performer.

ritual The recurring observance of set forms or rites by a collectivity.

rituals of solidarity An organizational tactic of social control serving to enhance members' sense of collectivity.

role The characteristic and expectable conduct truly expressive of an organizational position.

role bargaining Process through which the individual seeks to negotiate some compromise in the performances of his roles.

role choice An individual's choices of which role(s), within a set of competing or conflicting roles, shall be performed on a single occasion.

role compartmentalization Process through which two incompatible roles are confined to quite separate social arenas, with the result that the inevitable cross-pressures are more readily overlooked by all concerned.

role competition Demands on the individual performing two or more roles for limited amounts of time and other individual resources.

role conflict Conflict that arises when one role requires behavior which in some degree is incompatible with the behavior required by another role.

role expectations Expectations held by others and/or self concerning a social position within an organization. A person becomes subject to role expectations not as an individual but by virtue of occupying a particular social position.

role-identity The character an individual devises for himself as the occupant of an organizational position. These role-identities provide plans of action for the self as performer, evaluative standards for the self as audience, and communicable personal qualities for the self as character.

role-making Organizational and individual shaping of the character of the individual's organizational role through the systematic interlinkages of the five basic processes.

role negotiation The working-out of better role fits through bargaining and through conferring on joint ventures.

role scheduling An agenda or schedule of performances to provide for the satisfaction of all of an individual's roles within some appropriate time span.

role strain The subjective experience of competing and conflicting roles stemming from the competing and conflicting demands of various organizations with which the individual is involved.

role structure The primary social structure, or internal division of labor, of an organization.

role support The communicated support accorded to a performer by his audience for his claims concerning his role-identity. To gain role support, an individual is willing to incur certain costs.

satisfice To choose not necessarily the best possible action nor even the best relative to one's limited set of alternatives but rather to choose one that is "good enough."

secondary group Group in which the aspect of social structure is not sharply subordinated to the aspect of collectivity, more nearly resembling a voluntary association; groups on which the members are less broadly dependent.

secondary relationship Relationship in which the aspect of structure outweighs the aspect of collectivity and in which roles are more important than persons.

secondary social structure The pattern of suborganizations and the secondary dimensions of affect, conformity, and so on, within an organization.

segmental participation Participation in an organization that does not involve one's entire self or life.

selection A process of obtaining/sorting out/keeping desirable members while avoiding/refusing/ejecting undesirable members. For the individual, selection is a process of obtaining/maintaining desirable memberships and avoiding/relinquishing undesirable memberships.

self-fulfilling prophecy Expression coined by Robert K. Merton to denote the phenomenon that what is socially expected tends to come true.

self See social self

settlements Ecological (or economic) units.

sidepayments Selective sanctions to reward an individual's contributions to collective action and the collective good.

significant others Persons with whom the individual has deep personal bonds—mate, kin, friends, associates.

situs Cluster of related industries, such as manufacturing or transportation.

social change An independent variable marking the shift in social realities through time with attendant changed role prescriptions and role performances.

social community A community bounded by some socially defined characteristic of individuals, such as age-sex, language, race or ethnicity, religious affiliation, socioeconomic status, and occupation.

GLOSSARY

social construction of reality   The social process of jointly defining situations and generating social objects.

social control   Organizational process through which individuals' participation is constrained. The organization seeks both (1) to develop and sustain creative or at least conforming participation; and (2) to prevent and correct deviant participation.

social environment   The aggregate of commonly held meanings of persons, acts, and situations.

social exchange theory   Theory that envisions a market for the trading of performances, in which each participant gives some of his resources to another in return for somewhat different resources from the other.

social movement   A diffuse collectivity acting with some continuity to promote or resist some specific broad social change in the embedding organization.

social object   The meaning of a "thing" arrived at through the interaction process.

social position   One's place in the internal division-of-labor structure of any organization.

social process   The dynamic medium through which mutual influences between organizations and individuals are transmitted. The five basic social processes are: recruitment, socialization, interaction, innovation, and social control. A sixth process is logistics.

social role   A recipe for behavior, prescribing ideas, feelings, and behaviors appropriate for conduct in a given social situation.

social self   The integrative entity of a person; an organization of role-identities. Its three aspects are: (1) the "I," or self as performer (the active aspect); (2) the "me," or self as audience to that performer (the evaluative aspect); and (3) the self as character performed (the communicated aspect).

social structure   A socially differentiated pattern in which members not only play distinctive parts in the division of labor but also occupy distinct, though interdependent, social positions.

social validation   A viewpoint provided and communicated by a reference group or reference other; a source of comparison for measuring and adjudging oneself and other persons.

socialization   The organizational process through which an individual's participation is defined.

societal-level structures   Various imperfectly coincident collectivities—age-sex structure, speech community, polity, economy—that together delineate a national society.

Society   The web of organized social life in general; the dense and multidimensional web of interrelations among the countless number of specific social organizations.

special interest   An interest whose satisfaction by one member will necessarily diminish the satisfaction of that interest by other members.

specification of roles   The degree to which the actions of a position occupant are prescribed and proscribed clearly, consensually, and in detail.

speech community   The structured collectivity comprised of all those persons who speak and understand a particular language, organized to produce the fundamental collective good of communication.

sponsor   An individual member or suborganization that initiates an innovation and advocates it within the subsequent ratification procedings.

status   Worthiness based on the extent to which an individual's attributes, roles, and/or actions are recognized as contributing to the collective interests.

stigmatize   To collectively label an innovation as deviant (to be normatively proscribed or at best tolerated).

454

Glossary

stripping and substitution An organizational tactic of socialization whereby the individual has to unlearn deep-seated habits or attitudes and whereby those preferred by the organization are substituted.

subject Member of a polity. Subject-role interaction is a matter of observing or violating the law of the polity.

suborganization Collective secondary differentiation within a larger organization. Official suborganizations include departments, divisions, branches, and authorized committees. Unofficial suborganizations include factions and cliques. Either type coheres around special interests shared by some but not all members of the larger organization.

subversion A defensive action taken by an embedded group in the face of imposed or threatened innovations within the larger organization or in pursuit of special interests.

supplementation and revision A socialization tactic in which the individual's existing skills are adjusted to improve his ability to meet organizational role expectations.

supportive interchanges Interpersonal rituals serving to ratify and maintain a relationship.

surveillance The monitoring and evaluation of role performances of members in an organization by superiors and peers.

targets Those members of an organization whose roles are affected by another's innovative role performance and who stand to have their roles or social positions altered.

territory A bounded geographic area.

thing A bundle of stimuli. The same "thing" can present different meanings depending on different plans of action. In that most important case of persons as "things," the collective process of establishing the meaning of a person crucially involves arriving at some consensual identification of that person's current and latent social roles.

total institutions An association in which its clients' lives are almost completely controlled by the organization's staff. Total institutions may be either special types of bureaucracies or special types of voluntary associations.

training Extended organizational efforts toward the physical, emotional, and motivational development of the individual.

tribe A polity including all the bands (villages) of a speech community.

unofficial group A group that evolves within an organization on the basis of shared special interests.

values Slogans capable of providing the rationalization of action by encapsulating a positive attitude toward a purportedly beneficial state of affairs.

voluntary associations *See* associations, voluntary.

voluntary recruitment A social-exchange process in which neither the organization nor the individual has any special rights concerning membership.

working agreement Agreement upon the relevant social positions to which each person belongs for purposes of the present encounter. A working agreement can be said to exist when the cognitive processes of any participant, with respect to social identities, are not in gross conflict with the expressive processes of the other persons.

References

ADAMS, BERT N. 1968. *Kinship in an urban setting*. Chicago: Markham.

———. 1971. *The American family*. Chicago: Markham.

ALDOUS, JOAN. 1978. *Family careers: developmental change in families*. New York: Wiley.

ALDRICH, HOWARD E. 1979. *Organizations and environments*. Englewood Cliffs, N.J.: Prentice-Hall.

ALLAN, GRAHAM A. 1979. *A sociology of friendship and kinship*. London: Allen & Unwin.

ALLEN, HAROLD B., and GARY N. UNDERWOOD, eds. 1971. *Readings in American dialectology*. New York: Appleton-Century-Crofts.

ALLPORT, GORDON W. 1961. *Pattern and growth in personality*. New York: Holt, Rinehart & Winston.

———. 1968. The historical background of modern social psychology. Pp. 1–80 in G. Lindzey and E. Aronson, eds., *The handbook of social psychology* (2nd edition), vol. 1. Reading, Mass.: Addison-Wesley.

ALMOND, GABRIEL A., and SIDNEY VERBA. 1963. *The civic culture: political attitudes and democracy in five nations*. Princeton, N.J.: Princeton University Press.

ALTMAN, IRWIN, and DALMAS A. TAYLOR. 1973. *Social penetration: the development of interpersonal relationships*. New York: Holt, Rinehart & Winston.

AMES, LOUISE BATES. 1952. The sense of self in nursery school children as manifested by their verbal behavior. *Journal of Genetic Psychology*, 81: 193–232.

ANDERSON, JOHN R. 1976. *Language, memory, and thought*. Hillsdale, N.J.: Erlbaum.

ANDERSON, NELS. 1961. *Work and leisure*. New York: Free Press.

REFERENCES

ARCHIBALD, W. PETER, and RONALD L. COHEN. 1971. Self-presentation, embarrassment, and facework as a function of self-evaluation, conditions of self-presentation, and feedback from others. *Journal of Personality and Social Psychology,* 20: 287–297.

ARGYLE, MICHAEL, and MARK COOK. 1976. *Gaze and mutual gaze.* Cambridge: At the University Press.

ARGYRIS, CHRIS. 1964. *Integrating the individual and the organization.* New York: Wiley.

BABCHUK, NICHOLAS, and C. WAYNE GORDON. 1962. *The voluntary association in the slum.* Lincoln: University of Nebraska.

BACHRACH, PETER, ed. 1971. *Political elites in a democracy.* New York: Atherton.

BALDWIN, KAREN L. 1975. ''Down on Bugger Run: Family Group and the Social Basis of Folklore.'' Unpublished doctoral dissertation, University of Pennsylvania.

BALES, ROBERT F. 1950. *Interaction process analysis: a method for the study of small groups.* Reading, Mass.: Addison-Wesley.

BALES, ROBERT F., and PHILIP E. SLATER. 1955. Role differentiation. Pp. 259–306 in T. Parsons, R. F. Bales, et al., eds., *The family, socialization, and interaction process.* New York: Free Press.

BALTZELL, E. DIGBY. 1958. *Philadelphia gentlemen: the making of a national upper class.* New York: Free Press.

BANTON, MICHAEL P. 1964. *The policeman in the community.* London: Tavistock.

———. 1965. *Roles: an introduction to the study of social relations.* New York: Basic Books.

BARBER, BERNARD. 1961. Family status, local-community status, and social stratification: three types of social ranking. *Pacific Sociological Review,* 4: 3–10.

BARBER, BERNARD, and LYLE S. LOBEL. 1952. Fashion in women's clothes and the American stratification system. *Social Forces,* 31: 124–131.

BARBER, CHARLES. 1964. *Linguistic change in present-day English.* Birmingham: University of Alabama Press.

BARBER, JAMES D. 1965. *The lawmakers: recruitment and adaptation to legislation.* New Haven, Conn.: Yale University Press.

BARNOUW, VICTOR. 1979. *Culture and personality* (3rd edition). Homewood, Ill.: Dorsey.

BAUR, E. JACKSON. 1960. Public opinion and the primary group. *American Sociological Review,* 25: 210–219.

BAY, CHRISTIAN. 1968. Civil disobedience. Pp. 473–486 in D. L. Sills, ed., *International encyclopedia of the social sciences,* vol. 2. New York: Macmillan and Free Press.

BECKER, HOWARD S. 1952. The career of the Chicago public school teacher. *American Journal of Sociology,* 57: 470–477.

———. 1960. Notes on the concept of commitment. *American Journal of Sociology,* 66: 32–42.

———. 1963. *Outsiders.* New York: Free Press.

———. 1964. Personal change in adult life. *Sociometry,* 27: 40–53.

———. 1968. The self and adult socialization. In E. Norbeck, D. Price-Williams, and W. M. McCord, eds., *The study of personality: an interdisciplinary appraisal.* New York: Holt, Rinehart & Winston.

———. 1974. Art as collective action. *American Sociological Review,* 39: 767–776.

BECKER, HOWARD S., and JAMES CARPER. 1956a. The development of identification with an occupation. *American Journal of Sociology,* 61: 289–298.

References

———. 1956b. The elements of identification with an occupation. *American Sociological Review,* 21: 341–348.

BECKER, HOWARD S., BLANCHE GEER, EVERETT C. HUGHES, and ANSELM L. STRAUSS. 1961. *Boys in white: student culture in medical school.* Chicago: University of Chicago Press.

BECKER, HOWARD S., AND ANSELM L. STRAUSS. 1956. Careers, personality, and adult socialization. *American Journal of Sociology,* 62: 253–263.

BEHLING, ORLANDO, GEORGE LABOVITZ, and MARION GAINER. 1968. College recruiting: a theoretical base. *Personnel Journal,* 47: 13–19.

BELL, COLIN, and HOWARD NEWBY. 1973. *Community studies: an introduction to the sociology of the local community.* New York: Praeger.

BENEDICT, RUTH. 1946. *The chrysanthemum and the sword.* Boston: Houghton Mifflin.

BENNE, KENNETH D., and PAUL SHEATS. 1948. Functional roles of group members. *Journal of Social Issues,* 4: 41–49.

BENNIS, WARREN G., KENNETH BENNE, and ROBERT CHIN. 1969. *The planning of change* (2nd edition). New York: Holt, Rinehart & Winston.

BERLIN, BRENT, and PAUL KAY. 1969. *Basic color terms.* Berkeley: University of California Press.

BERNARD, H. Y. 1969. *Public officials, elected and appointed.* New York: Oceana.

BERNARD, JESSIE. 1962. *American community behavior.* New York: Holt, Rinehart & Winston.

———. 1981. *The female world.* New York: Free Press.

BERRY, BRIAN J. L. 1967. *Geography of market centers and retail distribution.* Englewood Cliffs, N.J.: Prentice-Hall.

BERRY, BRIAN J. L., and JOHN D. KASARDA. 1977. *Contemporary urban ecology.* New York: Macmillan.

BERSCHEID, ELLEN, and ELAINE WALSTER. 1969. *Interpersonal attraction.* Reading, Mass.: Addison-Wesley.

BERTRAND, ALVIN L., and ASSOCIATES. 1958. *Rural sociology: an analysis of contemporary rural life.* New York: McGraw-Hill.

BETTELHEIM, BRUNO. 1943. Individual and mass behavior in extreme situations. *Journal of Abnormal and Social Psychology,* 38:417–452.

BETTINGHAUS, ERWIN P. 1973. *Persuasive communication* (2nd edition). New York: Holt, Rinehart & Winston.

BIELBY, WILLIAM T., and ARNE L. KALLEBURG. 1975. *The differentiation of occupations.* Madison: University of Wisconsin Institute for Research on Poverty.

BIRDWHISTELL, RAY L. 1970. *Kinesics and context.* Philadelphia: University of Pennsylvania Press.

BLAU, PETER M. 1954. Cooperation and competition in a bureaucracy. *American Journal of Sociology,* 59: 530–535.

———. 1964. *Exchange and power in social life.* New York: Wiley.

BLAU, PETER M., and OTIS DUDLEY DUNCAN. 1978. *The American occupational structure* (2nd edition). New York: Free Press.

BLAU, PETER M., JOHN W. GUSTAD, RICHARD JESSOR, HERBERT S. PARNES, and RICHARD C. WILCOX. 1956. Occupational choice: a conceptual framework. *Industrial and Labor Relations Review,* 9: 531–543.

BLIXT, RAYMOND, and NORMAN PROVOST. 1971. *Youth culture on the urban scene.* New York: St. Mary's.

REFERENCES

BLOOMFIELD, LEONARD. 1933. *Language.* New York: Holt, Rinehart & Winston.

BLUM, RICHARD H., ed. 1972. *Surveillance and espionage in a free society.* New York: Praeger.

BLUMENTHAL, ALFRED. 1937. The nature of gossip. *Sociology and Social Research,* 22: 31–37.

BLUMER, HERBERT. 1948. Public opinion and public opinion polling. *American Sociological Review,* 13: 542–549.

———. 1962. Society as symbolic interaction. Pp. 179–192 in A. M. Rose, ed., *Human behavior and social processes.* Boston: Houghton Mifflin.

———. 1969. Fashion: from class differentiation to collective selection. *Sociological Quarterly,* 10: 275–291.

BLUMSTEIN, PHILLIP W. 1973. Audience, Machiavellianism, and tactics of identity bargaining. *Sociological Quarterly,* 36: 346–365.

BLUMSTEIN, PHILLIP W., KATHRYN GROVES CARSSOW, JANET HALL, BARBARA HAWKINS, RONALD HOFFMAN, ERNEST ISHEM, CAROLL PALMER MAURER, DANA SPENS, JOHN TAYLOR, and D. LEE ZIMMERMAN. 1974. The honoring of accounts. *American Sociological Review,* 39: 551–566.

BOCK, PHILIP K. 1980. *Continuities in psychological anthropology: a historical introduction.* San Francisco: W. H. Freeman.

BOSSEVAIN, JEREMY. 1974. *Friends of friends: networks, manipulators and coalitions.* Oxford: Blackwell.

BOLTON, CHARLES D. 1961. Mate selection as the development of a relationship. *Marriage and Family Living,* 23: 234–240.

BONJEAN, CHARLES M., and DAVID M. OLSON. 1964. Community leadership: directions of research. *Administrative Science Quarterly,* 9: 278–295.

BOSSARD, JAMES S., and ELEANOR S. BOLL. 1956. *Ritual in family living* (2nd edition). Philadelphia: University of Pennsylvania Press.

BOTT, ELIZABETH. 1971. *Family and social network* (2nd edition). New York: Free Press.

BOTTOMORE, THOMAS B. 1964. *Elites and society.* New York: Basic Books.

BOUTILIER, ROBERT G., J. CHRISTIAN ROED, and ANN C. SVENDSON. 1980. Crises in the two social psychologies: a critical comparison. *Social Psychology Quarterly,* 43: 5–17.

BRAGER, GEORGE A., and STEPHEN HOLLOWAY. 1978. *Changing human service organizations: politics and practice.* New York: Free Press.

BRAIBANTI, RALPH, and JOSEPH J. SPENGLER, eds. 1961. *Traditions, values and socio-economic development.* Durham, N.C.: Duke University Press.

BREED, WARREN. 1955. Social control in the newsroom: a functional analysis. *Social Forces,* 33: 326–335.

BRIM, ORVILLE G., JR. 1960. Personality development as role-learning. Pp. 127–159 in I. Iscoe and H. W. Stevenson, eds., *Personality development in children.* Austin: University of Texas Press.

BRIM, ORVILLE G., JR., and STANTON WHEELER. 1966. *Socialization after childhood.* New York: Wiley.

BRISSETT, DENNIS, and CHARLES EDGLEY, eds. 1974. *Life as theater: a dramaturgical sourcebook.* Chicago: Aldine.

BROOM, LEONARD, and PHILIP SELZNICK. 1963. *Sociology* (3rd edition). New York: Harper & Row.

BROWN, ROGER. 1958. *Words and things: an introduction to language.* New York: Free Press.

References

Burchard, Waldo W. 1954. Role conflicts of military chaplains. *American Sociological Review*, 19: 528–535.

Burgess, Ernest W. 1925. The growth of the city: an introduction to a research project. Pp. 47–62 in R. E. Park, E. W. Burgess, and R. D. McKenzie, eds., *The city.* Chicago: University of Chicago Press.

———. 1926. The family as a unity of interacting personalities. *The Family,* 7: 3–9.

Burke, Peter J. 1967. The development of task and social-emotional role differentiation. *Sociometry,* 30: 379–392.

———. 1968. Role differentiation and the legitimation of task activity. *Sociometry,* 31: 404–411.

———. 1969. Scapegoating: an alternative to role differentiation. *Sociometry,* 32: 159–168.

———. 1980. The self: measurement requirements from an interactionist perspective. *Social Psychology Quarterly,* 43: 18–29.

Burns, Tom. 1953. Friends, enemies and the polite fiction. *American Sociological Review,* 18: 654–662.

———. 1955. The reference of conduct in small groups: cliques and cabals in occupational milieux. *Human Relations,* 8: 467–486.

Burns, Tom, and G. M. Stalker. 1961. *The management of innovation.* London: Tavistock.

Byrne, Donn. 1971. *The attraction paradigm.* New York: Academic Press.

Caplow, Theodore. 1954. *The Sociology of work.* Minneapolis: University of Minnesota Press.

———. 1968. *Two against one: coalitions in triads.* Englewood Cliffs, N.J.: Prentice-Hall.

———. 1976. *How to run any organization: a manual of practical sociology.* New York: Holt, Rinehart & Winston.

Caplow, Theodore, and Reese McGee. 1958. *The academic marketplace.* New York: Basic Books.

Carlin, Jerome. 1962. *Lawyers on their own.* New Brunswick, N.J.: Rutgers University Press.

Carter, Launor F. 1954. Recording and evaluating the performance of individuals as members of small groups. *Personnel Psychology,* 7: 477–484.

Cartwright, Dorwin, and Alvin Zander, eds. 1968. *Group dynamics: research and theory* (3rd edition). New York: Harper & Row.

Chadwick-Jones, J. K. 1976. *Social exchange theory.* New York: Academic Press.

Chambliss, William J. 1965. The selection of friends. *Social Forces,* 43: 370–380.

Clark, Burton R. 1964. Sociology of education. Pp. 734–769 in R. E. L. Faris, ed., *Handbook of modern sociology.* Chicago: Rand McNally.

Clark, Carroll D. 1933. The concept of the public. *Southwestern Social Science Quarterly,* 13: 311–320.

Clark, Terry N. 1968. *Community structure and decision-making: comparative analyses.* San Francisco: Chandler.

Clarke, Kenneth, and Mary Clarke. 1963. *Introducing folklore.* New York: Holt, Rinehart & Winston.

Clausen, John A., ed. 1968. *Socialization and society.* Boston: Little, Brown.

Clemmer, Donald. 1958. *The prison community* (revised edition). New York: Rinehart.

Cohen, Albert K. 1955. *Delinquent boys.* New York: Free Press.

REFERENCES

COHN, NORMAN. 1957. *The pursuit of the millennium.* New York: Oxford University Press.

COLE, GEORGE F. 1973. *Politics and the administration of justice.* Beverly Hills, Calif.: Sage Publications.

COLEMAN, JAMES S. 1957. *Community conflict.* New York: Free Press.

———. 1971. *The adolescent society* (2nd edition). New York: Free Press.

COLLINS, ORVIS, MELVILLE DALTON, and DONALD ROY. 1946. Restriction of output and social cleavage in industry. *Applied Anthropology,* 5: 1–14.

COOLEY, CHARLES HORTON. 1902. *Human nature and the social order.* New York: Scribner's.

———. 1909. *Social organization.* New York: Scribner's.

COSER, LEWIS A. 1956. *The functions of social conflict.* New York: Free Press.

———. 1974. *Greedy institutions.* New York: Free Press.

COSER, ROSE LAUB. 1961. Insulation from observability and types of social conformity. *American Sociological Review,* 26: 28–39.

COTTRELL, W. FRED. 1940. *The railroader.* Stanford, Calif.: Stanford University Press.

CRAIN, ROBERT L., ELIHU KATZ, and DONALD ROSENTHAL. 1969. *The politics of community conflict.* Indianapolis: Bobbs-Merrill.

CRESSEY, DONALD R. 1973. Adult felons in prisons. Pp. 117–150 in L. E. Ohlin, ed., *Prisoners in America.* Englewood Cliffs, N.J.: Prentice-Hall.

CRESSEY, PAUL G. 1932. *The taxi-dance hall.* Chicago: University of Chicago Press.

CURTIS, SUSAN. 1977. *Genie: a psycholinguistic study of a modern-day "wild child."* New York: Academic Press.

DALTON, MELVILLE. 1950. Conflicts between staff and line managerial officers. *American Sociological Review,* 15: 342–351.

———. 1951. Informal factors in career achievement. *American Journal of Sociology,* 56: 407–415.

———. 1959. *Men who manage.* New York: Wiley.

DAVIS, F. JAMES, and RICHARD STIVERS. 1975. *Collective definition of deviance.* New York: Free Press.

DAVIS, KINGSLEY. 1947. Final note on a case of extreme isolation. *American Journal of Sociology,* 52: 432–437.

DAVIS, MURRAY S. 1973. *Intimate relations.* New York: Free Press.

DAWSON, ROBERT O. 1969. *Sentencing: the decision as to type, length, and conditions of sentence.* Boston: Little, Brown.

DENNIS, JACK, ed. 1973. *Socialization to politics: a reader.* New York: Wiley.

DENTLER, ROBERT A., and KAI T. ERIKSON. 1959. The functions of deviance in groups. *Social Problems,* 7: 98–107.

DEUTSCH, MORTON, and HAROLD B. GERARD. 1955. A study of normative and informational social influences upon individual judgment. *Journal of Abnormal and Social Psychology,* 51: 629–636.

deVILLIERS, JILL G., and PETER A. deVILLIERS. 1978. *Language acquisition.* Cambridge, Mass.: Harvard University Press.

DILLARD, J. L. 1972. *Black English: its history and usage in the United States.* New York: Random House.

DiRENZO, GORDON J., ed. 1974. *Personality and politics.* Garden City, N.Y.: Doubleday.

References

DITTES, JAMES E. 1969. Psychology of religion. Pp. 602–659 in G. Lindzey and E. Aronson, eds., *The handbook of social psychology* (2nd edition), vol. 5. Reading, Mass.: Addison-Wesley.

DORNBUSCH, SANFORD M. 1955. The military academy as an assimilating insitution. *Social Forces*, 33: 316–321.

DOUGLAS, JACK D., ed. 1970. *Deviance and respectability: the social construction of moral meanings.* New York: Basic Books.

DRUCKER, PETER F. 1974. *Management: tasks, responsibilities, practices.* New York: Harper & Row.

DUBIN, ROBERT. 1956. Industrial workers' worlds: a study of "central life interests" of industrial workers. *Social Problems*, 3: 131–142.

DUNCAN, OTIS DUDLEY. 1964. Social organization and the ecosystem. Pp. 36–82 in R. E. L. Faris, ed., *Handbook of modern sociology*. Chicago: Rand McNally.

DUNCAN, OTIS DUDLEY, and ALBERT J. REISS, JR. 1956. *Social characteristics of urban and rural communities, 1950.* New York: Wiley.

DUNCAN, STARKEY D., JR. 1972. Some signals and rules for taking speaking turns in conversations. *Journal of Personality and Social Psychology*, 23: 283–292.

———. 1973. Toward a grammar for dyadic conversations. *Semiotica*, 9: 29–46.

DUNCAN, STARKEY D., JR., and DONALD W. FISKE. 1977. *Face-to-face interaction.* Hillsdale, N. J.: Erlbaum.

DUNPHY, DEXTER. 1972. *The primary group.* New York: Appleton-Century-Crofts.

DURKHEIM, EMILE. 1933. *The division of labor in society* (translated by George Simpson). New York: Macmillan.

DUVERGER, MAURICE. 1962. *Political parties* (2nd edition). New York: Wiley.

EBERT, R. J., and T. R. MITCHELL. 1975. *Organizational decision processes.* New York: Crane, Russak.

ECKLAND, BRUCE K. 1968. Theories of mate selection. *Eugenics Quarterly*, 15: 78–80.

EDELMAN, MURRAY. 1977. *Political language.* New York: Academic Press.

EHRLICH, HOWARD J., JAMES W. RINEHART, and JOHN C. HOWELL. 1962. The study of role conflict: explorations in methodology. *Sociometry*, 25: 85–97.

EISENBERG, P. 1938. Judging expressive movement: I. Judgments of sex and dominance-feeling from handwriting samples of dominant and non-dominant men and women. *Journal of Applied Psychology*, 22: 480–486.

EISENSTADT, S. N. 1956. *From generation to generation: age groups and social structure.* New York: Free Press.

EISENSTEIN, JAMES, and HERBERT JACOB. 1977. *Felony justice: an organizational analysis of criminal courts.* Boston: Little, Brown.

EKMAN, PAUL, WALLACE V. FRIESEN, and PHOEBE ELLSWORTH. 1972. *Emotion in the human face: guidelines for research and an integration of findings.* Elmsford, N.Y.: Pergamon.

ELLWOOD, CHARLES A. 1925. *The psychology of human society.* New York: Appleton.

EMERSON, RICHARD M. 1962. Power-dependence relations. *American Sociological Review*, 27: 31–41.

———. 1976. Social exchange theory. *Annual Review of Sociology*, 2: 335–362.

ERIKSON, ERIK H. 1959. Identity and the life cycle. *Psychological Issues*, 1 (1).

ERIKSON, KAI T. 1966. *Wayward Puritans: a study in the sociology of deviance.* New York: Wiley.

REFERENCES

ERVIN-TRIPP, SUSAN M. 1964. An analysis of the interaction of language, topic and listener. *American Anthropologist,* 66 (6, part 2): 86–102.

ETZIONI, AMITAI. 1961. *A comparative analysis of complex organizations.* New York: Free Press.

———. 1965. Organizational control structure. Pp. 650–677 in J. G. March, ed., *Handbook of organizations.* Chicago: Rand McNally.

———. 1969. Social-psychological aspects of international relations. Pp. 538–601 in G. Lindzey and E. Aronson, eds., *The handbook of social psychology* (2nd edition), vol. 5. Reading, Mass.: Addison-Wesley.

EVAN, WILLIAM M. 1963. Peer group interaction and organizational socialization: a study of employee turnover. *American Sociological Review,* 28: 436–440.

———. 1972. An organization-set model of interorganizational relations. Pp. 181–200 in M. Tuite, M. Radnor, and R. Chisholm, eds., *Interorganizational decision-making.* Chicago: Aldine.

EXLINE, RALPH V. 1971. Visual interaction: the glances of power and preference. Pp. 163–206 in M. R. Jones, ed., *Nebraska symposium on motivation.* Lincoln: University of Nebraska Press.

FAULKNER, ROBERT B. 1973. Orchestra interaction: some factors of communication and authority in an artistic organization. *Sociological Quarterly,* 14: 147–157.

FAVA, SYLVIA F. 1958. Contrasts in neighboring: New York City and a suburban county. Pp. 124–131 in W. M. Dobriner, ed., *The suburban community.* New York: Putnam's.

FICHTER, JOSEPH H. 1961. *Religion as an occupation: a study of the sociology of professions.* Notre Dame, Ind.: University of Notre Dame Press.

FINE, GARY ALAN. 1979. Small groups and culture creation: the idioculture of Little League baseball teams. *American Sociological Review,* 44: 733–745.

FISCHER, CLAUDE S. 1975. The study of urban community and personality. *Annual Review of Sociology,* 1: 67–89.

FISHMAN, JOSHUA A. 1972. *The sociology of language.* Rowley, Mass.: Newbury House.

———. 1977. Language and ethnicity. Pp. 15–57 in H. Giles, ed., *Language, ethnicity and intergroup relations.* New York: Academic Press.

FISHMAN, JOSHUA A., ROBERT L. COOPER, and ANDREW W. CONRAD, eds. 1977. *The spread of English: the sociology of English as an additional language.* Rowley, Mass.: Newbury House.

FISKE, DONALD W. 1971. *Measuring the concepts of personality.* Chicago: Aldine.

FONER, ANNE, ed. 1975. *Age in society.* Beverly Hills, Calif.: Sage Publications.

FOOT, HUGH C., ANTONY J. CHAPMAN, and JEAN R. SMITH, eds. 1980. *Friendship and social relations in children.* New York: Wiley.

FOSS, DONALD J., and DAVID T. HAKES. 1978. *Psycholinguistics: an introduction to the psychology of language.* Englewood Cliffs, N.J.: Prentice-Hall.

FOX, MICHAEL W. 1971. *Behavior of wolves, dogs and related canids.* New York: Harper & Row.

FRAKE, CHARLES O. 1969. The ethnographic study of cognitive systems. Pp. 28–41 in S. A. Tyler, ed., *Cognitive anthropology.* New York: Holt, Rinehart & Winston.

FREIDSON, ELIOT. 1953. Communications research and the concept of the mass. *American Sociological Review,* 18: 313–317.

FREIDSON, ELIOT, and BUFORD RHEA. 1963. Processes of control in a company of equals. *Social Problems,* 11: 119–131.

References

FROHLICH, NORMAN, JOE A. OPPENHEIMER, and ORAN R. YOUNG. 1971. *Political leadership and collective goods*. Princeton, N.J.: Princeton University Press.

FRYKLUND, VERNE C. 1970. *Occupational analysis: techniques and procedures*. New York: Bruce Publishing Co.

GALPIN, C. J. 1915. The social anatomy of an agricultural community. Research Bulletin 34. Agricultural Experiment Station of the University of Wisconsin.

GANS, HERBERT J. 1962a. *The urban villagers*. New York: Free Press.

———. 1962b. Urbanism and suburbanism as ways of life: a re-evaluation of definitions. Pp. 625–648 in A. M. Rose, ed., *Human behavior and social processes*. Boston: Houghton Mifflin.

GARDNER, BURLEIGH, and WILLIAM F. WHYTE. 1945. The man in the middle: position and problems of the foreman. *Applied Anthropology,* 4: 1–28.

GARFINKEL, HAROLD. 1967. Passing and the managed achievement of sex status in an intersexed person. Pp. 116–185, 285–288 in H. Garfinkel, *Studies in ethnomethodology*. Englewood Cliffs, N.J.: Prentice-Hall.

GERSTL, JOEL E. 1961. Determinants of occupational community in high status occupations. *Sociological Quarterly,* 2: 37–48.

GINZBERG, ELI, SOL W. GINSBURG, SIDNEY AXELRAD, and JOHN L. HERMA. 1951. *Occupational choice*. New York: Columbia University Press.

GLASER, BARNEY G., ed. 1968. *Organizational careers: a sourcebook for theory*. Chicago: Aldine.

GLASER, BARNEY G., and ANSELM L. STRAUSS. 1971. *Status passage*. Chicago: Aldine-Atherton.

GLEASON, H. A., JR. 1961. *An introduction to descriptive linguistics* (revised edition). New York: Holt, Rinehart & Winston.

GLUCKMAN, MAX. 1963. Gossip and scandal. *Current Anthropology,* 4: 307–316.

GOFFMAN, ERVING. 1955. On face-work: an analysis of ritual elements in social interaction. *Psychiatry,* 18: 213–231.

———. 1956a. Embarrassment and social organization. *American Journal of Sociology,* 62: 264–274.

———. 1956b. The nature of deference and demeanor. *American Anthropologist,* 58: 473–502.

———. 1959a. The moral career of the mental patient. *Psychiatry,* 22: 123–142.

———. 1959b. *The presentation of self in everyday life*. Garden City, N.Y.: Doubleday Anchor.

———. 1961a. *Encounters: two studies in the sociology of interaction*. Indianapolis: Bobbs-Merrill.

———. 1961b. On the characteristics of total institutions. Pp. 1–124 in E. Goffman, *Asylums*. Garden City, N.Y.: Doubleday Anchor.

———. 1961c. The underlife of a public institution: a study of ways of making out in a mental hospital. Pp. 171–320 in E. Goffman, *Asylums*. Garden City, N.Y.: Doubleday Anchor.

———. 1963a. *Behavior in public places: notes on the social organization of gatherings*. New York: Free Press.

———. 1963b. *Stigma*. Englewood Cliffs, N.J.: Prentice-Hall.

———. 1967. *Interaction ritual*. Garden City, N.Y.: Doubleday Anchor.

———. 1971. *Relations in public: microstudies of the public order*. New York: Basic Books.

———. 1979. *Gender advertisements*. New York: Harper & Row.

REFERENCES

――――. 1981. *Forms of talk*. Philadelphia: University of Pennsylvania Press.

GOODE, WILLIAM J. 1960. A theory of role strain. *American Sociological Review,* 25: 483–496.

――――. 1979. *The celebration of heroes: prestige as a social control system*. Berkeley: University of California Press.

GOODGLASS, HAROLD, and SHEILA BLUMSTEIN, eds. 1973. *Psycholinguistics and aphasia*. Baltimore, Md.: Johns Hopkins University Press.

GORDON, CHAD. 1971. Role and value development across the life cycle. Pp. 65–105 in J. W. Jackson, ed., *Role*. Cambridge: At the University Press.

――――. 1976. Development of evaluated role identities. *Annual Review of Sociology,* 2: 405–433.

GOSLIN, DAVID A., ed. 1969. *Handbook of socialization theory and research*. Chicago: Rand McNally.

GOTTMAN, JOHN M. 1979. *Marital interaction: experimental investigations*. New York: Academic Press.

GOULD, ROGER L. 1978. *Transformations: growth and change in adult life*. New York: Simon & Schuster.

GOULDNER, ALVIN W. 1960. The norm of reciprocity: a preliminary statement. *American Sociological Review,* 25: 161–178.

GRAEN, GEORGE. 1976. Role-making processes within complex organizations. Pp. 1201–1245 in M. D. Dunnette, ed., *Handbook of industrial and organizational psychology*. Chicago: Rand McNally.

GRECO, BENEDETTO. 1975. *How to get the job that's right for you*. Homewood, Ill.: Dow Jones-Irwin.

GREELEY, ANDREW M. 1972. *The denominational society: a sociological approach to religion in America*. Glenview, Ill.: Scott Foresman.

GREENSTEIN, FRED I. 1965. *Children and politics*. New Haven, Conn.: Yale University Press.

――――. 1968. Political socialization. Pp. 551–555 in D. L. Sills, ed., *International encyclopedia of the social sciences,* vol. 14. New York: Macmillan and Free Press.

GREGORY, MICHAEL, and SUSANNE CARROLL. 1978. *Language and situation: language varieties and their social contexts*. London: Routledge & Kegan Paul.

GROSS, EDWARD. 1953. Some functional consequences of primary controls in formal work organizations. *American Sociological Review,* 18: 368–373.

GROSS, EDWARD, and GREGORY P. STONE. 1964. Embarrassment and the analysis of role requirements. *American Journal of Sociology,* 70: 1–15.

GRUSKY, OSCAR. 1970. The effects of succession: a comparative study of military and business organizations. Pp. 439–454 in O. Grusky and G. A. Miller, eds., *The sociology of organizations: basic studies*. New York: Free Press.

GUSFIELD, JOSEPH R., ed. 1970. *Protest, reform, and revolt: a reader in social movements*. New York: Wiley.

HAGE, JERALD, and MICHAEL AIKEN. 1970. *Social change in complex organizations*. New York: Random House.

HAGSTROM, WARREN O. 1975. *The scientific community*. Carbondale: Southern Illinois University Press.

HALL, DOUGLAS T. 1976. *Careers in organizations*. Santa Monica, Calif.: Goodyear.

HALL, EDWARD T. 1966. *The hidden dimension*. Garden City, N.Y.: Doubleday Anchor.

HALL, KENNETH, and ISOBEL MILLER. 1975. *Retraining and tradition: the skilled worker in an era of change*. London: Allen & Unwin.

References

HALL, OSWALD. 1946. The informal organization of the medical profession. *Canadian Journal of Economics and Political Science,* 49: 19–22.

———. 1948. The stages of a medical career. *American Journal of Sociology,* 53: 327–336.

———. 1949. Types of medical careers. *American Journal of Sociology,* 55: 243–253.

HALL, RICHARD H. 1975. *Occupations and the social structure* (2nd edition). Englewood Cliffs, N.J.: Prentice-Hall.

HALLOWELL, A. IRVING. 1954. *Culture and experience.* Philadelphia: University of Pennsylvania Press.

HAMILTON, DAVID. 1956. The ceremonial aspect of corporate organization. *American Journal of Economics and Sociology,* 16: 11–23.

HANNERZ, ULF. 1967. Gossip, networks and culture in a black American ghetto. *Ethnos,* 32: 35–60.

HARE, A. PAUL. 1976. *Handbook of small group research* (2nd edition). New York: Free Press.

HARGEN, JAMES. 1935. The psychology of prison language. *Journal of Abnormal and Social psychology,* 30: 359–365.

HARLOW, HARRY F., and MARGARET K. HARLOW. 1962. Social deprivation in monkeys. *Scientific American,* 207(11): 136–146.

HARRIS, ANTHONY R. 1976. Race, commitment to deviance, and spoiled identity. *American Sociological Review,* 41: 432–442.

HARRIS, MARVIN. 1964. *The nature of cultural things.* New York: Random House.

———. 1977. *Cannibals and kings: the origins of culture.* New York: Random House.

HARRISON, PAUL M. 1959. *Authority and power in the free church tradition.* Princeton, N.J.: Princeton University Press.

HART, H. L. 1976. *The concept of law.* New York: Oxford University Press.

HAUSKNECHT, MURRAY. 1962. *The joiners: a sociological description of voluntary association membership in the United States.* Totowa, N. J.: Bedminster Press.

HAWKINS, RICHARD, and GARY TIEDEMAN. 1975. *Creation of deviance: interpersonal and organizational determinants.* Columbus, Ohio: Merrill.

HAWLEY, WILLIS D., and FREDERICK M. WIRT, eds. 1974. *The search for community power* (revised edition). Englewood Cliffs, N.J.: Prentice-Hall.

HEAP, KEN. 1977. *Group theory for social workers.* Elmsford, N.Y.: Pergamon Press.

HEBB, D. O. 1955. The mammal and his environment. *American Journal of Psychiatry,* 111: 826–831.

HEDIGER, HEINI P. 1961. The evolution of territorial behavior. Pp. 34–57 in S. L. Washburn, ed., *The social life of early man.* New York: Viking Fund.

HEISS, JERROLD. 1981. *The social psychology of interaction.* Englewood Cliffs, N.J.: Prentice-Hall.

HENLEY, NANCY M. 1977. Status and sex: some touching observations. *Bulletin of the Psychonomic Society,* 2: 91–93.

HENRY, JULES. 1963. *Culture against man.* New York: Random House.

HERBERG, WILL. 1960. *Protestant-Catholic-Jew.* Garden City, N.Y.: Doubleday Anchor.

HERSKOVITS, MELVILLE J. 1952. *Economic anthropology.* New York: Knopf.

HIRSCH, PAUL M. 1972. Processing fads and fashions: an organization-set analysis of cultural industry systems. *American Journal of Sociology,* 77: 639–659.

REFERENCES

HOCHSCHILD, ARLIE R. 1973. *The unexpected community: portrait of an old age subculture.* Berkeley: University of California Press.

HOFFER, ERIC. 1951. *The true believer.* New York: Harper.

HOIJER, HARRY. 1954. *Language in culture.* Chicago: University of Chicago Press.

HOLLANDER, EDWARD P. 1958. Conformity, status, and idiosyncracy credit. *Psychological Review,* 65: 117-127.

HOMANS, GEORGE C. 1950. *The human group.* New York: Harcourt Brace & World.

———. 1974. *Social behavior: its elementary forms* (revised edition). New York: Harcourt Brace Jovanovich.

HOOS, IDA R. 1967. *Retraining the work force.* Berkeley: University of California Press.

HOPPER, REX D. 1950. The revolutionary process: a frame of reference for the study of revolutionary movements. *Social Forces,* 28: 270-279.

HOROBIN, G. W. 1957. Community and occupation in the Hull fishing industry. *British Journal of Sociology,* 8: 343-356.

HOSTETLER, JOHN A. 1980. *Amish society* (3rd edition). Baltimore, Md.: Johns Hopkins University Press.

HOUSE, JAMES S. 1977. The three faces of social psychology. *Sociometry,* 40: 161-171.

HOWTON, F. WILLIAM. 1969. *Functionaries.* Chicago: Quadrangle.

HUDSON, KENNETH. 1978. *The jargon of the professions.* London: Macmillan.

HUESMANN, L. ROWELL, and GEORGE LEVINGER. 1976. Incremental exchange theory: a formal model for progression in dyadic social interaction. Pp. 191-229 in L. Berkowitz and E. Walster, eds., *Advances in experimental social psychology,* vol. 9. New York: Academic Press.

HUGHES, EVERETT C. 1937. Institutional office and the person. *American Journal of Sociology,* 43: 404-413.

———. 1958. *Men and their work.* Chicago: Aldine.

———. 1971. *The sociological eye: selected papers.* Chicago: Aldine-Atherton.

HUNTER, ALBERT. 1974. *Symbolic communities: the persistence and change of Chicago's local communities.* Chicago: University of Chicago Press.

HURST, CHARLES E. 1979. *The anatomy of social inequality.* St. Louis: C. W. Mosby.

HUSTON, TED L., ed. 1974. *Foundations of interpersonal attraction.* New York: Academic Press.

HYMAN, HERBERT H., and ELEANOR D. SINGER, eds. 1968. *Readings in reference group theory and research.* New York: Free Press.

HYMES, DELL. 1962. The ethnography of speaking. Pp. 13-53 in T. Gladwin and W. C. Sturtevant, eds., *Anthropology and human behavior.* Washington, D. C.: Anthropology Society of Washington.

INKELES, ALEX, and DANIEL J. LEVINSON. 1969. National character: the study of modal personality and sociocultural systems. Pp. 418-506 in G. Lindzey and E. Aronson, eds., *The handbook of social psychology* (2nd edition), vol. 4. Reading, Mass.: Addison-Wesley.

IRWIN, JOHN. 1970. *The felon.* Englewood Cliffs, N.J.: Prentice-Hall.

JACKSON, JAY W. 1959. Reference group processes in a formal organization. *Sociometry,* 22: 307-327.

JAFFE, JOSEPH, and STANLEY FELDSTEIN. 1970. *Rhythms of dialogue.* New York: Academic Press.

JAMES, WILLIAM. 1890. *Principles of psychology* (2 vols.). New York: Holt.

References

JANES, ROBERT W. 1961. A note on the phases of the community role of the participant-observer. *American Sociological Review,* 26: 446–450.

JANIS, IRVING. 1973. *Victims of groupthink.* Boston: Houghton Mifflin.

JANOWITZ, MORRIS. 1960. *The professional soldier: a social and political portrait.* New York: Free Press.

———. 1967. *The community press in an urban setting: the social elements of urbanism* (2nd edition). Chicago: University of Chicago Press.

JENNINGS, HELEN H. 1950. *Leadership and isolation* (2nd edition). New York: Longmans, Green & Co.

JONES, RUSSELL A. 1977. *Self-fulfilling prophecies: social, psychological, and physiological effects of expectancies.* New York: Halsted Press.

JOOS, MARTIN. 1961. *The five clocks.* New York: Harcourt Brace & World.

KAHL, JOSEPH A. 1957. *The American class structure.* New York: Holt, Rinehart & Winston.

KAHN, ROBERT L., DONALD M. WOLFE, ROBERT P. QUINN, J. DIEDRICK SNOEK, and ROBERT A. ROSENTHAL. 1964. *Organizational stress: studies in role conflict and ambiguity.* New York: Wiley.

KANTROWITZ, NATHAN. 1973. *Ethnic and racial segregation in the New York metropolis.* New York: Praeger.

KAPLAN, SIDNEY J. 1959. Up from the ranks on a fast escalator. *American Sociological Review,* 24: 79–81.

KARP, DAVID A., GREGORY P. STONE, and WILLIAM C. YOELS. 1977. *Being urban: a social psychological view of city life.* Lexington, Mass.: D. C. Heath.

KARRACKER, WILLIAM. 1958. Teamwork and safety in flight. *Human Organization,* 17: 3–8.

KATZ, DANIEL, and ROBERT L. KAHN. 1978. *The social psychology of organizations* (2nd edition). New York: Wiley.

KATZ, ELIHU. 1957. The two-step flow of communication: an up-to-date report on an hypothesis. *Public Opinion Quarterly,* 21: 61–78.

KATZ, ELIHU, and PAUL F. LAZARSFELD. 1955. *Personal influence.* New York: Free Press.

KATZ, FRED E. 1968. *Autonomy and organization: the limits of social control.* Philadelphia, Pa.: Philadelphia Book Co.

KATZNER, KENNETH. 1975. *The languages of the world.* New York: Funk & Wagnalls.

KAUFMAN, HAROLD F. 1959. Toward an interactional conception of community. *Social Forces,* 38: 9–17.

KAVANAGH, DENNIS. 1972. *Political culture.* New York: Macmillan.

KEEFE, WILLIAM J., and MORRIS S. OGUL. 1964. *The American legislative process.* Englewood Cliffs, N.J.: Prentice-Hall.

KEESING, FELIX M. 1958. *Cultural anthropology: the science of custom.* New York: Holt, Rinehart & Winston.

KELLER, SUZANNE. 1968. *The urban neighborhood.* New York: Random House.

KELLEY, HAROLD H., and JOHN W. THIBAUT. 1978. *Interpersonal relations: a theory of interdependence.* New York: Wiley.

KENDON, ADAM. 1967. Some functions of gaze direction in social interaction. *Acta Psychologica,* 26: 22–63.

———. 1970. Movement coordination in social interaction. *Acta Psychologica,* 32: 100–125.

REFERENCES

————. 1972. Some relationships between body motion and speech. Pp. 177–210 in A. Siegman and B. Pope, eds., *Studies in dyadic communication.* Elmsford, N.Y.: Pergamon Press.

————. 1973. The role of visible behavior in the organization of social interaction. Pp. 29–74 in M. von Cranach and I. Vine, eds., *Social communication and movement.* London: Academic Press.

KENDON, ADAM, RICHARD M. HARRIS, and MARY RITCHIE KEY, eds. 1975. *Organization of behavior in face-to-face interaction.* The Hague: Mouton.

KEY, MARY RITCHIE. 1975. *Male/female language.* Metuchen, N.J.: Scarecrow Press.

KEY, V. O. 1961. *Public opinion and American democracy.* New York: Knopf.

KILLIAN, LEWIS A. 1964. Social movements. Pp. 426–455 in R. E. L. Faris, ed., *Handbook of modern sociology.* Chicago: Rand McNally.

KIMBERLY, JOHN R., ROBERT H. MILES, and ASSOCIATES. 1980. *The organizational life cycle: issues in the creation, transformation, and decline of organizations.* San Francisco: Jossey-Bass.

KLAPP, ORRIN E. 1962. *Heroes, villains, and fools.* Englewood Cliffs, N.J.: Prentice-Hall.

————. 1969. *Collective search for identity.* New York: Holt, Rinehart & Winston.

KLAPPER, JOSEPH T. 1961. *The effects of mass media.* New York: Free Press.

KLOSS, HEINZ. 1967. Types of multilingual communities: a discussion of variables. Pp. 7–17 in S. Lieberson, ed., *Explorations in sociolinguistics.* Bloomington: Indiana University Press.

KOHN, MELVIN L., and CARMI SCHOOLER. 1973. Occupational experience and psychological functioning: an assessment of reciprocal effects. *American Sociological Review,* 38: 97–118.

KONVITZ, MILTON R. 1946. *The alien and the Asiatic in American law.* Ithaca, N.Y.: Cornell University Press.

KORNBLUM, WILLIAM. 1974. *Blue collar community.* Chicago: University of Chicago Press.

KRIESBERG, MARTIN. 1949. Cross-pressures and attitudes: a study of the influence of conflicting propaganda on opinions regarding American-Soviet relations. *Public Opinion Quarterly,* 13: 5–16.

KUHN, MANFORD H. 1964. The reference group reconsidered. *Sociological Quarterly,* 5: 5–21.

KUHN, THOMAS S. 1970. *The structure of scientific revolutions* (2nd edition). Chicago: University of Chicago Press.

LABOV, WILLIAM. 1964. Stages in the acquisition of standard English. Pp. 77–103 in R. W. Shuy, ed., *Social dialects and language learning.* Champaign, Ill.: National Council of Teachers of English.

————. 1966. *The social stratification of English in New York City.* Washington, D. C.: Center for Applied Linguistics.

LA GAIPA, JOHN J. 1977. Testing a multidimensional approach to friendship. In S. W. Duck, ed., *Theory and practice in interpersonal attraction.* London: Academic Press.

LAKOFF, ROBIN. 1975. *Language and woman's place.* New York: Harper & Row.

LAMMERS, CORNELIS J., and DAVID J. HICKSON, eds. 1979. *Organizations alike and unlike: international and inter-institutional studies in the sociology of organizations.* London: Routledge & Kegan Paul.

LANE, ROBERT E. 1959. *Political life: why people get involved in politics.* New York: Free Press.

LANGTON, KENNETH P. 1969. *Political socialization.* New York: Oxford University Press.

LAVER, JOHN. 1975. Communicative functions of phatic communication. Pp. 215–238 in A. Kendon, R. M. Harris, and M. R. Key, eds., *Organization of behavior in face-to-face interaction.* The Hague: Mouton.

References

LAWLER, EDWARD E. 1976. Control systems in organizations. Pp. 1247–1291 in M. D. Dunnette, ed., *Handbook of industrial and organizational psychology*. Chicago: Rand McNally.

LAWRENCE, PAUL R., and JAY W. LORSCH. 1967. *Organization and environment.* Cambridge, Mass.: Harvard University Press.

LAZARSFELD, PAUL F., BERNARD BERELSON, and HAZEL GAUDET. 1948. *The people's choice: how the voter makes up his mind in a presidential campaign.* New York: Columbia University Press.

LAZARSFELD, PAUL F., and ROBERT K. MERTON. 1954. Friendship as a social process: a substantive and methodological analysis. Pp. 18–66 in M. Berger, T. Abel, and C. H. Page, eds., *Freedom and control in modern society.* New York: Van Nostrand.

LEECH, GEOFFREY. 1974. *Semantics.* Baltimore: Penguin Books.

LEMERT, EDWIN C. 1951. *Social pathology.* New York: McGraw-Hill.

LETKEMANN, PETER. 1973. *Crime as work.* Englewood Cliffs, N.J.: Prentice-Hall.

LEVENSON, BERNARD. 1961. Bureaucratic succession. Pp. 362–375 in A. Etzioni, ed., *Complex organizations: a sociological reader.* New York: Holt, Rinehart & Winston.

LEVINGER, GEORGE, and H. L. RAUSH, eds. 1977. *Close relationships: perspectives on the meaning of intimacy.* Amherst: University of Massachusetts Press.

LEVINGER, GEORGE and J. D. SNOEK. 1972. *Attraction in relationship: a new look at interpersonal attraction.* New York: General Learning Press.

LEVINSON, DANIEL. 1978. *The seasons of a man's life.* New York: Knopf.

LEWIN, KURT. 1948. *Resolving social conflicts: selected papers on group dynamics.* New York: Harper.

LIEBERSON, STANLEY. 1963. *Ethnic patterns in American cities.* New York: Free Press.

LINDESMITH, ALFRED R., and ANSELM L. STRAUSS. 1950. A critique of culture-personality writings. *American Sociological Review,* 15: 587–600.

LINDZEY, GARDNER, and DONN BYRNE. 1968. Measurement of social choice and interpersonal attractiveness. Pp. 452–525 in G. Lindzey and E. Aronson, eds., *The handbook of social psychology* (2nd edition). vol. 2, Reading, Mass.: Addison-Wesley.

LINTON, RALPH. 1940. A neglected aspect of social organization. *American Journal of Sociology,* 45: 870–886.

———. 1942. Age and sex categories. *American Sociological Review,* 7: 589–603.

LIPSET, SEYMOUR MARTIN, MARTIN TROW, and JAMES S. COLEMAN. 1956. *Union democracy.* New York: Free Press.

LISKA, ALLEN E. 1977. The dissipation of sociological social psychology. *American Sociologist,* 12: 2–8.

LITTLE, ROGER W. 1964. Buddy relations and combat performance. Pp. 195–223 in M. Janowitz, ed., *The new military.* New York: Russell Sage Foundation.

LITWAK, EUGENE, and IVAN SZELENYI. 1969. Primary group structures and their functions: kin, neighbors, and friends. *American Sociological Review,* 34: 465–481.

LIVINGSTON, J. STERLING. 1969. Pygmalion in management. *Harvard Business Review,* 47: 81–89.

LOFLAND, JOHN. 1969. *Deviance and identity.* Englewood Cliffs, N.J.: Prentice-Hall.

LOFLAND, LYN. 1973. *A world of strangers.* New York: Basic Books.

LORCH, ROBERT S. 1969. *Democratic process and administrative law.* Detroit, Mich.: Wayne State University Press.

LOTT, ALBERT J., and BERNICE E. LOTT. 1965. Group cohesiveness as interpersonal attraction: a review of relationships with antecedent and consequent variables. *Psychological Bulletin,* 64: 259–309.

REFERENCES

Lounsbury, Floyd G. 1964. The structural analysis of kinship semantics. Pp. 1073–1090 in H. G. Lunt, ed., *Proceedings of the IXth international congress of linguists.* The Hague: Mouton.

Lyman, Stanford M. 1974. *Chinese-Americans.* New York: Random House.

McCall, George J. 1964. Symbiosis: the case of hoodoo and the numbers racket. *Social Problems,* 10: 361–371.

———. 1974. A symbolic interactionist approach to attraction. Pp. 217–231 in T. L. Huston, ed., *Foundations of interpersonal attraction.* New York: Academic Press.

McCall, George J., Michal M. McCall, Norman K. Denzin, Gerald D. Suttles, and Suzanne B. Kurth. 1970. *Social relationships.* Chicago: Aldine.

McCall, George J., and J. L. Simmons. 1978. *Identities and interactions* (revised edition). New York: Free Press.

Maccoby, Eleanor E. ed. 1966. *The development of sex differences.* Stanford, Calif.: Stanford University Press.

McFeat, Tom. 1974. *Small-group cultures.* Elmsford, N.Y.: Pergamon Press.

McGrath, Joseph E. and Irwin Altman. 1966. *Small group research: a synthesis and critique of the field.* New York: Holt, Rinehart & Winston.

MacIver, Robert M. 1937. *Society.* New York: Farrar & Rinehart.

Mack, Raymond W., and Alan P. Merriam. 1960. The jazz community. *Social Forces,* 35: 211–222.

McTavish, Donald G. 1971. Perceptions of old people: a review of research methodologies and findings. *The Gerontologist Third Report, 1971–72,* Pp. 90–101.

Mann, Richard D., Graham S. Gibbard, and John J. Hartman. 1967. *Interpersonal styles and group development.* New York: Wiley.

March, James G., ed. 1965. *Handbook of organizations.* Chicago: Rand McNally.

Marcus, Philip M. 1977. Knowledge and power in bargaining for a marriage partner. Pp. 25–32 in J. P. Wiseman, ed., *People as partners* (2nd edition). San Francisco: Canfield Press.

Marks, Stephen R. 1977. Multiple roles and role strain: some notes on human energy, time and commitment. *American Sociological Review,* 42: 921–936.

Martindale, Don. 1960. *American social structure.* New York: Appleton-Century-Crofts.

Marvick, Dwaine, ed. 1961. *Political decision-makers.* New York: Free Press.

Maurer, David W. 1940. *The big con.* Indianapolis: Bobbs-Merrill.

Mayer, Robert R. 1972. *Social planning and social change.* Englewood Cliffs, N.J.: Prentice-Hall.

Mead, George Herbert. 1932. *The philosophy of the present.* Chicago: Open Court.

———. 1934. *Mind, self, and society.* Chicago: University of Chicago Press.

———. 1938. *The philosophy of the act.* Chicago: University of Chicago Press.

Meltzer, Leo. 1961. The need for a dual orientation in social psychology. *Journal of Social Psychology,* 55: 43–47.

Merton, Robert K. 1940. Bureaucratic structure and personality. *Social Forces,* 18: 32–40.

———. 1957. The self-fulfilling prophecy. Pp. 421–436 in R. K. Merton, *Social theory and social structure* (revised edition). New York: Free Press.

Metzger, Duayne. 1966. Procedures and results in the study of native categories: Tzeltal firewood. *American Anthropologist,* 68: 389–407.

References

MEYERSON, ROLF, and ELIHU KATZ. 1957. Notes on a natural history of fads. *American Journal of Sociology,* 62: 594–601.

MICHELS, ROBERT. 1949. *A summary and interpretation of political parties: a sociological study of the oligarchical tendencies of modern democracy.* New York: Free Press.

MICHELSON, WILLIAM. 1970. *Man and his urban environment: a sociological approach.* Reading, Mass.: Addison-Wesley.

MILBRATH, LESTER W., and M. LAL GOEL. 1977. *Political participation: how and why do people get involved in politics?* (2nd edition). Chicago: Rand McNally.

MILESKI, MAUREEN. 1971. Courtroom encounters: an observation study of a lower criminal court. *Law and Society Review,* 5: 473–538.

MILGRAM, STANLEY. 1970. The experience of living in cities. *Science,* 167: 1461–1468.

MILGRAM, STANLEY, and HANS TOCH. 1969. Collective behavior: crowds and social movements. Pp. 507–610 in G. Lindzey and E. Aronson, eds., *The handbook of social psychology* (2nd edition), vol. 4. Reading, Mass.: Addison-Wesley.

MILLER, DELBERT C., and WILLIAM H. FORM. 1964. *Industrial sociology.* New York: Harper & Row.

MILLER, DOROTHY, and MICHAEL SCHWARTZ. 1966. County lunacy hearings: some observations of commitments to a state mental hospital. *Social Problems,* 14: 26–35.

MILLER, GALE. 1978. *Odd jobs: the world of deviant work.* Englewood Cliffs, N.J.: Prentice-Hall.

MILLER, GEORGE A., and PHILLIP N. JOHNSON-LAIRD. 1976. *Language and perception.* Cambridge, Mass.: Harvard University Press.

MILLER, S. M., and FRANK RIESMANN. 1961. The working class subculture: a new view. *Social Problems,* 9: 86–97.

MILLER, WALTER B. 1958. Lower class culture as a generating milieu of gang delinquency. *Journal of Social Issues,* 14: 5–19.

MILLETT, JOHN D. 1962. *The academic community.* New York: McGraw-Hill.

MILNER, CHRISTINA, and RICHARD MILNER. 1972. *Black players: the secret world of black pimps.* Boston: Little, Brown.

MILLS, THEODORE M. 1957. *Group structure and the newcomer: an experimental study of group expansion.* Oslo: Universitetsforlaget.

MINAR, DAVID W., and SCOTT GREER., eds. 1969. *The concept of community: readings with interpretations.* Chicago: Aldine.

MINNIS, MHYRA S. 1953. Cleavage in women's organizations. *American Sociological Review,* 18: 47–53.

MONEY, JOHN, and A. EHRHARDT. 1972. *Man and woman, boy and girl: the differentiation and dimorphism of gender identity from conception to maturity.* Baltimore, Md.: Johns Hopkins University Press.

MOORE, WILBERT E. 1969. Occupational socialization. Pp. 861–883 in D. A. Goslin, ed., *Handbook of socialization theory and research.* Chicago: Rand McNally.

MORE, DOUGLAS M. 1962. Demotion. *Social Problems,* 9: 213–221.

MORRIS, DESMOND, PETER COLLETT, PETER MARSH, and MARIE O'SHAUGHNESSY. 1979. *Gestures: their origin and distribution.* New York: Stein & Day.

MURPHY, RAYMOND E. 1974. *The American city* (2nd edition). New York: McGraw-Hill.

MURSTEIN, BERNARD I., ed. 1971. *Theories of attraction and love.* New York: Springer Publications.

REFERENCES

MUTRAN, ELIZABETH, and PETER J. BURKE. 1979. Personalism as a component of old age identity. *Research on Aging,* 1: 37–63.

NADEL, S. F. 1951. *The theory of social structure.* New York: Free Press.

NEEDLER, MARTIN C. 1971. *Politics and society in Mexico.* Albuquerque: University of New Mexico Press.

NEUGARTEN, BERNICE L., JOAN W. MOORE, and JOHN C. LOWE. 1965. Age norms, age constraints, and adult socialization. *American Journal of Sociology,* 70: 710–717.

NEWCOMB, THEODORE M. 1948. The position of sociological theory. *American Sociological Review,* 13: 169–170.

———. 1961. *The acquaintance process.* New York: Holt, Rinehart & Winston.

NEWPORT, FRANK. 1979. The religious switcher in the United States. *American Sociological Review,* 44: 528–552.

NIERENBERG, GERARD I., and HENRY H. CALERO. 1971. *How to read a person like a book.* New York: Hawthorn Books.

NISBET, ROBERT A. 1962. *The quest for community.* New York: Oxford University Press.

NIXON, HOWARD L. 1979. *The small group.* Englewood Cliffs, N.J.: Prentice-Hall.

NOTTINGHAM, ELIZABETH E. 1971. *Religion: a sociological view.* New York: Random House.

OBERSCHALL, ANTHONY. 1973. *Social conflict and social movements.* Englewood Cliffs, N.J.: Prentice-Hall.

OLESON, VIRGINIA L., and ELVI W. WHITTAKER. 1968. *The silent dialogue: a study in the social psychology of professional socialization.* San Francisco: Jossey-Bass.

OLMSTEAD, MICHAEL S., and A. PAUL HARE. 1978. *The small group* (2nd edition). New York: Random House.

OLSON, MANCUR, JR. 1971. *The logic of collective action: public goods and the theory of groups* (revised edition). New York: Schocken.

OPIE, IONA, and PETER OPIE. 1959. *The lore and language of schoolchildren.* New York: Oxford University Press.

ORZACK, LOUIS. 1959. Work as a "central life interest" of professionals. *Social Problems,* 7: 125–132.

PARK, ROBERT E. 1915. *Principles of human behavior.* Chicago: The Zalaz Corporation.

———. 1926. The urban community as a spacial pattern and a moral order. Pp. 3–18 in E. W. Burgess, ed., *The urban community.* Chicago: University of Chicago Press.

———. 1927. Human nature and collective behavior. *American Journal of Sociology,* 32: 733–741.

———. 1931. Human nature, attitudes, and mores. Pp. 17–45 in K. Young, ed., *Social attitudes.* New York: Holt.

———. 1939. Symbiosis and socialization: a frame of reference for the study of society. *American Journal of Sociology,* 45: 1–25.

PERROW, CHARLES. 1970. Members as resources in voluntary organizations. Pp. 93–116 in W. R. Rosengren and M. Lefton, eds., *Organizations and clients.* Columbus, Ohio: Merrill.

PERRY, STEWART E., EARLE SILBER, and DONALD BLOCH. 1956. *The child and his family in disaster.* Washington, D.C.: National Academy of Sciences—National Research Council.

PETER, LAURENCE J., and RAYMOND HULL. 1969. *The Peter principle.* New York: Morrow.

PETERS, HERMAN J., and JAMES C. HANSEN, eds. 1971. *Vocational guidance and career development* (2nd edition). New York: Macmillan.

References

PETERSON, WARREN A., and NOEL P. GIST. 1951. Rumor and public opinion. *American Journal of Sociology,* 57: 159–167.

PLUMMER, KENNETH. 1975. *Sexual stigma: an interactionist account.* London: Routledge & Kegan Paul.

POLSKY, NED. 1969. *Hustlers, beats, and others* (revised edition). Garden City, N.Y.: Doubleday Anchor.

PORTER, LYMAN W., EDWARD E. LAWLER III, and J. RICHARD HACKMAN. 1975. *Behavior in organizations.* New York: McGraw-Hill.

PRESSEY, S. L., and R. G. KUHLEN. 1957. *Psychological development through the life-span.* New York: Harper.

PRESTHUS, ROBERT. 1978. *The organizational society* (revised edition). New York: St. Martin's.

PRUS, R. C. 1975. Resisting designations: an extension of attribution theory into a negotiated context. *Sociological Inquiry,* 45: 3–14.

PRYOR, FREDERIC. 1977. *The origins of the economy.* New York: Academic Press.

PUGH, DEREK, DAVID HICKSON, and ROBERT HININGS. 1969. The context of organizational structures. *Administrative Science Quarterly,* 14: 91–114.

QUANDT, IVAN. 1972. *Self-concept and reading.* New York: International Publishers.

REDFIELD, ROBERT. 1955. *The little community.* Chicago: University of Chicago Press.

REISS, ALBERT J., JR. 1961. *Occupations and social status.* New York: Free Press.

RESCHER, NICHOLAS. 1969. *Introduction to value theory.* Englewood Cliffs, N.J.: Prentice-Hall.

RIEBER, R. W. 1962. Stuttering and the self-concept. *Journal of Psychology,* 55: 307–311.

RILEY, MATILDA WHITE, MARILYN E. JOHNSON, and ANNE FONER. 1972. *Aging in society,* vol. 3, *A sociology of age stratification.* New York: Russell Sage Foundation.

ROBERTSON, THOMAS S. 1971. *Innovative behavior and communications.* New York: Holt, Rinehart & Winston.

RODMAN, HYMAN. 1968. Class culture. Pp. 332–337 in D. L. Sills, ed., *International encyclopedia of the social sciences,* vol. 15. New York: Macmillan and Free Press.

ROGERS, EVERETT M. 1962. *Diffusion of innovations.* New York: Free Press.

ROGERS, JOSEPH W., and M. D. BUFFALO. 1974. Fighting back: nine modes of adaptation to a deviant label. *Social Problems,* 22: 101–118.

ROHRER, JOHN H., and MUNRO S. EDMONSON. 1960. *The eighth generation: cultures and personalities of New Orleans Negroes.* New York: Harper & Row.

ROSE, ARNOLD M. 1967. *The power structure: political process in American society.* New York: Oxford University Press.

ROSE, ARNOLD M., and WARREN A. PETERSON, eds. 1965. *Older people and their social world: the subculture of the aging.* Philadelphia: F. A. Davis.

ROSENGREN, WILLIAM, and MARK LEFTON, eds. 1970. *Organization and clients: essays in the sociology of service.* Columbus, Ohio: Merrill.

ROSENKRANTZ, PAUL, SUSAN VOGEL, HELEN BEE, and INGE BROVERMAN. 1968. Sex-role stereotypes and self-concepts in college students. *Journal of Consulting and Clinical Psychology,* 32: 287–295.

ROSENTHAL, ROBERT, and LENORE JACOBSON. 1968. *Pygmalion in the classroom: teacher expectation and pupils' intellectual development.* New York: Holt, Rinehart & Winston.

ROSNOW, RALPH L., and GARY ALAN FINE. 1976. *Rumor and gossip: the social psychology of hearsay.* New York: Elsevier.

REFERENCES

Rosow, Irving. 1975. *Socialization to old age.* Berkeley: University of California Press.

Rossi, Peter. 1955. *Why families move: a study in the social psychology of urban residential mobility.* New York: Free Press.

Rotenburg, Mordechai. 1974. Self-labelling: a missing link in the "societal reaction" theory of deviation. *Sociological Review,* 22: 335-356.

Rothman, Robert A. 1978. *Inequality and stratification in the United States.* Englewood Cliffs, N.J.: Prentice-Hall.

Roy, Donald. 1954. Efficiency and "the fix": informal intergroup relations in a piecework machine shop. *American Journal of Sociology,* 60: 255-266.

Rubin, Joan, and Bjorn H. Jernudd, eds. 1971. *Can language be planned?.* Honolulu: University Press of Hawaii.

Rubin, Lillian B. 1976. *Worlds of pain: life in the working-class family.* New York: Basic Books.

Rubin, Zick. 1973. *Liking and loving: an invitation to social psychology.* New York: Holt, Rinehart & Winston.

———. 1980. *Children's friendships.* Cambridge, Mass.: Harvard University Press.

Safilios-Rothschild, Constantina. 1970. The study of family power structure: a review 1960-1969. *Journal of Marriage and the Family,* 32: 539-552.

Salaman, Graeme. 1974. *Community and occupation.* Cambridge: At the University Press.

Sapir, Edward. 1949. *Culture, language and personality.* Berkeley: University of California Press.

Sayles, Leonard R. 1958. *Behavior of industrial work groups.* New York: Wiley.

Scheflen, Albert E. 1964. The significance of posture in communication systems. *Psychiatry,* 27: 316-331.

———. 1972. *Body language and social order: communication as behavioral control.* Englewood Cliffs, N.J.: Prentice-Hall.

Schegloff, E. A. 1968. Sequencing in conversational openings. *American Anthropologist,* 70: 1075-1095.

Schein, Edgar H. 1956. The Chinese indoctrination program for prisoners of war: a study of attempted "brainwashing." *Psychiatry,* 19: 149-172.

———. 1968. Organizational socialization and the profession of management. *Industrial Management Review,* 9: 1-16.

———. 1971. The individual, the organization, and the career: a conceptual scheme. *Journal of Applied Behavioral Science,* 7: 401-426.

Schein, Edgar H., and Warren G. Bennis. 1965. *Personal and organizational change through group methods: the laboratory approach.* New York: Wiley.

Schelling, Thomas C. 1978. *Micromotives and macrobehavior.* New York: Norton.

Schmitt, Raymond L. 1972. *The reference other orientation: an extension of the reference group concept.* Carbondale: Southern Illinois University Press.

Schur, Edwin C. 1971. *Labeling deviant behavior.* New York: Harper & Row.

Schwartzman, Edward. 1973. *Campaign craftsmanship: a professional's guide to campaigning for elective office.* New York: Universe Books.

Scott, Marvin B., and Stanford M. Lyman. 1968. Accounts. *American Sociological Review,* 33: 46-62.

Scoville, James G. 1969. *The job context of the United States economy 1940-1970.* New York: McGraw-Hill.

References

SEBALD, HANS. 1968. *Adolescence: a sociological analysis.* New York: Appleton-Century-Crofts.

SECORD, PAUL F., and CARL W. BACKMAN. 1974. *Social psychology* (2nd edition). New York: McGraw-Hill.

SEDWICK, ROBERT C. 1974. *Interaction: interpersonal relations in organizations.* Englewood Cliffs, N.J.: Prentice-Hall.

SEGALL, MARSHALL, DONALD T. CAMPBELL, and MELVILLE HERSKOVITS. 1966. *The influence of culture on visual perception.* Indianapolis: Bobbs-Merrill.

SEWELL, WILLIAM H., ARCHIBALD G. HALLER, and GEORGE W. OHLENDORF. 1970. The educational and early occupational attainment process: replication and revision. *American Sociological Review,* 35: 1014–1027.

SHATZ, MARILYN, and ROCHELLE GELMAN. 1973. The development of communication skills. *Monographs of the Society for Research in Child Development,* 38: Serial No. 152.

SHEEHY, GAIL. 1976. *Passages: predictable crises of adult life.* New York: E. P. Dutton.

SHERIF, MUZAFER, O. J. HARVEY, B. J. WHITE, W. R. HOOD, and CAROLYN W. SHERIF. 1961. *Intergroup conflict and cooperation: the robbers cave experiment.* Norman, Okla.: University Book Exchange.

SHIBUTANI, TAMOTSU. 1955. Reference groups as perspectives. *American Journal of Sociology,* 60: 562–569.

———. 1966. *Improvised news: a sociological study of rumor.* Indianapolis: Bobbs-Merrill.

SHIBUTANI, TAMOTSU, and KIAN M. KWAN. 1965. *Ethnic stratification: a comparative approach.* New York: Macmillan.

SHIELDS, NANCY M. 1979. Accounts and other interpersonal strategies in a credibility detracting context. *Pacific Sociological Review,* 22: 255–272.

SHILS, EDWARD A. 1951. The study of the primary group. Pp. 44–69 in D. Lerner and H. D. Lasswell, eds., *The policy sciences.* Stanford, Calif.: Stanford University Press.

SHORT, JAMES F., and FRED L. STRODTBECK. 1965. *Group process and gang delinquency.* Chicago: University of Chicago Press.

SIEBER, SAM D. 1974. Toward a theory of role accumulation. *American Sociological Review,* 39: 567–578.

SILLS, DAVID L. 1957. *The volunteers.* New York: Free Press.

———. 1968. Voluntary associations: sociological aspects. Pp. 362–379 in D. L. Sills, ed., *International encyclopedia of the social sciences,* Vol. 16. New York: Macmillan and Free Press.

SIMMEL, GEORG. 1921. Sociology of the senses: visual interaction. Pp. 356–361 in R. E. Park and E. W. Burgess, *Introduction to the science of society.* Chicago: University of Chicago Press.

———. 1950. *The sociology of Georg Simmel* (translated by K. H. Wolff). New York: Free Press.

———. 1955. *Conflict and the web of group-affiliations* (translated by K. H. Wolff and R. Bendix). New York: Free Press.

SIMMONS, J. L. 1969. *Deviants.* Berkeley, Calif.: Glendessary Press.

SIMON, HERBERT A. 1957. *Administrative behavior* (2nd edition). New York: Macmillan.

SLATER, PHLIIP E. 1966. *Microcosm: structural, psychological and religious evolution in groups.* New York: Wiley.

SLOCUM, WALTER L. 1966. *Occupational careers: a sociological perspective.* Chicago: Aldine.

REFERENCES

SMIGEL, ERWIN O. 1960. The impact of recruitment on the organization of the large law firm. *American Sociological Review,* 25: 56–66.

SNOW, CATHERINE E., and CHARLES A. FERGUSON, eds. 1977. *Talking to children: language input and acquisition.* Cambridge: At the University Press.

SNOW, DAVID A., LOUIS A. ZURCHER, JR., and SHELDON EKLAND-OLSON. 1980. Social networks and social movements: a microstructural approach to differential recruitment. *American Sociological Review,* 45: 787–801.

SOMMER, ROBERT. 1965. Further studies of small group ecology. *Sociometry,* 28: 337–348.

SOUERWINE, ANDREW H. 1978. *Career strategies.* New York: AMACOM.

STEINER, GARY A., ed. 1965. *The creative organization.* Chicago: University of Chicago Press.

STEINMETZ, SUZANNE K., and MURRAY A. STRAUS, eds. 1974. *Violence in the family.* New York: Harper & Row.

STEWART, WILLIAM A. 1968. A sociolinguistic typology for describing national multilingualism. Pp. 531–545 in J. A. Fishman, ed., *Readings in the sociology of language.* The Hague: Mouton.

STOKES, RANDALL, and JOHN P. HEWITT. 1976. Aligning actions. *American Sociological Review,* 41: 838–849.

STRAUSS, ANSELM L. 1959. *Mirrors and masks: the search for identity.* New York: Free Press.

———. 1978. *Negotiations: varieties, contexts, processes, and social order.* San Francisco: Jossey-Bass.

STREIB, GORDON F., and CLEMENT J. SCHNEIDER. 1971. *Retirement in American society: impact and process.* Ithaca, N.Y.: Cornell University Press.

STRYKER, SHELDON. 1968. Identity salience and role performance. *Journal of Marriage and the Family,* 30: 558–564.

———. 1977. Developments in "two social psychologies": toward an appreciation of mutual relevance. *Sociometry,* 40: 145–160.

———. 1980. *Symbolic interactionism: a social structural version.* Menlo Park, Calif.: Benjamin/Cummings.

STUB, HOLGER R., ed. 1972. *Status communities in modern society.* Hinsdale, Ill.: Dryden Press.

STUEVE, C. ANN, and KATHLEEN GERSON. 1977. Personal relations across the life-cycle. Pp. 79–98 in C. S. Fischer, R. M. Jackson, C. A. Stueve, K. Gerson, L. M. Jones, and M. Baldassare, *Networks and places: social relations in the urban setting.* New York: Free Press.

SUPER, DONALD E. 1957. *The psychology of careers.* New York: Harper & Row.

SUPER, DONALD E., and MARTIN J. BOHN, JR. 1970. *Occupational psychology.* Belmont, Calif.: Wadsworth.

SUTTLES, GERALD D. 1968. *The social order of the slum.* Chicago: University of Chicago Press.

———. 1972. *The social construction of communities.* Chicago: University of Chicago Press.

SYKES, GRESHAM M. 1958. *The society of captives.* Princeton, N.J.: Princeton University Press.

TANNENBAUM, ARNOLD S. 1968. *Control in organizations.* New York: McGraw-Hill.

TAUSKY, CURT. 1970. *Work organizations: major theoretical perspectives.* Itasca. Ill.: F. E. Peacock.

TAX, SOL, ed. 1967. *Draft: a handbook of facts and alternatives.* Chicago: University of Chicago Press.

TAYLOR, DONALD W., and OLGA W. MCNEMAR. 1955. Problem solving and thinking. *Annual Review of Psychology,* 6: 455–482.

References

TAYLOR, IAN, and LAURIE TAYLOR, eds. 1973. *Politics and deviance.* Baltimore, Md.: Penguin Books.

TAYLOR, LEE. 1968. *Occupational sociology.* New York: Oxford University Press.

THOMPSON, DENNIS F. 1970. *The democratic citizen.* Cambridge: At the University Press.

THOMPSON, JAMES D., ed. 1966. *Approaches to organizational design.* Pittsburgh: University of Pittsburgh Press.

THOMPSON, JAMES D., ROBERT W. AVERY, and RICHARD CARLSON. 1962. *Occupations, personnel and careers.* Pittsburgh, Pa.: Administrative Science Center, University of Pittsburgh.

THRASHER, FREDERICK M. 1927. *The gang: a study of 1,313 gangs in Chicago.* Chicago: University of Chicago Press.

TIEDEMAN, DAVID V., and ROBERT P. O'HARA. 1963. *Career development: choice and adjustment.* New York: College Entrance Examination Board.

TOCH, HANS. 1965. *The social psychology of social movements.* Indianapolis: Bobbs-Merrill.

TOFFLER, ALVIN. 1980. *The third wave.* New York: Morrow.

TOM, VICTOR R. 1971. The role of personality and organizational images in the recruiting process. *Organizational Behavior and Human Performance,* 6: 573–592.

TRUMAN, DAVID B. 1951. *The government process: political interests and public opinion.* New York: Knopf.

TUNSTALL, JEREMY. 1969. *The fishermen: the sociology of an extreme occupation.* London: MacGibbon & Kee.

TURNER, RALPH H. 1962. Role-taking: process versus conformity. Pp. 20–40 in A. M. Rose, ed., *Human behavior and social processes.* Boston: Houghton Mifflin.

———. 1964. New theoretical frameworks. *Sociological Quarterly,* 5: 122–132.

———. 1970. *Family interaction.* New York: Wiley.

———. 1978. The role and the person. *American Journal of Sociology,* 84: 1–23.

TURNER, RALPH H., and LEWIS A. KILLIAN. 1957. *Collective behavior.* Englewood Cliffs, N.J.: Prentice-Hall.

———. 1972. *Collective behavior* (2nd edition). Englewood Cliffs, N.J.: Prentice-Hall.

VAN DEN BERGHE, PIERRE L. 1973. *Age and sex in human societies: a biosocial perspective.* Belmont, Calif.: Wadsworth.

VAN MAANEN, JOHN, ed. 1977. *Organizational careers: some new perspectives.* New York: Wiley.

VAN MAANEN, JOHN, and EDGAR H. SCHEIN. 1979. Toward a theory of organizational socialization. *Research in Organizational Behavior,* 1: 209–264.

VERBA, SIDNEY. 1961. *Small groups and political behavior: a study of leadership.* Princeton, N.J.: Princeton University Press.

VIDICH, ARTHUR J., and JOSEPH BENSMAN. 1968. *Small town in a mass society* (revised edition). Princeton, N.J.: Princeton University Press.

VROOM, VICTOR H. 1964. *Work and motivation.* New York: Wiley.

VROOM, VICTOR H., and PHILIP W. YETTON. 1973. *Leadership and decision-making.* Pittsburgh, Pa.: University of Pittsburgh Press.

WALLER, WILLARD. 1938. *The family: a dynamic interpretation.* New York: Holt.

WALLERSTEIN, IMMANUEL. 1974, 1980. *The modern world-system* (2 vols.). New York: Academic Press.

REFERENCES

WANOUS, JOHN P. 1980. *Organizational entry: recruitment, selection, and socialization of newcomers.* Reading, Mass.: Addison-Wesley.

WARREN, CAROL A. B. 1974. *Identity and community in the gay world.* New York: Wiley.

WARREN, ROLAND L. 1978. *The community in America* (3rd edition). Chicago: Rand McNally.

WATSON, O. M. 1970. *Proxemic behavior: a cross-cultural study.* The Hague: Mouton.

WEBER, MAX. 1946. Class, status, party. Pp. 180–195 in M. Weber, *From Max Weber: essays in sociology* (translated and edited by H. H. Gerth and C. W. Mills). New York: Oxford University Press.

———. 1947. *The theory of social and economic organization* (translated by A. M. Henderson and T. Parsons). New York: Free Press.

———. 1954. *Max Weber on law in economy and society* (translated and edited by M. Rheinstein and E. Shils). Cambridge, Mass.: Harvard University Press.

WEICK, KARL E. 1968. Systematic observational methods. Pp. 357–451 in G. Lindzey and E. Aronson, eds., *The handbook of social psychology* (2nd edition), vol. 2. Reading, Mass.: Addison-Wesley.

WEIGERT, ANDREW J., and ROSS HASTINGS. 1977. Identity loss, family, and social change. *American Journal of Sociology,* 82: 1171–1185.

WEINSTEIN, EUGENE A., and PAUL DEUTSCHBERGER. 1963. Some dimensions of altercasting. *Sociometry,* 26: 454–466.

———. 1964. Tasks, bargains, and identities in social interaction. *Social Forces,* 42: 451–456.

WEISS, ROBERT S. 1968. Materials for a theory of social relationships. Pp. 154–163 in W. G. Bennis, E. H. Schein, F. I. Steele, D. E. Berlew, eds., *Interpersonal dynamics* (revised edition). Homewood, Ill: Dorsey Press.

———. 1975. *Marital separation.* New York: Basic Books.

WHEELER, STANTON. 1966. The structure of formally organized socialization settings. Pp. 51–116 in O. G. Brim and S. Wheeler, *Socialization after childhood: two essays.* New York: Wiley.

WHITE, HARRISON C. 1970. *Chains of opportunity: systems models of mobility in organizations.* Cambridge, Mass.: Harvard University Press.

WHYTE, WILLIAM FOOTE. 1949. The social structure of the restaurant. *American Journal of Sociology,* 54: 302–310.

———. 1951. Small groups and large organizations. Pp. 297–312 in J. H. Rohrer and M. Sherif, eds., *Social psychology at the crossroads.* New York: Harper.

———. 1955. *Street corner society* (2nd edition). Chicago: University of Chicago Press.

WHYTE, WILLIAM H., JR. 1956. *The organization man.* New York: Simon & Schuster.

WILENSKY, HAROLD L. 1960. Work, careers, and social integration. *International Social Science Journal,* 12: 543–560.

———. 1969. *Organizational intelligence: knowledge and policy in government and industry.* New York: Basic Books.

WILENSKY, HAROLD L., and HUGH EDWARDS. 1959. The skidder: ideological adjustments of the downward mobile worker. *American Sociological Review,* 24: 215–231.

WILEY, NORBERT. 1967. The ethnic mobility trap and stratification theory. *Social Problems,* 15: 147–159.

References

WILLERMAN, LEE. 1979. *The psychology of individual and group differences.* San Francisco: W. H. Freeman.

WILLIAMS, ROBIN M., JR. 1977. *Mutual accommodation: ethnic conflict and cooperation.* Minneapolis: University of Minnesota Press.

WILLIAMS, THOMAS R., ed. 1975. *Socialization and communication in primary groups.* The Hague: Mouton.

WILLS, GORDON, and MARTIN CHRISTOPHER. 1973. What do we know about fashion dynamics? Pp. 11–24 in G. Wills and D. Midgley, eds., *Fashion marketing.* London: Allen & Unwin.

WILSON, JAMES Q. 1966. Innovation in organizations: notes toward a theory. Pp. 193–218 in J. D. Thompson, ed., *Approaches to organizational design.* Pittsburgh, Pa.: University of Pittsburgh Press.

WINTER, WILLIAM D., and ANTONIO J. FERREIRA, eds. 1969. *Research in family interaction.* Palo Alto, Calif.: Science and Behavior Books.

WIRTH, LOUIS. 1938. Urbanism as a way of life. *American Journal of Sociology,* 44: 8–20.

WOFFORD, JERRY C. 1977. *Organizational communication.* New York: McGraw-Hill.

WOLFRAM, WALTER A., and RALPH W. FASOLD. 1974. *The study of social dialects in American English.* Englewood Cliffs, N.J.: Prentice-Hall.

WRIGHT, PETER. 1974. *The language of British industry.* London: Macmillan.

WYNNE-EDWARDS, V. C. 1962. *Animal dispersion in relation to social behavior.* New York: Hafner.

YOUNISS, JAMES. 1980. *Parents and peers in social development.* Chicago: University of Chicago Press.

ZALD, MAYER N., and ROBERTA ASH. 1966. Social movement organizations: growth, decay and change. *Social Forces,* 44: 327–341.

ZALD, MAYER N., and MICHAEL A. BERGER. 1978. Social movements in organizations: coup d'état, insurgency, and mass movements. *American Journal of Sociology,* 83: 823–861.

ZALTMAN, GERALD, and ROBERT DUNCAN. 1977. *Strategies for planned change.* New York: Wiley.

ZELDITCH, MORRIS, JR. 1955. Role differentiation in the nuclear family: a comparative study. Pp. 307–351 in T. Parsons and R. F. Bales, eds., *Family socialization and interaction process.* New York: Free Press.

ZIVIN, GAIL, ed. 1979. *The development of self-regulation through private speech.* New York: Wiley.

NAME INDEX

Name Index

Aboud, F. E., 16
Adams, B., 364, 369, 405
Aiken, M., 341
Akey, D., 359
Aldous, J., 374, 379, 388, 391
Aldrich, H. E., 63, 66, 338, 359
Allan, G. A., 391, 405
Allen, H. B., 199
Allport, G. W., 8, 16, 35
Almond, G. A., 232, 237, 245
Altman, I., 372, 375, 398, 405
Ames, L. B., 206
Anderson, J. R., 205
Anderson, N., 262
Archibald, W. P., 419
Argyle, M., 415
Argyris, C., 359
Armistead, N., 16
Aronson, E., 16, 191, 301, 359, 422
Ash, R., 287–288
Avery, R. W., 261, 354
Axelrad, S., 259
Axline, A. W., 190

Babchuk, N., 340
Bachrach, P., 236

Backman, C. W., 16, 57, 365, 368–369, 390, 441–442
Baldassare, M., 404
Baldwin, K. L., 365
Bales, R. F., 368, 372
Baltes, P. B., 228
Baltzell, E. D., 266
Banton, M., 308, 426
Barber, B., 279, 315
Barber, C., 202
Barber, J. D., 241
Barnouw, V., 205, 211
Bauman, R., 210
Baur, E. J., 283, 292
Bay, C., 235
Becker, H. S., xx, 72–73, 107, 133–134, 161, 163, 166, 241, 260, 308, 315, 319, 321, 384
Bee, H., 225
Behling, O., 92
Bell, C., 311, 327
Bell, R. T., 210
Benedict, R., 243
Benne, K. D., 132, 366–367
Bennett, L. A., 190
Bennis, W. G., 132, 375, 379, 441
Bensman, J., 327
Berelson, B., 285, 301

NAME INDEX

Name Index

Name Index

NAME INDEX

Klapp, O. E., 151–152, 224, 298, 302
Klapper, J. T., 292, 375
Kloss, H., 265
Knapp, M. L., 422
Kohn, M. L., 259, 273
Konvitz, M. R., 233
Kornblum, W., 313
Kriesberg, M., 292
Kuhlen, R. G., 225
Kuhn, M. H., 23
Kuhn, T. S., 315
Kurth, S. B., 381, 404
Kwan, K. M., 265, 273

Labov, W., 199, 204, 207
Labovitz, G., 92
La Gaipa, J. J., 398
Lakein, A., 441
Lakoff, R., 216
Lammers, C. J., 337, 359
Lane, R. E., 238
Langton, K. P., 237
Laver, J., 414
Lawler, E. E., 55, 72, 81, 151, 162–163, 336–337, 355, 358
Lawrence, P. R., 63, 338
Lazarsfeld, P. F., 279, 283, 285, 379, 395
Lee, A. M., 301
Leech, G., 198, 210
Lefton, M., 344, 355
Lemert, E. C., 134
Letkemann, P., 258, 308
Levenson, B., 429
Levinger, G., 392, 398, 404–405
Levinson, D. J., 215, 225, 228, 243
Lewin, K., 370, 375
Lieberson, S., 313
Lindesmith, A. R., 266
Lindzey, G., 16, 191, 301, 359, 367, 422
Linton, R., 214, 228
Lipset, S. M., 308
Liska, A. E., xvii
Little, R. W., 391
Litwak, E., 401, 405
Livingston, J. S., 134
Lobel, L. J., 279
Lofland, J., 137

Lofland, L., 324
Lohisse, J., 301
Lorch, R. S., 238
Lorsch, J. W., 63, 338
Lott, A. J., 371
Lott, B. E., 371
Lounsbury, F. G., 199
Lowe, J. C., 224–225
Luckman, T., 42
Lyman, S. M., 42–43, 133, 308

McCall, G. J., 17, 25, 30, 33, 38, 42, 70, 381, 385–386, 388, 392, 404, 407, 417, 427, 429–430, 433–436, 441–442
McCall, M. M., xxi, 381, 404
McCarthy, J. D., 301
McCord, W. M., 166
McDougall, W., 8
McFeat, T., 365
McGee, R., 93, 321
McGrath, J. E., 372, 375
McLaughlin, B., 301–302
McNemar, O. W., 375
McTavish, D. G., 225
Maccoby, E. E., 220
MacIver, R. M., 49–51, 245, 306, 362–364, 371
Mack, R. W., 308
Mackenzie, W. J. M., 246
Mann, R. D., 373
March, J. G., 151, 358
Marcus, P. M., 394
Marks, S. R., 428, 433, 441
Marsh, P., 198
Martindale, D., 307
Marvick, D., 241
Marx, K., 252, 266
Maurer, C. P., 133
Maurer, D. W., 308, 314
Mayer, M., 190
Mayer, R. R., 238
Mead, G. H., xix, 25–28, 33–34, 363, 400, 438–439
Melton, J. G., 327
Meltzer, L., 7–8
Merriam, A. P., 308
Merton, R. K., 22, 114, 344, 355, 379, 395
Metzger, D., 199

490

Name Index

NAME INDEX

Redfield, R., 324
Reiss, A. J., 252, 310
Rescher, N., 53
Rhea, B., 152
Rieber, R. W., 207
Riesman, D., 422
Riesmann, F., 266
Riley, M. W., 224
Rinehart, J. W., 433
Rivers, W. L., 301
Robertson, T. S., 137
Rodman, H., 266
Roed, J. C., xvii, 16
Roethlisberger, F. J., 379
Rogers, E. M., 281-283, 293
Rogers, J. W., 134
Rohrer, J. H., 379, 435, 442
Rose, A. M., 72, 165, 220, 235
Rosenau, J. S., 190
Rosenberg, B. G., 405
Rosenberg, M., 42
Rosengren, W., 344, 355
Rosenkrantz, P., 225
Rosenne, S., 190
Rosenthal, D., 319
Rosenthal, R., 134, 427
Rosnow, R. L., 319-320
Rosow, I., 220
Ross, E. A., 8
Rossi, P., 320
Rostow, W. W., 190
Rotenburg, M., 134
Rothman, R. A., 262, 273
Roy, D., 151, 370
Rubin, J., 203
Rubin, L. R., 391
Rubin, Z., 363, 392, 404

Sachs, M. Y., 190
Safilios-Rothschild, C., 367
Salaman, G., 307-308, 322, 327
Samuelson, P. A., 272
Sapir, E., 199, 205
Sayles, L. R., 363, 379
Schaie, K. W., 228
Schatzman, L., 17
Scheflen, A. E., 415-416

Schegloff, E. A., 416
Schein, E. H., 73, 98, 107, 159-161, 165, 353, 375, 379, 441
Schelling, T. C., 66, 254
Schmitt, R. L., 25
Schneider, B., 93
Schneider, C. J., 262
Schooler, C., 259, 273
Schur, E. C., 37, 134, 241
Schwartz, M., 352
Schwartzman, E., 241
Scott, M. B., 42-43, 133
Scoville, J. G., 258
Seashore, S. E., 120
Sebald, H., 216
Secord, P. F., 16, 57, 365, 368-369, 390, 441-442
Sedwick, R. C., 120
Segall, M., 206
Selltiz, C., 17
Selznick, P., 306
Sewell, W. H., 259, 273
Shattuck, R., 41
Shatz, M., 218
Sheats, P., 366-367
Sheehy, G., 225
Sherif, C., 372
Sherif, M., 372, 379
Sherzer, J., 210
Shibutani, T., 24, 175, 265, 273, 319
Shields, N. M., xxi, 133
Shils, E. A., 369, 379
Short, J. F., 372
Sieber, S. D., 428
Silber, E., 371, 441
Sills, D. L., 334, 340-341, 352, 359
Simmel, G., xvii, 12-13, 323-324, 364, 381, 387, 394, 415, 438, 442
Simmons, J. L., 17, 25, 30, 33, 38, 42, 381, 386, 388, 407, 417, 427, 429-430, 433-436, 438, 441-442
Simmons, N., xxi, 443
Simon, H. A., 31
Singer, E., 24
Skolnikoff, E. B., 190
Slater, P. E., 368, 374
Slocum, W. L., 260, 273, 320
Smelser, N. J., 272
Smigel, E. O., 93

Name Index

493

NAME INDEX

SUBJECT INDEX

Subject Index

497

SUBJECT INDEX

Subject Index

Effects
  of career, 163-164, 166, 206-208, 225-226, 243,
    262-263, 267-270, 297-298, 323, 356, 376,
    401-402, 419
  of membership, 204-206, 225, 243-244, 261,
    265-269, 297-298, 321-325, 355, 375-376,
    400-402, 419-420
  of position/role, 163-164, 166, 204, 206-208, 225,
    242-243, 261-262, 265-269, 296-298, 321-323,
    355-356, 376, 401, 419-420
Elaboration, 58, 129-130, 332-337, 344
Embedded organizations, 63, 147, 149-150, 185,
  263, 275-276, 279, 282, 286, 288-289,
  296-298, 314, 317, 337, 369-370, 389, 391,
  407-408, 411-413 (*See also* Interorganizational
  relations)
Emotions, 19-20, 22-23, 42, 97, 205-206, 226, 262,
  265-270, 296-298, 324-325, 374-376, 401-402,
  419
Encounters, 62, 407-422
Environment, 9-11, 54, 62-63, 66, 98, 124,
  171-173, 181, 205, 249, 267, 309, 323-325,
  338, 345, 359, 370
Exchange theory, 30-33, 81-90, 254
Expectations, 22-23, 49, 54, 64, 82-84, 95-107,
  111-112, 118, 214, 220-221, 266-270
Expressive processes, 36-39, 96, 111, 392-394,
  417-418
  altercasting, 36-38, 96, 111, 417-418
  presentation of self, 80-81, 100, 111, 241
    393-394, 417-418

Fad, 278-279, 281
Fashion, 24, 276-282, 289-290, 296, 319
Feelings, 19-20, 22-23, 29, 42, 95, 205-206, 226,
  262, 265-270, 296-298, 324-325, 374-376,
  401-402, 419
Feral man, 19-20, 33, 41-42, 210, 228, 438-439
Formalization, 58-59, 129, 141, 231-232, 331-332,
  335, 341, 344-345, 348, 362-363, 366-367

Gatherings, 407-408, 412-414, 421-422
General roles, 426, 434
Gestures, 24, 28, 36-37, 198-199, 216, 415-417
Goals, personal (*See* Interests, personal)
Group determinism approach, 12-13

Groups, 61-62, 336-337, 361-379, 381-382,
  412-413
  institutionalized, 363, 366
  official, 61, 362-363, 366
  primary, 62, 283, 292-293, 362-364
  secondary, 62, 362-363
  unofficial, 61, 362-363, 366

Habits, 21-22, 24, 28, 82, 98, 243, 261, 265-270,
  375, 396, 410
Hierarchies of role-identities, 30, 394, 399, 433-436
  (*See also* Self, social)
  prominence, 30, 434-435
  salience, 30, 38, 435-436
Human ecology, 309-311, 328
Human nature, 19-20, 374-375

"I," 27-30, 399, 425, 439 (*See also* Self, social)
Identity (*See* Role-identities)
Independent roles, 426, 434
Individual goods, 47-48, 249
Innovation process, 113-115, 123-137, 155-158,
  188-189, 202-203, 222-223, 238-239, 257-258,
  276, 289, 294, 296, 318-319, 341-342, 346,
  351, 372, 397, 417-418
Interaction process, 109-120, 155-158, 188,
  201-202, 221-222, 237-238, 257, 294, 318,
  341, 346, 351, 371-372, 396-397, 415-417,
  428-433
Interactionism approach, 12-13, 266-267
Interest groups, 283-285, 287-288, 291-293
Interests
  collective, 49-51, 57-58, 82-90, 113-115, 131,
    196, 219, 232, 254, 267, 276-278, 282,
    285-289, 313-314, 332, 338, 343, 349,
    361-364, 368-369, 383-384, 408-409
  personal, 19, 21, 49-51, 56, 82-90, 100, 102,
    115-118, 206, 216-217, 225, 243, 261-262,
    265-270, 286, 296-298, 356, 376, 400-402,
    417, 419
  recruitment, 84-91, 100-101
  special, 50-51, 56, 82-90, 100, 115-117, 174,
    232, 267, 283, 286, 288, 313-314, 316, 338,
    364, 399, 411, 417
Interorganizational relations, 62-63, 66, 147,
  149-150, 174-175, 185-189, 263-265, 316-317,
  337-338, 359, 369-370, 391-392, 411-413, 425
Issues, 282-285, 287

SUBJECT INDEX

Subject Index

SUBJECT INDEX